Leisure for Canadians

Second Edition

Leisure for Canadians

Second Edition

edited by
Ron McCarville, Ph.D.
and
Kelly MacKay, Ph.D.

Venture Publishing, Inc.
State College, Pennsylvania

Venture Publishing, Inc.
1807 N. Federal Dr
Urbana, IL 61801
1-800-359-5940

Cover by StepUp Communications, Inc.

Library of Congress Catalogue Card Number: 2013954902
ISBN-10: 1-939476-02-X
ISBN-13: 978-1-939476-02-9
ISBN ebook: 978-1-57167-827-0

Contents

Preface

We are pleased to present you with the second edition of *Leisure for Canadians*. This edition builds on the work we started in our first effort published in 2007. In that edition, we began to explore leisure within Canadian society. Our goal was to expose the reader to the many roles played by leisure, the ways in which Canadians take part, and to explore what this means for leisure providers.

This second edition introduces a new theme within the larger leisure literature, that of sport and events management. We have added seven new chapters on various aspects of sport and event planning. There are several reasons for this addition. First, sport and events (ranging from festivals to games and tournaments) are pervasive. They are so pervasive that they often dominate much of the public attention devoted to leisure. As a result, we thought it appropriate to place them both within the larger discussion of leisure. Second, sport delivery and event planning can be complex and demanding in terms of expertise and resources. As a result, both are receiving increasing attention from educators and providers alike. We thought the new edition should reflect this increasing attention.

We have also added a chapter on the built environment and leisure behavior. It suggests the often profound effect of parks and trails on human behavior. Shopping malls offer another example of the importance of the built environment. We have added a chapter on the pervasive role of shopping in Canadian society today.

As was the case in the first edition, this text is comprised of chapters written by scholars from across Canada. All our contributors were asked to imagine they were talking with someone who asked, "What do we know about [your topic]?" The individual and collective goal was to bring the reader up to date on what is known on that topic. We believe these scholars have done a commendable job of bringing their respective topic areas to life for the reader.

We also asked authors who contributed to our first edition if they wished to update their respective chapters. Several have done so. Some of these changes represent updates of citations or statistics while others are more editorial in nature. In all cases, this second edition has been improved as a result of their efforts. We owe all our authors a great debt of gratitude.

The format of each chapter is generally consistent throughout the text. The authors each introduce their topic, outline why this topic is relevant to the leisure community, establish what we now know about that topic, and what is yet to be learned. There are a few variations on this theme, of course. For example, chapters focusing on historical background might be provided in a format that is a bit different from those reporting industry trends. In all cases, however, the goal is one of presenting the reader with our most current understanding of that topic.

We understand that this book is being used widely as an introductory textbook. Consequently, we wish to offer a bit of perspective on how this text might be used in the classroom. In his book *What the Best College Teachers Do* (2004), Ken Bain reports that many instructors simply assign chapter after chapter with no opportunity (or reason) for student debate and discourse. He found that the less effective instructors referred constantly to "covering the material." In those cases students were failing to truly understand or relate to the material.

Bain (2004) encouraged instructors to move beyond simply reporting material in class. He found that the best teachers were those who built student engagement around compelling questions. The best teachers structured their courses and indeed each lecture around interesting and challenging questions. Embedded in these questions were all the key concepts the instructors hoped to cover. This book lends itself to the approach suggested by Ken Bain. All our authors have provided reflective questions throughout their chapters to help readers apply this new knowledge to their understanding of leisure in their own society and in their own lives.

We encourage instructors to use these questions as they progress through the text. In this way, the ideas and issues will become more relevant, more tangible. The authors also offer text boxes (we call them "idea-" or "*i*-boxes") that highlight key issues and ideas that deserve special attention. Sometimes they are used to draw attention to an important study, while at other times they focus on a particular problem or challenge. In all cases, their goal is to provide a bit of additional perspective. Both the reflective questions and *i*-boxes can be used to initiate and structure class discussion.

We know too that the book contains more chapters than can be covered in a typical term or semester. We have done this to offer instructors choices regarding the topics they cover. We encourage instructors to pick and choose chapters they hope will encourage thought and debate among their students.

Finally, we feel this text is appropriate for new students to leisure hoping to grasp key issues as well as more advanced students seeking to explore leisure's complex role in our society. The contributors have worked hard to bring you the most current thinking on a wide variety of topics. Together they paint a picture of both the challenges and opportunities that leisure presents. We hope you embrace both as you seek to understand and enjoy leisure.

Ron McCarville
University of Waterloo
Waterloo, Ontario

Kelly MacKay
Ryerson University
Toronto, Ontario

INTRODUCTION

Cicero once observed that, "to be ignorant of what occurred before you, is to remain always a child." We couldn't agree more. That is why we open the book with a prologue prepared by Jiri Zuzanik on the history of leisure research. In preparing this book, the authors in this text have drawn heavily from the decades of leisure research, so it is appropriate that we begin with the origins of our research traditions. The rest of the book is separated into two distinctive parts or halves. We believe so strongly in Cicero's words that each of the book's two halves begins with more historical perspective. In both cases, the goal is to outline the origins of the ideas and traditions that are discussed in that particular section.

Part 1: Leisure in Canada

The first half of the text (Chapters 1–21) is devoted to the phenomenon of leisure. While Canadian society is the focus of this material, the discussion ranges widely across both space and time in its exploration of leisure. This portion of the book has three sections. The first section (Chapters 1–7) sets the stage for the rest of the text. It does so by first by offering definitions for leisure, recreation, and play and their respective roles in our society.

This section also introduces two themes that will recur throughout the text. The first theme focuses on the role of theory in helping us understand sport and leisure dynamics. The leisure literature generally, and this text in particular, are guided and directed by theory. It is the driving force that helps us make sense of all that we see and do. We thought this point should be emphasized early in the text. The second theme is that of politics and power. The authors in this text view sport and leisure as much more than benign, child-like activities. The discussion often draws attention to sport and leisure as potent forces in our individual and collective lives. These definitions and themes offer perspective on what is to come.

The second section (Chapters 8–19) begins to describe how Canadians spend their spare time. It is an exploration of those things we do when we are at leisure and play. This exploration offers a glimpse into the ways in which sport and leisure have become so much a part of everyday life. It suggests too the many things that influence the degree to which we are able to integrate sport and leisure into our everyday lives. What you learn about our leisure behaviours may surprise you.

The third section (Chapters 20–26) speaks to the diversity found within the Canadian social landscape. It becomes obvious that there is no one sport or leisure community. There are many groups and subgroups, each with its own challenges and perspectives. We cannot understand sport or leisure in our society without understanding these perspectives. The perspectives presented here are by no means comprehensive, but they do offer some insight into dominant themes within current discussions of sport and leisure in Canadian society.

Taken together, the material in the first half of the book suggests that both sport and leisure are complex and politically charged. They can be constrained by social group, work demands, income level, gender, disability, or age. They can represent central life interests and can become personally and collectively destructive. They can be actively sought by millions of Canadians daily in settings ranging from their living rooms to the Arctic and around the world. All this insight is useful only if it informs decision makers as they seek to facilitate leisure activity, so the second half is concerned with "What now?" It deals with ways in which sport and leisure services can be, and are, delivered across Canada.

Part 2: Leisure Delivery in Canada

The second half of this book is administrative in its focus. It offers the leisure provider with solutions to the challenges posed in the first half. The emphasis here is on much more than simply "how" to go about things. Our contributors offer ways of thinking about the role of providers as much as how to go about carrying out that role. The themes of empowerment and client focus come through time and time again.

Section 4 (Chapters 27–33) lays out the traditional approaches to leisure delivery. As was the case in the first half of the book, we begin with historical perspective. Chapter 27 provides a history of leisure provision over the past several hundred years here in Canada. In particular, it establishes why the public sector has adopted such a pervasive role in municipal leisure delivery. Chapter 28 then outlines the roles and challenges of private sector leisure delivery.

Section 5 (Chapters 34–41) discusses a variety of strategies that might be adopted in the delivery of leisure services. Again the emphasis is on empowerment and service to the community. The contributors insist that leisure management is not about the simple delivery of services. Rather, it is about deciding on where to place control of resources and how to best serve the community. These chapters also focus on traditional administrative challenges arising from the need to mobilize resources. The challenge is that of being both effective and efficient at the same time. This is not always an easy task, but this section should help.

It addresses program planning issues, human resource development (both paid and volunteer), financing, and marketing effort. These activities form the centerpiece of any administrative task, and each chapter offers both background and solutions to these challenges.

Prologue

Beginnings of Leisure Research in North America: A Forgotten Legacy?

Jiri Zuzanek, Ph.D.
University of Waterloo

Introduction

The beginnings of systematic leisure inquiry in North America and Europe lie in the 1950s and 1960s. In North America, they are closely associated with the names of David Riesman (1950), Max Kaplan (1960), Nels Anderson (1961), Sebastian de Grazia (1962), Rolf Meyersohn (1958, 1972), and others. In Europe, the onset of intensive and methodical study of leisure is associated primarily with the name of Joffre Dumazedier (1967). Yet, the work of these authors did not spring by magic out of nowhere. Rather, it grew out of traditions dating back to the late nineteenth century, the 1920s, and particularly the 1930s.

Leisure as an Educational, Policy, and Applied Concern

Social scientists were not necessarily the first who drove North Americans' attention to the importance of leisure phenomena. From the beginning of the twentieth century, but particularly since the 1920s, leisure has been often examined by authors operating from three perspectives: (a) educational and social-philosophical, (b) social problem/ social policy, and (c) applied.

Authors approaching leisure from educational and social–philosophical perspectives viewed leisure primarily as a moral issue and an action-oriented concern. They emphasized leisure's contribution to the person's "wholesome" development and constructive uses of leisure time. Many authors who contributed to this tradition had an educational background and examined leisure in the broader context of play or expressive behaviour. Most of them shared an optimistic view of leisure as an opportunity for personal growth and contrasted it with instrumentally oriented work activities.

Journalistic publications written from this perspective are marked by an almost religious belief in the developmental potentials of leisure and exhibit great zeal in advancing leisure's cause. Titles of selected articles from the 1920s and 1930s provide a fairly good idea of the orientation and beliefs shared by their authors, and include: "Education for the *Proper* Use of Leisure Time," "Training in the *Right* Use of Leisure," "Training for the *Wise* Use of Leisure," "Training for the *Profitable* Use of Leisure," "Guidance in the *Worthy* Use of Leisure Time," "Report of Committee on *Best* Use of Leisure Time," "Education and the *Larger* Leisure," "The *Wider* Use of Leisure," and "Significance of *Education* for Leisure" (emphases added).

Many influential books written from this perspective share a similarly apologetic view of leisure. In *The Education of the Whole Man* (1931), Jacks suggested that we should regard leisure as an "opportunity for exercising those creative and imaginative faculties, which the general standardization of labour tends to suppress" (p. 64). Leisure is called upon to educate not just parts of men, such as mind, soul, character, and body, but the "whole man as an inseparable unity of all four" (p. 69).

Burns carefully noted that his *Leisure in the Modern World* (1932) is not a "sermon," yet he structures the book as an extensive apology of leisure's contribution towards such worthy causes as "spontaneous enjoyment," "inner life," and "elimination of 'traditionalism,' 'localism,' and 'class distinctions.'" Overstreet's publication *A Guide to Civilized Leisure* (1934) centres upon the argument that "[i]n a world of scarcity, we have had to give our hostages to toil. Now, in an age of plenty, we can look forward to an increasing amount of time that is our own. We have, to an extent, grown work-wise. In the future, we shall grow leisure-wise" (p. 9).

Nash, in *The Philosophy of Recreation and Leisure* (1953), and Brightbill, in *The Challenge of Leisure* (1960), find in leisure a source of spontaneity, creativity, playfulness, community spirit, social equality, democracy, personal self-realization, and harmonious development of physical, intellectual, and artistic skills. Nash's "pyramid diagram" (see Figure 1), showing how man's uses of time progress from leisure inspired by the lowest instincts (delinquency) to the "peaks of creative achievement," probably best exemplifies this approach (Nash, 1953, p. 89). In short, leisure

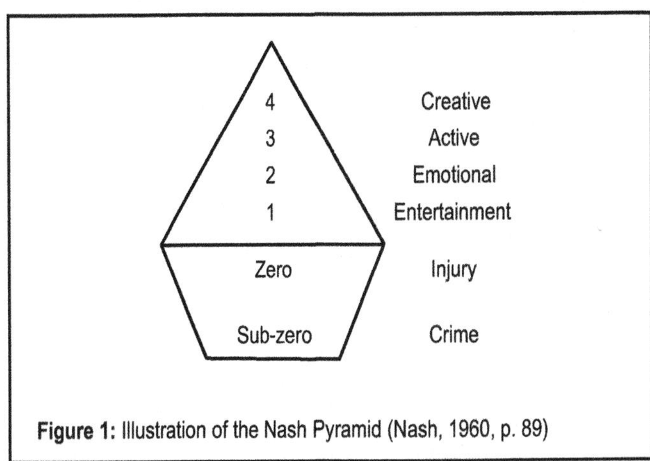

Figure 1: Illustration of the Nash Pyramid (Nash, 1960, p. 89)

has been heralded as a potential answer to most problems of modern civilization, capable of helping where work failed. This group of publications formulated some basic assumptions of subsequent leisure and recreational studies and programmes, and it still forms an integral part of readings in the numerous courses of the philosophy of leisure offered in North American universities.

The social problem/social policy approach toward leisure focuses on the challenges and pitfalls rather than the opportunities associated with leisure. This literature sees leisure, in essence, as problematic. It is dominated by moralistic concerns and regards growing amounts of leisure in modern societies as a source of alarming and disquieting developments, such as growing passivity, privatization, alienation, violence, or political corruption reminiscent of the late days of the Roman Empire ("bread and circuses"). A random selection of article titles from the 1920s and 1930s gives a good idea of the prevailing concerns of some of these writings: "*Delinquency* and Leisure," "The Curse of Leisure," "Our Need for *Wasting* More Time," "Tonic of *Disaster,*" "*Menace* of Leisure," "Leisure and *Crime,*" "*Dangers* in the New Leisure Area," "New Leisure—Blessing or *Curse*?" (emphases added).

Books such as Cutten's *The Threat of Leisure* (1926) and Durant's *The Problem of Leisure* (1938) exemplify well this approach toward leisure. Cutten, in particular, draws attention to the fact that, "While machinery has given opportunity for thought, the opportunity has not been grasped, and today leisure is chiefly … a cloak for idleness" (1926, p. 74). More categorically still, Cutten insists that, while leisure is the most precious gift that the past century has bestowed upon us, "it is also the most dangerous one" (p. 86). Coupled with the comfort and ease of modern life, leisure will result, according to Cutten, in "physical and mental degeneracy" (p. 89). An unlimited, unorganized, unled, and uncontrolled leisure is seen as "the greatest danger to which any nation was ever exposed" (p. 96). Cutten concludes his analyses by saying: "For a variety of reasons we are less prepared for leisure than any people since the beginning of time, and untrained and unready as we are, it may do more harm under present circumstances than it can do good" (p. 101).

A number of publications have highlighted the policy challenges of "new leisure." An early publication of Fulk, *The Municipalization of Play and Recreation* (1922), pointed out that "[t]he complicated and troublesome social situation of the city has forced some recognition of the problem of public leisure by municipal government" (p. 2). The book examines in great detail opportunity structures and policies of municipal recreation agencies in selected U.S. cities. Lies, in *The New Leisure Challenges for the Schools* (1933), examines policy issues associated with the introduction of education for leisure into school curricula and after-school activities.

As early as 1909–1911, several U.S. universities offered the first courses in recreation, park, and playground management, thus putting leisure study into the context of practical and applied interests (Van Doren & Hodges, 1975). Weir's book *Parks: A Manual of Municipal and County Parks* (1928) provided the first comprehensive introduction into park management and recreation administration. One also finds in the 1930s the first attempts to examine leisure from a social adjustment and therapeutic perspective, as in Davis's *Principles and Practice of Recreational Therapy* (1936) and *Play and Mental Health* (1938).

In general, social–philosophical, educational, social-problem, and applied studies of leisure published in the 1920s and 1930s contain interesting social observations and promising analyses of practical use and organization of leisure, but they are also often marked by superficial journalism, pedagogical moralizing, and wishful thinking.

Social Sciences and the Study of Leisure

Differently than educators or moral philosophers, social scientists examined leisure as a socially patterned behaviour rather than a moral issue or an object of social reform, although all groups regarded leisure as a major social policy concern. The work of four social scientists, spanning the period from the turn of the century to the 1930s is particularly interesting and influential in view of the subsequent development of leisure research in North America: Thorstein Veblen, author of *The Theory of the Leisure Class* (1899); Robert and Helen Lynds, authors of the *Middletown* (1929), and *Middletown in Transition* (1937); and George Lundberg, the leading author of *Leisure: A Suburban Study* (1934) [co-authored with Komarovsky and McInerny].

Thorstein Veblen:
The Theory of the Leisure Class

Veblen's classic, *The Theory of the Leisure Class* (1899), is America's first serious social inquiry of leisure. Although written by an economist, this is an eminently sociological book. In Rosenberg's words, Veblen received his formal training in philosophy, and is commonly regarded as an economist, yet "his vocation was truly that of a sociologist" (1970, p. 7).

Veblen was not a friend of leisure. His views of leisure were "tainted" by a strong Puritan bias, strengthened by his upbringing as a farmer's son from a family of hard-working Norwegian immigrants. Veblen stands out as a rare instance of an American scholar who does not partake in dominant liberal ideology with its appreciation of the values of discretion, spontaneity, and self-expression. Veblen neither embraced nor emphasized beneficial effects of leisure in his work. *The Theory of the Leisure Class* is a scathing and bitter attack on the lifestyles of American upper classes, the rich and the famous, for whom leisure was a status symbol, manifested by conspicuous consumption, vicarious leisure, waste, and snobbery. This being said, we should not underestimate Veblen's contribution to the social analysis of leisure. Veblen introduced an important theme into the sociology of leisure by examining the relationship between leisure, social status, and social stratification.

According to Veblen, leisure rather than work manifests and reinforces social differences. "In order to gain and to hold esteem, it is not sufficient merely to possess wealth and power. The wealth or power must be put in evidence" (1953, p. 42). Such evidence is provided by conspicuous consumption and vicarious leisure. "Since the consumption of more excellent goods is an evidence of wealth, it becomes honorific; and conversely the failure to consume in due quantity and quality becomes a mark of inferiority and demerit" (1953, pp. 63–64).

Veblen was nostalgic of the early stages of American history, that short period of time when status was associated with work rather than leisure, and leisure formed an integral part of the community life. Eventually work and leisure have split. A significant change occurred in the character of the American entrepreneurial classes. Speculation, absentee ownership, conspicuous consumption, and wasteful leisure betrayed the values of the early American Puritans and businessmen. Leisure became, according to Veblen, not honorific, but self-serving, senseless, and despicably unfair.

The Theory of the Leisure Class is an emotional and highly biased book written with passion and brilliance. Veblen exaggerates the idleness of the upper classes. According to Mills, "of course, there is and there has been a working upper class—in fact, a class of prodigiously active people" (1953, p. xv). Yet, Veblen did not approve of their work and ignored it. Veblen's violent condemnation of virtually all consumption, save the subsistence one, as conspicuous did not endear his views to modern economists. The latter are not prepared to accept Veblen's distinction between the "serviceable" (i.e., legitimate) and "non-serviceable" (i.e., wasteful needs). Yet even economists find Veblen's indignation with wasteful consumption morally and socially compelling (Wallich, 1965).

Paradoxically, Veblen may have drawn attention to developments that took reign in social life half a century after his book was published. His critique applies to the middle-class America of the 1930s, and the "mass society" of the post-World War II era (heralded as the end of class society), no less and possibly more than to the America of the late nineteenth century.

One is taken by surprise by the number of parallels between Veblen's analyses of the "leisure classes" and the discussion of social and club life in Lynds's *Middletown* (1929), Lundberg's (1934) analyses of organized leisure in Westchester suburbia, Riesman's (1950) penetrating examination of consumption's role in forming an "other-directed" personality of the mid-twentieth century, or Warner and Lunt's (1941) analyses of class and life-style distinctions in Yankee City. From Veblen's theories of competitive emulation as the motivating factor for consumption, there is only a step to Mills's distinction between the all-American values of "utility" and "workmanship" as opposed to those of the "world of the fast buck" (Mills, 1953, p. xi), Linder's (1970) theory of the "harried leisure class," or Hirsch's (1976) distinction between "conventional" and "positional" goods. Veblen is often remembered as the author of anecdotal references to the status-conferring role of leisure in distant history, such as Chinese Mandarin's long fingernails or Victorian ladies' corsets, but by examining leisure as a status symbol in America, Veblen focused researchers' attention to the social meaning and functions of leisure in modern societies and brought leisure into a broader context of studying contemporary society and social change.

Robert and Helen Lynd: *Middletown* and *Middletown in Transition*

The Lynds's studies, *Middletown* (1929) and *Middletown in Transition* (1937), contain some of the best-documented observations of America's leisure habits in the 1920s and 1930s. The first of these two volumes examines daily life in a medium-sized Midwest city—Muncie, Indiana—around 1924. The authors traced their analyses back to 1890. For this they collected considerable statistical and printed information from the 1890s. In his foreword to *Middletown,* Clark Wissler commended the authors for their "foresight in revealing the Middletown of 1890 as a genesis of the Middletown of today, not as its contrast" (1929, p. vi). When the book was published in 1929, the first year of the Great Depression, it met with instant success. The American ways of life were dramatically altered. This gave the Lynds an impetus to replicate their study under new conditions. The results of the second study, conducted in 1934–1935, form the basis of the *Middletown in Transition.*

Middletown and *Middletown in Transition* are social–anthropological studies. The Lynds did not focus in their books specifically on leisure phenomena. Rather, they examined the structure of everyday community life, including making a living, getting a home, training the young using leisure, and engaging in religious practices and leisure activities. The Lynds's analyses are based on the study of statistical evidence, published documents, observations, and extensive interviews. The *Middletown* volumes are filled with data, as well as cogent generalizations, and are regarded by many authors as classics among American community studies.

The Lynds' interest in leisure, unlike Veblen's, focused primarily on the relationships between leisure and social change, rather than leisure and social stratification. According to the Lynds, four factors contributed to the "remaking" of Middletown's leisure between 1890 and 1924: (a) shorter working hours; (b) proliferation of the automobile; (c) arrival of the movies; and (d) invention of the radio.

In 1924, daily work was an hour shorter than in 1890; half-day Saturday holidays were becoming a norm; and the word "vacation," virtually unknown in the 1890s, acquired its modern meaning, at least in the lives of the middle classes.

The automobile revolutionized Middletown's leisure more than anything else. It obliterated the horse culture of the 1890s, and made leisure a "regularly expected part of every day and week rather than an occasional event" (1929, p. 260). By 1923, there were 6,221 passenger cars in the city, or roughly two cars for every three families (1929, p. 253). Gone were carriage-riding and Sunday strolls. Walking for pleasure became practically extinct. On the 4th of July, Memorial Day, and Labor Day, people were leaving town rather than crowding its streets. Clergymen were competing with the automobile for Sunday church attendance.

Like the automobile, the motion picture meant more for Middletown than "just a new way of doing an old thing" (1929, p. 263). In 1890, there was only one opera house in Middletown. In 1923, nine motion picture theatres operated from 1:00 to 11:00 p.m., seven days a week, summer and winter.

These inventions, according to the Lynds, carried with them broader social and cultural connotations. More books were borrowed and periodicals sold in Middletown in the mid-1920s than in 1890. There were, however, fewer public debates focusing on new publications. Reading circles, rather active in the 1890s, mostly disappeared. Interest in music proliferated, but it took the form of listening rather than active participation. Phonograph and Victrola substituted for piano-playing and singing. The role of the neighbourhood and church declined. Associations and organized club groups gained in prominence (1929, p. 276). In 1890, people used to drop over in the evening. In 1923, they had to be invited "way ahead of the date to make a party of it" (1929, p. 275). Art and music served in the 1920s as a symbol of "belonging," rather than an expression of spontaneous artistic interest.

The developments after 1924 were also controversial. According to the Lynds, since 1925, Middletown had been through two periods with widely different implications for leisure.

> The first was big with both the promise and reality of leisure—golf, mid-winter trips to Florida, and the vague hope of "retiring" into that blessed land where "every day will be Sunday bye and bye" for the business class; and for the working class the tangible realities of automobiles, radio, and other tools for employing leisure. Then, swiftly, the second period, when enforced leisure drowned men with its once-coveted abundance, and its taste became sour and brackish. Today Middletown is emerging from the doldrums of the depression more than ever in recent years committed to the goodness of work.... Nobody is complaining nowadays about the former "smoke nuisance." (1937, p. 246)

Examination of the "bad" 1930s witnessed that Middletown read more books than the "good" pre-Depression years. The 1930s had also seen the end of Prohibition and the replacement of speakeasies with legal taverns serving, in the Lynds's words, as physical places for meeting new people and "institutionalizing spontaneity." The 1930s also experienced a spectacular rise of middle-class bridge game, hailed as the hostess's best friend and an "unparalleled device for an urban world that wants to avoid issues, to keep things impersonal, to enjoy people without laying oneself open or committing oneself to them, and to have fun in the process" (1937, p. 271). Last but not least, the 1930s were marked by a growth of public provisions for leisure needs provided mostly under emergency federal programs.

Drawing a summary balance for the Middletown's four years of prosperous growth and six years of Depression experience, the Lynds suggested that the community had not undergone a dramatic lifestyle change but rather had made some temporary adjustments.

> In the overwhelming majority of cases, the community has simply in the fat years bought more of the same kinds of leisure, and in the lean years made what curtailments it was forced to make and just marked time pending the return of the time when it could resume the doing of the familiar things. (1937, p. 293)

While the issue of social change is the focus of most of the Lynds' research attention, their analyses of the relationship between leisure and social class are also interesting, since they are done in the context of social change. Although the Lynds were aware of the advances of modern popular entertainment and approved of the growing provision of public recreational services to the lower-income groups, they were in no rush to conclude that leisure would obliterate class distinctions. For them, even in a modern society, leisure remains mostly a status game, perhaps slightly less ostentatious than it was in the earlier periods.

The Lynds clearly distinguish between the function of leisure in the lives of the business classes and the working classes. Their assessment of the role of leisure in the life of the upper classes differed from Veblen. According to the Lynds, in the lives of the business classes, particularly their male part, leisure is secondary to work.

> In this business-class world in which the job itself is so important to status ... men work not to get leisure but to get money, to "get ahead," to "get up in the world." The resulting spectacle—of some of the ablest members of society ... spending themselves unremittingly in work, denying themselves leisure and bending fine energies to the endless acquisition of the means of living a life they so often take insufficient leisure to live—is one factor leading certain contemporary psychiatrists to remark on the masochistic tendencies in our culture. (1937, p. 244)

The situation is quite different for the working classes. Here work does not, as a rule, provide an avenue for self-realization, while leisure provides some immediate gratifications, opportunity for socialization, entertainment, and possibly escape.

> Status in the workingman's world, where skill is yielding to the machine ... is increasingly beyond the worker's reach.... You have a job—if you're lucky—and you work.... Someday you're going to die. Meanwhile, leisure assumes a simple, direct, and important place in your scheme of things; it's when you live, and you get all of it you can—here, now, and all the time. (1937, p. 245)

The neighbourhood plays a more important role in the lives of the working classes than in the lives of the business classes, and so do many material possessions. "Only by understanding the different focus upon leisure in the lives of those living north and south of the tracks can one appreciate the tenacity with which the working man clings to his automobile" (1937, p. 245).

The Lynds's analyses of Middletown were at times labelled as "descriptive" (Mitchell, 1968). This critique is misdirected. The two Middletown volumes are by no means lacking insight or conceptualization. The Lynds do not shy away from interpretation. They combine judicious combination of statistical and survey data with what Weber called a "verstehen" (i.e., understanding) approach. The Lynds project themselves into the social and existential situation of their respondents, as if "reading their minds." Symptomatically, the authors of *Middletown* often use as their respondents well-informed individuals rather than random samples of indifferent populations. This makes for interesting reading, particularly since respondents are quoted verbatim.

Ideologically, the Lynds were not immune to the zeitgeist of the 1930s. Like so many other intellectuals, they were disturbed by the fallout of the Great Depression, and the fact that it could not be rationally explained or controlled. Their ire turned against the system and traditional establishment. They looked to the government for intervention. The moneyed culture of the middle classes appeared to the Lynds as shallow and pretentious rather than genuine and spontaneous, and in spite of their considerable attention to the working-class culture, it did not excite them either. Although less formal, it also has been affected by the all-American fascination with consumption. *Middletown* and *Middletown in Transition* are books written with mixed feelings. The authors seem to be longing for closer community ties typical of the gemeinschaft (i.e., community-bound) relationships of the 1890s, but they do not moralise about this issue or offer speculative remedies. Rather they faithfully report the pros and the cons of the new developments. Their work contains preciously unadulterated information about everyday life and leisure in the 1920s and 1930s and makes it one of the most interesting readings about America's life during this period.

George Lundberg:
Leisure—A Suburban Study

The book *Leisure—A Suburban Study* (1934) by Lundberg, Komarovsky, and McInerny is probably the first North American social science publication that uses the notion of leisure in its title in the modern sense, signifying discretionary time of large groups of urban and suburban population. In Lundberg's own words, he and his associates became interested in the problem of leisure because

> first, the amount of leisure time has been constantly increasing and seems destined to an even more rapid increase in the near future. Secondly, urban civilization and mechanical devices ... disrupted traditional leisure pursuits and the individual's control over his own spare time, thus compelling community recognition of the subject. (1934, p. 4)

The study on which Lundberg's publication rests was carried out between January 1932 and April 1933 in Westchester County, New York. It focused on a wealthy residential neighbourhood, a mixed suburb or satellite city, and a relatively poor residential neighbourhood. The authors' interest in suburbia was prompted by the fact that in the 1930s, suburbs in the United States were growing faster than the parent cities. Lundberg used modern survey techniques for the study of leisure, including time diaries and leisure participation questionnaires. A time-budget study of 2,460 individuals from Westchester County provided Lundberg with detailed information about the distribution of time between major daily and leisure activities among different occupational and gender groups.

Apart from the detailed information about the time use of America's urban and suburban population, the book covered a broad range of issues, such as organizational structure of community leisure and recreation, relationships between leisure and the family, leisure and church, leisure and school, and leisure and the arts. This produced a work that, in Meyersohn's words, has succeeded as no other study in "comprehending the social organization of leisure" (1969, p. 54).

According to Lundberg, the technological revolution and social changes in America profoundly affected leisure opportunities and activities.

> Spontaneous and informal neighbourhood life, which formerly provided a chief use of leisure, has largely disappeared as a result of the tremendous mobility of modern urban society. Neighbourhood life depends upon relative stability; it cannot flourish where a substantial part of the population moves every year or two. (1934, pp. 6–7)

Congested living quarters and the disappearance of the yard and other outdoor facilities have shifted recreation to the school, the club, and the commercial recreation place.

> Home and neighbourhood games and sports are supplanted by billiard "parlours" and public dance halls. Huge stadia offer a vicarious satisfaction for the urges that conditions no longer permit to fulfil directly. Instead of singing around the piano, we turn on the radio. (1934, pp. 6–7)

While some of these changes were disruptive, Lundberg did not see the situation as totally negative. In his opinion, the family was still the most stable nucleus of recreational activities in the suburb.

> Despite the inroads which clubs, sports, commercial amusements, the automobile, and the bridge game have made, the affectional and leisure functions of the family remain, even though many of the more overt recreational activities are carried on outside of the home. (1934, p. 189)

According to Lundberg, it is also doubtful whether modern leisure is more standardized than the leisure under simpler conditions. "The tremendous variety of products and facilities afforded by modern organizations, goods, and services, and the resulting opportunities for a broad latitude of choices, has probably offset the tendency toward standardization" (1934, p. 81).

The relationship between leisure and economy, and its social implications, concerned Lundberg greatly. Lundberg and his associates were aware of the arguments put forth by business and government, namely that intensified leisure consumption contributes to the flow of economic activities and stimulates production. They conceded that competitive consumption "undoubtedly keeps many out of mischief," yet, they could not suppress their uneasiness about this "charmed circle unpleasantly suggestive of a squirrel cage" (1934, p. 16). Leisure activities have, according to Lundberg, lost their essential nature as leisure. "One of the commonest of the ulterior ends toward which leisure activities tend to be perverted is that of competitive social status on a pecuniary basis" (1934, p. 82). As a result, an increasing number of people find themselves coerced into a meaningless round of "recreational" leisure activities, which they "heroically endure but which are devoid of capacity to minister to release of nervous tensions and to the development of personality" (1934, p. 17).

This analysis brings Lundberg logically to the conclusion that greater amounts of leisure time under existing conditions do not necessarily bring greater happiness. A shorter working day does not necessarily mean more leisure of a desired or desirable kind. Mere freedom from vigorous physical toil and long hours of labour, according to Lundberg, will not insure men against heavy and unhappy lives. "Clearly, something more than a short and easy working day, even with economic security, is needed before we have any assurance that the lives of men will be happier and lighter" (1934, p. 2).

The analysis of the conflict between the growing amounts of leisure and their poor use brings Lundberg and his associates into the realm of social policy. "It must be clear," Lundberg stated, "the main objects of striving are no longer to be attained through the mere accumulation of individual wealth. Health, personal security, and aesthetic satisfactions are increasingly dependent not upon individual wealth but upon community organization" (1934, p. 252). According to Lundberg, changing conditions of life made recreation a public concern "of the same basic character as education and health" (1934, p. 346).

Lundberg is a strong advocate of government intervention. He is not willing to concede leisure development to commercial recreation and competitive consumption. The issues are too complex to be treated on an individual or purely laissez-faire basis. Satisfaction of the leisure needs of one group increasingly infringes upon the interests of others or the larger interest of the community and culture. In this situation, the government is expected to engage experts, including social scientists, to ascertain societal priorities, and recommend means for their implementation.

> Public business has reached a degree of complexity where only expert professional administration should be tolerated in municipal and state, as well as in national, affairs. At present, the most profitable civic adult education is that which will convince people of their own incapacity to grasp many of the matters with which they are now struggling. (1934, p. 342)

This admirably frank, yet somewhat condescending, statement reflects the real complexities of modern-age management of public affairs, but unfortunately ignores the fact that experts' decisions are rarely independent and often bend to self-serving and special interests.

Lundberg was, perhaps, the first American social scientist before World War II to draw attention to the full impact of leisure on the future development of modern societies. He emphasized that the central problem before modern societies is that of "long hours of leisure for the masses of men" (1934, p. 10). He was aware, however, that it is not so much the amount of leisure time but the way it is or will be used that matter. The difference of greatest significance in the leisure of various groups is found, according to Lundberg, not in the total amount of leisure, nor in its distribution between different activities, but rather in the content and quality of its components.

Laying Foundations to Modern Studies of Leisure Phenomena

The post-World War II leisure research in North America (and to a certain extent in Europe) can be divided roughly into two periods: before and after 1965. The first period, from 1945 to the mid-1960s, is characterized by broad sociological conceptualizations and a widely shared consensus that leisure represents one of the focal concerns of modern civilization. The second period, after 1965, is characterized by a proliferation of specialized, technical, and applied studies, diversification of the disciplinary base of leisure research, and regretfully, a decline in the theoretical breadth of the analyses of leisure.

It is surprising to look at how much interest leisure generated among social scientists of the 1950s and 1960s. Relevant names include the following: David Riesman, Margaret Mead, Nels Anderson, Sebastian de Grazia, Martha Wolfenstein, Benett Berger, Robert Dubin, Harold Wilensky, Wilbert Moore, Rolf Meyersohn, and Max Kaplan in North America; Georges Friedmann, Pierre Naville, Jacques Ellul, and Joffre Dumazedier in France; and Reinhardt Wippler in the Netherlands. This was an extremely fruitful period for leisure research both intellectually and institutionally, as evidenced by the creation of the Chicago Centre for the Study of Leisure, the CNRS Group for the Study of Leisure and Popular Culture in Paris, and the UNESCO European Centre for Leisure and Education in Prague.

What are the links between the pre- and post-World War II research? What intellectual convergences or divergences does one discern when comparing these two periods? An attempt will be made to answer these questions by addressing three interrelated issues, which have "haunted" social scientists before and after World War II: (a) the relationships between leisure and social status, (b) the impact of cultural and technological factors on leisure, and (c) methodological challenges of capturing the role of leisure in modern societies.

Interest in the relationship between leisure and social status originated with Veblen. Few subsequent authors agreed with him. Most thought that Veblen erred in identifying leisure with social status. The Lynds, Lundberg, Riesman, Mills, and Wilensky have shown that upper classes in America were working hard rather than idling. According to Wilensky, "there is a general tendency for higher occupational strata to work long hours" (1963, p. 117). More specifically, "entrepreneurship is a powerful impetus to long hours of work" (1963, p. 120). Economists seemed to agree with Veblen about the role of social emulation in motivating consumption in modern societies, but rejected Veblen's moral critique of this phenomenon (Duesenberry, 1949; Hayek, 1965). Kaplan (1960) and Anderson (1961) in the United States, and Dumazedier (1957) in France, questioned Veblen's views of the status-conferral role of leisure, and emphasized instead mass leisure's contribution to greater equality in modern societies.

Yet Veblen's views continue to hold fascination with many students of leisure. One finds direct allusions to Veblen's views in the Lynds' analyses of Middletown's social life, in Lundberg's critique of the conspicuous consumption of New York suburbanites, and in Riesman's analyses of the fads and fashions of the "other-directed" America. Riesman did not consider himself a "devotee" of Veblen and downplayed Veblen's dismissal of supposedly vicarious needs, yet the "other-directed" America he so vividly portrayed, displays many Veblenesque features. "When I observe women on the beach or in the backyard suffering from sun, sand, and insects in order to become appropriately tanned," he wrote, "I sometimes wonder whether the management of corsets was more uncomfortable than of bare skin now" (1953, p. 177).

One recognizes Veblen's overtones in Berger's (1963) comments on Americans' fascination with cowboys, detectives, bull fighters, and sports-car racers as opposed to computer programmers, accountants, and executives, as well as in Seeley's (1956) analyses of the status-driven world of Crestwood Heights, or in Wilensky's (1964) discussion of the role of mass culture in the mass society. It seems that Veblen is more influential today than he is given credit for. He has created a "vision," a lens of sorts, and we can't help but see things through that lens. What was originally conceived by Veblen as a critique of the upper classes of nineteenth-century America became a telling metaphor of the middle classes and "mass society" of the twentieth century. Veblen's sarcasm may have been misdirected, but paradoxically, it turned prophetic.

American authors, unlike their European counterparts, often examined leisure in the context of cultural (value) change rather than technological progress. This is true of the Lynds, for whom changing leisure ways are as much a product of technical innovations and economic change, as they are a reflection of the newly emerging interests and values of the business and working classes. For Riesman, the changing role of leisure in modern America is tied foremost to the change in value orientations from those of inner-directedness to other-directedness, from production to consumption. The same theme is brilliantly addressed by Leo Lowenthal (1961) in his discussion of the shifts in Americans' reading allegiances from the "idols of production" to the "idols of consumption," and in Martha Wolfenstein's (1951) provocative comments about Americans' conversion to "fun morality." Margaret Mead (1957) associated leisure's growing importance in America with a shift of values from work to family, and Daniel Bell (1976) suggested that in the conflict between society's functional imperatives and its cultural values, the latter may have taken a lead in the 1960s.

Of course, greater emphasis on cultural values than on technological change is only a matter of degree. All of the aforementioned authors are aware of the importance of technical and economic changes, as well as of the impact of urbanization, industrialization, and mechanization on modern leisure. Yet cultural rather than technological and economic factors are in the forefront of their attention. Regretfully, this tradition may have ceased to inspire contemporary authors and we are missing an in-depth analysis of the cultural rather than technological underpinning of leisure trends at the turn of the two millennia.

Commenting on the sociological study of leisure of the 1960s, Bennett Berger pointed out its methodological shortcomings. According to Berger,

> theoretical relevance is precisely what is missing from most of the contemporary work in the sociology of leisure. The sociology of leisure today is little else than a reporting of survey data on what selected samples of individuals do with their time in which they are not working and the correlation of these data with conventional demographic variables. (1963, p. 28)

The situation described by Berger, contrasts sharply with that of the 1920s and 1930s, but unfortunately it very much resembles the one we face today. Although demographic variables used in today's analyses may be more varied than they were in the 1960s, much of current leisure discourse lacks theoretical breadth and conceptual anchorage.

The lack of theoretical focus, pointed out by Berger, may be in part related to an excessive emphasis put in modern survey research on random and representative sampling. According to Meyersohn, if the subject of leisure studies should shift from the duration to the process and meaning of leisure,

> the unit of analysis should shift from the disembodied individual, randomly selected, to the various communities which provide the relevant context for leisure activities. Above all, leisure is a social phenomenon: the meaning and importance of leisure activities are provided by the groups in which activities are shared. These groups are systematically ignored in random sampling of individuals and can only be captured in research designs which treat as their unit of analysis the groups in which particular leisure interests occur. (1972, p. 227)

In this regard books with a specific community or sub-cultural focus, born out of the *Middletown* tradition, such as Hollingshead's *Elmtown's Youth* (1949) and Seeley, Sim and Looseley's *Crestwood Heights* (1956), make survey data "meaningful through their linkage to a theory of community or class or subculture or whatever the dominant focus of the book in question happens to be" (Berger, 1963, p. 27).

In our discussion we tried to assess the relative contribution of educational and social science writings of the 1920s and the 1930s to our understanding of modern leisure. Our preference clearly lies with the analytical writings of social scientists rather than the moralistic and prescriptive writings of the educators. It lies with theoretical and conceptual relevancy rather than superficial social commentary, and with methodological complexity rather than shallow descriptiveness. It remains to be seen to what extent these qualities, present in the pre-World War II and early post-war leisure research, continue to inform our present-day leisure inquiry.

REFERENCES

Anderson, N. (1961). *Work and leisure*. London, UK: Routledge & Kegan Paul.

Bell, D. (1976). *The cultural contradictions of capitalism*. New York, NY: Basic Books.

Berger, B. M. (1963). The sociology of leisure: Some suggestions. In E. O. Smigel (Ed.), *Work and leisure*. New Haven, CT: College and University Press.

Brightbill, C. K. (1960). *The challenge of leisure*. Englewood Cliffs, NJ: Prentice Hall.

Burns, C. D. (1932). *Leisure in the modern world*. Washington, DC: McGrath Publishing.

Cutten, G. (1926). *The threat of leisure*. New Haven, CT: Yale University Press.

Davis, J. E. (1936). *Principles and practice of recreational therapy*. New York, NY: A. S. Barnes & Co.

Davis, J. E. (1938). *Play and mental health*. Washington, DC: McGrath Publishing.

Dubin, R. (1956). Industrial workers' worlds: A study of the "central life interests" of industrial workers. *Social Problems, 3*(3).

Dumazedier, J. (1957). Ambiguite du loisir et dynamique socioculturelle. *Cahiers Internationaux de Sociologie, No XXIII,* 75–76.

Dumazedier, J. (1967). *Toward a society of leisure*. New York, NY: The Free Press.

Durant, H. (1938). *The problem of leisure*. London, UK: Routledge.

Dusenberry, J. S. (1949). *Income, saving and the theory of consumer behavior.* Cambridge, MA: Harvard University Press.

Friedmann, G. (1961). *The anatomy of work: Labor, leisure and the implications of automation*. Glencoe, IL: The Free Press.

Fulk, J. R. (1922). *The municipalization of play and recreation*. Washington, DC: McGrath Publishing.

de Grazia, S. de. (1962). *Of time, work, and leisure*. New York, NY: The Twentieth Century Fund.

Hayek, F. A. (1965). The non sequitur of the "dependence effect." In E. S. Phelps (Ed.), *Private wants and public needs*. New York, NY: W. W. Norton.

Hirsch, F. (1976). *Social limits to growth*. New York, NY: The Twentieth Century Fund.

Hollingshead, A. (1949). *Elmtown's youth*. New York, NY: Wiley.

Jacks, L. P. (1931). *The education of the whole man*. New York, NY: Harper & Brothers.

Kaplan, M. (1960). *Leisure in America*. New York, NY: Wiley.

Larrabee, E., & Meyersohn, R. (Eds.). (1958). *Mass leisure*. Glencoe, IL: The Free Press.

Lies, E. T. (1933). *The new leisure challenges for the schools*. Washington, DC: McGrath Publishing.

Linder, S. B. (1970). *The harried leisure class*. New York, NY: Columbia University Press.

Lowenthal, L. (1961). *Literature, popular culture, and society*. Englewood Cliffs, NJ: Prentice Hall.

Lundberg, G. A., Komarovsky, M., & McInerny, M. A. (1934). *Leisure—A suburban study*. New York, NY: Columbia University Press.

Lynd, R. S., & Lynd, H. M. (1929). *Middletown: A study in contemporary American culture*. New York, NY: Harcourt, Brace & World.

Lynd, R. S., & Lynd, H. M. (1937). *Middletown in transition: A study in cultural conflicts*. New York, NY: Harcourt, Brace & World.

Mead, M. (1957). The pattern of leisure in contemporary American culture. *The Annals of the American Academy of Political and Social Science, 313*, 11–15.

Meyersohn, R. (1958). A comprehensive bibliography on leisure, 1900–1958. In E. Larrabee & R. Meyersohn (Eds.), *Mass leisure* (pp. 389–419). Glencoe, IL: The Free Press.

Meyersohn, R. (1969, Winter). The sociology of leisure in the United States: Introduction and bibliography, 1945–1965. *Journal of Leisure Research, 1*(1), 53–68.

Meyersohn, R. (1972). Leisure. In A. Campbell & P. E. Converse (Eds.), *The human meaning of social change*. New York, NY: Russell Sage Foundation.

Mills, C. W. (1953). Introduction to the mentor edition of Veblen's *The Theory of the Leisure Class*.

Mitchell, G. D. (1968). *A hundred years of sociology*. London, UK: Gerald Duckworth.

Moore, W. E. (1963). *Man, time, and society*. New York, NY: John Wiley and Sons.

Nash, J. B. (1953). *Philosophy of recreation and leisure*. St. Louis, MO: The C.V. Mosby Co.

Overstreet, A. B. (1934). *A guide to civilized leisure*. New York, NY: W. W. Norton.

Riesman, D. (1950). *The lonely crowd*. New Haven, CT: Yale University Press.

Riesman, D. (1953). *Thorstein Veblen: A critical interpretation*. NewYork, NY: Seabury Press.

Rosenberg, B. (Ed.). (1970). *Thorstein Veblen*. New York, NY: Thomas Y. Crowell.

Seeley, J. R., Sim, A. R., & Loosley, B. W. (1956). *Crestwood Heights*. New York, NY: Basic Books.

Van Doren C., & Hodges, L. (1975). *America's park and recreation heritage: A chronology*. Washington, DC: U.S. Government Printing Office.

Veblen, T. (1899). *The theory of the leisure class*. MacMillan (cited from the 1953 New York Mentor Book edition).

Wallich, H. C. (1965). Public versus private: Could Galbraith be wrong? In E. S. Phelps (Ed.), *Private wants and public needs*. New York, NY: W. W. Norton.

Warner W. L., & Lunt, P. S. (1941). *The social life of a modern community*. New Haven, CT: Yale University Press.

Weir, L. H. (1928). *Parks: A manual of municipal and county parks*. New York, NY: A. S. Barnes and Company.

Wilensky, H. (1963). The uneven distribution of leisure: The impact of economic growth on "free time." In E. O. Smigel (Ed.), *Work and leisure*. New Haven, CT: College and University Press.

Wilensky, H. (1964). Mass society and mass culture. *American Sociological Review, XXIX*, 173–197.

Wippler, R. (1970). Leisure behaviour: A multivariate approach. *Sociologia Neerlandica, VI*, 1.

Wissler C. (1929). Foreword to the 1929 edition of Lynds' *Middletown*. New York, NY: Harcourt, Brace & World.

Wolfenstein, M. (1951). The emergence of fun morality. *Journal of Social Issues, 7*(4), 15–25.

PART I: Leisure in Canada

Section A: Understanding Leisure

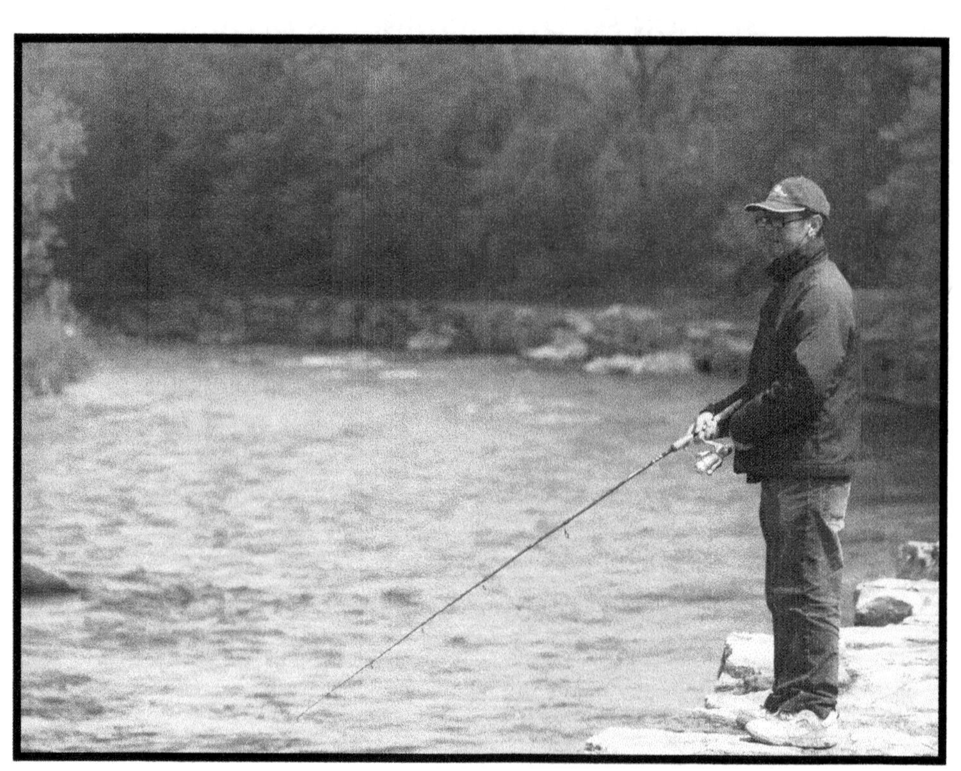

Chapter 1
Defining Leisure

Paul Heintzman, Ph.D.
University of Ottawa

Before you begin reading this chapter, take a few minutes and write down your own definition of leisure. As you read this chapter reflect on how your definition is similar to or different from those presented in the chapter.

Learning Objectives

After reading this chapter, students will be able to

1. Understand why it is important to define leisure.
2. Understand the major Western concepts of leisure.
3. Understand the historical evolution of the leisure concept.
4. Be aware of non-Western views of leisure.
5. Develop their own definition of leisure.

Introduction

> Imagine ... the bewilderment a naïve researcher suffers when discovering leisure may be free time, freedom, an activity, a state of mind, or a license of some sort... leisure studies is plagued by conceptual confusion... (Sylvester, 1990, p. 292)

In this chapter, we will not eliminate all the confusion, but hopefully by the end of the chapter, you will be able to understand the major ways that leisure has been defined in the Western world. Since Canada is an increasingly multicultural society we will very briefly introduce "non-Western" views of leisure, keeping in mind that we need to be cautious when equating non-Western views and words with Western views (see Chapter 21). Our approach will be historical in that we will start with earlier understandings of leisure and illustrate how the concept of leisure has evolved over time. An historical perspective helps us to understand how past ideas and events have shaped current ideas about leisure. The concepts in Table 1.1 will be covered.

Why should we define leisure? First, developing your own understanding of leisure has relevance for your life. Second, if you anticipate working in the leisure services field, it is important for you to develop an understanding of leisure as a foundation for your work. Third, an understanding of the common definitions of leisure will be helpful to you when working with a diversity of Canadians who hold a variety of understandings of leisure.

Table 1.1

Concept	Key idea(s)
Classical leisure	A state of being; an attitude
Leisure as activity	Non-work activity
Leisure as free time	Time after work and existence tasks
Leisure as a symbol of social class	Conspicuous consumption
Leisure as a state of mind	An optimal psychological experience
Feminist leisure	Meaningful experience; enjoyment
Holistic leisure	Leisure in all of life

Etymological Background of Leisure

Etymology is concerned with where a word came from and the development of its meaning. The English word "leisure" derives from the Latin *licere* by way of the French, *leisere*. The root word, *licere*, which means to be allowed and implies freedom from restraint, also evolved into the English word "license" (Owens, 1981). Literally, leisure meant permission in regard to the opportunity provided when one was free from legal occupation. Most Roman writers employed *otium* to denote the idea of leisure. *Otium* was linked with contemplation and opportunity for freedom from both time and occupation (Arnold, 1991). The Greek equivalent of Latin's *licere* and *otium* is *schole*, which can be traced to the same root as that of the Greek verb "to have" (Owens, 1981). de Grazia (1964, p. 10) elaborates: "The etymological root of *schole* meant to halt or cease, hence to have quiet or peace. Later it meant to have time to spare or, specially, time for oneself." The notion of leisure was expressed positively, signifying that it was valued more highly than work, while work was viewed negatively as *ascholia*. Likewise, in Latin, business was *negotium*.

Latin and Greek notions of leisure were closely associated with education: in Greek leisure is *schole* and in Latin, *schola*, the English "school." Therefore the word school, used to indicate the place where education takes place, comes from a word, which means leisure. Furthermore, the Greek concept of leisure is the origin of the division between the liberal arts and servile work. Liberal arts with the idea of education for its own sake, reflects the Greek notion of leisure.

The Classical View of Leisure: Leisure as a State of Being

The **classical view** emphasizes "contemplation, enjoyment of self in search of knowledge, debate, politics, and cultural enlightenment" (Murphy, 1974, p. 3). "Classical" refers to ancient civilizations, and, thus, in the Western world, it refers to the view of leisure in ancient societies such as Greece and Rome. In ancient Greece, there were clear distinctions between work, recreation, and leisure. Work was a means to provide for life's needs, recreation was rest from work, and leisure was the noblest pursuit in life. The ideal lifestyle consisted of leisure, but this lifestyle was dependent on a society where slaves, who made up 80% of the population, did most of the work.

The Greek philosopher Aristotle (384–322 BCE) believed that while work was important, leisure was an even more worthy endeavour: "Both occupation and leisure are necessary; but ... leisure is higher than occupation, and is the end to which occupation is directed" (*Politics*, trans. 1963, Book VIII, iii, 3). He wrote, "We do business in order that we may have leisure" (*Nicomachean Ethics*, trans. 1947, Book X, vii, 6). Rest and recreation were good, but not the highest good: "Happiness is not found in amusements.... For amusement is a form of rest; but we need rest because we are not able to go on working without a break, and therefore it is not an end, since we take it as a means to further activity" (*Nicomachean Ethics*, X, vi, 3).

Aristotle equated leisure with "freedom from the necessity of labour" (*Politics*, II, ix, 2), thus the person of leisure was free from the need to work for life's necessities and could focus on other things. For Aristotle, leisure, unlike recreation, was engaged in for its own sake: "We think of it [leisure] as having in itself intrinsic pleasure, intrinsic happiness, intrinsic felicity" (*Politics*, VIII, iii, 4). Leisure was closely related to *diagoge*, or cultivation of mind, and contemplation, or the search for truth. Aristotle viewed leisure as necessary for virtue, ethical development, and good government: "Leisure is a necessity, both for growth in goodness and for the pursuit of political activities" (*Politics*, VII, ix, 4). Education was to prepare a person for leisure and was to be distinguished from studies that prepared a person for work:

> There are some branches of learning and education which ought to be studied with a view to the proper use of leisure in the cultivation of the mind ... these studies should be regarded as ends in themselves, while studies pursued with a view to occupation should be regarded merely as a means and matters of necessity. (*Politics*, VIII, iii, 6)

Although Aristotle's view of leisure has received much attention, his view reflected that of aristocratic philosophers and a variety of perspectives on leisure probably existed in ancient Greek society (Sylvester, 1999).

How was Aristotle's view of leisure related to his understanding of (1) work, (2) recreation, and (3) education? Drawing a diagram might be a helpful way to understand these relationships.

While a criticism of the Greek ideal of leisure was that it was based on a society supported by slavery, as the classical view developed and evolved it did not necessarily continue to be associated with slavery. In Roman society, *otium,* the Latin word for leisure, was linked to contemplation and freedom; however, over time, *otium* was viewed for *negotium's* (work's) sake.

The Greek ideal of leisure was also modified in early Christianity where it became associated with the contemplative or spiritual life. Augustine (354–440 CE), a theologian and bishop, noted that there were three types of life: the life of leisure, the life of action, and the combined life of action and leisure. All of these lives were worthwhile as long as the life of leisure did not ignore the needs of one's neighbour and the life of action did not ignore the contemplation of God. For Augustine, leisure involved the "investigation and discovery of truth ... and no one is debarred from devoting himself to the pursuit of truth, for that involves a praiseworthy kind of leisure" (1972, Book XIX, ch. 19, p. 880).

Thomas Aquinas (1225–1274), a prominent theologian of the Middle Ages who brought together Aristotle's thought with Christian teachings, located Aristotle's notion of leisure and contemplation in the blessed vision of God. The contemplative understanding of leisure was also an important part of monastic culture, where the work of monks was united with the contemplative life of leisure (*otium*) (Leclerq, 1984). This tradition continued in the Roman Catholic theologian and philosopher Josef Pieper (1904–1997), who defined leisure as "a mental and spiritual attitude ... a condition of the soul ... a receptive attitude of mind, a contemplative attitude" in his book *Leisure: The Basis of Culture* (1963, pp. 40–41).

Today, the classical view of leisure is advocated by many in the Roman Catholic tradition (e.g., Doohan, 1990) who, like Pieper, see leisure as a spiritual attitude, and by leisure scholars, who see value in Aristotelian philosophy. For example, Sylvester (1990) has emphasized that classical leisure, unlike some more recent concepts of leisure, involved the virtue of moral judgment; it was important to use leisure rightly. Hemingway (1988) has highlighted that Aristotle viewed leisure as the arena through which an individual developed character and participated in the affairs of the community.

The classical Western view of leisure has some similarities with the classical Hindu view of leisure (Kashyap, 1991). In Hinduism, a distinction is made between *Pravritti*, the active life, and *Nivritti*, the contemplative life, which is associated with leisure. *Nishkam-karma-yoga* or inner leisure is characterized by a relaxing peace and a mind free from turmoil.

Is the classical view of leisure relevant to today's society?

Leisure as Activity

The **leisure as activity** view of leisure may be defined as "non-work activity in which people engage during their free time—apart from obligations of work, family and society" (Murphy, 1974, p. 4). Historically, the activity view of leisure was usually a utilitarian view, that is, the activity was engaged in to achieve a benefit such as physical health. In this view, leisure has often been subservient to work and associated with a rhythm to life of work and recreation. More recently, the leisure-as-activity concept has not necessarily been a utilitarian view.

As mentioned earlier, in Roman society *otium* (leisure) began to be for *negotium's* (work's) sake. Cicero (106–43 BCE) viewed leisure as "virtuous activities" by which a person "grows morally, intellectually, and spiritually" (as quoted by Stebbins, 1982, p. 268). Typical of Roman writers, he suggested a person is occupied in the work of the military, politics, or business and then re-creates (de Grazia, 1964). The classical view of leisure was gradually forgotten, work became the noblest activity, and leisure took the form of activity, or recreation, to re-create oneself to go back to work. This view was reinforced during the Renaissance (fourteenth to sixteenth century) and the Reformation (sixteenth century). During the Renaissance, as illustrated by the saying "a person is the measure of all things," there was a focus upon the unlimited potential of humans and on the present world rather than life after death. As a result, work was given greater value and non-work activities were seen as important to create a sound body and mind.

The Protestant reformers (sixteenth century) rejected the classical and medieval distinction between the active (secular) life and the contemplative (spiritual) life. For them, all of life and work was sacred. For the reformer Martin Luther (1483–1546) every activity, including non-work activities, could be used to glorify God (Luther, 1965). John Calvin (1509–1564) was opposed to excesses but approved of participation in the arts, games, and social parties as long as they contributed to the rhythm of life: "no where are we prohibited to laugh, or to be satiated with food, or to annex new possessions ... or to be delighted with musical harmony, or to drink wine" (1813, p. 316). The Puritans, who were enthusiastic reformers, frowned upon over-indulgence and destructive activities but celebrated life. While non-work activities often served work, as illustrated by Benjamin Colman's (1673–1747) comment that "we daily need some respite and diversion, without which, we dull our Powers; a little intermission sharpens 'em again" (as quoted in Miller & Johnson, 1963, p. 392), the use of leisure for instrumental purposes happily co-existed with enjoyment in the Puritan view (Johnson, 2009).

A modern proponent of the activity view of leisure was the French sociologist Joffre Dumazedier (1915–2002), who wrote: "Leisure is activity—apart from the obligations of work, family and society—to which the individual turns at will, for relaxation, diversion, or broadening his knowledge and his spontaneous social participation, the free exercise of his creative capacity" (1967, pp. 16–17).

Dumazedier believed that leisure had three functions: relaxation, entertainment, and development of personality.

Based upon an activity understanding of leisure, Robert Stebbins has recently developed the concepts of **serious leisure, casual leisure, and project-based leisure** (see Chapter 8). He defined serious leisure as "the systematic pursuit of ... an activity that participants find so substantial and interesting that ... they launch themselves on a career centered on acquiring and expressing its special skills, knowledge, and experience" (1999, p. 69). He identified three types of serious leisure: amateurs (e.g., amateur artists), hobbyists (e.g., collectors), and volunteers (e.g., social welfare volunteers). The distinctive qualities of serious leisure are as follows:

a. the need to persevere in the activity;
b. finding a career of achievement or involvement in the activity;
c. making a significant personal effort in the activity;
d. obtaining long-lasting tangible or intangible benefits or rewards through the activity;
e. strong identification with the chosen activity; and
f. a unique ethos or social world of the participants who engage in the activity.

In contrast, Stebbins defined casual leisure as "an immediately, intrinsically rewarding, relatively short-lived pleasurable activity requiring little or no special training to enjoy it" (1997, p. 18). Casual leisure may involve play, relaxation, passive or active entertainment, conversation, sensory stimulation, or casual volunteering. The central characteristic of casual leisure is pleasure.

Project-based leisure is "a short-term, moderately complicated, ...though infrequent, creative undertaking carried out in free time" (Stebbins, 2005, p. 2), which involves considerable effort and planning and sometimes knowledge and skill. These may be one-shot projects such as investigating one's genealogy or occasional projects such as decorating one's home for Christmas every year.

Defined as activity, leisure may have political or social purposes. Leisure may be seen as a form of political practice where everyday leisure activities can challenge or weaken dominant belief systems, thereby serving as a form of resistance (Shaw, 2001; see Chapter 7). Mair (2002/2003) has used the term civil leisure to describe people who use their non-work time for social activism concerning important societal issues.

The activity view of leisure has relevance in Islam (Martin & Mason, 2004). The prophet Mohammed (570–633 CE) stated: "Recreate your hearts hour after hour, for the tired hearts go blind" and "Teach your children swimming, shooting, and horseback riding" (Ibrahim, 1991, p. 206). In Islam, leisure activities fulfill three desires:

a. amusement, relaxation and, laughter;

b. rhythmic tunes and the experience of objects through the senses; and

c. the desire to wonder, learn, and gain knowledge.

What Is Recreation?

There is generally more consensus about the meaning of recreation than the meaning of leisure. The English word "recreation" is derived from the Latin word *recreatio*, which means restoration or recovery. This notion implies the re-creation of energy or the restoration of the ability to perform a specific function and therefore presupposes that some other activity has depleted one's energy or has negatively affected the ability to function.

de Grazia (1964) defined recreation as "activity that rests men from work often giving them a change (distraction, diversion) and restores (re-creates) them for work" (p. 233). Recreation may also be used to restore a person for volunteer, family, education, or health purposes. Unlike some understandings of leisure, such as the classical view where leisure is an end in itself, recreation is not engaged in "for its own sake," but represents a means to an end. For example, Kelly (1990) defined recreation as "voluntary non-work activity that is organized for the attainment of personal and social benefits including restoration and social cohesion" (p. 27). Therefore we can conclude that the concept of recreation is similar to the leisure as activity concept.

How do you see the relationship between the concepts of leisure and recreation?

Leisure as Free Time

We have also thought of leisure as **free time**. This is a quantitative perspective that defines leisure as "that portion of time which remains when time for work and basic requirements for existence have been satisfied" (Murphy, 1974, p. 3). Life may be divided into existence (taking care of biological needs such as sleeping and eating), subsistence (work), and leisure (discretionary or non-obligated time).

In preindustrial societies, time was viewed cyclically; that is, time was rooted in the rhythms of the natural world. People's lives revolved around sunrise and sunset, the change of seasons, and the planting and harvesting of crops. They were unlikely to separate work and leisure within their daily lives, and the demands of work were often lightened by songs and storytelling. Traditional gatherings like a barn-raising or a quilting bee possessed both leisure and work-like components. As a result, notions of work and leisure blended together.

The Industrial Revolution (1760–1830), however, changed everything. Unlike previous eras, the work of the industrial age was focused not on the farm, but in the factory. People began to move to the cities to tend the machines. Work was now situated *in space* at the factory and structured *in time* as the worker had to be at the workplace at a certain time to perform work duties. Facilitated by the development of clocks, work could be assigned to specific times, and work could be measured precisely. Time began to be viewed mechanically, and this linear notion of time began to influence and change people's understanding of leisure. Time away from work was free of the often unpleasant demands of the workspace, so it was called *free time*. This free time became synonymous with leisure.

When leisure is viewed as free time, the amount of leisure a person has depends on factors such as how long a person lives, when a person retires, the length of a person's work week, whether a person has a full-time job, a part-time job or a second job, the length of vacations and other paid time off. Furthermore, the size and timing of the units of free time are as important as the total amount of free time. For example, free time is different for a person who works eight hours a day for five days per week than a person who works ten hours a day for four days per week.

This view of leisure as free time influences how we think and talk about leisure today. We talk about leisure time as time away from work. Even the most rudimentary examination of our daily lives tells us that this view is overly simplistic. Is leisure simply the time when you are not eating, sleeping, studying, or in class? The free time view of leisure reduces leisure to a quantity of time and says nothing about the quality of that time. It assumes that more free time equates with more leisure.

The Jewish concept of Sabbath has some similarities to the notion of leisure as free time. The Jewish Scriptures command the Jewish people not to work on the Sabbath. For example, Exodus 20:8–11 reads, "Remember the Sabbath day by keeping it holy. Six days you shall labour and do all your work, but the seventh day is a Sabbath to the Lord your God." The Sabbath is a time of no work but also a time of celebration: "not a date but an atmosphere" (Heschel, 1951, p. 21). Thus, it does not completely fit within a quantitative free-time understanding of leisure but also includes a qualitative dimension (Heintzman, 2006). Sabbath was not only the foundation of Jewish life, but it also provided a more democratic form of leisure than in Greek society. Aristotle's leisure was based on the ancient Greek institution of slavery, whereas the Jewish Torah declared that everyone, including male and female servants, had an inalienable right to Sabbath (Gordis, 1982). The Jewish Sabbath was adopted and modified in the Christian Sunday and Islamic Friday. While it is often suggested that the roots of the Western concept of leisure are in ancient Greek society, some argue that it is equally rooted in the ancient Jewish tradition of the Sabbath with its organization of life into seven days and a valuing of leisure (Crabtree, 1982; Trafton, 1985).

Draw a circle for your average weekday. Divide the circle according to the time you devote to existence, subsistence, and leisure. List your main activities in each category.

Leisure as a Symbol of Social Class: Conspicuous Consumption

The concept of leisure as a **symbol of social class** views "leisure as a way of life for the rich elite" (Murphy, 1974, p. 92). In 1899, the American sociologist Thorstein Veblen wrote a classic book titled *The Theory of the Leisure Class* in which he questioned the intrinsic character of leisure activities and suggested that leisure behaviour was influenced by the desire to impress others and distinguish oneself from other people. He defined leisure as "non-productive consumption of time. Time is consumed non-productively (1) from a sense of the unworthiness of productive work, and (2) as an evidence of pecuniary ability to afford a life of idleness" (Veblen, 1899/1953, p. 46). He used the terms "conspicuous leisure" and "conspicuous consumption" to suggest that the visible display of leisure and consuming was more important than engaging in the leisure activity for its own sake. Thus, leisure had a symbolic nature. He suggested that wealthy classes throughout time have been identified by their possessions and by their use of leisure while lower classes emulate or imitate the wealthy classes so that society becomes increasingly consumptive (see Chapter 26). An article in the *Financial Post* titled "Ridiculously, Deliciously Conspicuous Consumption" reflects Veblen's theory (Siddiqi, 2003). The subtitle of the article illustrates the emulation principle: "Imagine that money's no object, that you're one of the elite making ultra-luxury goods the hot trend of the season. Now go ahead and drool." The items described included an $85,000 designer piano and bejewelled underwear worth $11 million.

In an ethnographic study titled *The Native Leisure Class: Consumption and Cultural Creativity in the Andes*, Rudi Colloredo-Mansfeld (1999) documents how the sale of textiles gave rise to an indigenous leisure class in Otavalo, a market town in northern Ecuador. The merchant elite has become a leisure class characterized by the consumption of both local (e.g., fajas) and global (e.g., televisions, automobiles) products. Wealthy Otavalena women show off their wealth by wearing a new faja (sash) for every social occasion, thereby creating an overt symbol of class division. Consumption has become culturally important and a primary way to obtain stature in that the wealthy display their identity through their conspicuous consumption rather than through their work.

Is the theory of the leisure class applicable to our society?

Leisure as a State of Mind: A Psychological Experience

The state of mind view of leisure, also known as **subjective leisure or leisure as psychological experience**, became prominent in the 1980s. It may be defined as "an experience that results from recreation engagements" (Driver & Tocher, 1970, p. 10); however, it often focuses on the optimal leisure experience. This psychological experience can include properties such as the following:

a. emotions and moods;

b. levels of intensity, such as relaxation, arousal, activation;

c. cognitive components, such as ideas and images;

d. perceptions of how quickly time is passing;

e. self-consciousness and self-awareness;

f. levels of absorption, attention, and concentration;

g. feelings of competence in regards to knowledge or skill;

h. and a sense of freedom. (Mannell & Kleiber, 1997)

The state-of-mind view defines leisure as an overriding experience that is not defined in contrast to work, but rather certain conditions are necessary to experience it.

The state-of-mind view is founded upon psychology. The psychologist William James introduced the term *stream of consciousness* in 1890 to refer to mental experiences or conscious states perceived as ever-changing and continuous. Another psychologist, Abraham Maslow, suggested that self-actualizers experienced peak experiences, which he defined as "moments of highest happiness and fulfillment" (1968, p. 73). Building on the work of psychologists, an early leisure scholar, John Neulinger defined pure leisure as: "A state of mind brought about by an activity freely engaged in and done for its own sake" (1981, p. 18). The two criteria for this experience are *perceived freedom* (the perception that a person is engaging in the activity because one has the choice to do so and desires to do it) and *intrinsic motivation*

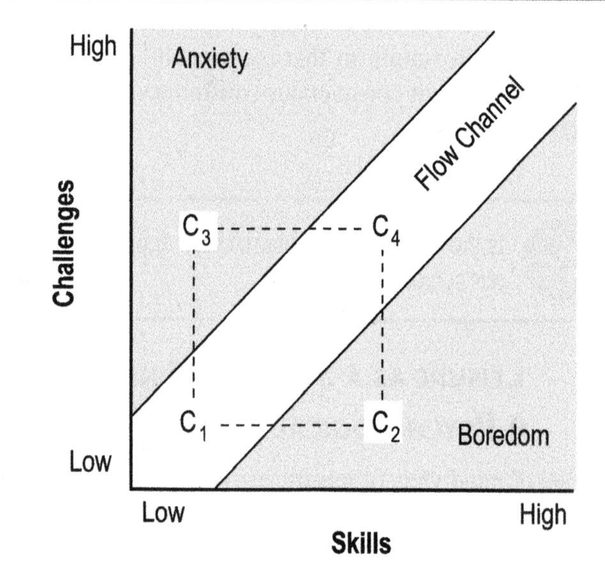

Figure 1.1 Csikszentmihalyi's Flow Model. Adapted from Mannell & Kleiber (1997).

What Is Play?

As we will see in Chapter 2 by Henle on play, leisure as a state of mind shares many traits with play: intrinsic motivation, free choice, suspension of reality, and positive affect.

Johann Huizinga (1955, p. 13) defined play as "a free activity standing quite consciously outside 'ordinary life' as being not 'serious' but at the same time absorbing the player intensely and utterly."

How do you see the relationship between the concepts of leisure and play?

(the individual gains satisfaction from the activity itself and not from an external reward).

Another psychological concept frequently associated with the state-of-mind view of leisure is the theory of *flow*. The social psychologist Mihalyi Csikszentmihalyi (1975) proposed that flow experiences were intensely absorbing experiences where the challenge of an activity matched the skill level of the individual so that the person lost track of both time and awareness of self (C_1 and C_4 on Figure 1.1). If a person's skills were much higher than the challenges of the activity, the person would experience boredom (C_2), while if the challenges were much higher than the skills a person would experience anxiety (C_3).

Jing Jie, the highest goal in life and highest pursuit of Chinese Taoist leisure, has been suggested to be similar to flow (Wang & Stringer, 2000). In Taoism, *Jing Jie*, an essence characterized by happiness and joyfulness that underlies all organic life, cannot be pursued but is a benefit of participation in activities such as martial arts, creative arts, or meditation. The Chinese experience of *rùmí*, a fascinating, enchanting, and absorbing experience, has also been shown to be similar to leisure as psychological experience (Walker & Deng, 2003/2004).

The state-of-mind view of leisure has been criticized as being concerned with private psychological experiences characterized by contentment, satisfaction, and well-being with little to say about the ethics and morality of these experiences (Sylvester, 1990). For example, participation in a criminal activity may provide an optimal psychological experience but not be ethical (see Chapter 18). Furthermore, the state-of-mind perspective has been criticized because of its emphasis upon optimal experience as an ideal outcome. This perspective seems to neglect the importance of less intense, but equally important, experiences like relaxation and "just being" (Kleiber, 2000). As Kleiber suggested, positive emotions can arise from relaxation as much as from action.

Do you agree with Sylvester's and Kleiber's critiques? Why or why not?

Feminist Leisure: Meaningful Experience

The contemporary women's movement emerged in the 1960s but it was not until the late 1980s that much attention was devoted to women's leisure (Henderson, Bialeschki, Shaw, & Freysinger, 1996; see Chapter 20). While there are a variety of feminist perspectives, all views stress that women are exploited and oppressed, and that women have a universal right to leisure. Feminist theory is critical of the traditional views of leisure (i.e., free time, activity) because they are built on premises that in many cases do not apply to women. For example, the free-time view of leisure is based on a duality of paid work and leisure that is not necessarily applicable to some women whose work is at home, nor even to those who work outside the home. Also some women feel they are not entitled to, or have, time for leisure. Feminist theory also critiques the activity concept of leisure because women often have obligations intertwined with "recreational activities"; for example, caring for children while swimming. Thus work and leisure may occur simultaneously, while leisure activities are frequently fragmented by the carrying out of responsibilities.

Furthermore, there are unique constraints on women's participation in leisure activities (see Chapter 9). Intrapersonal constraints include an ethic of care where women feel responsibility to care for others—their children, parents, spouse—sometimes to the point of feeling they have no right to leisure, ultimately limiting their leisure access. Interpersonal constraints, such as social control by others, and structural constraints, such as fear for personal safety and lack of provided opportunities to participate, also place limits on women's activity participation. Meanwhile, leisure as psychological experience is criticized as being focused too much on the individual with not enough recognition of situational and social factors (Henderson et al., 1996).

The result of much feminist research on leisure has led to an enhanced understanding of leisure as **meaningful experience** characterized by **enjoyment** (Henderson et al., 1996). These meaningful experiences may be found in many aspects of life. Often, meaningful experience is associated with time for self to relax and do nothing, affiliative leisure that involves relationships with other people such as friends and family, and autonomy where one can express oneself through self-determined (as opposed to determined by other people) or agentic leisure. Because meaningful experience is emphasized on this model, the activity, social setting, or physical location is seen as a leisure container in which the experience of leisure may take place. Feminists also speak of leisure enablers, the opposite of leisure constraints, which allow and facilitate leisure experiences. An example of a leisure enabler is a sense of entitlement to leisure. Leisure may also provide women with the opportunity to engage in acts of resistance that challenge the dominant values of society and thereby lead to women's empowerment.

Feminist observations about intrapersonal (e.g., ethic of care) and interpersonal (e.g., social control by others) constraints on women's leisure also exist in non-Western cultures. For example, Tsai (2006, 2008, 2010) used the feminist perspective to examine the leisure practices of Taiwanese women. Confucian teachings, prevalent in Taiwan, support a patriarchal society where a women's leisure is constrained by perceptions of women as passive and submissive, responsible for childrearing and domestic labour, and inherently and biologically inferior to men. Detailed regulations exist for women's leisure (e.g., women are discouraged from going out alone during leisure time) and leisure revolves around children and family. Thus, gender inequality in contemporary Taiwanese leisure settings is primarily due to premodern patriarchy and gender relations, and not lack of opportunity or individual obstacles. Despite the influence of Western feminism, Taiwanese women experience social pressure to conform to traditional roles in regards to leisure participation.

Do you agree with feminist theory's critique of traditional views of leisure? Why or why not?

Holistic Leisure: Leisure as a Total Way of Life

All of the definitions offered here suggest leisure is complex. It may be that there is more to leisure than any and all of these definitions suggest. Consider the notion of **holistic leisure**: within this understanding, **leisure is a total way of life** that eliminates the dichotomy between work and leisure. Holism recognizes that everything we do and how we do it is interrelated and affected by the other elements of our lives. Leisure may be experienced within the various contexts of life such as family, education, religion, or work. Leisure is fused with satisfying work and is continuous rather than fragmented. Thus, the holistic concept blends leisure as an end, as in the classical view, with leisure as a means, as in the activity view. It combines a focus on "being" with a focus on "doing" and thus reflects a return to a more traditional way of life (Kaplan, 1974).

The basis of holistic leisure has existed for centuries, but it was conceptualized during the 1960s and 1970s in response to a variety of social influences (Murphy, 1974), such as counter-cultural movements (e.g., the hippie movement), an increasing emphasis upon holistic understandings where the whole is seen as more than the sum of the parts, a crisis of identity and meaning when people were trying to find meaning in their work and in society, feelings of despair resulting from the Vietnam war, the fragmentation of life, and rapid change as documented in Toffler's (1971) book *Future Shock*. Historically societies tended to be holistic, but in the feudal and preindustrial period, social roles and elements of culture began to become distinguished and then in the industrial era work and leisure were clearly delineated. In many ways, holistic leisure returns to the preindustrial period in which work and leisure were simply different facets of everyday life.

A number of factors in the last few decades, most relating to the changing nature of work, have led to the possible development of a holistic integration of work and leisure (Goodale & Godbey, 1988; see also Chapter 11). These factors include the following:

- a search for authentic experiences at work and elsewhere
- the humanization of work
- a shift from the manufacturing to the service sector
- a rise in professionalism
- a broadening of the labour force with more women and more part-time workers
- removing of work from the workplace through technology such as computers, which reverses the trend of the Industrial Revolution when work was moved from the home to the factory

All of these factors make it more likely to experience elements of leisure in work and to integrate work and leisure into a holistic lifestyle.

Holistic expressions of leisure may be seen in preindustrial societies, such as ancient Israel when leisure involved components of time (Sabbath), activity (festivals), place (the Promised Land), attitude (faith), and state of being (physical and spiritual rest; Crabtree, 1982); in the monastic life where there was a unity of work and leisure as monks integrated both manual and intellectual work with the contemplative life of leisure *(otium)* (Leclerq, 1984); and in the lives of many women, especially those working at home for whom work and leisure coexist. Another example is North American aboriginal peoples who developed a culture based on a close association with the land and a cyclical, holistic world view. For aboriginal people, leisure is not a separate segment of life, but is linked to all life situations such as birth and death (Reid & Welke, 1998), and is reflected in cultural ceremonies, celebrations, and festivals (McDonald & McAvoy, 1997).

Is it possible to practice the holistic concept of leisure in contemporary North American society?

Conclusion

In this chapter, we reviewed several different definitions of leisure. Some of you have probably already developed your own understanding of leisure, while others may only be confused by the multiplicity of definitions. If so, how do you go about developing your own understanding of leisure? Here are a few suggestions: First, if you think semantic faithfulness is important—that is, that the etymological background of a word is important in deciding how we understand a word—then the classical view of leisure needs consideration. Second, some people suggest leisure is personally defined. Whether it is possible for leisure to be whatever one thinks it is may depend on the way you see the relationship between ideas and reality. Different possibilities exist: ideas and reality are the same; ideas approximate reality; and reality is determined by our mind. If you believe in the third possibility, then you are more likely to accept that leisure may be personally defined. This brings us to a third consideration: how important are shared definitions of leisure in determining your definition? Each of the definitions of leisure presented above is a shared definition of leisure, as numerous people have shaped each of them. If we do not have shared meanings then communication becomes difficult and confusion might result in the delivery of leisure services. It has been suggested that leisure is a postmodern concept with multiple meanings (Henderson, 2008). Is it possible to have more than one definition of leisure? Are all of the definitions presented in this chapter referring to the same phenomenon or are they describing related but different phenomenon? Can one word, "leisure," be used to describe a variety of related but different phenomena, or should we be more precise in our use of language? For example, as a person working in the leisure services field, one participant in your program might view leisure as free time and another participant might view leisure as a state of mind. Should we use the word "leisure" with both of them to describe these different phenomena? Perhaps the analogy of snow is helpful. For someone in a climate where snow is a rare occurrence such as the southernmost parts of Canada, one word might be sufficient to describe what snow is. But in the colder regions of Canada a variety of terms are used to describe it more specifically, terms such as powder snow, corn snow, fine-grained snow, and wet snow, which are helpful especially if we are waxing our skis. Similarly, should we be precise and when possible use terms such as "classical leisure," "leisure activity," "leisure time," "leisure as a symbol of social class," "leisure as a state of mind," "feminist leisure," and "holistic leisure," rather than simply use "leisure" to identify the phenomenon we are talking about? In other words, should we use different terms for different phenomena? Hopefully these considerations will be helpful to you in formulating and articulating your own understanding of leisure.

You began this chapter by writing your own definition of leisure. Now that you have read this chapter would you change your definition? How? Why?

Key Terms

Classical leisure
Feminist leisure
Holistic leisure
Leisure as activity
Leisure as free time
Leisure as a symbol of social class
Play
Recreation
State of mind leisure

References

Aristotle. (1947). *The Nicomachean ethics* (Trans. H. Rackham). Cambridge, MA: Harvard University Press.

Aristotle. (1963). *Politics* (Trans. E. Barker). London, UK: Oxford University Press.

Arnold, S. (1991). The dilemma of meaning. In T. L Goodale & P. A. Witt, (Eds.), *Recreation and leisure: Issues in an era of change* (pp. 5–20). State College, PA: Venture Publishing, Inc.

Augustine. (1972). *The city of God* (Trans. H. Bettenson). Markham, ON: Penguin.

Calvin, J. (1813). *Institutes of the Christian religion* (Trans. J. Allan). London, UK: J. Walker.

Colloredo-Mansfeld, R. (1999). *The native leisure class: Consumption and cultural creativity in the Andes.* Chicago, IL: University of Chicago Press.

Crabtree, R. D. (1982). *Leisure in ancient Israel.* (Unpublished doctoral dissertation). Texas A&M University, College Station, TX.

Csikszentmihalyi, M. (1975). *Beyond boredom and anxiety: The experience of play in work and games.* San Francisco, CA: Jossey-Bass.

de Grazia, S. (1964). *Of time, work and leisure.* New York, NY: Twentieth Century Fund.

Doohan, L. (1990). *Leisure: A spiritual need.* Notre Dame, IN: Ave Maria Press.

Driver, B. L., & Tocher, S. R. (1970). Toward a behavioural interpretation of recreational engagements, with implications for planning. In B. L. Driver (Ed.), *Elements of outdoor recreation planning* (pp. 9–31). Ann Arbor, MI: The University of Michigan Press.

Dumazedier, J. (1967). *Toward a society of leisure.* New York, NY: The Free Press.

Goodale, T. L., & Godbey, G. C. (1988). *The evolution of leisure: Historical and philosophical perspectives.* State College, PA: Venture Publishing, Inc.

Gordis, R. (1982, Winter). The Sabbath—Cornerstone and capstone of Jewish life. *Judaism, 31*, 6–11.

Heintzman, P. (2006). Implications for leisure from a review of the Biblical concepts of Sabbath and rest. In P. Heintzman, G. A. Van Andel, & T. L. Visker (Eds.), *Christianity and leisure: Issues in a pluralistic society* (Rev. ed., pp. 14–31). Sioux Center, IA: Dordt College Press.

Hemingway, J. L. (1988). Lesiure [sic] and civility: Reflections on a Greek ideal. *Leisure Sciences, 10*(3), 179–191.

Henderson, K. A. (2008). Expanding the meanings of *leisure* in a both/and world. *Loisir et Société, 31*(1), 15–30.

Henderson, K. A., Bialeschki, M. D., Shaw, S. M., & Freysinger, V. J. (1996). *Both gaps and gains: Feminist perspectives on women's leisure.* State College, PA: Venture Publishing, Inc.

Heschel, A. J. (1951). *The Sabbath.* New York, NY: Farrar, Straus & Giroux.

Huizinga, J. (1955). *Homo ludens.* Boston, MA: Beacon.

Ibrahim, H. (1991). Leisure and Islam. In G. S. Fain (Ed.), *Leisure and ethics: Reflections on the philosophy of leisure* (pp. 203–215). Reston, VA: American Association for the Study of Leisure and Recreation.

Johnson, K. E. (2009). Problematizing Puritan play. *Leisure/Loisir, 33*(1), 31–54.

Kaplan, M. (1974). New concepts of leisure today. In J. F. Murphy (Ed.), *Concepts of leisure: Philosophical implications* (pp. 229–236). Englewood Cliffs, NJ: Prentice Hall.

Kashyap, A. (1991). Leisure: An Indian classical perspective. *World Leisure and Recreation, 33*(2), 6–8.

Kelly, J. R. (1990). *Leisure* (2nd ed.). Englewood Cliffs, NJ: Prentice Hall.

Kleiber, D. A. (2000). The neglect of relaxation. *Journal of Leisure Research, 32*(1), 82–86.

Leclerq, J. (1984). Otium monasticum as a context for artistic creativity. In T. G. Verdun (Ed.), *Monasticism and the arts* (pp. 63–69). Syracuse, NY: Syracuse University Press.

Luther, M. (1965). *Luther's works,* vol. 53. (Ed. U.S. Leupold). Philadelphia, PA: Fortress.

Mair, H. (2002/2003). Civil leisure? Exploring the relationship between leisure, activism and social change. *Leisure/Loisir, 27*(3–4), 213–237.

Mannell, R. C., & Kleiber, D. A. (1997). *A social psychology of leisure*. State College, PA: Venture Publishing, Inc.

Martin, W. H., & Mason, S. (2004). Leisure in an Islamic context. *World Leisure, 46*(1), 4–13.

Maslow, A. H. (1968). *Toward a psychology of being* (2nd ed.). Toronto, ON: Van Nos Reinhold.

McDonald, D., & McAvoy, L. (1997). Native Americans and leisure: State of the research and future directions. *Journal of Leisure Research, 29*(2), 145–166.

Miller, P., & Johnson, T. H. (1963). *The Puritans* (Rev. ed., vol. 2). New York, NY: Harper Torchbooks.

Murphy, J. F. (1974). *Concepts of leisure: Philosophical implications*. Englewood Cliffs, NJ: Prentice Hall.

Neulinger, J. (1981). *The psychology of leisure*. Springfield, IL: Charles C. Thomas.

Owens, J. (1981, December). Aristotle on leisure. *Canadian Journal of Philosophy, 16*, 713–724.

Pieper, J. (1963). *Leisure: The basis of culture*. New York, NY: The New American Library.

Reid, D. G., & Welke, S. (1998). Leisure and traditional culture in First Nations communities. *Journal of Leisurability, 25*(1), 26–36.

Shaw, S. M. (2001). Conceptualizing resistance: Women's leisure as political practice. *Journal of Leisure Research, 33*(2), 186–201.

Siddiqi, M. (2003, December 20). Ridiculously, deliciously conspicuous consumption. *Financial Post*, p. IN1.

Stebbins, R. A. (1982). Serious leisure: A conceptual statement. *The Pacific Sociological Review, 25*(2), 251–272.

Stebbins, R. A. (1997). Casual leisure: A conceptual statement. *Leisure Studies, 16*(1), 17–25.

Stebbins, R. A. (1999). Serious leisure. In E. L. Jackson & T. L. Burton (Eds.), *Leisure studies: Prospects for the twenty-first century* (pp. 69–79). State College, PA: Venture Publishing, Inc.

Stebbins, R. A. (2005). Project-based leisure: Theoretical neglect of a common use of free time. *Leisure Studies, 24*, 1–11.

Sylvester, C. (1990). Interpretation and leisure science: A hermeneutical example of past and present oracles. *Journal of Leisure Research, 22*(4), 292–294.

Sylvester, C. (1999). The western idea of work and leisure: Traditions, transformations, and the future. In E. L. Jackson & T. L. Burton (Eds.), *Leisure studies: Prospects for the twenty-first century* (pp. 17–33). State College, PA: Venture Publishing, Inc.

Toffler, A. (1971). *Future shock.* New York, NY: Bantam.

Trafton, D. (1985). In praise of three traditional ideas of leisure. In B. G. Gunter, J. Stanley & R. St. Clair (Eds.), *Transitions to leisure: Conceptual and human issues* (pp. 23–31). Lanham, MD: University Press of America.

Tsai, C. L. (2006). Research note: The Influence of Confucianism on women's leisure in Taiwan. *Leisure Studies, 25*(4), 469–476.

Tsai, C. L. (2008). Women's leisure, leisurely women? Feminist perspectives on the leisure practice in Taiwan. *Asian Journal of Exercise and Sports Science, 5*(1), 39–47.

Tsai, C. L. (2010). A reflection on cultural conflicts in women's leisure. *Leisure Sciences, 32*(4), 386–390.

Veblen, T. (1899/1953). *The theory of the leisure class.* New York, NY: The New American Library.

Walker, G. J., & Deng, J. (2003/2004). Comparing leisure as a subjective experience with the Chinese experience of Rùmí. *Leisure/Loisir, 28*(3/4), 245–276.

Wang, J., & Stringer, L. A. (2000). The impact of Taoism on Chinese leisure. *World Leisure, 42*(3), 33–41.

Chapter 2
Introduction To Play

Steven Henle, Ph.D.
Concordia University

> I like nonsense, it wakes up the brain cells. Fantasy is a necessary ingredient in living. It's a way of looking at life through the wrong end of a telescope. Which is what I do, and that enables you to laugh at life's realities.
>
> *Ted Seuss Geisel (1901–1991), a.k.a. Dr. Seuss*

Learning Objectives

After reading this chapter, and after playful in-class experiences and reflection, students will be able to

1. Understand the power of play across the life span.
2. Think about play from multidimensional perspectives.
3. Experience authentic play to relate theory with practice.
4. Continue to explore the meaning of play.

Play and Your Education

How peculiar that you need to learn about play from a textbook. Did you play when you were a baby and a child? Did you continue to play as a young teenager? How did your play behaviour change when you turned eighteen? Do you still play? Will you play throughout the stages of your life? According to Cameron (2004) you may consider maintaining your youth, beyond your age, as a "kidult" or "adultescent" (Kay, 2003) and pre-occupy yourself by being playful, and never growing up. To learn about play and playfulness real life examples are helpful learning tools. You are encouraged from this point onward to use your life experiences as a personal case study. Through introspection about play in your life, you will experience rich learning.

What play-related activities can you organize to create experiential learning opportunities in your classroom?

Play has different meanings in different cultures. It is normal that individual nature (biology) and nurture (environment) shape experiences differently. The ideas presented in this chapter are ethnocentric and reflect a North American (Western) attitude and ideal about play and playfulness. It should be understood that the ideas presented have limited application when studying non-Western cultures.

Play Theory

Like all sciences, leisure requires a specific taxonomy so that we can better understand meanings and make distinctions between concepts (Reilly, 1981). Play requires a theory so that we can identify play, define play, and distinguish play from other human behaviours. To complicate the matter of finding an appropriate theory, people play in different contexts. For example, babies play peek-a-boo, children play in the park, and adolescents play through sexual exploration. What we all have in common is that healthy humans play. According to Lev Vygotsky (1976), a Russian born psychologist particularly interested in developmental psychology, child development and education, the problem with many play theories is that they over-intellectualize them, and this continues to be true. Therefore, understanding the theories of play is not a simplistic undertaking. The various theories provide insight into different aspects of human play behaviour. Early twentieth century theories about play are outdated and contradictory (even humorous). In early efforts to understand why we play, the following theories were postulated.

Surplus Energy Theory

The surplus energy theory explains that living creatures generate energy for survival, and after survival needs are satisfied there can be leftover energy. Leftover or surplus energy builds up and must be released, and it is through play that animals rid themselves of this excess energy. This theory, developed by a poet (Schiller) and a philosopher (Spencer) was popular and easy to accommodate to the human condition (Johnson, Christie, & Yawkey, 1987).

Recreation Theory

According to the recreation theory, people play for the benefit of restoring energy used in work. There are two ways to restore lost energy—one method is through sleep and the second method is by engaging in play. Of consequence, this theory assumes that work and play are opposites and recent research tells us that the opposite of play is not work (Marano, 1999).

The recreation theory and the surplus energy theory contradict each other. The recreation theory states that we play to regain lost energy, simultaneously the surplus energy theory states that we play because we have too much energy.

Recapitulation Theory

The roots of the recapitulation theory are derived from the development of the human embryo. As the embryo develops it seems to take on the appearance of lower level species and retraces human evolution. The recapitulation theory was, therefore, borrowed and adapted to explain children's play.

The recapitulation theory explains that children play to retrace the stages of human evolution and that the stages of play mimic human evolution. The purpose of play is to help children naturally expel their primitive instincts, which have become obsolete in a modern world (Johnson et al., 1987). To provide an insightful example, we might postulate that children play with playground equipment to mimic climbing and swinging which would recapitulate primates living in trees. Children engaged in organized sports are purging themselves of the primitive instinct to be part of a tribe engaged in battle with a competing tribe.

Practice Theory

The practice theory suggests that the purpose of play is to develop and refine the imperfect instincts that we are born with and that we will need in adult life. It is through play that a species young can refine skills in a safe environment. For example, when children play house, they are practicing skills that will be needed in adult life.

The recapitulation theory expresses the idea that humans re-live our ancestral evolution through play. In contradiction, the practice theory explains that the purpose of play provides the opportunity to practice skills during childhood that are essential over the life course.

The origins of play theory are contradictory; the surplus energy theory and the recreation theory try to explain play behaviour in terms of energy regulation while the recapitulation theory and the practice theory attempt to explain play behaviour in terms of human instinct. These four classical theories were developed without scientific research. Obviously these theories have liabilities that cannot be overcome. For example, in the recapitulation theory children play to rid themselves of primitive instincts; however, this theory does not account for children who play with space-related toys or who role-play as astronauts. The theories do provide a window for the modern researcher to learn about attitudes and values related to play. What is clearly evident in the classical theories is a paucity of ideas that play could be fun and engaged in for the pleasure of the experience, as Russell (2005) suggested, "Perhaps play does not occur because it is useful" (p. 54).

Modern theories of play have received more attention, and still researchers debate the benefit of one theory over another theory. To become adept at understanding play, the following theories can be considered as different lenses (Frost, Wortham, & Reifel, 2005) as a way to help comprehend the complicated concept of play from various points of view. More prevalent theories have the support of scientific research and include the psychoanalytic theory and the cognitive theory of play.

Psychoanalytic Theory

The history of the psychoanalytic theory is complex and various psychologists have contributed to the theory in relation to play behaviour. Sigmund Freud originally developed the psychoanalytic theory. Subsequently Lili E. Peller (1952) cautioned about interpreting the meaning of play behaviour. Erik Erikson (1963) also contributed information about children using play to reduce pressures associated with childhood. The psychoanalytic theory provides a lens into the emotional issues that children can struggle with, and play is a vehicle through which children communicate and work through their feelings (Scarlett, Naudeau, Salonius-Pasternak, & Ponte, 2005). If children are safe during play, it is an ideal opportunity to play and pretend that they are in control, to conjure up fantasy, and to begin to make meaning of an adult-directed world. In psychoanalysis, play is a useful tool to help children play out their feelings. There is debate, however, about whether children's play is a reflection of what children have experienced, or if play represents what children hope to experience. To understand children's play-related behaviour in the psychoanalytic perspective, it is therefore important to have knowledge about each individual child (Frost et al., 2005).

Cognitive Theory

The cognitive theory contends that play is linked with the mind and through play children are able to assimilate knowledge (Jean Piaget), problem-solve (Jerome Bruner), and create new knowledge (Lev Vygotsky). Each theorist viewed the relationship between play and cognitive process through a different lens, each contributed valuable insight to further our ability to understand children's play behaviour.

Jean Piaget was a famous Swiss scholar who based his early work on the observations of his three children. Piaget professed that children assimilate knowledge during play that has been acquired prior to play. Piaget established the very influential concept that children pass through (and re-visit) three different stages of play associated with a child's age. It is important to view the steps that Piaget recognized without putting emphasis on the related ages associated with the stages (Frost et al., 2005).

Stage one includes functional play. Stage two includes symbolic play, construction play, and sociodramatic play. Stage three represents the most complex stage and includes games with rules. At this level children function socially through rule-governed games. Examples of this may include games with predetermined rules (e.g., computer games, board games) and games in which the players are free to create their own rules.

Jerome Bruner (1975), an American psychologist who has contributed to cognitive psychology and cognitive learning theory in educational psychology, recognized the potential in play as a means to development. Specifically, his work focused on the utilitarian function of problem solving through play. According to Bruner, play allows children to develop skills for problem solving. By exploring through play, children can creatively find solutions to problems, test ideas, and develop skills. One of the benefits of problem solving through play is that when children make mistakes, the negative repercussions are minimized because the error was made during play and not during "real life."

Lev Vygotsky viewed play as useful to help children create new knowledge. His interest stems from "how children learn and how learning contributes to development" (Scarlett et al., 2005, p. 9). Vygotsky made a formidable impact on education by proposing that a zone of proximal development (ZPD) exists that promotes a child's development. There is a standard level at which a person can learn. However, to move beyond that comfort level three possible ZPD scenarios can be helpful; they are as follows:

1. through play to achieve higher learning. Play encourages a child to take risks knowing that the repercussions of error are not as serious during play as mistakes are during real life.
2. through social interaction with people who have greater skill levels.
3. through scaffolding to create an environment that supports the acquisition of knowledge or skills (similar to the way that scaffolding supports a building).

The psychoanalytic theory and the cognition theory provide insightful information about play. Other play-related theories have been developed that provide a more focused lens and detailed insight into play, including: the social theory of play (Smith, 2005), social intelligence (Bailey, 2002), play as creativity (Truhon, 1983), and play as therapy (Cooper, 2000). Russell (2005) briefly compares and contrasts eight common theories, including catharsis, behaviouristic, arousal seeking, and competence–effectance.

Taking into account your beliefs about play, find a theory that is meaningful to you. What emerging play theories can be found in the literature?

In-Depth Play-Related Research

Life-span	Casas (2003), Davis, Larkin and Graves (2002), Kariuki and Redman (1999)
Sexuality	Aune and Wong (2002), Baxter (1992)
Education	Bodrova and Leong (2005), Erickson (1985)
Socialization	Bailey (2002), Howe, Petrokos, Rinaldi, and LeFebvre (2005)
Research	Trevlas, Grammatikopoulos, Tsigilis, and Zachopoulou (2003)
Therapy	Cooper (2000), Miller and Reid (2003), Barrows (2002), Chethik (2000)
Creativity	Russ (2003), Truhorn (1983)

Defining Play

Having insight into play-related theories provides the learner with an understanding of the complexity of human play behaviour. The more challenging component is to understand the implication of the terms that define human play behaviour. If play is so easy to identify, why is it so difficult to define? Researchers agree on the value of play but cannot agree on a definition of play, which has resulted in multiple definitions of play, and therefore, play is inadequately defined (Cooper, 2000). How can we define play? Play is not synonymous with entertainment, games, sports, recreation, or leisure. The challenge is to provide a definition of play that is broad, not restrictive; the definition should focus on the "state of being" of the player instead of specific activities. This permits liberty, and allows for a range of behaviours and activities to fit within the definition. The compilation of definitions presented is commonly employed to help define play. Play definitions, therefore, may include some but not all of the terms described. To define play the following characteristics are commonly used: (a) intrinsic motivation, (b) free choice, (c) suspension of reality, (d) positive affect, (e) process over product, (f) play is active, (g) play is bound by rules, and (h) internal locus of control.

Intrinsic Motivation

Intrinsic motivation is a driving force to engage in the play behaviour or activity. In other words play is engaged in for

Quotes about Play

Play is the work of children.
Susan Isaacs (Isaacs, 1932)

A playful attitude is fundamental to creative thinking.
Johan Huizinga (Think Exist, 2005)

You can discover more about a person in an hour of play than in a year of conversation.
Plato (Think Exist, 2005)

All work and no play makes Jack a dull boy.
Proverb (Think Exist, 2005)

Play has been man's most useful preoccupation.
Frank Caplan (Think Exist, 2005)

"its own sake" (Johnson et al., 1987) for the purpose of pleasure for the player. The play is self-satisfying.

Free Choice

The freedom to participate and the freedom from obligation set the stage that helps create a state of mind that allows the individual to feel playful. According to Shelia Flaxman (2000), the freedom to choose to play promotes the enriching qualities of play. The notion of "freedom from obligation" and "freedom to play" are important determining factors (Dattilo, 1999). The engagement should be voluntary so that the players are not responding to external demands (Icenber & Jalongo, 1997).

Suspension of Reality

Suspension of reality allows the player to temporarily step outside of his/her reality and accept an imaginary self for the purpose of make believe (Levy, 1978). Play is transformational, allowing the player to change roles (Icenber & Jalongo, 1997).

Positive Affect

Play provides the player with positive experience and enjoyment (Johnson et al., 1987). Play is pleasurable (Icenber & Jalongo, 1997); in providing a positive affect it does not matter if the play is serious or frivolous.

Process over Product

Process over product stresses that the goal of play is the activity itself (or the pleasure from the activity); the end result, or the product are secondary concerns for the player (Johnson et al., 1987). Jacob Levy (1978) clearly illustrates that the product of play is not the purpose: "Only in play can we totally commit ourselves to the goal that minutes later is forgotten or irrelevant" (p. 10).

Play Is Active

The player(s) must be actively engaged in the activity (Icenber & Jalongo, 1997). Unlike entertainment during which people can assume an active or passive role, in play the player is active. Active behaviours may include but are not limited to exploration, experimentation, manipulation, make believe, and interaction with the environment.

Play Is Bound by Rules

Players accept that rules are part of play. The rules are self-imposed, regulated, and changed in accordance with the wishes of the players (Icenber & Jalongo, 1997). "During social pretend play children negotiate the rules of play" (Howe, Petrakos, Rinaldi, & LeFebvre, 2005, p. 784). When rules are dictated and enforced by authority figures who are not engaged in the play, the freedom to choose is eliminated and the activity is no longer play. Externally imposed rules, such as in organized sports, create a different environment from play-related activities. Hence organized sports and play, although both bound by rules, are different because of how the rules are created and managed.

Internal Locus of Control

Internal locus of control is the degree to which the players feel in control of their behaviours and the outcomes they experience. A player with a high internal locus of control perceives that s/he has control of her/his behaviour and destiny, while a person with a high external locus of control perceives that the outcomes in her/his life are beyond her/his control and rest with fate or the power of others.

Historically, many play theorists and researchers have combined various definitions of play in an attempt to create a comprehensive play definition. In 1978 Levy proposed a play behaviour model. The continuum was composed of non-play behaviours on the left and included characteristics such as extrinsic motivation, reality, and external locus of control. On the right side of the continuum were characteristics such as intrinsic motivation, suspension of reality and internal locus of control characterized play behaviour. The trend continues today as researchers combine various ideas in an ongoing effort to create a universally acceptable definition of play. Hara Estroff Marano (1999), Editor-at-Large of *Psychology Today,* quoted Sutton-Smith's definition of play "an autonomous, intrinsically motivated activity. We do it spontaneously, just because it's fun" (p. 68). Trevlas, Grammatikopoulos, Tsigilis and Zachopoulou (2003) tested the Children's Playfulness Scale and defined children's playfulness as a personality trait composed of "an internal predisposition to bring a playful quality to interactions within the environment..." (p. 33). Cooper (2000) borrowed a definition of play from other scholars, and added that the influence of culture impacts play:

> Play is a transaction between an individual and the environment that is intrinsically motivated, internally controlled, and free of many of the constraints of objective reality. Play is a special kind of activity or transaction that occurs between the individual child and the environment, influenced by cultural expectations, and engaged in because the child wants to, not because he or she has to (p. 262).

Al Gini (2003), Professor of Philosophy at Loyola University Chicago, captures the essence of play:

> For both children and adults, play is about awe, wonder, rapture and enthusiasm. Play is something we want to do, something we choose to do that is not work, that we enjoy and that gives us gratification and fun. In play, we drop inhibitions, give ourselves permission to imagine, to be creative, to be curious. Play, like laughter, is an end itself, something done without any other incentive except for the pleasure involved in the activity itself (p. 32).

Unfortunately, by adding the statement "...something we choose to do that is not work..." the notion is conveyed that play is the opposite of work, which limits the utility of the definition by making it impossible for people to experience play during work. Alternatively, the statement may be altered to read, "Play is something we want to do, a state of mind that we enjoy." This broadens the definition greatly and accommodates all activity based on the individual's perception (state of mind) of what is play.

In an attempt to convey the meaning of play, create your own definition by combining some of the ideas presented, then draw a model of your definition of play.

Play Therapy

The use of play as a therapeutic medium is evidenced in play theory and through current research. Play offers a glimpse into the player's world. Through play children express what they have experienced (Piaget), problem solve (Bruner), and reenact life stressors to make sense of the world (Freud and Erikson). If play is an important human component, and all healthy animals play (Frost et al., 2005), then we must examine the utility of play as a healing tool. Isenberg and Jalongo (1997) reported on some of the benefits of play: Play enables children to interpret their world, to develop social and cultural context, and to express feelings; encourages creative thinking; and promotes verbal and non-verbal communication. The benefits of play are unarguably beneficial and many approaches to play therapy have been put forward to promote play, or to use play as a tool for other therapeutic gains (Educational Play Therapy, 2006).

Miller and Reid (2003) investigated the value of virtual reality play for youth with cerebral palsy. Their findings indicate that research participants enjoyed participating and reported psychological, emotional, social and physical benefits. Participants also reported experiencing "flow." Flow is a theory developed by Mihalyi Csikszentmihalyi to explain the feelings that people sometimes experience during leisure (Dattilo, 1999). The flow sensation is described as a loss of awareness of time or being "in the zone" due in part to intense concentration, clear goals, immediate feedback, and appropriate challenge. This research is an example of using play activities to promote playful behaviour. Other research has focused on play therapy as a benefit to overcome other stressors. Occupational therapists often use play to help abused children deal with their trauma (Cooper, 2000). One advantage of play therapy is that the mental activity is not the direct goal, and therefore the player is unaware of the benefits play creates; it is as if the benefits associated with play "sneak in" while the player is preoccupied with the activity of playing (Marano, 1999).

The Role of Play in Education

Children first experience school as a place to play. During play children learn to socialize, spark creativity, foster bonds with teachers, and make the transition from life at home to life in the classroom with peers and teachers. Pramling-Samuelsson and Johansson (2006) suggested that the division between play and learning is blurred and that learning cannot happen without play and play leads to learning. This sentiment was suggested first by American psychologist, philosopher, and educational reformer, John Dewey in the 1920s. According to Reilly (1981) Dewey postulated that playful behaviour could only enhance the learners' education.

Making an argument to ensure that free-play is not eliminated from the school curriculum Flaxman (2000) suggested ten benefits of free-play:

1. fine motor development
2. gross motor development
3. social development
4. language acquisition

5. problem solving (and creative thinking)
6. exploration of cause-and-effect
7. therapeutic catharsis
8. self-talk
9. improved self-confidence
10. cooperation skills in a social context

In a curriculum guide, *The Kindergarten: Learning Through Play* (Education Québec, 2001), the benefits of play are exulted and it is suggested that play should have a central role in preschool education and the classroom environment should accommodate the play mandate. Play provides a solid foundation for education but requires increased awareness so that adults can provide meaningful play opportunities. If play is a powerful learning tool, why is the application of using play to increase learning limited to young children?

Play is a powerful learning medium, during which the players are focused and actively engaged, rather than passive observers (Coleman, 1976). Creating a playful learning environment manifests an authentic learning opportunity and engages learners to take ownership of their education. Surely it makes sense that the benefits associated with play and education are valuable beyond the primary grades. Recent studies suggest that there is an invaluable link between hands-on learning and motivation to learn (Martens, Gulikers, & Bastiaens, 2004; Van't Hooft, 2005). Experiential learning and authentic learning lead to greater exploration and knowledge for educators and learners (Murphy & Gazi, 2001). More research, however, is required to indicate if play creates authentic learning that leads to better knowledge, understanding, and thinking in education.

When you are acquiring new information how do you learn best, by reading, listening, watching, or doing? Can you recall "learning" during play?

Play for Life

By extrapolating the benefits of play behaviour it seems obvious that play should continue throughout life. The vocabulary used to describe play changes as people age; play is cited less frequently in the research phraseology and leisure and recreation are used more commonly. In a research study about free-time preferences and literacy by Nippold, Duthie, and Larsen (2005), early adolescents through early adults responded to the question, "How do you like to spend your free time?" As expected, "play" did not appear as a category, although playing computer or video games and playing sports were frequently listed.

In corporate Canada playful games are sometimes used in workshops to help motivate, train, and build team spirit among staff. Examples include adventure courses and initiative tasks used to improve corporate productivity (Dougherty & Takacs, 2004). Unfortunately, it seems that during adulthood play is not a priority and the benefits of play are, for the most part ignored, while "important" and "serious" matters of being grown-up are attended to. Later in life, there is a return to play. According to Dr. Melamed, "It may be that play in our culture is most accessible for children and older adults" (Melamed, 1990, p. 1).

Lanie Melamed (1928–2003) preached the virtues of play and acknowledged the dangers—the underside of play. According to Dr. Melamed being playful is related to age and stage of life, and as people age they tend to feel more self-confident. As a result, people become more willing to take risks, be inappropriate; in short, to play. The price for being a playful older adult may include going too far, social penalties for being playful, and resistance to authority. (Dr. Melamed was a member of the Raging Grannies.) However, the benefits of play outweigh the consequences. Dr. Melamed explained that being playful while growing older leads to inner feelings of self-worth, energy, and a sense of wellness; laughter and humour; openness to the unexpected and unknown; valuing the present; and hope and affirmation of life. In acknowledgement of some of Dr. Melamed's accomplishments, she is credited with promoting "play and fun in all its many guises."

Links to Playful Activities

http://www.albartus.com/motas
An adventure "mind" game and it is free (Albartus, 2005)

http://www.playsport.net
Teaching kids games by playing games, activities (The Ontario Physical and Health Education Association)

http://www.righttoplay.com
Promoting the right to play (The Right to Play)

http://www.inventionatplay.com
Linking play and innovation (The Lemeson Center)

http://www.puppetools.com
"Advancing the language of play" puppets for all ages (Puppetools, 2005)

Conclusion

Additional play-related topics will serve to increase your knowledge about play but are beyond the scope of this introductory chapter. Learners are encouraged to investigate themes related to play including but not limited to: gender, neurosciences, animal behaviour, obesity and active living, human sexuality, mental health, physical health, forensic science, technology (gaming), and cross-cultural studies.

Key Terms

Free choice
Internal locus of control
Intrinsic motivation
Play
Play theories
Suspension of reality

References

Albartus, J. (2005). Mystery of time and space. Retrieved from http://www.albartus.com

Aune, K., & Wong, N. (2002). Antecedents and consequences of adult play in romantic relationships. *Personality Relationships, 9*, 279–286.

Bailey, R. (2002). Playing social chess: Children's play and social intelligence. *Early Years, 22*(2), 163–173.

Bruner, J. (1975). Child development: Play is serious business. *Psychology Today*, 81–83.

Cameron, A. (2004). I'll never grow up, not me! *Maclean's, 117*(31), 56–57.

Cases, A. (2003). *Childhood playfulness as a predictor of adult playfulness and creativity.* Blacksburg, VA: Virginia Polytechnic Institute.

Chethik, M. (2000). *Techniques of child therapy* (2nd ed.). New York, NY: Guilford Press.

Coleman, J. (1976). Learning through games. In J. Bruner, A. Jolly, & K. Sylva (Eds.), *Play: Its role in development and evolution.* (pp. 460–463). New York, NY: Penguin Books.

Cooper, R. (2000). The impact of child abuse on children's play: A conceptual model. *Occupational Therapy International, 7*(4), 259–276.

Dattilo, J. (1999). *Leisure education program planning* (2nd ed.). State College, PA: Venture Publishing, Inc.

Davis, L., Larkin, E., & Graves, S. B. (2002). Intergenerational learning through play. *International Journal of Early Childhood, 34*(2), 42–49.

Dougherty, D., & Takacs, C. H. (2004). Team play: Heedful interrelating as the boundary for innovation. *International Journal of Strategic Management, 37*(6), 569–590.

Education Québec. (2001). *The kindergarten: Learning through play*. University of Québec in Montréal.

Educational Play Therapy. (2005). Educational play therapy. Retrieved from http://www.rch.org.au/ept/index.cfm?doc_id=1175

Erickson, E. H. (1963). *Childhood and society.* New York, NY: Norton.

Erickson, R. J. (1985). Play contributes to the full emotional development of the child. *Education, 105*(3), 261.

Flaxman, S. (2000). Play an endangered species. *Instructor, 110*(2), 39–41.

Frost, J., Wortham, S., & Reifel, S. (2005). *Play and child development* (2nd ed.). Upper Saddle River, NJ: Pearson Prentice Hall.

Dr. Seuss. Quotation #32247 from Michael Mancur's (cynical) quotations. Retrieved from http//www.quotationspage.com/quote/32247.html

Gini, A. (2003). *The importance of being lazy*. New York, NY: Routledge.

Howe, N., Petrakos, H., Rinaldi, C. M., & LeFebvre, R. (2005). "This is a bad dog, you know…": Constructing shared meanings during sibling pretend play. *Child Development, 76*(4), 783–794.

Icenber, J., & Jalongo, M. (1997). *Creative expression and play in early childhood* (2nd ed.). Upper Saddle River, NJ: Prentice Hall.

Isaacs, S. (1932). *The nursery years*. London, UK: Routledge & Kegan Paul.

Johnson, J., Christie, J., & Yawkey, T. (1987). *Play and early childhood development.* Glenview, IL: Scott Foresman.

Kay, B. (2003). 'Kidults' should grow up. Retrieved from http://www.liquidlewis.com/barb/archive/2003 1912kidults.htm

Levy, J. (1978). *Play behavior*. New York, NY: Wiley.

Marano, H. E. (1999, July/August). The power of play. *Psychology Today*, 36–40, 68–69.

Martens, R. L., Gulikers, J., & Bastiaens, T. (2004). The impact of intrinsic motivation on e-learning in authentic computer tasks. *Journal of Computer Assisted Learning, 20*(5), 368–376.

Melamed, L. (1990). *Learning about play*. Unpublished manuscript.

Miller, S., & Reid, D. (2003). Doing play: Competency, control, and expression. *CyberPsychology & Behavior, 6*(6), 623–632.

Murphy, K. L. & Gazi, Y. (2001). Role plays, panel discussions and simulations: Project-based learning in a web-based course. *Educational Media International, 38*(4), 261–270.

Nippold, M. A., Duthie, J. K., & Larsen, J. (2005). Literacy as a leisure activity: Free-time preferences of older children and young adolescents. *Language, Speech, and Hearing Services in Schools, 36*(2), 93–102.

Peller, L. (1952). Models of children's play. *Mental Hygiene, 36*, 66–83.

Pramling-Samuelsson, I., & Johansson, E. (2006). Play and learning—inseparable dimensions in preschool practice. *Early Child Development & Care, 176*(1), 47–65.

Puppetools. (2005). Retrieved from http://www.puppetools.com

Reilly, M. (1981). *Play as exploratory learning*. Beverly Hills, CA: Sage Publications.

Russ, S. (2003). Play and creativity: Developmental issues. *Scandinavian Journal of Educational Research, 47*(3), 291–303.

Russell, R. (2005). *Pastimes: The context of contemporary leisure* (3rd ed.). Champaign, IL: Sagamore Publishing.

Scarlett, W. G., Naudeau, S., Salonius-Pasternak, D., & Ponte, I. (2005). *Children's play*. Thousand Oaks, CA: Sage Publications.

Smith, P. K. (2005). Play: Types and functions in human development. In B. J. Ellis & D. F. Bjorklund (Eds.), *Origins of the social mind: Evolutionary psychology and child development* (pp. 271–291). New York, NY: Guilford Press.

The Lemeson Center. Invention at play. Retrieved from http://www.inventionatplay.org/

The Ontario Physical and Health Education Association. Play Sports. Retrieved from http://www.playsport.net/Ophea/PlaySport/index.cfm

The Quote Garden. (2006). Welcome to the Quote Garden. Retrieved from http://www.quotegarden.com/imagination.html

The Right to Play. Retrieved from http://www.righttoplay.com

Think Exist. (2005). ThinkExist.com. Retrieved from http://en.thinkexist.com

Trevlas, E., Grammatikopoulos, V., Tsigilis, N., & Zachoppolou, E. (2003). Evaluating playfulness: Construct validity of the children's playfulness scale. *Early Childhood Education Journal, 31*(1), 33–39.

Truhon, S. (1983). Playfulness, play, and creativity: A path analytic model. *The Journal of Genetic Psychology, 143*, 19–28.

Van't Hooft, M. (2005). The effect of the "Ohio schools going solar" project on student perceptions of the quality of learning in middle school science. *Journal of Research on Technology in Education, 37*(3), 221–243.

Vygotsky, L. (1976). Play and its role in the mental development of the child. In J. Bruner, A. Jolly, & K. Sylva (Eds.), *Play: Its role in development and evolution* (pp. 537–554). New York, NY: Penguin Books.

Chapter 3
Sport and the Community

Dawn E. Trussell, Ph.D.
Brock University

Learning Objectives

After reading this chapter, students will be able to

1. Understand how sports in the community are delivered and the significant role of volunteers.
2. Explore the social and cultural value of sport in the community.
3. Develop a broad understanding of some of the problems and exclusionary aspects of sport in the community.
4. Engage in critical discussion related to sport and salient issues that practitioners should consider in the provision of programs and services.

Introduction

It is a common belief that sport helps facilitate a healthy lifestyle; however, it also has many important features outside the sport domain. Sport provides the context in which local citizens may create and maintain social networks and can be the "focal points for community attention and involvement" (Coakley & Donnelly, 2009, p. 426). Sport can construct and promote a collective identity for towns, cities, and even nations. Sport also creates social spaces where aspects of community development—such as inclusion, integration, belonging, and connection—exist. At the same time, sport is not universally inclusive. That is, sport can also be exclusionary and reinforce social division among various social groups.

Sport is an important aspect of Canadian society and is structured and consumed through a variety of media. Slack (2003) outlined three levels of sport: community organizations and schools, intercollegiate sport, and highly professionalized leagues. Although all three areas are important in the leisure practices and experiences of Canadians, it is within sport in the community that many citizens will have the most involvement as participants, volunteers, and/or spectators.

The significance of community and recreational sport has received national priority. For example, the Canadian Sport Policy 2012 "sets direction for the period 2012–2022 for all governments, institutions, and organizations that are committed to realizing the positive impacts of sport on individuals, communities, and society" (p. 2). Recreational sport is identified as a policy goal whereby "Canadians have the opportunity to participate in sport for fun, health, social interaction, and relaxation" (p. 3). The facilitation of organized and/or unorganized sport programs or activities occurs through volunteers and salaried workers.

Sport in the community may also be where many future practitioners (such as you!) find life-long, rewarding careers. This chapter strives to present some of the salient issues in community sport, and it provides a critical look at some of the problems and issues confronting the delivery of recreational sport programs or activities.

How are Sports in the Community Delivered?

Canada's community sport system is a multisectoral and integrated system including public (federal, provincial, municipal), non-profit, private, commercial, and voluntary sectors. At the municipal level, recreation departments play an important role in the provision of major sporting facilities (e.g., playing fields, ice arenas, swimming pools, gymnasiums) as well as recreational sport programs. Other agencies such as the YMCA/YWCA and Boys and Girls Clubs also have facilities and develop and implement a variety of sport programs for children, adults, and families. Organizations and businesses within a community also contribute to sport through the provision of resources. For example, youth sport programs may be sponsored by volunteer service clubs such as Kinsmen, Lions, and Optimists. A wide variety of privately operated clubs with significant user fees (prevalent in sports such as tennis, golf, swimming, and gymnastics) and private businesses also provide facilities, equipment, and/or programs.

In response to economic, political, and social pressures, interorganizational linkages are becoming more popular in the provision of sport services (Thibault, Frisby & Kikulis, 1999). Schools and local governments have a long history of forming reciprocal agreements. Increasingly, all sectors (public, non-profit, and commercial) are working together to share resources in a fiscally constrained environment while they try to meet participants' expectations for higher quality sport programs and facilities (Cousens, Barnes, Stevens, Mallen, & Bradish, 2006). Moreover, with growing social concerns related to quality-of-life issues (e.g., obesity, crime, and violence) sport is seen as a vehicle to help address some of our greatest social ills. In response, joint initiatives between

How is Sport a Central Gathering Place?

Sports may be viewed as "sites for socialization experiences" (Coakley & Donnelly, 2009, p. 95). That is, sports are social spaces that provide rich memories (both positive and negative) and create meaningful personal, social, and cultural experiences for an individual. Sport also fosters larger social networks and a sense of community that unites individuals and families. In this sense, community sport is positioned as an important social hub and central gathering place that provides more than physical benefits (Tonts, 2005; Mair, 2009).

In rural communities, research has shown that there is an important connection between sport organizations and social structures. For example, sport clubs and venues may be the focal point of social interaction in small towns, in large part due to the lack of other cultural, entertainment, and leisure facilities (e.g., theatres, cinemas, large shopping centres, and health and fitness clubs) (Warner-Smith & Brown, 2002; Haugen & Villa, 2006). In many declining rural communities, sport clubs are also seen as the final pillar of social support that often outlast local pubs, shops, and even churches (Tonts, 2005), and as a vehicle to prepare children and future generations for a more urban or suburban lifestyle (Trussell & Shaw, 2009).

Yet, there are many barriers to participation that may be unique and/or heightened when providing sport and leisure services in a rural community. Rural communities are often physically and socially isolated (resulting in longer distances to sport facilities), have few resources and services (public transportation, childcare, education, and health services), and have higher rates of poverty and employment. How would these barriers affect one's sport (and leisure) participation? Can you think of strategies or program modifications to help overcome some of these difficulties? Why is it important that these modifications be made? In light of these difficulties, why is sport as a "social hub" so important in a rural community? What broader social implications does it have?

At the same time, what unique challenges might exist in an inner-city environment? How might the difficulties be the same as the rural context? How are they different? What modifications would need to be made in the delivery of sport programs and events? Considering your answers, why is sport as a "social hub" and central gathering place important in the inner-city context?

health and social institutions and traditional sport/leisure service providers have formed (for example, a Public Health Department and a Municipal Recreation Department).

Yet, with the emergence of new ways of doing business, new difficulties have also surfaced. As Thibault, Frisby, and Kikulis (1999) point out: "as a consequence, leisure service professionals are having to develop new skills to negotiate effectively with partners who often have different educational backgrounds, professional languages, and values" (p. 126). Some of the common problems that arise from these partnerships include a lack of guidelines, insufficient training, and poor coordination. For successful implementation, these undermanaged partnerships will require future practitioners to develop plans and strategies to adequately supervise and monitor new and existing agreements (Frisby, Thibault, & Kikulis, 2004).

The delivery of sport programs is also heavily reliant on individual citizens who volunteer their time and are instrumental to the successful operation of organizations. Indeed, "in all sports, volunteers are the 'life blood'—take away the volunteers and the sport dies" (de Cruz, 2005, p. 83). Volunteers are found at all levels (national, provincial, and local) and in various capacities (e.g., sport-governing body, coach, fundraiser). According to Doherty (2005), sport volunteers are one of the major volunteer sectors and represent 18% of total volunteerism in Canada.

In this textbook, Corbin (Chapter 40 on "Volunteering in Canada") discusses the heavy reliance on volunteers for sport and recreation groups as well as their primary motivations for volunteering. At the same time, there are slight differences when working with sport volunteers compared to non-sport volunteers. For example, sport volunteers are

Volunteers in sport organizations are facing many challenges. Sharpe's (2006) research on a grassroots baseball organization in Ontario revealed that there were several challenges/difficulties. Such challenges included "finding and mobilizing volunteers to contribute to the organizational work" (p. 394) and that "the organizational environment had changed, and had become more complex, regulated, and bureaucratic over time" (p. 395). Consequently, there were a small number of overworked volunteers who had knowledge about baseball, but little "professional competencies of administration such as marketing, accounting, or law" (p. 395). Nichols (2005) cited similar challenges, while Doherty (2005) also emphasized the under-representation of women and new Canadians in sport volunteering. In light of these difficulties, what strategies can you think of to help alleviate some of the challenges that are linked to volunteer management in sport?

more likely than non-sport volunteers to cite "instrumental rather than expressive or altruistic reasons for volunteering" (Cuskelly, 2005, p. 89). That is, sport volunteers are more likely to volunteer due to "personal or family involvement" in the sport organization, rather than reasons related to "helping others or the community" (albeit a sport volunteer may also be motivated by the latter at the same time). Many parents become involved in sport due to their children's participation and because they are asked by the organization to help out (Doherty, 2005). As volunteers are the backbone of the Canadian sport system (Harvey, Lévesque, & Donnelly, 2007) and many challenges exist (see text box), sport practitioners should be trained to understand how to effectively work with this group.

Is Youth Sport a Family Affair?

The increase in youth sport participation in North America since the 1950s has occurred primarily in adult-organized and agency-sponsored programs and has become a phenomenon of North American culture (Coakley, 2009; Coakley & Donnelly, 2009). Initially, most sport programs were developed for boys, and it was not until the 1970s that opportunities for girls' sport participation were created (Coakley & Donnelly, 2009). Organized youth sport is believed to facilitate important cultural lessons in the areas of character-building, teamwork, responsibility, cooperation, and competition—all attributes that are valued within a capitalist society (Dunn, Kinney, & Hofferth, 2003). Consequently, the emergence and popularity of children's sport organizations has added a new aspect to the socialization of children and the nature of their leisure.

Moreover, youth sport is more than child's play; it is a family affair that involves the entire family unit and has important implications for parenting practices. Children's participation in organized youth sport requires a great deal of the family's financial resources. Direct costs (e.g., registration fees) as well as "hidden," indirect costs (i.e., equipment, transportation, tournament fees, hotel rooms, and uniforms) are necessary to support children's organized sport participation. Townsend and Murphy (2001) reported that, on average, the cost per child per sporting activity is $500 per year. For competitive athletes, as much as $10,000 to $40,000 of the household income may be annually dedicated to sustain a child's sport-training experience (Coakley, 2009). This may create a social divide between those who can support their children's organized sport participation and those who cannot, such as low-income or single-parent households. Evidence has supported this proposition, as household income is a strong positive predictor of children's sport participation (Sport Canada, 2000; Trussell & McTeer, 2007). In fact, registration costs and/or lack of private transportation are significant barriers to children's sport participation (Lareau, 2003; Havitz, Morden, & Samdahl, 2004; Thompson, Rehman, & Humbert, 2005).

Kay (2000) suggested that the "time demands of sport affect the daily, weekly, and annual rhythms of family life" (p. 157). As such, family activities are often orchestrated with colour-coded calendars that control family activities, and mothers are often in charge of such coordination (Arendell, 2001). The time demands that organized sport may impose upon families often becomes a way of life, with parents feeling powerless to make changes and trapped by the demands placed upon them. Anderson and Doherty (2005) suggest that organized youth sport has facilitated the "over-scheduling of children and the consequent decline of family time" (p. 654). Some women have reported up to 20 hours per week dedicated to children's sport programs in transportation to practices, games, and fundraising initiatives (Trussell & Shaw, 2007). Further, Trussell and Shaw suggested that considerable tension and marital strain can develop as families try to negotiate career-dominated marriages while juggling children's participation in a number of activities. To help alleviate their stress, some families may make the decision to limit or discontinue their children's participation in organized sport programs.

At the same time, organized youth sport plays an important role in strengthening the family unit and gives them a sense of unity and shared family passion for a common interest. That is, organized sport can be crucial to the family members' construction of a "sense of family." Trussell (2009) suggested that parents believe that supporting their children's sport participation enhanced opportunities for communication with their children and facilitated a sense of family togetherness and belonging (whether it is time spent together in the vehicle, at the sport venue, or at home practicing). Trussell also found that sibling relationships were strengthened when children had a common sport interest, regardless of age or gender differences. This was illustrated through informal play opportunities connected to the type of sports they were involved in, as well as shared conversations about similar sport interests.

Sport and Diverse Populations

The common belief in Canada is that sport participation builds character and improves health and well-being. However, community sport is not without its problems and controversies. For example, researchers in Canada found that sport continues to reproduce racial hierarchies (Paraschak, 2007), social class barriers to participation (Donnelly & Harvey, 2007), dominant gender ideologies that constrain both females' and males' sport involvement (Schmalz & Kerstetter, 2006), and the preservation of

Adult-organized versus peer-organized sport: Is one better than the other for children?

The value of children's participation in organized sport is well documented and is believed to enhance children's physical and social growth and development. Yet, is too much of a good thing jeopardizing the development of other valuable skills? In some ways, children's perception of peer-organized and informal sports has been devalued with an increased emphasis on organized sport leagues (Trussell, 2009). Further, the ethical conduct of adults (parents and coaches) as well as participants and a "win at all cost" philosophy has compromised the integrity and quality of youth sport programs (Eitzen, 2009).

Let's consider some of the strengths of "shinny," or pick-up hockey, when comparing it to organized hockey leagues:

> inside an arena, inside cumbersome equipment, most of the players sit on the bench most of the time, behind which a pacing, anxious coach barks out orders, behind whom one or more idiot fans or parents take it way, way too seriously. The players are said to be *playing* hockey, but judging by the limited laughter and smiling, there is little play involved. Rather, organized hockey is about following instructions, executing set plays, confronting opponents, scoring, and winning. Open-air pickup hockey, on the other hand, is a game of endless variety, spontaneity, adaption, and unspoken rituals. With no coaches telling players what to do and no prescribed way to play, it lends itself to an often beautiful creativity. With no referees and few hard-and-fast rules, it insists on self-regulation and, in so doing, encourages accommodation and tolerance. Pickup hockey is always unpredictable and almost always instructive, even edifying, in a life-lessons kind of way. (Sanger as cited by Eitzen, 2009, p. 103).

After reading this passage, can you clearly identify three skills that are learned in peer-organized, informal sports? What are three skills that are emphasized in adult-organized, formal sports? What do you think: how can we promote the value and worth of both forms of sport participation, so that one is not sacrificed for the other—and children receive the benefits from both?

Sport can be divisive. Looking at three of the major hierarchies in society (class, race, and gender), sport plays a role in reproducing and reinforcing social divisions. Stereotypes can influence the type of sport involvement. What sports are traditionally male-dominated and female-dominated? Can you think of sports that have a high representation of one race? What role does social-class origin play? Are there any sports that are more dominated by one social class over another? What happens when a person who is "different" than the stereotypes tries to participate? When this social division happens, what broader consequences can it have, particularly when we think of the former text box and the role of sport as a central gathering place?

heteronormative values and encouragement of homophobia (Davison & Frank, 2007). In this sense, sport is not universally inclusive and can become a powerful divisive tool within a community. As Kay (2003) points out, sport can promote "white above black, male above female, physical prowess above alternative qualities, certain body types above others. And because of its pervasive presence, the divisions that arise through sport carry a social significance that reach far beyond sport itself" (p. 89). That is, these constructs of difference in sport may also, in turn, reinforce broader societal values outside of the sport domain.

Community sports may also be sites for change and resistance where individuals and groups can challenge the dominant norm, provide more inclusive spaces, and transform cultural values and beliefs. For example, as Shaw points out (see Chapter 7 on "The Politics of Leisure"), the simple act of participating in non-stereotypical sports that are thought to be traditionally masculine (e.g., boys in figure-skating) or feminine (e.g., girls in hockey) may affect and alter the attitudes of participants as well as other people (e.g., friends, teachers, parents, as well as the general public). Indeed, Kelly, Pomerantz, and Currie (2008) found that young girls' participation in the "non-traditional" sport of skateboarding challenged "boys' power and the ways in which girls are constructed through sexist and oppressive discourses" (p. 122). Traditionally, girls are thought to be the watchers, admirers, and supporters to boys' participation—unable to skateboard or not having what it takes. Yet, when presented with the opportunity, skateboarding provided the young girls with the opportunity to rewrite the oppressive rules of girlhood and emphasized femininity while creating powerful individual identities.

Sport also has the potential to break down social barriers based on race and ethnicity. Walseth (2006) pointed to the importance of sport for new immigrants to help facilitate integration into broader community life and create a sense of belonging and social support. Sport also provided a place of refuge where the young women could explore different forms of femininities than were presented in their home environment. However, Canadian research also emphasized that slight modifications may be required to successfully integrate two different cultures. For example, as Nakamura (2002) argued, to meet the needs of some Muslim women, steps may need to be taken such as: (i) a flexible dress code (allowing women to decide the degree to which they would like to be covered); (ii) an opportunity for sex-segregated programs (that some women may desire); and (iii) controlled access to the sport spaces (e.g., covering of doors and windows with paper during participation). These simple modifications could promote a more meaningful and inclusive environment and enhance sport-participation rates and experiences.

Other times, sport that is developed for a specific social group can promote a shared sense of community for individuals who have similar life experiences. For example, Goodwin et al. (2009) found that participation in wheelchair rugby provided the space for participants to be with other people in wheelchairs and to see their abilities and disabilities. Through this process they were able to explore identity alternatives and enhance social relations and emotional connections with others who have similar experiences. Wheelchair rugby also provided the venue in which participants could challenge the image of being fragile and passive via the hard hitting and aggressive nature of the sport. All of this was seen to enhance their psychological health and well-being.

Likewise, within different cultural groups, sport may also facilitate role models and social connections that promote cultural identity and provide the opportunity to pass on values and traditions. That is, sport can be a vehicle in which individuals and groups can (re)create and reinforce their cultural identities through sport. For example, sport can serve assimilationist and colonial agendas for Aboriginal youth, but it can also "provide an avenue through which these agendas can be challenged and subverted, thus allowing Northern youth to assert and maintain identities that differ from other Canadian youth" (Giles & Baker, 2008, p. 161). The Dene, Inuit Games, and North American Indigenous Games provide such examples. (Revisit Forsyth's chapter (22) on "Aboriginal Leisure in Canada" for a more detailed discussion).

Concluding Thoughts

This chapter presented some of the salient issues in community sport and provided a critical look at some of the problems and issues confronting the delivery of programs. Sport plays a central role in Canadian society in both positive and negative ways. It is a central hub or gathering place in bringing community members together. Sport can provide inclusive spaces that break down social barriers and allow people of difference to come together, and it can also provide the space to promote identity within social groups. Unfortunately, it can also be divisive and reinforce the social division among different social groups. To this end, organizations and community-based charitable groups are working toward providing accessible opportunities that will be more inclusive of Canada's diverse population and their sporting interests and needs.

Check out some of the many organizations that are working to break down social barriers and provide a more inclusive sport landscape for all Canadians. These organizations are also working to promote positive sporting experiences for all participants and help overcome the "darker side" of sport (e.g., drug abuse, sexual abuse, aggression, violence). See for example:

Canadian Association for the Advancement of Women and Sport and Physical Activity (CAAWS) - www.caaws.ca

The National Coaching Certification Program (NCCP) - www.coach.ca

True Sport - www.truesportpur.ca

What are some of these organizations' mandates and programs? What other organizations can you find?

Several challenges lay on the horizon for future practitioners. A multisectoral and integrated delivery system requires new skills to foster and manage the development and implementation of partnerships. An expectation for higher-quality programs and services, as well as time-stressed volunteers and families requires creative management frameworks. A developing interest for alternative sports, due to the exclusive structure and performance orientation of organized sports, may also provide some unique challenges. Alternative sports, or "action sports" such as skateboarding and parkour are coming into their own. How will these alternative sports fit into the sport delivery system? What should their emphasis be as we plan for our future facilities and programs in the public and private sectors? Finally, as the diverse makeup of Canada's population continues to grow and be recognized, how will practitioners respond to reflect the multiple and divergent needs of our communities? A critical reflection on these questions as well as the problems and issues confronting the delivery of sport programs is required, if we are to anticipate and plan for future sport research and practice.

Key Terms

Adult-organized sport
Diversity
Peer-organized sport
Sport delivery system
Volunteers
Youth sport

References

Anderson, J., & Doherty, W. (2005). Democratic community initiatives: The case of overscheduled children. *Family Relations, 54*, 654–665.

Arendell, T. (2001). The new care work of middle-class mothers: Managing childrearing, employment, and time. In K. Daly (Ed.), *Minding the time in family experience: Emerging perspectives and issues* (pp. 163–204). London, UK: Elsevier Science.

Canadian Sport Policy. (2012). Retrieved from Sport Information Resource Centre (SIRC) website: http://www:sirc.ca/CSPRenewal/documents/CSP2012_EN.pdf

Coakley, J. (2009). The good father: Parental expectations and youth sports. In T. Kay (Ed.), *Fathering through sport and leisure* (pp. 40–50). New York, NY: Routledge.

Coakley, J., & Donnelly, P. (2009). *Sports in society: Issues and controversies*. Toronto, ON: McGraw-Hill Ryerson.

Cousens, L., Barnes, M., Stevens, J., Mallen, C., & Bradish, C. (2006). "Who's your partner? Who's your ally?" Exploring the characteristics of public, private, and voluntary recreation linkages. *Journal of Park and Recreation Administration, 24*(1), 32–55.

Cuskelly, G. (2005). Volunteers in cricket. In G. Nichols & M. Collins (Eds.), *Volunteers in sports clubs* (pp. 83–86). LSA Publication No. 85.

de Cruz, C. (2005). Volunteer participation trends in Australian sport. In G. Nichols & M. Collins (Eds.), *Volunteers in sports clubs* (pp. 87–104). LSA Publication No. 85.

Davison, K., & Frank, B. (2007). Sexualities, genders, and bodies in sport: Changing practices of inequity. In K. Young & P. White (Eds.), *Sport and gender in Canada* (pp. 178–193). Toronto, ON: Oxford University Press.

Doherty, A. (2005). A profile of community sport volunteers. Report prepared for Parks and Recreation Ontario and Sport Alliance of Ontario.

Donnelly, P., & Harvey, J. (2007). Social class and gender: Intersections in sport and physical activity. In K. Young & P. White (Eds.), *Sport and gender in Canada* (pp. 95–119). Toronto, ON: Oxford University Press.

Dunn, J., Kinney, D., & Hofferth, S. (2003). Parental ideologies and children's after-school activities. *American Behavioral Scientist, 46*(10), 1359–1386.

Eitzen, D. (2009). *Fair and foul: Beyond the myths and paradoxes of sport* (4th ed.). Toronto, ON: Rowman & Littlefield.

Frisby, W., Thibault, L., & Kikulis, L. (2004). The organizational dynamics of under-managed partnerships in leisure service departments. *Leisure Studies, 23*(2), 109–126.

Giles, A., & Baker, A. (2008). Culture, colonialism, and competition: Youth sport culture in Canada's North. In M. Giardina & M. Donnelly (Eds.), *Youth culture and sport: Identity, power, and politics* (pp. 161–173). New York, NY: Routledge.

Goodwin, D., Johnston, K., Gustafson, P., Elliott, M., Thurmeier, R., & Kuttai, H. (2009). It's okay to be a quad: Wheelchair rugby players' sense of community. *Adapted Physical Activity Quarterly, 26*, 102–117.

Harvey, J., Lévesque, M., & Donnelly, P. (2007). Sport volunteerism and social capital. *Sociology of Sport Journal, 24*, 206–223.

Havitz, M., Morden, P., & Samdahl, D. (2004). *The diverse worlds of unemployed adults: Consequences for leisure, lifestyle, and well-being*. Waterloo, ON: Wilfrid Laurier University Press.

Haugen, M., & Villa, M. (2006). Rural idylls or boring places? In B. Bock & S. Shortall (Eds.), *Rural gender relations: Issues and case studies* (pp. 181–195). Cambridge, MA: CABI.

Kay, T. (2000). Sporting excellence: A family affair? *European physical education review, 6*(2), 151–169.

Kay, T. (2003). Sport and gender. In B. Houlihan (Ed.), *Sport and society* (pp. 89–104). Thousand Oaks, CA: Sage.

Kelly, D., Pomerantz, S., & Currie, D. (2008). "You can break so many more rules": The identity work and play of becoming skater girls. In M. Giardina & M. Donnelly (Eds.), *Youth culture and sport: Identity, power, and politics* (pp. 113–125). New York, NY: Routledge.

Lareau, A. (2003). *Unequal childhoods: Class, race, and family life*. Los Angeles, CA: University of California Press.

Mair, H. (2009). Club life: Third place and shared leisure in rural Canada. *Leisure Sciences, 31*, 450–465.

Nakamura, Y. (2002). Beyond the hijab: Female Muslims and physical activity. *Women in Sport and Physical Activity Journal, 11*(2), 21–48.

Nichols, G. (2005). Issues arising from Sport England's survey of volunteers in sport 2002–3. In G. Nichols & M. Collins (Eds.), *Volunteers in sports clubs* (pp. 1–14). LSA Publication No. 85.

Paraschak, V. (2007). Doing race, doing gender: First Nations, "sport" and gender relations. In K. Young & P. White (Eds.), *Sport and gender in Canada* (pp. 137–154). Toronto, ON: Oxford University Press.

Schmalz, D., & Kerstetter, D. (2006). Girlie girls and manly men: Children's stigma consciousness of gender in sports and physical activities. *Journal of Leisure Research, 38*(4), 536–557.

Sharpe, E. (2006). Resources at the grassroots of recreation: Organizational capacity and quality of experience in a community sport organization. *Leisure Sciences, 28*, 385–401.

Slack, T. (2003). Sport in the United States and Canada. In B. Houlihan (Ed.), *Sport and society* (pp. 295–311). Thousand Oaks, CA: Sage.

Sport Canada (2000). *Sport participation in Canada: 1998 Report.* Minister of Public Works and Government Services Canada (Catalogue No. CH24-1/2000-1E-IN).

Thibault, L., Frisby, W., & Kikulis, L. (1999). Interorganizational linkages in the delivery of local leisure services in Canada: Responding to economic, political and social pressures. *Managing Leisure, 4*, 125–141.

Thompson, A., Rehman, L., & Humbert, M. (2005). Factors influencing the physically active leisure of children and youth: A qualitative study. *Leisure Sciences, 27*, 421–438.

Tonts, M. (2005). Competitive sport and social capital in rural Australia. *Journal of Rural Studies, 21*(2), 137–149.

Townsend, M., & Murphy, G. (2001). "Roll up and spend your last dime": The Merry-go-round of children's extra-curricular activities in modern society. *ACHPER Healthy Lifestyles Journal, 48*(3–4), 10–13.

Trussell, D. (2009). *Organized youth sport, parenthood ideologies and gender relations: Parents' and children's experiences and the construction of "team family".* (Unpublished doctoral dissertation). University of Waterloo, Ontario.

Trussell, D., & McTeer, W. (2007). Children's sport participation in Canada: Is it a level playing field? *International Journal of Canadian Studies, 35*, 113–132.

Trussell, D., & Shaw, S. (2007). "Daddy's gone and he'll be back in October": Farm women's experiences of family leisure. *Journal of Leisure Research, 39*(2), 366–387.

Trussell, D., & Shaw, S. (2009). Changing family life in the rural context: Women's perspectives of family leisure on the farm. *Leisure Sciences, 31*(5), 434–449.

Walseth, K. (2006). Sport and belonging. *International Review for the Sociology of Sport, 41*(3–4), 447–464.

Warner-Smith, P., & Brown, P. (2002). "The town dictates what I do": The leisure, health and well-being of women in a small Australian country town. *Leisure Studies, 21*, 39–56.

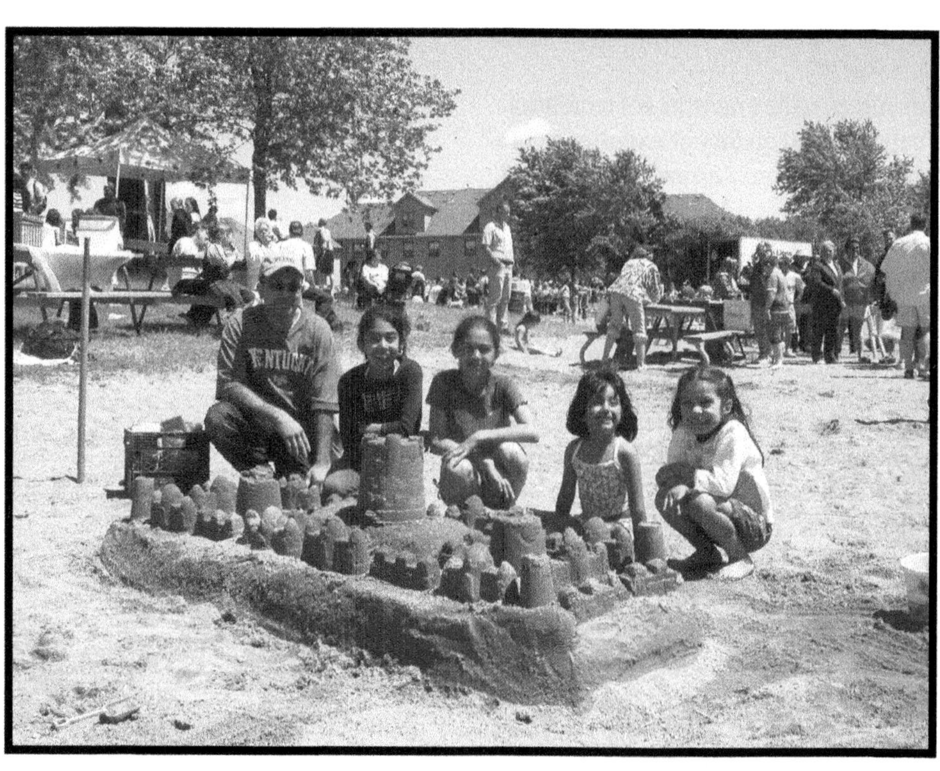

Chapter 4
Leisure's Many Roles

Charlene S. Shannon, Ph.D.
University of New Brunswick

Learning Objectives

After reading this chapter, students will be able to

1. Identify the roles of leisure for the individual, family, and society.
2. Recognize that leisure's influence can be both positive and negative.
3. Consider ways in which practitioners can maximize leisure's positive roles.

Introduction

The manner in which leisure interacts with aspects of our lives varies greatly depending on who we are, where we live, the circumstances existing in our lives, the opportunities available to us, and ultimately, the leisure choices we each make. In this chapter you will learn of leisure's many important functions at the individual, family, and societal levels. An exhaustive list of leisure's many roles is not provided, but specific examples illustrate how leisure interacts with the lives of individuals, families, and society as a whole. The numerous ways in which leisure can contribute to or enhances our lives will be discussed. You will discover that leisure's roles are not static, but rather they change and evolve with the circumstances in which we find ourselves. Finally, you will learn that these roles played by leisure are not always positive or constructive but can be destructive to an individual, family, community, and society.

Roles Related to the Individual

Considerable research within the field of recreation and leisure studies has focused on understanding leisure roles at the individual level. Some of these roles are more salient at particular stages of one's life while others are active across the lifespan (Freysinger, 1999). Life events can also alter the role that leisure plays in one's life. In this section, four key roles related to the individual are outlined and discussed. These roles relate to:

1. enjoyment,
2. identity development,
3. skill development, and
4. personal wellness

Let's consider each in turn.

Leisure is a source of enjoyment. Recall that leisure, loosely defined, is any activity or experience that (a) is freely chosen, (b) is intrinsically motivated (done for its own sake), and (c) provides the opportunity to use our own particular skills in interesting ways (Kelly, 1996). Engaging in leisure activities can have a variety of positive outcomes ranging from enhanced moods to feelings of accomplishment and mastery. All are related to what we would call satisfaction or enjoyment. The immediate benefit of such experiences is perhaps obvious. We all enjoy the satisfaction of having a good time and this feeling may last a very long time. Even recalling positive leisure experiences long after they have occurred can improve our moods (Iso-Ahola, 1994). Perhaps best of all, this enjoyment enhances how we feel about our lives. Those who take time to participate in leisure tend to report greater life satisfaction (Riddick, 1986).

Leisure interacts with identity development. Leisure plays a key role in helping individuals develop their own sense of self. It does so by offering the freedom to explore, experiment with, or "try on" different roles (Kelly, 1987). Like a stage in a play, leisure offers the opportunity to "present" ourselves to others and to gauge their reaction on our successes and failures. Through this process individuals' identities emerge. See the *i*-box "A Closer Look at Youth,

A Closer Look at Youth, Play, Games, and Identity

Children try on adulthood as they play house. Athletes of all ages become weekend warriors as they don the uniforms for any number of sports. All help build a sense of self and a sense of identity. Identity development is a particularly salient process in the lives of adolescents as they work to discover and define who they are and where they fit into society. An adolescent may try skateboarding simply out of curiosity. After gaining the ability to perform the tricks, learning the language associated with the sport, and connecting positively with other boarders, the adolescent may begin to identify himself or herself as a skateboarder. The youth may feel a sense of belonging to the skateboarding community and spend more time engaging in patterns of behaviour that will reinforce this new sense of identify and his or her connection to the group. Through such processes, identity evolves.

Play, Games, and Identity" to further consider the importance of leisure to identity development.

Leisure is also an avenue for discovering our individuality by providing opportunities for us to differentiate ourselves from others. This process is called *individuation* (Kleiber, 1999). Identities developed through leisure are beneficial long after childhood and adolescence. For example, during times of transition or through traumatic life events when an individual experiences loss of a work identity (such as through retirement, unemployment, or illness) a leisure identity can provide a continued sense of worth and value (Kelly, 1996). In such cases, leisure not only helps participants develop their own sense of self, but it can also provide a new sense of purpose. It is no surprise that leisure activities often become central life interests during times of change or personal turmoil.

Although leisure provides the freedom to explore and develop personal identities, it can also constrain individual identity formation. For example, societal expectations and stereotypes related to gender roles may limit perceptions of acceptable activities or experiences (Shaw, 1999). Girls are often discouraged from participating in physically demanding sports while boys are taught that domination of opponents is more important than fun in sport (Messner, 1998). Therefore, leisure experiences made available to these children may limit the identities that they may eventually develop (Henderson, 2005) (see Chapter 20).

In other cases, gay and lesbian youth may feel the need to conceal their sexual identities when participating in certain leisure contexts, especially public leisure. This can mean they are unable to fully experience or enjoy their leisure opportunities. Gay and lesbian youth may also avoid activities and experiences that reinforce heterosexuality or stereotypical male and female roles (Kivel & Kleiber, 2000).

Leisure contributes to skill development. Most leisure activities and experiences are rich with the potential for skill development. Leisure facilitates the development or improvement of interpersonal and communication skills. While hanging out with friends or participating on a sports team, children learn to share, compromise, negotiate, and be patient. Planning, problem solving, and decision-making skills can be developed through a variety of leisure experiences. Entertaining a group of friends with a backyard barbeque or taking a family camping vacation requires all of those skills. Volunteering, whether it is as a high school student council representative or as a Guide/Scout leader, offers an exceptional context for developing and practicing leadership skills.

Adults also use non-obligated time to try a variety of new activities, such as learning how to snowshoe, photograph scenery, or play a musical instrument. Once these skills are developed, they can serve other equally important roles. For example, once you are able to play a musical instrument, playing can be a source of personal pleasure and enjoyment. It can also function as an outlet for creative expression or a way to relax and relieve stress. Some skills developed through leisure may lead to employment (e.g., teaching piano) and even a career (e.g., being a musician).

Leisure interacts with dimensions of personal wellness. Wellness has many facets. We typically think of it in terms that are physical, social, emotional, intellectual, and spiritual. The literature indicates that leisure can play a positive role in all of them. For example, physically active leisure provides important health benefits and protects against the development of various illnesses and diseases (World Health Organization, 2003). The World Health Organization (WHO) notes, for example, that regular physical activity reduces the risk of premature death (especially from heart disease), from developing diabetes, from developing high blood pressure, and helps reduce these conditions among those who now have them. Even the incidence of many types of cancer is reduced by physical activity.

Leisure builds social wellness by offering space and opportunities to socialize, meet new people, as well as to develop and nurture friendships and relationships with family members (Kelly, 1993). This can help lead to emotional wellness. Emotional wellness implies having the ability to express emotions appropriately, cope with stress in a healthy way, and experience enjoyment in life regardless of the challenges it may present. Research has demonstrated that leisure experiences can serve as a healthy outlet for coping with stressful events (Iwasaki & Mannell, 2000) and expressing a wide range of emotions, including anger and sadness. Leisure can also be a source of pleasure and enjoyment during difficult life events such as illness (Shannon & Shaw, 2005). In these ways, leisure can contribute to emotional well-being (see Chapter 10).

Leisure activities and experiences provide the individual with opportunities to learn. Visiting a museum or historic site, travelling to a new place, attending an ethnic cooking class, or reading a book, all represent leisure activities that can engage the mind and promote intellectual wellness.

Finally, leisure can provide the opportunity for spiritual connection, spiritual maintenance, or expressions of spirituality (Heintzman & Mannell, 2003). As the religious philosopher Josef Pieper (1963) suggested, leisure can open one to the possibilities of a better life. Like Plato and Aristotle, he believed that through leisure we could let our minds open to new ideas, like flower buds opening to accept sunlight. This, he believed, was the basis of emotional and spiritual well-being.

Although leisure can contribute to virtually all the various dimensions of wellness, it is important to recognize that some of the leisure choices individuals make do not promote individual well-being. For example, recreational drug use and gambling are activities that can lead to addiction, which can in turn compromise physical, social, and emotional wellness (Hood & Peterson, 1991; see Chapter 18). Current trends related to video game play patterns and increased television viewing tell us that some of our more pervasive leisure activities encourage and contribute to passive lifestyles. Too much sedentary leisure can have negative individual health outcomes for anyone (Cameron, Craig, Stephens, & Ready, 2002) and diminish overall wellness.

Think about the role of leisure in your own life. When and how have the roles of your leisure changed? What is the most dominant role that leisure plays in your life right now? What changes can you anticipate in terms of leisure's role in your life in the future?

Roles Related to Family Functioning

Despite the changing structures and definitions of "family," it remains one of society's major institutions because of the functions it serves. Family is a basic unit of social life, and leisure is very much a part of the family dynamic. Much of the research conducted on leisure and family has focused on traditional, heterosexual families, therefore there is limited information on the role leisure plays in more diverse family forms. Consequently, leisure's roles in this section represent our understanding as it relates to the traditional family form.

Leisure provides opportunities for shared family experiences. Whether it is going out to a restaurant for dinner, bowling at a local alley, or playing a board game at home, leisure experiences provide opportunities for family members to be together. For example, parents' leisure with their children has been identified as one of the most satisfying forms of daily activity (Mannell & Zuzanek, 1995). Providing this context for shared family experiences, leisure serves many functions. First, it can facilitate family bonding and cohesion (Orthner & Mancini, 1991) and can reinforce relationships between parents and children. It can also develop a sense of family unity and connection to other family members and the family unit in general (Mactavish & Schleien, 1998).

Family leisure also represents a learning environment. During leisure, parents are often presented with the opportunity to pass along their own personal values (pointing out unacceptable or exemplary behaviour) along with their expectations related to their children's behaviours (Shaw & Dawson, 2001). They may not be able to sit with their child as they learn in school, but they can certainly be present as their children play board games or watch television. As opportunities arise they might praise any variety of noteworthy behaviours or offer alternative options as the situation demands. Through this shared family leisure, children develop leisure interests and behaviours that last a lifetime.

Family leisure is also a time of sharing. Family members may share their opinions, values, ideas, talents, and skills. In particular, leisure can be a time of sharing and passing on personal interests. For example, if a parent enjoys canoeing, that parent may introduce the activity to his or her partner and children. A child may involve a parent in building a *Star Wars* themed *Lego* masterpiece and in the process educate his or her parent about that particular pop culture phenomenon. Siblings often teach each other various leisure skills and activities so that they can pursue leisure experiences together.

Couple/family leisure can contribute to marital and family satisfaction. Family-based leisure has important implications for parents' satisfaction with their role as parents and with family life. For men, in particular, satisfaction with parenthood is greater when they have more frequent leisure interactions with their children (Freysinger, 1994). Leisure can also help improve marital satisfaction among couples who take part in leisure activities without their children being present (Hill, 1988). Trips or excursions without the kids, for example, are common as parents seek to escape the ongoing demands of parenthood and perhaps rediscover each other in the process.

Although shared family experiences can be beneficial for participants, family leisure can sometimes be a source of stress, frustration, and/or dissatisfaction for certain family members (Shaw & Dawson, 2003/2004). What may be an enjoyable and satisfying leisure experience for one family member may be perceived as unpleasant or work-like by another. For example, not all couple-based leisure contributes to martial satisfaction. It seems as though leisure activities that provide limited interaction (e.g., watching television together) can actually have a negative effect on marital satisfaction (Holman & Jacquart, 1988). Also, women experience family leisure differently from the rest of the family members because they often perform much of the "work" (e.g., planning and organizing activities) involved in family leisure experiences (Shaw, 1992).

Finally, the satisfaction that emerges from family leisure activities is not always shared evenly between parents and children (Zabriskie & McCormick, 2003). Children's satisfaction with family life is more narrowly related to their own personal satisfaction with the leisure activities in which the family engages. A toddler may find a family trip to a children's theme park a great adventure while a teen may find the same trip an exercise in embarrassment and boredom.

Leisure is an opportunity for transmitting family traditions and culture. A number of leisure experiences within the family occur through observing or celebrating various holidays and occasions together. Family celebrations are opportunities for the introduction and development of a variety of rituals or traditions. These rituals and traditions are believed to strengthen family ties and provide an outlet for expressions of family identity (Wolin & Bennett, 1984). As traditions are repeated and passed on from parents to children, those traditions serve to connect the generations, and foster continuity and family stability (Fiese et al., 2002). Hiding painted eggs in the backyard for children to find at Easter or roasting pumpkin seeds at Halloween may be traditions that families develop to celebrate major cultural events in their communities. Other family traditions may be less culture-specific and represent the unique priorities of the family. For example, leisure may include reading a story to a child each night before bed, camping at a particular provincial park each summer, or visiting and having dinner with grandparents every Friday evening. Such traditions help to clarify and communicate a family's values and build relationships between family members.

Certain leisure activities engaged in as a family also allow for the transmission of cultural values. Preparing a meal that represents the culture of a region, listening or playing music reflecting the culture of a particular ethnic group, or teaching a dance that is associated with a particular religious or cultural celebration are all leisure experiences that can help adults facilitate the development of cultural appreciation and understanding.

In what ways might becoming a parent change the way you participate in leisure activities? What roles might leisure play in blended, lone-parent, and same-sex couple families?

Roles Related to Society

Any society represents a large, relatively permanent, self-sufficient group of interacting people. Members of a society share:

1. a sense of belonging or identity
2. a body of shared values (deep seated, fundamental beliefs about what is right or wrong, good, or bad)
3. a system of social organization (e.g., democracy)
4. a sense of interdependency (members require the skills of others to thrive)

Without these shared values, interdependencies, and identities a society would cease to exist.

To survive, a society must transmit its values and its priorities to all its members. We call this transmission socialization. Socialization is the process through which group members internalize group values so that they can conform to group expectations. Throughout the ages, leisure has been used as a key socializing agent and is very much connected to social institutions such as the government, religious institutions, and education. They all use leisure to transmit culture and values (e.g., games can convey the importance of beliefs like competition, cooperation, and fair play while highlighting relevant symbols like trophies) and establish and promote social relationships. In many ways, these institutions influence the leisure in which Canadians engage. Consider within the examples offered next how leisure responds to the demands of socialization.

Leisure Reflects and Transmits Values and Norms of Society

Leisure performs an important socialization function by transmitting a society's values and norms (Kleiber, 1999). Values such as cooperation, responsibility, helping others, and respect can all be taught and developed through participation in various leisure activities. The leisure activities and experiences supported by government departments typically attempt to promote central value structures and belief systems. For example, in Canada we value the natural environment and open space; therefore, all three levels of government have established parks and protected areas to protect natural spaces for this and future generations of Canadians.

The relationship between society's values and leisure activity is dynamic. Just as leisure can influence adoption of societal norms, these norms can influence leisure participation patterns. For example, the work ethic in Canada undoubtedly influences the amount of time workers are willing to devote to leisure pursuits. Canadians learn in school how to work effectively and efficiently, but rarely learn how to play. When introduced to people for the first time, we are likely to wonder what this new friend does for a living, not what he or she does for entertainment. Many Canadians report that they would continue to work even if they were independently wealthy and lacked an economic incentive for doing so. Dominant Canadian values tend to

Through leisure, values and norms of a society are transmitted. Do you think it is also possible for leisure activities to influence the values or norms of a society?

revolve around work, and this will shape the way in which individuals then view leisure.

Leisure Contributes to the Economy

Leisure represents the world's largest single industry, and fulfils an economic function in two ways (Kelly & Godbey, 1992). First, individuals tend to consume leisure services and products in vast quantities. Billions of dollars of discretionary income is spent on leisure products and services. Going to the movies, eating out, purchasing video games or DVDs, taking instructional classes, travelling, purchasing sporting equipment, and buying scrap-booking supplies all involve investing in recreation and leisure and this influences a society's economic health. See *i*-box "A Closer Look at Leisure's Economic Role in the Community" for a specific example of how leisure can have an impact on the local economy.

Second, leisure activity has economic consequences because it aids production. Specifically, leisure is thought (a) to provide recuperative opportunities for workers by providing escape and novelty, (b) to improve the mental and physical well-being of workers to improve production schedules, and (c) to improve skill levels of the work force. The importance of leisure to production suggests that corporate and political leaders may be motivated to control leisure opportunities within their respective workforces. For example, corporate leaders may wish to encourage activities consistent with the corporate agenda—those pursuits that encourage cooperation, team work, competitive spirit, and even healthy lifestyle to "create" more motivated and productive workers.

A Closer Look at Leisure's Economic Role in the Community

Brian VanBlarcom, an economics professor at Acadia University, has conducted research related to understanding the economic impact of various recreation/leisure pursuits on communities in Nova Scotia. One study examined the spending of visitors hiking on the Cape Split Trail and in Blomidon Provincial Park, two key outdoor recreation attractions in Kings County, Nova Scotia. Using data collected and published by Gardner Pinfold Consulting Economists Limited in A Survey of Nova Scotia Hiking Trail Users 1999, it was estimated that over 15,000 non-residents who used the park in that year generated $560,000 in spending, $80,000 in direct wages, and $134,000 in total income (VanBlarcom & Ball, 2003).

Economic impact research helps us to understand how what individuals and families do as part of their leisure can affect the economy. In these examples, the economic impact was estimated in terms of the local community/region; however, leisure's economic role also functions at a societal level in many of the same ways, but on a larger scale. According to the World Travel and Tourism Council, the tourism, hospitality, and leisure industry is the largest industry in the world and accounts for almost 11% of the world gross domestic product. In Canada, tourism contributes approximately 2% to the country's Gross Domestic Product playing an important role in the health of the Canadian economy (Canadian Tourism Commission, 2004).

What leisure-related attractions, natural resources, or activities draw visitors and stimulate the local economy in the community in which you live?

Leisure Can Promote Group Solidarity

Canada is a multicultural society and its leisure profile reflects the diversity that multiculturalism offers. The origins of many of our favourite leisure activities are found in societies from all over the world. These activities promote solidarity in two ways. First, as noted earlier, activities promoted by the dominant culture tend to reflect the priorities of that culture. Groups and individuals who take part in those activities are "learning" and promoting those same priorities. In this way, solidarity is demonstrated and strengthened. Second, subgroups within the dominant culture can use leisure to promote and preserve their own cultural priorities. Many such groups use dance, art, and many forms of celebration to highlight what makes them unique within the larger society (Karlis, 1998). By doing so, they help build solidarity within the cultural group and awareness of their group among the larger community.

Not all subgroup cultures' leisure priorities are celebrated with equal enthusiasm. A few are actively discouraged because their practices are perceived to be inconsistent with the dominant values of the larger community. Consider, for example, the way in which the youth skateboard culture, one that sometimes projects a "bad boy" image, is often frowned upon by municipal recreation departments. Skateboard activities are often banned or criminalized and participants are fined for skating on public property (Heizer, 2004). Such restrictions arise because the values being promoted within that subgroup fail in some way to promote the values of dominant groups (in this case, adults) in society (Kloep & Hendry, 2003). Social institutions understand very well the

What leisure activities or behaviours do Canadians engage in that are "uniquely Canadian?"

influence of leisure activity and try hard to ensure that this influence is consistent with the dominant views of what is right and wrong, good and bad.

Leisure Can Promote Inclusion

There are a number of individuals and groups in our society who are socially marginalized—not considered part of mainstream society and therefore excluded from services that are offered commonly to others. Individuals with disabilities, youth at-risk, ethnic and racial minorities, and individuals who are gay or lesbian are among those individuals who typically have been on the margins. Some leisure researchers have focused on understanding the interactions between leisure and members of these marginalized groups. (Several chapters in this text pursue this theme in considerable detail.)

Leisure contexts can promote and develop equality as well as eliminate stereotypes associated with particular groups (Sable, 1995). Sport is one leisure context that has consistently brought people from different countries, cultures, and religions together to participate in common, universal activities. For example, sporting events are sometimes arranged between individuals with disabilities and those without disabilities. These events are noteworthy because they have the capacity to focus the attention of participants and spectators on the sport and not individual differences among the players. Such events promote integration and interaction between groups as players focus on learning the sport, developing skills, and cooperating toward common goals. These are the types of activities that build an inclusive community.

Unfortunately, leisure environments and experiences can also serve to perpetuate stereotypes and further promote exclusion and marginalization of certain groups in our society. Sports leagues have, in the past, often segregated one group from another. Sporting events often divided participants according to race, gender, and any number of divisive criteria. Such exclusion can deepen social divisions and conflicts. Typically, however, leisure is used to build understanding between participants and competitors (Coakley & Donnelly, 2004). The Olympic Games offer one striking example of the inclusive role played by leisure activity. They are intended to promote peace, cooperation, and serve as a positive force on the world stage. This is possible because, as suggested previously, special rules apply to leisure activities. Consequences are suspended and the joy of participation dominates. It seems unlikely that any activity other than leisure could fulfill this important task.

Implications for Practitioners

The many roles discussed here are not inherent in every leisure activity or experience, but rather represent the potential roles leisure can play as it contributes to and enhances individual lives, family life, and life in Canadian society. The challenge for recreation and leisure service providers is to help realize this potential. The goal is one of ensuring that leisure opportunities exist so that individuals, families, and society can enjoy the many positive outcomes that leisure has to offer. Knowledge of the positive potential for leisure is critical in working toward creating or facilitating opportunities and experiences that maximize or accentuate leisure's more positive contributions. Furthermore, a clear understanding of leisure's possible negative effects on an individual family, or society can help leisure services providers minimize the occasions or situations in which leisure's roles prove detrimental. This includes being sensitive to the practices of different cultures within our society, providing opportunities for families to engage in leisure that will meet a variety of needs, and regulating leisure behaviours that could be harmful to other individuals or society as a whole.

Finally, it is important to acknowledge that at times leisure's role may be consistently positive for the individual, family, and society. In other situations, however, the role played by leisure may be somewhat less than harmonious. Consider how leisure activities may contribute to an individual in some positive way, but may not play a positive role for family or society. An adolescent may pursue a leisure activity intended to develop his or her own individual identity (e.g., pursuing snowboarding as a serious leisure activity). If family members do not share the enjoyment of this activity or have difficulty financially supporting his or her involvement, this pursuit could detract from family cohesion and, in fact, be a source of family conflict. Furthermore, an activity like skateboarding, while it may provide participants with a valued sense of well-being, may still be perceived as a nuisance by members of the community or larger society.

Leisure is certainly a complicated topic. It has such a profound effect on all levels of society, yet many continue to think of leisure as non-serious activity suitable only for children. This chapter has shown that leisure activity can indeed be simplistic and even child-like, but its effects are sweeping and complex. Only a few of the societal influences that give shape and texture to our leisure repertoire are mentioned here. The goal of the chapter was to introduce the dynamic nature of the relationship between leisure and the society within which it takes place. A more comprehensive discussion on the complexity of this relationship takes place throughout the rest of this textbook.

Key Terms

Familial roles
Group solidarity
Identity development
Individuation
Individuals roles
Socialization
Societal roles

References

Cameron, C., Craig, C. A., Stephens, T., & Ready, T. A. (2002). *Increasing physical activity: Supporting an active workforce*. Ottawa, ON: Canadian Fitness and Lifestyle Research Institute.

Coakley, J., & Donnelly, P. (2004). *Sports in society: Issues and controversies* (1st Canadian ed.). Toronto, ON: McGraw-Hill Ryerson.

Fiese, B. H., Tomcho, T. J., Douglas, M., Josephs, K., Poltrock, S., & Baker, T. (2002). A review of 50 years of research on naturally occurring family routines and rituals: Cause for celebration? *Journal of Family Psychology, 16*, 381–390.

Freysinger, V. J. (1994). Leisure with children and parental satisfaction: Further evidence of a sex difference in the experience of adult roles and leisure. *Journal of Leisure Research, 26*, 212–226.

Freysinger, V. J. (1999). Life span and life course perspectives on leisure. In E. L. Jackson & T. L. Burton (Eds.), *Leisure studies: Prospects for the twenty-first century* (pp. 253–270). State College, PA: Venture Publishing, Inc.

Heintzman, P., & Mannell, R. C. (2003). Spiritual functions of leisure and spiritual well-being: Coping with time pressure. *Leisure Sciences, 25*, 207–230.

Heizer, C. (2004). Street smarts: A new brand of skatepark, called a skate plaza, hits the streets for boarders wanting to ride the rails. *Parks & Recreation, 39*(11), 74–79.

Henderson, K. A. (2005). What about girls? In P. A. Witt & L. L. Caldwell (Eds.), *Recreation and youth development* (pp. 407–423), State College, PA: Venture Publishing, Inc.

Hill, M. S. (1988). Marital stability and spouses' shared time. *Journal of Family Issues, 9*, 427–451.

Holman, T. B., & Jacquart, M. (1988). Leisure activity patterns and marital satisfaction: A further test. *Journal of Marriage and the Family, 50*, 69–78.

Hood, C. D., & Peterson, C. A. (1991). *Therapeutic recreation treatment needs during chemical dependency treatment*. Champaign, IL: Cooperative Extension Services.

Iso-Ahola, S. (1994). Leisure lifestyle and health. In D. Compton & S. Iso-Ahola (Eds.), *Leisure and mental health* (pp. 42–60). Park City, UT: Family Developmental Resources.

Iwasaki, Y., & Mannell, R. C. (2000). Hierarchical dimensions of leisure stress coping. *Leisure Sciences, 22*, 163–181.

Karlis, G. (1998). Social cohesion, social closure, and recreation: The ethnic experience in multicultural societies. *Journal of Applied Recreation Research, 23*(1), 3–21.

Kelly, J. R. (1987). *Freedom to be: A new sociology of leisure*. New York, NY: Macmillan.

Kelly, J. R. (1993). Leisure-family research: Old and new issues. *World Leisure and Recreation, 35*, 5–9.

Kelly, J. R. (1996). *Leisure* (3rd ed.). Boston, MA: Allyn & Bacon.

Kelly, J., & Godbey, G. (1992). *The sociology of leisure*. State College, PA: Venture Publishing, Inc.

Kivel, B. D., & Kleiber, D. A. (2000). Leisure in the identity formation of lesbian/gay youth: Personal, but not social. *Leisure Sciences, 2*, 215–232.

Kleiber, D. A. (1999). *Leisure experience and human development*. New York, NY: Basic Books.

Kloep, M., & Hendry, L. B. (2003). Adult control and adolescent challenge? Dilemmas and paradoxes in young people's leisure. *World Leisure Journal, 45*(3), 24–34.

Mactavish, J., & Schleien, S. (1998). Playing together growing together: Parents' perspectives on the benefits of family recreation in families that include children with a developmental disability. *Therapeutic Recreation Journal, 32*, 207–230.

Mannell, R. C., & Zuzanek, J. (1995). Married with children: Family leisure in daily life and satisfaction with family life. In *Symposium on Leisure Research* (p. 16). Arlington, VA: National Recreation and Park Association.

Messner, M. A. (1998). Boyhood organized sports, and the construction of masculinities. In M. S. Kimmel & M. A. Messner (Eds.), *Men's lives* (4th ed., pp. 109–121). Needham Heights, MA: Allyn & Bacon.

Orthner, D. K., & Mancini, J. A. (1991). Benefits of leisure for family bonding. In B. L. Driver, P. J. Brown, & G. L. Peterson, (Eds.), *Benefits of leisure* (pp. 215–301). State College, PA: Venture Publishing, Inc.

Pieper, J. (1963). *Leisure: The basis of culture*. New York, NY: Mentor Books.

Riddick, C. C. (1986). Leisure satisfaction precursors. *Journal of Leisure Research, 18*, 259–265.

Sable, J. R. (1995). Efficacy of physical integration, disability awareness, and adventure programming on adolescents' acceptance of individuals with disabilities. *Therapeutic Recreation Journal, 29*, 206–227.

Shannon, C. S., & Shaw, S. M. (2005). "If the dishes don't get done today, they'll get done tomorrow": Changes to women's leisure following a breast cancer experience. *Journal of Leisure Research, 37*(2), 195–215.

Shaw, S. M. (1992). Dereifying family leisure: An examination of women's and men's everyday experiences and perceptions of family time. *Leisure Sciences, 14*, 271–286.

Shaw, S. M. (1999). Gender and leisure. In E. L. Jackson & T. L. Burton (Eds.), *Leisure studies: Prospects for the twenty-first century* (pp. 271–281). State College, PA: Venture Publishing, Inc.

Shaw, S. M., & Dawson, D. (2001). Purposive leisure: Examining parental discourses on family activities. *Leisure Sciences, 23*, 217–231.

Shaw, S. M., & Dawson, D. (2003/2004). Contradictory aspects of family leisure: Idealization versus experience. *Leisure/Loisir, 28*(3–4), 179–201.

VanBlarcom, B., & Ball, M. (2003). *The economic impact of visitor hiking in Kings County, Nova Scotia.* Paper presented at the Annual Recreation Nova Scotia Conference, Oak Island, Nova Scotia.

Wolin, S. J., & Bennett, L. A. (1984). Family rituals. *Family Process, 23*, 401–420.

World Health Organization. (2003). *Health and development through physical activity and sport.* WHO/NHM/NPH/PAH/03.2. Geneva: WHO Document Production Services.

Zabriskie, R. B., & McCormick, B. P. (2003). Parent and child perspectives of family leisure involvement and satisfaction with family life. *Journal of Leisure Research, 35*, 163–189.

Chapter 5

Leveraging Sport Events to Achieve Health and Economic Benefits

Luke R. Potwarka, Ph.D.
University of Waterloo

Ryan Snelgrove, Ph.D.
University of Windsor

Learning Objectives

After reading this chapter, students will be able to

1. Explain how sport events can contribute to achieving health and economic benefits.
2. Describe some of the challenges associated with leveraging sport events.
3. Describe techniques that can be undertaken to leverage sports events.

Introduction

Sport events are often praised for their ability to deliver numerous benefits to the public. Most commonly, advocates claim that sport events can result in increased health and economic development (Chalip, 2006). These potential benefits are often used to place sport on the government agenda and support the use of public funds to host sport events. However, critics argue these benefits are largely overstated and never fully achieved. We advance the position that sport events can deliver health and economic benefits if they are managed with those outcomes in mind. In this chapter we discuss how sport events can contribute to improved health and economic development, and how they can be managed to ensure the realization of those benefits. Although much attention is given to international sport events such as the Olympics or FIFA World Cup, many of the concepts discussed in this chapter also apply to smaller-sized events.

Leveraging Sport Events for Health Benefits

Large-scale elite sporting events such as the Olympic Games or the FIFA World Cup of Soccer are often thought to have an impact on the activity levels of the general population (Murphy & Bauman, 2007). As such, government investments into hosting such events are often justified in terms of anticipated "trickle-down effects." These effects refer to an event's capacity to increase sport and/or physical activity (PA) levels across a community as a result of the extensive media coverage it generates (Hindson, Gidlow, & Peebles, 1994; Hogan & Norton, 2000). For instance, in a recent address to the House of Commons, England's Olympic Minister suggested that hosting the 2012 Summer Games would be "the catalyst that inspires people of all ages and all talents to lead more active lives" (Jewell, 2003). London 2012's official Olympic bid document predicted that "grassroots participation would be boosted. An already sports-mad nation would get fitter and healthier" (London 2012, 2005).

Have you ever been inspired to take up a sport after watching an elite athletic performance? If so, describe your experience.

There is some evidence in support of trickle-down effect claims. Surveys following the 1992 Summer Olympics, 1994 Soccer World Cup, and 2002 Winter Olympics reported increased sport club/organization memberships among host-region residents (Hindson et al., 1994). Such findings might be a function of improved access to newly developed sport infrastructure and/or podium success attained by a nation's athletes (Hogan & Norton, 2000; Lockhead, 2005). For instance, an annual survey conducted twelve months after the 2000 Sydney Olympics revealed increased rates for beach volleyball, water polo, and track and field, which were sports Australian athletes excelled at during the Games (Sweeny Sports Report, 2000/2001). However, these participation trends were not sustained over time (Sweeny Sports Report, 2000/2001).

There is also evidence to suggest that trickle-down effects are not a guaranteed outcome of mega-sporting events. For example, data collected after the Manchester 2002 Commonwealth Games found no impact on participation in sport-related activities or sport-club membership (MORI, 2004). In addition, surveys conducted in conjunction with the Sydney Olympics reported little change in citizens' general activity levels from pre- to post-event. In response to these types of reports, Veal (2003) concluded that the Olympics might actually have a "couch potato" effect on individuals because of the extensive television coverage of the event. In other words, he felt people are more likely motivated to passively observe mega-sport events than emulate the activities they are watching. This argument appears to be corroborated by a recent survey of Canadian citizens, which found that while the number of adults watching sports on television jumped 20% between 1998 and 2005, there was a simultaneous decline in sport participation over the seven-year period (Ifedi, 2008). Moreover, some researchers argue that mega-sport events might instead have a "discouragement effect" (Hindson et al., 1994), which occurs when members of the general population perceive elite athletes' performance levels to be unattainable. Indeed, the validity of trickle-down effect claims remains a heavily debated topic among leisure and sport professionals.

Do you think claims that a mega-sport event will result in a trickle-down effect are warranted? Why or why not?

Nevertheless, mega-sport events still constitute a prime opportunity to promote messages to the general population that inspire people of all ages to become physically fit (Soteriades et al. 2006). One reason for the lack of evidence of the trickle-down effect may be because public health and recreation sectors have generally failed to take advantage of the opportunities provided by mega-events to promote PA (Murphy & Bauman, 2007). Increased activity levels are more likely to result from the combined impact of staging the event and the implementation of sport and PA-related interventions (Coalter, 2004). However, few health professionals have leveraged sport events by designing, implementing, and evaluating programs that encourage people to become more active. One example is an initiative undertaken by the British Columbia Government called ActNow BC. This program coincided with the Vancouver Winter Olympics and used schools, local governments, employers, and communities to promote healthy active lifestyles. The goals of the program were to:

1. Increase the number of physically active people in the province by 20%.
2. Increase the percentage of adults who consume at least five servings of fruits and vegetables daily by 20%.
3. Reduce the number of adults in BC who are overweight by 20%.
4. Reduce tobacco usage by 20%.
5. Double the number of women who are counseled about the risks of alcohol and tobacco use during pregnancy. (ActNow BC, n.d.)

What can park and recreation agencies do to leverage the activity-related consequences of the Olympic Games? Describe a program they might run in tandem with the Olympics to make people more active.

When designing and implementing PA-related promotional campaigns in tandem with the Olympic Games, for example, health and recreation professionals might consider developing mass communication messages (e.g., television, print media, radio, Internet advertisements), which improve people's awareness of sporting opportunities in the community (Caville& Bauman, 2004). Moreover, Potwarka and McCarville (2010) outlined a number of other strategies that could be undertaken to leverage the Olympic Games in particular. Their recommendations included:

1. Health and recreation professionals could develop programs that connect Olympic athletes with predefined members of the general population to capitalize on the influence of athlete role models.
2. Health and recreation professionals could partner with school boards to design and implement physical education and sport curricula in tandem with mega-sport events that teach students the skills necessary to perform certain sports.
3. Event organizers and governments should strive to ensure that host residents have access to the sporting infrastructure created by the event.
4. At the policy level, health and recreation agencies can lobby local and national government officials to commit resources and develop strategies that facilitate increased sport and PA participation as a result of staging the sport event. In this way, municipal, provincial, and federal governments might consider making grass roots sport participation a funding priority in years leading up to and following the Olympics.

Large-scale participatory mass sport events such as city road races or triathlons are also thought to have an impact on the physical activity levels of the general population (Murphy & Bauman, 2007). To date, little research has examined the impact of mass participation sport events on subsequent sport and PA involvement. Events such as the Toronto, London, or Boston marathons continue to draw thousands of people each year. The London marathon, for example, draws spectator numbers in the range of 300,000 to 500,000 and television coverage is sold to over 100 countries (Murphy & Bauman, 2007). Those who participate in these kinds of events likely invest considerable time and effort into training and making preparations to compete. As well, some of these individuals might adhere to their training and nutrition regiments post-event.

People often travel from considerable distances to participate in such sport events. Over the years, opportunities to travel and take part in amateur level competitive sport events have become more pervasive (Kaplanidou & Gibson, 2010). The term "active sport tourist" has been ascribed to these event's competitors (Funk et al., 2007). Active sport tourism comprises two macro-forms, non-event (e.g., golf, skiing, water sports) and event-based such as travelling to participate in large scale events, such as city marathons or smaller scale events, such as local Senior Games events (Weed, 2009). Public health and sport professionals should continue to promote and encourage local residents and visitors to participate in these types of events.

Leveraging Sport Events for Economic Development

Many mid-to-large sized sport events receive subsidies from tax dollars to host the event. These subsidies are necessary because event profits often fail to cover costs. Event organizers and government officials argue for the use of public funds by claiming that the event will have a positive impact on the local economy. A positive economic impact is possible when the event creates *local* construction jobs to build new facilities or attracts out-of-town *visitors* to the event who then spend money at the event and in the community (Crompton, 1995). It is important to note that spending by local residents on the event or in the community during this time does not contribute to a positive impact because it is considered money that would have been spent on other forms of entertainment. Although spending by local residents does not contribute positively to the event's economic impact, it can take away from

If you lived in a city that was hosting a sport event would you be likely to stay in the area or escape to a quieter location? If you stayed in the area would you change where you went in the city?

positive gains achieved. This negative effect occurs when locals leave the area during the event and spend money elsewhere that would have otherwise been spent in their community (Chalip & Leyns, 2002). Thus, there is a need to attract sport tourists to the event while still meeting the needs of local residents.

There is much debate about the trustworthiness of studies commissioned by those who have promoted the event and the methodological techniques employed by researchers (Chalip & Leyns, 2002). Crompton (1995) reviewed sport-focused economic impact studies and found 11 major contributors to inaccurate analyses. These inaccuracies have led some researchers to suggest alternate ways of assessing benefits (Dwyer, Forsyth, & Spurr, 2004). Although the economic benefits claimed by event organizers or political elites are often significantly overstated, there is some evidence to suggest that at least minimal benefits can be achieved from hosting sport events (Chalip, 2006; Mules & Faulkner, 1996). While overall impacts may be positive, the event and certain sectors may realize more of the benefits than many small businesses (Putsis, 1998). Chalip and Leyns (2002) argue that such disparities are problematic because it would be expected that visitor spending, the essential driver of positive economic benefits, would occur at local businesses (e.g., restaurants, clothing shops). Hosting sport events can also lead to future economic gain when visitors return to the destination for other purposes or recommend the destination to friends and family (Taks, Chalip, Green, Kesenne, & Martyn, 2009).

Have you ever travelled to a sport event? How did you spend your money? Were you drawn to certain areas of the city over others?

To move beyond simply measuring the economic impact of sport events, researchers have advocated for a focus on how sport events can be actively managed to achieve desired economic benefits (e.g., Chalip, 2004; O'Brien, 2006). This process is known as leveraging.

In the case of sport events, the main tasks would be to find a way to increase overall visitor spending in the community, and expose visitors to the many attractions of the location to facilitate repeat visitation and word-of-mouth marketing (Snelgrove & Wood, 2010). Although it could be argued that strategies aimed at attracting visitors to a particular area or business may only serve to redistribute a fixed amount of visitor spending, the potential of leveraging exists in the supported idea that consumers make impulse purchases at events (Chalip & Leyns, 2002; Irwin & Sandler, 1998). Further, opportunities to shop are particularly salient for some sport-event visitors, meaning that helping those visitors fulfil that desire may increase overall satisfaction with the event and destination (Chalip & McGuirty, 2004).

Although the area of sport event leveraging is still new, there are some insights into effective leveraging strategies aimed at economic benefit. Important to recognize are the near and longer-term perspectives that should be taken in leveraging sport to achieve economic benefits. A common practice in many industries involves bundling services and/or products into a single package for a reduced price. Although largely successful as a marketing strategy in many situations, sport events have not commonly been bundled (Chalip & McGuirty, 2004). Bundling sport events with other destination attractions represents a strategic approach to leveraging sport events. Visitors may respond to bundling through increased awareness, simplification of information search and purchase decisions, perceived discounts on prices, and increased overall appeal of a destination (Naylor & Frank, 2001). Research suggests that people may spend more time in destinations before or after an event if the destination provides and promotes desired attractions (Taks et al., 2009). Chalip and McGuirty (2004) recommended a number of event and destination elements that could be bundled with sport events. In terms of event elements, they suggested (a) creating activities that allow attendees to celebrate event-related identities, and (b) adding music, dance, theatre or art exhibitions to sport events to appeal to event attendees not connected to the sport at-hand. Sport events could be bundled with destination elements such as those activities consistent with the participants' interests or the subculture represented by the event, organized sightseeing tours, and visits to specific attractions or shopping districts.

Although strategic initiatives can be undertaken to direct visitors to spending opportunities, small businesses need to also adopt strategies to capitalize on this opportunity and leverage the event. This is a crucial element as research has found that the economic impact of past events has been significantly limited because local businesses failed to appeal to visitors, leaving most attendees to make their only purchases at the event (Ahmed, Krohn, & Heller, 1996; Putsis, 1998). Chalip and Leyns (2002) showed that small businesses can be successful when they partner with other local business to create event-themed areas to allow for further celebration of the event's subculture, understand the preferences of consumers (See also the chapter by Wood and Snelgrove), and develop visitor-targeted promotional campaigns.

One of the ways that sport events can be leveraged is through the facilitation of future economic development within a host destination. O'Brien's (2006) research on the 2000 Sydney Olympic Games provides an excellent example of this possibility. As O'Brien explained, while visiting the Atlanta Games in 1996, government officials through the Australian Trade Commission saw an opportunity to connect the numerous business executives in attendance from around the world with the aim of creating future economic benefit for Australian companies. This initiative was the first-time a long-term program oriented towards developing business relationships was funded by a federal government. Specifically, Australia created Business Club Australia which was focused on leveraging the global focus of the Olympics to increase international trade. Specifically, Australia's Olympics leveraging plan was as follows (O'Brien, 2006, p. 247):

1. Generate public and private-sector support for a networking-based strategic business leveraging initiative.
2. Develop an initiative to facilitate business networking and relationship development between visiting international business leaders and their Australian counterparts before, during, and after the Sydney 2000 Olympic Games.
3. Make advance identification of, and contact with, international business leaders intending to visit Australia for the Games.
4. Market the initiative both domestically and internationally.
5. Implement the initiative.

The implementation first involved strengthening relationships amongst organizations within Australia and between the Australian commissions and Olympic organizing bodies. Next, a business centre was constructed and centrally positioned within the city (O'Brien, 2006). The centre provided full amenities including dining, social rooms, business rooms, and multilingual trade assistance and was designed as a "dating agency for business where, using specifically programmed networking functions, visiting internationals were 'matched' with potential Australian business partners" (O'Brien, 2006, p. 251). The initiative was largely viewed as a success, and was even replicated by other governments hosting sport events such as the 2002 Commonwealth Games in Manchester (O'Brien, 2006).

Conclusion

Numerous claims have been made about the benefits of hosting sport events. As discussed, the potential contributions of sport events lie in their active leveraging. Although this line of research continues to be developed, we provided some of the ways in which health and economic benefits can be achieved through the leveraging of sport events. Our hope is that this will inspire further creative strategies and move forward the contribution of sport in general.

Key Terms

Economic development
Leveraging sport
Promoting physical activity

References

ActNow BC. (n.d.). ActNow BC website. Retrieved from http://www.actnowbc.ca

Caville, N., & Bauman, A. (2004). Changing the way people think about health-enhancing physical activity: Do mass media campaigns have a role? *Journal of Sport Sciences, 22*, 771–790.

Chalip, L. (2004). Beyond impact: A general model for sport event leverage. In B.W. Ritchie & D. Adair (Eds.), *Sport tourism: Interrelationships, impacts, and issues* (pp. 226–252). Clevedon, UK: Channel View.

Chalip, L. (2006). Toward a distinctive sport management discipline. *Journal of Sport Management, 20*, 1–21.

Chalip, L.,& Leyns, A. (2002). Local business leveraging of a sport event: Managing an event for economic benefit. *Journal of Sport Management, 16*, 132–158.

Chalip, L., & McGuirty (2004). Bundling sport events with the host destination. *Journal of Sport & Tourism, 9*, 267–282.

Coalter, F. (2004). Stuck in the blocks? A sustainable sporting legacy? In A. Vigor, M. Mean, & C. Tims (Eds.), *After the goldrush: A sustainable Olympics for London* (pp. 91–108). London, UK: Institute for Public Policy Research/DEMOS.

Crompton, J. L. (1995). Economic impact analysis of sports facilities and events: Eleven sources of misapplication. *Journal of Sport Management, 9*, 14–35.

Dwyer, L., Forsyth, P., & Spurr, R. (2004). Evaluating tourism's economic effects: New and old approaches. *Tourism Management, 25*, 307–317.

Funk, D., Toohey, K., & Bruun, T. (2007). International sport event participation: prior sport involvement destination image, and travel motives. *European Sport Management Quarterly, 7*, 227–248.

Hindson, A., Gidlow, B., & Peebles, C. (1994). The "trickle-down" effect of top-level sport: Myth or reality? A case study of the Olympics. *Australian Journal of Leisure and Recreation, 4*, 16–24.

Hogan, K., & Norton, K. (2000). The price of Olympic gold. *The Journal of Science and Medicine in Sport, 3*, 203–218.

Ifedi, F. (2008). Sport participation in Canada, 2005. *Statistics Canada*. Ottawa, ON.

Irwin, R. L., & Sandler, M. A. (1998). An analysis of travel behaviour and event-induced expenditures among American collegiate championship patron groups. *Journal of Vacation Marketing, 4*, 78–90. doi: 10.1177/135676679800400107

Jewell, T. (2003). Statement to the House of Commons. Online at:www.culture.gove.uk/Reference_library/Press_notices/archive_2003/olympic_statement.htm

Kaplanidou, K., & Gibson, H. (2010). Predicting behavioral intentions of active event sport tourists: The case of a small scale recurring sports event. *Journal of Sport & Tourism, 15*, 163–179.

Lockhead, H. (2005). A new vision for Sydney Olympic park. *Urban Design International, 10*, 215–222.

London 2012. (2005). London 2012: A vision for the Olympic Games and Paralympic Games.

MORI (2004). *The sports development impact of the Commonwealth Games (2002): Post-Games research.* Research study conducted for UK Sport in Greater Manchester, Blackburn, Congleton and Liverpool: MORI.

Mules, T., & Faulkner, B. (1996).An economic perspective on special events. *Tourism Economics, 2*, 107–117.

Murphy, N. M., & Bauman, A. (2007). Mass sporting and physical activity events-are they "bread and circuses" or public health interventions to increase population levels of physical activity? *Journal of Physical Activity and Health, 4*, 193–202.

Naylor, G., & Frank, K. E. (2001).The effect of price bundling on consumer perceptions of value. *Journal of Services Marketing, 15*, 270–281.

O'Brien, D. (2006). Event business leveraging: The Sydney 2000 Olympic Games. *Annals of Tourism Research, 33*, 240–261.

Potwarka, L. R., & McCarville, R. E. (2010). Exploring the trickle-down effect of the Olympics on activity levels within host nations: Suggestions for research and practice. In C. Anagnostopoulos (Ed.), *International sport: A research synthesis* (pp. 179–190). Athens, Greece: Atiner Publishing.

Putsis, W. P. (1998). Winners and losers: Redistribution and the use of economic impact analysis in marketing. *Journal of Macromarketing, 18*, 24–33.

Snelgrove, R., Taks, M., Chalip, L., & Green, B. C. (2008). How visitors and locals at a sport event differ in motives and identity. *Journal of Sport & Tourism, 13*, 165–180.

Soteriades, E. S., Haddjichristodoulou, C., Kremastinou, J., Chelvatzoglou, F. C., Minogiannis, P. S., & Falagas, N. E. (2006). Health-promotion programs related to Athens 2004 Olympic and Para Olympic Games. *BMC Public Health, 6*(47). Retrieved from www.biomedcentral.com/1471-2458/6/47

Sweeny Sports Report (2000/2001). *The 14th annual survey of sporting interests and the* effectiveness of sponsorship. Melbourne, Victoria, Australia: Sweeny Sports.

Taks, M., Chalip, L., Green, B. C., Kesenne, S., & Martyn, S. (2009). Factors affecting repeat visitation and flow-on tourism as sources of event strategy sustainability. *Journal of Sport & Tourism, 14*, 121–142.

Veal, A. J. (2003).Tracking change: leisure participation and policy in Australia, 1985–2002. *Annals of Leisure Research, 6*, 245–277.

Weed, M. (2009). Progress in sport tourism research? A meta-review and exploration of futures. *Tourism Management, 30*, 615–628.

Chapter 6
Leisure Theory, Leisure Practice

Susan L. Hutchinson, Ph.D.
Dalhousie University

Learning Objectives

After reading this chapter, students will be able to

1. Understand what theory is and how it relates to leisure research and practice.
2. Understand how leisure theories have been developed.
3. Understand why theory is important to guide recreation practice.

Introduction

This text introduces you to a wide-ranging discussion of leisure, recreation, and play, providing you with information about the ways each can contribute to individual development and well-being, as well as to the healthy functioning of families, groups, communities, and society as a whole. Underpinning these definitions and concepts are leisure theories. The purpose of this chapter is to explain why knowing these definitions and concepts—and the theories and research underpinning them—is critical for leisure practice, whether in recreation management or therapeutic recreation settings.

I teach an undergraduate class on the topic of leisure theory. When faced with the prospect of having to learn theories most students will ask, "Why do I need to learn about theory? What does theory have to do with running recreation programs or providing services?" As one former student noted, "When I started this class I thought it was going to be pointless," a perspective that was likely shared by many of her classmates! Yet, as students begin to learn different leisure theories and, more importantly, start to think about how to apply these theories to solve real human problems in diverse recreation settings, they come to see the importance of knowing something about leisure theories to guide their future professional practice. Here are some examples of what students had to say by the end of one recent term when asked to reflect on whether their attitudes toward leisure theory had changed as a result of the class:

> When first getting into leisure I thought that theories were not important. Little did I know... theories are the driving force of knowledge. We must understand theories in general life, to better understand events. Theories in leisure are just as relevant and important as they are in other areas of life. (M. S., Recreation Management student)

> Before, I didn't have a very good sense of why leisure worked as treatment. Now I know that it's a lot more than playing and having fun. There are reasons for why different programs work and the reasons they're structured. (N. K., Therapeutic Recreation student)

> My attitudes towards leisure theory definitely changed as the semester went on. I realized how these theories can be applied to everyday life and serve as good guidelines when developing programs. (C. R., Recreation Management student)

> I now understand that in order to be successful, leisure and recreation programs should be based on leisure theory. (J. P., Recreation Management student)

> To be honest, I couldn't really understand what theory had to do with anything [before taking this class]. I kind of thought you just did it; you practiced based on models, step-by-step of how you were supposed to go about something. Now I know why people "think" things happen like they do. (E. L., Therapeutic Recreation student)

> Whether we know it or not, leisure theory guides a lot of actions and it is important for us to understand why, and how, this is. (M. S., Recreation Management student)

Now that some idea of how other students have come to view leisure theory has been given, my hope is that those who read this will also come to see its value for their own future professional practice. To provide help along the way, this chapter will focus on the following: (a) defining theory and its relationship to leisure research, and (b) explaining why theory is important to guide recreation practice. (For more in-depth explanations of leisure theories and theory-based programming in leisure/recreation settings, see the list of suggested readings at the end of the chapter.)

Thinking of a peak leisure or recreation experience you have had, reflect on the following:

- What contributed to making it so great (the people, the surroundings, the activity itself)?
- What motivated you to take part in this experience?
- What did you get out of the experience (e.g., any "benefits")?
- If you were responsible for creating a similar experience for others, what "theories" could help you make decisions about designing, marketing, or implementing a program/event?

Thinking about Theory

The *theory of recreation substitution* suggests that when people are unable to continue to participate in a preferred activity, they will substitute activities that provide similar psychological or social experiences, satisfactions, or benefits (Mannell & Kleiber, 1997). This theory may be useful when working with youth at risk, where their former leisure activities are no longer possible or desired.

What Is Theory?

Theory is the systematic explanation of some phenomena, based on evidence (typically scientific evidence, such as scholarly research) (Kelly, 1987). Theory specifies "relationships among concepts and actions… [and] suggests under what conditions something might happen" (Caldwell, 2001, p. 350). In other words, theories are often used to describe or explain relationships between two or more things or explain how and under what circumstances they are linked. Even though this sounds very technical, our lives are guided by our theories about what will happen in everyday situations, including leisure. For example, theory can be used to explain the relationship between television watching behaviours and boredom (if I watch television all weekend then I will be very bored). Everyone knows life is not so simple; however, there are many factors that shape leisure choices, behaviours, and experiences (e.g., motivations, gender, age, fitness level, etc.). Theory can help explain the conditions under which someone is likely to experience or do something. For example, if I am by myself watching television, and there is nothing I am interested in watching, then it is more likely that there will be a strong relationship between boredom and television watching than if I invite a group of friends over to watch a favourite program.

Theories can also help predict relationships between certain leisure behaviours and possible outcomes (e.g., benefits and risks) associated with these behaviours or experiences. For example, there has been some research about the risks associated with various leisure activities in adolescence, such as "hanging out" (Mahoney & Stattin, 2000). While most everyone has spent time hanging out with friends—and can therefore understand some of the possible risks (and benefits) of this form of unstructured leisure activity—there are theories that help provide explanations of how and why lack of structure and risk behaviours are related. Leisure professionals might want to use theories related to boredom and optimal experiences as examples to develop programs or social marketing strategies to help adolescents substitute hanging out and other unstructured activities with other, more active, activities that will still provide desired psychological benefits, satisfactions, or experiences (Caldwell, Darling, Payne, & Dowdy, 1999).

Kelly (1987) suggested that regardless of whether it is developed to understand some phenomena better or to guide decision making, theory is:

- an act of explanation that is communicated to others
- systematic, with presuppositions and evidence (observation/measurement)
- always subject to question and criticism
- selective and partial

Social scientists, including leisure researchers, develop theories to explain to others what they think might be going on in situations that are of importance to them. To build a rationale for their thinking, which is usually reflected in hypotheses or presuppositions, they conduct research (gather evidence). These ideas are then "put out there" (e.g., in a research article or book chapter) for others to think about, question, and criticize. Most often informed readers find they can understand how one theory might apply to a certain situation but not to others. In this way theories are always considered selective and partial. More research is always needed to apply the theories in different situations and with different populations to determine ultimately how useful they may be in guiding decision making to address particular social problems.

Where Do Leisure Theories Come From?

Several social science disciplines have influenced the development or application of theory in leisure studies. Psychological theories reflect efforts to understand individual's motivations, internal dispositions, experiences, and behaviour. Social psychology reflects an interest in the study of leisure behaviour of individuals in social situations or environments. Sociological perspectives stress the functions of leisure in relation to participation in, or maintenance of, social structures. Critical and feminist theories share this view but are interested in the ways that leisure is an instrument of social control, or affects (or is affected by) power relations (e.g., age or gender) in society. It is important to understand that, in everyday life, there are strong relationships between broader social forces (e.g., gender and age) and an individual's leisure motivation and behaviour.

Theories determine the emphasis given to social situations (external factors) versus person situations (internal psychological factors) to explain "what's happening" in a particular leisure-related situation (Mannell & Kleiber, 1997). For example, sociologists may be less interested in knowing about people's internal motivations or personality dispositions than the ways that social structures such as the family or economy affect free time use or access to community recreation opportunities. Interestingly, there are very few true leisure theories. Most theories that are used to understand leisure behaviour, experiences and time use, etc. have been adopted from other disciplines. Mannell and Kleiber suggested that social science theories can help leisure researchers and practitioners:

- Address problems that affect the health and well-being (risks and benefits) of individuals, families/groups, communities, and society.
- Understand the choices people make about leisure and how they affect and are affected by other aspects of life.
- Understand more about what people do and experience in their leisure and the factors that affect this.

In trying to learn leisure theories, it helps to frame thinking in relation to leisure-related problems or issues likely to be addressed in future work.

Thinking of the kind of work you want to do in the future, reflect on the following:

- What are the key issues related to leisure/recreation service delivery you will need to address?
- What is your hunch (presupposition/hypothesis) about what might be going on in this situation?
- What is the "level" at which your service delivery/intervention would be directed (e.g., individuals, families, groups, neighbourhoods, communities)?
- What kinds of theories might help you in addressing these issues?

Why Use Leisure Theory to Guide Leisure Practice?

As noted earlier, many students struggle to see the relationship between leisure research and theories and the kinds of work they see themselves doing in the future. There are several important reasons, however, for learning how to apply theories to guide leisure practice:

- to help assess/identify relevant needs
- to be accountable and provide a rationale for decisions
- to enhance outcomes for participants, agency, community
- to be able to communicate effectively with allied professionals
- to evaluate effectiveness of programs/services

Each is briefly described next.

Needs Assessment

Needs assessment is a fundamental part of the program planning process, whether working in community or therapeutic recreation settings. Needs (and strengths) assessment often involves identifying what is important or relevant in a situation (e.g., the problem being addressed) or factors affecting service delivery or leisure participation. In either case, theories can help in deciding what needs to be looked for as part of this assessment. For example, a genuine interest in designing a leisure program for older adults who have recently lost their spouse would likely lead to the desire to know not only their interests and past leisure participation, but also what might be stopping or preventing them from engaging in leisure currently. Leisure constraints theory (e.g., Jackson, 2005) can provide a framework for assessing perceived constraints as well as designing programs or services that can address these constraints. For example, we know that potential participants may be constrained by a variety of variables which arise from personal, group, or situational sources. We might wish to interview these adults to determine what kinds of variables most constrain them and then determine how to remove those constraints (see Chapter 9).

Provide Rationale and Increase Accountability

Theory can provide the rationale for decision making related to program policy, leadership development, and design. For example, if while working at a community recreation centre a request was received from town/city council to address problems of youth vandalism, it would be beneficial to provide strong theoretical reasons for undertaking any given program solution (with supporting research as evidence of their potential efficacy). This is called *theory-driven program design* or *evidence-based practice*. As a result of using theory and supporting evidence to guide program development and implementation, practitioners will be able to be more accountable to key "stakeholders" who may have invested in their programs (e.g., participants, funders, police/justice system, parents).

An example of how leisure and prevention researchers used social psychological theories to guide program development is provided by Caldwell, Baldwin, Walls, and Smith (2005) with their school-based TimeWise leisure education program. They used theories about boredom to identify problems associated with free time and self-determination theory to develop educational strategies to help kids develop the knowledge, skills, and awareness needed to "beat boredom" and become more self-determined in their free time activities. They argued that if adolescents developed these leisure-related skills, they would be less likely to engage in other risk-related behaviours in their free time (such as drinking and other substance use). Because they used theory to guide their program development, they were able to provide a strong rationale for why the program was needed and how it was designed. In turn, the theory helped guide program development, implementation and evaluation, assisting them to be more accountable to school administrators, who agreed to offer the program as part of their school curriculum, and the National Institute of Drug Abuse (NIDA), who funded program development and evaluation.

Enhance Outcomes

Most recreation practitioners must face situations where there are too few resources to do what is ideal. Within this reality, the practitioner will need to make decisions about the types of programs or services likely to be most effective in accomplishing goals or desired outcomes. Within many commercial or community recreation settings, a key outcome relates to customer satisfaction. It is important to consider the following questions: Are people leaving the program or service having had optimal experiences? Were their needs and wants not only met but exceeded? These issues become critical when trying to promote the benefits associated with various forms of leisure given limited resources.

As it relates to therapeutic recreation settings, practitioners need to demonstrate that the interventions that have been designed are likely to be most effective in reducing risks, promoting healthy lifestyle behaviours, or achieving other desired health and well-being outcomes. Theories help to link program processes and content to desired outcomes. For example, Hood and Carruthers (2002) used coping theories to design a substance use prevention program for women. Although they could use previous research (evidence) to help them understand the challenges faced by women to stay sober, coping skills theory provided a framework to focus program development. The theory they used suggested that there are two broad foci of coping efforts—reducing distress and increasing positive resources. Coping skill theory is helpful because it not only suggests key variables to address in their intervention (e.g., building positive resources such as social networks), but it also suggests the expected results of their interactions (when people develop positive social networks, they will feel better able to manage daily challenges associated with staying sober). Such insight is helpful to any provider hoping to make the most of limited resource levels.

Communication

Imagine going into a meeting with allied health professionals and trying to promote the development of a leisure education program for cancer survivors in the community. To simply go into this meeting and talk in generalities about leisure or recreation and what plans might be implemented and how they might work would most likely give rise to skepticism or even disapproval. To go into this same meeting and talk about issues related to personal control, self-efficacy, self-determination, coping, or other important social-psychological factors—and the theories that suggest how they are linked to health and well-being outcomes—would likely result in other health professionals listening with rapt interest, because a language is being spoken which is also important to them. Likewise, terms such as youth development or social capital resonate with key decision makers in communities. Although common terminology could be in both settings to communicate with important others without ever introducing theory, it is theory that helps create shared meaning regarding key variables and outcomes that are needed in order to take action (e.g., develop programs or policies).

Program Evaluation

Theory-driven program evaluation extends directly from theory-driven program planning (Baldwin, Hutchinson, & Magnusson, 2004). Program evaluation is critical to determine if your programs work (and why). Again, as it relates to issues of accountability and effectiveness, it must be determined if the programs or services designed are effective in achieving desired outcomes. Unfortunately, most program evaluation does not extend beyond asking people if they enjoyed themselves or what they liked about the program. These generic forms of evaluation will help little in knowing whether or not the program achieved the intended outcomes. Incorporating theory into every aspect of the program planning process allows for "beginning with the end in mind" by linking program evaluation tools with specific program goals and procedures. Results can be measured against predictions so that it can be known whether the program has succeeded or failed in its objectives.

For example, it might be decided upon to offer an adventure program for youth-at-risk with the goal of improving self-efficacy (Bandura, 1986) or beliefs about one's ability to take personal control in situations that matter. Self-efficacy theory suggests that people will perceive themselves as more capable of learning new tasks or taking on new challenges when they (1) have had the chance to develop (and practice) requisite skills, (2) see others similar to them being successful, and (3) are provided with task-specific feedback. Using this theory, programmers can measure the degree to which these three variables ware addressed in the program and the results of the initiative. Evaluating participants' self-efficacy before and after the program can help determine whether or not components of the program designed to address self-efficacy actually worked.

Summary

An entire volume of books would be needed to comprehensively represent the range of theories and supporting research that have been examined in recreation and leisure studies! This book, however, gives an introduction to many of them. For example, "Purple leisure" is a concept framed by theorizing about deviance and risk behaviour in leisure and is discussed in this book. Chapters on leisure constraints theory and stress-coping theory help provide a framework for program development in health-related settings. Other chapters examine research and theories regarding the relationships between leisure and work, gender, ethnicity, disability, and social class. These chapters reflect theories used to describe and explain broad social factors that shape leisure behaviour and experiences at individual, group, and community levels.

Although it is beyond the scope of this chapter to explain how to use theory to guide program design and evaluation, Baldwin et al. (2004) and Caldwell (2001) provide excellent examples of how to apply theory to program design in therapeutic recreation. Baldwin, Caldwell and Witt (2005) have detailed the steps involved in theory-based programming for recreation and youth development. In the areas of health promotion or health-related behaviour change, several other useful examples of theory-driven programming and evaluation are available (e.g., Bickman, 1996; Chen, 2005). The first step is to believe that knowing something about theory will aid in a future within the recreation profession. The next time these theories present themselves it should be asked, "How can these theories help in the development of effective programs and services?"

Key Terms

Leisure practice
Leisure theory
Theory-driven programming

Suggested Readings

Baldwin, C. K., Hutchinson, S. L., & Magnusson, D. R. (2004). Program theory: A framework for theory-driven programming and evaluation. *Therapeutic Recreation Journal, 38*(1), 16–31.

Baldwin, C. K., Caldwell, L. L., & Witt, P. A. (2005). Deliberate programming with logic models: From theory to outcomes. In P. A. Witt & L. L. Caldwell (Eds.), *Recreation and youth development* (pp. 219–239). State College, PA: Venture Publishing, Inc.

Caldwell, L. (2001). The role of theory in therapeutic recreation: A practical approach. In N. Stumbo (Ed.), *Professional issues in therapeutic recreation: On competence and outcomes* (pp. 349–364). Champaign, IL: Sagamore Publishing.

Chen, H.-T. (2005). *Practical program evaluation: Assessing and improving planning, implementation, and effectiveness.* Thousand Oaks, CA: Sage Publications.

Mannell, R. C., & Kleiber, D. A. (1997). *A social psychology of leisure.* State College, PA: Venture Publishing, Inc.

References

Baldwin, C. K., Hutchinson, S. L., & Magnusson, D. R. (2004). Program theory: A framework for theory-driven programming and evaluation. *Therapeutic Recreation Journal, 38*(1), 16–31.

Baldwin, C. K., Caldwell, L. L., & Witt, P. A. (2005). Deliberate programming with logic models: From theory to outcomes. In P. A. Witt & L. L. Caldwell (Eds.), *Recreation and youth development* (pp. 219–239). State College, PA: Venture Publishing, Inc.

Bandura, A. (1986). The explanatory and predictive scope of self-efficacy theory. *Journal of Social and Clinical Psychology, 4*, 359–373.

Bickman, L. (1996). The application of program theory to the evaluation of a managed mental health care system. *Evaluation and Program Planning, 19*(2), 111–119.

Caldwell, L. (2001). The role of theory in therapeutic recreation: A practical approach. In N. Stumbo (Ed.), *Professional issues in therapeutic recreation: On competence and outcomes* (pp. 349–364). Champaign, IL: Sagamore Publishing.

Caldwell, L. L., Baldwin, C. K., Walls, T., & Smith, E. (2004). Preliminary effects of a leisure education program to promote healthy use of free time among middle school adolescents. *Journal of Leisure Research, 36*(3), 310–335.

Caldwell, L. L., Darling, N., Payne, L. L., & Dowdy, B. (1999). "Why are you bored?": An examination of psychological and social control causes of boredom among adolescents. *Journal of Leisure Research, 31*, 103–121.

de Grazia, S. (1964). *Of time, work, and leisure*. Garden City, NY: Anchor.

Dumazedier, J. (1974). *The sociology of leisure*. New York, NY: Elsevier.

Hood, C. D., & Carruthers, C. P. (2002). Coping skills theory as an underlying framework for therapeutic recreation services. *Therapeutic Recreation Journal, 36*(2), 137–153.

Iso-Ahola, S. E. (1980). *Social psychological perspectives on leisure and recreation*. Springfield, IL: Charles C. Thomas.

Jackson, E. L. (Ed.). (2005). *Constraints to leisure*. State College, PA: Venture Publishing, Inc.

Kelly, J. R. (1987). *Freedom to be: A new sociology of leisure*. New York, NY: Macmillan Publishing.

Mahoney, J. L., & Stattin, H. (2000). Leisure activities and adolescent antisocial behavior: The role of structure and context. *Journal of Adolescence, 23*, 113–127.

Mannell, R. C., & Kleiber, D. A. (1997). *A social psychology of leisure*. State College, PA: Venture Publishing, Inc.

Pieper, J. (1964). *Leisure, the basis of culture*. New York, NY; Pantheon Books.

Chapter 7
The Politics of Leisure

Susan M. Shaw, Ph.D.
University of Waterloo

Learning Objectives

After reading this chapter, students will be able to

1. Have an understanding of the meaning of power and politics in social life.
2. Understand the political significance of leisure.
3. Distinguish different ways in which leisure is political.
4. Provide a variety of examples of the political nature of leisure.

Introduction

It might be surprising to see a chapter on the politics of leisure in this textbook. Leisure is often thought of as a non-serious part of life—that is, as a time for having fun or simply for relaxing, away from the responsibilities associated with school, work, or family. The benefits of leisure are frequently recognized, not only because of the enjoyment leisure can provide, but also for the positive physical and psychological health outcomes associated with participation in particular leisure activities. Leisure, though, is rarely thought of as "political," even by people who work in the recreation and leisure studies field, and the political nature of leisure is rarely debated. This chapter strives to challenge the perception that leisure is apolitical or "innocent" (Green, Hebron, & Woodward, 1990), and suggests that there are important political aspects to leisure that deserve our attention. In particular, the suggestion will be made that there are two different ways in which leisure and leisure practices are political in nature. One of these is an "overt" (or clearly visible) form of politics, relating primarily to governmental processes. The other is more "covert," and is a political aspect of leisure that often remains hidden or unrecognized.

Before presenting these two components of leisure politics in more detail, it is helpful to think about the meaning of politics or what it is that makes a situation "political." *The Dictionary of the Social Sciences* (Thomson-Nelson) defines politics in the following way:

> **Politics:** This can be narrowly defined as all that relates to the way a society is governed. Politics is the process by which the community makes decisions and establishes values that are binding upon its members. This definition comes from the original Greek meaning of "politics," the government of the city state. In general speech, politics refers much more widely to processes that involve the exercise of power, status or influence in making decisions or establishing social relationships. This latter meaning is implied by the idea of "office politics" or "sexual politics" (as used by Kate Millet) or the claim that "the personal is political" (http://socialsciencedictionary.nelson.com/ssd/SocialDict.jsp).

Based on this definition it is clear, first of all, that politics is about power and the use of power. Governments, for example, whether they are federal, provincial, or municipal governments, wield power by making decisions that affect people living within their respective jurisdictions. These decisions relate not only to defining legal or illegal activities, but also to the distribution of resources, particularly financial resources, and the level of economic support given to different groups and agencies. From the definition above it is also clear that individuals can exercise power, and that this personal power (a term used by the famous social philosopher, Michel Foucault, 1980) can influence decision making and/or relationships. This is the basis of the idea of "office politics" and "sexual politics." Furthermore, the definition establishes that politics is also about values. Government decisions are based upon spoken (or sometimes unspoken) values about what issues are important and what activities or services are worthy of economic support. Personal power relates to values too, and the use of that power is often directed towards persuading others to change their values, attitudes, or behaviours.

The dictionary definition gives some indication of the two different ways in which leisure can be seen as political. First, leisure is political because of the decisions that are made, often by governmental bodies, which affect leisure policy and leisure opportunities by determining or limiting the resources and the levels of economic and non-economic support that are available. This reflects the overt or formal political aspect of leisure. Second, leisure practices and leisure activities may themselves influence values, beliefs and attitudes, and in this way leisure can be seen as a venue for exercising personal power. This role of leisure as a form of political influence is often subtle in nature and can represent a "hidden" form of power in that it may not be recognized by others and may not even be intentional. This, then, is the covert aspect of leisure as political and reflects the claim that "the personal is political."

In this chapter, the two aspects of political processes associated with leisure are described and discussed in more detail. The purpose is not only to illustrate the political nature of leisure but also to persuade the reader that it is important to recognize and understand these processes. If leisure is indeed political, and if leisure practice has political consequences, then it is important to be aware of how these processes work. Awareness and understanding could encourage more people, and particularly leisure professionals, to participate in the debate about the role and significance of leisure and perhaps influence political processes in beneficial ways.

Leisure and the Political System

Recreation, Parks, and Tourism Services

Most any debate about leisure politics probably relates to recreation, parks, or tourism services. Many of these leisure-related services are supported financially by one or more levels of government and sometimes governments become directly involved in policy debates and policy-related decision making that directly affect leisure service delivery. National and provincial parks are a good example. The preservation of our system of parks is inevitably political because parks are expensive to run and maintain, and because preservation means by definition that new developments (e.g., new housing areas or new businesses) are not allowed or are strictly controlled by the government. In addition, the successful formation and maintenance of a parks system requires some explicit values statements about purposes and goals (Eagles & McCool, 2002). For example, are parks created primarily for the purpose of maintaining natural environments and the preservation of endangered species? Or, are they there primarily for people's enjoyment? Can these two purposes exist side by side? Or is there likely to be tension and even conflict if both purposes are regarded as equally important?

Perhaps these debates are familiar, and perhaps the opinions of some of friends and classmates are also known. Some Canadians favour the idea of environmental protectionism as the overriding value and some support the idea of "parks for people." Also, there are differences of opinion with respect to the kinds of activities that people should be allowed to do in parks, and particularly whether activities that cause higher levels of environmental damage or noise pollution should be banned. If these debates are familiar, it might benefit the reader to consider where and when the discussions of such values and policies were heard. Were they heard on television or on other media outlets? Readers should also consider their familiarity with the policies and platforms of Canada's major political parties. Although these issues are political, and their resolution depends to a fairly large extent on government decision making, Thus it seems appropriate, at this time, to give more attention to the political implications of leisure.

What are, or should be, the values, goals, and purposes of our park system? Should there be more public debate about this?

Similar issues about the politics of leisure can be raised with respect to recreation programs, facilities, and services. These services are usually managed at the local or municipal level, so the local government is involved in the allocation of economic and other resources. People who work in the recreation services field are probably very aware of many of the issues regarding resources and budgets, but generally the debate is narrowly proscribed and there is little public involvement in discussions. The politics of recreation service provision may not be seen as a pressing political issue and may not be seen as a political issue at all by some people, but there are clearly a number of important questions that depend on values and political decision making. For example, who are, or who should be, the recipients of such services? Should it be those individuals and families who can afford to pay? Or should the services be available to everybody, regardless of income? What about those people who are in particular need for such services, such as single-parent families, or people with health-related problems or with disabilities? Should these members of the community be given special consideration?

Have you heard any discussion of the politics of recreation service provision? If so, was this in a public or private forum? What issues were discussed? What issues should be discussed?

In some ways political questions related to tourism services are closely connected to those surrounding the politics of parks and recreation, but in other ways the debate here is different and involves different interest groups. Probably the main reason for this difference is the economic significance of the tourism industry (see Chapter 12). Thus, while governments get involved with and are interested in tourism service provision, the economic questions predominate, as opposed to questions of service provision for particular population groups or questions of environmental protection. Sometimes social policy issues come into play, such as concern about the social impact of tourism on local communities and on community development. For tourism, though, as for other areas of recreation and leisure, the political aspects of services and resources do not get a lot of public attention or recognition.

Should more attention be given to political decision making and the role of governments related to leisure? How can this be accomplished? Should political parties be asked about their leisure-related platforms?

Other Social Policies and Services Affecting Leisure

Apart from recreation, parks, and tourism, there are other areas of social and economic policies and government decision making that have important implications for leisure as well. Perhaps the most obvious policy area that affects leisure is that of work-related (or labour-related) policy. Legislation about working hours and conditions, about part-time work, about overtime, and about vacation time, all have important implications for the availability of leisure and free time, and by extension to levels of participation and enjoyment of leisure. Labour legislation and any proposed changes to such legislation are often hotly debated by politicians and by labour leaders as well as by employees. Typically, the issue of leisure or free time is not part of the debate and certainly not central to the debate. There is plenty of evidence, however, that working time and the demands of work are major factors affecting leisure time and leisure involvement. We know, for example, that hours of work have increased in recent years for many people (Zuzanek & Smale, 1997) and that work-life stress has increased at the same time (Duxbury & Higgins, 2002), making it difficult for many people to find the time for desired leisure pursuits. Employed parents (especially mothers) find it particularly difficult to balance the demands of work and family, and often give up—if reluctantly—on the idea of personal leisure (Shaw, Johnson, & Andrey, 2003). In some ways part-time work can be seen as a solution to this problem; however, low remuneration for part-time work and the lack of benefits and job security (because many legislative labour requirements do not apply to part-time employees) make this option unattractive or unrealistic for many employees. As a result we as a society, like the United States, seem to be experiencing a loss of leisure time (see Chapter 11 and Schor, 1991).

The link between work time, labour legislation, and opportunities for leisure may be obvious to those who study these issues and have discovered that many people are either too time-stressed or too tired (or both) to become involved in meaningful leisure (Green et al., 1990; Shaw & Dawson, 2001; Swan & Cooper, 2005); however, leisure is rarely part of the consideration in discussions of labour laws. Does this imply that leisure is not a particularly significant issue in the lives of Canadians? Or are there other reasons why the issue of leisure is overlooked by politicians?

There are other work-related policies that also have implications for leisure and leisure time. These include policies related to mandatory versus optional retirement, maternity and paternity leave options, and the provision of day care services. Mandatory retirement has now been banned in several Canadian provinces, and it seems likely that the remaining provinces will follow suit. This move provides more options for the worker, but it may mean that many older workers will work for longer (giving up on some of the leisure benefits typically associated with retirement). Also younger workers may find it more difficult to find paid work or will be more likely to face unemployment. This could lead to more free time, although unemployment does not typically lead to a life of leisure (Havitz, Morden, & Samdahl, 2004). Maternity, paternity, and parental leave policies, on the other hand, provide benefits for parents (both mothers and fathers) that might help them to balance the demands of work and family and still find time for some leisure. Interestingly, day care was a major issue in the January 2006 federal election, one that may also affect leisure availability, even though leisure was not part of the political debate at the time. Consideration should be given to whether day care is a leisure-related issue or not.

How many different social and economic policies can you think of that affect leisure, leisure resources, and/or leisure opportunities? How important is it for leisure to be incorporated into the debates about these policies?

The argument here, then, is not that leisure is a central issue in public political debates, but rather that leisure availability is affected by a range of legislative actions and social policy initiatives that are determined by one or another level of government. Labour-related policy is just one example, and you may be able to think of other types of social and economic policy that affect leisure in some way. Indeed, leisure practice is affected in many ways by governmental policy because leisure is an integrated part of life and is not a separate or distinct sphere. This is another reason why we should perhaps not be surprised by the idea that leisure is political.

The Politicization of Leisure Activities

The discussion of the influence of politics on leisure should not be left without giving some consideration to the way in which particular leisure activities sometimes become "politicized." Perhaps the most obvious example is that of the Olympic Games. Are the Olympic Games a "political" event? Certainly they have been used for political purposes in the past, including Hitler's deliberate use of the

Berlin Olympics in the summer of 1936 to promote his political philosophy of Aryan supremacy and his version of National Socialism (Nazism). Several decades later (in 1972) a major terrorism attack occurred at the Olympic Games in Munich in which eleven Israeli athletes were murdered (an event which was featured in the movie *Munich*, 2005). Clearly the Games were used for this attack to ensure attention by the international media.

Are You Interested in the Politics of Sport?

If so, check out the Center for the Study of Sport in Society (http://www.sportinsociety.org/), located at Northeastern University in Boston, Massachusetts. Since 1989 the Center has been publishing *The Racial and Gender Report Card* analyzing progress in hiring women and people of colour in sports positions in the United States, and it has developed a range of programs including the Mentors in Violence Prevention (MVP) program, the Athletes for Human Rights initiative, and the Disability in Sport program. The Founder and Director Emeritus of the Center, Dr. Richard Lapchick, is best known for his work on sport and politics. One of his many publications is his chapter on the history of the modern Olympic Games (Lapchick, 1996) which concludes with, "politics is and has always been part of the Olympic movement" (p. 269). A more recent book by Dr. Lapchick, *Smashing Barriers: Race and Sport in the New Millennium* (Lapchick, 2002), discusses the politics of race and sport, examining the ways in which sport can be both discriminatory and liberatory. Lots of interesting reading here!

Another event that was hotly debated at the time was the protest by a group of African American athletes at the 1968 Games in Mexico City. These athletes used peaceful means to protest the continuing problems and discrimination facing Blacks in the United States, but they also used the Games as a political venue to get their message across to the public and to the international community. The African American protesters were widely criticized for making the Games "political" (Lapchick, 1996), and the dominant opinion in the United States (and perhaps elsewhere) was that the Games are and should be a celebration of sports and of achievement, and should not be politicized.

While many might agree with this stance, an argument can be made that the Games have become politicized in a number of ways and that this politicization may be difficult, if not impossible, to reverse. The economic implications of the Games alone, and the importance placed on hosting the Games by many state governments, businesses, and sporting communities, suggests that the Olympics are not free of political interest and political involvement. In addition, many state governments (including some with very small budgets) have put vast resources into their top-level athletic programs to enhance their chances of winning Olympic medals. In Canada, the funding of Olympic athletes and programs has been somewhat controversial with some arguing that medals are important in terms of our national pride (largely a political reason), while others argue that sports and sports excellence are a matter of personal choice (largely a leisure reason) and that our relatively scarce economic resources could be better used elsewhere (for another purpose).

What do you think about the politicization of the Olympic Games? Are the Games inevitably political or should they be kept free of political influence? Can you think of other leisure activities or sports events that have become "politicized"? Is the politicization of leisure activities and events a good thing, a bad thing, or a bit of both?

Leisure and Power Relations

Structured Relations of Power

The notion of the covert or hidden political aspects of leisure refers to the ways in which leisure plays a role in challenging (or alternatively reinforcing) the structured relations of power in society. This goes beyond the formal political processes discussed earlier to address the question of which individuals and groups in our society have power and influence, and which groups are marginalized or lacking in power. Of particular significance is whether these relations of power can be changed or modified through certain types of leisure practice.

To understand this aspect of leisure, you need to know what is meant by the term "power relations" or "structured relations of power." These are terms that sociologists use to describe the unequal access to power and resources for different people or groups of people in a particular society. The differences are not individual or random, but relate to individuals' characteristics that raise or lower their potential access to power. For example, someone born into a very low income or destitute family has a much reduced chance of accessing a good education, a good job, a high income, or a position of power compared to someone born into a wealthy, educated, and well-connected family. Similarly, Anglo-Canadians have easier access to power and resources compared to Canadians who are members of visible minority groups. Aboriginal Canadians often face problems, such as discrimination and cultural devaluation, that are much less likely to constrain non-Aboriginals in seeking positions associated with power and status. In addition, a person's access to power is also affected by his or her gender, age, sexual orientation, health and disability status, and other factors. This does not mean that people who grow up in, or find themselves in disadvantageous circumstances cannot become empowered. It does mean, though, that such people are likely to face more challenges and difficulties in accessing power and resources than people from other more advantaged groups.

The factors that affect access to power, or the characteristics that put an individual in a more advantageous or disadvantageous position can be seen as societal structures, and the individual is "positioned" in relation to these power structures based on his or her demographic, cultural, or other characteristics. Although these societal structures obviously cannot be seen, the effects of these relations of power can be, and have been, documented and analyzed (Stewart, 2001). The question to be addressed in the following sections is: What role does leisure play, or can it potentially play, with respect to these power structures? If leisure or leisure practice has some influence on societal power relations, clearly this would mean that leisure has some form of political significance above and beyond its relationship to formal or government political systems.

Leisure and Resistance

In recent years a number of leisure researchers have been examining the ways in which leisure participation and leisure practice can resist or challenge structured relations of power and potentially empower disadvantaged individuals and groups (e.g., Freysinger & Flannery, 1992; Shaw, 2001; Wearing, 1998). These researchers have come to the conclusion that leisure is an important site for this type of resistance and that certain forms of resistant leisure practice can lead to positive social change. Moreover, because this type of change involves changes in the distribution of power, status and access to resources, it represents a form of political change as well.

One of the reasons that leisure is thought to be significant in terms of this form of political and social change has to do with the nature of leisure itself. Resisting disadvantage, constraint or oppression requires some degree of freedom to act independently and thus enable an individual to challenge societal expectations and stereotypes. Because leisure, by definition, involves freedom of choice and self-expression, it can be seen as an "ideal" place where this type of resistance can occur. For example, someone who feels constrained by a physical or mental disability, and by the social stigma that can be associated with being disabled, may use leisure to challenge these constraints, to show independence of spirit, to challenge stereotypes, and to develop a new sense of self. In other words, simply by making choices and taking control over that area of social life, an individual can experience a sense of personal empowerment. Furthermore, this empowerment may also spill over into other areas of his or her life, thus challenging the devaluation of persons with a disability in a number of different ways.

A second reason why leisure may be a prime location for resistance is that particular types of leisure activities and practices can challenge societal beliefs and orthodoxies that are constraining. It is these societal ideologies or orthodoxies that help to perpetuate unequal power relations. For example, negative beliefs about the abilities of people of colour or people belonging to certain social classes may affect their chances of obtaining a job with a high degree of power and responsibility. Likewise, stereotypes and social expectations about gender roles and traditional beliefs about the nature of femininity may constrain girls' and women's hopes and aspirations. This, in turn, can negatively affect their opportunities and their self-concepts. Some leisure activities, it is argued, can be used by people of colour, women, and others from disadvantaged groups to challenge these societal stereotypes. Sports are one type of potentially empowering activity since they project an image of power and competence, and so can become a form of resistance. Social leisure can also facilitate resistance because it involves interaction with others in a relaxed setting, and because socializing often involves humour, which can challenge attitudes and enhances social cohesion (Green, 1998). These individual acts of resistance may also affect other people's attitudes and lead to new ways of thinking about gender, race, social class, age, disability, etc.

Resistance, Gender, and Beyond

Most of the research on resistance to date has focused on gender (see Chapter 20), particularly on the ways in which women sometimes use leisure to challenge traditional beliefs or ideologies about femininity. For example, a classic study by Wearing (1990) showed how mothers of new babies challenged the dominant ideology (or set of beliefs) of motherhood, which expects mothers to dedicate their lives to the care of their child without thinking of their own personal needs. For the mothers in Wearing's study, simply claiming the right to some leisure for themselves was an act of resistance.

Another form of resistance for women relates to the specific activity in which they choose to become involved. For example, studies have looked at whether participation in activities traditionally thought to be "masculine" pursuits—such as hockey (Theberge, 2000), motorcycling (Auster, 2001), and bodybuilding (Guthrie & Castelnuovo, 1992)—can be seen as a form of resistance. Sometimes the resistance associated with these activities is not deliberate or intentional; that is, the participants did not set out to challenge notions of femininity, but simply wanted to enjoy the activity. Regardless, the simple act of participation could affect the attitudes of these participants as well as other people (e.g., friends, boyfriends, teachers, parents). Participation could influence the beliefs and attitudes of the general public, as could newspaper and television coverage.

> Do you think girls' and women's increased participation in sports is a result of and/or a cause of changing beliefs about gender? For example, do you think that the success of the Canadian women's hockey team in recent years is a reflection of changing attitudes or has it also influenced these attitudes?

Of course, men can also challenge traditional and constraining views of masculinity as well by participating in non-stereotypical activities. One researcher (Davis, 1990) examined male cheerleading as a potential form of resistance for these male athletes. Other types of resistance through leisure include resistance to dominant orthodoxies about aging through participation in Masters athletic competitions (Dionigi, 2004), or resistance to heterosexism through participation in Gay Pride parades (Pronger, 2000). To the extent that such activities challenge negative attitudes and beliefs, they have the potential to act as a form of resistance that can change power relations in society. The research on resistance, though, is still in its infancy and clearly more work needs to be done. Researchers may yet uncover many other ways in which leisure functions as a form of resistance.

> Can you think of other examples or ways in which leisure can challenge dominant ideologies or orthodoxies about particular groups of people in our society?

Leisure and Social Reproduction

Of course, not all leisure activities can be seen as resistance, and some can be seen as a form of reproduction or reinforcement of dominant belief systems. For example, leisure can be disempowering to people from marginalized groups by perpetuating or reinforcing negative attitudes and stereotypes. This can occur, for instance, through racist or homophobic jokes in leisure settings, or through activities that sexualize women and girls in derogatory ways. There is a considerable body of research conducted over many years on the perpetuation of sexism, racism, and homophobia through television programs, such as "sitcoms" (Wober & Gunder, 1988). Video games, too, have been criticized not only for their violent content but also for their racist and sexist depictions of characters and their sexualized violence (Delamere, 2004). These kinds of media representations contribute to the way in which negative ideas about gender, race, or sexuality are perpetuated or, in other words, how stereotypes are reinforced.

Another form of social reproduction through leisure is the role of sports in the social construction of attitudes and beliefs about masculinity. A number of sports sociologists have done extensive research on boys' and men's participation in sports (e.g., see McKay, Messner, & Sabo, 2000; Messner & Sabo, 1990). These sociologists have argued that the male sports system reinforces gender hierarchies and makes these hierarchies seem "natural" or inevitable. At the same time, the traditional views of masculinity that are perpetuated through sports can be constraining on male leisure because sports can become a "compulsory" form of activity for boys, even for those boys who are not interested and not athletically inclined (see Messner, 1998). Moreover, a stigma continues to be attached to boy's participation in activities traditionally thought of as "feminine" (e.g., ballet dancing), and this has a constraining effect on boys' leisure options.

How Do Organized Sports for Boys Construct Masculinities?

Michael Messner, a well-known sports sociologist from the University of Southern California, conducted interviews with 30 male former athletes. His study, published in the book *Men's Lives* (Messner, 1998), revealed the insecurities and loneliness that many of these athletes had experienced as young boys, and how they learned about the importance of winning (or "beating others") to gain a sense of self-worth.

Messner concluded that organized sports for boys teaches lessons about masculinity and what it means to be a successful male, at least in American society. The lessons and values learned indicate that sport is a "gendering" institution that reinforces hierarchies and inequalities and thus tends to perpetuate traditional, and often restrictive, views of masculinity.

> Do you think that boys' sport in Canada also reproduces traditional notions of masculinity? Is the masculine culture similar in all boys' sports or does it vary from sport to sport or from community to community? To what extent is sports participation a "right of passage" for boys today if they want to be seen as successful and popular?

What are some other examples of reproduction through leisure? Examples can probably be found in many different forms of leisure, including not only sports but also in cultural activities, different forms of media activities, and social and interactional leisure, such as parties. In thinking of these and other examples of reproduction, as well as examples of resistance, and through discussion of these examples with friends and classmates, it is likely that an awareness of the problems will quickly arise in attempting to categorize any one form of leisure as either "clearly resistance" or "clearly reproduction." This is because resistance and reproduction sometimes coexist, and both processes are often contradictory and incomplete. Dionigi's (2004) research on Master athletes, for example, showed that older adults are capable of competing in physically intense sports and are not "weak" or "over the hill." At the same time, this form of leisure participation also seemed to reinforce some negative attitudes towards aging as well, and encouraged denial of the aging process. Another interesting study (Tye & Powers, 1998) addressed the question of whether the rise of bachelorette parties as an alternative to traditional bridal showers is a form of gender resistance and/or whether such parties perpetuate negative stereotypes about women. Again, this illustrates the mix or resistance and reproduction that can occur within any one type of leisure activity.

Bridal Showers, Bachelorette Parties, Stag Parties: Innocent Fun? Liberation? or a New Conformity?

If you are female, you may well have been to a bridal shower. Or perhaps you have been to a bachelorette party. Which did you prefer? If you are male, you have likely attended a stag party. Did you enjoy it? Was it a significant event or just an excuse to have fun?

A study by two sociologists in Atlantic Canada took a close look at bachelorette parties, otherwise known as "stagette parties" or "girls' night out," and they came up with some interesting observations (Tye & Powers, 1998). The authors argue that bachelorette parties can be seen as a form of gender resistance, particularly resistance to the traditional role expectations associated with being a wife and mother. At the same time, bachelorette parties can also be seen to reinforce some traditional images and stereotypes, and especially the sexual objectification of women. This would suggest that these parties may not be fully liberatory, but may, perhaps, reflect a new version of conformity.

What do you think? Would you want a bachelorette party for yourself? or for your future spouse? How do they compare with stag parties?

In struggling to understand this complex mix of resistance and reproduction in leisure, it is clear that any one form of leisure practice can be contradictory because: (1) it may involve a range of different intentions or motivations on the part of participants, (2) it may involve different behaviours and thus send out different images and messages, and (3) people may respond to these messages and images in different ways (Shaw, 2001). Nevertheless, it is clear that both resistance and reproduction processes occur within leisure settings and that these processes can be seen as political processes in that they challenge and/or reinforce dominant ideologies and power structures. Because such processes may or may not be recognized by participants or observers, resistance and reproduction can be seen as a subtle—and often hidden or covert—political aspect of leisure.

Can you think of examples of reproduction and resistance in your life, or in the lives of people that you know? How important do you think leisure is in terms of enhancing positive social change and/or perpetuating negative social conditions?

Concluding Thoughts: Do Politics Matter?

The argument developed in this chapter is that the political aspects of leisure are important because leisure plays a number of significant political roles, both negative and positive, in our society. Politics and political decision making influence opportunities for and access to leisure. At the same time, everyday leisure practices affect power dynamics in society because of their influence on dominant systems of belief that affect people's lives, opportunities, and access to power and status.

To date, the political aspects of leisure have not been widely recognized. The role of governments and political decision making, and the influence of this form of politics on leisure have not gained much attention in the media, or among leisure scholars. The implications for leisure of other social and economic policies have garnered even less attention. Moreover, although a number of researchers have explored the more covert political aspects of leisure, such as resistance and reproduction processes and their influence on power relations, discussion of these issues has not extended beyond the academic realm.

At this point it may be time to give more attention to the political implications of leisure. One reason to seek to extend and widen the debate would be to gain more recognition for the value and significance of leisure both in people's lives and for society in general. A second would be that discussion of the political aspects of leisure would lead to recognition of both the positive and negative aspects of leisure practice, and this, in turn, could lead to finding ways of enhancing the positive aspects and minimizing the negative ones. Last but not least, understanding the politics of leisure can help people make decisions about their own lives, and could also help professional leisure service providers address these issues, too.

Key Terms

Governmental power
Personal power
Politics
Power
Resistance
Reproduction

References

Auster, C. J. (2001). Transcending potential antecedent leisure constraints: The case of women motorcycle operators. *Journal of Leisure Research, 33*(3), 272–298.

Davis, L. R. (1990). Male cheerleaders and the naturalization of gender. In M. A. Messner & D. F. Sabo (Eds.), *Sport, men and the gender order* (pp. 153–161). Champaign, IL: Human Kinetics.

Delamere, F. M. (2004). "It's just really fun to play!" A constructionist perspective of violence and gender representations in violent video games. University of Waterloo, ON.

Dionigi, R. A. (2004). *Competing for life: Older people and competitive sport.* Callaghan, NSW, Australia: University of Newcastle.

Duxbury, L., & Higgins, C. (2002). *The 2001 national work-life conflict study: Final report.* Ottawa, ON: Health Canada.

Eagles, P. F. J., & McCool, S. F. (2002). *Tourism in national parks and protected areas: Planning and management.* Wallingford, UK: CABI Publishing.

Foucault, M. (1980). *Power-Knowledge: Selected interviews and other writings 1972–1977.* New York, NY: Pantheon Books.

Freysinger, V., & Flannery, D. (1992). Women's leisure: Affiliation, self-determination, empowerment and resistance? *Loisir et Société, 15*(1), 303–321.

Green, E. (1998). "Women doing friendship": An analysis of women's leisure as a site of identity construction, empowerment and resistance. *Leisure Studies, 17*(3), 171–185.

Green, E., Hebron, S., & Woodward, E. (1990). *Women's leisure: What leisure?* Basingstoke, Hampshire, UK: Macmillan.

Guthrie, S. R., & Castelnuovo, S. (1992). Elite women bodybuilders: Models of resistance or compliance? *Play and Culture, 5*, 401–408.

Havitz, M. E., Morden, P. A., & Samdahl, D. M. (2004). *The diverse worlds of unemployed adults: Consequences for leisure, lifestyle, and well-being.* Waterloo, ON: Wilfrid Laurier University Press.

Lapchick, R. E. (1996). The modern Olympic Games: A political cauldron. In R. E. Lapchick (Ed.), *Sport in society: Equal opportunity or business as usual?* (pp. 253–271). Thousand Islands, CA: Sage Publications.

Lapchick, R. E. (2002). *Smashing barriers: Race and sport in the new millennium.* Lanham, MA: Madison Books.

McKay, J., Messner, M. A., & Sabo, D. F. (Eds.). (2000). *Masculinities, gender relations, and sport.* Thousand Oaks, CA: Sage Publications.

Messner, M. A. (1998). Boyhood, organized sports, and the construction of masculinities. In M. S. Kimmel & M. A. Messner (Eds.), *Men's lives* (4th ed., pp. 109–121). Boston, MA: Allyn & Bacon.

Messner, M. A., & Sabo, D. F. (Eds.). (1990). *Sport, men, and the gender order: Critical feminist perspectives.* Champaign, IL: Human Kinetics.

Pronger, B. (2000). Homosexuality and sport: Who's winning? In J. McKay, M. A. Messner, & D. F. Sabo (Eds.), *Masculinities, gender relations, and sport* (pp. 222–244). Thousand Oaks, CA: Sage Publications.

Schor, J. B. (1991). *The overworked American: The unexpected decline of leisure.* New York, NY: Basic Books.

Shaw, S. M. (2001). Conceptualizing resistance: Women's leisure as political practice. *Journal of Leisure Research, 33*(2), 186–201.

Shaw, S. M., & Dawson, D. (2001). Purposive leisure: Examining parental discourses on family activities. *Leisure Sciences, 23*(4), 217–231.

Shaw, S. M., Johnson, L. C., & Andrey, J. (2003). The struggle for life balance: Work, family, and leisure in the lives of women teleworkers. *World Leisure, 45*(4), 15–29.

Stewart, A. (2001). *Theories of power and domination.* London, UK: Sage Publications.

Swan, J., & Cooper, C. L. (2005). *Time, health and the family: What working families want.* London, UK: Working Families Group.

Theberge, N. (2000). *Higher goals: Women's ice hockey and the politics of gender.* Albany, NY: State University of New York Press.

Thomson-Nelson. *The dictionary of the social sciences.* Retrieved from http://socialsciencedictionary.nelson.com/ssd/main.html

Tye, D., & Powers, A. M. (1998). Gender, resistance and play: Bachelorette parties in Atlantic Canada. *Women's Studies International Forum, 21*(5), 551–561.

Wearing, B. M. (1990). Beyond the ideology of motherhood: Leisure as resistance. *Australian and New Zealand Journal of Sociology, 26*, 36–58.

Wearing, B. M. (1998). *Leisure and feminist theory.* London, UK: Sage Publications.

Wober, M., & Gunder, B. (1988). *Television and social control.* New York, NY: St. Martin's Press.

Zuzanek, J., & Smale, B. J. A. (1997). More work—less leisure? Changing allocations of time in Canada, 1981 to 1992. *Loisir et Société/Society and Leisure, 20*(1), 73–106.

Section B: Canadians and Their Leisure

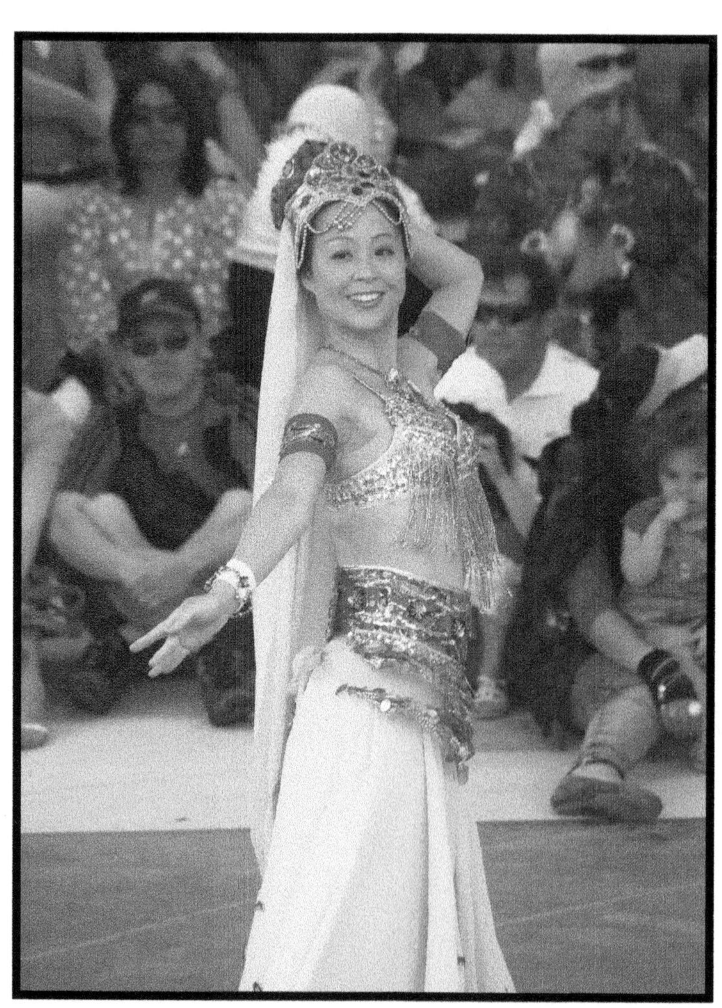

Chapter 8

Leisure Lifestyles

Robert A. Stebbins, Ph.D.
University of Calgary

Learning Objectives

After reading this chapter, students will be able to

1. Understand three forms of leisure: serious, casual, and project-based.
2. Understand discretionary time commitment.
3. Understand leisure lifestyle and how it is related to objectives (1) and (2).

As a concept, lifestyle has many applications, most notably in life in general, in work, and in leisure. In everyday usage these three tend to blend, as "way of life," "work/life balance," "daily routine," and similar expressions are talked about. The definition of lifestyle that fits well with these broad conceptions is: a distinctive set of shared patterns of tangible behaviour organized around a set of coherent interests or social conditions or both, and can be explained and justified by a set of related values, attitudes, and orientations and which, under certain conditions, becomes the basis for a separate, common social identity for its participants (Stebbins, 1997a).

Leisure studies specialists have studied and theorized about lifestyle in at least four ways. One, they have shown an interest in how participants mobilize the resources needed to engage in a leisure activity (e.g., time, money, social support). Two, they have examined participants' ties to the social world and constituent organizations of a particular core leisure activity and how these sometimes facilitate and sometimes hinder involvement in that world. Three, some lifestyle analyses have centred on how the core leisure activity serves as a basis for personal and social identification with it. Four, the costs and rewards of such activity have been studied as these are experienced not only while participating in the activity itself, but also while participating in the broader social milieu in which it is embedded. All four approaches are considered in the following discussion of discretionary time commitment and the ways both it and leisure lifestyle vary according to serious, casual, and project-based leisure.

Types of Leisure Lifestyles

Kelly (1999, pp. 144–147) noted that, since leisure easily lends itself to stereotyping, its classification according to stereotyped lifestyle has become a convenience. Thus many lifestyle classifications are based on a single factor such as passive worker, "jock," artist, high-risk enthusiast, outdoors person, and so on. One critical weakness of such typologies is their assumption that leisure is segregated; that a specialized area of free time is pursued independently of the rest of life. Apart from this way of developing typologies, there exists a variety of types based on peoples' patterns of consumption, which, as Kelly observes, have been constructed primarily to serve commercial marketing interests.

Thus theoretically based typologies in leisure are comparatively rare. Gunter and Gunter (1980) developed one that merits wider citation than it has received. They considered leisure activities along two dimensions: (a) time/choice/structure and type, and (b) degree of psychological involvement in a particular activity. By cross-classifying these two dimensions, they generated four types.

1. First there is pure leisure, which the authors see more as an experience than as a specific type. Here there is little institutional structure constraining high involvement in the leisure activity, as in the thrill of the roller coaster ride or the flow felt in alpine skiing (assuming skier competence on the hill).
2. An anomic leisure lifestyle results when a highly structured institutional environment frames low involvement in leisure. This leads to disengagement, exemplified in recreational drug and alcohol use.
3. Organized leisure is my term for the Gunters' category of activities found in highly structured institutional environments that are, however, highly absorbing psychologically. The leisure of group-based amateurism falls here (e.g., community theatre, sporting teams, amateur orchestras and jazz ensembles).
4. An alienated leisure lifestyle arises from a weakly structured institutional environment, wherein leisure involvement is correspondingly low. This is the classificatory home of passive entertainment, as seen in the inveterate consumer of television and the regular patron at a neighbourhood bar.

Discretionary Time Commitment

In leisure studies free time has long been considered a key resource for the individual, to manipulate to his or her personal ends. Discretionary time commitment is an, essentially, non-coerced, allocation of a certain number of minutes, hours, days, or other measure of time that a person devotes, or would like to devote, to carrying out an activity. Such commitment is both process and product. That is, people either set (process) their own time commitments (products) or willingly accept such commitments (i.e., agreeable obligations) set for them by others. Individuals setting personal time commitments by establishing which hours of the day will be devoted to specific activities, such as learning to play an instrument or train for a sport, are examples of this. Volunteers accept commitments when they agree to come to a school on a certain day to help a teacher with a classroom project. It follows that disagreeable obligations, which are invariably forced on individuals by others or by circumstances, fail to constitute discretionary time commitments, since the latter, as process, rest on personal agency, or determination. In short, discretionary time commitment finds expression in leisure and the agreeable sides of work (which, in effect, are experienced as leisure).

What discretionary time commitments have you made in the past seven days?

Note, however, that time can be, and often is, allocated to carrying out disagreeable activities, whether at work or outside it. Such commitments—call them coerced time commitments—are, obviously, not discretionary. Hence they fall beyond the scope of this discussion and, with some interesting exceptions, beyond the scope of leisure (but see a later statement on leisure costs).

What coerced time commitments have you made in the past seven days?

More generally past, present, and future time commitments are spoken of (discretionary and coerced) at work, leisure, and in the realm of non-work obligations. The kinds of time commitments people make help shape their work and leisure lifestyles, and constitute part of the patterning of those lifestyles. In leisure the nature of such commitments varies substantially across its three forms: serious, casual, and project-based leisure.

Serious Leisure

Serious leisure is the systematic pursuit of an amateur, hobbyist, or volunteer activity that participants find so substantial, interesting, and fulfilling that they typically launch themselves on a (leisure) career centred on acquiring and expressing its special skills, knowledge, and experience (Stebbins, 1992, 2001b). The term was coined by the author to express the way the people he interviewed and observed viewed the importance of these three kinds of activity in their everyday lives. The adjective "serious" (a word the respondents often used) embodies such qualities as earnestness, sincerity, importance, and carefulness, rather than gravity, solemnity, joylessness, distress, and anxiety. The idea of "career" in this definition follows sociological tradition, where careers are seen as available in all substantial, complex roles, including those in leisure.

Amateurs are found in art, science, sport, and entertainment, where they are invariably linked in a variety of ways with professional counterparts. The two can be distinguished descriptively in that the activity in question (e.g., acting, astronomy, hockey, stand-up comedy) constitutes a livelihood for its professionals but not its amateurs. Furthermore, most professionals work full-time at the activity whereas all amateurs pursue it part-time. The part-time professionals in art (e.g., poetry) and entertainment (e.g., ballroom dancing) complicate this picture; although they work part-time, their work is judged by other professionals and by the amateurs as of professional quality. Amateurs and professionals are locked in and therefore defined by a system of relations linking them and their publics— the professional-amateur-public, or P-A-P system. Examples include amateurs pitching batting practice for a professional baseball team, helping round out a section in a professional orchestra for a particular concert, and collecting data on variable stars for analysis by professional astronomers (see Chapter 4 and Stebbins, 1992). Hobbyists lack this professional alter ego, suggesting that, historically, all amateurs were hobbyists before their fields professionalized. Hobbyists are classified according to five categories:

1. collectors
2. makers and tinkerers (e.g., building furniture, making quilts, fixing old clocks)
3. activity participants (in non-competitive, rule-based, pursuits, e.g., fishing and barbershop singing)
4. players of sports and games (in competitive, rule-based activities with no professional counterparts, e.g., long-distance running and competitive swimming)
5. the enthusiasts of the liberal arts hobbies, which are primarily prodigious reading pursuits in such areas as a genre of literature or a period of history

Amateurs and hobbyists are drawn to their leisure pursuits significantly more by self-interest than by altruism.

Volunteers, by contrast, engage in activities fired by a more or less equal blend of these two motives. Volunteering is uncoerced help offered either formally or informally with, at most, token pay and done for the benefit of other people (beyond the volunteer's family) and the volunteer. This conception of volunteering revolves largely around a central subjective motivational question; that is, it must be determined whether volunteers feel they are engaging in: (a) enjoyable casual leisure (as in handing out leaflets, stuffing envelopes); (b) fulfilling serious leisure (e.g., guiding at the zoo, mentoring for adolescents); or (c) enjoyable or fulfilling project-based leisure (ushering for a barbershop singers' convention, preparing a PowerPoint presentation for a surprise birthday party), a core activity that they have had the option to accept or reject on their own terms. A key element in the leisure conception of volunteering is the felt absence of moral coercion to do the volunteer activity, an element that, in "marginal volunteering" (e.g., working in the food bank as part of a class assignment) may be experienced in degrees, as more or less coercive.

Serious leisure is further defined by six distinctive qualities that are found uniformly among its amateurs, hobbyists, and volunteers. One is the occasional need to persevere. Participants who want to continue experiencing the same level of fulfillment in the activity have to meet certain challenges from time to time. Thus, musicians must practice assiduously to master difficult musical passages, baseball players must throw repeatedly to perfect favourite pitches, and volunteers must search their imaginations for new approaches with which to help children with reading problems. For all three types of serious leisure the deepest fulfillment sometimes comes at the end of the activity rather than during it: from sticking with it through thick and thin, from conquering adversity.

Another quality distinguishing all three types of serious leisure is the opportunity to follow a (leisure) career in the endeavour: a career shaped by its own special contingencies, turning points, and stages of achievement and involvement. Nevertheless, in some fields, notably certain arts and sports, this career choice may include decline. Moreover, most, if not all, careers here owe their existence to a third quality; serious leisure participants put forth significant personal effort using their specially acquired knowledge, training, or skill and, indeed at times, all three. Careers for serious leisure participants unfold along lines of their efforts to achieve, for instance, a high level of showmanship, athletic prowess, or scientific knowledge, or to accumulate formative experiences in a volunteer role.

Serious leisure is further distinguished by numerous durable benefits, or tangible, salutary outcomes that such activity delivers to its participants. They are self-actualization, self-enrichment, self-expression, regeneration or renewal of self, feelings of accomplishment, enhancement of self-image, social interaction and sense of belonging, and lasting physical products of the activity (e.g., a painting, a scientific paper, a piece of furniture). A further benefit—self-gratification, or pure fun, by far the most evanescent in this list—is also enjoyed by casual leisure participants. The possibility of realizing such benefits constitutes a powerful goal in serious leisure.

Fifth, serious leisure is distinguished by a unique ethos that emerges in connection with each expression of it. This ethos is the spirit of the community of serious leisure participants, as manifested in shared attitudes, practices, values, beliefs, goals, and so on. The social world of the participants is the organizational milieu in which the associated ethos is expressed (as attitudes, beliefs, values) or realized (as practices, goals). According to Unruh (1980) every social world has its characteristic groups, events, routines, practices, and organizations. It is held together, to an important degree, by semiformal, or mediated, communication. In other words, social worlds are typically neither heavily bureaucratized nor substantially organized through intense face-to-face interaction. Rather, communication is commonly mediated by newsletters, posted notices, telephone messages, mass mailings, radio and television announcements, and similar means.

The social world is a diffuse, amorphous entity to be sure, but nevertheless one of great importance in the impersonal, segmented life of the modern urban community. Its importance is further amplified by a parallel element of this special ethos, which is missing from Unruh's conception, namely that such worlds are also made up of a rich subculture. One function of this subculture is to interrelate the many components of this diffuse and amorphous entity. In other words, there is associated with each social world a set of special norms, values, beliefs, styles, moral principles, performance standards, and similar shared representations.

The sixth quality—participants in serious leisure tend to identify strongly with their chosen pursuits—springs from the presence of the other five distinctive qualities. In contrast, most casual leisure, although not usually humiliating or despicable, is nonetheless too fleeting, mundane, and commonplace to become the basis for a distinctive identity for most people.

Furthermore, certain rewards and costs come with pursuing a hobbyist, amateur, or volunteer activity. As the *i*-box list on the following page shows, the rewards are predominantly personal.

The costs are a distinctive combination of tensions, dislikes, and disappointments, which each participant confronts in his or her own way within every serious leisure activity. Tensions and dislikes develop within the activity or through its imperfect mesh with work, family, and other

Rewards of Serious Leisure

Personal

1. Personal enrichment (cherished experiences)
2. Self-actualization (developing skills, abilities, knowledge)
3. Self-expression (expressing skills, abilities, knowledge already developed)
4. Self-image (known to others as a particular kind of serious leisure participant)
5. Self-gratification (combination of superficial enjoyment and deep satisfaction)
6. Re-creation (regeneration) of oneself through serious leisure after a day's work
7. Financial return (from a serious leisure activity)

Social

8. Social attraction (associating with other serious leisure participants, with clients as a volunteer, participating in the social world of the activity)
9. Group accomplishment (group effort in accomplishing a serious leisure project; senses of helping, being needed, being altruistic)
10. Contribution to the maintenance and development of the group (including senses of helping, being needed, being altruistic in making the contribution)

leisure interests. Put more precisely, the goal of gaining fulfillment in serious leisure is the drive to experience the rewards of a given leisure activity, such that its costs are seen by the participant as more or less insignificant by comparison.

Casual Leisure

Casual leisure is an immediately and intrinsically rewarding, relatively short-lived and pleasurable activity requiring little or no special training to enjoy it. It is fundamentally hedonic, pursued for its significant level of pure enjoyment, or pleasure. The term was coined by the author in the 1982 conceptual statement about serious leisure, which at the time, depicted its casual counterpart as all activity not classifiable as serious (project-based leisure has since been added as a third form, see next section). As a scientific concept, casual leisure languished in this residual status, until Stebbins (1997b), belatedly recognizing its centrality and importance in leisure studies, sought to elaborate the idea (see Rojek, 1997). It is considerably less substantial and offers no career of the sort found in serious leisure.

Its eight types include play (e.g., dabbling), relaxation (e.g., sitting, napping, strolling), passive entertainment (e.g., watching TV, reading books, recording music), active entertainment (e.g., playing games of chance, playing party games), sociable conversation (e.g., gossip and "idle chatter"), sensory stimulation (e.g., sex, eating, drinking), and casual volunteering (as opposed to serious leisure, or career, volunteering). The last and newest type—pleasurable aerobic activity—refers to physical activities that require effort sufficient to cause marked increase in respiration and heart rate.

This refers to "aerobic activity" in the broad sense, to all activity that calls for such effort, including the routines pursued collectively in (narrowly conceived of) aerobics classes and those pursued individually by way of televised or videotaped aerobics programs (Stebbins, 2004). Yet, as with its passive and active cousins in entertainment, pleasurable aerobic activity is basically casual leisure; that is, to do such activity requires little more than minimal skill, knowledge, or experience. Examples include the game of the Hash House Harriers (a type of treasure hunt in the outdoors), kickball (a cross between soccer and baseball), and such children's games as hide-and-seek. It is likely that people pursue the different types of casual leisure in combinations of two and three at least as often as they pursue them separately.

Notwithstanding its hedonic nature, casual leisure is by no means wholly frivolous, for some clear costs and benefits accrue from pursuing it. Moreover, in contrast to the evanescent, hedonic property of casual leisure itself, these costs and benefits are enduring. The benefits include serendipitous creativity and discovery in play, regeneration from early intense activity, and development and maintenance of interpersonal relationships (Stebbins, 2001a). Some of its costs are rooted in lack of variety as manifested in boredom. Moreover, casual leisure alone is unlikely to produce a distinctive and valued leisure identity.

List your present serious and casual leisure activities.

Project-Based Leisure

Project-based leisure (Stebbins, 2005)—a third form of leisure activity—requires considerable planning, effort, and sometimes skill or knowledge, but is after all neither serious leisure nor intended to develop into such. Examples include planning surprise birthday parties, making elaborate preparations for a major holiday, and volunteering for sports events. Though only a rudimentary social world springs up around the project, in its own particular way it brings together friends, neighbours, or relatives (e.g., through a genealogical project or Christmas celebrations), or draws the individual participant into an organizational milieu (e.g., through volunteering for a sports event or major convention). Project-based leisure is not all the same. Whereas systematic exploration may reveal others, two types are presently evident: one-shot projects and occasional projects.

One-Shot Projects

In all these projects people generally use the talents and knowledge they have at hand, even though for some projects they may seek certain instruction beforehand, possibly by way of reading a book or taking a short course. Some projects resembling hobbyist activity participation may require a modicum of preliminary conditioning. The goal is to always successfully undertake the one-shot project and nothing more; sometimes a small amount of background preparation is necessary for this. A survey might show that most project-based leisure is hobbyist in character seconded by a kind of volunteering. First, the following hobbyist-like projects have been identified so far:

Making and Tinkering

- Interlacing, interlocking, and knot-making from kits
- Other kit assembly projects (e.g., stereo tuner, craft store projects)
- Do-it-yourself projects done primarily for fulfillment, some of which may even be undertaken with minimal skill and knowledge (e.g., build a rock wall or a fence, finish a room in the basement, plant a special garden). This could turn into an irregular series of such projects, spread over many years, possibly even transforming the participant into a hobbyist.

Liberal Arts

- Genealogy (not as ongoing hobby)
- Tourism: special trip, not as part of an extensive personal tour program, to visit different parts of a region, a continent, or much of the world

Activity participation

- Long back-packing trip, canoe trip; one-shot mountain ascent (e.g., Fuji, Rainier, Kilimanjaro)

One-shot volunteering projects are also common, though possibly somewhat less so than hobbyist-like projects. Less common than either are the amateur-like projects, which seem to concentrate in the sphere of theatre.

Volunteering

- Volunteer at a convention or conference, whether local, national, or international in scope.
- Volunteer at a sporting competition, whether local, national, or international in scope.
- Volunteer at an arts festival or special exhibition mounted in a museum.
- Volunteer to help restore human life or wildlife after a natural or human-made disaster, for instance, a hurricane, earthquake, oil spill, or industrial accident.

Entertainment Theatre

- Produce a skit (a form of sketch) or one-shot community pageant; create a puppet show; prepare a home film or a set of videos, slides, or photos; prepare a public talk.

Occasional Projects

The occasional projects seem more likely to originate in or be motivated by agreeable obligation than their one-shot cousins. Examples of occasional projects include the sum of the culinary, decorative, or other creative activities undertaken at home or at work for a religious occasion or someone's birthday. Likewise, national holidays and similar celebrations sometimes inspire individuals to mount occasional projects consisting of an ensemble of inventive elements.

Unlike one-shot projects, occasional projects have the potential to become routinized, which happens when new creative possibilities no longer come to mind as the participant arrives at a fulfilling formula wanting no further modification. North Americans who decorate their homes the same way each Christmas season exemplify this situation. Indeed, it can happen that over the years such projects may lose their appeal but not their necessity, thereby becoming disagreeable obligations which their authors no longer define as leisure.

One-shot projects also hold the possibility of becoming unpleasant. Thus, the hobbyist genealogist gets overwhelmed with the details of family history and the difficulty of verifying dates. The thought of an individual putting in time and effort doing something once considered leisure but has since turned into a dreaded chore makes no sense. Likewise, volunteering for a project may turn sour, creating in the volunteer a sense of being faced with a disagreeable obligation, which however, must still be honoured. This is leisure no more.

Time Use in Leisure

Discretionary time commitment differs across and within these three forms of leisure. Generally speaking, serious leisure requires its participants to allocate more time than participants in the other two forms, if for no other reason than, of the three, it is pursued over the longest span of time. In addition, certain qualities of serious leisure, including especially perseverance, commitment, effort, and career, tend to make amateurs, hobbyists, and volunteers particularly cognizant of how they allocate their free time, the amount of that time they use for their serious leisure, and the ways they do this.

Describe a leisure project you would like to carry out. Describe the last time you engaged in project-based leisure or were involved in someone else's leisure project. What type of project was it?

Consider some examples. Amateur and hobbyist activities based on the development and polishing of physical skills (e.g., learning how to juggle, figure skate, make quilts, play the piano) require the aspiring entertainer, skater, quilter, and so on to commit a fair amount of time on a regular basis, sometimes over several years, to acquiring necessary skills. Once acquired, the skills and related physical conditioning must be maintained through use. Additionally some serious leisure enthusiasts take on (agreeable) obligations that demand their presence at certain places at certain times (e.g., rehearsals, matches, meetings, events). But, most importantly, the core activity, which is the essence of a person's serious leisure, is so attractive that this individual very much wants to set aside sufficient time to engage in it. In other words, serious leisure often borders on becoming uncontrollable; it engenders in its practitioners a desire to pursue the activity beyond the time or the money (if not both) available for it. So, even though hobbies such as collecting stamps or making furniture usually have few schedules or appointments to meet, they are nonetheless enormously appealing to some, and as such encourage these collectors and makers to allocate time whenever possible for this leisure.

Project-based leisure tends to carry with it similar demands. There are often scheduled meetings or responsibilities, if not both, and though of short-range, the condition of uncontrollability can also be a concern. However, project-based leisure does not, by definition, involve developing, polishing, and maintaining physical skills, which is one of the key differences in use of discretionary time that separates it from serious leisure. Furthermore, with project-based leisure comes a unique sense of time allocation: time use is more or less intense but limited to a known and definite period of the calendar (e.g., when the games are over, when the stone wall is built, when the surprise birthday party has taken place). Indeed, one of the attractions of projects for some people is that no long-term commitment of time is foreseen.

Would you say that any of your leisure is uncontrollable in terms of discretionary time commitment?

Finally, casual leisure may, in its own way, generate time commitments, as in the desire to set aside an hour each week to watch a television program or participate as often as possible in a neighbourhood coffee klatch. Furthermore, some casual leisure, famously watching television, is attractive, in part, because it is often available on a moment's notice—call it "spontaneous discretionary time commitment"; it can fill in gaps between discretionary and coerced time commitments, and in the process, stave off boredom. Additionally, casual volunteering commonly has temporal requirements, as in joining an environmental clean-up crew over the weekend, serving free meals to the poor on Thanksgiving Day, or collecting money for a charity by going door-to-door or soliciting on a street corner.

The discretionary allocation of time in leisure is, then, hugely complicated. So, when broaching the subject, we must be sure to specify the form and, within the form, the type of leisure in question. Time allocation differs substantially from amateur boxing to hobbyist barbershop singing to volunteer fire fighting and from genealogical projects to casual people-watching from a streetside cafe. The complexity of the allocation of leisure time may also be affected by significant others. Not infrequently such allocation is negotiated with spouses, partners, friends, and relatives. The leisure participant may want to devote more time than these people will accept, since the latter want the former to spend time (perhaps money too) with them. Enter, again, the issue of uncontrollability.

By understanding how discretionary time commitment varies across the three forms of leisure, we overcome an undesirable, idiographic tendency in lifestyle research. This tendency is to report in detail on a particular lifestyle, say of amateur tennis players, volunteer fire fighters, or soap opera devotees, while making little effort to generalize that lifestyle to the broader category into which these enthusiasts fall of athlete, service volunteer, and television viewer. Linking time allocation to the three forms of leisure facilitates generalization.

Would you say that you have an optimal leisure lifestyle? Explain.

Key Terms

Amateur
Casual leisure
Career
Discretionary time commitment
Hobbyist
Identity
Lifestyle
Project-based leisure
Serious leisure
Social world
Volunteer

References

Gunter, G. B., & Gunter, N. C. (1980). Leisure styles: A conceptual framework for modern leisure. *The Sociological Quarterly, 21*, 361–374.

Kelly, J. R. (1999). Leisure behaviors and styles: Social, economic, and cultural factors. In E. L. Jackson & T. L. Burton (Eds.), *Leisure studies: Prospects for the twenty-first century* (pp. 135–150). State College, PA: Venture Publishing, Inc.

Rojek, C. (1997). Leisure theory: Retrospect and prospect. *Loisir et Société/Society and Leisure, 20*, 383–400.

Stebbins, R. A. (1992). *Amateurs, professionals, and serious leisure*. Montréal, Québec and Kingston, ON: McGill-Queen's University Press.

Stebbins, R. A. (1997a). Lifestyle as a generic concept in ethnographic research. *Quality & Quantity, 31*, 347–360.

Stebbins, R. A. (1997b). Casual leisure: A conceptual statement. *Leisure Studies, 16*, 17–25.

Stebbins, R. A. (2001a). The costs and benefits of hedonism: Some consequences of taking casual leisure seriously. *Leisure Studies, 20*, 305–309.

Stebbins, R. A. (2001b). *New directions in the theory and research of serious leisure*. Lewiston, NY: Edwin Mellen.

Stebbins, R. A. (2004). Pleasurable aerobic activity: A type of casual leisure with salubrious implications. *World Leisure Journal, 46*(4), 55–58.

Stebbins, R. A. (2005). Project-based leisure: Theoretical neglect of a common use of free time. *Leisure Studies, 24*, 1–11.

Unruh, D. R. (1980). The nature of social worlds. *Pacific Sociological Review, 23*, 271–296.

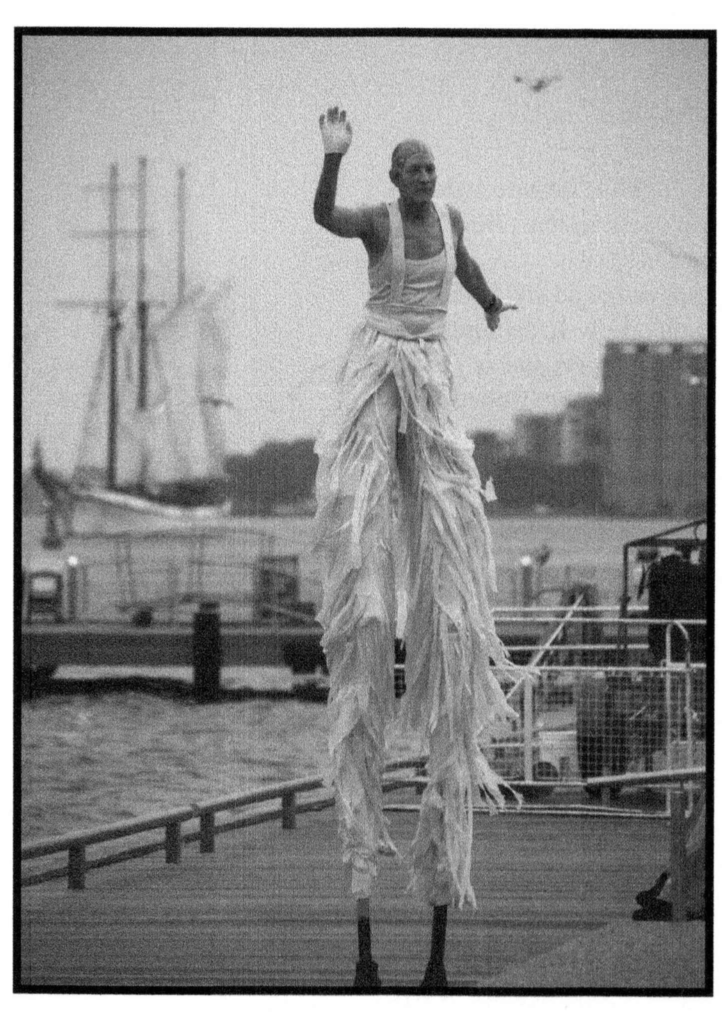

Chapter 9
Leisure Constraints

Edgar L. Jackson, Ph.D.
University of Alberta

Learning Objectives

After reading this chapter, students will be able to

1. Connect their own daily lives with the concepts and findings of leisure constraints research.
2. Know the purposes and value of the field.
3. Articulate the main stages in the development of leisure constraints research, and why these occurred.
4. Be aware of the key models used to understand constraints, and how these evolved in relation to changing assumptions and new empirical evidence.
5. Know the main findings in leisure constraints research and how these relate to the choice of methods.
6. Understand the main recent changes in leisure constraints research and likely developments in the future.

Leisure and Constraints in Your Everyday Life

Suppose you are having coffee with a group of friends one mid-week February morning on a Canadian campus. Most of the group, about six or seven in all, both men and women, are winter-sports enthusiasts (downhill skiing and snowboarding). An avid boarder yourself, you suggest to the others a skiing/boarding weekend at an alpine resort some two hundred kilometres away.

> "Not me," says one. "I'm not interested in that any more."
>
> "Nor me," says another, "I have to work on Saturday, and besides, I don't have that kind of money right now."

A third mentions a date she has plans for Friday night, while a fourth says she doesn't like that particular resort or the people who tend to go there. A fifth is still recovering from a sprained ankle. By the time the weekend comes around, you do in fact go on the trip, but accompanied by only one of your friends. The trip costs more than you had planned because you can't share the costs among as many people as you'd expected, and it turns out to be less fun than you'd hoped because most of your friends aren't there.

The point of this hypothetical scenario is that it describes a common episode of recreation and leisure that leisure scholars might approach from a variety of perspectives. It suggests issues of interest, preferences, participation, non-participation, and enjoyment; motivations and their strengths are clearly another element; social relations are obviously a third aspect; yet another might be the spatial geography of origins (home), destinations (the location and attractiveness of the resort), and the distance separating the two, with implications for costs and balancing time commitments.

The scenario also suggests how our leisure behaviours might be influenced by several types of leisure constraints (see later for definitions): intrapersonal constraints (which could explain lack of interest); interpersonal constraints (the date, as well as the absence of friends); and structural constraints (costs, lack of time, other commitments, perceptions of recreation resources and facilities, etc.). In addition, the "story" illustrates two other themes about leisure constraints. First, constraints not only influence recreation preferences and participation but also leisure enjoyment; and second, the negotiation of constraints—the fact that, in some instances, people try to alleviate or overcome the influence of constraints. In these cases, participation still occurs but in a way that probably differs from what would have happened if the constraints had been absent. In this sense, the concept of constraints can be thought of as a sort of "conceptual glue" that holds together a number of superficially different and apparently disconnected aspects of leisure behaviour. It does not *replace* other approaches to describing and understanding leisure, but rather is *complementary* to them, offering a host of novel concepts, questions and interpretations on issues that otherwise might be only partially understood. It is this simultaneously cohesive and complementary role that has produced a large and ongoing amount of attention to leisure constraints by leisure scholars over the last two to three decades.

Thinking about your own leisure, what constraints do you encounter in achieving your leisure goals? Are these constraints intermittent or permanent? Is there anything you try to do to overcome or alleviate the effects of these constraints? Do you think that your leisure would be different if the constraints were not present to begin with? If so, how? If not, why not?

The Purpose and Value of Leisure Constraints Research

To state things rather more formally than in the previous anecdote, leisure constraints research aims to "investigate factors that are assumed by researchers and/or perceived or experienced by individuals to limit the formation of leisure preferences and/or to inhibit or prohibit participation and enjoyment in leisure" (Jackson, 2000, p. 62). There are essentially three general justifications for leisure constraints research. To begin, the topic is of interest and value in and of itself: understanding individuals' leisure choices and behaviour requires investigation of all the factors, both positive (e.g., motivations, anticipated benefits) and negative (constraints) that influence those choices. Studies of constraints can also help to explain why observed relationships among values and attitudes, leisure preferences, and overt leisure behaviour are frequently tenuous. Second, constraints research has assisted in generating new insights into aspects of leisure previously thought to be well-understood, such as leisure participation, motivations, satisfactions, and recreational conflict. Third, the field has turned out to be a useful device to enhance communication among scholars with diverse disciplinary training, topical interests, and methodological orientations.

If people are not aware of a barrier to their leisure, and its effects, is this still a constraint? In other words, does something have to be *perceived* as a constraint to *be* a constraint?

A Brief Overview of the Development of Leisure Constraints Research

Systematic research on leisure constraints has existed as a distinct subfield of investigation within leisure studies for about two and a half decades, beginning with some key papers that were published in the early 1980s (Boothby, Tungatt, & Townsend, 1981; Francken & van Raaij, 1981; Romsa & Hoffman, 1980; Witt & Goodale, 1981). Most of the research conducted in the 1980s was empirical, being based on theory at only the deepest and most implicit level (Stockdale, 1989). Consequently, researchers tended to make certain assumptions about constraints and their impacts on people's leisure and recreation that were not uncovered as limiting the development of the field until much later. Among the early assumptions the two most important were as follows: (1) constraints are immovable, static obstacles to participation; and (2) the most significant, if perhaps not the only, effect of constraints on leisure is to block or limit participation. In other words, the absence or presence of constraints would explain why a person does or does not participate in an activity. To use subsequent language, structural constraints (those that intervene between preferences and participation) were thought to be the only significant type of constraint. As a corollary, the emphasis was on activities and participation as outcomes of constraints, which, like the constraints items, were the most easily quantifiable and measurable aspects of leisure to investigate.

The picture changed considerably in several ways in the late 1980s and after. The field began to be characterized by more explicit and increasingly sophisticated theorizing, as researchers began to uncover previous false assumptions and explore new concepts. There were two facets to this development: innovative interpretation of new and more

Early Assumptions about Constraints

The basic assumption in early research on "barriers to participation" (using the terminology that was prevalent at the time) was that a person is presumed to have a preference, desire, or demand for a leisure activity, but fulfillment of this preference may be compromised by the presence of a constraint. This type of thinking is summarized in the model shown in Figure 9.1a. A slightly more sophisticated model is shown in Figure 9.1b: participation results from the absence of constraints, but the outcome of encountering a constraint is non-participation. Little if any attention was paid to outcomes of constraints other than non-participation, nor were constraints acknowledged to affect preferences. Thus, a non-participant was assumed to be constrained in some way but a participant was not constrained. These assumptions have been rejected in subsequent research.

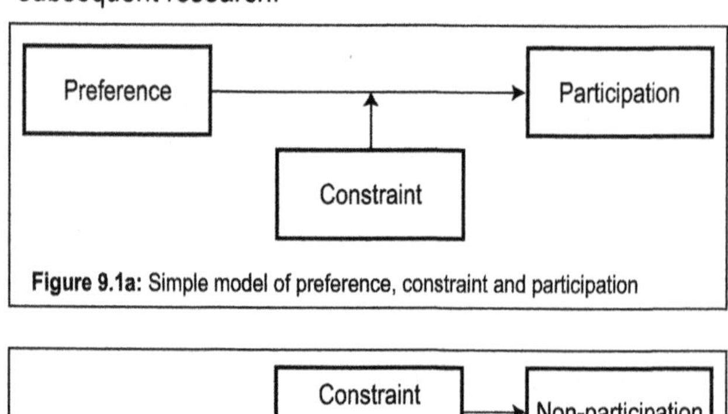

Figure 9.1a: Simple model of preference, constraint and participation

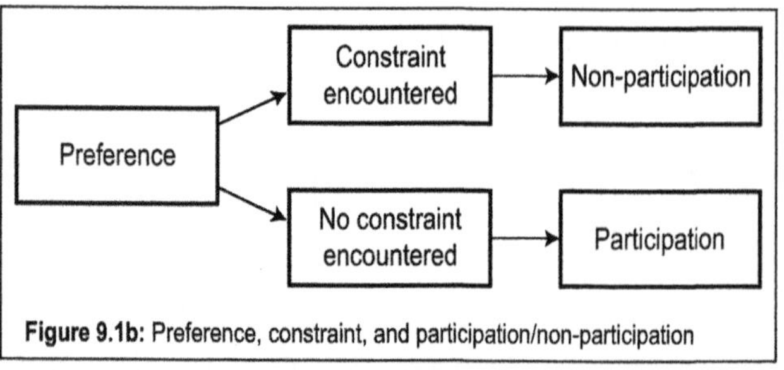

Figure 9.1b: Preference, constraint, and participation/non-participation

complex empirical research; and the emergence of a series of theoretical, model-based articles that challenged previous assumptions and attempted to set the stage for the more sophisticated empirical research that was to follow. The language changed too. The word "constraints" replaced "barriers"; "leisure" replaced "recreation"; and the word "participation" was dropped. The array of methods was widened, in particular with the incorporation of qualitative methods (see following) and the declining domination of the questionnaire (as, of course, was also happening more widely in leisure studies and indeed in the social sciences as a whole). Criticism began to be aired about constraints research and concepts, which generated a vigorous and healthy scholarly debate about the value and accuracy of the insights to be gained from research conducted using a constraints-based perspective (see, e.g., Samdahl & Jekubovich, 1997a, followed by replies from Henderson, 1997 and Jackson, 1997, and a rebuttal by Samdahl & Jekubovich, 1997b).

Changes in the Terminology of Leisure Constraints Research

In the early 1980s, the field of leisure constraints research, had it been recognized as distinct within leisure studies, would have been referred to as "barriers to recreation participation." The current conventional terminology is "constraints to leisure," a change that represents much more than a semantic difference: it is indicative of three fundamental shifts in focus and conceptualization.

The more inclusive term "constraints" is now preferred to "barriers," because the latter fails to capture the entire range of explanations of constrained leisure behaviour. Moreover, the word "barrier" tends to direct researchers' attention toward only one type of constraint, that which intervenes between preferences and participation ("structural constraints"). Today, however, a much more comprehensive and complex range of constraints is recognized.

Replacement of the word "recreation" with leisure simultaneously represented both broadening the focus of investigation and forging closer links than before with the mainstream of thinking in leisure studies.

Dropping the word "participation" was based on recognition that constraints influence far more than the choice to participate or not. It was also consistent with the evolution of definitions of leisure, away from activity- and time-based conceptualizations and toward the meaning of leisure as experienced by the participant rather than as defined by the researcher.

Source: Modified from Jackson and Scott, 1999

Theories and Models

Three specific developments occurred between about 1987 and 1991 that challenged the somewhat naïve thinking of early constraints research and changed its course. First, stimulated in part by an integrative review (Jackson, 1988), there was an increase in new empirical research activity coupled with a growing awareness among leisure scholars of the pervasive importance of constraints, both in people's leisure lives and in diverse areas of leisure studies in which constraints had not previously been investigated. For example, and related to Crawford and Godbey's (1987) work on expanding the range of constraints, some initial attempts were made to go beyond the simple preferences/constraints/participation model and investigate what were called "antecedent constraints" at the time—limiting factors thought to shape the development of interests and preferences (e.g., Henderson, Stalnaker, & Taylor, 1988; Jackson, 1990a, 1990b).

Secondly, some very innovative research was published that later proved to be the foundation for subsequent theoretical exploration of the concept of "leisure constraints negotiation." For example, Scott (1991), in a qualitative study of contract bridge, showed that people often take quite innovative steps to negotiate the constraints they face (this, in fact, was the first time the term "negotiation" appeared in the constraints literature). Kay and Jackson (1991) demonstrated how many people manage to participate in their chosen leisure activities "despite constraint." Shaw, Bonen, and McCabe (1991), having identified the counter-intuitive finding that it is often the more constrained people who participate more frequently than the less constrained, questioned the assumption that "more constraints mean less leisure."

The third development—new theorizing and the construction of models—which in fact was intimately connected with the other two, and which indeed would likely not have occurred had it not been for the stimulus of the articles by Scott, Kay and Jackson, and Shaw et al., among others, was the publication of an increasingly sophisticated set of models of leisure and constraints.

In retrospect the single most important conceptual development in leisure constraints research in the 1980s was the publication in *Leisure Sciences* of a seminal paper by Crawford and Godbey (1987), "Barriers to family leisure." Crawford and Godbey made two main contributions, which have been adopted as axiomatic by subsequent leisure constraints researchers. First, they argued that it was not only participation and non-participation that were affected by constraints, but also preferences—in other words, lack of desire for an activity or lack of awareness could also be subject to and therefore explained in part by constraints. Secondly, and in a sense a corollary of the first contribution, they broadened the range of constraints that could be recognized as affecting leisure behaviour. Thus, not only do constraints *intervene* between preferences and participation, as shown in *i*-box "The Negotiation Thesis," referred to as "structural constraints" by Crawford and Godbey, but they also *affect* preferences in several significant ways, most notably through the operation of what Crawford and Godbey refer to as "intrapersonal" and "interpersonal constraints." The next step in the modelling process occurred in the form of a "hierarchical model" in which Crawford, Jackson, and Godbey (1991) recast the thinking that had gone into the Crawford and Godbey paper in terms of a sequential hierarchy of constraints. They argued that, although most research attention had been paid to structural constraints, these are probably the least important in shaping leisure behaviour, whereas intra- and interpersonal constraints are likely to be more important influences on leisure. The notion that people might negotiate through these sequentially arranged constraints was only implicit in the hierarchical model, but became more explicit as the focus of attention in a subsequent article by Jackson, Crawford, and Godbey (1993). The "negotiation thesis," as it came to be known, was based on the idea, derived from Kay and Jackson (1991) and Scott (1991) that, despite experiencing constraints, people do find ways to participate in and enjoy leisure, even if such participation and enjoyment may differ from what they would have been in the absence of constraints.

**The Negotiation Thesis—
Model and Propositions**

The negotiation thesis was summarized in a flow-diagram model (Figure 9.2), and six specific propositions were presented, namely:

1. Participation is dependent not on the absence of constraints (although this may be true for some people) but on negotiation through them. Such negotiation may modify rather than foreclose participation.
2. Variations in the reporting of constraints can be viewed not only as variations in the experience of constraints but also as variations in success in negotiating them.
3. Absence of the desire to change current leisure behaviour may be partly explained by prior successful negotiation of structural constraints.
4. Anticipation of one or more insurmountable interpersonal or structural constraints may suppress the desire for participation.
5. Anticipation consists not simply of the anticipation of the presence or intensity of a constraint but also of anticipation of the ability to negotiate it.
6. Both the initiation and outcome of the negotiation process are dependent on the relative strength of, and interactions between, constraints on participating in an activity and motivations for such participation.

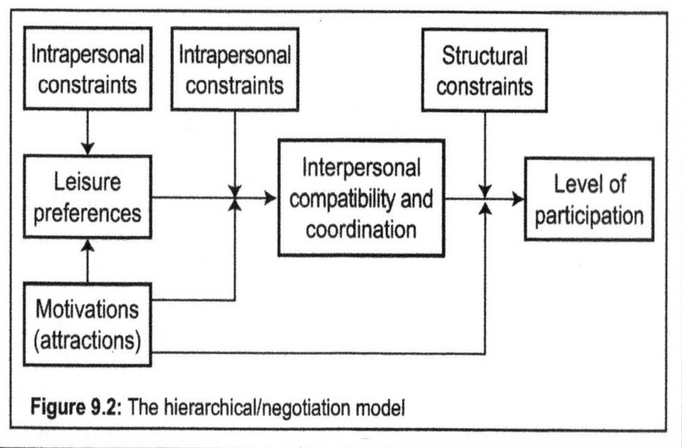

Figure 9.2: The hierarchical/negotiation model

Does theory matter in leisure constraints research and practice? Isn't it just a process of collecting data about the barriers and constraints that people experience and developing practices to alleviate them? If theory does matter in leisure constraints research, which of the theories outlined elsewhere in this book would be the most helpful in advancing the field?

What Do We Know about Constraints?

Any attempt to summarize knowledge presented in dozens, if not hundreds, of academic research papers on leisure constraints published over a two- to three-decade period is inevitably compromised by the need to leave out a great deal of detail, painting only the broadest picture of what we know. Nonetheless, there are four important themes that we can focus on here to give a general sense of what the field is all about: (1) research on structural constraints, (2) alternative measures of constrained leisure, (3) the hierarchical model and the negotiation of constraints, and (4) the contributions of qualitative research.

Research on Structural Constraints

Although the situation is changing, the bulk of published empirical research on constraints to leisure has focused on what Crawford and Godbey (1987) called "structural constraints." Moreover, in the early stages of research much of the analysis was conducted on an item-by-item basis, consisting essentially of cross-sectional correlations between scores of constraints items and two other sets of variables: measures of participation and non-participation, and socio-economic and demographic variables. Following the lead of McGuire (1984), however, methods to reduce the complexity of item-by-item analysis were introduced into the field, such as factor analysis (e.g., Hawkins & Freeman, 1993), cluster analysis (Jackson, 1993; Norman, 1995), and multidimensional scaling (Hultsman, 1995).

Alternative Measures of Constrained Leisure

As most empirical constraints research up to the late 1980s addressed structural constraints, it is not surprising that the body of research typically emphasized non-participation

Key Findings from the Analysis of Structural Constraints

There is a stable and virtually universal range of categories of structural constraints to leisure, typically consisting of the following: (1) the costs of participating; (2) time and other commitments; (3) problems with facilities; (4) isolation (sometimes subdivided into social isolation and geographical isolation); and (5) lack of skills and abilities. With minor variations, these dimensions are representative of the kinds of empirical groupings commonly reported in quantitative (usually factor analysis-based) classifications of constraints items and scales.

No constraint or type of constraint is experienced with equal intensity by everyone, although time- and cost-related constraints rank among the most widely and intensely experienced inhibitors of the achievement of leisure goals and a balanced lifestyle.

The experience of constraints varies among individuals and groups: no sub-group of the population, and probably no individual, is entirely free from constraints to leisure.

Relationships between categories of constraints and personal characteristics such as age and income also tend to be stable. The idealized composite graph shown in Figure 9.3 is a good example both of the kinds of the analysis and the graphic presentation of quantitative data that typically emerge from questionnaire surveys, in which respondents are asked to rate the importance of varying numbers of constraints items (such as being too busy with their family, the costs of participating) in relation to aspects of constrained leisure. As the graph shows, when analyzed and presented at this highly aggregate and general level, some interesting and stable patterns emerge about apparent changes in constraints across the life cycle. Moreover, each category of constraint not coincidentally exhibits a distinct pattern of association with age. Thus, a lack of skills and abilities, although consistently rated as least important among every age group when averaged across a survey sample, gradually increases in importance as the life cycle progresses. In contrast— both in terms of the relative importance of the constraint and the direction of the relationship—costs as a negative influence on participation decline with advancing age. Perhaps not surprisingly, because the category of constraints may be viewed as "external" to the individual, most studies have shown that the amount and quality of facilities as a constraint to leisure do not vary with age. As far as the remaining two categories are concerned, isolation is typically characterized by a U-shaped relationship with age, meaning that it is most important in the early stages of the life cycle, declines until early middle age, and increases once again in the later stages of life. In dramatic contrast, commitments and time constraints are usually characterized by a very strong inverted, U-shaped relationship.

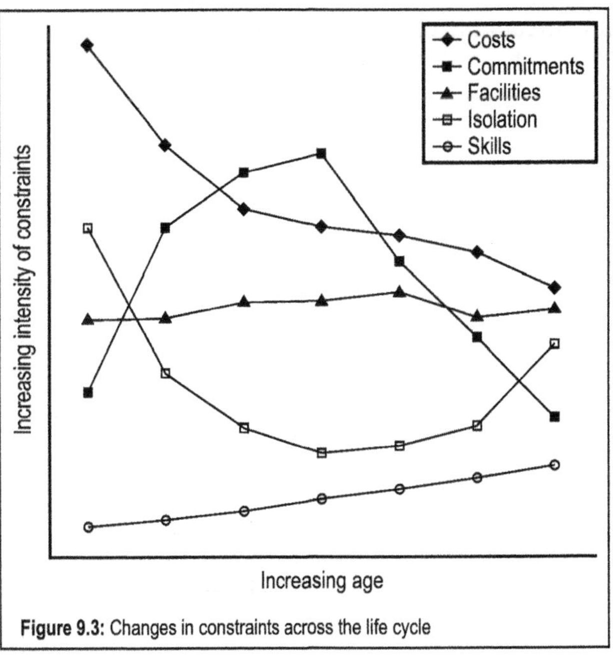

Figure 9.3: Changes in constraints across the life cycle

A similar picture emerges when variations in the reporting of constraints are analyzed by income. As one might expect, the costs of participation decline with increasing income. However, time commitments increase, a trend that can be interpreted to suggest not only that increasing income is achieved at the cost of giving up free time, but also that individuals make conscious choices about trade-offs between free time and disposable income.

Allowing for the limitations of drawing developmental-like inferences about individuals from cross-sectional aggregate data, what appears to emerge from the kinds of findings displayed in Figure 9.3 is that not only is there change in the individual constraints and combinations of constraints that people experience as they move through the life-cycle or through income categories, but also a process of exchange—of one combination of constraints for another.

Source: Based on Jackson, 2000

Look at the graph in Figure 9.3. Does the ranking of constraints for young people (costs, social and geographical isolation, facilities, commitments, and skills) reflect the constraints you experience in your own leisure? How do you think the relative importance of your leisure constraints will change as you grow older? Ask a middle-aged person and an elderly person to comment on the constraints they experience in relation to the graph. Do you think the patterns of constraints shown by the lines in the graph would be different for females and males?

and the desire to participate in leisure in general or in a specific activity as the main aspects of leisure against which to investigate the operation of constraints (e.g., Jackson 1990a; Jackson & Dunn 1991; Jackson & Searle 1983; Searle & Jackson 1985). Since then, a variety of other aspects of leisure have been used against which to measure the impact of constraints. These include the inability to maintain participation at or increase it to desired levels, ceasing participation in former activities, the non-use of public leisure services, and insufficient enjoyment of current activities.

Some researchers have questioned whether the arrays of constraints associated with these different aspects of leisure are similar or different. Do work commitments, for example, impact people's desire to participate in leisure activities with the same intensity as people's desire to continue participating? Research has shown that, while there is a common core of constraints that tends to emerge regardless of the aspects of leisure chosen to be studied, the relative strength and importance of items and dimensions vary sufficiently among aspects of leisure to warrant caution in assuming that, say, barriers to participation in leisure in general or in a specific activity are the same as the reasons why people cease participating or are unable to devote more time to leisure.

This finding implies that academic researchers must be very careful when designing research. Preferably, they should select two or more aspects of leisure for inclusion in a single study of leisure constraints. Practitioners, too, need to clearly articulate which problematic aspects of leisure they wish to tackle when modifying the delivery of services to alleviate constraints. For example, there would be little point in building a new facility on the assumption that supply is not meeting demand, when the real problem is the fee structure or substandard existing facilities.

The Hierarchical Model and the Negotiation of Constraints

There has been less research on the other types of constraints besides the structural category, although there have been exceptions (e.g., Gilbert & Hudson, 2000; Hawkins, Peng, Hsieh, & Eklund, 1999). The empirical evidence to date supports the validity of distinguishing among intrapersonal, interpersonal, and structural constraints, and that these are arranged in a sequential hierarchy (see, for example, Raymore, Godbey, & Crawford, 1994; and Raymore, Godbey, Crawford, & von Eye, 1993). Research has also shown that people adopt strategies to negotiate through the various levels to fulfill their leisure. For example Scott (1991), in his study of participants in contract bridge, identified three main options: acquisition of information about limited opportunities for play; altered scheduling of games to adjust to reduced group membership and individuals' time commitments; and skill development to permit participation in advanced play. Strategies to adjust to time and financial constraints on leisure in general, identified by Kay and Jackson (1991), included reducing (but not entirely foregoing) participation, saving money to participate, trying to find the cheapest opportunity, making other (non-leisure-related) economies, reducing the amount of time spent on household tasks, and reducing work time. Similarly, Samdahl and Jekubovich (1997a) described how people change work schedules, alter their routines, and select activities that can meet their leisure goals. At a more general level, Jackson and Rucks (1995) distinguished between cognitive and behavioural strategies, the latter being subdivided into modifications of leisure and of non-leisure, and further categorized into modifying the use of time, acquiring skills, changing interpersonal relations, improving finances, physical therapy, and changing leisure aspirations.

The Contributions of Qualitative Research

Although some social scientists would argue that it is anachronistic to separate research conducted using quantitative and qualitative methods, the unique contributions of the latter to leisure constraints research are worthy of a brief but distinct discussion. In sharp contrast to the predominantly quantitative, usually survey-based research of the 1980s, there is now a growing body of qualitative constraints research. Its proponents and practitioners have made many contributions, but three are particularly noteworthy.

Firstly, qualitative researchers have greatly extended the identification of the range of constraints that affect people's leisure and, indeed, their lives as a whole. It is no coincidence that this strand in leisure constraints research has been contributed mainly if not exclusively by female researchers, usually working within a feminist framework (see Henderson, 1991; Henderson, Bialeschki, Shaw, & Freysinger, 1996; Shaw, 1994), and no doubt influenced by counterpart work from the UK, such as Deem (1986) and

Wimbush and Talbot (1988). Thus, much of the work on constraints from a qualitative perspective was initially aimed at uncovering constraints that were thought to be particularly pertinent to women, but which had been overlooked in previous quantitative research based on constraints items and scales stemming from the assumptions of predominantly male researchers. Consequently, a substantial number of research articles appeared beginning in the early 1990s, contributed by researchers such as Susan Shaw, Karla Henderson, and Deborah Bialeschki, and their associates and students. Their research examined constraints such as ethic of care (Henderson & Allen, 1991), lack of a sense of entitlement to leisure (Henderson & Bialeschki, 1991), fear (Whyte & Shaw, 1994), and body image (Frederick & Shaw, 1995), or focused on particular aspects or circumstances of women's lives, such as immigration, language difficulties and isolation (Rublee & Shaw, 1991), ethnicity and adolescence (Tirone & Shaw, 1997), maturation of children (Bialeschki & Michener, 1994), menopause (Parry & Shaw, 1999), and the death of a spouse (Patterson & Carpenter, 1994), to name just a few examples. It is worth noting, however, that based on this new knowledge, there is an emerging recognition that much of what has been learned about women, leisure, and constraints may apply equally well to men. Thus, we are now witnessing the appearance of pieces such as Shaw and Henderson's (2003) conference paper entitled *Leisure research about gender and men: The weakest link?* In addition, a recent chapter by these authors adopts a gender-based perspective that encompasses both women and men (Shaw & Henderson, 2005).

A second important contribution from qualitative researchers has been to challenge the conventional wisdom derived from the conclusions and inferences from quantitative survey research. This has occurred on several levels:

1. questioning the validity of the supposed hierarchical sequence in the experience of constraints proposed by Crawford et al. (1991), both from an empirical perspective (e.g., Gilbert & Hudson, 2000; Ravenscroft, 2004) and a theoretical perspective (Henderson & Bialeschki, 1993);
2. a somewhat broader critique of terminology and its hidden implications (e.g., Samdahl, Hutchinson, & Jacobson, 1999, on "navigation" versus "negotiation"); and
3. outright skepticism about the value of approaching leisure from a constraints-based perspective (Samdahl, 2005; Samdahl & Jekubovich, 1997a).

One need not agree with these challenges, especially the last, to acknowledge their value in generating debate and prompting other researchers to clarify and sharpen their concepts.

The third contribution from qualitative research has been to provide a much clearer sense of context at both the micro scale (individual people's lives) and the macro scale (society) for understanding the experience and effects of constraints. Quantitative surveys provide cross-sectional, instantaneous data that are equivalent to a narrowly framed, slightly out-of-focus, black-and-white snapshot of a tiny slice of people's lives. Constraints surveys tell us very little if anything about the rest of people's lives, except indirectly and at an aggregate level by using statistical methods to correlate constraints with various socioeconomic and demographic variables. In short, much constraints research is bereft of context, whether this is at the personal, familial, or societal levels. It is almost as if we have said to our survey respondents, "Tell us about your leisure and constraints, but don't tell us about anything else that is important in your life." There is also no question that we have not achieved much understanding of the leisure of people whose very lives may consist almost entirely of constraint: the poor, many unemployed people, single parents, the elderly, some members of some minority groups, and so on. If such people have been included in our surveys (and one wonders here about response rates and how far we can generalize from, say, 40% questionnaire return rates if the other 60% may, because of personal circumstances, be precisely those who are most constrained), we have typically asked them what, for them, must be viewed as superficial and trivial questions that are met with puzzlement if not outright derision or anger.

Qualitative research has done much to redress these problems, weaving a far richer tapestry of how constraints fit into the context of people's lives, and of how these in turn are shaped and affected by the broader social, political, economic, and environmental milieu within which we live. Although it typically begins with the individual—as does most quantitative research—the qualitative orientation is far better placed to examine the antecedents and context of constraints. Moreover, this overall trend does much toward helping to "close the gap" between the predominantly social-psychological orientation of most North American leisure research and the more sociological approach typically adopted in Britain and western Europe, as presented by Coalter (1997, 1999; see also Beckers, 1995; Mommaas, 1997; Ravenscroft, Church, & Gilchrist, 2005; and Shaw, 1997). As a result, North American leisure constraints research—and indirectly leisure studies—is far better placed to incorporate, adapt, and be enriched by alternative perspectives, approaches, concepts and theory from outside the continent, and thus to alleviate the detrimental intellectual and geographical isolation that has recently been decried in the literature (Jackson, 2004; Samdahl & Kelly, 1999; Valentine, Allison, & Schneider, 1999).

Suppose you choose recreation management as a career after you graduate. How would knowledge about people's leisure constraints help you to serve your clientele better? If you had to commission a study of your clientele's preferences and constraints, would you choose a quantitative method or a qualitative method? What are the advantages and disadvantages of each method?

Conclusions: The State of Research on Constraints to Leisure

It is impossible to do justice to the breadth, depth, and complexity of research on constraints to leisure in a short chapter such as this. If you want to understand the field in more detail, then the best source to consult is a recent book, *Constraints to Leisure* (Jackson, 2005), which consists of 22 chapters written by some 40 leading researchers and grouped into four main sections. The first is "Impacts and Experiences of Constraints Among Diverse Populations." These chapters summarize what we know about the populations who are often thought to be the most affected by constraints to their leisure. The second section, "New Approaches to the Study of Constraints," begins with theory and concludes with method, while in between there is consideration of broad issues of culture, time, outdoor recreation, disciplinary foundations and interdisciplinary connections, new concepts (affordance) and an integrating framework (benefits and constraints). Section three, "Constraints Research and Practice," is comprised of three chapters that focus largely on applications, and the book concludes with a section entitled "Critique," which consists of two chapters that in a sense "stand back" from everything that has preceded them. There has been an increasing recognition in recent years that there is a "North American paradigm" in leisure research on this side of the Atlantic; this is equally true of leisure constraints research as it is of the broader field of which it is a part. Thus, the first of the two chapters in the "Critique" section reminds us that there are other approaches. Finally, to forestall the idea that there is universal agreement about the value and contributions of leisure constraints research, the last chapter adopts an intentionally critical posture toward the field.

To conclude, considerable progress has been made in the understanding of constraints to leisure over the last two or three decades. Very little empirical research devoid of a theoretical basis is now being conducted, and the empirical and theoretical "branches" are not as isolated from each other as they used to be. Indeed, the most recent developments in leisure constraints research reflect an intimate intertwining of theoretical thinking and empirical analysis, with the field moving ahead as new findings stimulate new interpretations, which in turn power the next stages of empirical research (see, for example, the studies reported by Hubbard & Mannell, 2001, and Mannell & Loucks-Atkinson, 2005).

Leisure constraints research is now well-established as a recognizable and distinct subfield within leisure studies, and thinking about constraints has also been assimilated into leisure research that is not overtly directed towards the specific goal of understanding leisure constraints. These developments provide significant and exciting opportunities for future research and practice.

One approach to leisure in North American leisure studies has been to define it as "perceived freedom." However, if virtually all people are constrained to some extent in their leisure, doesn't this call into question the value of the "perceived freedom" concept? To put it another way, is there a conflict between concepts of freedom and constraint in leisure and, if so, how can they be reconciled?

Key Terms

Barriers
Leisure constraints
Leisure models
Leisure non-participation
Negotiation of constraints

References

Beckers, T. (1995). Back to basics: International communication in leisure research. *Leisure Sciences, 17*, 327–336.

Bialeschki, M. D., & Michener, S. (1994). Re-entering leisure: Transition within the role of motherhood. *Journal of Leisure Research, 26*, 57–74.

Boothby, J., Tungatt, M. F., & Townsend, A. R. (1981). Ceasing participation in sports activity: Reported reasons and their implications. *Journal of Leisure Research, 13*, 1–14.

Coalter, F. (1997). Leisure sciences and leisure studies: Different concept, same crisis? *Leisure Sciences, 19*, 255–268.

Coalter, F. (1999). Leisure sciences and leisure studies: The challenge of meaning. In E. L. Jackson & T. L.

Burton (Eds.), *Leisure studies: Prospects for the twenty-first century* (pp. 507–519). State College, PA: Venture Publishing, Inc.

Crawford, D. W., & Godbey, G. (1987). Reconceptualizing barriers to family leisure. *Leisure Sciences, 9*, 119–127.

Crawford, D. W., Jackson, E. L., & Godbey, G. (1991). A hierarchical model of leisure constraints. *Leisure Sciences, 13*, 309–320.

Deem, R. (1986). *All work and no play? The sociology of women and leisure*. Milton Keynes, UK: Open University Press.

Francken, D. A., & Van Raiij, M. F. (1981). Satisfaction with leisure time activities. *Journal of Leisure Research, 13*, 337–352.

Frederick, C. J., & Shaw, S. M. (1995). Body image as a leisure constraint: Examining the experience of aerobic exercise classes for young adults. *Leisure Sciences, 17*, 57–89.

Gilbert, D., & Hudson, S. (2000). Tourism demand constraints: A skiing participation. *Annals of Tourism Research, 27*, 906–925.

Hawkins, B. A., & Freeman, P. (1993). *Factor analysis of leisure constraints for aging adults with mental retardation*. Paper presented at the NRPA Symposium on Leisure Research, San Jose, CA.

Hawkins, B. A., Peng, J., Hsieh, C.-M., & Eklund, S. J. (1999). Leisure constraints: A replication and extension of construct development. *Leisure Sciences, 21*, 179–192.

Henderson, K. A. (1991). The contribution of feminism to an understanding of leisure constraints. *Journal of Leisure Research, 23*, 363–377.

Henderson, K. A. (1997). A critique of constraints theory: A response. *Journal of Leisure Research, 29*, 453–457.

Henderson, K. A., & Allen, K. (1991). The ethic of care: Leisure possibilities and constraints for women. *Loisir et Société/Society and Leisure, 14*(1), 97–113.

Henderson, K. A., & Bialeschki, M. D. (1991). A sense of entitlement to leisure as constraint and empowerment for women. *Leisure Sciences, 13*, 51–65.

Henderson, K. A., & Bialeschki, M. D. (1993). Exploring an expanded model of women's leisure constraints. *Journal of Applied Recreation Research, 18*, 229–252.

Henderson, K. A., Bialeschki, M. D., Shaw, S. M., & Freysinger, V. J. (1996). *Both gains and gaps*. State College, PA: Venture Publishing, Inc.

Henderson, K. A., Stalnaker, D., & Taylor, G. (1988). The relationship between barriers to recreation and gender-role personality traits for women. *Journal of Leisure Research, 20*, 69–80.

Hubbard, J., & Mannell, R. (2001). Testing competing models of the leisure constraint negotiation process in a corporate employee recreation setting. *Leisure Sciences, 23*, 145–163.

Hultsman, W. Z. (1995). Recognizing patterns of leisure constraints: An extension of the exploration of dimensionality. *Journal of Leisure Research, 27*, 228–244.

Jackson, E. L. (1983). Activity specific barriers to recreation participation. *Leisure Sciences, 6*, 47–60.

Jackson, E. L. (1988). Leisure constraints: A survey of past research. *Leisure Sciences, 10*, 203–215.

Jackson, E. L. (1990a). Variations in the desire to begin a leisure activity: Evidence of antecedent constraints? *Journal of Leisure Research, 22*, 55–70.

Jackson, E. L. (1990b). Trends in leisure preferences: Alternative constraints-related explanations. *Journal of Applied Recreation Research, 15*(3), 129–145.

Jackson, E. L. (1993). Recognizing patterns of leisure constraints: Results from alternative analyses. *Journal of Leisure Research, 25*, 129–149.

Jackson, E. L. (1997). In the eye of the beholder: A comment on Samdahl & Jekubovich (1997), "A critique of leisure constraints: Comparative analyses and understandings." *Journal of Leisure Research, 29*, 458–468.

Jackson, E. L. (2000). Will research on leisure constraints still be relevant in the twenty-first century? *Journal of Leisure Research, 32*, 62–68.

Jackson, E. L. (2004). Individual and institutional concentration of leisure research in North America. *Leisure Sciences, 26*, 323–348.

Jackson, E. L. (2005). (Ed.). *Constraints to leisure*. State College, PA: Venture Publishing, Inc.

Jackson, E. L., Crawford, D. W., & Godbey, G. (1993). Negotiation of leisure constraints. *Leisure Sciences, 15*, 1–11.

Jackson, E. L., & Dunn, E. (1991). Is constrained leisure an internally homogeneous concept? *Leisure Sciences, 13*, 167–184.

Jackson, E. L., & Rucks, V. C. (1993). Reasons for ceasing participation and barriers to participation: Further examination of constrained leisure as an internally homogeneous concept. *Leisure Sciences, 15*, 217–230.

Jackson, E. L., & Rucks, V. C. (1995). Negotiation of leisure constraints by junior-high and high-school students: An exploratory study. *Journal of Leisure Research, 27*, 85–105.

Jackson, E. L., & Scott, D. (1999). Constraints to leisure. In E. Jackson & T. Burton (Eds.), *Leisure studies: Prospects for the twenty-first century* (pp. 299–321). State College, PA: Venture Publishing, Inc.

Jackson, E. L., & Searle, M. S. (1983). Recreation non-participation: Variables related to the desire for new recreational activities. *Recreation Research Review, 10*(2), 5–12.

Kay, T., & Jackson, G. (1991). Leisure despite constraint: The impact of leisure constraints on leisure participation. *Journal of Leisure Research, 23*, 301–313.

Mannell, R. C., & Loucks-Atkinson, A. (2005). Why don't people do what's "good" for them? Cross-fertilization among the psychologies of non-participation in leisure, health, and exercise behaviors. In E. L. Jackson (Ed.), *Constraints to leisure* (pp. 221–232). State College, PA: Venture Publishing, Inc.

McGuire, F. A. (1984). A factor analytic study of leisure constraints in advanced adulthood. *Leisure Sciences, 6*, 313–326.

Mommaas, H. (1997). European leisure studies at the crossroads? A history of leisure research in Europe. *Leisure Sciences, 19*, 241–255.

Norman, W. (1995). *Perceived constraints: A new approach to segmenting the vacation travel market.* Paper presented at the NRPA Symposium on Leisure Research, San Antonio, TX.

Parry, D. C., & Shaw, S. M. (1999). The role of leisure in women's experiences of menopause and mid-life. *Leisure Sciences, 21*, 197–212.

Patterson, I., & Carpenter, G. (1994). Participation in leisure activities after the death of a spouse. *Leisure Sciences, 16*, 105–117.

Ravenscroft, N. (2004). Tales from the tracks: Discourses of constraint in the use of mixed cycle and walking routes. *International Review for the Sociology of Sport, 39*(1), 27–44.

Ravenscroft, N., Church, A., & Gilchrist, P. (2005). The ontology of exclusion: A European perspective on leisure constraints research. In E. L. Jackson (Ed.), *Constraints to leisure* (pp. 321–335). State College, PA: Venture Publishing, Inc.

Raymore, L. A., Godbey, G. C., & Crawford, D. W. (1994). Self-esteem, gender, and socioeconomic status: Their relation to perceptions of constraint on leisure among adolescents. *Journal of Leisure Research 26*, 99–118.

Raymore, L. A., Godbey, G. C., Crawford, D. W., & von Eye, A. (1993). Nature and process of leisure constraints: An empirical test. *Leisure Sciences, 15*, 99–113.

Romsa, G., & Hoffman, W. (1980). An application of non-participation data in recreation research: Testing the opportunity theory. *Journal of Leisure Research, 12*, 321–328.

Rublee, C. B., & Shaw, S. M. (1991). Constraints on the leisure and community participation of immigrant women: Implications for social integration. *Loisir et Société/Society and Leisure, 14*(1), 133–150.

Samdahl, D. M., (2005). Making room for "silly" debate: Reflections on leisure constraints research. In E. L. Jackson (Ed.), *Constraints to leisure* (pp. 337–349). State College, PA: Venture Publishing, Inc.

Samdahl, D. M., Hutchinson, S. L., & Jacobson, S. (1999). *Navigating constraints? A critical commentary on negotiation in leisure studies.* Paper presented at the Ninth Canadian Congress on Leisure Research, Acadia University, Wolfville, NS.

Samdahl, D., & Jekubovich, N. (1997a). A critique of leisure constraints: Comparative analyses and understandings. *Journal of Leisure Research, 29*, 430–452.

Samdahl, D., & Jekubovich, N. (1997b). A rejoinder to Henderson's and Jackson's commentaries on "A critique of leisure constraints," *Journal of Leisure Research, 29*, 469–471.

Samdahl, D. M., & Kelly, J. J. (1999). Speaking only to ourselves? Citation analysis of Journal of Leisure Research and Leisure Sciences. *Journal of Leisure Research, 31*, 171–180.

Scott, D. (1991). The problematic nature of participation in contract bridge: A qualitative study of group-related constraints. *Leisure Sciences, 13*, 321–336.

Searle, M. S., & Brayley, R. E. (1992). *Is constrained leisure an internally homogeneous concept? A further examination.* Paper presented at the NRPA Symposium on Leisure Research, Cincinnati, OH.

Searle, M. S., & Jackson, E. L. (1985). Socioeconomic variations in perceived barriers to recreation participation among would-be participants. *Leisure Sciences, 7*, 227–249.

Shaw, S. M. (1994). Gender, leisure, and constraint: Towards a framework for the analysis of women's leisure. *Journal of Leisure Research, 26*, 8–22.

Shaw, S. M. (1997). Cultural determination, diversity, and coalition in leisure research: A commentary on Coalter and Mommaas. *Leisure Sciences, 19*, 277–279.

Shaw, S. M., Bonen, A., & McCabe, J. F. (1991). Do more constraints mean less leisure? Examining the relationship between constraints and participation. *Journal of Leisure Research, 23*, 286–300.

Shaw, S. M., & Henderson, K. A. (2003). *Leisure research about gender and men: The weaker link?* Paper presented at the NRPA Symposium on Leisure Research, St. Louis, MO.

Shaw, S. M., & Henderson, K. (2005). Gender analysis and leisure constraints: An uneasy alliance. In E. L. Jackson (Ed.), *Constraints to leisure* (pp. 23–34). State College, PA: Venture Publishing, Inc.

Stockdale, J. E. (1989). Concepts and measures of leisure participation and preference. In E. L. Jackson & T. L. Burton (Eds.), *Understanding leisure and recreation: Mapping the past, charting the future* (pp. 113–150). State College, PA: Venture Publishing, Inc.

Tirone, S. C., & Shaw, S. M. (1997). At the center of their lives: Indo Canadian women, their families and leisure. *Journal of Leisure Research, 29*, 225–244.

Valentine, K., Allison, M. T., & Schneider, I. (1999). The one-way mirror of leisure research: A need for cross-national social scientific perspectives. *Leisure Sciences, 21*, 241–246.

Whyte, L. B., & Shaw, S. M. (1994). Women's leisure: An exploratory study of fear of violence as a leisure constraint. *Journal of Applied Recreation Research, 19*, 5–21.

Wimbush, E. , & Talbot, M. (1988). *Relative freedoms: Women and leisure*. Milton Keynes, UK: Open University Press.

Witt, P. A., & Goodale, T. L. (1981). The relationship between barriers to leisure enjoyment and family stages. *Leisure Sciences, 4*, 29–49.

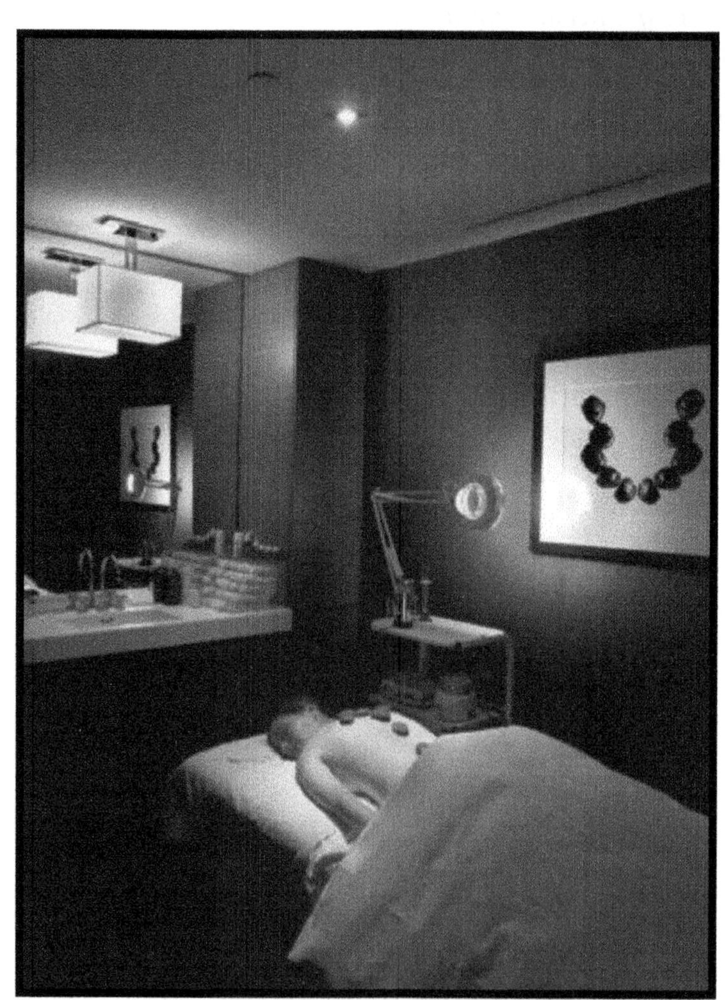

Chapter 10
Stressful Living and Leisure as a Meaningful Stress-Coping Pursuit

Yoshitaka Iwasaki, Ph.D.
University of Alberta

Learning Objectives

After reading this chapter, students will be able to

1. Understand the prevalence, significance, and nature of stress in people's lives in our diverse society.
2. Understand the role and mechanisms of leisure in dealing with stress.
3. Recognize the contribution of leisure as a stress-coping device to our health and life quality.

Introduction and Overview

Have you ever felt stress in your life? When observing people around you, including family and friends, does it appear that stress is prevalent in many Canadians' lives? In contemporary society, many people seem pressed for time (Cushman, Veal, & Zuzanek, 2005), and "I am busy," is a common expression often heard in everyday conversations. Besides time pressure, many have multiple demands in various life domains (Jackson, 2005). For example, many college or university students are often obliged to "juggle" multiple tasks, such as part-time (or even full-time) jobs, family responsibilities, commitments to partners and friends, and community involvements, in addition to being a student. Also, considering the structure of our society, "power imbalance" could be a source of stress for some individuals (Raphael, 2004). For example, discrimination based on one's background and uniqueness could generate stress, particularly among non-dominant and often marginalized individuals. Women in general tend to experience more gender-based discrimination than do men (i.e., sexism), while ethnic minorities often encounter racism. The other forms of discrimination due to power imbalance in society include ageism, classism, ableism, and homophobia/heterosexism (Garnets, 2002). These "isms" are often experienced as a major source of stress in our diverse society (Iwasaki, Bartlett, MacKay, Mactavish, & Ristock, 2005). Thus, the nature of stress is very complex and encompasses individual, social, and structural aspects. Given the complex and broad nature of stress, research has shown that many people, including Canadians, often feel stress (Shields, 2003).

In this chapter, several key aspects and issues about stress will be examined, as will, more importantly, the role of leisure in dealing with stress in our lives. As noted in the previous chapters, not only does leisure have various meanings (e.g., personal, social, spiritual, cultural) for different people under different contexts, but the roles of leisure in people's lives are also very diverse. Of the various roles, many people value leisure as a way to cope with stress. To understand leisure's function as a stress-reliever or a stress-coping activity, it is important to first recognize the nature of stress, or more specifically, to understand what stress is, what makes us feel stress, and how stress impacts our lives. Researchers have begun to identify key mechanisms by which leisure can facilitate dealing with stress, and the contribution of leisure to managing stress appears to be a major benefit of leisure for many people (Iwasaki & Schneider, 2003). In the last section of this chapter, critical issues and questions about these topics will be explored, by emphasizing how this knowledge can be applied to personal and practical situations.

Importance and Relevance of Stress-Related Concepts to Our Lives

Stress is prevalent and has a significant presence in many people's lives, and as a result, studies of stress and its influences on people and society have been a "hot" area of academic research (Moos, Holahan, & Beutler, 2003). The notions of stress and coping (including leisure as an important stress-coping pursuit), however, are not simply academic concepts. Stress is experienced first-hand by many people on a daily basis; and because of the centrality of stress in our lives, many are very concerned with how to deal with or "buffer" stress. The use of stress-coping strategies appears essential not only to "surviving" but also to one's "thriving" (Caldwell, 2005). Research has begun to show that many people are knowledgeable, creative, and resilient in coping effectively with stress (Iwasaki, Bartlett, et al., 2005; Klitzing, 2004). This is good news because we also know that by successfully overcoming stressful encounters (e.g., loss of a loved one or health problems) with coping strategies including leisure, people can gain important personal, social, cultural, or spiritual insights into their own lives (Hutchinson, 2004; Iwasaki, MacKay, Mactavish, Ristock, & Bartlett, 2006). Gaining or finding valued meanings through leisure can also lead to other positive outcomes, such as enhanced quality of life and human development as a result of stress-coping endeavours (Kleiber, Hutchinson, & Williams, 2002). For the purposes of this chapter it is important to highlight the significance of stress and coping through meaningful leisure pursuits in people's everyday lives. It is equally important to note the importance of policy-making and service-provision to the coping process. As more is learned about stress and coping, policies and services that aid in the coping process can begin to be created. For example, managing stress through leisure can be an important therapeutic device, which can in turn be integrated into leisure education or counselling programs (Caldwell, 2005). Such insights are helpful to both the leisure participant and the provider.

What Is Known about Stress, Coping, and Leisure

What is stress? What makes us feel stressed? What impacts does stress have on our lives? These are the key questions addressed in the first part of this section. In the second part of this section, primary questions include: (a) How do people use leisure as a way of dealing with stress? and (b) What are the main mechanisms by which leisure can facilitate coping with stress in our lives?

What Is Stress? What Makes Us Feel Stress?

We often feel stress when we realize the demands that we are facing are overwhelming or challenging. This typically involves a person's appraisal of a demand (e.g., test, assignment with a deadline) that is presented by her or his situation or environment (e.g., school). Consistent with this idea, Lazarus and Folkman (1984) defined stress as "a particular relationship between the person and the environment that is appraised by the person as taxing or exceeding his or her resources and engendering his or her well-being" (p. 19). Based on our own appraisal of a demand or challenge in our lives, we often seek to find out whether we have sufficient resources to deal with it effectively. These resources can be our personal competence and strategies (e.g., planning ahead, acting appropriately), support from others (e.g., family, friends, teachers), and anything that helps to manage the demand or challenge. Given the complex nature of our society, we often face a multitude of demands, challenges, or difficulties in our lives. For example, each of us plays multiple roles in life, such as being a student, employee, family member, parent, community member, and/or spouse/partner. Also, we sometimes encounter negative life events such as health problems, injuries, relationship problems, work-related problems, financial difficulties, and the loss of a loved one. These roles and events may be overwhelming and make us feel stressed.

It is important, however, to recognize that some sources of stress are chronic in nature and can have a prolonged effect on one's well-being. For example, discrimination based on an individual's gender, race/ethnicity, class, age, disability, and/or sexual orientation tends to have a substantial impact on individuals throughout their lives (Garnets, 2002). Discrimination is experienced at various levels including personal, social, political, and historical. Racism, for instance, against Aboriginal peoples and some ethnic minorities has operated institutionally and politically many years, and has operated institutionally and politically (e.g., through government policy), creating a power imbalance in our societal system. Despite recent efforts to correct it, this power imbalance still prevails and has a significant impact on personal experiences, social relationships, and everyday lives of those who are affected by racism (Raphael, 2004). Considerable stress may be experienced as a result of such experiences.

Many of us have multiple identities (related to gender, race, class, etc.), which could be another major source of stress. To illustrate this point, consider the multiple identities and life circumstances of the following three groups of women: (a) Aboriginal women with diabetes, (b) older women with a disability living in poverty, and (c) racial minority lesbians. These three groups of women demonstrate unique combinations of identities that reflect different experiences of social power. The first group of women identify themselves as being Aboriginal, being women, and having diabetes, while the second group has a different combination of identities—being women, elderly, living with a disability, and in a low socioeconomic class. The third group has a unique combination of multiple identities including being female, of a racial minority, and lesbian. Stress as experienced by these three groups of women, appears complex and different perhaps as a function of their unique combinations of identities. Some researchers have attempted to describe these unique experiences as "multiple jeopardy" (Bowleg, Huang, Brooks, Black, & Burkholder, 2003). Thus, to understand the nature of stress, it is necessary to recognize the diversity within our society.

There is also extensive evidence that stress can have a negative impact on our health, life quality, and daily living (Lazarus, 1999). For example, it has been shown that many of the leading causes of death in our society are, either directly or indirectly, stress-related. These causes include coronary heart disease, cancer, lung illness, accidental injuries, and suicide (Sachs, 1991). More recently, a Canadian-based study has concluded that stress is one of the key social determinants of health (Raphael, 2004); although it is important to recognize that there are some positive aspects of stress such as being a motivator to produce a positive outcome.

How Does Leisure Help Us Deal with Stress?

As shown, a stress-free life is almost impossible for many, so a variety of resources and strategies are often used to deal with stress and maintain good health and well-being. In fact, research evidence has increasingly supported the idea that leisure can make an important contribution to coping with stress (Caldwell, 2005; Iwasaki & Schneider, 2003).

Let's examine some of the key mechanisms by which leisure can help people cope with stress. First, leisure can be used as a means of taking a break or having a time-out from stressful, everyday life. Having a coffee break, a lunch break, or a weekend getaway are some examples of this function. People often feel refreshed or rejuvenated as a result of a leisure-time break or time-out (e.g., a quick workout, a winter get-away for Canadians). Second, leisure can provide an opportunity for balance in life. Taking a leisurely walk in an urban park, appreciating the outdoors, spending quality time with family or friends, and doing other leisure activities (e.g., physical activity, volunteering, creating or appreciating art) can all play an important role in maintaining balance in life. Thus, leisure is considered an important element of balanced lifestyles for many individuals.

Leisure also helps us cope with stress by helping create valued meanings in life. In this context, meanings refer to psychological, spiritual, social, and/or cultural signification and expressions that are important and essential for one's life (Baumeister and Vohs, 2002). Such meanings are critical to our individual and collective well-being. As Frankl (1985) suggested, for many individuals "searching for meaning is the primary motivation in life" (p. 121). Recent leisure literature has emphasized the significant role of leisure in meaning-making (Juniu & Henderson, 2001). For example, Hutchinson (2004) argued that leisure can create "a range of personal, familial, social, and cultural meanings, including a sense of connection, accomplishment, self/relationship/cultural affirmation, hope, control, etc." (p. 31).

A point worth emphasizing here is that it is leisure's unique characteristics that make it an ideal setting in which to discover personal meaning. As Caldwell (2005) tells us, several, intertwined aspects of leisure generate such meaning. These aspects include "a context for self-determined and autonomous behaviour, competence and social relationships, a time for self-reflection, an opportunity for identity development, and a way to transcend negative life events and engage in a re-birth of spirit" (pp. 18–19). Think of the many ways leisure can help each of us create meaning in our lives. Social leisure (e.g., family picnic) can provide an opportunity to develop social meaning (e.g., family cohesiveness), while cultural leisure-like activities (e.g., Aboriginal dancing and music) can facilitate cultural and spiritual meanings (in this case, for Aboriginal peoples) by helping them affirm their cultural identity. Meaning may emerge from any variety of leisure activities. One of the most popular is that of volunteering. By volunteering, participants can create a sense of altruism (by helping others in a community event, for example), enhance their self-identity or self-esteem, and/or gain a sense of competence and accomplishment.

Leisure can even help us understand and appreciate our place in the universe. For example, from a unique cultural perspective, Gong (1998) suggested that facilitating tranquillity and peace of mind is an essential element of leisure for many Chinese people (e.g., through hiking in the mountains, visiting a temple, or drinking tea or wine). The respite offered by such leisure activities served to help participants in understanding the meaning of life.

As implied in Caldwell's point, engaging in leisure to cope with stressors in life can also provide the potential for human development and positive transformation. This growth-oriented benefit of stress-coping through leisure highlights the strengths and resilience of people. Despite stressful and sometimes traumatic experiences in life, many people are able to overcome the difficulties and challenges they encounter in life. Research has shown that leisure can be an important source of affirming and demonstrating human strengths (Kleiber et al., 2002). For example, dealing with a traumatic injury through leisure may provide an opportunity to discover new potential about oneself. Coping with loss of a loved one through leisure may enable one to develop a new, exciting social connection with others. Also, engaging in leisure to deal with a disappointment in life may facilitate personal reflection about oneself and one's life. All of these functions of leisure can then lead to the discovery of new self and hope for life, which is tied closely to positive transformation and human growth throughout the life-span (Hutchinson & Kleiber, 2005). In a context of life-long learning, Spector and Cohen-Gewerc (2001) argued that leisure is a "journey" of discovering one's uniqueness to grow and experience a meaningful and enriched life because "in leisure, one can be oneself" (p. 53).

Illustrating the relevance of the above ideas about leisure as a means of coping with stress, the first *i*-box (p. 94) presents some selected direct quotes/comments from Canadians, reported in a recent study conducted in Winnipeg, Manitoba (Iwasaki et al., 2006). The second *i*-box (p. 94) highlights findings of selected recent studies to show culturally unique aspects of leisure for dealing with challenges in life or promoting life quality in global, international contexts.

Findings from a Recent Study Conducted in Winnipeg, Manitoba (Iwasaki et al., 2006)

The investigators found that culture (based on ethnicity) and subculture (based on disability or sexual orientation) play a key role in describing lived experiences of stress and coping, particularly in the contribution of leisure-like activities in coping with stress. The following quotes from their study participants (with pseudonyms) illustrate several examples of the stress-coping mechanisms through leisure covered in this chapter:

> Belonging to groups, just for get-togethers. They're all my culture, they're all Native. Even just going sitting there, listening to them talk. I always come home with such a light feeling because they share so many wonderful stories with me. It's nice to be with them, and it makes me feel happy. (Karen, First Nations woman with a disability)
>
> A lot of my work is generally in front of computer, I'm always sitting. So the gym is a big part. It's physical and my body is moving and it's my form of exercise and it's healthy for me. Yeah, it's a balance. (Madison, lesbian)
>
> The mind and body work together... I think dance is really important to relieve stress. You try to jig for a couple of hours. It takes away stress. (Susan, Métis woman)
>
> I started exercising just two years ago. I did it as a response to save my sanity from a whole pile of stress that was on me at the time. I do cycling, some laps, and some weights. I realized that I started to feel a lot better physically. But, perseverance, it changed how I thought about things—it changed my response to really horrible situations and it let me move on. I did get much stronger—the incredible benefits. (Allison, woman with a disability)

International Examples of Leisure and Stress-Coping

Leisure is a global phenomenon (Cushman et al., 2005); therefore, it is important to give attention to the nature of leisure pursuits in international contexts, beyond European and North American contexts. Particularly, research evidence about leisure from developing countries is useful to recognize unique cultural contexts in which leisure takes place and the culturally grounded ways in which leisure can contribute to coping with stress and promoting life quality.

For example, as described by Yau and Packer (2002), tai chi as a form of Chinese martial art provides an opportunity for deep meditation to develop an inner calmness and strength, which can help to deal with challenges in life. Nagla (2005) indicated that despite hardships (e.g., poverty) experienced by many people in developing countries, dining in third-world villages represents a "leisurely collective ritual" (p. 25). In these villages, extended families and sometimes entire villages congregate for celebrations such as religious festivals, weddings, and birthdays, and food is always central on these occasions (Nagla). Salzman and Halloran (2004) and Wearing (1998) showed that in spite of the oppressive colonial systems burdened on Indigenous peoples throughout the world, they are regaining cultural and spiritual recovery and meaning through Indigenous dance and music, arts and crafts, storytelling and literature, traditional rituals, and the use of humour and laughter. Shalhoub-Kevorkian (2003) found that despite the trauma of losing a child, Palestinian women "did not break down" and proactively became "creators of safety nets" and showed strengths in the company of other women, through being involved in such activities as songs, gatherings, praying, poetry, and writing (p. 404). Finally, for young Botswanans who are faced with a multitude of obstacles such as the lack of basic infrastructures for living, Amusa, Wikesa, Adolph, Kalui, Busang, and Thaga (2001) emphasized the importance of leisure education, particularly the use of leisure (e.g., Indigenous games, pastimes, and sports) as a developmental tool, and its contribution to strengthening their cultural identity and life quality.

Critical Issues and Questions: Application to Personal and Practical Situations

The final section of this chapter presents some critical issues and questions, which should be personally relevant to the lives of many readers. This section explores how we can apply the knowledge about stress and coping to our lives. The first issue to be addressed is the stress-coping role of leisure in our health and life quality. The second issue deals with the use of leisure as a therapeutic device.

Knowledge about stress and the role of leisure in dealing with stress seems very useful to our daily living. Knowledge of potentially effective coping resources can make us better equipped to manage stress. Although some people may have underestimated the value of leisure as a stress-coping activity, research has shown tremendous potential and power of leisure, particularly, the constructive use of meaningful leisure pursuits, as a life-survival and thriving technique (Iwasaki, Mactavish, & MacKay, 2005; Kleiber, 2004). Such use of leisure for health promotion and life-quality enhancement has also been emphasized. Use the following questions to reflect critically on your own life to

Reflect on your life and respond to the following questions relevant to the content of this chapter:

1. Identify and list things in your life that make you feel stress. Think about various domains of your life including: academic, interpersonal (e.g., family, friends), employment, and community. Have you recently experienced major negative life events such as loss of a loved one, health problems, injuries, financial difficulties, etc.? Have you ever felt discriminated or oppressed because of your personal uniqueness (e.g., gender, race/ethnicity, disability, age, sexual orientation), which could be a source of stress?
2. Considering your leisure preferences, what types of leisure pursuits can make you feel good, happy, or are enjoyable to buffer against stress? Have you ever had some meaningful, rewarding experience from your leisure activity? How about social leisure, cultural leisure, spiritual leisure, leisure travel, nature-based recreation, or volunteering as a leisure activity, besides physically active leisure?
3. Based on the things you have learned from reading this chapter, how would you use your leisure in a different way to cope better with stress? Have you ever thought about the potential contribution of leisure to meaning-making, transcending negative life difficulties, or human development/growth?

identify a personally meaningful leisure activity (e.g., running, social leisure, arts, cultural leisure) to deal effectively with stressors in various settings such as school, interpersonal (e.g., family, friends), employment, and community settings.

Another important area of application involves the contribution of leisure to stress-coping as a therapeutic device from practical perspectives. This application is relevant to a wide range of individuals under stress, regardless of their age, ability, health, or social status. Particularly, engagement in enjoyable and meaningful leisure activities seems to have a "therapeutic" impact on adjusting to, recovering from, and/or transcending life difficulties and challenges in a constructive way (Caldwell, 2005). This idea is very useful to the area of therapeutic recreation, particularly in leisure education and counselling. For example, recreation programs for youth-at-risk or elderly persons can incorporate the use of client-relevant and meaningful leisure activities as a therapeutic stress-coping device. In fact, such use of leisure is appropriate to and useful in an interdisciplinary health care system, given that effective health care requires the adoption of a holistic concept of health. In addition to clinical-based medical services to patients or clients (e.g., elderly care, mental health care, rehabilitation), it is important to provide a more holistic, humanistic, and balanced approach to the services rather than just focusing strictly on "fixing" the problem from a negative perspective. Potentially, the therapeutic, stress-coping function of constructive, enjoyable, and meaningful leisure can be a key element of a humanistic and balanced approach to patient or client care. The value and benefits of leisure are enormous and should not be underestimated in health, social, and community services. Use the last set of reflection questions to think critically about the application of knowledge gained from this chapter in a practical situation. This situation deals with the delivery of a therapeutic recreation program for under-privileged groups of people.

As emphasized in the text, the idea of leisure as a means of coping with stress seems useful and important in practical settings. Assume that you are in the position to develop and deliver a therapeutic recreation program for the following groups of people in your community. To help these people better cope with stress and promote their health and life quality, what kind of program would you implement? What would be the goal and focus of this program (e.g., social context, competence and identity development, mental health such as self-esteem and happiness)? What sort of recreation activities would you provide to achieve the goal of the program?

a. Older people
b. Individuals with disabilities
c. Socioeconomically disadvantaged individuals
d. Youth-at-risk
e. Aboriginal peoples
f. Recent immigrants

Key Terms

Coping
Health
Human development
Leisure
Quality of life
Stress

References

Amusa, L. O., Wekesa, M., Adolph, T. L., Kalui, B., Busang, E., & Thaga, K. (2001). Providing leisure and recreation needs for a developing economy: The case of Botswana. In F. H. Fu & H. Ruskin (Eds.), *Physical fitness and activity in the context of leisure education* (pp. 269–291). Hong Kong, China: Dr. Stephen Hui Research

Centre for Physical Education and Wellness, Hong Kong Baptist University.

Baumeister, R. F., & Vohs, K. D. (2002). The pursuit of meaningfulness. In C. R. Snyder & S. J. Lopez (Eds.), *Handbook of positive psychology* (pp. 608–618). London, UK: Oxford Press.

Bowleg, L., Huang, J., Brooks, K., Black, A., & Burkholder, G. (2003). Triple jeopardy and beyond: Multiple minority stress and resilience among Black lesbians. *Journal of Lesbian Studies, 7*(4), 87–108.

Caldwell, L. L. (2005). Leisure and health: Why is leisure therapeutic? *British Journal of Guidance and Counselling, 33*(1), 7–26.

Cushman, G., Veal, A. J., & Zuzanek, J. (Eds.). (2005). *Free time and leisure participation: International perspectives.* Cambridge, MA: CABI Publishing.

Frankl, V. (1985). Man's search for meaning. New York, NY: Washington Square Press.

Garnets, L. D. (2002). Sexual orientations in perspective. *Cultural Diversity and Ethnic Minority Psychology, 8*(2), 115–129.

Gong, B. (1998). *Chinese leisure.* Shanghai: Shanghai Antique Press.

Hutchinson, S. L. (2004). Negative life events and the creation of meaning in leisure. In F. H. Fu, D. Markus, & T. K. Tong (Eds.), *Negative events in the life cycle: Leisure and recreation as a counteraction* (pp. 22–33). Hong Kong, China: Dr. Stephen Hui Research Centre for Physical Education and Wellness, Hong Kong Baptist University.

Hutchinson, S. L., & Kleiber, D. (2005). Leisure, constraints, and negative events: Paradox and possibilities. In E. L. Jackson (Ed.), *Constraints to leisure* (pp. 137–152). State College, PA: Venture Publishing, Inc.

Iwasaki, Y., Bartlett, J., MacKay, K., Mactavish, J., & Ristock, J. (2005). Social exclusion and resilience as frameworks of stress and coping among selected non-dominant groups. *International Journal of Mental Health Promotion, 7*(3), 4–17.

Iwasaki, Y., MacKay, K., Mactavish, J., Ristock, J., & Bartlett, J. (2006). Voices from the margins: Stress, active living, and leisure as a contributor to coping with stress. *Leisure Sciences, 28*, 163–180.

Iwasaki, Y., Mactavish, J., & MacKay, K. (2005). Building on strengths and resilience: Leisure as a stress survival strategy. *British Journal of Guidance and Counselling, 33*(1), 81–100.

Iwasaki, Y., & Schneider, I. E. (2003). Leisure, stress, and coping: An evolving area of inquiry. *Special issue of Leisure Sciences on leisure, stress, and coping, 25*, 107–114.

Jackson, E. L. (Ed.). (2005). *Constraints to leisure.* State College, PA: Venture Publishing, Inc.

Juniu, S., & Henderson, K. A. (2001). Problems in researching leisure and women: Global considerations. *World Leisure Journal, 43*(4), 3–10.

Kleiber, D. A. (2004). Reconstructing self and leisure in the wake of negative life events: When acute distress gives way to possibility. In F. H. Fu, D. Markus, & T. K. Tong (Eds.), *Negative events in the life cycle: Leisure and recreation as a counteraction* (pp. 2–21). Hong Kong, China: Dr. Stephen Hui Research Centre for Physical Education and Wellness, Hong Kong Baptist University.

Kleiber, D. A., Hutchinson, S. L., & Williams, R. (2002). Leisure as a resource in transcending negative life events: Self-protection, self-restoration, and personal transformation. *Leisure Sciences, 24*, 219–235.

Klitzing, S. W. (2004). Women living in a homeless shelter: Stress, coping and leisure. *Journal of Leisure Research, 36*, 483–512.

Lazarus, R. S. (1999). *Stress and emotion: A new synthesis.* New York, NY: Springer.

Lazarus, R. S. and Folkman, S. (1984). *Stress, appraisal and coping.* New York, NY: Springer.

Moos, R. H., Holahan, C. L., & Beutler, L. E. (Eds.). (2003). Special issue on coping. *Journal of Clinical Psychology, 59*(12), 1257–1403.

Nagla, M. (2005). Leisure, food, and health: Practices and attitudes of rural and urban people in India. *World Leisure Journal, 47*(1), 24–31.

Raphael, D. (Ed.). (2004). *Social determinants of health: Canadian perspectives.* Toronto, ON: Canadian Scholars Press.

Sachs, B. C. (1991). Coping with stress. *Stress Medicine, 7*, 61–63.

Salzman, M. B., & Halloran, M. J. (2004). Cultural trauma and recovery: Cultural meaning, self-esteem, and the reconstruction of the cultural anxiety buffer. In J. Greenberg, S. L. Koole, & T. Pyszczynski (Eds.), *Handbook of experimental existential psychology* (pp. 231–246). New York, NY: Guilford Press.

Shalhoub-Kevorkian, N. (2003). Liberating voices: The political implications of Palestinian mothers narrating their loss. *Women's Studies International Forum, 26*(5), 391–407.

Shields, M. (2003). Stress, health and the benefit of social support. *Health reports, Catalogue Number 82-003-XPE, Vol. 15*(1). Ottawa, ON: Statistics Canada.

Spector, C., & Cohen-Gewerc, E. (2001). From education to initiation: Leisure as a second chance. *World Leisure Journal, 43*(3), 48–53.

Yau, M. K.-S., & Packer, T. L. (2002). Health and well-being through t'ai chi: Perceptions of older adults in Hong Kong. *Leisure Studies, 21*, 163–178.

Wearing, B. (1998). *Leisure and feminist theory.* London, UK: Sage Publications.

Chapter 11
Leisure and the Changing Workplace

Margo Hilbrecht, Ph.D.
University of Guelph

Learning Objectives

After reading this chapter, students will be able to

1. Consider the relationship between work and leisure.
2. Explore the evolving nature of the Canadian workplace.
3. Develop an understanding of how non-traditional work arrangements may influence leisure opportunities.
4. Reflect upon sociodemographic changes in the workforce with implications for leisure services.
5. Consider the contribution of leisure to work-life integration.

Introduction

This chapter explores the changing Canadian work environment and the relationship of work and leisure. Many people think of leisure as the opposite of work—a time away from employment responsibilities for relaxing and enjoying their favourite activities once other needs and commitments have been met. From this vantage point, weekends, evenings, and holidays are the main blocks of time for leisure. For increasing numbers of Canadians though, workplace trends dictate different daily and weekly patterns. Technological innovations combined with an increasingly globalized economy contribute to a different work environment compared to previous generations. Many employment schedules no longer follow a Monday-to-Friday daytime routine. Alternative arrangements such as telework, flexible hours, shift work, and evening and weekend work hours have become more prevalent. This creates challenges both for employees in accessing leisure and for recreation professionals in providing services and programs. As our society moves from a manufacturing to a knowledge-based economy, it is not uncommon to find business organizations where employees are encouraged to be "unconditional workers" by starting early, leaving late, taking work home, and being constantly accessible through e-mail, mobile phones, and other forms of technology (Perlow, 1998; Christensen, Schneider, & Waite, 2005). Part-time hours, contract work, and self-employment have increased during the past decade. With fewer and/or sometimes unpredictable work hours, it may be difficult to plan or pay for leisure activities. This means people may feel less "free" to choose how they spend their free time.

At the same time, the workforce continually undergoes demographic changes that reflect the composition of our society. In Canada, there are more new immigrants, dual-earner families, and seniors working beyond the traditional age of retirement than there were a decade ago. When considering these trends, think about how they may affect opportunities for leisure for an individual, a family, or for community involvement. Also, keep in mind what some of the most pressing challenges might be for recreation professionals.

Defining Work

In the first chapter, readers were introduced to a broad range of meanings and definitions for leisure. Like leisure, there are almost as many different ways of understanding *work*. The meaning of work can differ according to a variety of situational and life-cycle factors. For example, some may think of work only as paid employment, but others might define work as studying, looking for work, unpaid housework or caregiving. Additionally, what seems like work to one person may feel like leisure to another, and the reverse can be true too (Shaw, 1985). In this chapter work is broadly defined as *employment activities undertaken by an individual for financial compensation.*

> Work is often seen as a polar opposite to leisure both in allocation of time and state of mind; however, the notion of "separate spheres" may not be true for everyone. Some people have enjoyable, challenging, rewarding jobs that include many qualities normally associated with leisure. What may create the distinction between work and leisure is the reward factor. For leisure, rewards have intrinsic, not monetary values whereas for work, the primary motivation is monetary even though there may be intrinsic rewards too (Reid, 1995).

The Relationship between Work and Leisure

The work–leisure relationship has been of interest to social scientists for many years. More than 40 years ago, technological advancements in the workplace led to predictions of greater amounts of free time. It was believed that increasing automation would decrease the length of the workday, and there were concerns about how this anticipated increase in leisure might be used for the greater social good. French sociologist Joffre Dumazedier theorized that a "leisure society" was emerging. He saw increased workplace automation as a catalyst for boredom, alienation, and a loss of meaning in one's work, especially among the working class. Because of unsatisfying work experiences and more free time, leisure would replace work as the central focus in people's lives. Individuals would choose where to work based on recreation opportunities provided both in the local community and by the employer (Dumazedier, 1967). The work–leisure relationship began to be viewed as an important issue for society, and several theories were advanced to help understand this relationship.

Most of these theories gave work primacy over leisure; in other words, to understand people's leisure choices and patterns it is important to look at what they do at work. Among the better-known foundational theories are the *spillover and compensation hypotheses* (Wilensky, 1960). The *spillover hypothesis* proposed that qualities, characteristics and attitudes toward tasks at work are carried over or reflected in leisure choices. Spillover can be either *optimistic* or *pessimistic*. *Spillover–optimistic* describes the leisure of individuals highly engaged in their work who become actively involved in a variety of personally and/or socially beneficial leisure activities. *Spillover–pessimistic* is most commonly embraced by critics of industrial society who focus on the alienation—or disconnection—of individuals from their work. Wilensky proposed that these negative attitudes and experiences would extend to leisure. For instance, people who are bored and find little meaning in their work would be drawn to activities requiring minimal input in terms of planning, effort, or variation from a set routine (e.g., collapsing onto the couch after work, switching on the TV, too tired to plan anything different and too bored to care).

On the other hand, the *compensation hypothesis* suggested that leisure activities are chosen to satisfy psychosocial needs not met in the work environment. Compensation can be either *aggressive* or *upgrading*. An example of *compensation–aggression* might be the fast-food worker who engages in violent or risk-taking leisure activities to compensate for a dull and meaningless workday routine. A *compensation–upgrading* leisure experience could occur if the worker instead chose activities allowing some measure of creativity or meaning not found in work. For example, a parking-lot attendant who also has musical abilities might play in a band during his or her leisure time. This would provide an enjoyable, creative outlet for interests and skills not required or valued by his or her employer.

Other ways of understanding the work–leisure relationship have included *time-budget studies* that allow researchers to quantify the amount of time devoted to work and leisure. Time diary information is usually gathered by national statistics agencies. People are asked what activities they do throughout the day, as well as where and with whom the activities take place. Since there are only 24 hours each day, when time for one activity such as work or caregiving is increased there is a corresponding decrease in time spent in other activities like leisure. Time diaries of different groups of people are compared on the basis of characteristics such as age, gender, life-cycle stage, occupation and other demographic factors. The influence of each factor can be identified when looking at average amounts of time devoted to work and leisure. This makes time-budget studies well suited to analyses of historical trends (Zuzanek & Smale, 1999), as well as different cultural emphases on work, leisure, and other activities.

The *socioeconomic perspective* is concerned with trade-offs between having more leisure, fewer work hours and a lower income; or, having less leisure, longer work hours, and more money (Gratton & Taylor, 2004). A problem with this approach is that it fails to consider other factors such as non-work obligations like caregiving and domestic responsibilities, which are still disproportionately done by women (Lewis, 2003). Moreover, the "ideal worker norm" (J. Williams, 2000) where long hours on the job are viewed as a demonstration of employee loyalty and commitment can inhibit "choice" in the trade-off between leisure and income (Perlow, 1998). Still, there are people who *downshift* in an attempt to lead a more fulfilling life. They resist the pervasive materialism characteristic of many industrialized societies by working fewer hours, decreasing consumption, and enjoying greater amounts of free time (Hamilton & Mail, 2003). Of particular interest in this chapter is the *socioorganizational and planning perspective*. Originally outlined by Zuzanek and Mannell (1983), it explores the impact of non-traditional work schedules and alternative employment models on leisure. Recent economic and workplace trends have made this approach increasingly relevant for recreation professionals. To understand why this is so, it is important to think about how the workplace has changed and who is affected.

The Changing Workplace

As mentioned earlier, technological advances and other factors allow work to be performed in settings other than offices or factories. Many people now work from home (e.g., telework) or as mobile office workers in other locations.

Changes have occurred in the structure of jobs, too, with a growth in casual work, part-time jobs, and self-employment. This has implications for leisure opportunities at all levels because of issues related to job security, financial stability, and time commitments. In this section, we explore some workplace trends relevant to leisure participation.

Models of Employment

In the post-war era, jobs generally followed a *traditional employment model.* Most workers had a full-time, year-round job, a regular Monday-to-Friday workweek, and an expectation of continued employment (Vosko, Zukewich, & Cranford, 2003). This model remains the basis of most labour laws and policies even though other employment models have emerged during the past few decades. These models are termed *non-standard* or *precarious employment* and broadly categorized as: part-time work (less than 30 hours per week), temporary employment (contract, seasonal, casual, or any other arrangement with a pre-determined end date), self-employment (with no paid employees), and multiple job-holders (two or more jobs at the same time) (Krahn, 1995). The proportion of Canadians working part-time is now almost one in five (Statistics Canada, 2011). Temporary work comprises 13% of paid employment. Multiple-job holders have quadrupled since 1976 and are especially prevalent among younger workers (Statistics Canada, 2009). Working in non-standard or precarious employment can have economic consequences such as a lower wages and fewer employee benefits (Vosko et al., 2003). Consequently, this group—who represent a sizable proportion of the labour force—is less likely to have a large discretionary income that can be allocated to leisure.

> ? In addition to having less discretionary income, how else might leisure be affected by non-standard work? Remember to consider all four categories: part-time, temporary, self-employment, and multiple-job-holding. What benefits or drawbacks do you see with each type of employment in relation to leisure opportunities? Do you think recreation providers take different employment arrangements into account when developing programs and services?

Thinking about Time

In this section, readers are asked to consider how *time* (number of work hours) and *timing* (when work occurs) influence the work-leisure relationship. Long hours, unpredictable or "anti-social" work schedules, and the expectation of constant availability to employers and customers can all play a role in leisure patterns.

Time. In Canada, maximum weekly work hours are determined by provincial legislation. For example, a regular workweek for employees in Ontario is 44 hours and they cannot be *required* to work more than 48 hours per week. Still, certain occupations are exempt from these standards including managers, professionals, and emergency workers. Additionally, in sectors such as the tourism industry, special rules apply (Ontario Ministry of Labour, 2010). Other provinces have similar regulations. For this reason (and likely others) in 2007, 22.6% of workers reported paid or unpaid overtime hours, with an average of 8.6 hours per week more than their usual work hours (Statistics Canada, 2009). The time-budget approach to work and leisure suggests that with the equivalent of an additional day of work per week, there will be a trade-off resulting in less time for leisure or other activities.

Timing. Economic changes have resulted in many workplaces expanding their hours of operation. For example, retail stores used to close on Sundays, but this is no longer the case. Evening and weekend shifts mean that work schedules can be at odds with those of family and friends. These "anti-social" work hours can affect not only the range of available activities, but also the choice of leisure companions. This is important to consider since almost one-third of employed Canadians work something other than a traditional weekday schedule, with most having rotating or irregular shifts (C. Williams, 2008). Research largely substantiates that a worker's social life, family life, marital stability, quality of health, and the range and frequency of participation in leisure activities are adversely affected by a non-standard work schedule. (LaValle, Arthur, Millward, Scott, & Clayden, 2002; Presser, 2003; Barnes, Bryson, & Smith, 2006; Kalil, Ziol-Guest, & Levin Epstein, 2010).

Unpredictable schedules can also present difficulties when trying to regularly pursue organized leisure activities. Workers may not know their work schedule for the following week more than a few days in advance. When they will be working, on what days, for how many hours or, indeed, whether they will be needed at work at all can vary widely from week to week. Unpredictable schedules are sometimes associated with retail sales, fast food restaurants,

> It can be challenging to provide access to leisure programs, services, and facilities when people work unusual hours. Some smaller, private fitness clubs have responded by providing members with a key to the facility—although there may be obstacles such as liability issues that make this difficult for organizations with limited resources. Can you suggest other ways that recreation professionals or employers might respond to the needs of employers working mainly evening and night shifts?

and manufacturers who follow a "just-in-time" production model, where workers are scheduled in response to sales and customer demand. Although more research is needed on irregular schedules and leisure participation, people with highly variable work hours appear to have lower job quality, higher levels of stress and lower levels of self-assessed health than workers with traditional, set work schedules (Heisz & LaRochelle-Cote, 2006).

Fortunately, there are other employment arrangements with the potential to make it easier for workers to participate in leisure activities. These may include *flextime*—when employees begin and end their workday around a "core" work time, *job sharing*—where two or more workers share the same job on a part-time basis, and *telework*—when a person works from home or at another location for all or some of their work time using file sharing, e-mail, and instant messaging to perform their job. These arrangements allow employees greater control over when (and sometimes where) they work so they can optimally schedule their daily activities. Flexible work hours seem particularly beneficial for accessing leisure. A study of parents with flexible work hours indicated that mothers spend more time on physically active leisure and report higher levels of satisfaction with work–life balance, health, and life in general (Hilbrecht & Shaw, 2010).

> The pace, or tempo, of life is also worth considering. In *Faster: The Acceleration of Just about Everything* (1999), author James Gleick tells us that North Americans live in a culture marked by speed, intensity, and efficiency. In this environment, what is the role of leisure? Do we place more value on activities that mirror the ever-increasing tempo of society (i.e., the "work hard—play hard" approach), or are we more likely to seek refuge in a more relaxing approach to our leisure?

In summary, changes in the economy and the structure of the workplace can influence the work–leisure relationship. In the next section, we explore some sociodemographic shifts in the workforce during the past three decades and consider how they might effect the provision of leisure and recreation services.

The Changing Workforce

The labour force composition is of interest to policymakers and government officials concerned with a healthy, productive workforce. Human Resources and Skills Development Canada recognizes the implications of understanding recent workforce changes with respect to providing relevant employment policies:

> The most remarkable changes include greater labour market participation of women, the increase in dual-wage earner families, the rise in numbers of lone-parent families, the aging of the population, changing immigration patterns, the growth of non-standard work, and new working arrangements. . . . Existing Canadian workplace practices and regulatory models remain largely based on an old industrial model and a social pattern of the able-bodied white male principal income earner working for a single employer on a full-time permanent basis. This model does not reflect or correspond to the realities and complexities of the new workforce. (HRSDC, 2005, introduction, para. 1)

It is beyond the scope of this chapter to address how all of these changes influence leisure. Therefore, in this section, we will consider only two important trends—women's workforce participation, and the aging workforce.

The Female Workforce

In 2009, women's labour force participation reached 58.3%, up from 41.9% in 1976 (Ferrao, 2010). Although more men than women work for pay, the gap is considerably smaller than in previous generations (see Figure 11.1). Women's workforce participation may not seem new for those born after the 1970s, but government policies and workplace cultures have been slow to recognize and respond to issues facing employed women. Many women face a "second

> Cultural expectations of parents to provide a range of organized leisure activities for children also contributes to mothers' decreased leisure time. Arendell (2001) reported that the movement toward more structured childhoods has changed the nature of traditional maternal care and increased women's workloads through added activities such as planning, scheduling, coordinating, and monitoring children's "free" time. Although both parents in dual-earner families in her study were committed to this structured approach to raising children, women were expected to be in charge of carrying it out. Organizing children's leisure has become a new gender-based activity that reduces mothers' time for their own activities and needs. Shaw (2008) extends these sentiments to family leisure, adding that family leisure activities compound women's workloads—whether employed or not—since women "consistently shoulder the major portion of this work, including the organizational work, the clean-up work and the 'emotion work' of facilitating positive experiences" (p.10).

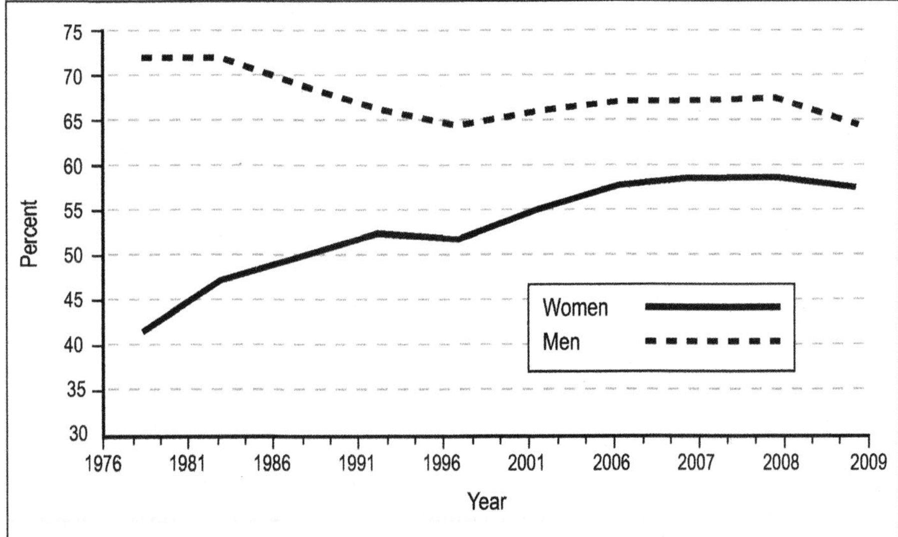

Figure 11.1: Canadian labour force participation rates of women and men, 1976–2009
Source: Ferrao, V. (2010). Paid work. *Women in Canada: A gender-based statistical report* (6th ed.)(Catalogue No. 89-503-X). Ottawa, ON: Minister of Industry, Statistics Canada, p. 6.

shift" of domestic work when they finish their paid workday (Hochschild, 1989), leaving little time for leisure. Although men are contributing more to some types of childcare, the gender gap remains significant in most Canadian families (Hilbrecht, 2009). Married women in dual-earner couples still spend significantly more time than men doing housework and caring for children (Marshall, 2006). Not surprisingly, employed women have less leisure time per day than men throughout the lifecycle (Fast & Frederick, 2004). Over a lifetime, this can add up to a remarkable imbalance in access to leisure.

The Aging Workforce

The largest population group in Canada is beginning to reach the traditional retirement age of 65. Because of their large numbers, baby boomers—those born during the 20-year period between 1946 and 1966—exert a tremendous influence on social and economic trends. Mandatory retirement is now considered discriminatory and has been abolished relatively recently in most provinces. This will affect rates of labour force participation and the consumption of leisure services. In 2006, about one in ten seniors was working for pay. The decision not to retire can be related to financial status and obligations, educational attainment, and health status (Uppal, 2010). No doubt there are other reasons too, such as job satisfaction, a sense of purpose, and social factors. With this in mind, retirement may no longer be the option of choice for increasing numbers of seniors. It is important to recognize these trends and how they might affect the demand for public and private leisure services.

Whether the baby boom generation decides to retire before, at, or after age 65, there will be implications for recreation practitioners. Think about some possible scenarios. For instance, if many baby boomers chose early retirement, will there be a greater demand for leisure services? Considering lifecycle and lifestyle factors, what type of activities might be in greatest demand? Remember to think about the influence of income and health status. Will this have an impact on the traditional approach to recreation provision for seniors?

Women's greater workforce participation and the aging workforce are just two of many changes contributing to a different work environment from over 40 years ago. At that time, concerns were related to technology's impact on work and how increased automation might transform the relationship of work and leisure in industrialized societies. Concerns about technology's transformative effect still exist but have taken a different form. Newer digital technologies can contribute to a blurring of boundaries between work, home, and leisure, with the potential to influence the nature and quality of experiences in each domain. Work easily intrudes on a worker's personal life when he or she is expected to be constantly available through mobile phones and other electronic technology, and it can work in the opposite direction too. Not only do families complain about an individual's refusal to turn off a work-issued Blackberry while at home or on vacation, but employees have also been fired for excessive personal Internet use at work. This raises questions about how to best integrate or separate different life spheres such as work and leisure; or, how technology can either add to or reduce work–life conflict and stress related to managing different commitments and responsibilities. These are challenging questions and have contributed in part to perceptions of time pressure and, sometimes, excessive workplace demands. In the final section of this chapter, we explore the potential of leisure to play a role in work–life integration and evaluate earlier predictions of a leisure society.

Leisure and Work–Life Integration

The term *work–life integration* has started to replace *work–life balance* in describing how people mesh their job with the rest of their life. Many believe that *balance* may not be the best metaphor to describe how people attend to their various commitments, responsibilities, and priorities without undue stress. One reason is that balance is fleeting and never easily attained. Another is that a person's ability to balance seems to place responsibility firmly on the individual and their time-management skills (or lack thereof). Yet many things—such as unpredictable work hours, employer's demands, or different expectations of mothers and fathers at home—are not easily managed, controlled, or slotted into a daily routine. This makes balance almost impossible to achieve. Balance conjures up an image of scales with one side (work) creating an imbalance with the other (family). This two-sided model overlooks other activities that contribute to a healthy, fulfilling life including leisure, volunteering, religious or spiritual activities, and sleep. One might also question the dominant assumption that striving for balance is always a good thing. There could be some circumstances where imbalance may be preferable (Bickenbach & Glass, 2009), and more time and energy should be directed to one area more so than others. For example, a worker who also cares for an elderly parent may work more efficiently if he or she is allowed a reduced workload when a family member is experiencing a health crisis.

Work–life integration takes a wider view than work–life balance, understanding that everyone has different capacities, responsibilities, and interests. It recognizes that in order for individuals to be effective at work and in other areas of their lives, there are contributing factors that also need to be addressed at a broader social level by organizations and governments (Lero & Lewis, 2008). Work–life integration is also a type of spillover theory that focusses on positive attitudes carried over between work and the rest of life that can enrich each of an individual's many roles (Greenhaus & Parasuaraman, 1999). This more holistic approach questions assumptions about work–life balance being primarily a women's issue or relevant only when people have families. People at all stages face challenges finding adequate time and other resources to meet their work (or school), health, home, and relationship needs with a minimum of stress or conflict.

In North America, the role of leisure in work–life integration has been somewhat overlooked but the positive association with health, coping, and life satisfaction strongly suggests it should be given more attention. Roberts (2011) contends that leisure's contribution to the well-being of individuals and societies is one of its most important consequences. Leisure has beneficial health effects for those experiencing time pressure, job instability, and irregular employment associated with changing economic conditions (Cartwright & Warner-Smith, 2003), and has been identified as a coping mechanism for stressful situations at work (Iwasaki, 2003). Having opportunities to interact with family members, one's partner, neighbours, and friends is related to stronger perceptions of well-being (Helliwell & Putnam, 2005). Others stress the necessity of considering the long arm of the job and its effect on time for friendships and quality of life generally. As Lewis (2003) comments, "if work is taking over from leisure and other personal activities on a wide scale, we need to examine the broader and long-term effects on individual well-being, families, and communities" (pp. 353–354). By highlighting leisure's contribution to health and well-being, and the association with fewer sick days and greater productivity (sometimes referred to as the *business case*) employers might be encouraged to support workplace policies that create time and space for leisure (Danna & Griffin, 1999). More importantly, individuals and organizations may be more inclined to adopt workplace policies and practices that are helpful to all employees—not just those with children at home—that would enhance work–life integration.

Think about your own life and all of your responsibilities and commitments. How much of a priority is leisure? How does that fit in with school, work, or family commitments? Are you satisfied with your level of work–life integration? If not, how might it be improved?

Remember that work–life integration emphasizes the contribution of cultural expectations and organizations' policies, rather than focussing exclusively on individuals and how they manage their time. How could *others* (e.g., employers, professors, or family members) help?

It seems that changes in the economy, both locally and internationally, and in the workforce itself have mitigated against the "leisure society." There is no agreement that free time has greatly increased (Jacobs & Gerson, 2004), or that leisure has replaced work as the central focus among employed Canadians. Whether due to the nature of the work itself, its role as means of identity development and self-esteem, or simply because of the extrinsic monetary rewards, work continues to dominate most people's lives and remains a central life interest and necessity for much of the population. Therefore, while the "leisure society" may not have materialized in Canada—at least for the time being—the influence of leisure on work is important to consider in the context of Canadian workers' perceptions of well-being and work–life integration.

Conclusion

The workplace and labour force are constantly evolving, dynamic entities. The work of earlier theorists laid a foundation for the analysis of the work–leisure relationship. Some of their hypotheses remain relevant, while others have fallen out of favour with the passage of time. Recreation professionals should consider how employment factors affect leisure programming, accessibility, and opportunities for workers and their families. In this chapter, we have explored the work–leisure relationship from a theoretical perspective and thought about some of the practical applications. We have also examined changes in the way we work, as well as influential developments in workforce demographics. By monitoring Canadian labour market trends and workplace practices, leisure providers can be more focused on and responsive to individual, family, and community needs.

Key Terms

Compensation hypothesis
Compensation–aggression
Compensation–upgrading
Spillover hypothesis
Spillover–optimistic
Spillover–pessimistic
Leisure society
Time-budget studies
Socioeconomic perspective
Socioorganizational and planning perspective
Ideal worker
Downshift
Traditional employment model
Non-traditional or precarious employment
Anti-social work hours
Unpredictable schedules
Work–life balance
Work–life integration

References

Arendell, T. (2001). The new care work of middle class mothers: Managing childrearing, employment, and time. In K. J. Daly (Ed.), *Minding the time in family experience: Emerging perspectives and issues* (pp. 163–204). Oxford, UK: Elsevier Science.

Barnes, M., Bryson, C., & Smith, R. (2006). *Working atypical hours: What happens to "family life"?* London, UK: National Centre for Social Research.

Bickenbach, J. E., & Glass, T. A. (2009). Life balance: The meaning and the menace in a metaphor. In K. Matuska & C. H. Christiansen (Eds.), *Life balance: Multidisciplinary theories and research* (pp. 13–22). Thorofare, NJ: SLACK Inc. and AOTA Press.

Cartwright, S., & Warner-Smith, P. (2003). "Melt down": Young women's talk of time and its implications for health, well-being and identity in late modernity. *Annals of Leisure Research, 6*(4), 318–338.

Christensen, K. E., Schneider, B., & Waite, L. J. (2005). Achieving work–life balance: Strategies for dual-earner families. In B. Schneider & L. J. Waite (Eds.), *Being together, working apart: Dual career families and the work-life balance* (pp. 449–457). Cambridge, UK: Cambridge University Press.

Danna, K., & Griffin, R. W. (1999). Health and well-being in the workplace: A review and synthesis of the literature. *Journal of Management, 25*(3), 357–384.

Dumazedier, J. (1967). *Toward a society of leisure*. New York, NY: The Free Press.

Fast, J., & Frederick, J. (2004). *The time of our lives: Juggling work and leisure over the life cycle* (Catalogue no. 89-584-MIE, No. 4). Ottawa, ON: Statistics Canada, Minister of Industry.

Ferrao, V. (2010). Paid work. *Women in Canada: A gender-based statistical report* (6th ed.). Ottawa, ON: Minister of Industry, Statistics Canada.

Gratton, C., & Taylor, P. (2004). The economics of work and leisure. In J. T. Haworth & A. J. Veal (Eds.), *Work and leisure* (pp. 85–106). East Sussex, UK: Routledge.

Greenhaus, J. H., & Parasuaraman, S. (1999). Research on work, family, and gender: Current status and future directions. In G. N. Powell (Ed.), *Handbook of gender & work* (pp. 391–412). Newbury Park, CA: Sage.

Hamilton, C., & Mail, E. (2003). Downshifting in Australia: A sea-change in the pursuit of happiness (Discussion Paper No. 50). Canberra, AU: The Australia Institute.

Heisz, A., & LaRochelle-Cote, S. (2006). *Summary of: Work hours instability in Canada* (Catalogue No. 11F0019MIE, No. 279). Ottawa, ON: Statistics Canada, Business and Labour Market Analysis Division.

Helliwell, J. F., & Putnam, R. D. (2005). The social context of well-being. In F. A. Huppert, N. Baylis, & B. Keverne (Eds.), *The science of well-being* (pp. 435–360). Oxford, UK: Oxford University Press.

Hilbrecht, M. (2009). *Living in real time: Parents, work, gender and well-being*. Germany: Verlag VDM.

Hilbrecht, M., & Shaw, S. M. (2010). *Flexible schedules and parents' health: Does gender matter?* Paper presented at the Canadian Association for Research on

Work and Health Conference: Worker Health in a Changing World of Work, May 25–26, Toronto, ON.

Iwasaki, Y. (2003). The impact of leisure coping beliefs and strategies on adaptive outcomes. *Leisure Studies, 22*(2), 93–108.

Jacobs, J. A., & Gerson, K. (2004). *The time divide: Work, family, and gender inequality.* Cambridge, MA: Harvard University Press.

Kalil, A., Ziol-Guest, K. M., & Levin Epstein, J. (2010). Nonstandard work and marital instability: Evidence from the National Longitudinal Survey of Youth. [10.1111/j.1741-3737.2010.00765.x]. *Journal of Marriage and Family, 72*(5), 1289–1300.

Krahn, H. (1995). Non-standard work on the rise. *Perspectives on Labour and Income, 7*(4) (Statistics Canada Cat. 75-001E), 35–42.

LaValle, I., Arthur, S., Millward, C., Scott, J., & Clayden, M. (2002). *Happy families? Atypical work and its influence on family life.* Bristol, UK: Policy.

Lero, D. S., & Lewis, S. (2008). Assumptions, research gaps and emerging issues: Implications for research, policy and practice. In D. S. Lero, K. Korabik, & D. L. Whitehead (Eds.), *Handbook of work–family integration* (pp. 371–397). San Diego, CA: Elsevier.

Lewis, S. (2003). The integration of paid work and the rest of life. Is post-industrial work the new leisure? *Leisure Studies, 22*(4), 343–345, DOI:10.1080/02614360310001594131

Marshall, K. (2006). Converging gender roles. *Perspectives on Labour and Income* (Catalogue. No. 75-001-XIE), *18*(3), 5–17.

Ontario Ministry of Labour (2010). Industries and jobs with special exemptions and/or special rules. Retrieved from http://www.labour.gov.on.ca/english/es/pubs/guide/special.php#managerial

Perlow, L. (1998). Boundary control: The social ordering of work and family time in a high tech organization. *Administrative Science Quarterly, 43*, 328–357.

Presser, H. B. (2003). *Working in a 24/7 economy: Challenges for American families.* New York, NY: Russell Sage Foundation.

Reid, D. G. (1995). *Work and leisure in the 21st century: From production to citizenship.* Toronto, ON: Wall & Emerson.

Roberts, K. (2011). Leisure: the importance of being inconsequential. *Leisure Studies, 30*(1), 5–20.

Shaw, S. M. (1985). The meaning of leisure in everyday life. *Leisure Sciences, 7*(1), 1–24.

Shaw, S. M. (2008). Family leisure and changing ideologies of parenthood. *Sociology Compass, 2*, 1–16.

Statistics Canada (2009). *The Canadian labour market at a glance—2007.* (Catalogue no. 71-222-X). Ottawa, ON: Minister of Industry. Retrieved from http://www.statcan.gc.ca/pub/71-222-x/2008001/section-a-eng.htm

Statistics Canada (2011). Full-time and part-time employment by sex and age group, CANSIM table 282-0002. Retrieved from http://www40.statcan.gc.ca/l01/cst01/labor12-eng.htm

Uppal, S. (2010). Labour market activity among seniors. *Perspectives on Labour and Income, 11*(7), 5–18.

Vosko, L. F., Zukewich, N., & Cranford, C. (2003). Precarious jobs: A new typology of employment. *Perspectives on Labour and Income, 4*(10), 16–26.

Williams, C. (2008). Work-life balance of shift workers. *Perspectives on Labour and Income, 20*(3), 5–16.

Williams, J. (2000). *Unbending gender: Why work and family conflict and what to do about it.* Oxford, UK: Oxford University Press.

Zuzanek, J., & Mannell, R. (1983). Work–leisure relationships from a sociological and social psychological perspective. *Leisure Studies, 2*, 327–344.

Zuzanek, J., & Smale, B. (1999). Life-cycle and across-the-week allocation of time to daily activities. In W. E. Pentland, A. S. Harvey, M. P. Lawton, & M. A. McColl (Eds.), *Time use research in the social sciences* (pp. 127–153). New York, NY: Kluwer Academic/Plenum Publishers.

Chapter 12
Leisure Travel

Stephen Smith, Ph.D.
University of Waterloo

Learning Objectives

After reading this chapter, students will be able to

1. Understand the definition of tourism and how leisure travel fits within the broader concept of tourism.
2. Appreciate the contributions of tourism to the Canadian economy.
3. Be able to describe basic characteristics of Canadian leisure travellers.
4. Understand some forces shaping leisure travel.
5. Discuss some of the future trends in tourism.

Introduction

Tourism is an important leisure activity for many Canadians—about 6 out of 10 Canadians take a tourism trip in any given year. Tourism is an important contributor to the quality of life for many Canadians, and is a direct source of employment for over 600,000 Canadians. Thus, even more than something people do when they are not working, for many Canadians, tourism is something they do for work. It also receives substantial media attention whenever something like a terrorist attack, hurricane, or a health warning occurs that stop people from visiting a city or country. What exactly, though, is tourism? How big is it in Canada? What are the characteristics of visitors? This chapter explores the answers to these and other questions.

Defining Tourism

Unlike "recreation" or "leisure," there is an official definition of tourism. It was developed by the World Tourism Organization (UNWTO) and has been adopted by the United Nations Statistical Commission. The UNWTO defines tourism as the activities of persons away from their usual environment for a period of no more than one year, and for almost any purpose of travel except commuting to work or school. In Canada, the phrase "outside the usual environment" normally means travel at least 80 km away from home or travel across an international border. This distance threshold is somewhat arbitrary, but it reflects the outer limit of commuting or routine trips for most people. Tourism trips may last a few hours only, or extend over weeks or even months.

People engage in tourism for a wide range of trip purposes. These include travel for work (such as going to a business meeting), travel to conferences, travel for medical purposes, travel for religious purposes, travel for personal matters (such as attending a wedding), visiting friends or family, as well as pleasure travel (or what we call "leisure travel" in this chapter).

Persons engaged in tourism are referred to as "visitors" by the UNWTO (1994). Visitors who stay away overnight are called "tourists"; those who go on a tourism trip and return the same day are called, logically enough, "same-day visitors."

Tourism is sometimes called the world's largest industry—generating over 1 trillion U.S. dollars globally in international travel, plus unknown trillions in domestic travel (UNWTO, 2003). However, as you can infer from the UNWTO definition, tourism is not really an industry—it is something that people do. An industry is a group of businesses that produce essentially the same product using essentially the same technology. Thus, an industry is generally known by the type of product or service it produces. The automobile industry, for example, produces automobiles. In the case of tourism, the businesses that produce tourism services include accommodation services, which provide people a place to stay and sleep as well as transportation services, which people use to move around. In other words, there is no single, distinctive product or service that can be said to be "tourism." Rather, there are many different types of tourism products, produced by many different types of industries. While one cannot meaningfully speak of tourism as a single industry, there are tourism industries. These are industries that produce services heavily used by people engaged in tourism:

- Transportation
- Accommodation
- Food and beverage services
- Recreation and entertainment
- Travel agencies and tour operators
- Sightseeing companies
- Convention services

Each of these industries would exist in a substantially smaller form than they currently do if tourism did not exist.

The services or products produced by each of these tourism industries will sound similar to the industry name—the transportation industry produces transportation services, the food and beverage industry produces food and beverage services. Products and services that draw a significant portion of their sales from visitors are called tourism commodities. Like tourism industries, tourism commodities would exist only in a greatly reduced degree if tourism did not exist. It is important to remember the distinction between the industry and the product. A tourism commodity can be produced by different industries. Airlines also sell meals, hotels often sell meals as well, plus dry cleaning services, telephone services, spa services, and so on.

The main tourism commodities used by visitors include:

- Transportation
    - » Passenger air
    - » Passenger rail
    - » Inter-urban bus
    - » Vehicle rentals
    - » Vehicle repairs and parts
    - » Vehicle fuel
- Accommodation
    - » Hotels, motels, and inns
    - » Resorts and lodges
    - » Cabins and cottages
    - » B&Bs, guest houses
    - » Campground and RV parks
- Food and beverage services
    - » Full-service restaurants
    - » Limited-service restaurants
    - » Drinking establishments
    - » Caterers
- Other tourism commodities
    - » Recreation and entertainment
    - » Travel agency services
    - » Convention fees

> Most tourism souvenirs, such as t-shirts, are not considered to be tourism commodities. This is because souvenirs are classified as retail goods, along with all forms of clothing, household items, jewelry, and so on. Only 2–3% of all retail goods are purchased by people engaged in tourism. Thus, the total volume of sales of retail goods from visitors is too small to classify them as a tourism commodity.

How Big is Tourism in Canada?

Canadians love to travel. In 2009, they made 227.1 million trips (same-day and overnight), spending $33.7 billion dollars in Canada alone. Domestic destinations—places in Canada—are the most popular places to visit, accounting for over 75% of spending and over 85% of all the trips Canadians take. In terms of international travel, not surprisingly perhaps, the United States is the most frequently visited foreign country because of its proximity to Canada (see Table 12.1). In fact, about 80% of Canadians live within 200 km of the Canada–United States border. The most popular overseas country to visit is the Mexico, because of its proximity, well-developed resorts, and good value (See Table 12.2).

Table 12.1: Top 10 States Visited by Canadians: 2008

State	Overnight visits (thousands)	Total nights (thousands)	Spending (million $)
New York	3,077	8,652	956
Florida	2,872	48,524	3,242
Washington	2,142	6,078	484
Michigan	1,422	3,577	321
California	1,257	10,774	1,129
Nevada	1,059	4,936	930
Maine	885	2,972	282
Pennsylvania	786	1,965	158
Vermont	758	2,342	172
North Dakota	722	1,520	196

Source: Statistics Canada. 2008 International Travel Survey

> Note that many of the states in the top 10 are those that share a border with Canada. Are these the states where Canadians spend the longest time and the most money? If not, what do you think the reason is for the difference?

Overall, tourism in Canada in 2008 generated $72.8 billion dollars in total receipts. Approximately $55.4 billion was spent by Canadians travelling in their country; the rest was spent by international visitors. This was spent in a variety of different industries, as shown in Table 12.3. The levels of spending shown are specific to tourism, and do not include spending in other industries from people engaged

Table 12.2: Top Ten Overseas Countries Visited by Canadians: 2008

Country	Overnight visits (thousands)	Total nights (thousands)	Spending (million $)
Mexico	1,125	11,518	1,186
United Kingdom	1,017	12,406	1,277
Cuba	932	7,806	791
France	809	9,779	1,057
Dominican Republic	763	6,319	651
Germany	362	3,333	312
Italy	338	3,471	456
Netherlands	274	2,173	212
China	250	5,403	452
Spain	216	2,261	266

Source: Statistics Canada. 2008 International Travel Survey

Look at the list of the 10 most popular overseas nations visited and suggest two different motives for Canadians to travel overseas.

in tourism, such as the purchase of clothing or food from grocery stores. Total spending in each industry by Canadians is always larger than spending by visitors, sometimes much larger because many customers of certain types of businesses include people who are not engaged in tourism. For example, while visitors spent $10.6 billion on food and beverage services ($8.2 billion by Canadians) in the course of tourism trips during 2009, total spending in restaurants was actually $53.7 billion. In other words, about 20¢ of every dollar earned by Canadian restaurants was spent by a visitor.

Table 12.3: Domestic Visitor Spending and Tourism Employment by Major Tourism Industry: 2008

Industry	Spending (billions $)	Employment (thousands of jobs)
Transportation	22.4	72.3
Accommodation	6.8	162.4
Food and beverage services	8.2	149.7
Other tourism commodities (e.g., recreation and entertainment, conventions, travel agency fees)	9.2	113.1
Other commodities (e.g., souvenirs, food from grocery stores)	8.8	119.3
Total	**55.4**	**616.8**

Source: Statistics Canada. 2010 National Tourism Indicators

Profiles of Leisure Travellers

Table 12.4 (p. 112) describes some of the characteristics of same-day leisure travellers and overnight leisure travellers as well as the general Canadian population. Marital status has relatively little impact on the tendency to take leisure trips, whether same-day or overnight. However, several other characteristics make a major difference. People who have not graduated from high school are much less likely to take a leisure trip. For example, about 6% of Canadians have less than 9 years of formal education, and they make only about 3% of same-day and overnight trips. In contrast, those with a university degree are much more likely to travel. About 21% of Canadians have a university degree, but they produce 29% of same-day trips and a similar percentage of overnight trips.

Why do people who have higher educations tend to travel more than those with less education?

Having a job is important, too. People who are not in the labour force—full-time students, homemakers not working outside the household, retirees—are much less likely to take a trip than those people who are employed. Not surprisingly, income also plays an important role. Households earning under $40,000 do not take many trips, while those earning more take more trips. As incomes rise, the likelihood of taking both same-day and overnight trips increases. For example, about 17% of Canadians earn $80,000 or more, but they generate 25% of all same-day trips and 34% of overnight trips. This is the only group that is more likely to make overnight trips than same-day trips. All other income groups make more same-day trips than overnight trips.

Why are people who are in the highest income group more likely to take overnight trips, while all other incomes groups are more likely to take same-day trips?

Family structure—the number of adults and children—also plays a role in leisure travel. Adults who live alone are not as likely to travel for leisure as adults who live with other adults. Those who live in households with three or more adults—such as grown-up children or who have grandparents living with them—are much more likely to take either a same-day trip or an overnight trip than adults in other households. Having children in a house reduces the likelihood that the household will take leisure trips. Households with no children are about 50% more likely to travel for leisure than those with children.

Table 12.5 (p. 112) describes some of the characteristics of same-day and overnight leisure trips. It will not be a surprise to see that the family car is the most common mode of travel for both. Buses are the second most common mode for same-day travel, but they are used by only a very small portion of travellers. Airlines are the second most common

Table 12.4: Travellers' Characteristics

Characteristic	Same-day leisure travellers %	Overnight leisure travellers %	General population (2006 census) %
Marital status			
Married/common-law	54	54	49
Never married	38	39	48
Widowed/separated/ divorced	8	7	3
Education			
Less than high school	4	3	6
High school diploma	9	11	26
College diploma	52	51	42
Univeristy certificate or diploma below bachelor's level	5	7	5
University degree	29	27	21
Labour force status			
Employed	68	74	67
Unemployed	5	4	8
Not in labour force	26	23	25
Number of adults in household			
One adult	11	10	27
Two adults	56	57	56
Three adults or more	33	33	17
Number of children in household			
No children	56	57	38
One child	16	15	27
Two children	20	20	24
Three children or more	8	8	10
Household income			
<$20,000	8	7	10
$20,000–$39,999	22	18	25
$40,000–$59,999	24	21	30
$60,000–$79,999	19	19	18
$80,000 or over	25	34	17

Source: Statistics Canada. 2008 Travel Survey of Residents of Canada; 2006 Canadian Census

Table 12.5: Trip Characteristics

Characteristic	Same-day leisure travellers %	Overnight leisure travellers %	General population %
Main mode of transportation			
Auto	95.6	83.2	n/a
Air	0.1	11.9	n/a
Bus	3.1	2.8	n/a
Rail	0.2	0.6	n/a
Boat	0.2	0.9	n/a
Other	0.9	0.7	n/a
Nights away			
1	n/a	70.4	n/a
2–3	n/a	16.5	n/a
4–7	n/a	9.8	n/a
8 or more	n/a	3.3	n/a
Season of trip			
Winter	21.6	15.9	n/a
Spring	24.1	20.5	n/a
Summer	31.1	48.4	n/a
Autumn	23.1	15.2	n/a
Province of residence			
Newfoundland & Labrador	1.8	1.9	1.7
Prince Edward Island	0.5	0.5	0.5
Nova Scotia	5.1	3.0	3.0
New Brunswick	3.1	2.0	2.4
Quebec	22.9	23.3	24.1
Ontario	39.7	40.1	38.0
Manitoba	3.5	4.0	3.7
Saskatchewan	3.6	2.9	3.3
Alberta	9.5	10.5	9.9
British Columbia	10.2	11.7	13.0
Yukon	n/a	n/a	<0.1
Northwest Territories	n/a	n/a	<0.1
Nunavut	n/a	n/a	<0.1
Province of destination			
Newfoundland & Labrador	1.9	1.9	n/a
Prince Edward Island	0.5	1.0	n/a
Nova Scotia	5.3	3.7	n/a
New Brunswick	3.7	2.5	n/a
Quebec	22.6	24.6	n/a
Ontario	39.7	37.6	n/a
Manitoba	3.5	3.2	n/a
Saskatchewan	3.5	3.1	n/a
Alberta	9.4	9.2	n/a
British Columbia	10.1	13.0	n/a
Yukon	n/a	<0.1	n/a
Northwest Territories	n/a	<0.1	n/a

Source: Statistics Canada. 2008 Travel Survey of Residents of Canada; 2006 Census of Canada

Are leisure trips, whether same-day or overnight, important in the upbringing of a child? If you think so, what could be done to encourage more parents to take trips with their children?

What sorts of people are most likely to take overnight trips that last longer than one week?

form of travel for overnight trips, largely because of the very long distances associated with much travel in Canada.

Most overnight travel is only for a short time. About 7 out of 10 overnight trips are one night only, and about 1 out of 6 last only two nights. The traditional two-week vacation common a generation ago has virtually disappeared because of time pressures for most working people.

The Quebec poet Gilles Vigneault writes in his song, "Mon Pays," "Mon pays ce n'est pas un pays, c'est l'hiver" (My country is not a country, it is winter). Canada's four seasons do affect our travel habits, especially for overnight travel. Nearly half of all overnight trips are taken during the summer. After an active travel season, most Canadians stop taking overnight trips after Labour Day and remain close to home until Victoria Day. The pattern of overnight trips by season makes it appear that Canada has a three-month summer, followed by a six-month winter, and a slow thawing in the spring. Same-day travel, though, does not show a dramatic seasonal pattern. While summer is still the most common time for same-day trips, Canadians make same-day trips frequently in all seasons.

Seasonality

Seasonality is a dominant force in Canadian tourism. The concentration of business in only a few months, usually the summer, can make it difficult for a business to be run profitably over an entire year. Some businesses have to shut down during their low season—the time when few visitors come—to save costs. Very high use levels in short periods of time can cause environmental problems, inefficient use of resources, and create headaches trying to hire enough staff for the peak period.

However, the tendency of visitors to concentrate in one season of the year is not always a problem. Low seasons allow businesses and communities to do maintenance without affecting large numbers of visitors. Low seasons can also allow tourism entrepreneurs to take time off for their own vacations.

Seasonality is caused by a variety of forces. Weather, of course is a major factor. However, institutional factors such as school holidays, the timing of religious or secular holidays, as well as traditions, are also factors. Different countries have different seasonality patterns. Countries in the Southern Hemisphere, of course, have their seasons reversed from those in those in the Northern Hemisphere. Travel in China, in contrast, is focused on three national holiday periods—a week-long celebration around the National Day (October 1), another week around Labour Day (May 1), and two weeks around the Chinese Lunar New Year.

What are some actions businesses or destinations can take to reduce seasonality in tourism?

The very low rate of inter-provincial travel for Newfoundland and Labrador is not surprising, given that the province is an island and the only modes of travel off the island are by air and ferry. Why do you think that residents of British Columbia are no more likely to travel inter-provincially than those of Newfoundland and Labrador?

There are only slight provincial variations in the propensity of Canadians to make same-day or overnight trips. By comparing the percent of same-day or overnight trips generated by each province to that province's percent of the Canadian population, you can get a sense of which provinces are more or less likely to travel than the national average. Residents of Nova Scotia are the most likely to take same-day trips: about 5% of trips are made by the 3% of Canadians who live in that province. In other words, Nova Scotians are about 1.8 times (5.3/3.0) more likely to make a same-day trip than the average Canadian. Ontarians are also more likely than the average to travel. In contrast, Quebecers and British Columbians are noticeably less likely to take same-day trips.

Ontarians are the most likely to make overnight trips, and British Columbians are the least likely. The provincial patterns for same-day and overnight destinations roughly mirror the same pattern as province of origin. This reflects the fact that most Canadians do not travel outside their own province. This observation can be verified by looking at Table 12.6, a summary of intra- and inter-provincial travel for overnight pleasure trips. Look at any province as a destination for its residents. With the exception of Prince Edward Island, a majority of Canadians do not take trips outside their home province in any given year. In fact, over 90% of residents of Newfoundland and Labrador, and of British Columbia travel only in their own province. The reason for the exception of Prince Edward Island is, of course, the very small size of that province. The most common destination of Islanders is New Brunswick—the province at the other end of Confederation Bridge. If you add the percent of Islanders travelling only within PEI and the percent that travel across the bridge to New Brunswick, you have accounted for a majority of all trips by Islanders.

What do Canadians like to do on their trips? Table 12.7 (p. 114) reports the percentage of persons engaged in a variety of activities during same-day and overnight trips. Shopping is the most popular same-day trip activity, followed closely by participating in sport. Both are engaged in by more than one out of three travellers. It should be noted that the definition of sport is a very broad one including swimming, hiking, cycling, and golf. Some participation rates in individual sports are also shown. Sightseeing is the third most common same-day activity, with about one in four Canadians

Table 12.6: Patterns of Inter-Provincial Travel: Percentage of Person Trips by Province of Destination, 2008

Province of origin	Province of destination									
	NF	PE	NS	NB	QC	ON	MB	SK	AB	BC
NF	90.5	0.7	3.4	1.4	0.3	3.1	0.1	0.0	0.2	0.4
PE	0.2	18.0	36.0	40.9	2.3	1.6	0.0	0.0	1.2	0.8
NS	1.4	11.3	73.4	8.3	1.5	3.4	0.1	0.0	0.5	0.3
NB	1.1	8.9	15.7	60.8	9.4	3.1	0.0	0.0	0.8	0.3
QC	0.1	0.3	0.1	2.2	88.9	7.7	0.0	0.0	0.3	0.3
ON	0.5	0.7	0.7	0.3	8.6	87.1	0.4	0.1	0.4	1.2
MB	0.0	0.0	0.3	0.1	0.3	8.5	72.1	12.3	4.6	2.7
SK	0.0	0.0	0.3	0.1	0.5	1.2	4.0	70.1	18.2	5.6
AB	0.1	0.0	0.1	0.2	0.3	1.7	0.4	6.2	66.2	24.8
BC	0.0	0.0	0.4	0.6	0.5	1.6	0.1	0.5	5.8	90.5

Source: Statistics Canada. 2008 Travel Survey of Residents of Canada

reporting sightseeing on a same-day trip. Sightseeing is rarely the primary purpose for taking a trip, but it can be an important secondary activity. Visiting friends or relatives is also very popular; together, these two activities are engaged in by more than one-third of Canadians on same-day trips.

These same activities are also the most popular ones for overnight trips, although the percentage of people reporting participation is higher for overnight trips. That makes sense because people have more time to engage in activities, and thus typically do more different things on overnight trips. In fact, participation in every activity is higher for overnight trips with the exception of downhill skiing. This tends to be an activity that is more popular with same-day travellers than overnight travellers. The right-hand column of Table 12.7 shows the ratio between participation in overnight activities and same-day activities.

Cruising shows the greatest difference in participation rates—people are more than five times as likely to go on a cruise for an overnight trip than to take one as a same-day outing. Some of the other activities that show a big difference

Table 12.7: Trip Activities

Activities	Same-day leisure travellers %	Overnight leisure travellers %	Ratio between same-day and overnight participation
Visited friends	18.1	34.8	0.5
Visited relatives	15.7	29.5	0.5
Went shopping	38.2	45.5	0.8
Went sightseeing	26.7	45.7	0.6
Went to a festival	5.1	9.4	0.5
Went to a cultural performance	5.1	9.9	0.5
Went to an aboriginal activity	0.5	2.4	0.2
Went to a museum	4.2	12.1	0.3
Went to a zoo	4.1	6.9	0.6
Went to a theme park	4.5	7.8	0.6
Went to a national park	8.8	17.6	0.5
Went to an historic site	6.1	15.0	0.4
Went to a bar or nightclub	7.1	19.0	0.4
Went to a casino	3.8	6.4	0.6
Went on a cruise	1.5	8.7	0.2
Participated in sports	36.1	54.9	0.7
Went swimming	9.1	23.9	0.4
Went boating	4.4	15.5	0.3
Participated in other water sports	1.5	6.2	0.2
Went golfing	2.7	7.1	0.4
Went hunting	0.6	0.9	0.7
Went fishing	4.4	10.1	0.4
Went bird-watching	2.1	6.9	0.3
Went cross-country skiing	0.6	1.1	0.5
Went downhill skiing	3.9	3.1	1.3
Went snowmobiling	0.7	1.2	0.6
Went walking	12.7	28.5	0.4
Went cycling	2.5	7.2	0.3

Source: Statistics Canada. 2008 Travel Survey of Residents of Canada

Why is downhill skiing a more common activity for Canadians making same-day trips than overnight trips?

are cultural—going to an aboriginal activity, going to a museum, or going to an historic site. Water-based activities such as boating and participating in water sports (such as water skiing or scuba diving) are more likely to be done on overnight trips than on same-day trips. People are also more likely to go to a bar or nightclub as part of an overnight trip. This is probably to be expected because having to drive back home at least 80 km after going to a bar is not something most people want to do.

Trip activities may be either "primary"—they are the main reason for the trip—or "secondary"—they are activities done on a trip taken for other reasons. Which of the activities shown in Table 12.7 are more likely to be primary activities than secondary activities?

Factors Shaping Leisure Travel

Canadian travel patterns are shaped by many forces, and the styles of travel are changing. Some of the more important trends are discussed below.

Time Pressures

Many Canadians feel they have little free time, and that traditional two-week vacations are something they cannot manage due to pressures from jobs. As a result, short getaways (1–3 nights) are becoming more common, with many people taking several long weekends over the year rather than one long vacation. More and more Canadian households have two working adults, and the complications of arranging joint vacation schedules also encourages couples to make numerous short trips rather than to arrange one longer vacation. Also, people are now making decisions about their trips much closer to the time of the trip. Canadians once planned trips six months or even a year in advance; now most trips are planned less than a month before the trips. Sometimes the lead time is only a week or two. The Internet makes last-minute trip planning easier, and the growing trend to take long weekend trips rather than a week or two requires less advance planning.

A *USA Today* report in 2006 estimated that over 50% of workers in full-time jobs took 30 minutes or less on their lunch hour. (Armour, 2006)

Increasingly Sophisticated Travellers

Just hanging out on a sunny, warm salt-water beach used to be a very popular vacation. It still is, especially during our long Canadian winters. However, as people travel more, they begin to want more from their getaways and vacations. There is increasing interest in what is called "experiential travel," travel that allows you to immerse yourself in a culture or activity so that you learn, grow, and discover new things about yourself. Trips that provide the opportunity to experience new cultures, learn new skills, to be pampered at a spa, or to devote yourself to a favourite activity are increasingly popular.

Economic Conditions

Leisure travel requires not only discretionary time, but also discretionary income. Over time, Canadian incomes have risen, allowing more Canadians the opportunity to travel. However, most Canadians are still very conscious of price and look to get a good value in their travel. When the Canadian dollar rises in value against the U.S. dollar, Canadians tend to travel more to the U.S.; when the dollar falls, Canadians tend to stay home. Rising fuel prices also tend to keep people closer to home, as travellers try to control how much they spend on gasoline. Rising fuel costs also hit air travel hard; fuel costs are one of the biggest components in the cost of an airline ticket. The 2008–2010 recession did not reduce overall demand for travel by Canadians, but it did shift demand to closer destinations reachable by car, and often where one could stay with family or friends to reduce costs.

Airline Deregulation

In 1987, the Government of Canada passed the "Freedom to Move Act." One of the major features of this act was to allow airlines the freedom to set their own rates and schedules without having to get them approved by Transport Canada. The Act also allowed any group of investors who had the capital, and were, in the words of the Act, "fit, willing, and able" to start an airline. This meant they had to show that they could acquire insurance and meet safety and aircraft maintenance regulations. The changes meant that the marketplace would generally determine which airlines would succeed or fail, not government policy.

The result has been a dramatic reshaping of the Canadian airline industry. Canadian Airlines International was forced into bankruptcy, allowing Air Canada to emerge as the dominant carrier. However, deregulation encouraged low-cost carriers such as WestJet to enter the market. The airline industry continues to go through restructuring, but deregulation has increased choices for Canadians in terms of domestic flights and substantially reduced air ticket costs. However, this has come at the cost of reduced service; passengers are willing to accept lower service standards in return for cheap prices.

While the dominant trend in the Canadian airline industry is to reduce service in order to reduce the price of tickets, Air Canada has added services in its Executive First cabins. For those people who want a more comfortable environment and are willing to pay for it, Air Canada offers for its international flights a lie-flat bed, an innovative seating arrangement that allows everyone to have direct access to the aisle, privacy screens between seats, more comfortable seats, an oversized tray-table for working, and in-seat power for portable electronic devices.

Internet

The Internet has been one of the most significant changes in tourism marketing in the last decade. Travellers are able to surf the Internet for information on virtually any destination and a great many tourism businesses around the world. A destination or tourism business without a website is at a serious disadvantage in trying to compete for customers. The more sophisticated tourism websites not only provide visitors with current and detailed information, they are designed to encourage people to register on the site—providing information on travel interests and preferences as well as contact information. In return, they are able to receive e-mails offering customized packages or information on travel specials. Some tourism websites allow the user to do a virtual tour of the resort or hotel, golf course, or to observe current conditions through webcams strategically placed at scenic spots.

Potential travellers can often make reservations directly on the Internet with a hotel, airline, rental car company, rail company, or bus company, and they can even order tickets from attractions. Online travel agencies such as Expedia, Orbitz, Hotels.com, Priceline, and Destina consolidate hotel and air travel offerings to offer travellers discount prices. This has created challenges for some companies who have allocated a certain portion of their airline seats or their hotel rooms to these discounters. Consumers increasingly demand access to the fares advertised by the third-party operators, even when booking directly with the original tourism supplier. This situation caused Air Canada, for example, to revise its website to make the range of airfares and associated conditions very clear to the consumer. Air Canada also guarantees that no other website will offer a lower fare than the Air Canada site.

The Internet also allows for more efficient communication among travellers who may have complaints about bad travel experiences, or who simply want to keep in touch with family and friends through e-mail and the sending of digital photographs. The writing of travel blogs or the posting of reviews of hotels and resorts is an increasingly popular activity among traveller and such postings are a growing influence on travel decisions.

Accessibility Concerns

Persons with physical disabilities also like to travel. However, many Canadian businesses and facilities still have work to do in improving the accessibility of their facilities to visitors who might be in wheelchairs, use helper dogs, or have other limitations on their ability to travel. Ensuring accessible design means more than simply providing a wheelchair ramp. Washrooms, for example, need to be designed to meet the needs of persons in wheelchairs. Airplanes, trains, ferries, motor coaches, subways, and other forms of public transportation need to be able to accommodate the needs of travellers with a variety of limitations on mobility. Safety alarms in hotels and other public building should be capable of being perceived by individuals who may be either blind, deaf, or both. Thus, multiple alarm systems are needed. As the Canadian population ages, the need for more accessible tourism facilities and services will grow.

Security Concerns

The rise of terrorist attacks in many parts of the world has made air travel more difficult. There are tighter restrictions on what you can take on board a plane, and security checkpoints at airports often pose a bottleneck to the smooth flow of travellers. If your flight is to the United States and you have to pre-clear customs at the airport, the combination of security clearances and customs clearances can sometimes take up to two hours. Some travellers now claim that they are reducing their use of air carriers for pleasure travel because the hassles have become too onerous.

Land-based international travel has also become more tedious. While land crossings into the United States are still often fairly speedy, with no more than a 10- or 15-minute wait, crossings on holidays or at times of a security alert can hold you up for three or four hours. In the autumn of 2005, Canadian custom officers walked off the job for an entire afternoon as a protest to be allowed to carry firearms to protect themselves against possible terrorists. Their actions shut down some of the busiest crossings between Canada and the United States for hours, creating substantial resentment in the travelling public.

The Western Hemisphere Travel Initiative (WHTI) requires anyone entering the United States from a foreign country—including American citizens returning home—to have a passport. The new regulations temporarily reduced the number of trips made by Canadians to the United States by 2008, but the rising Canadian dollar offset the losses by encouraging Canadians to travel in this country. However, the number of Americans coming to Canada has dropped dramatically. There are numerous reasons for this, but concerns over border-crossing formalities is a major contributor. The WHTI will likely encourage more Canadians to travel domestically, although the increase in domestic Canadian travel will not likely offset the losses from reduced American travel to Canada.

Even before the increase in terrorism attacks, Americans were less likely than Canadians to travel internationally. Historically, only about 20% of Americans carried passports. This has risen to 34% in 2005. Many of these do not use the passport for international travel, but use it as a secure form of proof of identity. Over 40% of Canadians have passports, and this rises to 70% of those who travel to the U.S. by car.

A study by Smith and Xie (2003) looked at the impact of the border on the travel patterns of U.S. residents to Canada. They found that, depending on the state, the Canada–United States border acted as if it added from 500 to 3,700 km of travel to the trip. In other words, the number of trips by American from one state to the Canadian province just across the border was reduced by an amount equal to the effect of having to travel up to an additional 3,700 km.

The Future of Leisure Travel

Tourism continues to evolve. As we have already discussed, one of the forces shaping travel in recent years has been the experience of "time poverty," the sense that people are unable to take the time for longer trips. This will continue to be a concern into the future, although as the baby boom generation retires, a large portion of the population will begin to have more discretionary time. This is a generation that has discovered the pleasures of travel and as long as their health and finances permit, they are likely to travel even more. As experienced and sophisticated travellers, they will be looking for novel experiences, personalized attention, and excellent value. They are knowledgeable consumers and tourism businesses will need to be sure to provide them with credible information and to deliver on promises. Many will be interested in travelling to offshore destinations, as long as security and health concerns can be addressed. Many of the children of the baby boom generation, "Gen-X" have grown up with travel as a normal part of their lives. They will travel more than their parents did at the same age. Thus, we can expect to see continued long-term growth in the tourism sector.

Packaging—the combining of accommodation, transportation, and activities into a single tourism offering—will also continue to grow in importance. However, as many destinations and tour companies have already learned, many experienced travellers do not necessarily want pre-packaged tours. The market for the traditional escorted tour will continue to decline as more people gain experience and confidence in making their own travel decisions and purposes. Travellers increasingly want to be able to create customized packages that cater to their specific needs and interests. The Internet will be a powerful tool to help this happen.

There will be increasing diversity in the range of products offered to Canadian leisure travellers. Tourism businesses are under continuous pressure to come up with new experiences and products to attract repeat business as well as to draw new customers. The whole range of emerging tourism experiences is too great to discuss here, but some of the trends that are already emerging include the following.

A growing number of hotel guests seek small-scale, luxury hotels (known as boutique hotels) that provide their guests with highly trained hotel staff and upscale amenities. These hotels, usually with only 20 or 30 rooms, focus on providing discreet, personalized service including fine dining, beautiful rooms with very high quality mattresses and appointments, luxury bathroom furnishings, and attentive staff trained to respond to their customers' requests for show tickets, flowers and wine in the room, individually chosen music CDs and movie DVDs, and spa services. The feeling of the guests who can afford this type of service is that, having earned their money to pay for an upscale getaway, they are entitled to the best service possible.

Another tourism product that emphasizes service and convenience is the cruise industry. Cruising has been around since the early 1970s, as the market for trans-Atlantic liners collapsed when commercial jet travel across the Atlantic began. The cruise lines had to reposition their liners from being a form of transportation to becoming floating resorts. Only 15% of North Americans have been on a cruise (Kerstetter et al., 2005) yet many say this is a dream vacation for them, so there is substantial potential for the market to grow. Cruise ships vary in size, market position, and experiences offered. At one end are small luxury ships that may carry only 100 passengers, such as those of Le Lavant, which sails the Great Lakes. Le Lavant and similar cruise lines feature educational cruises as well as honeymoon packages for two weeks or longer. At the other end are mega-ships carrying thousands of passengers, on trips lasting from one- or two-night "booze cruises" to month-long cruises. Royal Caribbean's *Oasis of the Seas* is, at the time of writing, the world's largest cruise ship, carrying over 6,000 passengers.

The cruise industry knows that if they can get you to take one cruise, you will likely come back for other cruises, eventually taking more expensive and longer trips. So the variety of products offered not only allows them to cater to different market segments, it is a way of attracting new cruise passengers knowing they will likely become confirmed "cruisers."

Cruising has traditionally been associated with places like the Caribbean, Mexico, and the Mediterranean. However, Alaskan cruises have grown substantially in recent years with many ships stopping in Vancouver on their way north. Atlantic Canada has also seen the start of a cruise industry, with ships stopping at Halifax, Saint John, and as far inland as Quebec City. The next stage of development will be the expansion of Great Lake cruises as a niche cruising product.

Spa tourism is one of the most rapidly growing product segments in Canadian tourism, driven by the rising interest in health and alternative treatments to ensure a healthy life. Spas are particularly popular with middle-aged, well-educated women, but men are now beginning to patronize spas more frequently. For women, the focus is on aesthetics, nutrition, and health. Men tend to patronize spas for relaxation and for stress relief. Most spas are day spas, drawing people for a few hours from the immediate area. However, there are an increasing number of destination spas where guests stay from one to three nights. Some are located in hotels such as those in the Fairmont Hotels and Resorts chain; others are independent establishments, usually located in attractive rural settings. Destination spas offer a range of aesthetic treatments such as facials, pedicures, and body wraps; various forms of massage; exercise programs; educational programs, usually on some aspect of healthy living; and fine dining. Sports such as golf, tennis, swimming, and horseback riding may also be available.

One of the newest tourism experiences to emerge in Canada is culinary tourism. Culinary tourism refers to any tourism trip during which the consumption, tasting, appreciation, or purchase of Canadian food products is an important component. Thus, visiting a winery during a trip and tasting wines would be a form of culinary tourism. So, too, would be dining at a restaurant featuring dishes made with local foods, visiting farmers markets, going to a cooking school, visiting a pick-your-own farm operation, or attending a food festival. The central feature of culinary tourism is that it centres on local or regional foods. In other words, it is not simply dining at well-known or expensive restaurants. Rather, the focus is on experiencing the foods produced in a given region as part of the culture of that region.

What food or drink products are produced in the region in which you live? Do restaurants feature these on their menus? If not, what do you think the reasons are?

Culinary tourism has long been associated with certain places such as Tuscany, Italy; Guangzhou, China; Provence, France; and New Orleans, United States. Unlike these places that have distinctive styles of cooking that are known worldwide, Canada lacks any distinctive cuisine. However, what we do have are hundreds very high quality local ingredients, including grains, vegetables, fruits, fish, meats, cheeses, beer, and wines. Quebec has the best developed culinary tourism products, including excellent local beers, artisinal cheeses and breads, specialty meats, and, of course, many superb restaurants featuring local products. British Columbia, especially on Vancouver Island and in the Okanagan, has also begun to promote local products as part of the visit to those regions. Seafood, wines, cheeses, and vegetables produced and sold locally through farmers markets, shops, and restaurants have become important tourism draws for visitors. Now other provinces are recognizing the potential of food and drink as a way of attracting visitors as well as helping to generate income for family farms. Further, by buying local ingredients, consumers can help reduce the environmental impacts associated with restaurants and stores having to ship in products from perhaps thousands of kilometres.

Once the stuff of science fiction, the idea of people making leisure trips into outer space has come true. Only three people (Dennis Tito, an American investment banker; Mark Shuttleworth, a South African Internet entrepreneur; and Greg Olsen, an American businessman and amateur scientist, have ventured into space. All three flew on the Russian Soyez rocket to the International Space Station, at the cost of $20 million per trip. At that price, there won't be many people making the trip, but there is substantial demand if the price comes down. A study in 1997 in the U.S. National Leisure Travel Monitor found that of 1,500 people surveyed, 42% said they would like to travel into space and would pay an average of $10,800. Would you go into space if given the chance, and how much would you be willing to pay?

For more information on space tourism, check out the Space Tourism Society at *www.spacetourismsociety.org*

Conclusion

Leisure travel is an important form of leisure behaviour for many Canadians and is done in every part of Canada. Taking trips, whether same-day or overnight, is a way for people to relax, learn about their country, enjoy new experiences and favourite activities, and to keep in touch with family and friends. Leisure travel also contributes to the Canadian economy, generating tens of billions of dollars in revenues and supporting hundreds of thousands of jobs. Activities associated with leisure travel can also create environmental and social impacts. Air pollution from cars, traffic congestion, and overuse of popular tourism sites or environmentally sensitive areas can often be seen as effects created by leisure travel. On the other hand, the ability to visit and enjoy historic and scenic areas can help generate the political pressure to save them for future use.

Social impacts can also be both positive and negative. Travel allows people to get to know other individuals and cultures. This can help overcome mistrust or misunderstanding between different groups. On the other hand, the presence of too many strangers in small towns, especially if the visitors do not show respect for local culture and customs can cause anger and resentment.

While leisure travel is usually very enjoyable and sometimes seen as glamorous and exciting, it needs research and careful management to ensure that as more and more Canadians travel, they and the places they visit will be able to enjoy the benefits leisure travel can bring. At the same time, research and management is needed to minimize and control the problems leisure travel can cause.

Key Terms

Tourism
Visitor
Same-day travel
Overnight travel
Tourism industry
Tourism commodity
Tourism trends

References

Armour, S. (2006). Lunch break becomes briefer as lunch "hour" shrinks. *USA Today.* Retrieved from http://www.usatoday.com/money/economy/employment/2006-06-11-no-lunch-hour-usat_x.htm

Kerstetter, D. L., Yen, I-Y., & Yarnal, C. M. (2005). Plowing uncharted waters: A study of perceived constraints to cruise travel. *Tourism Analysis, 10*, 137–150.

Smith, S. L. J., & Xie, P. (2003). Estimating the distance equivalence of the Canada–U.S. border on U.S.-to-Canada visitor flows. *Journal of Travel Research, 42*, 191–194.

Statistics Canada. (2006). *Census of Canada*. Ottawa, ON: Statistics Canada.

Statistics Canada. (2008a). *Travel survey of residents of Canada*. Ottawa, ON: Statistics Canada.

Statistics Canada. (2008b). *International Travel Survey*. Ottawa, ON: Statistics Canada.

World Tourism Organization. (1994). *Recommendations on tourism statistics*. Madrid, Spain: World Tourism Organization.

World Tourism Organization. (2003). *Tourism highlights*. Madrid, Spain: World Tourism Organization.

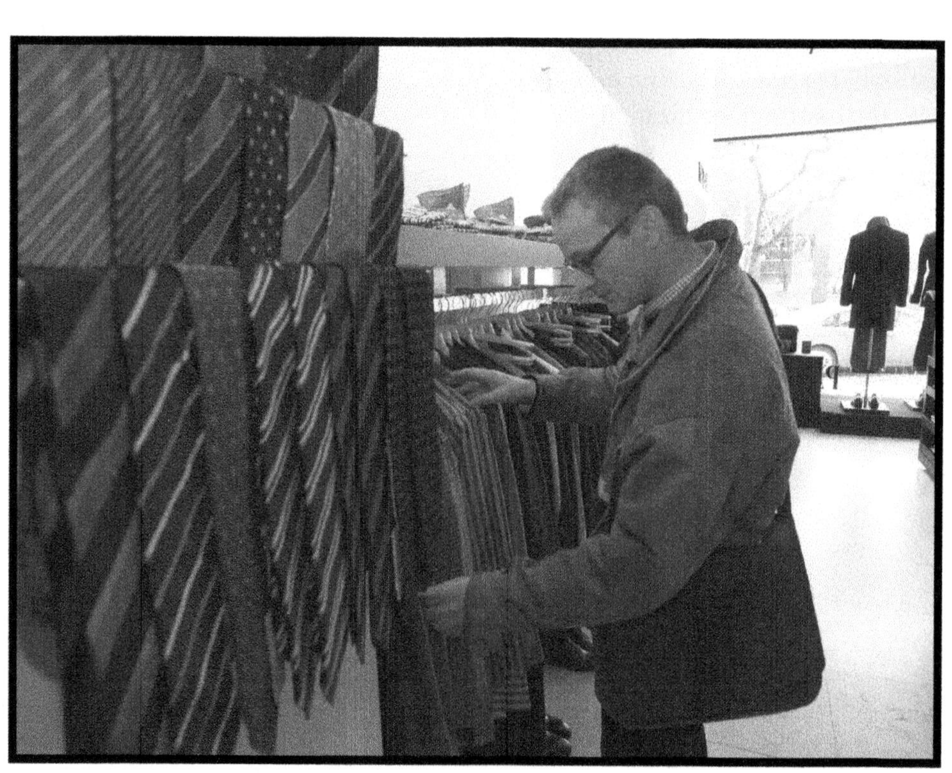

Chapter 13
Shopping as Leisure

Ron McCarville, Ph.D.
University of Waterloo

Learning Objectives

After reading this chapter, students will be able to

1. Understand some of the complexity surrounding leisure in everyday living.
2. Understand how shopping can be considered as both work and leisure.
3. Understand the bases for shopping's leisure (hedonic) designation.
4. Understand the potentially dark side of shopping.

Introduction

The chapters in this textbook explore the complexity of leisure in everyday life. The purpose of this chapter is to discuss how leisure activity, something that might appear simple and straightforward, can be complex and even contradictory. The topic of this chapter, shopping, offers a case in point. When you think about it, shopping should be a chore. Shopping is a way to acquire those things we want and need. It is a search for what consumer behaviorists call a payoff (Bloch, Ridgway, & Sherrell, 1989). We seek the benefits offered by goods and services, and shopping is the time we spend searching for these things in outlets, both real and virtual.

From this perspective, shopping seems very work-like. Indeed, people often talk about the drudgery of shopping. For example, Miller (1998) conducted a year-long ethnography of shopping within 76 North London (England) households and discovered that any "pleasure of shopping was non-existent because … shopping was always carried out under the constraints of competition for the time spent shopping" (p. 69). Miller went on to observe that even retired persons felt pressed for time while shopping, so the task seemed universally onerous.

Even the most casual observer, though, would tell you that shopping is not all drudgery. Gill (2005) recalls standing in front of St. Peter's Basilica in Rome, where he observed an Italian teenager wearing a T-shirt with the slogan "shopping makes me happy" (p. 79). This teen was clearly not alone. Schor (2004) reports a national U.S. study in which "more than a third of all children aged nine to fourteen would rather spend time buying things than doing almost anything else" (p. 37).

While shopping has its detractors, we cannot ignore the extent of shopping behavior in our society. Shopping is a pervasive daily activity in which millions of Canadians take part. For example, 22 million people visit the West Edmonton Mall each year, a number that is 7 times the population of Alberta (TripleFive Group of Companies, 2008). The number of participants far exceeds those who take part in other "types" of leisure settings. Given that thousands of malls and retail outlets dot the landscape throughout the industrialized world, one begins to appreciate the scope of shopping activity within Western society.

What is your shopping profile? How often do you shop? What is your favourite shopping location? How long did your last shopping trip last?

The leisure literature has often speculated that shopping could be leisure. In their essay on leisure as symbolic consumption, Dimanche and Samdahl (1994) discussed "shopping during leisure" and "leisure shopping" (p. 123). They concluded that shopping was a legitimate leisure activity in which identity and self-expression might be pursued. Another early effort by Johnson and Mannell (1983) studied the shopping mall as a leisure environment. Each of these efforts draws attention to the leisure potential within shopping experiences and settings.

Klaffke (2003) observed that "For some shopping is an art; for others, it's a sport. It can be a vice and it can be a cause. Some love it. Some hate it. Rarely is someone indifferent" (p. 1). Why does shopping create such an emotional response among shoppers and non-shoppers alike?

As we ponder everyday activities like shopping, it is important for us to ask questions like "why?" Why and when can an activity that some describe as drudgery also be considered as fun? This chapter seeks to answer that question. Let's explore the dynamics of the shopping experience, looking for the why and when.

The Dark Side of Shopping

We should first acknowledge that any discussion of shopping is complicated by the politically charged nature of the activity itself. Shopping involves much more than the simple collection of goods and services. Indeed, it "carries with it anti-feminist, anti-environmental, and anti-intellectual baggage" (McCracken, 1990, p. 15). Think about it. The shopping experience is largely controlled by commercial forces. Commercialism is the process through which goods, services, and even experiences are reduced to the status of commodities, something to be bought and sold (Butsch, 1990). Butsch suggests that such efforts represent a process of exploitation that seeks to objectify and control experiences. Such exploitation may be inconsistent with notions of leisure.

That is why Hemingway (1996) argued that commercialism and leisure form an unhappy pairing. He notes that over the last century, commercial forces have commodified leisure "to be marketed and sold as any other commodity" (p. 34). He laments that leisure has been transformed from a force for liberation and change to one of social control. Where once leisure was intended to emancipate, it has been reduced to the status of a novelty designed to amuse and distract.

The influence of commercialism is noteworthy. Over the last century, "American business began to create a new set of commercial enticements—a commercial aesthetic—to move and sell goods in volume . . . offering a vision of the good life and of paradise" (Leach, 1993, p. 9). This vision "pushed out all others" (Leach, p. xv). Since that time, "a very different concept of society ... emerged—a consuming public, defined and developed by individual acquisition and the use of mass-produced goods" (Cross, 2000, p. 1). The emergence of mass consumerism is tied to a variety of conditions, ranging from resource depletion, global warming, and waste (Cohen, 2003) to a collective sense of unhappiness (Scitovsky, 1992). For these reasons, many leisure scholars are unhappy when we speak of shopping activity as leisure activity.

Further, there seems an implicit understanding that shopping is linked to materialism, the belief that possessions give meaning to our lives (Schor, 2004). Individuals described as materialistic tend to link pleasure, status, and satisfaction with the acquisition of possessions. In fact, materialism is negatively correlated with life satisfaction (Wang & Wallendorf, 2006). The more we seek meaning through buying things, the less satisfied we become. In the end, materialism can lead to meaningless spending, environmental damage, and unhappy populations. It is perhaps little wonder that "We know from popular opinion and social scientific study that our materialism is one of the things that is most wrong with our society, and one of the most significant causes of our modern difficulties" (McCracken, 1990, p. 1). As a result, materialistic pursuits are viewed as poor substitutes for more legitimate forms of leisure (Scitovsky, 1992).

It gets worse. Shopping activity raises many gender-based concerns. Specifically, the task of shopping is often imposed on women. Fiske (1989) reports that

> as capitalism developed throughout the nineteenth century it produced and naturalized first the nuclear family as the foundation social unit, and second a new and specific role for women within this unit and thus within the social formation at large. The woman became the domestic manager of both the economic and emotional resources of the family. (pp. 311–312)

This pattern has not been lost on corporate advertisers who, over much of the last hundred years, maintained a steady stream of messages designed to cajole women into purchasing their products. They have done so primarily by "spread[ing] the word that a woman who did not purchase the growing array of consumer goods was jeopardizing her family, and missing out on the best life had to offer" (Schor, 1991, p. 97).

Taken together, these perspectives suggest that shopping can be inconsistent with positive and meaningful leisure experience. Consequently, leisure researchers often dismiss consumption-based activities like shopping in favor of more "constructive" forms of leisure (Cook, 2006). This chapter takes the position that, given its complexity, shopping is exactly the sort of leisure activity we should be exploring. To ignore it creates what Cook (2006) labels an "existentialist" debate in which issues are discussed as good or bad, right or wrong. He notes that such a debate fails to capture the complexity of daily living. McCracken (1990) agrees, suggesting that efforts to, for example, demonize consumption present a "familiar and entirely wrongheaded idea [that] helps keep us from seeing the cultural significances of consumption plainly" (p. 1). Both Cook (2006) and Deem (1999) suggest that consumptive activities (like shopping) may provide fertile ground for better understanding the complexity of the leisure experience.

In this chapter, I take the perspective that shopping is "not inherently good or bad, but it is deeply human" (Hine, 2002, p. 2). I view the act of shopping not through a "consumerism" lens but from an experiential perspective. My goal is to explore shopping, not as an exercise in consumption, but rather as a potential leisure experience. I will separate shopping from its consumerism and materialistic baggage and explore it as a pursuit often chosen by people in their leisure time. The focus here will be on the experience itself.

What Other Fields Are Saying about Shopping

To begin, shopping is very much a part of everyday living. That is why it has been studied for years in the anthropological (McCracken, 1990), consumer behavior (Arnold & Reynolds, 2003), and tourism (Hsieh & Chang, 2006) literatures. Each literature recognizes the recreational potential of the shopping experience, and all place the activity within sociocultural, experiential, or symbolic contexts as they seek to understand the activity (Backstrom, 2006). The anthropological perspective has attempted to discuss shopping activity within the larger social fabric of the community. Discussions on the topic have been far-reaching. Some, like Hine (2002), discuss the importance of shopping as a means of simple acquisition. We shop to acquire new things. Others, like McCracken (1990), deal with the more symbolic elements of shopping activity. These researchers consider why we buy name-brand products or why we shop in some stores and not others. They seek to discover why one brand becomes popular while another fades.

Still other researchers have focused on the collective and individual results of shopping (Schor & Holt, 2000). This line of research focuses on the effects of materialism and mass consumption. Are people who shop happier or more content that those who shop less? Is shopping linked to well-being?

The intent within all these approaches seems generally to be one of understanding the role, place, and meaning of shopping within the larger social context. The overwhelming conclusion of anthropological research on shopping suggests that shopping represents a profoundly political ground upon which norms are reproduced and resisted, where identities are shaped, and rewards are negotiated. It represents an arena where the "micro-politics of everyday life" (Raisborough & Bhatti, 2007) are played out. Hine (2002) sums up the anthropological view when he observes that "the acquisition and use of objects, while not unique to our species, is one of our defining characteristics" (Hine, 2002, p. x).

The consumer behavior and tourism literatures have focused more directly on understanding the motives, search patterns, and preferences of the shopper. These literatures have long assumed that shopping has a "fun side" (Babin, Darden, & Griffin, 1994; Hsieh & Chang, 2006). Within this more commercially based literature, the shopping experience has been described in terms of excitement (Wakefield & Baker, 1998), satisfaction (Westbrook & Oliver, 1991), pleasure (Machleit & Eroglu, 2000), and exploration (Miller, 1998). Each of these characteristics seems consistent with notions of leisure and recreation (Unger & Kernan, 1983; Mannell & Kleiber, 1997; Schulz & Watkins, 2007; Watkins & Bond, 2007). Let's explore, in more detail, the origins of shopping's fun side.

When is Leisure Thought to Occur?

The theme I have been exploring in this chapter is the potential of shopping to be both work and play. Why might the same activity (shopping) be labeled as drudgery in one case and as leisure in another? To answer this question we must understand what constitutes a leisure experience. Considerable effort within the social psychological research community has focused on the definitional characteristics of leisure. The goal of this research thread has been one of delineating conditions under which participants would consider leisure to be present (Mannell & Kleiber, 1997). Generally, this literature tells us that leisure is a subjective experience (Neulinger, 1974). Specifically, participants are more likely to regard an experience as leisure when they believe that specific conditions have been fulfilled. Once they define the experience as leisure, it becomes leisure.

Early discussions of these conditions focused on perceptions of relative freedom or choice, intrinsic motivation, and pleasurable involvement (Unger & Kernan, 1983). For example, Jansen-Verbeke (1987) observed that shopping could be a leisure activity when it was undertaken "by one's own free choice" (p. 71). In other words, shopping could be a leisure activity if it was freely chosen by the participant. If the activity is freely chosen, then it is more likely to be considered as leisure activity (Mannell & Kleiber, 1997).

Since that time the basic "attributes" (Mannell & Kleiber) or "properties" (Watkins & Bond, 2007) that characterize a leisure event have emerged. They include sense of separation or escape, opportunity for identity development, spontaneity, and adventure or exploration. The presence of these attributes or properties is indicative of a leisure episode. This is the case regardless of the setting. Consequently, even work activity can be considered as leisure when these conditions are present (Mannell & Kleiber, 1997).

The Importance of Meaning

Leisure scholars also tell us that the meaning we assign to an activity can also make it seem more or less leisure-like. Meaning refers to the individual's subjective reaction to an activity or event (Szalay & Bryson, 1974). Meaning arises from the actual experience and the way in which symbols within the experience are interpreted. It is this interpretation of events that establishes the leisure potential of any given episode. For example, Dupuis and Smale (2000) reported that female caregivers could view caregiving as emotionally draining but also as a source of identity and power. The same activity could have very different meanings for the participant. This may help explain why shopping can be both work and leisure. Different subjective assessments by the participants encourage different conclusions by those participants.

One explanation for the differential application of meanings is that of positioning. Positioning is a process "through which individuals locate themselves through existing (and shifting) identities" (Raisborough & Bhatti, 2007, p. 472). Shoppers may position a shopping episode as an obligation forced on them by family commitments or as an opportunity to seek out new possibilities. By doing so, they actively negotiate between "various possibilities and restraints created and imposed by others" (Raisborough & Bhatti, 2007, p. 472). As you might imagine, the position that is adopted can have a dramatic influence on the way the shopper views shopping activity.

Consequently, shopping settings would seem to offer a fertile time and space for positioning. Within the shopping context, shoppers can adopt various roles and identities, express their individuality, and exercise choices that explore who they are and want to be. Doing so may help them "piece together a coherent selfhood" (Kelly, 1983, p. 103). Shoppers can search for items that help them express who they are and who they hope to be. This may be the case even if shopping is obligatory. They may have to shop, but if they position it as an opportunity for self-expression, the shopping activity may become less work-like.

Let's consider now the various elements of a shopping experience. As we link together these elements, think of reasons why they might influence shoppers' assessment of that event.

Types of Shopping

The business literature suggests two basic shopping categories. The first is economic or utilitarian shopping undertaken for extrinsically motivated reasons. This is shopping done to complete a task. The shopper might be picking up paint or bread. The goal is to simply fulfill a requirement. This type of shopping is thought to be work-like in its orientation and experientially unsatisfying (Backstrom, 2006).

Conversely, hedonic (pleasurable) or recreational shopping is motivated more by the search for fun than the search for value (Babin et al., 1994). We know, for example, that during recreational shopping, the purchase of goods is sometimes incidental to the larger shopping experience. Indeed, positive emotional responses may emerge even in the absence of purchase behavior (Langrehr, 1991). Hirschman (1980) speculated that, for recreational shoppers, the acquisition of products may be less important than the opportunity to spend time with friends or to enjoy the sensory stimulation offered by many retail environments. In such cases, shoppers may seek what Downs (1961) called non-purchase pay-offs. They are taking part in order to experience emotional and hedonistic benefits rather than goods and services. Sherry (1990) suggests that the importance of these emotional experiences may "prove far more significant than the mere acquisition of products" (p. 27). It is not surprising, then, that shopping can be an intensely emotional experience.

The Importance of the Setting

McIntyre and Roggenbuck (1998) suggest that leisure potential emerges from person–environment interactions. Shoppers typically visit retail settings in order to search for those things they desire. As they process all the stimuli they see and hear and smell, they help create their own experiences. One shopper may see a mall as noisy, crowded, and chaotic, whereas another views the same mall as an opportunity for fun and adventure. As such, participants are not passive subjects who simply react to the characteristics of the setting in which they find themselves. Instead, they take an active role in interpreting and manipulating stimuli from their environment. In this way, a retail setting is similar to more traditional leisure settings. It offers the opportunity for participants to actively create experiences in which personal goals are sought and sense of self is explored.

Much of the modern shopping experience is characterized by the prominent display of objects for sale wrapped in an often dramatic setting. The intended effect is to offer shoppers the opportunity to pursue fantasy fulfillment and escape (Babin et al., 1994). The current trend is often traced to the Great Crystal Palace Exhibition of 1851. The exhibition was housed in a dramatic glass and iron structure, built on 14 acres in Hyde Park in London, with over 772,784 square feet of floor space (Klaffke, 2003).

> Never before had the public been aware that there were so many things to need or want or . . . buy. The Great Exhibition filled the minds of the masses with images of cultural wares, practical goods which incorporated new technologies, and—most importantly—frivolous things they didn't previously know they craved. (Klaffke, 2003, p. 27)

Klaffke (2003) goes on to note that the exhibition introduced an element of wonder and fun into the often mundane process of shopping. The interest generated in the exhibit was not lost on retailers. They were quick to respond:

> By 1900 department store retailers tried to conceal from customers the bleaker parts of the stores, not only with mirrors but also by segregating the bookkeeping floors ... clearly from the merchandising ones. As late as World War I, Macy's in New York was still struggling to complete the isolation of its "nonselling employees" on the undecorated high floors. (Leach, 1993, p. 75)

By doing so, retailers are engaged in what Gieryn (2000) classified as "place-making." They are attempting to create a space that is not simply visited, but rather experienced by the shopper. They do so by filling their respective spaces with novelty, opportunity, and stimulation (Bloch, et al., 1989). As a result, shopping venues serve not only a utilitarian but also a hedonic function (Johnson & Mannell, 1983).

Shopping as a Means of Values Clarification

Of particular interest to this discussion, shopping has been linked to values clarification and identity development. For example, Miller (1998) found that values manifested through shopping (thrift, respectability, conscientiousness, etc.) often conformed to shoppers' values in other domains of life. In other words, shopping offered a way to express and reinforce values.

For some shoppers, shopping offers a potentially unique setting for resisting expectations imposed on them by others. Miller (1998) offered the example of Mary who, while living in poverty, used shopping as a way to resist the daily demands that were being placed upon her. While she knew that she was expected to be careful with the little money she had, she would sometimes resist such expectations by spending money on non-essential objects and services. As Miller notes, "while she understands that thrift is admired as a skill, she simply does not desire to be that kind of person" (p. 64). She used shopping as a way of resisting expectations that had been placed on her.

Shopping may even involve lifestyle clarification for the shopper and for those around the shopper. As Miller (1998) again suggests, while shopping for loved ones, "The shopper is not merely buying goods for others, but hoping to influence these others into becoming the kind of people who would be the appropriate recipients for that which is being bought" (p. 8). This suggests that behavioral choices within the shopping experience are influenced by self-referenced meanings (Dimanche & Samdahl, 1994). Shopping activity can help clarify and support the image we wish to present to others (and to ourselves).

Think of your own shopping choices. Do your shopping choices serve to meet or resist the expectations of others?

Shopping as a Source of Achievement

The search for mastery within uncertain or complex settings has been highlighted in a variety of theoretical perspectives ranging from the concept of flow (Csikszentmihalyi, 1990) to the arousal-seeking model (Ellis, 1973). It seems clear that pleasure can result when participants use their own skill to succeed in uncertain situations. As a mountain climber once observed, "The climber likes difficult pitches, even those which tax him [sic] to the utmost, but in such cases, it is as pleasant for him to feel safe, in his heart of hearts, as it is unpleasant to go beyond his resources, to run a risk, or to incur some climbing hazard" (Mitchell, 1983, p. 157).

The appeal, it seems, is in applying knowledge and skill such that complexity is reduced and issues are resolved. In this way, decisions and consequences are linked. Competence is tested and, if successful, achievement is enjoyed. A "pleasant" sensation results (Manfredo, Driver, & Tarrant, 1996; Watkins & Bond, 2007). This sensation can have a profound effect upon participants' sense of well-being and future behavior patterns (Ryff, 1989; Propst & Koesler, 1998; Sylvia-Bobiak & Caldwell, 2006).

We know that shopping is an activity that can be characterized by many feelings of accomplishment. It offers an interactive setting presenting the shopper with both challenges and opportunities. As Hine (2002) suggests, the shopper must constantly answer the questions of everyday living: "What will we feed our families? How will they be clothed? What tools are needed to survive and prosper?" (p. x). Given that shopping is, at its core, a search for value (Babin et al., 1994), it represents an ongoing negotiation between spending and saving, between acquisition and loss.

Participants must constantly search the environment for opportunities to acquire that which they desire without giving up too much in the process. Success while doing so may generate perceptions of mastery. For example, shoppers interviewed by Miller (1998) took considerable pride in applying the principle of thrift during their shopping endeavors. Indeed, he referred to thrifty shopping as a "skill" (p. 63) that was much sought after by the vast majority of his informants: "It is . . . reasonable to see thrift as an end in itself—that is, people are going shopping in order to have the experience of saving money. For some the thrill is in the bargain and it almost doesn't matter how much one spends in order to achieve it [and] thrift itself is as important a factor in shopping for the wealthy as it is for the poor" (p. 61).

This notion of the bargain may be particularly appealing for some shoppers. They may receive considerable satisfaction from something as simple as redeeming coupons (Larson, 1994). Larson found that such redemptions assured the shoppers that discounts had been gained and their sense of value was enhanced. When savings are enjoyed, perceptions of value are increased (Holbrook, 1986), and a positive emotional response is likely (Oliver, 1993). It seems clear that shopping, like more traditional leisure activities, has the potential to create profound feelings of achievement.

Concluding Comments

Taken together, these insights suggest that shopping can be both problematic and compelling. It is problematic because it is inherently consumptive. Further, retail settings, within which shopping typically occurs, are controlled by commercial forces. These forces have, for decades, been promoting the appeal of shopping and fueling a largely materialistic vision among shoppers. We know too that the obligation to shop is often imposed on women, who must already fight for and negotiate personal leisure time (Raisborough & Bhatti, 2007).

We must also acknowledge, though, that shopping can be compelling. There are many reasons for its appeal. It occurs in novelty-rich environments (Bloch et al., 1989). It represents a search and involves choice. Both can help clarify and support personal value systems. As a result, shopping carries with it the potential to diminish as well as empower the individual. It can add novelty as we pursue the demands of work, family, and relationships. Parameters between obligation and leisure are blurred; work and leisure were blended as roles are fulfilled and leisure is experienced (Kelly & Kelly, 1994). In the case of hedonic shopping, both work and leisure seem to be blended so that one activity is indistinguishable from the other. While shopping may be a form of work, it also represents an important leisure setting. The best leisure experiences offer fulfillment, the potential to escape pressure, to exercise choice, and to pass time (Watkins & Bond, 2007). All seem possible within shopping activities.

Reproduction and Resistance

As suggested above, shopping seems an activity laden with gender expectations. Women often shop for family members as part of their roles as household managers. In this way, shopping activities seem very much an exercise in conformity. Shopping activities serve to perpetuate the role expectations that have traditionally been imposed on women. For some, then, shopping activity tends to "reproduce" and encourage stereotypical roles for women.

In other ways, however, shopping activities may represent an opportunity to resist traditional role obligations; to reclaim time and space for participants' own purposes. Household demands may have started the shopping ball rolling, as it were, but the exercise need not end there. Parry (2005) observed that "active creation of leisure spaces, times, and activities may empower or otherwise support women to resist [dominant] ideology" (p. 133). The literature suggests that hedonic shopping can facilitate such "active creation." As such, shopping may both reproduce and resist traditional role expectations. Raisborough and Bhatti (2007) use the story of Joy, who blended both homemaking and gardening activities in ways that offered a creative repositioning of gendered norms. Such repositioning involved "negotiations and interactions with others within shifting power relations of social contexts and rhythms of the life course" (p. 460). They conclude that women's agency may have a "more complex and negotiated nature than can be realized from reproduction/resistance frameworks" (p. 460).

Shopping activity is often a result of obligation, and this obligation is not randomly distributed within the traditional household. It is a task typically assigned to women within that household. How do such expectations play out for women shoppers? Do they shop as a result of obligation or is there something more at work? Under what conditions might shopping activities reproduce or resist stereotypical role expectations for women shoppers?

Key Terms

Consumption
Consumerism
Commercialism
Leisure
Hedonic shopping
Utilitarian shopping
Values clarification
Achievement

References

Arnold, M. J., & Reynolds, K. E. (2003). Hedonic shopping motivations. *Journal of Retailing, 79*, 77–95.

Babin, B. J., Darden, W. R., & Griffin, M. (1994). Work and/or fun: Measuring hedonic and utilitarian shopping value. *Journal of Consumer Research, 20*, 644–656.

Backstrom, K. (2006). Understanding recreational shopping: A new approach. *International Review of Retail, Distribution, and Consumer Research, 16*, 143–158.

Bloch, P. H., Ridgway, N. M., & Sherrell, D. L. (1989). Extending the concept of shopping: An investigation of browsing activity. *Academy of Marketing Science, 17*, 13.

Butsch, R. (1990). Leisure and hegemony in America. In R. Butsch (Ed.), *For fun and profit: The transformation of leisure into consumption* (pp. 3–27). Philadelphia, PA: Temple University Press.

Cohen, L. (2003). *A consumers' republic: The politics of mass consumption in postwar America*. New York, NY: Alfred A. Knopf.

Cook, D. T. (2006). Problematizing consumption, community, and leisure: Some thoughts on moving beyond essentialist thinking. *Leisure, 30*, 455–466.

Cross, G. (2000). *An all-consuming century: Why commercialism won in modern America*. New York, NY: Columbia University Press.

Csikszentmihalyi, M. (1990). *Flow: The psychology of optimal experience*. New York, NY: Harper & Row Publishers.

Deem, R. (1999). How do we get out of the ghetto? Strategies for research on gender and leisure for the twenty-first century. *Leisure Studies, 18*, 161–177.

Dimanche, F., & Samdahl, D. (1994). Leisure as symbolic consumption: A conceptualization and prospectus for future research. *Leisure Sciences, 16*, 119–129.

Downs, Anthony. (1961). A theory of consumer efficiency. *Journal of Retailing, 37*, 6–12, 50.

Dupuis, S. L., & Smale, B. J. (2000). Bittersweet journeys: Meanings of leisure in the institution-based caregiving context. *Journal of Leisure Research, 32*, 303–340.

Ellis, M. J. (1973). *Why people play*. Englewood Cliffs, NJ: Prentice Hall.

Fiske, John (1989). Shopping for pleasure: Malls, power and resistance. In J. B. Schor and D. B. Holt (Eds.), *The consumer society* (pp. 306-328). New York, NY: The New Press.

Gieryn, T. F. (2000). A space for place in sociology. *Annual Review of Sociology, 26*, 463–496.

Gill, A. (2005, December). The future of shopping. *Air Canada EnRoute Magazine*, pp. 12, 78–83.

Guiry, M., Magi, A. W., & Lutz, R. J. (2006). Defining and measuring recreational shopper identity. *Journal of the Academy of Marketing Science, 34*, 74–83.

Hemingway, J. L. (1996). Emancipating leisure: The recovery of freedom in leisure. *Journal of Leisure Research, 28*, 27–43.

Hine, T. (2002). *I want that! How we all became shoppers*. New York, NY: Harper Collins.

Hirschman, E. C. (1980). Innovativeness, novelty seeking, and consumer creativity. *Journal of Consumer Research, 7*(3), 283–295.

Holbrook, M. B. (1986). Emotion in the consumption experience: Toward a new model of the human consumer. In R. Peterson, W. Hoyer, & W. Wilson (Eds.), *The Role of affect in consumer behavior: Emerging theories and applications* (pp. 17–52). Lexington, MA: Lexington Books.

Hsieh, A., & Chang, J. (2006). Shopping and tourism night markets in Taiwan. *Tourism Management, 27*, 138–145.

Jansen-Verbeke, M. (1987). Women, shopping, and leisure. *Leisure Studies, 6*, 71–86.

Johnson, R. C., & Mannell, R. C. (1983). The relationship of crowd density and environmental amenities to perceptions of malls as leisure and shopping environments. *Recreation Research Review, 10*, 18–23.

Kelly, J. R. (1983). *Leisure identities and interactions*. London, UK: George Allen & Unwin.

Kelly, J. R., & Kelly, J. R. (1994). Multiple dimensions of meaning in the domains of work, family, and leisure. *Journal of Leisure Research, 26*, 250–274.

Klaffke, P. (2003). *Spree: A cultural history of shopping*. Vancouver, BC: Arsenal Pulp Press.

Langrehr, F. W. (1991). Retail shopping mall semiotics and hedonistic consumption. *Advances in Consumer Research, 18*, 428–433.

Larson, C. (1994). Discount coupons: Beyond the price discount effect. In E. W. Goddard & D. S. Taylor (Eds.), *Proceedings of the NEC-63 Conference on promotion in the marketing mix: What works, where, and why* (pp. 42–52). Guelph, Ontario: University of Guelph.

Leach, W. (1993). *Land of desire*. New York, NY: Random House.

Machleit, K. A., & Eroglu, S. A. (2000). Describing and measuring emotional response to shopping experience. *Journal of Business Research, 49*, 101–111.

Manfredo, M. J., Driver, B. L., & Tarrant, M. A. (1996). Measuring leisure motivation: A meta-analysis of the recreation experience preference scales. *Journal of Leisure Research, 28*, 188–213.

Mannell, R. C., & Kleiber, D. A. (1997). *A social psychology of leisure*. State College, PA: Venture Publishing, Inc.

McCracken, G. (1990). *Culture and consumption: New approaches to the symbolic character of consumer goods and activities*. Bloomington, IN: Indiana University Press.

McIntyre, N., & Roggenbuck, J. W. (1998). Nature/person transactions during an outdoor adventure experience: A multi-phasic analysis. *Journal of Leisure Research, 30*, 401–422.

Miller, D. (1998). *A theory of shopping*. New York, NY: Cornell University Press.

Mitchell, R. (1983). *Mountain experience: The psychology and sociology of adventure*. Chicago, IL: University of Chicago Press.

Neulinger, J. (1974). *The psychology of leisure: Research approaches to the study of leisure*. Springfield, IL: Charles C. Thomas.

Oliver, R. L. (1993). Cognitive, affective, and attribute bases of the satisfaction response. *Journal of Consumer Research, 20*, 418–430.

Parry, D. C. (2005). Women's leisure as resistance to pronatalist ideology. *Journal of Leisure Research, 37*, 133–151.

Propst, D. B., & Koesler, R. A. (1998). Bandura goes outdoors: Role of self-efficacy in the outdoor leadership development process. *Leisure Sciences, 20*, 319–344.

Raisborough, J., & Bhatti, M. (2007). Women's leisure and auto/biography: Empowerment and resistance in the garden. *Journal of Leisure Research, 39*, 459–476.

Ryff, C. D. (1989). Happiness is everything, or is it? Exploration on the meaning of psychological well-being. *Journal of Personality and Social Psychology, 57*, 1069–1081.

Schor, J. B. (1991). *The overworked American: The expected decline of leisure*. New York, NY: Basic.

Schor, J. B. (2004). *Born to buy*. New York, NY: Scribner.

Schor, J. B., & Holt, D. B. (2000). *The consumer society reader*. New York, NY: New Press.

Schulz, J., & Watkins, M. (2007). The development of leisure meaning inventory. *Journal of Leisure Research, 39*, 477–497.

Scitovsky, T. (1992). *The joyless economy*. Oxford, UK: Oxford University Press.

Sherry, J. (1990). A sociocultural analysis of a midwestern flea market. *Journal of Consumer Research, 17*, 13–30.

Sylvia-Bobiak, S., & Caldwell, L. (2006). Factors related to physically active leisure among college students. *Leisure Sciences, 28*, 73–89.

Szalay, L. B., & Bryson, J. A. (1974). Psychological meaning: Comparative analyses and theoretical implications. *Journal of Personality and Social Psychology, 30*, 860–870.

TripleFive Group of Companies. (2008). *West Edmonton Mall: World's largest (Guinness world records), The greatest indoor show on Earth*. Retrieved from http://triplefive.com/en/pages/wem

Unger, L. S., & Kernan, J. B. (1983). On the meaning of leisure: An investigation of some determinants of the subjective experience. *Journal of Consumer Research, 9*, 381–392.

Wakefield, K. L., & Baker, J. (1998). Excitement at the mall: Determinants and effects on shopping response. *Journal of Retailing, 74*, 515–539.

Wang, J., & Wallendorf, M. (2006). Materialism, status signaling, and product satisfaction. *Journal of the Academy of Marketing Science, 34*, 494–505.

Watkins, M., & Bond, C. (2007). Ways of experiencing leisure. *Leisure Sciences, 29*, 287–307.

Westbrook, R. A., & Oliver, R. L. (1991). The dimensionality of consumption emotion patterns and consumer satisfaction. *Journal of Consumer Research, 18*, 84–91.

Chapter 14
Consumer Behaviour in Sport

Laura Wood, Ph.D.
University of Western Ontario

Ryan Snelgrove, Ph.D.
University of Waterloo

Learning Objectives

After reading this chapter, students will be able to

1. Describe the ways in which sport is consumed and some of the major trends within each form of consumption.
2. Explain how sport consumers can be segmented and discuss the strengths and limitations of each approach.
3. Describe the process of initiation, continuance, and discontinuation in sport and the factors associated with movement between stages.

Introduction

Understanding consumers is an important basis for effective marketing decisions. Designing programs, products, and event experiences; setting prices; creating promotion strategies; and distributing services or products all benefit from understanding consumers. Central to this process is an understanding of how consumers differ and why some people become dedicated consumers whereas others do not. In this chapter we describe how sport is consumed; detail segments of sport consumers; and explain the sport-consumer process including initiation, continuation and intensification, and discontinuation.

How Sport is Consumed

Sport is consumed in a variety of ways. This section provides an overview of the most common types of sport consumption such as game and special-event attendance, TV viewership, merchandise purchases, sport tourism, and sport participation.

Game and Special Event Attendance

Sport consumers attend sport games, matches, and sport events, such as the Olympics and Canadian Games. These games and events occur at both the professional (e.g., Major league sports such as NHL, NBA, MLB) and the amateur or recreational level (e.g., university athletics, Pan Am Games, high school games, recreational hockey league). When people consume sport by attending sport games they are commonly referred to as spectators. Interestingly, Canadians are increasingly consuming amateur sport as spectators. More specifically, in 2005 approximately 9 million Canadian adults were spectators for amateur sport, a 20% increase from 1998 (Statistics Canada, 2008a).

TV Viewership

In addition to attending games or events in person, consumers can view many games or events on television or the Internet. Viewing can occur in the comfort of one's own home, at a friend's place, or at any location that has television or the Internet. In fact, the success of sport television over the years (e.g., ESPN, TSN, Sportsnet) has resulted in the development of more specialized sports viewing for consumers including sport specific channels, such as the Golf Channel, Leafs TV, and other speciality channels including the Outdoor Life Network. Overall, Canadians spend 6% to 8% of their TV viewing time watching sports (Statistics Canada, 2006). Males aged 18 and older spend the greatest amount of television viewing time watching sports at 11% to 14%.

Merchandise Purchases

Purchasing sport merchandise is another form of sport consumption. This involves purchasing sport equipment (e.g., skis, snowshoes, golf clubs), apparel (e.g., team uniform, shorts, golf shirts), professional and amateur sport team and athlete merchandise (e.g., Calgary Flames jersey, Sidney Crosby poster), sports magazines (e.g., Sports Illustrated) and/or event related merchandise (e.g., Vancouver 2010 Olympics t-shirt, Super Bowl XLV hat).

Sport Tourism

Sport consumers also travel to attend sport events taking place within the province, across the country, or in other parts of the world. In doing so, consumers may travel to a destination they may not have visited otherwise (Snelgrove, Taks, Chalip, & Green, 2008). While in the destination consumers may also engage in additional tourist activities and spend money in the community on hotels, food, and other entertainment. In fact, sport tourism has been described as the fastest growing segment in Canada's tourism industry. Sport tourism spending within Canada has been undertaken primarily by Canadians as they have accounted for

85% of total spending (Canadian Heritage, 2007). In 2007, sport tourists from overseas spent approximately $195 million in Canada, while sport tourists from the United States spent approximately $118 million (Canadian Heritage, 2007).

Sport Participation

Participation in competitive or recreational sport is also a form of sport consumption. Sport participation varies between more formally organized sport (e.g., participation in a scheduled game or event) and less formally organized sport (e.g., a pick-up game, spontaneous play with friends). Alarmingly, organized sport participation in Canada has declined over the past 20 years. In 2005, nearly 3 in every 10 Canadians (15 years and older) regularly participated in one or more sports (Statistics Canada, 2008a). This rate of involvement is significantly lower than rates in 1990 when almost 5 in 10 people participated in sport (Statistics Canada, 2008a). Further, this decline in sport participation is evident across age, gender, educational level, income, and provinces (Statistics Canada, 2008a). Overall, golf is the most played sport, surpassing hockey in popularity in 1998. Although golf is the most played sport, it is predominately played by men (75% men). Hockey is the second most popular sport followed by swimming, soccer, basketball, baseball, and volleyball (Statistics Canada, 2008a). In 2004, 51% of children aged 5 to 14 regularly played a sport (Statistics Canada, 2008b). Boys tend to participate in organized sport more often than girls; however, this gap appears to be decreasing. For children the most played organized sport is soccer.

Why do you think sport participation is declining in Canada?

Although discussed independently, sport can be consumed in a number of ways by the same consumer. For example, a hockey fan may watch their favourite team on television, purchase team related merchandise, participate in fantasy sports, attend games, and in some cases play the sport themselves. Marketers are increasingly becoming aware of the value of leveraging one type of consumption to increase spending or involvement in another area. For example, the professional sports leagues like the NFL have promoted fantasy sports as a way of deepening connections between consumers and the league. Interestingly though, researchers have found very little connection between those who watch a sport and those who play a sport. Thus, not all people consume sport in the same way, necessitating recognition of different groups or segments of consumers who have varied needs and interests.

Approaches to Segmenting Sport Consumers

Segmentation involves separating larger heterogeneous markets into smaller homogenous segments. This process enables marketers to target smaller segments more efficiently with products or services that meet specific consumers' needs and interests. Depending on the sport organization's strategy they may choose to focus on one particular market segment, or attempt to appeal to a number of segments at the same time. This section provides examples of the most common ways of segmenting consumer markets, including demographic and geographic, behavioural, benefits, and lifestyle. Each of these approaches to segmentation is based on the idea that people's consumption can be explained by these factors. It is important to note that marketers often use multiple methods of segmentation simultaneously to develop even smaller and more specific segments.

Demographics and Geographic

Demographics based segmentation is the most common approach used by organizations and involves separating the market for a service or product based on information such as age, sex, income, occupation, education, religion, and race. One reason for its popularity is the ease in which these variables can be measured. Geographic segmentation involves the division of consumers based on geographical location such as country, province, city, town, or neighbourhood. Geography plays an important role in segmentation for sport organizations. For example, sport-equipment companies selling winter sports gear would not expect to have large consumer markets in warm-weather locations.

Ethnicity themed nights at basketball games in the NBA is one example of demographic segmentation. These nights, such as Asian Heritage night, are created to attract a specific demographic (i.e., people of Asian descent) to the games. In hosting these types of nights, teams are especially interested in attracting people who would not have been interested in attending the game otherwise. Of particular focus is the promotion of a player who has a certain ethnic background, and the incorporation of cultural elements into the event. For example, in the fall of 2010 The Golden State Warriors had cultural performances at the game, created special Asian Heritage seating sections, and had a portion of the proceeds from ticket sales benefit local Asian organizations in the community (Golden State Warriors, n.d.).

Similarly, recreational-sport facilities may focus on consumers living within a certain area.

Behavioural

Segmentation based on behavioural information is most commonly undertaken by sport marketers using consumers' usage patterns. Consumers can differ on their levels of consumption ranging from non- or light users to heavy users of a product or service. Marketers can use this information to target each of these groups separately with different pricing or advertising, or choose to focus on a particular group. For example, a professional sports team may want to focus on heavy users because they are responsible for the majority of total consumption. Alternatively, a recreational sports centre may have an interest in getting more people active in the community and would target non- or light users specifically. In many cases though, it may be best to strive to satisfy the needs of most of these usage groups to ensure a continuous level of light, medium, and heavy users (Mullin, Hardy, & Sutton, 2007). Doing so recognizes that light users may eventually become medium or heavy users over time. Although marketers often focus on heavy consumers of products, or the hardcore fans of sport, Trenberth and Garlan (2007) argued that it is also important to consider how "sport marketers [can] reach new sport consumers and turn them into sports fanatics before their attention and disposable income are diverted to other forms of entertainment" (p. 97). However, the behavioural usage approach does little to explain why people move from one stage of usage to another.

Benefits

Sport marketers can also segment based on the benefits sought from a product or service. This approach to segmentation is based on the idea that consumers are motivated by the potential benefits that may arise from their consumption. McDonald, Milne and Hong (2002) reviewed existing research and identified 13 of the most common benefits derived from sport consumption including: physical fitness, risk taking, stress reduction, aggression, affiliation, social facilitation, self-esteem, competition, achievement, skill mastery, aesthetics, value development, and self-actualization. Organizations can satisfy existing consumers by creating opportunities to achieve desired benefits, or redesign existing products or services to meet the desired benefits of new consumers. Potential benefits can also be featured prominently in advertisements that let consumers know about the benefits derived from sport services or products. Although benefits may be an important aspect of understanding consumption they do not fully capture the social influences involved in consumption initiation or continuance. Further, some researchers have argued that benefits or motivations are mostly after-the-fact reasons people attribute to their consumption rather than driving factors (Stevenson, 2002).

Sport Lifestyle

Lifestyle segmentation involves considering how sport is consumed directly by examining sport subcultures and documenting their norms, styles, and use of language in conjunction with sport participation. For example, well-documented subcultures exist in youth culture around snowboarding and skateboarding that differentiate these groups from adults who also participate in similar sports. This approach to segmentation can be differentiated from previous ones in a number of ways. Although *social connections* may be a common benefit reported amongst various snowboarders, analyzing subcultures provides further detail around norms related to communication styles and preferences (Green & Chalip, 1998). Similarly, different segments are more likely to respond when marketers use appropriate language and understand the meaning of

As mentioned earlier, marketers may use a combination of approaches to segment a market. For example, Wood, Snelgrove, and Danylchuk (2010) were interested in identifying segments at a charity sport event (i.e., the RONA MS Bike Tour) and used demographics, behavioural, and lifestyle variables. They found that four groups existed which they labelled event enthusiasts, cause fundraisers, road warriors, and non-identifiers. A summary of these findings appear in the following table.

Variables	Event enthusiasts	Cause fundraisers	Road warriors	Non-identifiers
Cycling identity (Think of themselves as cyclists)	High	Low	High	Low
Fundrasing identity (Think of themselves as fundraisers for MS)	High	High	Low	Low
Amount fundraised	High ($950)	Moderate to High ($611)	Moderate ($491)	Moderate ($411)
Event History	Long (~7 years)	Minimal (~3 years)	Minimal (~3 years)	Minimal (~2 years)
Age	45 years old	36 years old	41 years old	41 years old
Gender	63% male	63% male	63% male	63% male
% of total respondents	31%	13%	36%	20%

> Recognizing the MS Society of Canada's goal of maximizing the amount of money fundraised each year and retaining participants, answer the following questions: Which group(s) would you target if you were in charge of organizing the charity sport event and why?

particular products (Wood, Taks, & Danylchuk, 2008). Studies of adult subcultures around surfing demonstrate variations in approaches to the sport, lifestyle centrality, and adoptions of norms within the same age groups (e.g., Wheaton, 2000), indicating that age in isolation often fails to provide insight into consumption.

Initiation, Continuation, and Discontinuation in Sport

To attract new sport consumers, marketers need to understand why some people become and continue to be consumers of sport and others do not. As you will recall, the previous section described four common approaches used to segment the market of current sport consumers. Although these approaches may be a useful basis for segmentation, not all of them are helpful in explaining initiation or continuation in sport. Although certain demographics are associated with sport consumption, these demographics tell us little about the process of becoming or staying a sport consumer. Further, not all people of a certain gender, ethnicity, or age become or continue to be consumers of sport. Similarly, people may report certain benefits of consumption, but these benefits do not fully explain initial involvement or how people form attachments to sport. For example, people may indicate they value the health benefits or camaraderie derived from playing basketball in a recreational league, but that does little to explain how they came to be involved in the sport or how they became aware of the league. Further, the circumstances surrounding initial involvement may have little to do with ongoing consumption or discontinued consumption. Below we outline a framework that provides a way of understanding the sport-consumption process in terms more complex than demographics or benefits approaches.

Getting Started

People become involved in sport in one of three ways. That is, they are either recruited by others, seek out sport to fulfill particular needs, or feel forced or pressured to become involved in sport (Prus, 1996; Stevenson, 2002). A common way of being recruited into sport is through one's parents. This may involve taking a child to a sports game for the first time, teaching them how to play, or purchasing sport logoed clothing. Research has found that fathers, in particular, often introduce their children to sports and sports teams through conversations and watching sports and specific teams on television together (James, 2001). Peers, media, and school activities also influence children's initial sport activity and team preferences. Adults also become involved in sport in the same ways in that they are often recruited by family, friends, and co-workers, seek out ways of fulfilling needs such as the desire to be physically fit, and sometimes feel obligated to participate in sport because of family members' interests (e.g., Green & Chalip, 1997; Wood, 2010). Although many people become aware of sports and teams and are influenced by others to initiate sport consumption, not all people do become consumers. In many cases, personal and social risks associated with initial involvement may be too high to warrant initiation or continuation beyond an initial experience (Prus, 1996). Risks are numerous and could include things such as a perceived lack of skills, having a body image perceived to be incongruent with a sport, or potential negative feedback from friends or family.

Sustaining and Intensifying Involvements

When people do start and continue past initial experiences, their continuation or intensification can be explained in a number of ways. For example, fans may become more attached to their team when being a fan fulfills desired needs such as vicarious achievement or enhanced social status (Funk & James, 2001). The concept of a sport lifestyle is also important to understanding continued involvement as a sports fan or participant. For example, when sport becomes a central part of people's lives they are less likely to end related friendships made through sport (Prus, 1996). Also, people are often resistant to change already established identities (e.g., being known as a runner or Toronto Maple Leafs fan) because of what others might think of them. Collective participation in sport also provides a means of supporting each other and negotiating constraints that otherwise might lead to discontinuation (e.g., skill development) (Wood, 2010). By way of example, Stevenson (2002) found that Master's swimmers were more likely to continue participating when they were able to successfully "modify parts of their lifestyles to accommodate their swimming, including adapting to the schedule of practice times, making preparations for morning swims, taking care of obligations as parent or caregiver, and adjusting their work obligations" (p. 138).

Discontinuing Involvements

Over time consumers involved in sport, through spectatorship or participation, may become disinvolved. Although much less research has been conducted in this area, as compared to initiating and intensifying sport involvements (Funk & James, 2001), research suggests a number of reasons for disengagement. There are simply too many factors that influence disengagement to be listed here, but we will describe some of the more common ones. For some people, playing a sport or being a fan of a particular team no longer fit with how they would like to be viewed by others. As a result, these people stop consuming sport to alter their image. In other cases, people may stop being a fan of a team because they become frustrated with a team's performance, disapprove of a certain player's actions, or dislike that their favourite player was traded. With respect to sport participation, people may stop playing a sport when it is no longer viewed by others as popular, when it is no longer enjoyable or physically possible to play, when friends have stopped playing, when opportunities to play no longer exist, or when it becomes less preferable than other sport activities or family life.

Conclusion

The process of understanding sport consumers is a complex endeavour. In this chapter we provided an overview of how and why sport is consumed and the different ways in which sport marketers can segment the larger market of consumers. Undoubtedly many factors are at play in the consumption process. This complexity necessitates that most sport organizations focus on some of the most prominent factors. Although the approach taken by a particular organization will be better informed by theories of sport consumption, it will always be limited by the resources available to the organization (e.g., finances, expertise) and its overall mission.

Key Terms

Benefits of sport
Market segmentation
Sport initiation and continuance
Sport lifestyles

References

Canadian Heritage. (2007). *Report on economic impacts of cultural and sport tourism in Canada 2007.* Retrieved from http://www.pch.gc.ca/pc-ch/org/sectr/inter/econ_impct2007/101-eng.cfm

Funk, D. C., & James, J. (2001). The psychological continuum model: A conceptual framework for understanding an individual's psychological connection to sport. *Sport Management Review, 4*, 119–150.

Golden State Warriors, (n.d.). Asian community night. Retrieved from https://www.gs-warriors.com/forms/secure/fct_1011_asian.html

Green, B. C., & Chalip, L. (1997). Enduring involvement in youth soccer: The socialization of parent and child. *Journal of Leisure Research, 29*, 61–77.

Green, B. C., & Chalip, L. (1998). Sport tourism as the celebration of subculture. *Annals of Tourism Research, 25*, 275-291.

James, J. D. (2001). The role of cognitive development and socialization in the initial development of team loyalty. *Leisure Sciences, 23*, 233–261.

McDonald, M. A., Milne, G. R., & Hong J. (2002). Motivational factors for evaluating sport spectator and participant markets. *Sport Marketing Quarterly, 11*, 100–113.

Mullin, B. J., Hardy, S., & Sutton, W. A. (2007). *Sport marketing* (3rd ed.). Champaign, IL: Human Kinetics.

Prus, R. (1996). *Symbolic interaction and ethnographic research: Intersubjectivity and the study of human lived experience.* New York: State University of New York Press.

Snelgrove, R., Taks, M., Chalip, L., & Green, B. C. (2008). How visitors and locals at a sport event differ in motives and identity. *Journal of Sport & Tourism, 13*, 165–180.

Statistics Canada. (2006). TV Viewership. Retrieved from http://www.statcan.gc.ca/daily-quotidien/060331/dq060331b-eng.htm

Statistics Canada (2008a). Participation in sports. Retrieved from http://www.statcan.gc.ca/daily-quotidien/080207/dq080207b-eng.htm

Statistics Canada (2008b). Canadian social trends (No. 85): Kids' sports. Retrieved from http://www.statcan.gc.ca/pub/11-008-x/2008001/article/10573-eng.htm

Stevenson, C. L. (2002). Seeking identities: Towards an understanding of the athletic careers of masters swimmers. *International Review for the Sociology of Sport, 37*, 131–146.

Trenberth, L., & Garland, R. (2007). Sport and consumer buying behaviour. In J. Beech & S. Chadwick (Eds.), *The marketing of sport* (pp. 83–101). London, UK: Prentice Hall.

Wheaton, B. (2000). "Just do it": Consumption, commitment, and identity in the windsurfing subculture. *Sociology of Sport Journal, 17*, 254–274.

Wood, L. (2010). Playing our way: The role of social groups in women's loyalty to sport participation. Presented at the 25th annual conference of the North American Society for Sport Management (NASSM), Tampa Bay, FL.

Wood, L., Snelgrove, R., & Danylchuk, K. (2010). Segmenting volunteer fundraisers at a charity sport event. *Journal of Nonprofit & Public Sector Marketing, 22*(1), 38–54.

Wood, L., Taks, M., & Danylchuk, K. (2008). Communicating with young people in the sport industry: Practitioners' insights. *International Journal of Sport Communication, 1*, 286–300.

Chapter 15
Urban Recreation

Ron Johnson, Ph.D.
University of Waterloo

Scott Forrester, Ph.D.
Brock University

Learning Objectives

After reading this chapter, students will be able to

1. Identify the providers of recreation within an urban context and cite examples of programs provided by each of the three sectors.
2. Identify trends affecting urban recreation.
3. Explain the factors contributing to the increasing prevalence of home-based leisure and provide examples of recreation in the home.
4. List and describe four forms of urban recreation.
5. Describe five issues facing urban recreation.

Introduction

Despite the vastness of Canada and the images many people have of open space and sparsely populated areas, Canada is an urban nation. More than 80% of Canada's population resides in urban environments (Statistics Canada, 2006). In urban areas people face unique challenges that affect their choice of recreation. The demand for more open space, shrinking tax dollars, deterioration of urban infrastructures, safety, and crime concerns are some of the issues influencing recreation provision and choice. How providers and residents react to these issues greatly influences the recreation landscape of urban Canada.

The Providers

Within the context of the urban environment, the delivery of recreation services and programs falls under the mandate of three groups: (1) the public sector, (2) the commercial sector, and (3) the private (not-for profit) sector. Although all three providers have a distinct role to play in supplying recreation opportunity, there are occasions when their activities overlap and at times may even conflict. To understand their specific roles and see how they contribute to the overall recreation fabric, it is necessary to examine how each one operates within the urban context.

Public Sector

The public sector's mandate, in recreation and other areas of service provision, is primarily to promote the overall well being of society. Within the urban context, the municipal government is responsible for the provision of recreation. Given that the public sector obtains its funds from tax-supported activities or taxes via municipal budgets, it is incumbent upon the public sector to serve all members of society. Historically public recreation has been available to all citizens; however, there is a further caveat that the public sector should specifically address issues that face marginalized or needier members of society. Given this mandate, public recreation has provided such activities and programs as libraries, parks, sports fields, open space, minor sports, community centres, pools, arenas, as well as leisure oriented classes and instruction. In addition, cultural and community activities have fallen under their jurisdiction. In all such endeavours the overall theme that drives public recreation is the public good.

In a perfect world, public recreation would meet the needs and wishes of all citizens; however, the reality is that the public sector is limited by financial constraints. As demands for more recreation continue to increase, some municipalities have found themselves unable to meet the growing demands. Given the finite amount of resources available, municipal governments have had to make hard choices about what they could or could not offer and who could or could not receive services within the context of budgets. This has led to a retrenchment of offerings in some cities and an attempt to ration opportunities (see Chapters 29 and 38).

Commercial Sector

The commercial sector provides recreation opportunities that are primarily based on the potential for creating a profit. Unlike the public sector, equity and social value are not key issues in deciding what recreation opportunities to offer. This does not mean that public or voluntary cannot generate revenue: in fact they often do. The difference is in the motivation for providing the service or activity, and the disposition of the revenue. In public and not for profit sectors, revenues are primarily for reinvestment for the benefits of their clients, whereas in the commercial recreation sector revenues are to a great degree viewed as profit.

Because profit is the primary motive of the commercial sector it is not restricted in terms of whom they serve or what the service is (within the confines of the law). The urban environment is the ideal place for commercial operators to exist because that is where the population numbers exist for a client base. Commercial recreation forms an important part of the overall recreation landscape of the urban environment. They provide opportunities like bowling alleys, arcades, movie theatres, fitness clubs, clubs, restaurants, and bars. Obviously, such facilities require a clientele base sufficient to support the enterprise; therefore, such facilities are more common and are found in large numbers in the urban environments.

Private

The third area is neither profit-motivated nor operated by government. The private sector is usually aimed at a particular population segment or offers a service that is important to the community but is not adequately provided by the other sectors. Examples of organizations in this private, not-for-profit sector would be churches, service clubs, YM-YWCA, sport governing bodies, Boys and Girls clubs, etc.

The three sectors do not operate in isolation. Often there will be overlap of recreation provision. For example, one might find a golf course or fitness centre being operated by either the commercial or public sectors. Ideally this provides more choice for the public, therefore, enhancing the recreation opportunity in the urban area. When such operations are the result of cooperation and coordination this can be positive. If, however, direct competition exists, conflict can result.

Cite examples of recreation that represent the three providers in your home town.

Trends in Urban Recreation

There are a variety of trends that tend to work against the viability of urban recreation providers. Recent surveys and publications by recreation professionals and futurists have identified several major trends and issues that need to be addressed to maintain the roles of recreation providers. Some of the more significant trends are listed in Table 15.1.

These trends offer major challenges to recreation providers and unfortunately there aren't any simplistic solutions. This means that many of the resources available to recreation provision will be consumed by social and fiscal issues, leaving even fewer resources aimed at the implementation of recreation opportunity.

How has the urban area nearest to where you live responded to these issues?

Table 15.1: Major Trends Affecting Provision of Recreation

- Deteriorating Park and Recreation Infrastructures
- Increasing Crime Rates/Urban Fear
- Increasing Demand for Safety
- Increasing Use of the Home as a Recreation Centre
- Increasing Demand for Recreation Services
- Changing Demographics—Aging, Family Structure
- Increasing Awareness of Health, Wellness and Obesity
- Increased Immigration and Cultural Diversity
- Increased Demand for Public Accountability

Recreation in the Urban Fortress

Despite the presence of the three major recreation providers vying for their time and/or dollars, the primary place of recreation for most people is at home. The importance of the home is not a new phenomenon. It has been a major part of recreation activity throughout the eras of parlour games, radio, television, and the burgeoning home entertainment industries. What is new is the degree to which the home has come to dominate people's leisure lives and the complexity of home-based recreation opportunity. The importance of the home in terms of dominance is illustrated by the fact that most families will have at least on occasion or as a regular occurrence chosen to eat in front of the TV. The dominance of the home was brought to light in the 1990s by Faith Popcorn, well known futurist and founder of the trend identifying Brain Reserve, when she focused on the growing phenomenon of "cocooning" (Popcorn, 1991). Cocooning describes the phenomenon of people retreating to their homes for a significant portion of their daily lives, including recreation. Spurred on by advances in technology, which allowed people access to high quality and convenient entertainment in the confines of their own homes and the growing phenomenon of urban fear (statistics suggest this fear may be more a result or more a perception than a reality) many people have chosen to make their homes the ultimate centre for their recreation. Home, for many, acts as a sanctuary to isolate one from criminals, pollution, terrorists, or other forms of external threat. The need for such a sanctuary seems exacerbated by media practices that make the home appear more inviting and a lot safer than the outside world. With the introduction of technological entertainment, such as the iPod and the Xbox, outside entertainment becomes less significant. Whether a person is actually cocooning or simply using home as a technological entertainment centre, the home becomes a dominant part of one's recreation experience.

Cocooning, or variations thereof, has created a lot of spin-off reactions that in turn have an impact on urban recreation. We have been warned of the tendency toward declining physical fitness, obesity, or deteriorating social skills as people isolate themselves in the confines of their homes. In fact, urban home design itself has undergone changes to meet the new demands. We now have gourmet kitchens, entertainment rooms, and bathrooms that double as self-contained spas. Why leave home when it is filled with such amenities?

Social trends, like cocooning, in turn influence public, commercial, and private not-for-profit recreation delivery. Where does public recreation fit if many of its former clients no longer use its services? What can commercial recreation do to keep its business base? To combat this trend, safety and quality have to be at the forefront.

What recreation opportunities do you have in your own home?

Expressions of Urban Recreation

Festivals

It is hard to imagine an urban area in Canada that does not have at least one festival. Toronto has Caribana, Kitchener has Octoberfest, Calgary has the Stampede, and so on. Why so many, and why are they so important to the host area? Those who advocate for the festivals view them as providing a variety of desirable outcomes: increased tourist dollars; prestige; community cohesiveness; cultural awareness, etc. Seldom does one hear anything negative regarding the festival concept, unless it is the immediate neighbours complaining of the noise and resulting garbage. The increase in the number of festivals over the years is understandable. The success of the most popular festivals leads to imitation, and in many instances the spin-offs have also been successful. There are, in fact, festivals for almost every imaginable interest group and population segment. The biggest drawback is that with so many festivals, there are serious questions of "over competition" and quality. Even for the ones that may be of questionable quality there are those who would fight for their continuance. This is especially true if the event promotes certain social or political agendas, profits a particular segment of society, or has been entrenched as part of the heritage of the area.

Sport

From the earliest cities, sport has formed an integral part of the recreation fabric of urban areas. From the time of Greece and Rome when the Olympics, the coliseum, and blood sports dominated the urban scene to the modern North American city, sport has ruled. Heroes and urban myths have arisen from the heroics of the athlete in urban Canada. The Maple Leafs, Les Canadiens, Bill Barilko, the 1972 summit series, the Saddledome, BC Place, and the Grey Cup all symbolize the importance of sport to the life of cities. People value sport as a cultural expression and identity. Whether in the stands at a Grey Cup game, watching the Maple Leafs or participating in a game of street hockey, many Canadians make sport part of their daily lives.

The whole sport experience also includes the ambience and tertiary activities, such as, the hot dogs and souvenirs, the pre-game anticipation and the post-game refreshments, the games' thrills and the next day analysis. All these are part of the urban sport experience. Even when there are no games, the architectural reminders keep sport in the minds of the cities' citizens. How many tourists visiting Toronto seek to visit the Sky Dome or the Hockey Hall of Fame? It matters little if a team is playing or if hall of fame members are in attendance. These facilities draw attention simply because they exist. No other form of recreation opportunity holds as many people in its grip. Sports teams are important to the urban area. Whether because of prestige, image boosterism, or the realization of tourist dollars and economic spin offs, sports teams play an integral role in the life of cities.

Cultural Opportunities and the City

Cultural expressions frequently are divided into two categories: high culture and popular (mass) culture. High culture can be defined as the customs, leisure pursuits, and practices of the wealthy or elite. Popular or mass culture relates to the customs, leisure pursuits, and practices of the general population. Generally high culture consists of things, events, or presentations that are not intended for mass consumption, and because of cost or other barriers, such as education or special abilities, only a select few will pursue such opportunities. To meet audience requirements (critical mass of users) high culture is usually restricted to urban areas. Examples of high culture would include opera, ballet, theatres, galleries, and museums. Given the nature of these events, they generally do not create a profit. As a result, high culture is usually supported through patrons, sponsorships, and government grants, as well as admission fees (i.e., ticket sales).

Although popular culture facilities and activities require a lower population base to be successful, the presence of a large number of people in urban areas also encourages their establishment. For this reason, the city becomes the focal point for a variety of popular culture opportunities. Therefore, an abundance of movie theatres, gyms, billiard halls, bowling alleys, restaurants, pubs, and other popular culture establishments exist in urban areas, usually under the ownership of the commercial sector. In the urban environment, the large base of population helps ensure the commercial success of these opportunities.

Both high culture and popular culture activities play an important role in the overall well-being of the urban structure. It is obvious that as a city grows and becomes more dynamic, both forms of cultural expression will grow with it to meet increased demand. But, cultural activities, both high and popular, also play a critical role in stimulating urban growth and healthy urban environments. For this reason urban planners and community developers have used cultural amenities to attract people to a city to play, work, or live. Successful urban renewal has depended heavily upon recreation as a key factor in anchoring a rebirth of urban life. Recreation opportunity and a healthy city seem to go hand in hand.

Simulated Leisure Environments

The urban landscape lends itself to bold new initiatives that deal with a number of the major trends/issues affecting the provision of recreation such as safety, crowding, and a desire for entertainment. Urban areas, like Las Vegas, NV for example are almost entirely simulated. From pyramid-shaped hotels, to the re-creation of the New York city skyline, or the waterways of Venice, urban areas like Las Vegas, NV are almost entirely simulated. Most cities, while not as obvious as Las Vegas, are beginning to incorporate many simulated leisure environments (SLEs) into the urban recreation mix. Zoos and aquariums have offered city dwellers the opportunity to experience the marine world and animal kingdom safely for decades. Indoor rock climbing walls have been common for years and many fitness facilities, sports domes, and arcades are beginning to introduce indoor golf simulators.

Downtown beaches are being created worldwide that allow urbanites the opportunity to get to the beach without ever leaving the city. Stretches of sand are being brought in to urban riverfronts to create the feeling of a lazy, sunny day at the beach, "just a seashell's throw from the buildings, shops, and busy streets of Paris, Amsterdam, Brussels, Budapest, Rome, and Berlin" (*The Tribune*, Sat July 9, 2005, p. C2). Artificial white-water rivers, in South Bend, IN for example, are increasingly being included in urban recreation planning as a catalyst toward re-development of decaying urban downtowns. Many Canadian cities, like St. Catharines, Ontario, for example, are in the planning stages of developing similar artificial white water rivers. More recently, indoor ski domes that resemble sports arenas or airport hangars, albeit situated on stilts, as high as 12 stories tall, are increasingly being incorporated into urban areas (Tokyo, Japan), mega shopping malls (Madrid, Spain), and sports centres (Dubai, United Arab Emirates). These indoor domes can measure up to 2,000 feet long and span over 300 feet wide usually containing one slope likely divided into a couple of runs. Lastly, indoor beach domes (presently located in Miyazaki, Japan and Berlin, Germany) are a more extreme example of urban SLEs, consisting of artificial oceans washing over indoor beaches complete with fake palm trees, plastic rainforests, erupting volcanoes, boardwalks, restaurants, and cafes. See *i*-box (p. 143).

How long will it be until similar indoor ski slopes or indoor beach domes are incorporated into the Edmonton Mall or other urban areas in Canada? What are the effects of these commercialized simulations of leisure environments? Is simulated leisure still leisure? Will the fast, over-scheduled pace of life, increase the attraction of these SLEs as a more convenient and accessible option, providing vicarious experiences with more immediate gratification? What consequences/benefits might SLEs have on the environment, life satisfaction, or quality of life?

Urban Recreation and "Fantasy City"

Increasingly, cities all over the globe are transforming their downtown environments into urban entertainment destination sites that aim to produce high value-added experiences (Howell, 2005). Hannigan (1998) first described this trend with the term "Fantasy City" which is bound and defined by the following central features:

1. Theme-o-centric: Many entertainment venues follow a scripted theme, normally drawn from sports, history, or popular entertainment. Either a single theme is used or "theme enhancement" is employed in which an atmosphere is created around a distinctive geographic locale, historical period, or type of cultural activity. "Multi-theming" is often implemented for larger entertainment sites in which the site is divided into a series of zones, each with its own thematic focus.

2. Branded: Urban entertainment destinations and leisure sites are often combined with pre-existing consumer and show business brands (e.g., Nike, Universal, Coca-Cola, ViaCom) based on the expectation of creating a profitable synergy.

3. Day and night: Fantasy City operates day and night, much like casinos in Las Vegas, trying to reach its intended market of baby boomer and Generation X adults in search of leisure, sociability, and entertainment. While suburban shopping malls close by nine or ten o'clock at night, these urban entertainment centres encourage late night activities which range from

Why Simulated? The Case of Artificial White-Water Rivers

Since the majority of natural white-water rivers are inaccessible for the greater part of the world's population, Goodman and Parr (1994) offer the following list as typical reasons for building an artificial course:

- to satisfy the increasing demand for white-water canoeing by introducing the sport into areas where no natural facilities exist
- to create more sites for white-water recreation, training, and competition
- to lessen the need for long journeys to remote river sites
- to relieve pressure on natural sites where most slalom events are presently held
- to allow easier access to slalom sites for the ever-increasing numbers of spectators
- to provide alternatives for canoeing when natural white-water rivers are reserved exclusively for fishing
- to create a focal point for other outdoor activities
- to create a focal point for civic pride and to increase financial investments in an area (p. 192)

Furthermore, when natural waterways suffer from low water levels, commonplace over the past several years (Peters, 2000), water flow is constant and can be controlled in artificial white-water rivers. This further increases the accessibility of these rivers by creating conditions conducive to the differing needs of rafters, kayakers, canoeists, and tubers. By controlling the water flow and adjusting rock and boulder placements, artificial courses can be used for slalom races, rodeo boating, instruction, and swift water rescue training which appeals to both beginners and international calibre athletes.

Currently, ten U.S. cities and towns already have white-water kayak parks, and thirteen more are looking into them, including four in the state of North Carolina alone (Miller, 2001). According to figures from the Outdoor Industry Association (OIA) (Peters, 2000) artificial white-water rivers will likely be prominent features in metropolitan areas in the future. The OIA monitors participation in 15 outdoor activities such as bicycling, rock climbing, backpacking and hiking, and although these activities have plateaued recently, kayaking is one of three activities exhibiting dynamic growth. A recent survey by the OIA revealed that 6.4 million Americans kayaked in the year 2000, a 50% increase over a two-year period.

Additionally, the number of individuals who reported that they kayaked at least 10 times during the year increased 150% over the same period. As most natural white-water rivers are inaccessible for the majority of the world's population, artificial white-water rivers will likely be a prominent feature in urban areas in the future. While no artificial white water rivers currently exist in Canada, at least one city (St. Catharines, Ontario) is in the planning stages of such a development.

themed night clubs to after hours entertainment "destinations" in tourist areas.

4. Modular: Fantasy City mixes and matches an increasingly standard array of components in various configurations. Typically, an urban entertainment destination will contain one or more themed restaurants (Hard Rock Café, Planet Hollywood, Rainforest Café), a megaplex cinema, an IMAX theatre, record (HMV, Virgin, Tower) and book (Chapters, Barnes and Noble, Borders) megastores, and modern arcades with interactive virtual reality games and ride simulators. Public sector examples of recreation common to most urban areas might include aquariums, arenas, theatres, or museums.
5. Solipsistic: Fantasy City is isolated from surrounding neighbourhoods physically, economically, and culturally. Boyer (1993) has referred to this as the "city of illusion"—a metropolis which ignores the reality of homelessness, unemployment, social injustice and crime, while eagerly transforming sites and channels of public expression into promotional spaces" (Hannigan, p. 4).
6. Post-modern: Fantasy City is also post-modern in that it is developed based on technologies of simulation, virtual reality, and the thrill of the spectacle. As these "simulation technologies" become increasingly advanced, producing a new generation of attractions that are largely simulated, the space between authenticity and illusion recedes, creating the condition of "hyper-reality"—in which the difference between the natural and the synthetic becomes increasingly blurred.

Viewing urban areas as entertainment destinations certainly changes the traditional interpretation of cities, whose identity was historically defined by the types of industry (transportation, manufacturing, finance, etc.) with recreation/leisure being peripheral to its overall character. Hannigan's (1998) Fantasy City concept places leisure at the forefront – the central defining point of the city itself.

How have these trends influenced cities in which you have lived or have visited?

Issues Facing Urban Recreation

To list all the issues facing recreation within the urban context would take far more space than we could possibly cover in one chapter. Below are some of the most relevant issues that either challenge or threaten the delivery of recreation and leisure services in urban areas.

The Role of Public Recreation in the Urban Context?

The role of recreation in the urban context is multi-dimensional and has changed over time and in relation to particular urban areas. Historically, recreation has its roots in providing a service that helped to ameliorate social problems. The early recreation leaders viewed recreation as a means to teach ethics and create citizens who would blend into and function effectively in society. More recently city leaders have looked to recreation to help solve social problems or act as a means of social control. For example, the recent spate of gun deaths in Toronto has led to suggestions of using recreation to foster a more positive environment for disenfranchised youth, and in so doing turn them away from gangs, drugs and guns. But, overriding the social implications is the fact that recreation is enjoyable. We live in a self-gratifying environment: unless people find the recreation provided to be pleasurable they simply will not buy into it.

Outdoor Recreation in Urban Areas

Urban governments have traditionally offered parks and open spaces intended for the well being of citizens. Since Frederick Law Olmsted gave us Central Park in New York and Mount Royal in Montréal, the concept of an urban "park" has been central to most cities. These have usually been viewed as spaces where a person could escape the brick, concrete, and asphalt of the urban environment and find repose in a semi-rural setting—an urban oasis. For most of our history these areas have been provided for passive outdoor activities or as settings for sports fields and children's playgrounds. A more recent trend has been to provide outdoor environments that can accommodate activities that traditionally have not been part of urban outdoor settings.

Many outdoor recreation activities which are conventionally thought of as occurring in predominantly "natural" recreation settings or "wilderness" are now occurring in urban environments (Batt, 2004). Examples include climbing, abseiling, and base jumping on/from buildings, monuments, and quarry faces; technical/ high speed mountain biking in urban parks; off-road motorcycling in urban and near-urban parks; horseback riding on roads with high speed motor vehicle traffic; and jet-skiing and white-water kayaking in suburban creeks and storm water drains. As urban areas expand into or surround adjoining rural lands, forestry areas, water catchments, and protected areas, subsequently reducing the natural or wilderness that previously supported these activities, and as participation increases, the pursuit of these outdoor recreation activities in urban settings is becoming increasingly problematic (Batt).

Are the risk management, ecological impact, visitor satisfaction policies, or planning and management tools that have been developed for these activities where they occur in predominantly "natural" recreation settings effective for urban environments?

Family Structure/Demographics

Urban areas represent the greatest variety and clustering of demographic characteristics. Single parents, blended families, same sex couples, yuppies, DINKS (Double Income No Kids), and other family variations all have different needs that require unique solutions. This entails a wide variety of recreation opportunities to meet each distinct need. In some circumstances these groups are clustered, which makes service delivery easier. The reality is that old style programs no longer are satisfactory.

Economically Disadvantaged and Unemployed Persons

Poverty is not unique to the urban environment, but its concentration makes the problem more obvious. Toronto, for example, has been grappling with the presence of homeless people, a seemingly unsolvable problem. While governments and advocates grapple with definitions and potential solutions, the problem remains. From a recreation standpoint the issues of who falls into this category, what does this mean to the individual, and what are the impacts on these people raise questions in terms of what can recreation do. Recreation cannot solve the problems created by poverty and unemployment but it can alleviate symptoms and overcome some of the negatives. Through providing meaningful experiences, developing social skills and values, a significant urban problem can be partially alleviated.

The Automobile, the Environment, and Recreation

There is no question that recreation uses resources. Either by travelling to and from activities, or the direct consumption of resources, recreation can be unnecessarily consumptive and a cause of pollution. Most views of recreation's negative impact on the environment conjure up images of SUVs tearing up environmentally sensitive landscapes or recreationists destroying natural habitat. But recreation can be just as harmful in the urban environment and given the larger number of people even more so. The single leading cause of harm/damage is the automobile. For most urban dwellers, mass transit has not become their primary mode of transportation. The automobile has become part of a person's daily life. To illustrate this, consider the drive-through restaurant/coffee shop (a very large part of a person's leisure is spent either in recreational shopping or recreational food consumption). Not only is the "recreationist" driving to the coffee shop, they spend much of their time idling in line, contributing to resource waste and air pollution.

Not only has the automobile been identified as a major contributor to environmental degradation, it has had a profound affect on the overall landscape of cities. The automobile allowed people the opportunity to turn to the suburban shopping mall for their retail needs and it allowed businesses to locate outside the city core. As businesses fled to the suburbs and shopping malls, the central cities suffered decline. Within the context of recreation this meant decreased visitors to downtown. Formerly vibrant recreation locations either fled with the other businesses or degenerated. What remained were lower quality recreation opportunities taking advantage of the ensuing lower rents.

Conclusions

Urban environments offer a complex and varied range of recreation opportunities. Regardless of one's socioeconomic or ethnic background, there are recreation opportunities available to satisfy a variety of desires. The present urban recreation scene is a multi-faceted evolution of recreation opportunities created to meet the contemporary demands of the public. The wide variety of demands, to a great degree have been the result of the diversity of population, whether in terms of ethnic or social background, economic or family status, cultural or educational background, now commonplace in most cities. Added to this has been an increase in type of opportunity due to technological advances and the growing economy. The result is an unparalleled number of recreation choices for the urban dweller.

There are, of course, a number of traditional types of recreation practices that have been part of the urban scene for many years. The actual format they follow and the sophistication with which they are presented may have changed, but these practices continue to be an important part of the urban scene. For example, sports and festivals have a long-standing tradition in urban recreation. These are still part of the scene although the economic impact they generate and social role they play has changed.

Two modern cultural expressions that have had a marked presence are the home based urban fortress/cocooning concept and the Fantasy City. The first of these is an extension of home-based recreation accentuated because of technology and urban fear. The second is an attempt to capitalize on the public's willingness to spend on recreation and city officials looking for ways to "improve" their city.

Many issues face recreation providers in urban settings. The reality of urban life means there will be poor and unemployed people, disenfranchised citizens, urban crime, and environmental degradation. Equity for all citizens, a long sought after goal in the public sector, has been an elusive dream. Recreation must face these issues. Although recreation may not solve urban problems, it can tackle such issues and create a better place to live.

Key Terms

Cocooning
Culture (high and popular)
Fantasy City
Festivals
Providers
Sectors
Simulated leisure environments
Trends
Urban recreation

References

Batt, D. (2004, September). Outdoor recreation in urban environments. Paper presented at the World Leisure Congress, Brisbane, Australia.

Boyer, M. C. (1993). The city of illusion: New York's public places. In P. Knox (Ed.), *The restless urban landscape*. Englewood Cliffs, NJ: Prentice Hall.

Goodman, F. R., & Parr, G. B. (1994). The design of artificial white-water canoeing courses. Paper presented at the Proceedings of the Institute of Civil Engineers.

Hannigan, J. (1998). *Fantasy city: Pleasure and profit in the postmodern metropolis*. New York, NY: Routledge.

Howell, J. (2005). Manufacturing experience: Urban development, sport and recreation. *International Journal of Management and Marketing, 1*(1–2), 56–68.

Miller, J. (2001, November 4). Whitewater parks offer thrilling twist and turn in city planning. *The News and Observer*, pp. 1A, 14A.

Peters, D. (2000). St. Catharines group pioneering innovative whitewater venue. Rapid, 2, 14.

Popcorn, F. (1991). *The popcorn report: Faith Popcorn on the future of your company, your worlds, your life*. New York, NY: Doubleday.

Raitz, K. (1995). *The theater of sport*. Baltimore, MD: Johns Hopkins University Press.

Sand in the city: Urban beaches a la Paris Plage sprout all over Europe. (2005, July 9). *The Welland Tribune,* p. C2.

Storman, W. (2000). The death of Olmstedian vision of public space. *Journal of Leisure Research, 2*(1), 166–170.

Statistics Canada (2006). *Census of population, 2006.* Ottawa, ON: Government of Canada.

Chapter 16
The Built Environment and Leisure Behaviour

Andrew T. Kaczynski, Ph.D.
University of South Carolina

Laurene Rehman, Ph.D.
Dalhousie University

Learning Objectives

After reading this chapter, students will be able to

1. Define the concept of the built environment.
2. Understand the relationship between leisure behaviour and the built environment.
3. Recognize ways the built environment may influence individual and community health and well-being.

Introduction

The neighbourhoods and communities we live in have a significant impact on our leisure behaviour and our health and well-being. This seems like a simple enough idea, but until recently, health behaviours and outcomes were primarily viewed as individual choices (King, Stokols, Talen, Brassington, & Killingsworth, 2002). If a person spent excessive amounts of time in front of the television, he or she was regarded as lazy or not capable or confident enough to exercise. If he or she was a pack-a-day smoker, it was because of a personal choice or a lack of willpower. Now, however, researchers and professionals in leisure studies, parks and recreation, public health, and other fields generally accept that both personal attitudes and beliefs as well as environmental factors shape our behaviours and the outcomes of those actions (Sallis, Owen, & Fisher, 200; Dustin, Bricker, & Schwab, 2010). Explanations such as unethical target marketing and advertising or a lack of sidewalks in neighbourhoods are now viewed as plausible contributors to a teenager taking up smoking or a parent keeping their child from walking to the local park. Working from this broader perspective, this chapter will explore the value of social ecological models in understanding and promoting positive health behaviours. We will also describe the importance of the built environment to community health and how diverse elements of our surroundings impact our physical and social well-being. Better understanding how the contexts in which we live influence our actions and behaviours can help to inform practices and policies aimed at changing leisure and community settings to improve our quality of life and population health.

Social Ecological Approaches to Health Promotion

Figure 16.1 provides a social ecological model showing the five levels of factors commonly thought to influence health behaviours (McLeroy, Bibeau, Steckler, & Glanz, 1988). Social ecological models are valuable because they emphasize that complex health behaviours such as physical inactivity, healthy eating, or smoking are best understood and addressed using a multi-level approach (Sallis, Owen, & Fisher, 2008). Furthermore, health promotion professionals recognize that interactions between levels should also be taken into account (e.g., how confidence in one's ability to be more active, a personal factor, may be influenced by living close to an attractive park, an environmental factor). Finally, social ecological models help us to remember that targeting multiple types and levels of influences is a daunting task and will require collaboration among academics and professionals from numerous disciplines to plan, implement, and evaluate health promotion initiatives.

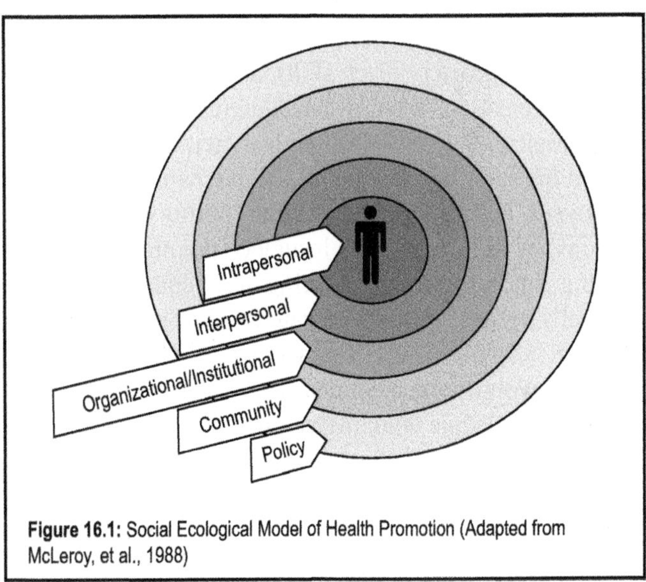

Figure 16.1: Social Ecological Model of Health Promotion (Adapted from McLeroy, et al., 1988)

Within the social ecological model, *intrapersonal* factors are the influences most proximal to the individual and include knowledge, skills, attitudes, and other attributes within the person whose leisure or health behaviour we are concerned with. For example, although we certainly want to be wary of stereotyping, sociodemographic characteristics, such as gender, age, race, education, income, or family situation, are often strongly related to an individual's likelihood of engaging in various positive (e.g., physical activity) or negative (e.g., smoking) behaviours. Other important intrapersonal factors may include psychological constructs such as my self-efficacy to be physically active or my beliefs about how my body looks to my friends and family.

The next level of the social ecological model addresses *interpersonal* factors. These include the relationships one forms with friends, family, classmates, or co-workers, and how these interactions promote or impede actions related to leisure and health. For example, I may perceive increased social support to quit drinking because my neighbour offers to watch my children while I attend a substance abuse program. Likewise, a group of co-workers may have greater success losing weight if they pursue this goal collectively rather than on their own.

The third level in Figure 16.1 refers to *organizational* or *institutional* factors. We spend much of our days interacting within organizations or institutions and, consequently, these settings are key influences on our leisure, work, and health behaviours. Within these locations, both the physical and social environment are important. For example, a school with a big yard and an engaging playground, a policy mandating 60 minutes of physical education every day, and vending machines filled with nutritious snacks sends a strong message about the importance of living a healthy lifestyle and supports opportunities to easily do so. Local churches or other religious centers often provide a place for people to worship and practice their faith, mingle with others and build relationships, learn or teach skills, and engage in active or passive recreation, thereby encouraging spiritual, social, psychological, and physical health all at the same time. Finally, a business might support positive habits amongst its employees by offering lunch hour nutrition counseling sessions, by reducing health insurance premiums for those quitting smoking, or by placing aesthetically pleasing stairwells (rather than dark elevators) at the entrances to its building. All of these types of actions can change both the physical layout of organizations or institutions and the social norms of the people who interact there.

A fourth type of influence that may impact leisure and health behaviours are *community* factors. This is the level within the social ecological model where the built environment plays the greatest role. As discussed later, the built environment impacts our behaviours and health in a wide variety of ways (Frank et al., 2006). For example, sidewalks serve as infrastructure to move people safely from point A to point B while also providing a venue for children's play or casual conversations between neighbours. A nearby park, depending on its availability, proximity, and design, can be a space for an intense soccer match among friends or a relaxing afternoon with a novel, while also acting as an environmental resource that helps to reduce urban temperatures and air pollution. On the other hand, negative attributes of a neighbourhood, such as the presence of vandalism or unsavory businesses (e.g., strip bars, cigarette stores), can encourage crime or unhealthy habits while also making the environment less pleasing for being active or interacting with others.

Finally, *public policy* plays a critical role in shaping leisure and health behaviours. Policies can exist within many different arenas—schools, businesses, communities, etc.—and can promote or impede healthy behaviours. They can also be formal (e.g., a city law) or informal (e.g., an employee code of conduct) and have a direct or indirect impact on an individual's actions. For example, many municipalities require a minimum number of parking spots depending on the size of a business, but have no such guidelines or laws related to sidewalk or bike lane construction in new developments. Likewise, some provinces are investigating the use of financial incentives, often in the form of tax exemptions or write-offs, for things like purchasing physical activity equipment or public transit passes, building fitness facilities into a business site, or registering children for active recreation programs. Many communities have enacted bylaws banning smoking in public places (e.g., bars, restaurants, parks) or restricting the locations of alcohol-selling outlets away from schools. When implemented thoughtfully and with regard for all parties who may be affected, public policies can often have a significant positive impact on the leisure and health behaviours of a large number of people.

Pick a health behaviour in your own life, like physical activity or healthy eating. Can you think of one or more factors within each of the five levels of the social ecological model that influences that behaviour?

The Built Environment and Community Health

Although multiple factors and levels within the social ecological model help to shape our behaviours, the primary focus of this chapter is on how the built environment influences our leisure and health. The built environment is a term that is increasingly used by professionals and researchers in a wide range of disciplines. But what exactly do we mean by this? According to the definition put forth by Health Canada (as stated by Srinivasan et al., 2003), the built environment:

> includes our homes, schools, workplaces, parks/recreation areas, business areas, and roads. It extends overhead in the form of electric transmission lines, underground in the form of waste disposal sites and subway trains, and across the country in the form of highways. The built environment encompasses all buildings, spaces, and products that are created or modified by people. It impacts indoor and outdoor physical environments (e.g., climatic conditions and indoor/outdoor air quality), as well as social environments (e.g., civic participation, community capacity, and investment) and subsequently our health and quality of life (p. 1446).

This is a valuable definition in several respects. To begin with, it is comprehensive in recognizing that both manufactured (e.g., streets) as well as natural (e.g., parks) features of our surroundings influence our health behaviours and outcomes. As well, it implicitly acknowledges the interconnectedness between different elements of our built environment, such as when excessive car use affects air quality and when poor air quality reduces the desire to walk or bike instead of drive. Finally, Health Canada's definition mentions both physical and social environments as being important in shaping the ways we behave and the health and quality of life we achieve. In the next section, we provide a brief overview of the myriad of ways the built environment influences health and well-being and the diverse factors within our neighbourhoods and communities that can promote or restrict healthy behaviours.

Before continuing, however, it is useful to consider why targeting the built environment to improve health is a valuable strategy. After all, as discussed above, social ecological models recommend that there are numerous settings and levels at which we can intervene to try to change health behaviours. The truth is a multilevel approach is likely to be most effective, but targeting the built environment as a key component of such a strategy has a number of considerable advantages (Sallis et al., 2006). Firstly, built environment changes usually impact a large number of people. For example, the addition of a family restroom and a splash pad to a park may benefit all the children and parents in a neighbourhood, while zoning fast-food restaurants away from schools prevents a substantial number of youth from being overexposed to unhealthy food choices. In contrast, a group or individual-based program at a local community center or school to promote physical activity or healthy eating likely won't be able to serve as many members of the targeted population.

Secondly, built environment improvements such as constructing sidewalks or adding streetlights to a neighbourhood usually last 10, 20, 30, or even 100 years. These relatively permanent effects have the potential to benefit multiple generations. By offering individual counseling sessions or support groups, we may achieve some immediate gains in physical activity or other healthy behaviours, but research shows the effects of such intra- and interpersonal programs fade considerably within a short period of time (Marcus & Forsyth, 1999).

Finally, changing the built environment can often impact multiple health behaviours simultaneously. For example, if a grocery store is built nearby, my accessibility to fruits, vegetables, and other positive food options would likely increase dramatically; however, I may also be more likely to walk to the store rather than drive and perhaps on a daily or biweekly basis. Moreover, because of my more frequent visits, I am probably going to purchase a greater percentage of fresh foods that are more nutritious, rather than packaged or processed foods that last longer. Given these powerful synergies across behaviours, researchers and health promotion professionals have started to recognize the many ways the built environment can influence health and well-being.

Think about the different features of the built environment in your own neighbourhood. Do they encourage or discourage healthy behaviours like biking and walking?

How Does the Built Environment Influence Health and Well-Being?

Given the broad range of elements that encompass the built environment, it is not difficult to imagine the variety of ways our surroundings can influence leisure and health behaviours (Dannenburg et al., 2003). For example, neighbourhoods that are well kept with tree-lined streets, have abundant green space for relaxation and recreation, and are free of noise pollution can promote reduced stress and improved mental health. Likewise, trees and parks can help to deal with air and water pollution and such pollutants are less prevalent to begin with when people are able to walk or bike rather than drive to school, work, or other destinations. The design of the built environment has an impact on crime and violence in communities, which can undoubtedly impact our physical and mental health. In the remainder of this section, we examine two behaviours or outcomes in particular—active living and social cohesion—that have strong connections with individual and community health.

The Built Environment and Active Living

There is strong support for the importance that physical activity or active living plays in a healthy lifestyle (Global Advocacy Council for Physical Activity, 2010). We can all think of how good we personally feel after participating in a physical activity (such as running, playing a sport, hiking, swimming, etc.) but there are a variety of benefits beyond simply feeling better. Specifically, regular "physical activity promotes well-being, physical and mental health, prevents disease, improves social connectedness and quality of life, provides economic benefits, and contributes to environmental sustainability" (Global Advocacy Council for Physical Activity, 2010, p. 1). Although there are tremendous benefits to a physically active lifestyle, most people are not obtaining sufficient activity. The recent Canadian Health Measures Survey (CHMS) by Statistics Canada reported only 15% of adults and 7% of children are obtaining sufficient activity for health benefits (Colley et al., 2011a; Colley et al., 2011b). So what is causing this reduced physical activity? The built environment provides some guidance both in terms of challenges and solutions.

> "In the old cities, getting enough physical activity during one's day wasn't an issue because it was as much a part of life as eating or sleeping. Today, physical activity has been engineered out of most aspects of life.... The modern city has changed all of this creating environment in which it is less and less common to work physical activity into the everyday patterns of life." (Frank, Engelke, & Schmid, 2003, p. 3)

When examining how the built environment influences physical activity, there are several dimensions or categories that have been considered. Within this chapter, we will use three main categories: land use, urban design, and transportation (Frank, Engelke, & Schmid, 2003).

Imagine your typical day. Can you think of three ways that physical activity has been engineered out of your life because of modern conveniences?

Land use refers to the patterns or groupings of places in the built environment and how they may or may not support physical activity. For example, work places, residential homes, restaurants, recreation facilities, parks, grocery stores, and other destinations may be within easily accessible, close arrangements or patterns that encourage active transportation (such as walking or cycling). On the other hand, they may be poorly connected and dispersed over large distances that instead promote driving and discourage active modes of transport (Handy et al., 2002). Poorly connected spaces have often occurred as a result of "urban sprawl." "Urban sprawl uses large quantities of land, tends to separate housing from stores, schools and workplaces, and encourages dependency on automobiles. Key features of urban sprawl include communities that have:

> new housing developments at the edges of, or well outside of, established community areas; have housing that is relatively isolated from shops, services, workplaces, and schools and that have lower numbers of residents per square kilometre ("low density"); encourage dependency on automobiles to get around and to travel between housing, shops, services, schools and workplaces; have longer commuting times for residents from their homes to school and/or work; have curved, unconnected residential street patterns and wide, busy commercial streets that may pose a safety risk to pedestrians and cyclists; and are not particularly pedestrian friendly due to a lack of sidewalks and/or narrow sidewalks that are located close to busy streets with lots of automobiles nearby. (Heart and Stroke Foundation, 2011, p. 1)

Therefore, careful consideration of land use patterns is an important element of the built environment that can support and actually encourage physically active leisure. Research has found that residents in neighbourhoods with physical activity facilities, shops and services within walking distance, sidewalks or footpaths, and quality parks have an increased likelihood of being physically active (Kaczynski & Henderson 2007; Saelens & Handy, 2008). Another element of the built environment linked to physical activity is urban design.

The last time you went out shopping, did you drive or use some form of active transportation (including public transit)? What about when you went to work or school? What influenced your choice of transportation mode?

Urban design considers people's perception of the built environment (Frank, Engelke, & Schmid, 2003). It may include aspects such as aesthetic qualities and safety (Handy, Boarnet, Ewing, & Killingsworth, 2002). Areas where we enjoy participating will encourage more frequent usage. Consider for example your own neighbourhood. Now think about it in the winter—or the summer—how does it differ? What makes it easy to navigate? What makes it difficult? What about your friends' neighbourhoods? How do they differ? What are the sidewalks like? What are the natural spaces within the area? Is it easy to walk or more challenging? If you could picture your ideal space, what would that look like? What would be in your ideal neighbourhood? Each space will influence our capacity for physical activity and health opportunities.

In which settings would you be more interested in going for a walk? People are more naturally drawn to visually appealing spaces and features. They will be more likely to walk or cycle in their communities if they perceive them as attractive and safe. Regardless of the actual level of crime in the community, people develop a perception of its safety (Nova Scotia Justice, 2007). Parents often cite road safety as the key reason they will not allow their children to walk or cycle (Salmon, Salmon, Crawford, Hume, & Timperio, 2007). Attitudes and perceptions will greatly influence usage of the built environment, especially during times of the day when it may be dark outside or in low-lit areas, which may thereby be perceived as even more unsafe.

How safe do you feel in your neighbourhood? What features or lack of features makes it feel safer or more dangerous?

The final element to consider in the built environment is *transportation* (Frank et al., 2003). This refers to the connections among each element of the built environment or its street connectivity and scale. The more fluidly a person can move between spaces in the built environment, the greater the likelihood that they will do so. See the case study of a walking community in Brantford, Ontario. Communities that are well connected in terms of trails, sidewalks, and bike lanes will encourage people to use more active forms of transportation in their daily patterns. Some communities have actually made changes to their transportation plans to encourage such development and also discourage automobile usage in certain areas. For example, one-way or pedestrian-only streets will actively encourage walking or cycling.

Case Study: Brantford, ON—A walking community

"Brantford is the best walking city in Ontario according to the Canadian Federation of Podiatric medicine. Brantford City Council was one of the first in Ontario to endorse the International Charter for Walking, and Mayor Mike Hancock signed it in October 2007 as part of a city-wide commitment to supporting the proclamation of walking month in the city. The signed charter is now on prominent display in the downtown public library" (Source: Green Communities, Canada Walks, 2011).

Similarly, community design characterized by large distances between facilities and an absence of good locations for walking will encourage people to drive more often. "Green routes" are one such example of where communities may designate active transit routes. Therefore, the spaces, design, and connections among the various elements of our built environment greatly influence the potential for physical activity. Each aspect plays a role in how people will move around within their built environment and whether or not they will choose more active methods of doing so.

The Built Environment and Social Cohesion

In addition to physical activity, our built environment also affects opportunities to interact with others or to develop social cohesion. Indeed, some of the elements in the built environment that promote physical activity may also encourage social activity among neighbours and friends. For example, land use planning, transportation planning, and the level of walkability can encourage people to interact with others in their communities through active use of sidewalks, playgrounds, parks, and trails. Similarly, poorly designed and disconnected communities can discourage interaction by residents each driving in their own automobiles and only socializing, at most, with the members of their own household. This will lead to low levels of social capital in communities. Social capital is a term often used to describe how connected we are with other people and our community, and it has been shown to have significant implications for health (Kawachi & Berkman, 2000). Community design that impedes social capital can produce a lack of awareness and connection with one's neighbours, thereby potentially leading to feelings of distrust, uncertainty, and even fear.

A few studies have directly examined the associations between neighbourhood walkability and constructs related to neighbourhood connectedness. Leyden (2003) reported that people living in more walkable neighbourhoods, as measured by proximity to nine facilities or services, were more likely to know their neighbours, participate politically, have greater trust and faith in people, and be more socially engaged. Another study looked at environmental variables in exclusively suburban areas and residents' perceptions of social capital (Wood et al., 2008). They found that participants living in a suburban area with a conventional suburban street pattern (i.e., cul-de-sacs and curved layout) had greater social capital than persons living in suburbs with traditional (i.e., predominantly grid-like) or hybrid (i.e., mix of grid and cul-de-sacs) street patterns. The authors also looked at the number and specific types of destinations within a half-mile of participants and concluded that "more is not necessarily better and that there may be an optimum number of destinations required to generate feelings of safety and social capital, with greater consideration needed to be given also to the type and quality of destinations rather than simply the quantity" (Wood et al., 2008, p. 24). Indeed, Cohen and colleagues (2008) reported that certain neighbourhood features, such as more parks and fewer alcohol outlets, were associated with individuals' ratings of collective efficacy (i.e., their perceptions of trust and of neighbours' willingness to help each other).

In addition to being influenced by the built environment, social cohesion is an element that can affect how people actively participate in their community or environment. For example, in a national study of over 62,000 U.S. children ages 6–17, those with low neighbourhood social capital—as measured via four questions about parents' perceptions of neighbourhood social cohesion, trust, and reciprocity—had a 66% greater chance of being inactive (no days of vigorous physical activity in the past week) and a 33% lower chance of being classified as active (3 or more days of vigorous physical activity in the past week) than children with high neighbourhood social capital (Singh, Kogan, & van Dyck, 2008). Additionally, Brennan, Baker, Haire-Joshu, and Brownson (2003) constructed an 18-item protective social factors scale, based on dimensions such as social participation, cohesion, trust, reciprocity, and safety. They found that greater perceptions of protective social factors were related to an increased probability of meeting physical activity recommendations, especially among lower income people. Other research has likewise reported that greater levels of social capital, community satisfaction, and community participation, among other indicators of social cohesion, are related to increased physical activity participation (Greiner, Li, Kawachi, Hunt, & Ahluwalia, 2004; Kim, Subramanian, Gortmaker, & Kawachi, 2006).

How many of your neighbours do you know? Is this more or less than the neighbourhood in which you grew up? What elements of your neighbourhood contribute to or detract from developing connections with other people in your area?

Conclusion

The built environment is increasingly recognized as a key factor that influences our everyday actions, including those related to leisure and health. This is reflected in the wealth of organizations that are taking an active interest in issues related to healthy community design and its impact on behaviours (see *i*-box for a list of related websites). Improving the design of our communities will not happen overnight and will require the collaboration of researchers and professionals in multiple disciplines—planning, transportation, architecture, parks and recreation, public health, education, economics, political science, and public policy, just to name a few. Studies show there is increasing demand for traditionally designed neighbourhoods as people realize the physical, social, economic, and environmental benefits these types of designs can provide (Handy et al., 2008). Through careful planning that takes into account diverse transportation and recreation preferences, we can develop healthy communities where people of all ages can live, work, and play in settings that promote both leisure and overall well-being.

Websites Related to Healthy Community Design

8-80 Cities–Walk & Bike • Parks & Streets • For All:
http://www.8-80cities.org

Active & Safe Routes to School:
http://www.saferoutestoschool.ca

Active Living Research:
http://www.activelivingresearch.org

Key Terms

Built environment
Leisure behaviours
Health and well-being
Physical activity
Individual and community health

References

Brennan, L. K., Baker, E. A., Haire-Joshu, D., & Brownson, R. C. (2003). Linking perceptions of the community to behavior: Are protective social factors associated with physical activity? *Health Education & Behavior, 30*(6), 740–755.

Cohen, D. A., Inagami, S., & Finch, B. (2008). The built environment and collective efficacy. *Health & Place, 14*(2), 198–208.

Colley, R. C., Garriguet, D., Janssen, I., Craig, C. L., Clarke, J., & Tremblay, M. S. (2011a). Physical activity of Canadian adults: Accelerometer data from the 2007 to 2009 Canadian Health Measures Survey. *Statistics Canada, Health Reports, 22* (1), Catalogue no. 82-003-XPE

Colley, R. C., Garriguet, D., Janssen, I., Craig, C. L., Clarke, J., & Tremblay, M. S. (2011b). Physical activity of Canadian children and youth: Accelerometer data from the 2007 to 2009 Canadian Health Measures Survey. *Statistics Canada, Health Reports, 22* (1), Catalogue no. 82-003-XPE.

Dannenburg, A. L., Jackson, R. J., Frumkin, H., Schieber, R. A., Pratt, M., Kochtitzky, C., & Tilson, H. H. (2003). The impact of community design and land-use choices on public health: A scientific research agenda. *American Journal of Public Health, 93*(9), 1500–1508.

Dustin, D. L., Bricker, K. S., & Schwab, K. A. (2010). People and nature: Toward an ecological model of health promotion. *Leisure Sciences, 32*(1), 3–14.

Frank, L. D., Engelke, P. O., & Schmid, T. L. (2003). *Health and community design: The impact of the built environment on physical activity*. Washington, DC: Island Press.

Frank, L. D., Sallis, J. F., Conway, T. L., Chapman, J. E., Saelens, B. E., & Bachman, W. (2006). Many pathways from land use to health-Associations between neighborhood walkability and active transportation, body mass index, and air quality. *Journal of the American Planning Association, 72*(1), 75–87.

Global Advocacy Council for Physical Activity (2010). International Society for Physical Activity and Health. Retrieved from http://www.globalpa.org.uk

Greiner, K. A., Li, C. Y., Kawachi, I., Hunt, D. C., & Ahluwalia, J. S. (2004). The relationships of social participation and community ratings to health and health behaviors in areas with high and low population density. *Social Science & Medicine, 59*(11), 2303–2312.

Handy, S. L., Boarnet, M. G., Ewing, R., & Killingsworth, R. E. (2002). How the built environment affects physical activity: Views from urban planning. *American Journal of Preventive Medicine, 23*(2 supplement), 64–73.

Handy, S., Sallis, J. F., Weber, D., Maibach, E., & Hollander, M. (2008). Is support for traditionally designed communities growing? Evidence from two national surveys. *Journal of the American Planning Association, 74*(2), 209–221.

Heart and Stroke Foundation. (2011). *Heart and Stroke Foundation of Canada Position Statement: The built environment, physical activity, heart disease, and stroke.* Retrieved from http://www.heartandstroke.com

Kaczynski, A. T., & Henderson, K. (2007). Environmental correlates of physical activity: A review of evidence about parks and recreation. *Leisure Sciences, 29*, 315–354.

Kawachi, I., & Berkman, L. (2000). Social cohesion, social capital, and health. In L. F. Berkman & I. Kawachi (Eds.), *Social epidemiology* (pp. 174–190). London, UK: Oxford University Press.

Kim, D., Subramanian, S. V., Gortmaker, S. L., & Kawachi, I. (2006). U.S. state- and county-level social capital in relation to obesity and physical inactivity: A multilevel, multivariable analysis. *Social Science Medicine, 63*(4), 1045–1059.

King, A. C., Stokols, D., Talen, E., Brassington, G. S., & Killingsworth, R. (2002). Theoretical approaches to the promotion of physical activity: Forging a transdisciplinary paradigm. *American Journal of Preventive Medicine*, 23(2S), 15–25.

Leyden, K. M. (2003). Social capital and the built environment: The importance of walkable neighborhoods. *American Journal of Public Health, 93*(9), 1546–1551.

Marcus, B. H., & Forsyth, L. H. (1999). How are we doing with physical activity? *American Journal of Health Promotion, 14*(2), 118–124.

McLeroy, K. R., Bibeau, D., Steckler, A., & Glanz, K. (1988). An ecological perspective on health promotion programs. *Health Education Quarterly, 15*(4), 351–377.

Nova Scotia Justice (2007). Government of Nova Scotia. Retrieved from http://www.gov.ns.ca/just/

Saelens, B. E., & Handy, S. L. (2008). Built environment correlates of walking: A review. *Medicine and Science in Sports and Exercise, 40*(7), S550–566.

Sallis, J. F., Cervero, R. B., Ascher, W., Henderson, K. A., Kraft, M. K., & Kerr, J. (2006). An ecological approach to creating active living communities. *Annual Review of Public Health, 27*, 297–322.

Sallis, J. F., Owen, N., & Fisher, E. B. (2008). Ecological models of health behavior. In K. Glanz, B. K. Rimer, & K. Viswanath (Eds.), *Health behavior and health education: Theory, research, and practice* (4th ed., pp. 465–485). San Francisco, CA: Jossey-Bass.

Salmon, J., Salmon, L., Crawford, D. A., Hume, C., & Timperio, A. (2007). Associations among individual, social, and environmental barriers and children's walking or cycling to school. *American Journal of Health Promotion, 22*(2), 107–114.

Singh, G. K., Kogan, M. D., & van Dyck, P. C. (2008). A multilevel analysis of state and regional disparities in childhood and adolescent obesity in the United States. *Journal of Community Health, 33*(2), 90–102.

Srinivasan, S., O'Fallon, L. R., & Dearry, A. (2003). Creating healthy communities, healthy homes, healthy people: Initiating a research agenda on the built environment and public health. *American Journal of Public Health, 93*(9), 1446–1450.

Wood, L., Shannon, T., Bulsara, M., Pikora, T., McCormack, G., & Giles-Corti, B. (2008). The anatomy of the safe and social suburb: An exploratory study of the built environment, social capital and residents' perceptions of safety. *Health & Place, 14*(1), 15–31.

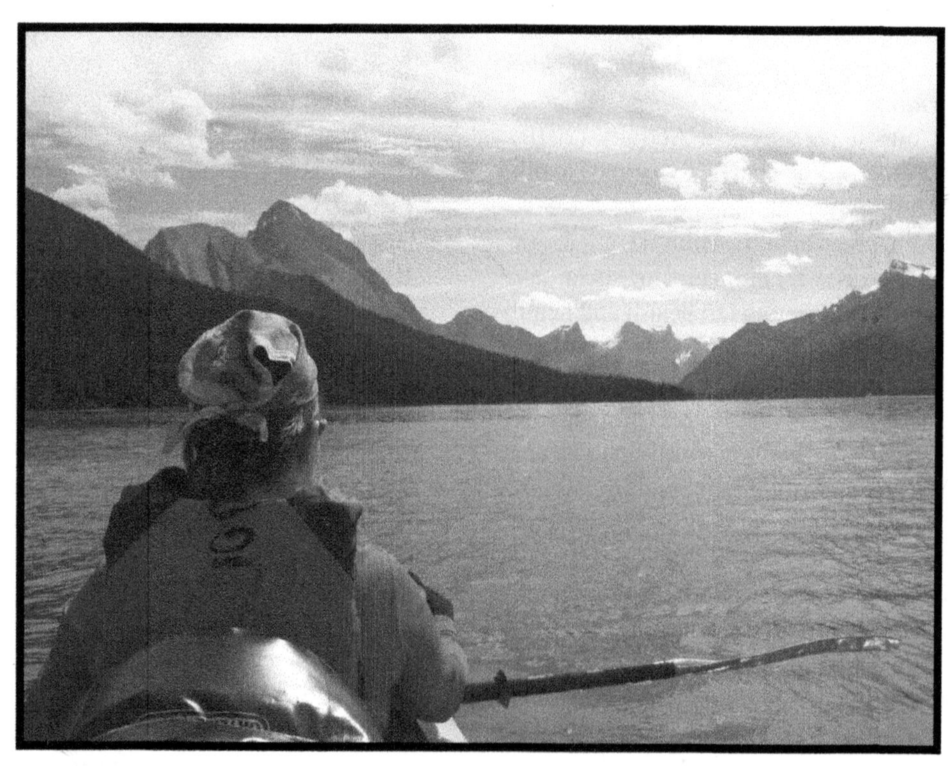

Chapter 17
Leisure in Natural Settings

J. Michael Campbell, Ph.D.
University of Manitoba

Learning Objectives

After reading this chapter, students will be able to

1. Understand the various means by which outdoor recreation can be classified and the role of nature in these classification schemes.
2. Describe the multi-phasic nature of the outdoor recreation experience.
3. Understand the role of motivation in the outdoor recreation experience.
4. Be familiar with some of the basic outdoor recreation management concepts and their applications.
5. Be aware of the potential impacts that outdoor recreation can have upon the environment and how management deals with these issues.

Introduction

As you read through this text you might be surprised to find a chapter dedicated to outdoor recreation. What is it about outdoor recreation that necessitates an entire chapter dedicated to it alone? Don't the general principles learned in other chapters apply equally to outdoor recreation? Just what is outdoor recreation? What makes it "different" from other forms of recreation and leisure? While initially outdoor recreation might appear to be little more than recreational activities in the out of doors, outdoor recreation satisfies needs and motives that other forms of recreation cannot. The human species has evolved over millennia as a part of the natural environment and it is only relatively recently in our history that we have become "domesticated." The need to reconnect and find our natural roots runs deep and may vary in strength from individual to individual, but it is nevertheless an important connection to our past. Indeed, many traditional forms of outdoor recreation (e.g., hunting, fishing, berry picking, collecting wood) are re-enactments of earlier human lifestyles—a re-creation of life more in tune with the environment and our ancestors. Results of numerous studies on the importance of nature to Canadians (DuWors, Villeneuve, & Filion, 1999; Filion, DuWors, & Boxall et al., 1993; Filion, DuWors & Jasquemont et al., 1987; and Filion, James et al., 1983) show that leisure in the natural environment is very important to Canadians across the country. The most recent survey conducted in 1996 indicates that 86% of Canadians participate in some form of leisure in the natural environment and that the economic value of these activities exceeds 11 billion dollars a year (DuWors et al., 1999).

Classifying Leisure in Natural Settings

Outdoor recreation and leisure can be any number of diverse activities and experiences that take place in the natural environment. A Statistics Canada study identified 17 activities in natural settings along with wildlife viewing, hunting, fishing, and residential wildlife related activities.

Table 17.1: Leisure in Natural Settings, Canadian response rates (percent)

Relaxing in an outdoor setting	32.4
Picnicking	26.0
Camping	18.8
Photographing in natural areas	15.9
Canoeing/Kayaking/Sailing	9.9
Cycling in natural areas	8.6
Climbing	4.3
Off-road vehicle use	3.4
Horseback riding	1.6
Sightseeing in natural areas	31.1
Swimming/beach activity	23.7
Hiking/Backpacking	18.5
Gathering nuts, berries, firewood	11.0
Power boating	9.3
Downhill skiing	4.7
X-country skiing/Snowshoeing	3.5
Snowmobiling	2.5

What do you think constitutes leisure in natural settings? Researchers who study leisure in natural environments have developed a number of means of classifying leisure in natural environments based on various criteria. Develop a list of all the activities and experiences that you consider to be leisure or recreation in natural settings. In looking at your list can you group the activities based upon similarities and differences (e.g., are they linked by things such as location, outcome, purpose, equipment?). After considering some of the classification schemes presented below, can you identify where the activities you listed would fall on the spectrum?

While there are a number of characteristics that can be used to classify outdoor recreation perhaps the most relevant is based upon the relationship to nature and the natural environment. In the first instance we consider whether the focus of the leisure pursuit is the natural environment. That is, is nature the primary focus of the activity or merely the location or space in which it takes place? Many activities that are conducted outdoors appear to have little connection to nature as part of the experience. In this example we could consider two pursuits at opposite ends of the spectrum, for example wilderness canoeing and all-terrain vehicle riding. Both of these activities take place outdoors and clearly require access to land, and yet the degree to which nature is the focus may vary. For example, one could imagine that ATV riding might not require a complete and functioning ecosystem and could be conducted in any number of outdoor locations with various degrees of modification (e.g. old gravel quarry, recent clear cut, power transmission line). In contrast, wilderness canoeing clearly depends upon the existence of large relatively undisturbed tracts of land and water. Moreover, the desires and motives of the participants in each of these activities may be quite different. This apparent contradiction highlights one of the key concerns in utilizing the list of activities approach to understanding and management of recreation in the natural environment.

Another means by which outdoor recreation can be characterized is whether it is facility-based or nature-based. In this characterization the chief difference is based upon the degree to which the outdoor activity depends upon the existence of facilities. Some very obvious examples of activities that are facility-based include activities such as downhill skiing, golfing, or visiting an interpretive centre. Each of these activities depends to various degrees upon some form of built facility. At the other end of the spectrum are experiences and activities that require little or no facilities; activities such as backpacking, canoe tripping, and picking wild berries. These activities in contrast depend quite heavily upon having an appropriate natural environment to enjoy them; after all it's pretty hard to pick berries if there are no bushes. Between these two extremes are leisure pursuits that depend to some degree upon the existence of facilities, the most obvious (and one we rarely think about as such) is camping in a campground. Many outdoor activities that we currently consider being facility-based began with more direct connections to the natural landscape.

> Can you identify any nature-based recreational pursuits that have become increasingly facility-based? Are there some activities that you no longer consider to be nature-based but once were?

Outdoor recreation activities can also be classified as to whether they are nature-oriented or user-oriented. In this classification the key element is whether the participant places emphasis on experience of nature or experience of the activity as evidenced in their performance. Any number of outdoor activities may lie at a range of locations along this spectrum, depending solely upon the motivations of the participants. For example, a person could be mountain biking for the sole purpose of any of the following: to experience the wilderness; to socialize in nature with friends and family; to access the backcountry; to improve physical fitness; or to compete in a cross-country bike race. Most of these motives might include some focus on nature but it is clear that the degree of focus is different in each and, in some cases, personal performance or competition is the primary motive.

Finally, the classification of outdoor activities as consumptive or non-consumptive is another means of understanding outdoor recreation behaviour. Consumptive activities are those in which physical elements of the natural world are collected, such as game, fish, fossils, or berries. Non-consumptive activities, for example hiking or whale watching, are those activities in which nothing is physically taken from nature.

The preceding discussion on classification of nature-based recreation suggests that it is not so much the activities themselves as the motives behind them and the manner in which they are conducted that is the most important determinant in their relationship to nature. This presents quite a challenge for researchers. In the past, research into outdoor activity has often used surveys that focussed on general participation patterns. Lists of activities were produced from these surveys but we now know they often failed to provide answers needed to plan and manage recreation properly in natural settings. In addition, lists of activities do not provide information about preferences. Lists often focus upon rates or frequency of participation not on which activities people prefer so they may mask constraints that limit participation. For example, your favourite outdoor activity might be downhill skiing but if you live in Manitoba, you will have limited opportunities to participate. Understanding the motives behind participation in nature-based recreation and the goals of the participants is essential to providing opportunities to satisfy the full spectrum of nature-based recreation, as well as, reducing conflict between users.

The Five Components of Outdoor Recreation

Aldo Leopold, the one-time head of the United States Forest Service, identified five components of the experience of outdoor recreation: (1) collection of physical objects; (2) feelings of isolation in nature; (3) experiencing fresh air and scenery; (4) perception of nature; and (5) development of a sense of husbandry. They are not necessarily discrete and any or all of them may form a part of a single outdoor experience.

The collection of physical evidence of the experience can be characterized as the youthful stage in the development of outdoor recreation experiences. If you think back to your own youth and some of your first outdoor activities you might recall the pleasure you felt when bringing home the frogs, tadpole, bugs, and other evidence of your outdoor activities (often our mothers weren't quite so pleased and had us remove them from the house). This collection provides us with a "certificate" of our experience and is evidenced also in the photo collection of the avid nature photographer or the life list of the birder. There is some concern over this component of the outdoor experience. The concern is over the inherently consumptive nature of this activity. As we collect, we tend to consume these items as trophies. Some suggest the danger in this is not the taking of the trophy so much as the potential that the trophy becomes the sole reason for the outdoor recreation experience.

The need to experience isolation in nature is not something everyone desires and yet some people have a very deep need to experience this component. In fact, many people are terrified of the idea of being alone in nature. Ironically, as this need increases there are fewer and fewer places where that need can be met, as more and more people flock to the few small green spots on the map. This simple arithmetic suggests why we must manage our outdoor recreation opportunities to provide for a variety of experiences.

The simple experience of fresh air and scenery, Leopold's third component, is unique because it can be enjoyed by many without interfering with others doing the same. A drive along the Cabot Trail in Nova Scotia or the Bow Valley Parkway in Alberta provides the opportunity for many to see the same landscape and breathe the fresh air without necessarily diminishing the experience of others doing the same.

In perception of nature Leopold saw the nascent development of husbandry through recreationists developing understanding and perception of nature's rhythms. By doing so, he believed we could achieve harmony with nature. Perception requires a keen awareness of nature and natural processes and is much more than simply being entertained but being really involved.

Finally, the feeling of husbandry or a responsibility or obligation to the environment is the final and most important of Leopold's five components. In husbandry the recreationist with keen perception more than perceives nature's rhythms but seeks to become a steward of the land community ensuring its existence for the future. Clearly the development of a sense of husbandry represents the maturation of the relationship with nature and recognition of one's place and responsibility in the land community. The development of perception and stewardship should be the ultimate goal of all outdoor recreation programs.

The Total Recreation Experience

Researchers have attempted to describe the many stages or phases in a typical outdoor leisure experience. Together these phases represent the Total Recreation Experience. This experience is comprised of four phases: (1) anticipation; (2) planning; (3) participation; and (4) recollection. Anticipation is the point at which we begin to dream about our recreation experience, imagining all the possibilities and deciding to participate. In the planning phase, as the name implies, we begin to make preparations for our participation. This preparation might include finding others to participate, collecting maps, securing permits, and more complex preparations like ensuring we have the requisite skills or certification for the activity. The participation phase, the actual conduct of the activity, is clearly the phase most of us think of when we are asked about outdoor recreation. The final phase, recollection, is comprised of the memories we retain from our experience and is often an important element that we share with others (Clawson & Knetch, 1963).

Supply, or Where the Experience Occurs

Where do Canadians participate in outdoor recreation? Well the obvious answer is outdoors, and, as a nation, Canada is truly blessed with tremendous access to natural settings. From national parks to provincial parks to local conservations areas, most Canadians have relatively easy access to the natural environment.

National Parks

Canada currently has 41 national parks representing 30 of 39 natural regions. Canada was the third nation to establish a national park with the creation of Rocky Mountain National Park (now Banff) in 1887 (set aside in 1885). At the time of its creation the park consisted of 25 square kilometers surrounding the Cave and Basin hot springs. The development of the Banff Springs Hotel resulted in Banff initially being an "outpost of civilization amidst limitless wilderness" (Sandford, 1999). Now, for many national parks the reverse is the case and many parks are islands of wilderness in a sea of development. As a result, the focus of parks' management has changed over the 100 plus years of their existence. The initial act of creating a national park in Canada was largely an economic activity and early management of the park was as a tourism attraction (Lothian, 1987). Now in many parts of the country national parks are the last vestiges of wilderness and as such, important for wildlife habitat.

National parks are managed both to protect the natural environment and to provide Canadians with opportunities to enjoy the outdoor recreation and leisure opportunities they provide. Parks Canada utilizes a variety of management strategies and frameworks to manage the parks and ensure that use of the parks does not damage them for future generations.

Heritage Rivers

Rivers have been important features of Canada for millennia, providing transportation routes for Canada's first peoples and subsequently the trade routes of the voyageurs and the fur trade, indeed molding the country and its people. Canada's national river conservation program, the Canadian Heritage Rivers System, promotes, protects and enhances Canada's river heritage. A river recognized as a Canadian Heritage River must represent an outstanding example of the natural and/or cultural values and provide quality recreational opportunities. This recognition of the importance of a river's recreational value is unique to the Heritage Rivers System and highlights the important role rivers play in outdoor recreation in Canada. There are currently 39 Canadian Heritage Rivers across the country and more are added each year. Heritage Rivers in Canada cover a wide spectrum: from canals, such as the Rideau, to the broad swift sub arctic rivers, like the Seal and the Thelon.

Provincial Parks

In contrast to national parks, provincial parks fulfill a wider variety of roles and like the Heritage Rivers often place opportunities for recreation as a priority. Again the diversity of opportunities is a key element in the development of a provincial park system. The Ontario provincial parks system is, arguably, the most comprehensive of the provincial systems in terms of its attention to providing a range of opportunities to visitors across the province and ensuring that, as much as is practicable, residents of all regions have access to all types of opportunity.

While most of us think of major parks and protected areas when we envision outdoor recreation, as noted in Chapter 15 on urban recreation, most outdoor recreation takes place in far less dramatic locations such as neighbourhood green spaces. According to the Survey on the Importance of Nature to Canadians, 77% of Canadians engage in domestic nature related activities near or on their own property (Duwors et al., 1999). It is the opportunity to experience nature near to home that ensures that all Canadians have access to these meaningful experiences.

Management Concepts

One of the earliest outdoor recreation management concepts is that of *carrying capacity*. This is a concept borrowed and adapted from the management of cattle. When applied to recreation, carrying capacity refers to the maximum number of recreationists that a given area can accommodate without having a negative impact on the environment or the experiences of other recreationists. Like its use in range science, the maximum number of recreationists is quite variable and is dependent upon the amount, type, and timing of the activity. Indeed with respect to recreation, carrying capacity is even more fluid or elastic as it has physical, ecological, and psychological components.

Physical carrying capacity refers to the capacity of the built environment to accommodate users. How many cars can fit in the Moraine Lake parking lot at Banff National Park? How many people can stand on the viewing platform at Niagara Falls? Physical carrying capacity is often fixed and to a large degree known, unlike ecological and psychological carrying capacity.

Ecological carrying capacity refers to the amount of impact the biological and physical components of the environment can accommodate without negative effect. Examples of measures of ecological carrying capacity include; changes or reduction in vegetation cover, habituation, or other changes in animal behaviour, trail braiding, and erosion.

Psychological carrying capacity refers to the impact of people on other people. This concept is often discussed in terms of goal interference whereby one person's pursuit of his/her outdoor goals interferes with the pursuits of others. One early Canadian study of psychological carrying capacity focussed on conflict between cross-country skiers and snowmobilers (Jackson & Wong, 1982). The researchers discovered that threats to psychological carrying capacity are not always experienced to the same degree by all concerned. In this case, the skiers experienced more goal interference than did the snowmobilers. As such, there were two (and quite possibly more) different carrying capacities at work on the trails shared by the two groups. This asymmetry causes problems in the application of carrying capacity to the management of outdoor recreation in the natural environment. Despite these problems the idea of carrying capacity has led to the development of a number of successful management schema.

Management Frameworks

The Recreational Opportunity Spectrum (ROS) was introduced by the United States Forest Service as means to plan for, and provide management direction to, outdoor recreation opportunities on public lands. The spectrum is based on the idea that differing types of outdoor recreation require different types of environments. It sets out to identify the level of management, facilities, access, and services required to satisfy the needs of the different types of recreational use. Put another way, no one park can be all things to all people. Generally, the spectrum component of the model identifies six classes of recreational opportunity, ranging from primitive through rustic to modern. The level of services and management is specified for each class of opportunity and ranges from little to no services and access in the primitive opportunity class to paved roads and many of the conveniences of home in the modern opportunity class.

Can you identify some of the outdoor recreation areas in your region based upon the opportunity spectrum? What features of the sites lead you to this conclusion? For example how do you gain access to the site, how evident is management, what type of facilities are provided?

Many park systems have employed the principles of the ROS as it provides a framework for planning and identifying the level of management interventions in any particular park class. (See the Ontario provincial park system for an excellent example of the principles of ROS applied system wide at http://www.ontarioparks.on/english/pdf/bluebook.pdf.)

The ROS does not, however, address the need to plan any individual park for a variety of uses. Instead managers use zoning within individual parks. They know that not all activities are appropriate to all areas of the park. This is particularly important in multi-use parks that attempt to provide a variety of visitor experiences. Zoning enables managers to create, in the same park, a zone for wilderness or backcountry, one for natural environment, one for outdoor recreation of a more developed type, and another for visitor services. The use of zoning allows park managers to protect particularly vulnerable features of the park from use or overuse. Parks Canada employs a five-zone model that recognizes:

1. special preservation;
2. wilderness;
3. natural environment;
4. outdoor recreation; and
5. park services

Special preservation zones are areas in the park that contain rare, threatened, or endangered features and species. In general, access to these regions is strictly controlled and many members of the public are not aware of their existence. The wilderness zone makes up the largest percentage of most national parks in Canada and provides the habitat needs of the park's wildlife and opportunities for recreation of a primitive nature.

A number of other management frameworks have been developed such as; the Limits of Acceptable Change, Visitor Impact Management, and Visitor Experience and Resource Protection. Based upon the principles of carrying capacity, they attempt to include both ecological and recreation carrying capacity in the management process. Parks Canada's Visitor Activity Management Process, while not directly based on carrying capacity, does consider motives and demographic factors in guiding visitor management and has been employed to provide insight to identifying appropriate activities in National Parks (Payne & Nilson, 2002). See *i*-box, Strategies for Limiting Use, p. 162.

Environmental Impacts of Outdoor Recreation

While it is undeniable that outdoor recreation provides many benefits to individuals, society, and the environment, it is not without its negative impacts. In the following section we consider the impacts of recreation on the environment.

Clearly large numbers of people recreating in natural environments will, in the absence of mitigating measures, result in damage to the environment. Examples include air and water pollution, litter, damage to vegetation and soils, and changes to wildlife behaviour. Large numbers of visitors can seriously stress water treatment facilities and may result in significant water pollution. The same large numbers of visitors also contribute to noise and light pollution in parks and protected areas. Even the greenest activities such as wilderness canoeing can cause significant environmental damage. Canoes made of plastics and other synthetics produce toxic by-products and waste during their manufacture, and we burn fossil fuels flying to remote lakes and rivers or driving our cars to the destination point. Most of us are unaware of our impacts on the natural environment and while it is impossible to prevent impacts altogether while enjoying the natural world, it is important to try to minimize them. A number of management strategies have been developed in an attempt to mitigate against negative impacts.

Litter

One of the most obvious impacts of human use of the natural environment is litter and means of reducing or

Strategies for Limiting Use (Manning, 1999)

	Lottery	Reservation	Queue	Pricing	Merit
Process	Random draw	Reduces numbers by requiring pre-planning	First come, first served	Charge entrance fee. Employ differential fees	Require evidence of ability
Effect	Reduces numbers. No identifiable group benefits, but does not reflect demand	Reduces numbers. Can impact those who are unwilling or unable to plan	Reduces numbers. Provides some measure of value as reflected in lost time. Benefits locals	Reduces numbers by controlling distribution of use	Some reduction in numbers. Reduced per capita impact
History or experience	Little used, has been applied for big game hunting	Main type of rationing used. Increasing uses in Canada, including wilderness areas	Used in conjunction with reservation	Little used. Entrance fees not necessarily intended to limit use	Little used as level of proficiency and certification requirements vary
Example	Manitoba Elk draw	West Coast Trail reservation	West Coast Trail	Pricing structure of campgrounds in Banff NP	

eliminating it have been studied for over 50 years. Recent research in Riding Mountain National Park determined that litter is the one impact that most park visitors are capable of identifying (MacKay & Campbell, 2004). The impacts of litter extend beyond the visual and can have many negative impacts upon wildlife. Birds, animals, and fish may ingest litter or may become entangled in it. Bears may be drawn into occupied campsites because of food-based litter. In all such cases, these natural inhabitants will suffer the consequences.

Impacts on Soil and Vegetation

The principal effect of recreation on vegetation results from the cumulative effects of trampling. These effects can be amplified by recreational activities and equipment (e.g., hiking versus horseback riding, and wearing heavy hard soled boots as opposed to running shoes) and during wetter periods. In addition, wet conditions cause many trail users to attempt to skirt the wet areas resulting in expansion of the impact. These effects are even more significant at campsites as people tend to spend more time in camp than on any one portion of trail.

Impacts on Wildlife

Wildlife is impacted both directly and indirectly by the pursuit of leisure in natural areas. Other than direct mortality the most significant effects on wildlife are changes in wildlife behaviour resulting from various human recreation activities. These behavioural changes can be classified as habituation, attraction, and avoidance (Knight & Cole, 1995). Habituated animals no longer display their natural responses to the presence of humans. Elk in Banff no longer flee when humans approach and, as a result, endanger both humans and themselves. Animals that associate people with food can become attracted to humans and facilities. The squirrel that begs for food at the campground is exhibiting attraction behaviour and while many consider it cute, this type of behaviour can be dangerous to humans and wildlife. When the attracted animal is larger (e.g., a bear) the threat is greatly increased both to humans and the bear; it could be said that a fed bear is a dead bear.

Which of the management techniques identified in the Strategies *i*-box above would you apply to a trail that was becoming eroded? What information would you need to determine the best approach?

Trends and the Future of Outdoor Recreation

As we have seen, leisure in natural settings is both a very important element in many people's lives and a complex phenomenon. It is unlikely that the desire to participate in nature-based recreation will abate in the near future, and many researchers believe that demand will continue to increase as we become increasingly urbanised and our lifestyles and employment become more oriented to technology. The so-called leisure revolution predicted in the 1960s has never been realized; however, as our day-to-day lives provide less interaction with the natural world, the need for leisure in natural settings is sure to grow. To meet this demand there will need to be greater commitment to providing access to natural environments and green spaces to urban residents.

As more people seek solitude in natural environments we will increasingly have to find ways to ration use (see Strategies *i*-box). Currently, many remote areas of Canada see very little or indeed no recreational use. These areas will continue to offer the opportunity for solitude to those able to reach them for years to come. For those without the skill, free time, or necessary financial resources to visit these remote regions however, solitude will be increasingly difficult to discover.

Technology

Technology affects leisure in natural settings through a variety of means including: advances in equipment, the

Technology, Bicycles, and Outdoor Recreation

For many of the students reading this text, the idea that there was a time without mountain bikes might come as a surprise, but in fact mountain bikes are widely identified as having developed in Marin County, California in the late 1970s and only became widely available commercially in the mid 1980s. Continued technological advances have resulted in the bikes of today, which are built specifically for cross-country, free-riding and downhill. Mountain bikes have had wide ranging impacts on park management and managers have been forced to adapt to an entirely new type of use. The mountain bike has afforded people greatly increased access to the backcountry with riders travelling easily up to 60–70 kilometres in a day, a distance a hiker would take three days to cover. As a result some backcountry areas are increasingly becoming day use areas (Campbell & MacKay, 2004). In Banff National Park the use of mountain bikes coupled with the encroachment of logging roads on the Park's borders, have allowed fishers day use access to remote lakes that previously required overnight stays. This has changed the nature of the fishery by allowing fishers to take a limit of fish home when in the past most fishers might keep one fish to eat and release the remainder. The result was over-fishing and a decline in the quality of the fishery (Pacas, 2003).

development of new recreational pursuits, increasing access to information regarding opportunities and conditions, online reservations, and effectively "shrinking the globe."

Advances in equipment have had an enormous impact on how recreation is carried out in natural settings, and will continue to do so in the future. It is a rare outdoor recreational pursuit that has not in some way been affected by technological advances. Modern synthetic materials have significantly decreased the weight of all outdoor gear, allowing people to travel farther, longer, and faster with obvious consequences to the environment. The development of the shaped ski is widely credited with renewing interest in downhill skiing, an activity that had seen its popularity flatten in recent years as the younger generation embraced snowboarding. Advances in lift technology get more people up the mountain faster, while advances in grooming and snow-making ensure consistent conditions and increase safety.

Computers and the Internet have had enormous impacts on people and society. Access to information is only a mouse click away, greatly altering the anticipation and planning phases of our recreational experience. Every aspect of our recreation experience, including virtual participation (see Chapter 15), can be conducted from the comfort of our homes. We can check on snow conditions at any number of ski resorts, monitor the weather forecasts, while evaluating the slopes and lifts, and booking our trip online. Many park agencies now have online booking of campsites and provide a host of information regarding trail conditions, interpretive programming etc., facilitating people's leisure experiences.

Climate

Perhaps the greatest potential threat to the environment upon which leisure in natural areas depends is that of global climate change. While considerable uncertainty exists as to the exact outcome of global climate changes, the majority of climate researchers suggest that the average global temperature will increase and that the greatest increases will occur in the higher latitudes. Based upon suggested temperature and precipitation changes for Ontario, Wall (1988) examined the impact upon a variety of outdoor recreation activities and found that a number of winter activities would be in danger of being eliminated and many others could become marginal.

Given the uncertainty regarding the actual nature of any climate changes that might occur, it is difficult to state with precision how leisure in natural settings will be affected. It is undeniable that environmental issues and concerns will have a significant impact on leisure in natural areas.

Concluding Thoughts

As we have seen in this chapter, outdoor recreation encompasses a diverse array of activities and experiences, and for many Canadians it is the only means by which they interact with the natural environment. This "reconnection" or "re-recreation" of our relationship with the natural environment is perhaps the most important element of the outdoor recreation experience. It is through direct contact with nature that we come to understand, appreciate, and ultimately develop a sense of stewardship for the natural environment. Given the general decrease in our connection with nature as part of our daily life, the value of and demand for quality outdoor experiences will only increase, thus necessitating informed management of our parks and natural areas along with the public's expectations of what these special places are able to provide.

Key Terms

Anticipation
Attraction
Avoidance
Carrying capacity

Consumptive
Facility-based
Habituation
Heritage Rivers
Litter
Motivations
Nature-based
Non-consumptive
Recreational Opportunity Spectrum
Supply
Zoning

References

Campbell, J. M., & MacKay, K. J. (2004). The role of people, place and process in implementing a promising backcountry monitoring program: Riding Mountain National Park. *Environments, 32*(1), 31–45.

Clawson, M., & Knetch, J. (1963). Outdoor recreation research: Some concepts and suggested areas of study. *Natural Resources Journal, 3*, 250–275.

DuWors, E., Villeneuve, M., & Filion, F. L. (1999). *The importance of nature to Canadians: Survey highlights.* Ottawa, ON: Environment Canada.

Filion, F. L., DuWors, E., Boxall, P., Bouchard, Reid, R., Gray, P.A., et al. (1993). *The importance of wildlife to Canadians: Highlights of the 1991 survey.* Ottawa, ON: Canadian Wildlife Service, Environment Canada.

Filion, F. L., DuWors, E., Jasquemot, P., Boxall, P., Gray, P.A., & Reid, R. (1987). *The importance of wildlife to Canadians in 1987: Highlights of natural survey.* Ottawa, ON: Canadian Wildlife Service, Environment Canada.

Filion, F. L., James, S.W., Ducharme, J. L., Pepper, W., Reid, R., Boxall, P., & Teillet, D. (1983). *The importance of wildlife to Canadians: highlights of the 1981 national survey.* Ottawa, ON: Canadian Wildlife Service, Environment Canada.

Jackson, E., & Wong, R. (1982). Perceived conflict between urban cross-country skiers and snowmobilers in Alberta. *Journal of Leisure Research, 14*, 47–62.

Knight, R. L., & Cole, D. N. (1995). Wildlife responses to recreationists. In R. L. Knight & K. J. Guttzwiller (Eds.), *Wildlife and recreationists: Coexistence through management and research* (pp. 51–70). Washington, DC: Island Press.

Leopold, A. (1969). *A sand county almanac: With other essays on conservation from Round River.* New York, NY: Oxford University Press.

Lothian, W. F. (1987). *A brief history of Canada's national parks.* Ottawa, ON: Environment Canada.

MacKay, K. J., & Campbell, J. M. (2004). A mixed method approach for measuring environmental impacts in nature based tourism and outdoor recreation settings. *Tourism Analysis, 9*, 141–152.

Manning, R. E. (1999). *Studies in outdoor recreation: Search and research for satisfaction.* Corvallis, OR: Oregon State University Press.

Pacas, C. (2003). Aquatic ecosystem scientist Banff National Park, personal communication.

Payne R., & Nilsen, P. (2002). Visitor Planning and Management. In P. Dearden & R. Rollins, *Parks and protected areas in Canada: Planning and management* (2nd ed, pp. 97–114). Don Mills, ON: Oxford University Press.

Sandford, R. W. (1999, June 3). The Banff heritage tourism strategy presentation. Banff Visitor Centre.

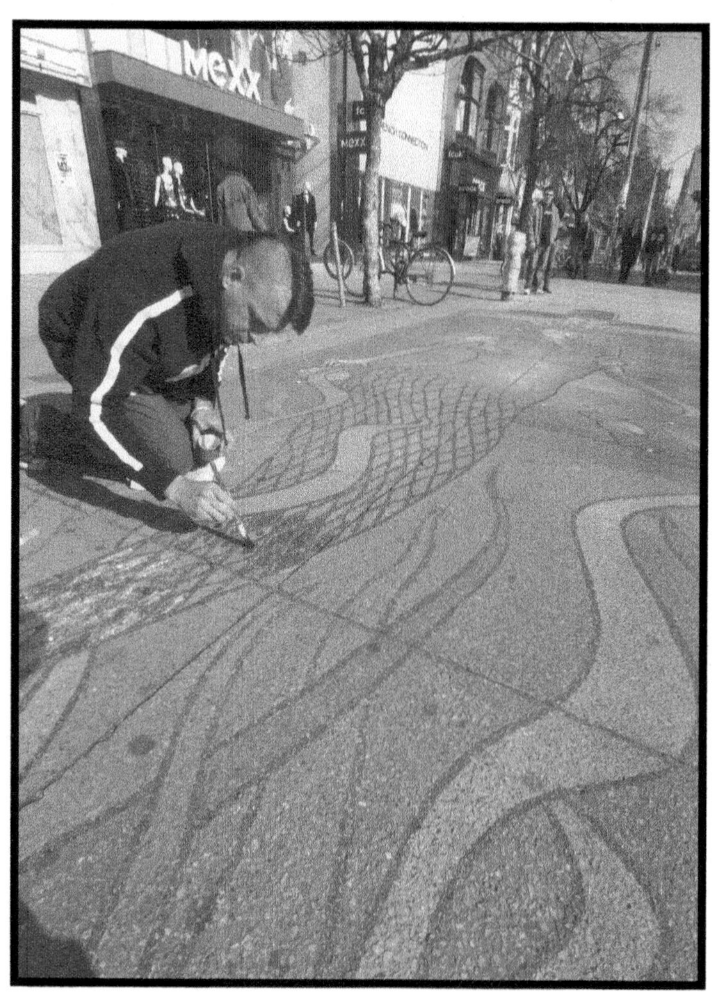
Mexx
MEXX

Chapter 18
Exploring Leisure's Boundaries

Anne-Marie Sullivan, Ph.D. and Danielle LeDrew, B.Kin.
Memorial University of Newfoundland

Learning Objectives

After reading this chapter, students will be able to

1. Understand the complexity of marginal leisure;
2. Know what constitutes tolerable and intolerable deviance.
3. Understand activities viewed as marginal or deviant in our society.
4. Be aware of the wide range of activities encompassed within marginal leisure.
5. Know classification systems developed to identify good and bad forms of leisure.
6. Be aware of some of the common theoretical explanations of marginal and deviant behaviour.
7. Understand why marginal leisure is an important area of inquiry for leisure studies.

Introduction

Almost all people participate in some form of leisure that is not immediately identified as a typical leisure activity and most participate in some form of leisure that is "on the margins" or termed deviant. These activities can range from overindulging during the holidays and obsessive exercise, to stalking and even serial killing. In this chapter, we will examine deviant leisure in all its forms.

What comes to mind when you hear the word *leisure*? What are some of the images that immediately pop into your head? In all likelihood, your thoughts are positive ones. The term leisure brings about images of fun, relaxation, spending time with loved ones, and all types of meaningful activity. Now think of all the things that you do in your leisure time. Does the image stay the same? If not, how does it change?

What Is Leisure?

What does the term leisure mean to the majority of people in Canadian society? As discussed in early chapters of this textbook, leisure is incredibly varied. Leisure may be challenging or relaxing, solitary or social, organized or spontaneous. Some people think in terms of time outside of work, family, and personal obligation; others think in terms of activity; still others think in terms of the experience itself. The meaning of leisure depends on the eye of the beholder.

There is unlikely to be one *best* definition for leisure (Freysinger & Kelly, 2004). How leisure is defined depends on the individual as well as the need and context of the definition. There are a number of common leisure themes including freedom, enjoyment, and intrinsic meaning for the individual. What is clear is that leisure is not solely determined by the activity itself, such that almost anything at any time may constitute leisure for someone. At first glance, leisure may seem to be somewhat secondary in comparison to other domains of life including family, work, and education; however, when given careful consideration, it is quickly evident that leisure is much more than what happens in the time leftover from the rest of life.

A review of the major journals in the field of leisure studies would suggest that leisure is typically viewed in positive terms. Rojek (1999) has suggested that the main concern for leisure researchers has been that of promoting social order and/or improving social and cultural conditions. The benefits of leisure are well researched and promoted in the field (Driver, Brown, & Peterson 1991).

Leisure continues to be "conceptualized in the literature as a positive realm of activity in which there are a myriad of benefits to participants and non-participants alike, both directly and indirectly" (Glover, 2003, p. 308). Leisure is accepted universally as a positive experience marked by freedom of choice and intrinsic motivation. As is the case for any activity, however, there is a questionable side that also demands consideration. This destructive side of leisure has come to include activities such as alcohol and drug use, gambling, sex tourism, and prostitution (Rojek, 1999).

Given that some leisure may be dangerous, destructive, and wasteful, it is surprising that academic interest in such questionable leisure has been negligible. As noted above, it has been suggested that leisure research tends to focus on the positive elements of leisure such as the benefits of participation for the individual as well as for the rest of society. Many leisure researchers are hesitant to acknowledge that people may participate in socially intolerant or distasteful activities as leisure because "most of them are emotionally involved with the belief that leisure is unquestionably a social benefit" (Rojek, 1999, p. 29). Rojek (1999) goes on to suggest that, "such is the strong association between leisure and positive experience, many leisure professionals will hold that the study of transgressive and infractious behaviour is better left to medical practitioners, psychoanalysts, and criminologists" (p. 33).

Leisure is generally considered to be activity carried out in harmony with the main values of the larger society (Kaplan, 1960). It is also assumed that "leisure has the potential to contribute positively to the quality of individuals' lives" (Glover, 2003, p. 307). Such sentiments have led many leisure researchers to focus solely on the benefits of leisure (Driver, Brown, & Peterson, 1991). Nevertheless, the idea that leisure behaviour sometimes goes against the moral grain of society has been increasingly recognized and explored. Stebbins (1996), Rojek (1997; 1999), and Cantwell (2003) posit that there can also be a questionable side to leisure. Rojek (1999) further notes that very little attention has been given to undesirable forms of leisure in the field of leisure research. In recent years there has been some research conducted on specific deviant activities, much of which was carried out by university students. For example, Glover (2003) focused on the rave scene while Shinew and Parry (2005) examined alcohol and substance use by college students and Sullivan (2006) explored gambling motivations of university students. Further examples include Shaw's (1999) article on pornography, Smith, Volberg, and Wynne's (1994) article on uncontrolled gambling practices, and Clift and Carter's (2000) edited book on prostitution and sex tourism.

Leisure and Deviance

As noted previously, leisure is not always warm and fuzzy. The notion that leisure can be considered deviant is not a new idea. It is important to note that like leisure, deviance is dependent on the eye of the beholder. Deviant behaviour can be defined as "conduct that is perceived by others as violating institutionalised expectations that are widely shared as legitimate with the society" (Bynum & Thompson, 1996, p. 16). This tells us that depending on the expectations of each individual society, deviant behaviours will vary, so what may be banned in one society may be part of everyday living in another. There is no one act that is universally condemned by all societies (not even murder or incest). Even within a given society, behaviour defined as deviant continually undergoes redefinition so what may be considered deviant today may become accepted tomorrow. A recent example of this is gambling. Not that long ago most forms of gambling were illegal, yet today not only is most gambling a legal activity, it is an ever growing recreational activity for many in our society.

According to Stebbins (1996) deviant behaviour can take two basic forms: tolerable and intolerable. *Tolerable behaviours* are those where the threat to the community is perceived to be quite low, and subsequently the activity is tolerated by members of the community. Unless the behaviour escalates to a point where they feel a threat related to the activity, community members adopt a position of passive acceptance regarding the activity. If a threat is felt, however, members of the community will take an active position to prevent the behaviour from occurring. Many forms of casual leisure, such as gambling, recreational drug use, consumption of alcohol, and some forms of sexual behaviour, can be classified as *tolerable deviance* (Stebbins, 1996).

Intolerable behaviour is "behaviour in violation of powerful criminal and non-criminal moral norms" (Stebbins, 1996, p. 6). Included here are behaviours or actions such as theft, assault, rape, suicide, substance abuse, and compulsive gambling. It is important to note that some activities, such as alcohol consumption and gambling, are seen as tolerable until they reach certain levels and the consequences related to the activity are detrimental to the individual and others in society.

What Is Marginal or Deviant Leisure?

So what then constitutes marginal leisure? This question is in fact rather challenging to answer, as once again, it depends on the eye of the beholder. It has been referred to as "deviant" or "the other side of leisure" (Freysinger & Kelly, 2004). The term *deviant* has been considered problematic because of the emotional baggage it carries. As a result, the term *marginal* is often used in this chapter. Regardless of the terminology used, there has been some debate over what to include in this category. This type of activity, which is not considered socially acceptable, has been referred to as *purple recreation* (Curtis, 1988) to indicate the "off-colour" nature of the activity. Russell (2002) suggested the term *taboo recreation* because these activities generally challenge societal norms, laws or belief systems. The terms "marginal," "questionable," "problematic," and "deviant" have been used to refer to this other side of leisure—or the dark side of leisure.

There are many reasons given why people choose to participate in a class of behaviours designated as "deviant" within society but experienced as "leisure" to the individual. Some people engage in this kind of behaviour to attempt to control outcomes, as can be seen in gambling. According to Katz (1988), some people are simply attracted to drinking, smoking, and partying for the pursuit of pleasure; people enjoy deviant behaviours.

Substance Use

Substance use is an activity that has gone from illegal to legal depending on the substance. For example, during the Prohibition of the 1920s alcohol consumption was illegal, yet today it is a widely accepted part of many leisure experiences. In Canada today, there is a great deal of discussion surrounding the de-criminalization of marijuana use. It is known that marijuana is less harmful in many respects than alcohol, yet it remains illegal while alcohol is readily available for consumption. If you travel to Amsterdam, essentially anything goes, and marijuana contributes to the economy and is considered a reasonable form of pleasure. In Canada and the United States, millions of dollars are spent on the war against marijuana. Who is right and who is wrong?

"Substance abuse is perhaps the most prevalent type of taboo recreation" (Russell, 2002, p. 202). The use of drugs and alcohol as a recreational activity is not a new phenomenon. So why is this form of leisure such a popular one? Perhaps substance use allows us to escape from everyday life. Under many circumstances, substances are combined with other recreational activities to increase the excitement of the primary activity. How often do people drink socially when out for a meal? Another possible explanation for the increase in substance use may be its growing availability. No one would argue that peer pressure has not contributed to the increase in drug and alcohol use, especially in people who are underage. Youth of all ages try things to be cool and fit in with peer groups. Today, people in their early teens, and often younger, have already experienced their first time using some drug or taking their first drink. At what point does occasional drinking and drug use turn from leisure activity into an addictive problem? When a person has no control over whether he or she uses a drug or drinks, they have become addicted. A person who has reached this stage believes that he or she has to have it. Addiction can be physical, psychological, or both. Anyone can fall victim to addiction. Because an initially social recreational activity has become an addiction, does this mean we, as leisure researchers, should no longer consider this as a viable topic of concern for the field of leisure studies?

Gambling

A second activity that has gone from illegal status to legal is gambling. Still, it is challenging to accurately estimate statistics on gambling because of the amount that is carried out illegally. In addition, it has been suggested that many individuals underestimate gambling behaviour because of the misconceptions people hold regarding this type of activity. There are any number of reasons why people gamble, but for many it is a recreational activity. Many forms of gambling were illegal until recent years, and because of the illegal nature of the activity, gambling was viewed as deviant. In today's society, gambling is a mainstream recreational activity, meaning the majority of adults have gambled at some point in their lives and do not consider it a problem—it has become a form of tolerable deviance.

In some instances however, gambling becomes a problem for an individual and subsequently impacts not only the individual, but also those associated with the individual, such as family and friends, and society as a whole. Such pathological gambling remains viewed by many as intolerable deviance and many attempts are made to control and prohibit such gambling. Since gambling is only a problem for a small percentage of those who participate and it results in such large revenues for those promoting gambling (in Canada this includes provincial governments), it will be nearly impossible to restrict gambling as has been done in the past.

How would you respond to the question "Do you gamble?" Have you ever scratched a lottery ticket or bought a raffle ticket on a prize? What about placing bets with friends on the outcome of a sports event or game? Have you ever bought a Lotto 649 ticket just to see what might happen? Now, how would you answer the question "Do you gamble?"

According to Smith and his colleagues (1994), gambling is an example of "leisure behaviour on the edge" (p. 233). Furthermore, a number of leisure theorists have included gambling as a form of less than desirable leisure. Lahey (1993) identified gambling as a form of "dark play" (p. 79) while Freysinger and Kelly (2004) include it in their discussion of the other side of leisure. This makes gambling a tricky area of inquiry for leisure researchers; because depending on the nature of the gambling being studied, it may be a form of deviance or it may be a commonplace recreational activity. Based on this divided view, it is vital that gambling be included in leisure research to gain a better understanding of what constitutes a leisure activity and what happens when leisure becomes destructive.

Criminal Activity

Most individuals make every attempt to lead their lives within the parameters set by the legal community. Some of the activities previously mentioned such as marijuana use, while illegal, are generally tolerated because they do not usually have any major implications for the majority.

How far is too far? Where do we draw the line between good and evil? leisure and non-leisure? Who actually draws the line? A major challenge for leisure researchers lies in defining leisure. As noted at the start of the chapter, leisure lies in the eye of the beholder. Does that mean that anything can be considered leisure? Does that mean that serial killing can be leisure the same as taking your dog for a walk?

In other instances, depending on the perspective of the majority, illegal behaviour is tolerated in certain contexts (Stebbins, 1996). For example, people have been acquitted or received a lesser sentence in crimes of passion. Some have argued that completely unacceptable criminal activity may have elements of leisure (Gunn & Caissie, 2006).

For example, Gunn and Caissie (2006) made the argument that serial murder can be considered leisure to those committing the crimes. They examined male-female team serial murder and identified a number of common leisure activities that occurred alongside the act of killing including photography, collecting "souvenirs," and video-recording. Furthermore, the activity of killing happened "during the team killers' free time; the activities were freely chosen, and had a number of benefits for the team killers such as enjoyment, thrill, excitement; there was a building of social cohesion; there was an element of risk... pursuing their activities at all costs even if others become victims of their leisure; defiance of societal norms and values; and so on" (Gunn & Caissie, 2006, p. 47). While not all illegal forms of deviant leisure are this severe it is important to recognize that there are elements of leisure in a number of less than desirable and illegal activities.

Classifying Leisure as Deviance

In an attempt to describe the relationship between leisure and deviance, there have been two classification systems proposed to distinguish destructive forms of leisure from more constructive choices. J. B. Nash was one of the first leisure researchers to examine the difference between "bad" and "good" leisure pursuits. In doing so he created a system known as the Nash Pyramid (Nash, 1953) to classify deviant forms of leisure. Joseph Curtis followed suit in 1979 through the development of The Curtis Scale, a second formal way of classifying deviant leisure.

Nash (1953) created the Nash Pyramid (Figure 18.1) to demonstrate a hierarchy of leisure values. In this illustration he describes "zero" levels of leisure time use as those activities that cause "injury or detriment to self" and "subzero" levels of leisure pursuits such as "acts performed against society" (Nash, 1960, p. 89). The levels above zero range from 1 to 4. Level 1 represents activities done for entertainment or enjoyment: leisure that allows the individual to "kill time" such as watching television. Level 4 activities include those that allow for creative participation such as composing music or painting. According to this system, people should aim to be involved in higher level activities more often than lower level and subzero level activities. Participation in too many activities low on this scale can impede personal growth and development.

When he coined the term *purple recreation*, Curtis (1979, 1988) also developed a system (see Figure 18.2) for classifying recreation activities, purple recreation in particular. This system included what he defined as delinquent activities, those activities that provide pleasure for the participant but are viewed as negative uses of free time by others in society. This system is essentially a continuum from bad to good. The far left on the scale represents those activ-

Everyday Activities Gone Wild

Often times when we think of deviant leisure activities we think of those discussed above; however, in addition to these activities, many everyday activities also have a more destructive side. In fact, many of us engage in some form of deviant leisure on a regular basis.

Consider the Sunday driver—is this activity a form of leisure for that individual? Most of us would likely say yes. The annoying thing about such an activity is most often the low speed of the driver. What about the driver who speeds, swerves in and out of traffic and drag races with other drivers? While many people would view this as a dangerous and unnecessary activity, for some it is a thrill and something they enjoy as part of their leisure repertoire. For others, driving often leads to "road rage" and places drivers in high stress situations. In these instances, people have been known to harm others because of an intentional or more often unintentional act of the other driver.

There is also a wide range of acceptable to deviant behaviour in relation to sexual activity. While the majority of sexual behaviour occurring between two adults is consensual and part of a relationship, there is also a great deal of sexual behaviour that is part of a power struggle and some forms of this behaviour are in fact illegal. Examples of deviant sexual acts include fetishism, exhibitionism, voyeurism, rape, and prostitution (Bynum & Thompson, 1996).

Even activities that are usually viewed as positive forms of leisure can take a nasty turn due to overindulgence. Consider the number of people who overeat at different times. What about those individuals who become so obsessed with being physically active that other aspects of their lives begin to take a backseat? Is watching television always a constructive use of free time? Most would think it is necessary to consider what types of programs the individual is watching. When any one activity takes over, this activity becomes problematic and hence can take on elements of deviant leisure.

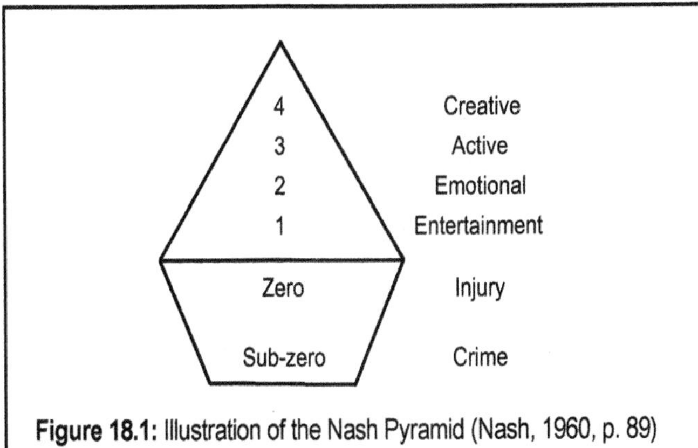

Figure 18.1: Illustration of the Nash Pyramid (Nash, 1960, p. 89)

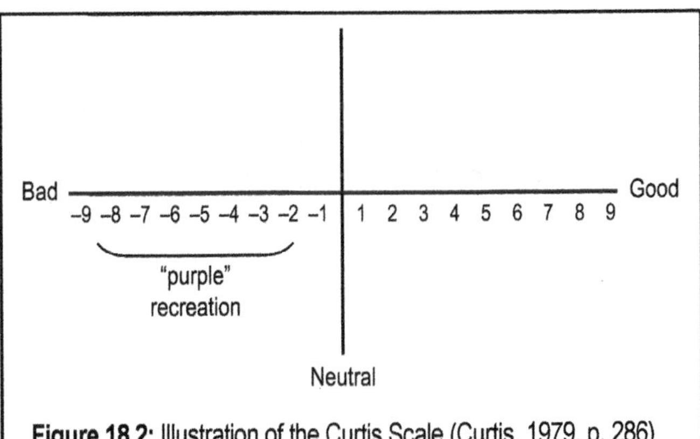

Figure 18.2: Illustration of the Curtis Scale (Curtis, 1979, p. 286)

ities that are extremely negative including murder, torture, and brutality to vulnerable individuals and groups. The far right represents those activities that are extremely positive such as generosity, pure love and selflessness. Most conventional recreation activities fall somewhere between –3 and +6, with off colour movies, and average to heavy drinking at the –3 mark and gardening and artistic pursuits at the +6 mark. Pub crawling falls around the –1 mark while social drinking and card playing has been ranked at approximately the +1 mark. It is important to note that this classification system was devised in the late 1970s meaning that some of these activities may be ranked differently in today's world. For example, at that time, most forms of gambling were illegal activities; while today, most gambling is legal and part of mainstream recreation for the majority of our society.

The discussion to this point demonstrates that it is challenging to determine what is good and what is bad because the definition of deviance is continuously changing. Many factors, including the society in question, the political environment, the historical context of the activity, and the majority viewpoint will impact whether an activity is viewed as deviant or not. Essentially almost any activity can have negative elements.

How Has Participation in Marginal Leisure Been Explained?

As with most forms of behaviour a number of explanations have been posited in an attempt to explain such behaviours. Marginal behaviour in the form of leisure is no different. A number of psychological and sociological theories have been used to understand deviance and why people choose to participate in marginal forms of behaviour. For a brief discussion of some of these theories, see Table 18.1 (p. 172).

What are some of the outstanding issues? (Why is marginal leisure important?)

Rojek (1997) suggests that deviance has been largely ignored in leisure research. Due to lack of available evidence, those interested in deviant leisure are forced to go to other disciplines for published information including psychiatry, psychology, sociology, and criminology for further understanding (Rojek, 1999, 2000; Stiefvater & Suren, 2004). Although the use of various disciplines can enhance understanding of deviance, Cantwell (2003) highlighted the need for further deviance research within the field of leisure studies to illuminate the meaning of deviance as it relates to leisure participation. Currently, some deviant forms of leisure, including gambling, substance use, and sex tourism, have been understood as resulting from a combination of biological, psychological, and sociological factors. Still, the majority of leisure researchers have yet to give substantial attention to the possibility that leisure may enhance understanding of these behaviours (Rojek, 1999, 2000). The first formal attempt from leisure researchers to acknowledge the value in studying these less desirable forms of leisure came in the form of a special issue of *Leisure/Loisir* entitled "Deviant Leisure" (Stebbins, Rojek, & Sullivan, 2006). This special issue addresses issues including serial murder (Gunn & Caissie, 2006), gambling as tolerable deviance (Sullivan, 2006), the playing of violent video games (Delamere, 2006), visiting strip clubs (Bowen & Daniels, 2006), and binge drinking (Crabbe, 2006).

It is also important to study deviant behaviour as a form of leisure because deviant leisure is increasing in our society, and it is vital that this area be explored further in depth. In addition to the desire to reduce deviance in our communities, the body of knowledge in the area of leisure research cannot be complete without a clear understanding of all forms of leisure, including that considered deviant. For example, Williams and Walker (2006) suggested that improvements in crime prevention and rehabilitation efforts could be enhanced if leisure among offenders were examined in enough detail to lead to a more in-depth understanding of criminal behaviour.

Table 18.1: Theoretical explanations of marginal behaviour

Sensation seeking (Zuckerman, 1979)	According to Zuckerman, sensation seeking can be defined as "the need for varied, novel, and complex sensations and experiences and the willingness to take physical and social risks for the sake of such experiences" (p. 10). People seek out leisure opportunities to meet their sensation-seeking needs including bungee jumping, rock climbing and sky-diving; others use acts of deviance to meet these needs.
Theory of differential association (Sutherland, 1947)	This theory states that behaviour is learned through elements and patterns present and rewarded in the individual's physical and social environment. The likelihood then of engaging in deviant behaviour depends on the pro-deviance to anti-deviance messages the individual receives; the higher the number of pro-deviance messages received, the more likely deviant behaviour will follow. Although the individual may struggle with messages from these relationships and the expectations of society, because intimate relationships have more meaning in the individual's life, those definitions of behaviour are likely to dominate the person's thinking and subsequently behaviour.
Theory of differential reinforcement (Burgess & Akers, 1966)	This theory states that individuals are motivated to behave in particular ways based on rewards and punishments received as a result of these behaviours. Within this framework, individuals participating in deviant behaviours are doing so because of the rewards they perceive to be associated with participation. These individuals are likely interacting with other individuals that they may view as role models. Consequently they then imitate these behaviours in search of the rewards provided by these models.
Social bond theory (Hirschi, 1969)	Unlike the majority of early theorists in this area, Hirshi was not attempting to explain why people participate in delinquent behaviours, but rather why some do not. This theory posits that the strength of social bonds individuals feel towards conventional institutions will determine variations in rates of deviance. Such conventional bonds restrict individuals' impulses toward nonconformity. Therefore, weakly bonded individuals are more likely to engage in deviant acts if the behaviour appears beneficial.
Anomie (Durkheim, 1951)	Durkheim posited that during periods of severe societal changes and times of uncertainty, the usual rules that restrain individuals from participating in generally unacceptable behaviours are weakened resulting in increased engagement in these objectionable activities. Merton (1957) expanded Durkheim's theory to be more representative of various forms of delinquent behaviour rather than focusing on suicide. Merton suggests that anomie can explain deviant behaviours because it arises from a sense of inconsistency between the aspirations of individuals and the means available to achieve these goals. That is, "the social structure strains the cultural values, making action in accord with them readily possible for those occupying certain statuses within society and difficult or impossible for others" (Merton, 1957, p.162). When such contradictions occur, people cannot be expected to know what is acceptable in this unbalanced society.

In summary, there are several forms of leisure that are questionable and in some cases, illegal. All of these less desirable forms of leisure are referred to as deviant leisure (Cantwell, 2003; Rojek, 1999; Russell, 2002; Stebbins, 1987; Stiefvater & Suren, 2004). Specific examples of deviant leisure that have been studied include juvenile auto theft (Drozda, 2006), pornography (Shaw, 1999), gambling (Smith, Volberg, & Wynne, 1994; Sullivan, 2006), binge drinking (Crabbe, 2006), sex tourism (Oppermann, 1998), and violent video games (Delamere, 2006). According to Stebbins (1987), many of these behaviours could be described as tolerable deviance, because in most instances, people will tolerate these activities even if they would never participate themselves (Stebbins, 1987). It is also important to note, however, that activities can shift from being tolerable to intolerable depending on many societal factors including political changes, the perceived impact of the activity on members of society, or a change in legal status of some of these activities. To enhance understanding of the full spectrum of leisure behaviour and its consequences, it is vital that leisure researchers begin to move past the idea that leisure is inherently good.

In 1999 Tibor Scitovsky stated that, just as hunger is a sign of the need for food, boredom signals people's need for mental or physical activity: something to keep them occupied and to vent their energy. Just as starvation can make people steal if they have no money to buy food, boredom can lead to violence if they can find no other activity to keep them occupied.

Key Terms

Deviant leisure
Intolerable deviance
Tolerable deviance

References

Bowen, H. E., & Daniels, M. J. (2006). Beyond body: Buying and selling attitude and fantasy [Special issue on deviant leisure]. *Leisure/Loisir, 30*(1), 87–109.

Burgess, E. W., & Akers, R. L. (1966). A differential association reinforcement theory of criminal behavior. *Social Problems, 14*, 128–147.

Bynum, J. E., & Thompson, W. E. (1996). *Juvenile delinquency: A sociological approach* (3rd ed.). Needham Heights, MA: Allyn & Bacon.

Cantwell, A. M. (2003). Deviant behavior. In J. Jenkins & J. J. Pigram (Eds.), *Encyclopaedia of leisure and outdoor recreation.* London, UK: Routledge.

Clift, S., & Carter, S. (2000). *Tourism and sex: Culture, commerce and coercion.* London, UK: Pinter.

Crabbe, T. (2006). Bingers: The performativity and consumption of 'deviant' leisure [Special issue on deviant leisure]. *Leisure/Loisir, 30*(1), 149–169.

Curtis, J. E. (1979). *Recreation theory and practice.* St. Louis, MO: The C. V. Mosby Company.

Curtis, J. E. (1988). Purple Recreation. *SPRE Annual on Education, 3*, 73–77.

Delamere, F., & Shaw, S. M. (2006). Playing with violence: Gamers' social construction of violent video game play as tolerable deviance [Special issue on deviant leisure]. *Leisure/Loisir, 30*(1), 7–25.

Driver, B. L., Brown, P. J., & Peterson, G. L. (1991). *Benefits of leisure.* State College, PA: Venture Publishing, Inc.

Drozda, C. (2006). Juveniles performing auto theft: An exploratory study into a deviant leisure lifestyle [Special issue on deviant leisure]. *Leisure/Loisir, 30*(1), 111–132.

Durkheim, E. (1951). *Suicide: A study in sociology* (Trans. J. A. Spaulding & G. Simpson). New York, NY: The Free Press.

Freysinger, V. J., & Kelly, J. R. (2004). *21st century leisure: Current issues.* State College, PA: Venture Publishing, Inc.

Glover, T. D. (2003). Regulating the rave scene: Policy alternatives of government. *Leisure Sciences, 25*(4), 307–325.

Gunn, L., & Caissie, L. T. (2006). Deviant leisure and serial murder: Exploring the unknown [Special issue on deviant leisure]. *Leisure/Loisir, 30*(1), 27–54.

Hirschi, T. (1969). *Causes of delinquency.* Berkeley, CA University of California Press.

Kaplan, M. (1960). *Leisure in America.* New York, NY: John Wiley.

Katz, J. (1988). *The seductions of crime.* New York, NY: Basic Books.

Lahey, M. (1993). Playing in the dark. In K. Fox (Ed.), *The 7th Canadian Congress on Leisure Research.* University of Manitoba Printing Services.

Merton, R. K. (1957). *Social theory and social structure* (2nd ed.). New York, NY: The Free Press.

Nash, J. B. (1953). *Philosophy of recreation and leisure.* Dubuque, IA: Wm. C. Brown.

Oppermann, M. (1998). *Sex tourism and prostitution: Aspects of leisure, recreation and work.* Elmsford, NY: Cognizant Communication Corp.

Rojek, C. (1997). Leisure theory: Retrospect and prospect. *Loisir et Société/Society and Leisure, 20*, 383–400.

Rojek, C. (2000). *Leisure and culture.* New York, NY: Palgrave.

Rojek, C. (1999). Abnormal leisure: Invasive, mephitic, and wild forms. *Loisir et Société/Society & Leisure, 22*, 21–37.

Russell, R. V. (2002). *Pastimes: The context of contemporary leisure* (2nd ed.). Champaign, IL: Sagamore Publishing.

Shaw, S. M. (1999). Men's leisure and women's lives: The impact of pornography on women. *Leisure Studies, 18*, 197–212.

Shinew, K. J., & Parry, D. C. (2005). Examining college students' participation in the leisure pursuits of drinking and illegal drug use. *Journal of Leisure Research, 37*, 364–386.

Smith, G. J., Volberg, R. A., & Wynne, H. J. (1994). Leisure behaviour on the edge: Differences between controlled and uncontrolled gambling practices. *Loisir et Société/Society and Leisure, 17*, 233–248.

Stebbins, R. A. (1987). *Sociology: The study of society.* New York: Harper & Row, Publishers.

Stebbins, R. A. (1996). *Tolerable differences: Living with deviance* (2nd ed.). Toronto, ON: McGraw-Hill Ryerson.

Stebbins, R. A., Rojek, C., & Sullivan, A. M. (2006). Editorial [Special issue on deviant leisure]. *Leisure/Loisir, 30*(1), 3–5.

Stiefvater, R., & Suren, A. T. (2004). The role of deviant recreation in the curriculum of recreation students: A confessional tale. *Journal of Recreation and Leisure*. Retrieved from http://yellow.byu.edu/~grayh/swdaahperd/2004journal.html#role

Sullivan, A. M. (2006). I am not a gambler, you are a gambler: Distinguishing between tolerable and intolerable gambling [Special issue on deviant leisure]. *Leisure/Loisir, 30*(1), 171–192.

Sutherland, E. H. (1947). *Principles of criminology*. Philadelphia, PA: Lippincott.

Williams, D. J., & Walker, G. J. (2006). Leisure, deviant leisure, and crime: 'Caution: Objects may be closer than they appear.' [Special issue on deviant leisure]. *Leisure/Loisir, 30*(1), 193–218.

Zuckerman, M. (1979). *Sensation seeking: Beyond the optimal level of arousal*. Hillsdale, NJ: Lawrence Erlbaum Associates, Inc.

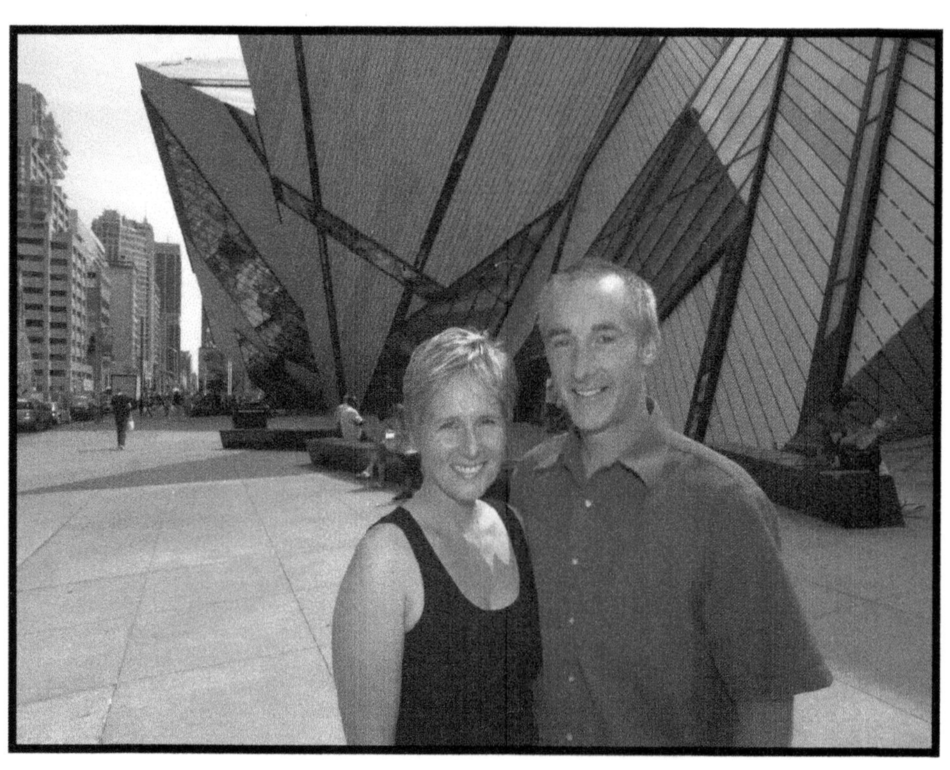

Chapter 19
Sex, Sexuality, and Leisure

Glenn J. Meaney, B.A. (Hon) and B. J. Rye, Ph.D.
St. Jerome's University at the University of Waterloo

Learning Objectives

After reading this chapter, students will be able to

1. Understand the connection between sexuality and leisure.
2. Understand the complexities involved with sexuality and leisure.
3. Know that sex is sometimes not a leisure activity.
4. Understand sexuality as a key component of personal development.
5. Understand sexuality as a key component of interpersonal relationships.
6. Understand sexuality as a social phenomenon.
7. Know how and why sexuality is controlled by social institutions.
8. Know how sexuality fits into diverse ethical frameworks.
9. Understand that sex can be a fun and healthy activity that can be defined as leisure or as play.

Introduction

Leisure can be defined as discretionary time; that is, time that is not invested in work, fulfilling obligations, or other mandatory activities. Perhaps more precisely, leisure can be defined as activities performed by choice during discretionary time. It has been noted, however, that leisure activities are engaged to fulfill personal needs; in the optimal case, the pursuit of leisure can lead to self-actualization (Karlis, 2004). It would seem that sex fits the definition of a leisure activity quite well. Most people engage in sexual activity by choice, choose specific sexual partners, and experience sex as pleasurable. However, there may be cases where sex is not a leisure activity; that is, participation may be mandatory, serve to fulfill obligations, or may not lead to self-satisfaction. In fact, just as the concept of leisure has proven difficult to nail down, sex and sexuality are difficult terms to define. Once defined, the place of sex in society is complicated and its classification as a leisure activity is still more complex. Perhaps the best way to approach this classification is to start with definitions of sex and sexuality, then discuss when sex is not leisure, and finally, elucidate how sexuality does fit into a leisure framework.

Defining Sex and Sexuality

In its simplest form, sex classifies a group of activities, engaged in alone or with one or more others, which involve stimulation of the genitals and other sensitive parts of the body (e.g., breasts). This stimulation often, but not necessarily, leads to orgasm by one or more of the participants. Orgasm is a physiological reflex that is experienced by most people as pleasurable. Sexuality is more complex and inclusive, referring not only to sex in itself, but also to the complex of understandings, meanings, and constructions around sexual activity. At the individual level, sexuality can be a defining feature of personality or central trait; for some, sexuality may be a cardinal trait (see *i*-box on Allport's classifications). At the interpersonal level, sexuality can define relationships between people (e.g., sex is generally considered a component of marriage and similar intimate relationships). At the social level, sexuality encompasses a set of roles, obligations, and duties that are prescribed (or proscribed) by society. For example, in Canadian society, it is expected that people will not have sex outside of their primary relationships; otherwise, we tend to characterize the

Allport's Classifications of Personality Traits

Gordon Allport, a famous psychologist, devised a scheme for classifying personality traits. Unlike many of his contemporaries, Allport believed that personality was best determined by studying individuals in great depth, rather than by analysis of group averages. As a result of his investigations, Allport (1937) classified personality traits into the following three broad categories.

1. Cardinal traits are personality traits that dominate a person's life and pursuits. In the TV show *Sex in the City*, for example, Samantha's sexuality could be seen as a cardinal trait, because sexuality is the dominant force in her life. Not all people have a cardinal trait but for those who do, this one personality trait is the primary driving force in the person's life. That is, most major decisions in the person's life will be made around their cardinal trait.

continued >>

(continued)

2. Central traits are the few characteristics that can be used to describe yourself or someone you know. Typically, people are seen to have four or five central traits that give a picture of their personality. You may describe a good friend as being warm, trustworthy, loyal, intelligent, and fair. Central traits help to form an overall impression of a person. This might be thought of as a self-schema in relation to the self or another-schema in relation to others. Sexuality may be a central trait for many; while it does not dominate their lives like a cardinal trait, it may be a consistent aspect of behaviour.
3. Secondary traits are characteristics that may be less obvious, less important, or less noticeable. Secondary traits may be transitory (e.g., you may see yourself as a university student, but this will change when you graduate), or permanent but difficult to notice (e.g., you may express sexuality by engaging in sexual fantasy, which others would not see). Secondary traits are generally evident in behaviour.

How might cardinal traits interact with prejudice? What are the differences among cardinal, central, and secondary traits? What is *sex*? What is *sexuality*? How are the two distinguished?

person as having an affair or cheating. All aspects of sexuality determine its status as leisure.

When Sex Is Not Leisure

Sex may not be leisure when it is not a voluntary activity, when it is part of an obligatory duty, or when it is work. Sex workers, such as prostitutes and exotic dancers, are unlikely to see sex as a leisure activity; rather, sex is a job that fulfills the same purposes that employment serves for other people. The complication here is that the meaning of sex may be contextual: Sex is work in some cases, and leisure in others. For example, when an exotic dancer goes home to her partner, the intimacy of the relationship may replace work as the motivation for engaging in sexual activity. Sex within a relationship may still not be leisurely; however, in some times and places, sex is seen as a wife's or husband's duty, something that must be present for the sake of the relationship. In such cases, sex is not leisure, but an obligation (see Hawkes, 1996, Chapter 6), and a husband or wife may feel compelled to have sex with her or his partner. Sometimes, the person initiating sexual contact may not experience sex as leisure, but as a source of great distress, particularly in the case of paraphilias (see the Paraphilias *i*-box). Lack of choice most clearly speaks against sex as leisure. In extreme cases, such as sexual assault, sex is clearly not a form of leisure, at least not for the victim; the perpetrator may consider the assault to be a form of leisure (or not, if the behaviour is compulsive).

Paraphilias

Paraphilia is a class of disorders defined by the American Psychiatric Association (2000) as sexual urges, fantasies, or behaviours that cause significant distress or impairment and involve unusual objects, activities, or situations. Common examples of paraphilias are:

1. Fetishism: the attainment of sexual pleasure through objects that are not generally sexual. For example, a man who cannot have an orgasm without wearing women's underwear but wearing women's underwear strains his marriage has a fetish.
2. Sexual sadism: the attainment of sexual pleasure through the infliction of pain or humiliation. For example, a man who has no interest in consensual sexual activity and can only have an orgasm by forcing sex upon his partner—sexual assault—would be diagnosed as a sexual sadist.
3. Voyeurism: the attainment of sexual pleasure through watching another person nude or disrobing—the voyeur typically desires to watch without consent (see Rye & Meaney, in press, for a discussion of the complexity of voyeurism).

It is important to note that paraphilias can often represent behaviours that are normal and healthy (e.g., Laumann, Gagnon, Michael, & Michaels, 1994, found that many people enjoy watching their consenting partners undress), except when they are taken to an extreme (e.g., non-consenting partners), become compulsive (e.g., the person desires more conventional activities, but is not aroused by them), or cause distress or social impairment.

How would being a prostitute impact sex in a meaningful relationship? What are paraphilias and how are they distinguished from healthy sexuality?

Sexuality can itself be used as a form of social control; that is, certain kinds of sexual activity may be outright proscribed, or restricted only to particular contexts. In Canadian society, for example, people are only allowed to have one spouse at a time (monogamy; Criminal Code, Part VII, §290(1), §293(1)); however, other societies (e.g., sub-Saharan African Countries such as Senegal & Mali; Lardoux,

2004; Tertlit, 2005) are polygamous, allowing one person to have many wives, and a few societies (e.g., the Toda of India, the Marquesans of Polynesia; Ford & Beach, 1951; Levine & Sangree, 1980) are polyandrous, allowing one person to have many husbands (see Middleton, 2002). Society exerts many levels of control over sexuality, and this restricts and complicates the choices that can be made by individuals. Once again, the leisure aspect of sex is curtailed by the complications of social circumstances. For example, marital rape is illegal in Canada (Criminal Code, Part VIII, §278), but some countries allow it (see Bennice & Resick, 2003). In many countries, sexual activity is restricted, implicitly or explicitly, to specific kinds of relationships, generally some variant of marriage. So people who wish to have sex must either get married (which often involves waiting to reach an appropriate age) or must have sex illicitly. Either way, sex can become a source of anxiety. If getting married is not a choice in itself, sex within the marriage may be transformed to an onerous duty; having sex illicitly may be punished by legal sanctions, social exclusion, or guilt. Perhaps you may remember the popular Emmy-winning children's television show *Pee Wee's Playhouse*. Paul Reubens, who both created and portrayed the title character, Pee Wee Herman, was arrested in 1991 for masturbating in an adult theatre (charged with misdemeanour indecent exposure). Many people might say that this is a victimless crime and that this type of behaviour is expected in a darkened adult theatre where sexually explicit films are shown. On the other hand, Reubens suffered socially from being the butt of many jokes, the network stopped televising reruns of his show, and his business career was severely curtailed. This case illustrates the severe consequences of engaging in socially proscribed behaviours. This is a turning point where sex that was pursued for leisure purposes is transformed by social convention into something other than leisure.

Under what circumstances might sex not be considered leisure? How can sexuality be a form of social control? Why are we so interested in the sexuality of public figures?

When Sex Is Leisure

Sex can be considered leisure when it is voluntary, it is not work, and it serves some personal, rather than social or moral, need for the individual or individuals involved. Even when sexuality is leisure, it is still complex. Sexual activity may be play; that is, the activity may be joyful in itself. Or, engaging in sexual activity may be a re-affirmation of one's identity. Alternatively, it may meet important personal needs in relation to a significant other. In this sense, sex is about more than simply physical pleasure, although the physical pleasure may be a prime motivator for engaging in sex (see Abramson & Pinkerton, 1995). We will attempt to discuss sex as leisure from the simplest aspects to the most complicated aspects, but it must be understood that sexuality is complex at every stage (see Foucault, 1976/1978).

At its simplest, sex can be seen as a source of simple physical pleasure and release of tension. Orgasm serves these purposes in itself and is largely independent of circumstance. In this sense, sex is fun and playful, and can be enjoyed by an individual alone (masturbation) or by a couple or group. In its simplest form, sexual activity may take the form of fantasy, which may only involve thinking about sex, or may expand into complex scenarios; sexual fantasy is often accompanied by self-stimulation to orgasm. Even at this level, sexual pleasure can be accompanied by feelings of guilt or anxiety. For example, while many people report masturbating (Pinkerton, Bogart, Cecil, & Abramson, 2002; Rye, 2006), it is rarely discussed openly and such discussion is considered in poor taste (Coleman, 2002). Sexual pleasure becomes even more complicated when another person (or other people) is involved. Mutual consent can be a particularly prickly issue; rarely do we say to another person, "I would like to have sex now," and have the person respond, "Me, too." Generally, one person is more interested and may have to convince the other. Resolving this tension between the pursuit of pleasure and the complications it sometimes entails can lead to a complex set of attitudes and decisions about when and with whom to have sex.

How does sexuality fit into a framework of leisure activities?

Sex as a Leisure Activity

Sexuality as Personal Development

Sexuality can be a defining factor of personality (thus, a cardinal trait or a central trait) or it can be a direct expression of personality traits (i.e., a generally dominant person may seek out positions of dominance in sexual activity). Sexuality can be a key component of personality development by determining activities in which one will engage and with whom these will be engaged. Sexuality is a particular concern of adolescents, who are experiencing physical sexual growth and defining their future personalities; decisions made during adolescence then carry through the entire life-cycle. Sexuality can become a cardinal trait, or an organizing principle, of a person's life. This may be particularly true of those who belong to sexual minorities (e.g., gay, lesbian, bisexual, or transgender people; see

Cardinal Trait *i*-box) or who have atypical or little known sexual interests, such as sadomasochism. When sexuality is a cardinal trait, people may go through a great deal of trouble to engage in their chosen sexual activities. Even if an individual does not define sexuality as a cardinal trait, other people may see it as one and may make judgments based on that perception. So, when we learn something about someone's sexuality, we feel as if we know the person on an intimate level; this may explain the popularity of sexual scandals involving political figures and celebrities. Consider Bill Clinton's oral sex affair with Monica Lewinsky: This "marital infidelity" was thought to influence Clinton's ability to govern the United States. The popular logic was: if he is a "cheat" in this aspect of his life, he will cheat in all aspects of his life—and he was impeached from the presidency because of it. Even when sexuality is not a cardinal, or dominating trait, it may be a central trait—one of the few characteristics used by the self and others to define personality.

Cardinal Trait: Cardinal Virtue or Cardinal Vice

Consider the following statements made by a lesbian about how her sexual orientation becomes a cardinal trait, both for herself and for others: "...once people know I am a lesbian that becomes all I am.... they judge everything I do through that lens..."

Having information about someone's sexual identity, particularly if the person is gay, lesbian, or bisexual, can lead people to ignore all other aspects of personality; for example, "...if I treat someone coldly, I am not having a bad day; I am being a typical cold-hearted dyke... even the gender stereotype is ignored."

On the other hand, sexuality as a cardinal trait can be self-defined: "...sometimes, I disappear on my 'straight' friends for months at a time... to be around gay people.... I need to be with my own 'type' for a while...." In this sense, reaffirmation of one's personal identity through a cardinal trait can become a source of confidence and self-esteem.

To the extent that sexuality is a crucial component of personality, it can be a tool for self-actualization. Expressing important personality traits reinforces and redefines a sense of identity. Sexual pursuits can not only express an existing personality trait, but may also serve to broaden one's horizons by experimenting with different activities. Consider the following hypothetical journey of a young woman: 1) At 14, she believes she will be a virgin until she marries because these are the values she has learned; 2) At 16, she has sex with a boy for the first time and discovers that sex is pleasurable and she would like to try more things; 3) At 18, she has had multiple sexual partners to further explore the experience; and, 4) At 26, she decides on a partner she enjoys, sexually and otherwise, and enters a monogamous marriage. This experimentation can lead to a greater understanding of one's most intimate likes and dislikes: knowledge that allows individuals to enhance their own leisure experience(s) and allows people to define themselves in sexual terms. This self-knowledge, in turn, may lead to solidification of the sexual component of personality (i.e., sexual self-schema) and may also result in sexual self-actualization: the pinnacle of development of the sexual self. The experiential component of sexuality allows people to feel more comfortable and feel more in touch with their bodies. Of course, this experience may be both enhanced and complicated by pursuing sexual relations with other people.

How can healthy sex lead to self-actualization?

Sexuality and Relationships

Relationships can place restrictions on sexuality: In most cultures, sex is considered an integral part of some types of relationships and is forbidden in all other relationships. Typically, sex is an expected or required component of marriage and similar romantic relationships (e.g., cohabitation, steady boyfriend/girlfriend). This can have a positive and a negative impact on the people involved. Sex can be a physical display of emotional intimacy that expresses the joy of sharing oneself with another special person. On the other hand, sexual activity is restricted to "approved" relationships and people who have sex outside of those relationships can become heavily stigmatized. In many societies, for example, sexual behaviour is expected to occur only within heterosexual marriages. Those who wish to engage in sex with a consenting same-sex partner are often punished by social, or even legal, sanctions. In the United States, for example, some states make anal intercourse illegal in any case, while others prohibit anal sex between men only. In Canada, anal sex is restricted to those 18 years and older or those in a heterosexual marriage (Criminal Code, Part V, §159(1), §159(2), but this law has been contested, see "Equalize the age..." 2006 [unauthored newspaper article]; Lewis, 2006; compare with Weston, 2006), while there are no such restrictions on vaginal intercourse. A similar, but lesser, disapproval is held for those who have sex with other-sex or same-sex partners outside the context of an intimate relationship. There is evidence, however, that Canadians have become increasingly accepting of a diversity of both sexual activities and relationships in which sex is permissible (e.g., DeLamater & Hyde, 2003; Gagnon &

How can sexuality function to express love and intimacy in a long-term relationship?

Smith, 1987). This greater diversity allows more people to pursue leisure in ways that are satisfying to them.

Sexuality as Social Identity

Sexual identity not only determines the particular sexual activities a person enjoys and with whom they are enjoyed, but also leads to the formation of larger social groups. Belonging to a group, in turn, helps individuals to develop and further explore their own identity. Peer groups tend to consist of like-minded individuals pursuing common goals. Young women and men, in particular, tend to discuss their sexual experiences with their peers and sometimes cooperate in seeking out sexual encounters. This process allows for not only reaffirmation of sexual identity, but also for social cohesion. While this bonding is (generally) not sexual in itself, it can be centred on sexual activity. This, then, encourages other kinds of non-sexual sharing and the common pursuit of other, leisure related goals. The role of sexual identity in group bonding is particularly important among adolescents, who are only beginning to form personal, interpersonal, and social identities. It is also important to members of sexual minorities or those who pursue atypical sexual activities, who may have few non-group peers with whom to share their experiences. In fact, bonding with others who have similar sexual interests can be so important to people that they will sometimes go through great lengths to meet like-minded individuals.

Shared experience centred directly on sexual activity can be seen in social groups that are directly focused on sexual activities of choice. There are many such examples, but we will discuss only one such case. Sadomasochism involves two types of sexual behaviour, sadism and masochism. Sadism is the attainment of sexual pleasure from the infliction of pain or humiliation on another; masochism is the attainment of sexual pleasure from having pain or humiliation inflicted on oneself. While sadomasochism may seem to many to be weird or unusual, a substantial minority of the population enjoys these behaviours. This portion of the population is large enough to foster the development of clubs for people who wish to indulge their sadomasochistic impulses. Like other kinds of social clubs, sadomasochism clubs tend to have heavily enforced rules. For example, there may be safe words used to stop sadistic participants from inflicting harmful and undesired amounts of pain and humiliation. Acceptance by club members depends on adhering to the prescribed regulations. While accepted behaviours may be more loosely defined, most sadomasochistic clubs share a number of common characteristics.

How do shared sexual experiences contribute to a sense of social and personal identity?

A Continuum of Normal and Abnormal Sexual Behaviours

While we discussed sadism and masochism as paraphilias, most people who engage in sadomasochism do so in a "non-paraphilic" way. That is, sadomasochism is paraphilic when it is a compulsive behaviour ('the participants cannot help themselves'), when either of the participants is non-consenting, or when the urge to engage in sadism or masochism is so great that it interferes with the participants' lives and/or functioning. Non-paraphilic or non-clinical sadomasochism is much more common. Most people who engage in these behaviours do not have to do so for all or even most of their sexual encounters (Sandnabba, Santtila, & Nordling, 1999). Both partners are active, consenting participants who enjoy sadomasochism (Alison, Santtila, Sandnabba, & Nordling, 2001; Sandnabba et al., 1999). This distinction reflects the continuum that is often seen in the classification of abnormal behaviours: Behaviours that are normal and healthy become abnormal or unhealthy when they become extreme, compulsive, or harmful (see Chapter 18).

Sadomasochism tends to be heavily scripted (the participants act out pre-arranged scenarios), and typically involves fetishistic equipment (e.g., whips, chains, and leather outfits) and ritualistic situations (e.g., bondage). As a whole, the sadomasochism scene is perhaps best defined as fantasy-oriented and role-playing (Alison et al., 2001; Sandnabba et al., 1999). Participation in club activities leads to a sense of social identity through association with similar others. In this sense, the particular sexual behaviours have their own value, but also serve leisure needs (e.g., personal, relational, and social) beyond sexual pleasure (i.e., feelings of belonging, feeling normal, lessening potential stigma). The choice of particular activities however, emphasizes the driving motivation not of group identity, but of sexual pleasure in itself.

How do sexual activities, such as sadomasochism, contribute to understanding of the cultural importance of sexuality?

Sex and Society: Social Control and Sexual Ethics

While sexuality can be both healthy and leisurely, individual expressions of sexuality have consequences for other people and for society as a whole; therefore, there has been a persistent need for some control of sexuality in all societies. Most societies, perhaps surprisingly, have very similar rules regarding sexuality (Baumeister & Tice, 2001, Chapter 4), indicating that the same panorama of sexual behaviours and the same need for social control of sexuality is present in all human societies. The form of social control, however, varies to a degree, and defines how sexuality can be seen as a leisure activity. Social control over sexuality is expressed in the form of sexual ethics, and three distinct types of ethical frameworks can be distinguished: the ethics of divinity, community, and autonomy (Shweder, Much, Mahapatra, & Park, 1997).

Ethics of divinity (which include, but are not limited to, most religious belief systems) are based on a fundamental belief in some natural law; those who break the natural law are seen as "sinful," "unclean," or "blasphemous." Such an ethic may decree, for example, that the sole purpose of sex is reproduction; any other sexual behaviours that do not contribute to reproduction would be proscribed. The ethic of divinity does not hold the wishes or preferences of any individual or group (except, perhaps, the ruling group) in high regard; the individual is largely ignored except to the degree that she or he conforms to the natural order. Sexuality as leisure, and, in fact, any form of leisure may be difficult or impossible to attain under the ethic of divinity.

Ethics of community are based on the fundamental importance of society as a whole. Individuals are valued and recognized to the extent that they contribute to the "greater good" of the community; those who do not contribute to the community are considered selfish and may be subject to shame, humiliation, and ostracization. Such an ethic may punish a man for masturbating because he is engaging in "selfish" pleasure rather than bonding with another member of the group. On the other hand, group sex may be allowed to the extent that it contributes to bonding among members of the group. Sexuality as leisure may be more attainable under community than divinity because self-satisfaction may result from performing one's duty to the community. Still, self-satisfaction and personal development must not be goals in themselves, and leisure may remain elusive.

Ethics of autonomy are based on fundamental beliefs about the value and rights of the individual; those who do not respect the rights of other individuals are subject to legal or social sanctions. Such an ethic allows the individual to pursue her own preferences and meet her own needs to the extent that she does not interfere with the rights of other people. Same-sex sexual contact, for example, is perfectly permissible because it does no harm. Harm and consent are key components of the ethic of autonomy. Rape is not tolerated under autonomy because the rapist does not seek the victim's consent. Unlike divinity and community, autonomy recognizes leisure as an important pursuit in itself because it plays a role in personal well-being. Sexuality as leisure is most attainable under an ethic of autonomy.

These ethical frameworks are based on different value systems and, in the extreme, are mutually exclusive; however, most societies tend to have elements of all three frameworks. While contemporary Canadian society shows evidence of divinity and community (e.g., public nudity is illegal if it offends "public decency," whether or not it does any harm; Criminal Code, §174(1), §174(2)), there is evidence that we are moving toward an ethic of autonomy. For example, the Criminal Code (§163(8)) defines obscene publication as one whose "...dominant characteristic is the undue exploitation of sex, [combinations of sex and crime], horror, cruelty, and violence." These materials are illegal, not because sex is "unnatural" or "offensive," but because these portrayals carry the potential for great harm. On the other hand, any involvement with child pornography (Criminal Code, §163, §164) is illegal because of the particular harm inherent in the exploitation of children. Canadian laws are much less focused on disallowing particular acts, and much more focused on consent (are the participants willing?) and potential for harm (is anyone getting hurt?). As we move closer to an ethic of autonomy, Canadian society becomes more consistent with a view of sex as leisure, or even as play.

How does sexuality meet the goals of leisure activities? How might sexuality differ from other activities in how those goals are met?

Sex Is Fun

While sex can serve to meet many needs, perhaps the most essential reason for engaging in sexual activity is that sex is pleasurable. In this sense, sex is a kind of play. The pleasure that can be achieved not only through sexual stimulation but also through the sexual stimulation of others may be the most fundamental source of pleasure (see Abramson & Pinkerton, 1995a). Abramson and Pinkerton (1995b) argue that sex is pleasure. It may be that all of the personal, interpersonal, and social benefits and consequences of sexuality arise from the simple pursuit of the well-being that can result from engaging in behaviours that we enjoy.

How does sexuality as a leisure activity fit into each of the three ethical frameworks of divinity, community, and authority?

Key Terms

Cardinal trait
Central trait
Ethic of autonomy
Ethic of community
Ethic of divinity
Monogamy
Paraphilia
Polyandry
Polygyny
Schema
Secondary traits
Self-actualization
Sex
Sexual fantasy
Sexuality
Social control

References

Abramson, P. R., & Pinkerton, S. D. (Eds.). (1995a). *Sexual nature/sexual culture*. Chicago, IL: University of Chicago Press.

Abramson, P. R., & Pinkerton, S. D. (1995b). *With pleasure: Thoughts on the nature of human sexuality*. New York, NY: Oxford University Press.

Alison, L., Santtila, P., Sandnabba, N. K., & Nordling, N. (2001). Sadomasochistically oriented behavior: Diversity in practice and meaning. *Archives of Sexual Behavior, 30*(1), 1–12.

Allport, G. (1937). *Personality: A psychological interpretation*. New York, NY: Holt.

American Psychiatric Association. (2000). *Diagnostic and statistical manual of mental disorders* (4th ed., text revision). Washington, DC: Author.

Baumeister, R. F., & Tice, D. M. (2001). *The social dimension of sex*. Toronto, ON: Allyn & Bacon.

Bennice, J. A., & Resick, P. A. (2003). Marital rape: History, research, and practice. *Trauma, Violence, & Abuse, 4*(3), 228–246.

Buss, D. M. (1994). *The evolution of desire: Strategies of human mating*. New York, NY: Basic Books.

Coleman, E. (2002). Masturbation as a means of achieving sexual health. *Journal of Psychology and Human Sexuality, 14*(2/3), 5–16.

DeLamater, J. D., & Hyde, J. S. (2003). Sexuality. In J. J. Ponzetti, Jr. (Ed.), *International encyclopedia of marriage and family, Vol. 3*. (2nd ed., pp. 1456–1462). New York, NY: Macmillian/Thomson Gale.

Equalize the age of consent. (2006, February 11). *Winnipeg Free Press*, p. A11.

Ford, C. S., & Beach, F. A. (1951). *Patterns of sexual behavior*. New York, NY: Harper & Row and Hueber Medical Divisions.

Foucault, M. (1978). *The history of sexuality: Vol. 1. An introduction* (R. Hurley, Trans.). New York, NY: Pantheon. (Original work published 1976)

Gagnon, J. H., & Simon, W. (1987). The sexual scripting of oral genital contacts. *Archives of Sexual Behavior, 16*(1), 1–25.

Hawkes, G. (1996). *A sociology of sex and sexuality*. Philadelphia, PA: Open University Press.

Karlis, G. (2004). *Leisure and recreation in Canadian society: An introduction*. Toronto, ON: Thompson Educational.

Lardoux, S. (2004). Polygyny, first marriage and fertility in Senegal and Mali. *Dissertation Abstracts International, A: The Humanities and Social Sciences, 65*(11), 4359-A. (UMI No. 3152073).

Laumann, E., Gagnon, J., Michael, R., & Michaels, S, (1994). *The social organization of sexuality*. Chicago, IL: The University of Chicago Press

Levine, N. E., & Sangree, W. H. (1980). Asian and African systems of polyandry. *Journal of Comparative Family Studies, 11*(3), 385–410.

Lewis, K. (2006, February 10). Gay activists seek uniform age of consent: At present, the ages are different for heterosexuals and homosexuals. *Vancouver Sun*, p. A5.

Middleton, D. R. (2002). *Exotics and erotics: Human cultural and sexual diversity*. Prospect Heights, IL: Waveland Press.

Pinkerton, S. D., Bogart, L. M., Cecil, H., & Abramson, P. R. (2002). Factors associated with masturbation in a collegiate sample. *Journal of Psychology and Human Sexuality, 14*(2/3), 103–121.

Rye, B. J. (2006). [A survey of sexual attitudes and behaviours]. Unpublished raw data.

Rye, B. J., & Meaney, G. J. (in press). Voyeurism: It is good as long as we do not get caught. *Journal of Psychology and Human Sexuality.*

Sandnabba, N. K., Santtila, P., & Nordling, N. (1999). Sexual behavior and social adaptation among sadomasochistically-oriented males. *Journal of Sex Research, 36*(3), 273–282.

Shweder, R. A., Much, N. C., Mahapatra, M., & Park, L. (1997). The "big three" of morality (autonomy, community, divinity) and the "big three" explanations of suffering. In A. M. Brandt & P. Rozin (Eds.), *Morality and health* (pp. 119–169). Florence, KY: Taylor & Frances/Routledge.

Tertlit, M. (2005). Polygyny, fertility, and savings. *Journal of Political Economy, 113*(6), 1341–1371.

Weston, J-H. (2006, February 14). Gay activists ask Canada to lower age of consent for anal sex, National Post agrees. Retrieved from http://www.lifesite.net/ldn/2006/feb/06021403.html

Section C: Leisure in a Diverse Canada

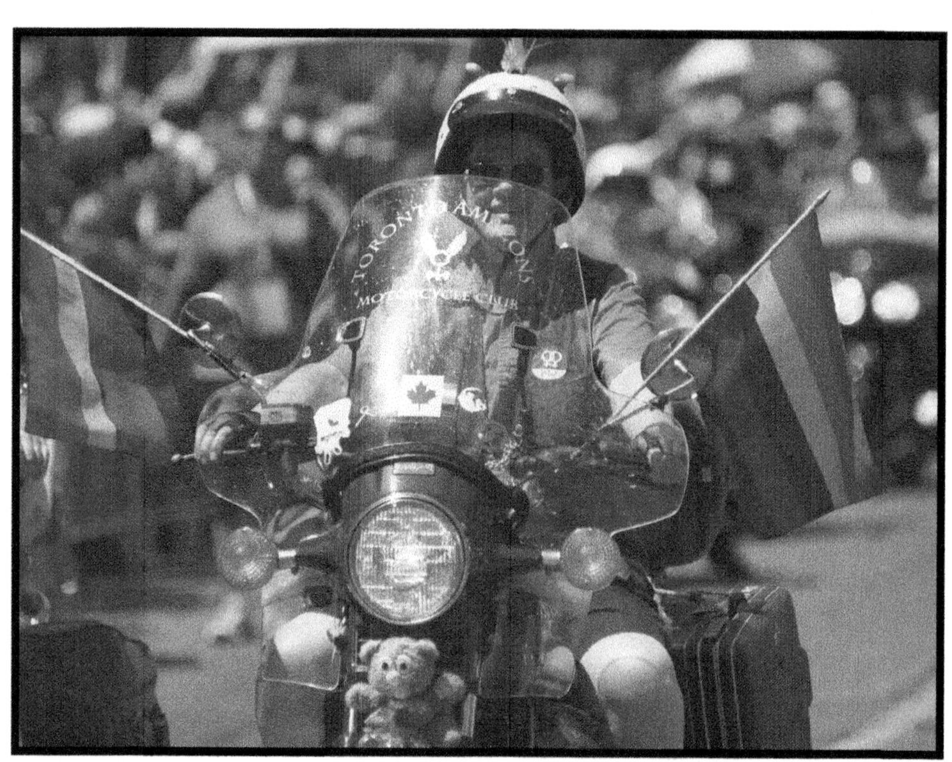

Chapter 20

Gender and Leisure

Diana C. Parry, Ph.D.
University of Waterloo

Learning Objectives

After reading this chapter, students will be able to

1. Appreciate the difference between sex and gender.
2. Understand the historical evolution of gender research within leisure studies.
3. Be familiar with feminist theory, which has guided much gender research within leisure studies to date.
4. Realize how gender serves to reproduce gender roles, relations, and expectations for both women and men.
5. Recognize how leisure may be a context for women and men to resist traditional gender roles, expectations and stereotypes.
6. Identify areas that warrant future attention from a gender perspective.
7. Value the role recreation practitioners play in shaping gender experiences.

Introduction

Magazine headlines such as, "The Female Chauvinist Pig: How It Became Cool to Treat Yourself Like a Piece of Meat" (Timson, 2005) and "The Age of the Wuss: The Sad Slump of North American Manhood" (Gillis, 2005) are drawing attention to gender issues within Canadian society. Gender is so pervasive it often takes popular press headlines or some other deliberate disruption to draw our attention to the gendered nature of society (Lorber, 2006). Once that disruption occurs, it is evident that we all live in a gendered society. On a macro level discussion, the influence of gender is evident in our social structures including the family, work, and public policies. Similarly, on a micro scale, the influence of gender is evident in the daily routines and practices of people, including child rearing practices, sports, and television shows (Henderson, Bialeschki, Shaw, & Freysinger, 1996). Given the pervasive nature of gender in society, it is no surprise that leisure activities are also inextricably linked to gender. Over the past two decades, the link between leisure and gender has developed into a large and growing body of literature. The purpose of this chapter is to introduce students to this exciting area of leisure studies and to help students appreciate the link between gender and leisure.

Gender Versus Sex

One of the original contributions of gender research was the differentiation between gender and sex. Gender refers to the examination of men and women within a cultural and social context. Unlike sex, which refers to one's biological assignment of male or female, gender "refers to how society determines expectations and behaviour regarding masculinity and femininity. One's biological sex leads to a lifetime of relationships and expectations based on gender" (Henderson et al., 1996, p. 17). For example, we expect baby girls to be dressed in pink, while baby boys are dressed in blue to display their sex assignment. Based upon that display, people interact with the baby in certain ways—more aggressive, rough and tumble play with boys and more vocal, gentle play with girls. These differences stem from notions of "masculinity" (tough, aggressive, heterosexual) and "femininity" (soft, nurturing, compassionate). Our conceptualizations of "masculinity" and "femininity" then translate into gender role expectations. For example, Henderson and Shaw (under review) note how conceptualizations of masculinity translate into roles including "fatherhood, male bonding, and the acceptance of economic… responsibility" (p. 6). Notions of "femininity" translate into roles as well, such as motherhood, female socialization, and the acceptance of household and emotional responsibility. Toward this end, Henderson et al. (2002) commented, "people have learned to take on certain roles in their lives because of a hegemonic world where individuals react to values and beliefs that support, often unconsciously, social relationships and structures of power" (p. 259). With this in mind, Lorber (2006) explains gender is not "in our genes," but rather is a social process that is constantly created and recreated through human interaction and social life. In this

Hegemony refers to "the predominant influence, as of a state, region, or group, over another or others" (Dictionary.com)

Does gender difference imply inequality between men and women?

sense, gender is commonly referred to as a social construction, meaning that humans produce and reproduce it in their social interactions as opposed to it being biologically determined, as sex is.

The Evolution of Gender Research with Leisure Studies

Gender issues have been discussed in varying degrees in leisure literature over the past twenty years. Henderson (1994) noted gender research in leisure studies has evolved through several stages over the years. Henderson's review demonstrated that initially, leisure research was "male scholarship" whereby women were invisible and it was assumed there was a universal leisure experience. The findings of research conducted on men's leisure were assumed to be applicable to the leisure lives of women. The second step in the evolution of gender research was the compensatory phase (Henderson, 1994). During this stage of research, scholarship was still defined by men, but it was recognized that women ought to be a research consideration as well. This compensatory stage is commonly referred to as the "add women and stir" stage (Wimbush & Talbot, 1988) and resulted in sex being added to other demographic's variables such as age, race, and income levels.

"Bifocal scholarship" that documented differences in women's and men's leisure habits and patterns was the focus of the third stage (Henderson, 1994). Most of the research in this stage focused on documenting sex differences, which meant biological characteristics became a primary focus in leisure literature. While this research is credited as a starting point for the inclusion of women's leisure experiences, "sex cannot be divorced from gender with its cultural construction of roles based on birth assignment as female or male" (Henderson, 1990, p. 230). As such, most of the research conducted in this stage was limited in its contribution to understanding how gender influenced leisure experiences.

The fourth stage resulted in woman-centred research, or feminist scholarship, that focused on the conditions women face in their day-to-day lives and framed those experiences within a broader social context (Henderson, 1994). Research conducted during this stage was primarily conducted by, for, and with women. Following this woman-centred approach a fifth stage coined 'new scholarship' or 'gender scholarship' emerged. Henderson (1994) noted, "a premise underlying this phase of scholarship is that all of us (men and women) live in a totally gendered society so behaviour can be better understood by examining the experiences of women and men within that framework. Furthermore, this new gender scholarship extends feminist scholarship by suggesting that the leisure of women cannot be universalized and no one female or male voice exists" (pp. 3–4). Thus, one outcome of gender scholarship has been the appreciation of diversity within and between groups of men and women (Shaw, 1999). More specifically, the social and cultural foci of gender research have highlighted the differences that occur within groups due to factors such as age, ethno-cultural considerations, race, and sexual orientation. Having said that, the gender approach also incorporates overarching commonalities among people of the same gender due to societal beliefs, expectations, roles, and relations (Shaw, 1999). In sum, gender scholarship appreciates that both men and women are affected by the cultural connotations of gender, which has implications for the leisure of both groups.

Feminist Theory in Leisure Research

Much of the gender scholarship has adopted a feminist theoretical framework. While not all feminists focus on the same political struggles, most feminists are dedicated to eliminating patriarchal social systems through which the distribution of power, benefits, and burdens are not equal (Kirkley, 2000). Patriarchy is defined in terms of hierarchical thinking whereby the status of one group, namely men, is placed over that of another, namely women. Patriarchy is depicted by privilege, power and domination (Kirkley, 2000). One key component of patriarchy is the oppression of women; most feminists would agree that women are wrongly oppressed. Jaggar (1988) stated, "feminism is used to refer to all those who seek, no matter on what grounds, to end women's subordination" (p. 5). What feminists disagree on is the source of the oppression and what needs to be done to abolish it, which has lead to different feminist theories (Kirkley, 2000). Although there are a number of different feminist theories that vary according to the emphasis placed on different issues and strategies (Tuana & Tong, 1995), four main approaches can be identified: liberal, Marxist, radical, and socialist.

In addition to these four main approaches, a more general overarching perspective of feminism can also be identified and is often utilized within leisure research (Henderson et al., 1996). Within this perspective, feminism has been has been defined as a framework that embodies "equity, empowerment, and social change for men and women" (Henderson et al., 1996, p. 13). Feminist theorists typically place emphasis on women's freedom of choice through control over their bodies and over other aspects of their lives (The Boston Women's Health Book Collective, 2005). They also recognize the pervasive nature of gender and the impact of gender relations on everyday life (Shaw, 1994). Researchers working within a general feminist paradigm are concerned that women and men be allowed to

Why do you think feminism has been labelled the new "F word?" What are your thoughts on "feminism?" Are you a feminist? Why/why not? Can men be feminists? Support your position.

speak with their own voices, that all aspects of their lives be taken into account, and that the research process facilitates personal empowerment and positive social change as well as improved theoretical understanding (Sapiro, 1994).

Feminist theory has offered a valuable and insightful way to study leisure. Henderson et al. (1996) note as scholars adopt feminist theory, leisure researchers address specific experiences of men and women "and build theory upon this information, [so] a comprehensive understanding of leisure behaviour will be formed" (p. 95). Indeed, a comprehensive understanding of leisure as it connects to gender is evident in the current understanding of the roles of leisure in reproducing and resisting gender roles, expectations, and relations.

The Role of Leisure in Reproducing Gender

Much of our current understanding regarding gender stems from research that has examined how gender influences leisure choices and activities. We now appreciate that when women and men make choices about their leisure, they do so within a broad cultural and social context that communicates what types of activities and experiences are appropriate for women and men in society. Indeed, the influence of gender can be seen in the extent to which activities are stereotyped according to gender. Auster (2001) noted the "sex-typing and sex segregation of leisure activities is reflected in, for example, the disproportionate number of men compared to women joining ice hockey and football teams and the disproportionate number of women compared to men signing up for dancing and quilting classes" (p. 273). The earliest work in this area was conducted by Metheny (1967)—a sociologist who studied the gender stereotyping of sports. She found that the majority of sports to be considered appropriate for men or "masculine" pursuits, but a number of sports were considered more appropriate for women. Metheny argues the gender stereotyping of sports is based upon gendered roles and expectations. Accordingly, specific sports can be categorized as either "masculine" or "feminine" depending upon physicality, bodily contact, and the aesthetics of the sport. More current research in this area has found the gendered nature of sports still exists. For example, Wiley, Shaw, and Havitz (2000) noted football, ice hockey, and boxing are considered appropriate sports for men while dance, gymnastics, figure skating, and other non-contact sports are considered appropriate for women. Wiley et al., concluded, "this stereotyping of activities clearly affects participation choices, with most men restricting their participation to masculine activities that conform to male gender role expectations, and the majority of women participants also conforming by choosing activities that are thought of as feminine" (p. 22).

"A *stereotype* is a structured set of beliefs about the way a group of people think and act" (Matlin, 1992, p. 588).

Do you think our society is changing with respect to gender appropriate activities? If so, provide some examples of activity that demonstrates such change.

Although men and women both face the gender stereotyping of leisure activities, some research suggests men may face more restrictive choices because, as a society, we tend to be more accepting of women crossing over into non-traditional gender activities, like riding motorcycles (Auster, 2001). Having said that, many people do not cross traditional gender lines because "conforming activities that are deemed to be gender-appropriate provides females and males with higher social status compared with participation in non-conforming or gender inappropriate sports" (Wiley et al., 2000, p. 22). In short, the influence of gender on leisure is evident in the reproduction of pursuits considered appropriate for men and those considered appropriate for women.

The influence of gender can also be seen in the gendered nature of leisure constraints. Constraints are those factors/issues that limit our access to leisure or in some way reduce our enjoyment of leisure. More specifically, Shaw (1999) defined constraints as "factors [that] may prevent, reduce, or modify participation, or may adversely affect the quality or enjoyment of the leisure activities" (p. 274). Within the gender scholarship of leisure studies, much of the research on constraints has focused on women. The body of research on women's leisure constraints has been explored from two main approaches. The first approach focused on the "ways in which women are disadvantaged or oppressed within a patriarchal society, and how their subordinate status within society limits their access to, and enjoyment of, leisure" (Shaw, 1994, p. 8). For example, Bialeschki and Michener (1994) studied the transitions women face in their leisure lives throughout motherhood and found that at some point in their mothering careers, women felt constrained by an ethic of care. They commented, "from a negative standpoint, an ethic of care was perceived as a constraint to leisure for mothers because of the expectations that family leisure needs would be the highest priority" (p. 68). In other words, women were constrained by feeling as though they needed to provide or facilitate leisure for others, while neglecting their own leisure needs.

Closely linked to an ethic of care, is a sense of entitlement to leisure. Henderson (1990) found women are constrained by not feeling entitled to their own leisure because of their need to facilitate it for others. Women are also constrained by household and childcare responsibilities. Hochschild (1989) studied women's leisure in reference to their employment status and coined the term *second shift* to reflect the housework and child care women did when they came home after a full day of paid of employment. The second shift was found to create a major gap between men's and women's leisure that in many cases is still prevalent today (Willming & Gibson, 2000). Perhaps Kay (2000) summed up this perspective best when she stated, "prevailing ideologies of motherhood and womanhood have been extensively recognized as fundamental influences on women's leisure" (pp. 249, 255) and allow more leisure time and opportunities for men.

The second approach to women's leisure constraints examined leisure activities themselves as constraining because they reinforce and reproduce oppressive gender structures or relations (Shaw, 1994). For example, Shaw (1997) studied pornography as a male leisure pursuit and its impact upon women's lives. She found pornography elicited fear in women, had a negative impact on their relationships and their identities, and was seen to reinforce sexist attitudes amongst men, yet "many of the women felt their opinions were not 'legitimate,' and overt resistance to pornography was often muted" (p. 197). Delamere (2005) studied the gendered nature of violent video games. She found violent video games reproduced stereotypical gender roles in the gaming content and character representations. Delamere stated, "a large portion of the violence in the games is gendered violence targeted towards female characters or any other non-hegemonic forms of masculinity (i.e., disempowered characters based on race or sexuality)" (p. 138).

Even though most of the literature on constraints has focused on women, men also face leisure constraints. Shaw and Henderson (2000) suggested that men "may feel constrained by their paid work activities and the social pressure to be "successful." Many men may also feel too embarrassed or inhibited to participate in activities that are deemed to be 'feminine'" (p. 1). Similarly, Kay (2006) studied men's experiences with fatherhood and noted that men are constrained by the role of breadwinner, which limits their time for family leisure experiences. Kimmel (2006) stated men are constrained in their lives and leisure by what he refers to as the traditional recipe for masculinity: self-control, exclusion, and escape. Kimmel's recipe for masculinity is particularly evident in sports. Indeed, Messner (1998) argued that sport participation is seen as compulsory for young boys to demonstrate their masculinity. Toward this end, Lorber (2000) argued "competitive sports have become, for boys and men, as players and spectators, a way of constructing a masculine identity, a legitimate outlet for violence and aggression, and an avenue for upward mobility" (p. 15). The values and ideologies associated with sports, such as toughness, aggression, and competition, are consistent with, and act to reinforce, hegemonic notions of masculinity (Messner, 1998). Hegemonic activities are those that reinforce and reproduce self-control, aggression, violence, etc. In other words, hegemonic activities construct a masculine identity. Based upon these ideals, sports are a complex terrain for men to negotiate. On the one hand, there are men who do not live up to these notions of hegemonic masculinity. Such men are not welcome or do not desire to play sports and are therefore not considered "real" men. On the other hand, men are being constrained into participating in sports to demonstrate their masculinity (Henderson & Shaw, under review). In sum, leisure pursuits may be considered constraining to both men and women given their role in reinforcing and reproducing oppressive gender structures or relations (Shaw, 1994). (See Chapter 9.)

How does gender shape your own leisure choices?

The Role of Leisure in Resisting Gender Stereotypes, Expectations, and Ideals

Although it is important to understand how leisure contributes to the reproduction of traditional gender relations, it is equally important to understand how leisure may be a context for people to resist such ideals. The notion of leisure as resistance is based on the idea that leisure practices, experiences, satisfactions, choices, and activities are linked to power and power relations in the social world (Shaw, 2001). Leisure, defined broadly, when conceptualized as resistance, is seen as a site for people, either individually or in groups, to challenge unequal power distributions or the ways that power is implemented. Under this premise, leisure becomes one arena where power is gained, maintained, reinforced, diminished or lost (Shaw, 2001). The notion of resistance is applicable to all marginalized groups. As with the research on constraints, however, much of the gender scholarship on resistance has been conducted with women. Indeed, the notion of resistance emerged in research where women were found to use their leisure or gain from their leisure a sense of empowerment. In particular, leisure was found to enhance women's power by challenging dominant patriarchal power structures in society and the resultant gendered relations (Deem, 1999).

Empowerment refers to "one's capacity to acquire understanding and control over personal, social, and political forces to improve life situations" (Braithwaite, 2000, p. 193).

In this sense, women's leisure as resistance is based on two theoretical assumptions: first, the idea of agency, which "allows for the view that women (and men) are social actors who perceive and interpret social situations and actively determine, in each setting, how they will respond" (Shaw, 1994, p. 15). The second assumption is the notion that leisure experiences are relatively freely chosen. Specifically, two key characteristics of leisure, personal choice and self-determination, have been associated with resistance to traditionally prescribed gender identities, stereotypes, and roles propagated through dominant patriarchal culture by enabling women to exert personal control and power (Shaw, 2001).

"Broadly understood, the term *agency* signals the capacity for individuals to perceive their situation, reason about it, consciously monitor their action, form motives, and so on" (Schwandt, 2000, p. 4).

First time mothers, for example, were found to use leisure as a form of resistance to socialized gender roles by seeking experiences based on a need for increased sense of autonomy and self-value, which is not expected of mothers in a patriarchal society (Wearing, 1990). Green (1998) explored women's friendships in relationship to resistance. She found that women-only leisure contexts facilitated feelings of empowerment and resistance to stereotyped gender roles. In particular, Green (1998) found that in their friendship groups, women used humour as "spaces for re-working gender identities via resistance to stereotyped gender roles" (p. 181) enabling them to partake in liberating experiences. Auster (2001) studied women motorcycle operators: a stereotypically masculine leisure pursuit. In her study of 453 female motorcyclists, Auster found that partaking in non-traditional leisure pursuits allowed women to transcend constraints, again providing women with the opportunity to feel empowered through leisure. Wearing and Wearing (2000) studied why young girls choose to smoke cigarettes as a leisure activity. They concluded that smoking provided a way for them to resist "prissy, confining 'good girl' images" (p. 47). Clearly, through their leisure, women can resist "societal views about women's expected roles and behaviours" (Shaw, 2001, p. 187). Similarly, given the constraints that men are facing in their leisure, the ways that men might use their leisure to resist hegemonic notions of masculinity is an area that warrants investigation as well.

What modern social practices in Canadian society help to reinforce society's perception of women as the "weaker sex" thus impacting and in some cases restricting their leisure choices?

Future Perspectives on Gender and Leisure

An overview of the type of research that has been conducted in the past gives us an idea of what types of studies need to be conducted in the future. For example, our examination of the gender scholarship within leisure studies demonstrates much of this research has examined women as "gendered beings." The focus on women led Wearing (1998) to ask, "Has feminist theory contributed to an understanding of leisure in general?" (p. 155). Kimmel and Messner (1998) remind us men are "gendered beings" too and warrant study from a gender perspective. In their words:

> Men are also "gendered," and this gendering process, the transformation of biological males into socially interacting men, is a central experience for men. That we are unaware of it only helps to perpetuate the inequities based on gender in our society (p. xv).

Leisure scholars need to understand the gendered nature of men's lives, including their leisure. Kay (2006) stated, leisure studies "offers a particularly rich contribution to social science literature on gender, family and the domestic sphere [but] offers little detailed analysis of men's experiences in these contexts" (p. 135). Miller (2005) argued the male body and notions of masculinity "are up for grabs" as recently signified by the term "metrosexual." Clearly, this aspect of men's lives and its link to leisure warrant attention. Henderson and Shaw (under review) note, however, the challenge in researching men as gendered beings is to "retain a critical feminist edge that can be applied to both the study of men and women, and avoid the tendency to superimpose a simple gender analysis" (p. 7).

A second area for future research is how leisure experiences and activities serve to influence gender relations and expectations. More specifically, previous research has done an excellent job in demonstrating the effect of gender on leisure. Much less is understood, however, about how leisure contexts may influence or affect gender relations or ideologies, even though leisure is generally credited as an important site for doing so (Henderson, Hodges, & Kivel, 2002). For example, in discussing her research on women motorcycle operators, Auster (2001) asked, "Would gender stereotypes affect individuals' perceptions of and willingness to participate in such leisure activities? Would various aspects of a decision to participate reflect the impact of gender role expectation and stereotypes of leisure activities?" (p. 293). These types of questions speak to the need for research that examines how leisure pursuits in non-conforming activities influence societal perceptions of gender roles and expectations. In short, how does leisure affect gender roles and expectations?

A third area for future research that warrants attention is mixed gender settings. Little leisure research has explored how leisure pursuits that involve both men and women influences gender relations. Parry, Glover and Shinew (2005) studied gender roles and expectations within the leisure context of a community garden wherein there were both men and women working together. Their research demonstrated how gender roles were simultaneously reproduced and resisted. As Shaw (2001) stated, the flip side of resistance is reproduction "and the two processes are seen to work continuously and contiguously, in opposite directions, often with one or the other process being dominant at any one time" (p. 188). For example, in the community garden, women took on leadership roles, which resisted gender stereotypes, but they also reproduced gender roles by seeking out men to perform some of the physically demanding jobs such as heavy lifting. More research is needed to explore how leisure contexts, such as neighbourhood associations, influence gender roles and expectations. Toward this end Shaw (1999) stated, "interactions with others during leisure, including interactions with people of the same as well as the opposite gender, also reflect, reinforce, and sometimes challenge ideas about appropriate behaviour for women and men" (p. 276). More research on different leisure contexts would shed light on this complex process.

A fourth area for study would be to examine those who fall outside the traditional sex assigned of "male" and "female." Although Western society is deeply committed to the idea that there are only two sexes, Fausto-Sterling (2006) argued that male and female is simply not enough. In her words, "there are many gradations running from female to male; and depending on how one calls the shots, one can argue that along that spectrum lie at least five sexes—and perhaps even more" (p. 87). According to Fausto-Sterling, the term inter-sex refers to those who embody a mixture of male and female characteristics and include hermaphrodites, male pseudo-hermaphrodites, and female pseudo-hermaphrodites. Similarly, Grossman, O'Connell, and D'Augelli (2005) noted transgender people have received scant attention in the leisure literature or elsewhere. Transgender—transsexuals, cross-dressers, gender benders/blenders—"challenge recreation and leisure professionals because their gender identity and expressions differ from society's role expectations of what it means to be male or female. These... people confront traditional 'girl-boy' activities associated with gender stereotyping" (Grossman, O'Connell, & D'Augelli, 2005, p. 5). Clearly this is an area of gender and leisure research that deserves more attention.

"hermaphrodites... possess one testis and one ovary, male pseudo-hermaphrodites have male testes and some aspects of the female genitalia but no ovaries, and the female pseudo-hermaphrodites have ovaries and some aspect of the male genitalia but lack testes" (Fausto-Serling, 2006, p. 87).

A final area for future research is how men and women negotiate gendered constraints. James (2000) examined adolescent girls at swimming pools and found they were constrained in their participation by feeling self-conscious and embarrassed by their bodies, which affected both the frequency of their participation and their enjoyment. Of the girls interviewed, 29% said they would use swimming pools more often if boys were not around. This is not to suggest that these girls gave up swimming as a leisure pursuit. Many found ways of negotiating their constraints, such as wearing t-shirts while swimming or covering themselves up with a towel until right before they jumped into the pool, so as to continue their participation. Whyte and Shaw (1994) studied fear of violence as a leisure constraint. Their results showed that women's fear of violence resulted in them having fewer leisure choices and reduced enjoyment of leisure because of heightened anxiety levels. Whyte and Shaw (1994) also found, however, the women in their study developed strategies to negotiate these constraints to continue their participation in desired pursuits. These studies, amongst others, demonstrate that people do not simply accept constraints, but rather negotiate around them (see Chapter 9). More research in this area would clarify the gendered nature of constraints and how people react to them to keep leisure in their lives. In so doing, research might identify what types of changes might be made to facilitate different leisure opportunities or experiences for women and men.

Select and describe one aspect of women's or men's leisure that is still a concern for you. How could this issue be addressed in the future?

Conclusion and Implications for Practice

Clearly, there is a link between gender and leisure that has implications for both professionals working in recreation and leisure, but also for the lives of individuals. Information on the gendered nature of leisure can help leisure service providers become aware of the influence of gender on the lives of both men and women. Indeed, one of the original purposes of public recreation was to "advance girls' and women's chances for social equality" (Tillotson, 2000, p. 3). Opportunities for a variety of leisure experiences are needed and attention should be directed towards providing environments that enable men and women to resist traditional gender roles, expectations, and relations. Indeed, recreation and leisure professionals are in the unique positions of being able to contribute to social change—either on an individual or broader level—in regard to gender roles, expectations and relations through the provision of leisure pursuits that are not divided along gender lines. For example, in facilitating sport opportunities, instead of starting with two presumed distinct categories (male, female) it might be more useful to group people according to ability (Lorber, 2000). In addition to the people working in the leisure industry, the chapter is applicable to us as individuals. Recognizing the influence of gender often helps people understand their leisure choices and think about what type of choices they make and why. In sum, the relationship between gender and leisure has implications for both professional practice and personal lives.

What are two of the most important lessons you are taking from this text with respect to gender and leisure?

Key Terms

Gender
Leisure
Reproduction
Resistance

References

Auster, C. J. (2001). Transcending potential antecedent leisure constraints: The case of women motorcycle operators. *Journal of Leisure Research, 33*(3), 272–298.

Bialeschki, M. D., & Michener, S. (1994). Re-entering leisure: Transition within the role of motherhood. *Journal of Leisure Research, 26*(1), 57–74.

The Boston Women's Health Book Collective (2005). *Our bodies, ourselves.* New York, NY: Simon and Schuster.

Braithwaite, R. L. (2000). Empowerment. In A. E. Kazdin (Ed.), *Encyclopedia of psychology* (pp. 193–194). New York, NY: Oxford University Press.

Brown, W. (1995). Liberalism's family values. In W. Brown (Ed.), *States of injury: Power and freedom in late modernity* (pp. 135–165). Princeton, NJ: Princeton University Press.

Deem, R. (1999). How do we get out of the ghetto? Strategies for research on gender and leisure for the twenty-first century. *Leisure Studies, 18*(3), 161–177.

Delamere, F. M. (2005). Violent video games play: A gendered experience. Paper presented at the eleventh Canadian Congress on Leisure Research, Nanaimo, British Columbia.

Fausto-Sterling, A. (2006). The five sexes: Why male and female is not enough. In K. E. Rosenblum & T. C. Travis (Eds.), *The meaning of difference: American constructions of race, sex and gender, social class, and sexual orientation.* New York, NY: McGraw-Hill.

Gillis, C. (2005, October 31). The age of the wuss. The sad slump of North American manhood. *Maclean's Magazine, 118*(44), 28–32.

Green, E. (1998). 'Women doing friendship': An analysis of women's leisure as a site of identity construction, empowerment and resistance. *Leisure Studies, 17,* 171–185.

Grossman, A. H., O'Connell, T. S., & D'Augelli, A. R. (2005). Leisure and recreational "girl-boy" activities: Studying the unique challenges provided by transgendered young people. *Leisure/Loisir, 29*(1), 5–26.

Hochschild, A. (1989). The second shift: Working parents and the revolution at home. New York, NY: Viking.

Henderson, K. A. (1994). Broadening an understanding of women, gender, and leisure. *Journal of Leisure Research, 26*(1), 1–7.

Henderson, K. A. (1990). Anatomy is not destiny: A feminist analysis of the scholarship on women's leisure. *Leisure Sciences, 12,* 229–239.

Henderson, K. A., Bialeschki, M. D., Shaw, S. M., & Freysinger, V. (1996). *Both gains and gaps: Feminist perspectives on women's leisure.* State College, PA: Venture Publishing, Inc.

Henderson, K. A., Hodges, S., & Kivel, B. D. (2002). Context and dialogue in research on women and leisure. *Journal of Leisure Research, 34*(3), 253–271.

Henderson, K. A., & Shaw, S. M. (2004). *Leisure research about gender and men? A Research note.* Manuscript submitted for publication.

Jaggar, A. M. (1988). *Feminist politics and human nature.* Totowa, NJ: Rowan and Littlefield.

James, K. (2000). "You can feel them looking at you": The experiences of adolescent girls at swimming pools. *Journal of Leisure Research, 32*(2), 262–280.

Kay, T. (2006). Where's Dad? Fatherhood in leisure studies. *Leisure Studies, 25*(2), 133–152.

Kay, T. (2000). Leisure, gender and family: The influence of social policy. *Leisure Studies, 19*, 247–265.

Kimmel, M. S. (2006). *Manhood in America: A cultural history*. New York, NY: Oxford University Press.

Kimmel, M. S., & Messner, M. A. (2001). Editors' introduction. In Kimmel, M. S., & Messner, M. A. (Eds.), *Men's lives*. (5th ed., pp. ix-xvii). Boston, MA: Allyn & Bacon.

Kirkley, D. (2000). Is motherhood good for women? A feminist exploration. *Journal of Obstetric, Gynecologic and Neonatal Nursing, 29*(5), 459–465.

Lorber, J. (2006). The social construction of gender. In T. E Ore (Ed.), *The social construction of difference and inequality: Race, class, and gender* (3rd ed.). New York, NY: McGraw-Hill.

Lorber, J. (2000). Believing is seeing: Biology as ideology. In Zinn, M. B., Hondagneu-Sotelo, P., & Messner, M. A. (Eds.), *Gender through the prism of difference*. (2nd ed., pp. 13–22). Boston, MA: Allyn & Bacon.

Matlin, M. W. (1992). *Psychology*. New York, NY: Holt, Rinehart and Winston.

Messner, M. A. (1998). Boyhood, organized sports, and the construction of masculinities. In M. S. Kimmel & M. A. Messner (Eds.), *Men's lives* (4th ed., pp. 109–121). Boston, MA: Allyn & Bacon.

Metheny, E. (1967). *Connotations of movement in sport and dance*. Dubuque, IA: William C. Brown.

Miller, T. (2005). A meterosexual eye on the queer guy. GLQ: *A Journal of Lesbian and Gay Studies, 11*(1), 112–117.

Parry, D. C., Glover, T. D., & Shinew, K. J. (2005). "Mary, Mary Quite Contrary, How Does Your Garden Grow?" Examining Gender Roles and Relations in Community Gardens. *Leisure Studies, 24*(2), 177–192.

Sapiro, V. (1994) *Women in American society*. Mountain View, CA: Mayfield Publishing.

Schwandt, T. (2001). *Dictionary of qualitative inquiry* (2nd ed.). Thousand Oaks, CA: Sage Publications.

Shaw, S. M. (1994). Gender, leisure, and constraint: Towards a framework for the analysis of women's leisure. *Journal of Leisure Research, 26*, 8–22.

Shaw, S. M. (1997). Men's leisure and women's lives: The impact of pornography on women. *Leisure Studies, 18*, 197–212.

Shaw, S. M. (1999). Gender and leisure. In E. L. Jackson & T. L. Burton (Eds.), *Leisure studies: Prospects for the twenty-first century* (pp. 271–279). State College, PA: Venture Publishing, Inc.

Shaw, S. M. (2001). Conceptualizing resistance: Women's leisure as political practice. *Journal of Leisure Research, 33*(2), 186–201.

Timson, J. (2005, September 26). The female chauvinist pig. How it became cool to treat yourself like a piece of meat. *MacLean's Magazine, 118*(39), 37–41.

Tillotson, S. (2000). *The public at play: Gender and the politics of recreation in post-war Ontario*. Toronto, ON: University of Toronto Press.

Tong, R. (1989). Radical feminism on reproduction and mothering. In R. Tong, *Feminist thought: A comprehensive introduction* (pp. 71–94), Boulder, CO: Westview Press.

Tuana, N., & Tong, R. (1995). Socialist feminist perspectives. In N. Tuana & R. Tong (Eds.), *Feminism and philosophy: Essential readings in theory, reinterpretation, and application* (pp. 261–264). Boulder, CO: Westview Press.

Wearing, B. (1998). Personal leisure spaces: Poststructuralist theories. In *Leisure and feminist theory* (pp. 143–161). London, UK: Sage Publications.

Wearing, S., & Wearing, B. (2000). Smoking as a fashion accessory in the 90s: Conspicuous consumption, identity and adolescent women's leisure choices. *Leisure Studies, 19*(1), 45–58.

Whyte, L. B., & Shaw, S. M. (1994). Women's leisure: An explanatory study of fear of violence as a leisure constraint. *Journal of Applied Recreation Research, 19*(1), 5–21.

Wiley, C. G. E., Shaw, S. M., & Havitz, M. E. (2000). Men's and women's involvement in sports: An examination of the gendered aspects of leisure involvement. *Leisure Sciences, 22*, 19–31.

Willming, C., & Gibson, H. (2000). A view of leisure and patterns of family life in the late 1990s. *Loisir et Société/ Society and Leisure, 23*(1), 121–144.

Wimbush, E., & Talbot, M. (Eds.). (1988). *Relative freedoms*. Milton Keynes, UK: Open University Press.

Chapter 21
Multicultural Perspectives

Gordon J. Walker, Ph.D.
University of Alberta

Learning Objectives

After reading this chapter, students will be able to

1. Understand the terms *race*, *ethnicity*, and *visible minority group*.
2. Know two important trends affecting Canada's composition.
3. Be able to provide six explanations for why ethnic and visible minority groups sometimes participate in different activities or at different levels.
4. Understand how leisure constraints and leisure motivations can vary, and how self-construal can affect these two factors.
5. Learn about three programming considerations leisure practitioners who work with ethnic and visible minority group members should know.

Multicultural Perspectives

One of the questions post-secondary students often ask themselves is "Who am I?" Students can answer in many ways, including based on sociodemographic factors such as their gender (e.g., "I am a woman"), social class ("I am from a working-class family"), ethnicity (e.g., "I am Chinese Canadian"), or based on their leisure behaviour (e.g., "I am a rugby player," "I am a Gleek"). Not surprisingly, these two types of answers are often related to, for example, how ethnic identity affects people's leisure behaviour, and how people's leisure behaviour reinforces their sense of ethnic identity. Before this relationship can be examined more fully, however, it is first necessary to explain what ethnicity is, how it is similar to and different from some other identity-descriptive terms, and what two of the key ethnicity-associated trends are in Canada.

Topic's Importance/Relevance

Race and ethnicity are not identical concepts; race is concerned with shared physical features (e.g., skin colour, eye shape), ethnicity with common cultural characteristics (e.g., language, religion, traditions, ancestral origin, family patterns, value systems). These descriptors occasionally overlap, however. For example, a person who self-identifies as "Chinese" is describing him- or herself in terms of both race and ethnicity. Omi and Winant (1994) called this "racialized ethnicity." An individual may also self-identify with more than one ethnic group, such as Irish and Scottish or Chinese and Canadian, or even a combination of the two (e.g., Chinese Canadian). Finally, people who are "non-Caucasian in race or non-White in colour" but who are also not Aboriginal are sometimes referred to as members of a "visible minority group" (Statistics Canada, 2003a).

Although ethnicity and visible minority group are broad concepts, their use does provide us with insight into Canada's recent and future composition. According to the 2006 census (Statistics Canada, 2008a), over 10 million people reported their ethnic ancestry as being Canadian, either alone (5.7 million) or in combination with other ethnicities (4.3 million). Next was English (6.6 million), followed by French (4.9 million), Scottish (4.7 million), and Irish (4.4 million). Interestingly, the number of people reporting being only Canadian grew from 2.8% in 1991 to 18.4% in 2006 (Statistics Canada, 2008b). According to Thomas (2005), this "ethnic realignment" is the result of a variety of factors, including: changes in how the census is conducted; Canada's particular democratic institutions and collective achievements (e.g., the Charter of Rights, universal health care, multiculturalism); and a desire to differentiate oneself from both Americans and recent immigrants (most of whom are visible minority group members).

In 2006, 16.2% of Canadians were visible minority group members (Statistics Canada, 2008a). South Asians were the largest group (24.9%) followed by Chinese (18.2%), Blacks (15.5%), Filipinos (8.1%), and Latin Americans (6.0%). (It is important to note here, however, that some of these categories are comprised of multiple distinct subgroups, with South Asians for instance including East Indians, Sri Lankans, Pakistanis, etc.). Visible minority group members are expected to nearly double in less than 20 years, from 16.2% in 2006 to 30.6% in 2031 (Statistics Canada, 2010). At this time, approximately 8.7% of Canadians will be South Asian, 6.4% will be Chinese, and 2.4% will be Filipino (Statistics Canada, 2010).

In summary, in addition to the increasing Aboriginal population (see Chapter 22 on Aboriginal leisure), it appears that there are two other major trends transforming Canadian society: (1) the growing number of visible minority group members, with South Asians and Chinese as the largest sub-groups; and (2) the growing number of people who say they are either solely or partly Canadian. Unfortunately, the effect of these trends on leisure studies in our country is unclear, but we do have some insight into the relationship between ethnic and visible minority groups and their leisure behaviour (see *i*-box).

"Ethnic Ancestry and Ethnic Identity"

1. How would you answer the following question, modified slightly from the 2006 census (Statistics Canada, 2005)?

What were the ethnic or cultural origins of your ancestors? An ancestor is usually more distant than a grandparent. For example, Canadian, English, French, Chinese, Italian, German, Scottish, East Indian, Irish, Cree, Mi'kmaq (Micmac), Metis, Inuit (Eskimo), Ukrainian, Dutch, Filipino, Polish, Portuguese, Jewish, Greek, Jamaican, Vietnamese, Lebanese, Chilean, Salvadorean, Somali, etc. Specify as many origins as applicable:

a) ______________________________
b) ______________________________
c) ______________________________
d) ______________________________

2. How would you answer the following question, from a typical leisure study (e.g., Walker, Deng, & Dieser, 2001)?

What ethnic or cultural group do you belong to? For example, Canadian, English, French, Chinese, Italian, German, Scottish, East Indian, Irish, Cree, Mi'kmaq (Micmac), Metis, Inuit (Eskimo), Ukrainian, Dutch, Filipino, Polish, Portuguese, Jewish, Greek, Jamaican, Vietnamese, Lebanese, Chilean, Salvadorean, Somali, etc. Specify as many groups as applicable:

a) ______________________________
b) ______________________________
c) ______________________________
d) ______________________________

3. Did the answers you gave in question 1 (i.e., ethnic ancestry) affect the answers you gave in question 2 (i.e., ethnic identity)? Are there other factors besides ethnic ancestry that affect what you perceive as being your ethnic identity? Did you use only one space, and if so, did you write "Canadian"? Why?

What We Now Know

To date there has been relatively little research conducted on ethnic and visible minority groups and leisure behaviour in Canada. In terms of leisure participation differences, for example, Hall and Rhyne (1989) considered 17 ethnic groups in Ontario. Among their findings was that Chinese were more likely to participate in passive activities (e.g., watching television, visiting libraries) compared with those in other groups. Similarly, Walker and Chapman (2001) found that Chinese Canadians visiting a Canadian national park in Alberta were more likely to report viewing wildlife and scenery as their top activities, while Euro-North Americans (e.g., visitors who said they were English, Irish, Scottish, German, Canadian, or a combination) were more likely to report camping and day-hiking. Hung (2003) noted that while Asians constitute a large portion of the Greater Vancouver metropolitan area, they were much less likely to participate in outdoor recreation activities or to visit regional or provincial parks.

Based on research largely conducted in the United States, there are at least six explanations for why differences in leisure participation exist. Two of the earliest explanations put forth were the marginality and subcultural (or "ethnicity") hypotheses. According to Washburne (1978) "underparticipation" in an activity occurred either when members of an ethnic or visible minority group are marginalized because of "poverty and the various consequences of socioeconomic discrimination [e.g., inadequate transportation, lack of nearby facilities]" (p. 177), or when group members' cultural norms, values, and leisure socialization patterns were not congruent with that activity. Although both hypotheses have garnered some support both have also been criticized (Gramann & Allison, 1999); which has led to two other, discrimination-based explanations being put forward.

The first discrimination explanation suggests that leisure participation decreases when an ethnic or visible minority group member perceives he or she is being discriminated against either by other recreationists or by recreation agency staff (i.e., perceived personal discrimination). Although a Statistics Canada study (2003b) found that 35% (15% rarely, 17% sometimes, and 3% often) of visible minority group members felt discriminated against in the previous five years, we do not know if or how often this happened during their leisure. On the other hand, Tirone (1999) discovered that South Asian Canadian teenagers reported experiencing numerous discriminatory acts during community recreation programs and competitive sport activities, and at YMCAs and summer camps. In contrast, Stodolska and Jackson (1998) found that Polish immigrants in Edmonton reported markedly *less* personal discrimination in leisure settings than in other settings (e.g., schools, the workplace, government offices)—a result the researchers believe may have been because Polish people, being racially White, were less easily identifiable and therefore less often targeted than visible minority group members.

The second explanation for discrimination occurs when "organizationally or community prescribed practices, motivated by neither prejudice nor intent to harm that nevertheless have a negative and differential impact on members of a subordinate group" (i.e., institutional discrimination; Feagin & Eckbert, 1980, p. 12). Although there has been no leisure research on this topic in Canada to date, Scott (2005) suggested four ways in which public parks and recreation agencies can unintentionally commit institutional discrimination, including: (1) a too "entrepreneurial" approach, due to which a focus on fees, marketing, and privatization may mean social equity is overlooked; (2) too much emphasis on customer loyalty may mean that social equity and inclusion are overlooked; (3) a lack of staff diversity, and a general failure of diversity training; and (4) too narrow a conception of need and the assumption that it is equally easy for everyone to "just do it."

> Have you or any of your friends ever felt discriminated against during your leisure? Was it perceived personal discrimination or institutional discrimination? What did you do?

Kleiber, Walker, and Mannell (2011) have recently identified two additional reasons why differences in leisure participation might exist. First, positive emotion (or affect) is one of the properties often associated with leisure. But while measuring how people actually feel (or what Tsai, Knutson, & Fung, 2006, call "actual affect") is useful, measuring how people want to feel (or what they call "ideal affect") is equally so. According to these researchers, people often try to reduce the discrepancy between their actual and ideal affect by participating in specific mood-producing behaviours, including leisure activities (Tsai, Miao, & Seppala, 2007). Because the type of affect an individual considers ideal is dependent on his or her cultural background, however, this in turn can influence which kind of leisure activity he or she wants to participate in. For example, Tsai et al. (2006) found that European Americans preferred high-arousal positive affect (or HAP, including elated, excited, and enthusiastic) more than Hong Kong Chinese, while Hong Kong Chinese preferred low-arousal positive affect (or LAP, including calm, relaxed, and peaceful) more than European Americans. Based on these preferences, we would expect to find Canadians and/or Euro Canadians are more inclined to engage in HAP-producing leisure activities (e.g., snowboarding) while Chinese and/or Chinese Canadians are more inclined to engage in LAP-producing leisure activities (e.g., reading).

Acculturation, the second reason Kleiber and colleagues (2011) identified, is most applicable for immigrants and their children. Acculturation refers to the changes an individual or cultural group experiences as a result of contact with another cultural group (Berry, Poortinga, Segall, & Dasen, 2002). Besides *assimilation* (where a person prefers to become absorbed into the "mainstream" culture and so shed her or his heritage culture) and *separation* (where a person prefers to hold on to his or her heritage culture and tries to keep the mainstream culture largely at bay), two other acculturative "strategies" are possible: *integration* (where a person prefers to maintain his or her heritage culture and to be involved in the mainstream culture) and *marginalization* (where a person is not only unable or unwilling to maintain her or his heritage culture, but also unable or unwilling to be involved in the mainstream culture). (See Figure 21.1 below, based on Berry's et al. Model.)

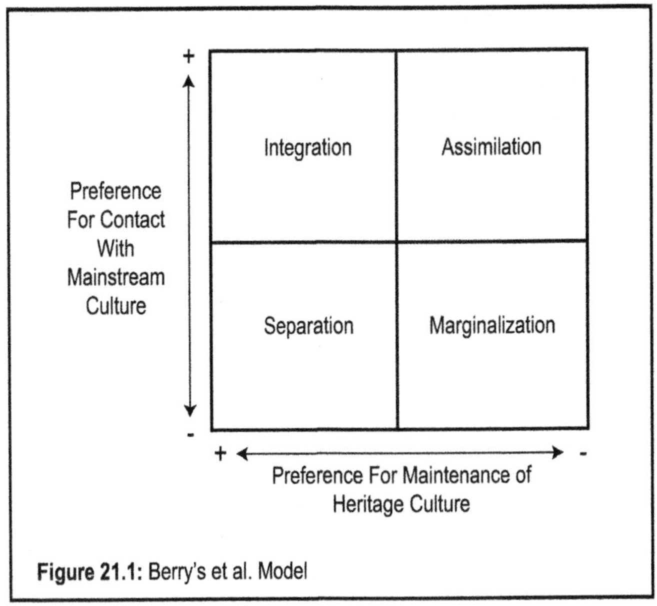

Figure 21.1: Berry's et al. Model

In terms of acculturation and leisure participation specifically, a recent study (Walker, 2011) of Mainland Chinese immigrants to Canada found that individuals: (a) who were either assimilated or integrated were more likely to participate in fitness activities than those who were separated; (b) who were integrated were more likely to participate in media activities than those who were either separated or marginalized; and (c) who were assimilated were more likely to participate in spectator sports than those who were separated.

In summary, research in this area continues to generate considerable debate. Floyd (1998), for instance, argued that other aspects of leisure behaviour besides participation needed to be examined. Hutchison (2000) agreed, but he also thought we should focus less on *describing* what leisure differences exist and focus more on *explaining* why these differences exist. In part because of such concerns, there has been growing interest in ethnic and visible minority group members' leisure constraints and motivations.

As Jackson described in his chapter, there are three kinds of leisure constraints: (1) *intrapersonal*, which are individual psychological qualities that affect the formation of leisure preferences; (2) *interpersonal*, which are social factors that affect the formation of leisure preferences; and (3) *structural*, which occur after leisure preferences are formed but before actual leisure participation takes place. Arguably, three of the explanations outlined above (i.e., marginality, perceived personal, and institutional discrimination) appear to be structural constraints. In contrast, the subcultural hypothesis and acculturation seem to be intrapersonal constraints, as this barrier includes individual psychological states. Other types of intrapersonal constraints include a person's prior experience, and perceived skill, in a specific leisure activity; his or her attitudes about the appropriateness and availability of that activity; and significant others' attitudes about the appropriateness and availability of the activity as well (Crawford & Godbey, 1987).

A person's attitudes about a specific activity may be influenced by how he or she feels and thinks about leisure in general, or what is sometimes called "leisure attitude." Studies have found that leisure attitude does vary across ethnic and visible minority groups. For example, in the previously mentioned study of 17 Ontario groups, Hall and Rhyne (1989) also found that Chinese, Portuguese, South Asian, and West Indian participants were less likely to value having free time, while British, Jewish, and Scandinavian participants were more likely to value having free time. Of the 17 groups studied, those who described themselves as Chinese valued free time the least. This finding is supported by a study (Deng, Walker, & Swinnerton, 2005) that found that Chinese in Canada rated affective (e.g., "my leisure pursuits are interesting") and cognitive (e.g., "leisure pursuits are beneficial to individuals and society") attitude items lower than Anglo-Canadians (i.e., those who indicated they were English, Irish, Scottish, Welsh, Canadian, or a combination).

In their study, Deng et al. (2005) also examined the effect of acculturation on leisure attitudes and, contrary to expectations, they found that more acculturated Chinese (e.g., those who were more likely to speak English) were actually *less* positive about the beneficial aspects of leisure than less acculturated Chinese (e.g., those who were more likely to speak Mandarin). The researchers believed this result may have been due to an "overshoot" effect being present whereby less acculturated and likely more recent immigrants adopted a Euro Canadian perspective and, in doing so, went well beyond the group standard.

Are there other types of intrapersonal and structural constraints you think ethnic and visible minority group members face? How might acculturation affect these?

In the same way that leisure constraints may vary both within and among ethnic and visible minority groups, so too can leisure motivations. Walker, Deng, and Dieser (2001) compared the motivations of Chinese Canadians and Euro Canadians visiting a Canadian national park in Alberta. Of the nine motivations measured, Euro-North Americans rated higher experiencing nature, peace, and calm and being free to make their own choices, while Chinese Canadians were more concerned with feeling they were part of the group and being perceived as humble and modest by their companions. To better understand the reasons for these differences, researchers found that self-construal, a concept that reflects how people think about themselves in relation to others, was helpful. According to Markus and Kitayama (1991), while Euro-North Americans are more likely to have *independent* selves—and therefore to value being unique, internal attributes (like personality traits), and asserting oneself—people in or from Asia and Africa are more likely to have *interdependent* selves—and therefore to value belonging, external attributes (like roles and statuses), and restraining oneself. Potentially, the type of self-construal a person has affects his or her cognitions, emotions, and motivations (Markus & Kitayama, 1991). Walker et al. (2001) found for example that: (1) Chinese Canadian national park visitors were more interdependent and Euro Canadians visitors were more independent; and (2) visitors who were more interdependent were also more motivated to try to feel they were part of the group than were visitors who were more independent.

In a follow-up article, Walker, Deng, and Dieser (2005) described how self-construal could affect intrinsic motivation—a quality common in leisure but rare elsewhere (Russell, 2002). According to Ryan and Deci (2000), "extrinsic motivation refers to the performance of an activity in order to attain some separable outcome and, thus, contrasts with intrinsic motivation, which refers to doing an activity for the inherent satisfaction of the activity itself" (p. 71). To date, most leisure theorists (e.g., Neulinger, 1981; Iso-Ahola, 1999) have held that freedom or personal choice is *the* key factor affecting intrinsic motivation, and, in the case of independent selves Walker et al. agree. But they also believe that for interdependent selves *the* key factor affecting intrinsic motivation is, instead, a feeling of belongingness. As they add, however, because even the most independent person is interdependent to some degree, these individuals also likely engage in "interdependent" leisure activities on

Would you say you are more independent or interdependent? Can you give an example of a leisure activity you do that would be independent? that would be interdependent?

occasion (e.g., when they are a "role" player on a sports team) and, similarly, interdependent selves sometimes engage in "independent" leisure activities as well (e.g., when they are at an informal party with close friends).

In the same way ethnicity can affect one's leisure behaviour, so too can leisure affect one's sense of ethnicity. Xu, Shim, Lotz, and Almeida (2004) found that Asian American students' ethnic identity was higher depending upon the degree of interaction they had with Asian American friends, and that this "ethnic-friendship orientation" had a positive effect on the frequency they ate ethnic foods, listened to ethnic music, and attended ethnic movies. Although Xu's et al. (2004) study did not find that consumption of these ethnic leisure activities also positively affected participants' sense of ethnic identity, the researchers felt that this relationship was possible over longer periods of time. One of the ways this might happen is through participation in ethnic community organizations (Breton, Reitz, & Valentine, 1980). Karlis (2004) believed that this is where many people practice their ethnic heritage and engage in ethnic-specific recreation activities.

Have you ever been in a leisure setting where your sense of ethnic identity was more noticeable than usual? When it was less noticeable than usual?

Outstanding Issues/Questions

As mentioned earlier, there has been relatively little research conducted in Canada on ethnic and visible minority groups' leisure behaviour. This gap is particularly important as the number of visible minority group members continues to increase. At the same time the number of people reporting being solely or partly Canadian has also grown considerably due, at least in part, as a reaction against the growing number of visible minority group members (Thomas, 2005). Although more research is clearly needed, it must take into account Floyd (1998) and Hutchison's (2000) concerns regarding the need to move beyond leisure participation, and to explain as well as describe both similarities and differences in leisure behaviour. Additionally, Walker and Wang (2005) cautioned against simply assuming that explanations developed in the United States apply in Canada. This country's ethnic and visible minority group composition, the ways in which we think of ourselves in relation to others (i.e., our self-construals), and the government policies and societal attitudes that exist (i.e., multiculturalism vs. "the melting pot" in the United States), are considerably different from one country to the next.

How do you think leisure might be similar and different in Canada and the United States? What explanations would you use to explain these differences?

Unfortunately, the lack of research on ethnic and visible minority groups' leisure behaviour also means that little is known about how best to plan and manage recreation programs, services, and facilities for members of these groups. Beyond Scott's (2005) suggestions for how to avoid committing acts of institutional discrimination, current leisure practitioners should consider: (1) conducting multilingual needs assessments, focus groups, and face-to-face interviews to learn more about ethnic and visible minority group members' wants and desires; (2) developing programs that allow members of these groups to recreate among themselves, with members of other ethnic and visible minority groups, and with majority group members, as they so choose; and (3) taking into account the structural constraints ethnic and visible minority group members face, including low income, lack of equipment, and limited English language proficiency. Finally, as a post-secondary student who will soon become a leisure practitioner, you should strongly consider taking a social science course that examines race, ethnicity, and culture or, even better, talking to your instructor about a recreation course specifically on this topic being offered. Doing so will better prepare you for a Canada that is much more ethnically and racially diverse than the one earlier recreation professionals encountered, but a country that is also much less multicultural than it will become in the future.

How would you design a recreation opportunity that takes into account ethnic and visible minority group concerns? For example, plan a badminton program for Chinese immigrants; or a trip to a provincial/national park for a group of Pakistani parents and their children; or a concert for a group of ethnically diverse seniors living in a care home.

Keywords

Acculturation
Attitude
Constraint

Ethnicity
Leisure
Motivation
Multiculturalism
Participation
Visible Minority Group

References

Berry, J. W., Poortinga, Y. H., Segall, M. H., & Dasen, P. R. (2002). *Cross-cultural psychology: Research and applications* (2nd ed.). New York, NY: Cambridge University Press.

Breton, R., Reitz, J., & Valentine, V. (1980). *Cultural boundaries and the cohesion of Canada.* Montreal: The Institute for Research on Public Policy.

Crawford, D., & Godbey, G. (1987). Reconceptualizing barriers to family leisure. *Leisure Sciences, 9*, 119–127.

Deng, J., Walker, G. J., & Swinnerton, G. (2005). Leisure attitudes: A comparison between Chinese in Canada and Anglo-Canadians. *Leisure/Loisir, 29*, 239–273.

Feagin, J. R., & Eckbert, D. L. (1980). Discrimination: Motivation, action, effects, and context. *Annual Review of Sociology, 6*, 1–20.

Floyd, M. (1998). Getting beyond marginality and ethnicity: The challenge for race and ethnic studies in leisure research. *Journal of Leisure Research, 30*, 3–22.

Gramann, J. H., & Allison, M. T. (1999). Ethnicity, race, and leisure. In E. Jackson & T. Burton (Eds.), *Leisure studies: Prospects for the twenty-first century* (pp. 283–297). State College, PA: Venture Publishing, Inc.

Hall, M. H., & Rhyne, D. (1989). *Leisure behaviour and recreation needs of Ontario's ethnocultural populations.* Toronto, ON: Ministry of Tourism and Recreation.

Hung, K. (2003). *Achieving cultural diversity in wilderness recreation: A study of the Chinese in Vancouver.* (Unpublished master's thesis). University of Waterloo, Waterloo, Ontario, Canada.

Hutchison, R. (2000). Race and ethnicity in leisure studies. In W. C. Gartner & D. W. Lime (Eds.), *Trends in outdoor recreation, leisure and tourism* (pp. 63–71). New York, NY: CABI.

Iso-Ahola, S. E. (1999). Motivational foundations of leisure. In E. Jackson & T. Burton (Eds.), *Leisure studies: Prospects for the twenty-first century* (pp. 35–51). State College, PA: Venture Publishing, Inc.

Karlis, G. (2004). *Leisure & recreation in Canadian society: An introduction.* Toronto, ON: Thompson Educational.

Kleiber, D. A., Walker, G. J., & Mannell, R. C. (2011). *A social psychology of leisure* (2nd ed.). State College, PA: Venture Publishing, Inc.

Markus, H., & Kitayama, S. (1991). Culture and the self: Implications for cognition, emotion, and motivation. *Psychological Review, 98*, 224–253.

Neulinger, J. (1981). *The psychology of leisure* (2nd ed.). Springfield, IL: Charles C. Thomas.

Omi, M., & Winant, H. (1994). Racial *formation in the United States.* New York, NY: Routledge.

Russell, R. (2002). *Pastimes: The context of contemporary leisure* (2nd ed.). Champaign, IL: Sagamore.

Ryan, R., & Deci, E. (2000). Self-Determination Theory and the facilitation of intrinsic motivation, social development, & well-being. *American Psychologist, 55*, 68–78.

Scott, D. (2005). The relevance of constraints research to leisure service delivery. In E. L. Jackson (Ed.), *Constraints to leisure* (pp. 279–293). State College, PA: Venture Publishing, Inc.

Statistics Canada. (2003a). *Canada's ethnocultural portrait: The changing mosaic.* Retrieved from http://www12.statcan.ca/english/census01/Products/Analytic/companion/etoimm/canada.cfm

Statistics Canada. (2003b). *Ethnic diversity survey.* Retrieved from http://www.statcan.ca/Daily/English/030929/d030929a.htm

Statistics Canada. (2005). *2006 census questions.* Retrieved from http://www12.statcan.ca/english/census06/info/questions/index.cfm

Statistics Canada. (2008a). *Canada's ethnocultural mosaic, 2006 Census: National picture—More than 200 different ethnic origins.* Retrieved from http://www12.statcan.ca/english/census06/analysis/ethnicorigin/more.cfm

Statistics Canada. (2008a). *Canada's ethnocultural mosaic, 2006 Census: National picture—South Asians surpass Chinese as the largest visible minority.* Retrieved from http://www12.statcan.ca/english/census06/analysis/ethnicorigin/south.cfm

Statistics Canada. (2010). *Projections of the diversity of the Canadian population, 2006 to 2031* (Catalogue No. 91-551-X). Retrieved from http://www.statcan.gc.ca/pub/91-551-x/91-551-x2010001-eng.pdf

Stodolska, M., & Jackson, E. L. (1998). Discrimination in leisure and work experienced by a White ethnic minority group. *Journal of Leisure Research, 30*, 23–46.

Thomas, D. (2005). "I am Canadian." *Canadian Social Trends, Spring*, 2–7.

Tirone, S. (1999). Racism, indifference and the leisure experience of South Asian Canadian teens. *Leisure/Loisir 24*, 89–114.

Tsai, J., Knutson, B., & Fung, H. (2006). Cultural variation in affect valuation. *Journal of Personality and Social Psychology, 90*, 288–307.

Tsai, J., Miao, F., & Seppala, E. (2007). Good feelings in Christianity and Buddhism: Religious differences in ideal affect. *Personality and Social Psychology Bulletin, 33*, 409–421.

Walker, G. J. (2011, May). *Chinese-Canadian immigrants' acculturation strategies and leisure participation.* Paper presented at the Thirteenth Canadian Congress on Leisure Research, St. Catharines, Ontario.

Walker, G. J., & Chapman, R. (2001). Visitor motivation. *Parks Canada's Research Links: A Forum for Natural, Cultural and Social Studies, 9*, 3.

Walker, G. J., Deng, J., & Dieser, R. (2001). Ethnicity, acculturation, self-construal, and motivations for outdoor recreation. *Leisure Sciences, 23*, 263–283.

Walker, G. J., Deng, J., & Dieser, R. (2005). Culture, self-construal, and leisure theory and practice. *Journal of Leisure Research,* 37, 77–99.

Walker, G. J., & Wang, X. (2005). Further considerations on culture, self-construal, and leisure theory and practice. *Book of abstracts: Eleventh Canadian Congress on Leisure Research; 2005 May 18-20* [CD]. Nanaimo, BC: Canadian Association for Leisure Studies.

Washburne, R. (1978). Black under participation in wildland recreation: Alternative explanations. *Leisure Sciences, 1*, 175–189.

Xu, J., Shim, S., Lotz, S., & Almeida, D. (2004). Ethnic identity, socialization factors, and culture-specific consumption behaviour. *Psychology & Marketing, 21*, 93–112.

Chapter 22
Aboriginal Leisure in Canada

Janice Forsyth, Ph.D.
University of Western

Learning Objectives

After reading this chapter, students will be able to

1. Understand the purpose of historical knowledge and its relationship to leisure theory and practice in contemporary society.
2. Explain why gaining an understanding of historical context is an important element for guiding leisure theory and practice.
3. Generate more informed questions about Aboriginal leisure practices in Canada.

Introduction

Leisure is a social practice that is constructed and reconstructed over time. To people living one hundred years ago, the types of leisure activities that we engage in today would perhaps seem strange and irrational. Similar thoughts might be held by our contemporaries about older leisure practices. What did people do before the advent of nightclubs, fitness facilities, provincial and national parks, television, and video games? What was the role of leisure before the rise of industrialization and modern technology? How did these historical events shape our leisure patterns? Obviously, these transformations did not happen naturally, that is, without public intervention. Both individually and collectively, we adapted to the changes taking place around us and found ways to integrate leisure into our lives. One connection that can thus be drawn between our modern practices and those of our ancestors is that we each adapted our leisure patterns to our changing world, thereby ensuring the continuity of meaningful and relevant activities.

Like all Canadians, Aboriginal people have a long and rich history in leisure. Part of this record has been told by historians, sociologists, and anthropologists in various journals and books on sport and recreation. In recent years, the emergence of "leisure studies" as a legitimate area of research has opened up the field to a wider range of scholars, although there remains a dearth of information on issues pertaining to Aboriginal people. What information does exist generally focuses on two broad themes: (1) how Aboriginal leisure preferences either enhance traditional Aboriginal values and beliefs or facilitate Aboriginal integration into mainstream society and (2) issues in tourism, especially as they relate to Aboriginal festivals as well as access to, and management of, provincial and national parks. While these perspectives help illuminate some of the issues which impact on Aboriginal leisure in Canada, the narrow emphasis on cultural preferences and tourism limits our understanding of the different ways Aboriginal people engage in leisure and the factors that affect their participation. To address this weakness in the literature, this chapter will introduce readers to some of the key historical factors that influenced Aboriginal leisure practices in Canada and examine some of the contemporary issues that Aboriginal people face in working towards their own goals for meaningful leisure.

Historical Perspectives

Students may wonder about the relevance of understanding the way people historically engaged in leisure. What purpose does history serve in a field that emphasizes current issues? What value can be attached to learning about the way leisure was organized in the past? What utility does this knowledge serve in our contemporary world? These are, arguably, reasonable questions; after all, the field of leisure is a relatively new area of study that is gaining legitimacy within many academic institutions in Canada. Proponents must therefore carve out a niche for themselves by distinguishing their field from more established areas like history, sociology, and anthropology.

This is not to suggest that the focus on current issues be replaced with a mountain of historical analyses, but, rather, that historical interpretations be woven more purposefully into classroom discussions about contemporary leisure practices. If the present historical moment is informed by the past, then we must take into account how we, as a society, arrived at this particular moment in time. This approach to knowledge acquisition should lead us to ask more pertinent questions about leisure and, as a consequence, help us to make more informed decisions about policy and practice. Consider the role of historical questioning when working through the following issue. What is the historical relationship between Aboriginal people, the creation of reservations, and the development of provincial and national parks in Canada? How have these relationships shaped the way Aboriginal people utilize these protected areas? Similarly, how have these relationships influenced the development and management of parks? Who has benefited most from these relationships? Throughout this chapter, students are encouraged to consider carefully how historically rooted questions, such as those identified here, can help generate a deeper understanding of the current issues in leisure studies.

What follows is an overview of three significant issues that shaped Aboriginal leisure practices in Canada from the mid-nineteenth to the mid-twentieth century. They are:

1. cultural regulation
2. sports and games at residential schools
3. mainstream sporting practices. Students should pay close attention to the way ideas about race, class, and gender shaped the types of activities that were made available for Aboriginal people, and how Aboriginal people responded in turn (see Chapters 20 and 21).

Cultural Regulation

The history of cultural regulation in Canada begins in the late nineteenth century when the federal government embarked on a campaign to prohibit traditional Aboriginal religious practices. At that time, there was a widespread belief among government and church officials that as long as Aboriginal religious systems remained intact, Aboriginal people would never realize the spiritual benefits of Christianity or learn how to engage in productive labour. Church and state thus attempted to replace traditional practices, like the Potlatch and Sundance ceremonies, with secular activities, relying on Euro-Canadian sports and games to help them accomplish this task (Pettipas, 1994). This process of cultural regulation and replacement facilitated an understanding of Euro-Canadian sports and games as modern and appropriate behaviours while positioning Aboriginal physical practices as uncivilized and undesirable, thus providing a basis on which to eradicate traditional activities (Paraschak, 1998).

During this era, "sports days" emerged as appropriate forms of social activities for Aboriginal people, and were often held in conjunction with national celebrations, like Dominion Day, thereby symbolically linking sports to Canadian citizenship and patriotic duty. The inclusion of sports days at Euro-Canadian styled gatherings, like white-sponsored stampedes, agricultural exhibitions and fairs, and government-approved community celebrations, also suggested that Euro-Canadian sports and games would help usher Aboriginal people into the twentieth-century through hard work and patriotic play.

The objective of assimilation was often challenged by Aboriginal participants, such that sports days served contradictory purposes. On the one hand, they were opportunities for Aboriginal people to engage in friendly competition, a practice that was already well-established among the people throughout the land. On the other hand, they were opportunities for Aboriginal people to host traditional religious ceremonies, as some people took advantage of these hectic and boisterous meetings to engage in their old time practices. For example, Daniel Kennedy, an Assiniboine Chief from Saskatchewan, recalls how his elders used him as a spokesperson to convince Department of Indian Affairs officials to host local dances under cover of sports days and other Euro-Canadian celebrations (Gresko, 1986). Thus, Aboriginal people integrated Euro-Canadian sports and games into their everyday lives, and at least some people did so as a way to divert attention away from the practice of their traditional pursuits.

Physical Games and Contests in Northern Canada

The Dene and Athabaskan participated in a variety of games to develop strength, speed, power, flexibility, and endurance. Both men and women joined in activities emphasizing the gendered nature of their roles, which entailed differently strenuous tasks. As one fur trader noted at Fort Resolution around 1800, "It is true the men have to undergo the fatigue of the chase, but still the women must carry the meat home" (Heine, 1999, p. I-15).

The Inuit, whose traditional territory spans the most northerly reaches of the continent, played and competed in events that developed the same skills as the Dene but with an additional emphasis on pain tolerance, such as the knuckle hop, mouth pull, and ear lift, to mentally and physically prepare them for the harsh realities of life on the land (Heine, 1998, p. I-25).

The Impact of Residential Schooling

The prohibitions against traditional Aboriginal cultural practices were bolstered by the development of the residential school system, where traditional activities were viewed as counter-productive to the federal goal of assimilation. Aboriginal and non-Aboriginal writers have produced detailed and disturbing accounts of the environment within these schools, and there is no doubt that the residential system ruptured Aboriginal cultural life in Canada (e.g., Milloy, 1999; Fournier, 1997; Grant, 1996).

To be sure, this institutionalized form of education was considerably different than traditional Aboriginal forms of teaching. Before Europeans settled on the continent, Aboriginal people received their education by learning how to survive on the land, and physical games and contests were central to their training. For example, the Dene and Inuit engaged in a variety of games and contests to increase their tolerance to pain, physical endurance, and dexterity. See the first *i*-box for examples. In addition to the physical conditioning these activities provided, traditional sports and games were also key sites for reinforcing the social, political, economic, and spiritual aspects of life. Among the Iroquois, lacrosse was used to cement social ties, prepare the men for war, engage in economic relations, connect with the spiritual world, and have fun (Mitchell, 1978). No matter what their form, traditional physical activities were crucial for maintaining Aboriginal cultural identities and ensuring basic survival. The establishment of the residential school system would forever change the way Aboriginal people would relate to their land and their physical cultural practices.

In the residential schools, Euro-Canadian sports and games played a pivotal role in the assimilative process as the federal government looked to popular Euro-Canadian sports and games to help bring about fundamental changes in the values and behaviours of its students. It was believed that participation in Euro-Canadian activities would contribute to the breakdown of communal values by fostering a competitive spirit among the pupils, and hopefully, through regulated instruction, the skills they learned would translate into a desire for individual achievement and wealth (Canada, Volume 1, 1996).

In the first half of the twentieth century, callisthenic programs and military drills were popular features in the schools, including institutions situated in the far north, such as the Hay River Mission School, located on the southern tip of Great Slave Lake in the Northwest Territories (Heine, 1995). The link between military training and nationalism was unmistakable as the drills were designed to replace tribal allegiances with a newfound sense of loyalty to the Canadian state. In the latter half of the twentieth century, competitive amateur sport became a more pronounced feature of the residential schools. Federal officials believed these contests would help facilitate the integration of Aboriginal students into the public school system, and encouraged residential school staff to promote participation, especially in team sports (e.g., Dewar, 1986; Johnston, 1988).

Another outcome of this 'lived' experience was that Euro-Canadian sports and games constructed and reinforced popular notions about gender. To be sure, Aboriginal people had their own well established notions about appropriate male and female behaviour, which differed among Aboriginal groups as well as from Euro-Canadian views. For example, prior to colonization, Aboriginal women participated in a wide variety of sports and games such as double ball, handball, and football—events that were traditionally reserved for females (Paraschak, 2001). After settlement, Euro-Canadian styles of play reinforced the notion that Euro-Canadian interpretations of gender were the most appropriate forms of behaviour. As was the case in the public school system, male students were provided with opportunities to participate in vigorous activities that developed their manly character, while female students were encouraged to participate in gentle, healthful exercises that were deemed appropriate for young women, despite the fact that they were required to demonstrate incredible strength and stamina as the housekeepers of entire institutions (Miller, 1996).

Clearly, Euro-Canadian sports and games served a variety of purposes within the residential schools. Students should take a moment to consider the role of sports and games in the public school system today. In addition to providing health benefits, what type of values and behaviours are being promoted through physical education, varsity sports, as well as after-school and intramural programs? Consider the role of sports and games in constructing, reinforcing, and challenging dominant ideas about race, class, gender, (dis)ability, etc. Reflect on your experience in school and draw on personal examples to shed light on this discussion.

Mainstream Sporting Practices

Aboriginal leisure practices were also influenced by the emerging mainstream sport system, where formal and informal discrimination was part of the environment. Organizers assumed Aboriginal athletes possessed natural athletic abilities and channelled Aboriginal participants into segregated "Indian" events so as to preserve and protect white conceptions about their own social and cultural superiority. In early nineteenth-century Montréal, for example, it was generally understood among the local snowshoeing clubs that Aboriginal athletes were not allowed to compete against white athletes in organized events (Morrow, 1988). Derision was not limited wholly to the men. For instance, in the early twentieth century in the sport of rodeo, Aboriginal women were relegated to so-called "Squaw" events to distinguish their performances as being outside the "norm" for participation (Paraschak, 2001, p. 790).

In the late nineteenth century, formal rules for participation were developed by sport organizers in central and eastern Canada, who attempted to restrict their competitions to participants of gentlemanly status by codifying the concept of an "amateur" athlete. Originally, an "amateur" referred to a gentleman of the leisured class, someone who had the time and money to travel and compete; however, with the emergence of a strong middle class presence in sport, the concept of amateurism took on explicitly "classist" and racist dimensions as organizers sought to define their distinctiveness from those whom they believed were the less desirable elements of society (Cosentino, 1975, 1998). For example, in 1880, the National Amateur Lacrosse Association prohibited Aboriginal participation in an effort to ensure their sport, appropriated from the Iroquois, remained an activity where middle and upper class men could engage in their gentlemanly pursuits (Fisher, 2002).

The paradox of these events—cultural repression, residential schooling, and derision and exclusion in the emerging mainstream sport system—is that they led to the reaffirmation of Aboriginal cultural institutions and identities. In other words, Aboriginal people survived and adapted their cultures to the changing world around them. Thus, as active participants in contemporary society, the role that Aboriginal people played and continue to play in shaping contemporary leisure practices in Canada cannot be ignored.

Given this perspective on Canadian history, students are encouraged to think about the types of activities that are promoted at the various gatherings they have attended. Consider the range of activities that are offered during school breaks, regional celebrations, and national holidays. What might you conclude from the selection that is made available to the public? Whose traditions are reinforced and legitimized? Whose traditions are excluded or marginalized? What does this tell us about our present state of Canadian multiculturalism?

Contemporary Issues

After World War II, Aboriginal people began to organize themselves politically and assert their right to control the policies and programs that affected their lives. This move towards self-determination was expressed through various leisure practices, such as the revitalization of powwows and traditional dancing (Paraschak, 1996a). Efforts toward self-determination continue today, as Aboriginal people seek to increase their opportunities for leisure in traditional and contemporary style, in both the all-Aboriginal and mainstream setting.

Such efforts are visible in sport, where Aboriginal people have been working towards the development of an all-Aboriginal sport system since the 1970s. Problems such as racism on and off the playing field, and the unequal provision of sport and recreation services to Aboriginal communities served as the impetus for the development of the all-Aboriginal system. Motivated by these concerns, Aboriginal people sought the development of an all-Aboriginal sport system that would remain distinct from, while simultaneously being connected to, the mainstream system. The term *double helix* is sometimes used to refer to the bond that exists between the two systems. See the Double Helix *i*-box for a description of this relationship. The emergence of the term double helix is significant because it shows how Aboriginal people, by "naming" their preferred structure for sport, are asserting their belief that the all-Aboriginal system, and the activities which it fosters, are a legitimate and vital component of the Canadian sport system.

The Double Helix

In recent years, the term *double helix* has been used to describe the relationship between the all-Aboriginal and mainstream sport systems. The double helix consists of parallel strands joined by cross-links. The parallel strands represent the all-Aboriginal and mainstream sport systems each operating independently from each other; the cross-links represent the sites where the two systems connect. The image of the double helix is useful for two reasons. First, it draws attention to the existence of an all-Aboriginal sport system in Canada. Second, it highlights specific sites where Aboriginal sport connects to, and remains distinct from, the mainstream sport model. This model is thus a useful tool for conceptualizing the relationship between the all-Aboriginal and mainstream systems. It also draws our attention to the way Aboriginal sport leaders have been trying to build the all-Aboriginal sport system in Canada and, at the same time it provide opportunities for Aboriginal athletes to integrate into the mainstream sport system in ways that enhance their Aboriginal cultural identities.

The development of the all-Aboriginal sport system has not been easy. Historically, federal and provincial governments were reluctant to fund the development of separate opportunities for Aboriginal people. For example, beginning in 1972, the federal government, through Fitness and Amateur Sport, now Sport Canada, began providing grants to Aboriginal political organizations through the Native Sport and Recreation Program. With federal funding, Aboriginal programs flourished as activities in a wide range of events were hosted at the local, regional, and national level throughout the country. Despite the program's success, it was terminated in 1981 when the federal government shifted its priorities from mass participation to elite sport development. With the new focus on competitive outcomes, reviewers concluded that the programs that Aboriginal organizers had developed would not produce the high performance results desired by the federal government (Paraschak, 1995a).

Despite recurring setbacks, like the demise of the Native Sport and Recreation Program, Aboriginal people continue to push forward, utilizing both traditional and contemporary forms of participation, as well as the all-Aboriginal and mainstream system to work towards their goals for leisure. Ample evidence of Aboriginal self-determination exists, albeit only two visible examples are provided here in brief. They are: (1) the inclusion of traditional

Dene and Inuit activities in the Arctic Winter Games, and (2) the emergence of the North American Indigenous Games.

Dene and Inuit Games

In the far north, the Inuit and Dene have successfully lobbied for the inclusion of their traditional events in the Arctic Winter Games, a major multi-sport competition for athletes in the circumpolar region of the globe. These games are truly an international event, attracting athletes from countries such as Russia, Greenland, Iceland, and northern Europe. In 1974, several traditional Inuit contests were incorporated as legitimate sporting events into the Arctic Winter Games. In 1990, a Dene Games category was created, thus adding four Dene events to the nine Inuit contests, which now constitute the "Arctic Sports" competition in the Arctic Winter Games (Paraschak, 1997).

While Inuit and Dene games are part of the official sport program in northern games and festivals, in southern events, like the Canada Games, they are often framed as "cultural" activities. Such framing places the Inuit and Dene games outside of the boundaries for what constitutes legitimate "sport." Meanwhile, mainstream activities like basketball and volleyball are accepted uncritically as "sport" and, as a result, receive ongoing financial support for increased athlete and coaching development (Paraschak, 1996b). Although the Inuit and Dene are finding ways to incorporate their sports into the mainstream model, the challenge remains for them to do this in a way that resists the commodification of their cultural practices and strengthens their cultural identities (Heine & Young, 1997). This challenge will not be easy; however, the development of instructional materials such as the traditional Dene and Inuit games manuals—and the inclusion of these activities in northern schools—may facilitate this transition.

Other researchers have pointed to the ongoing issue of gender in Inuit and Dene games. For example, female participants do not hold the same status as men in traditional hand games. Oftentimes, females are banned from competing in this event; however, within the context of the Arctic Winter Games, where females are allowed to participate in the junior age category, finding female participants to take part in an event that challenges traditional norms of participation can be tricky. As Audrey Giles points out, the decision to include a gender equity policy to level the playing field for female participants is one that must be negotiated carefully with the Aboriginal northerners (Giles, 2002).

North American Indigenous Games

Another example of Aboriginal people working towards their own vision for sport is the North American Indigenous Games (NAIG), a major multi-sport and cultural festival for the Aboriginal people of Canada and the United States. The purpose of the NAIG is to bring Aboriginal people together to celebrate their cultures, express their identities in their own preferred manner, provide opportunities to excel in sport, and have fun. First held in 1990, the NAIG has evolved into the single largest sporting venue for Aboriginal athletes, with approximately five thousand participants taking part in both the 1997 and 2002 Games (Forsyth, 2004). Previous NAIG have been held in Edmonton, Alberta (1990); Prince Albert, Saskatchewan (1993); Blain, Minnesota (1995); Victoria, British Columbia (1997); and Winnipeg, Manitoba (2002).

With the development of the all-Aboriginal sport system, in particular the NAIG, controversies surrounding the construction of a segregated sport system surfaced, thus challenging the provision of services for Aboriginal people only. Some scholars have responded to this challenge, commenting on the need for a separate system based on the notion of equality of opportunity (fairness in the provision of programs and services)—not equal opportunity (identical programs and services)—for social and cultural reasons—many of which are historically rooted. For example, sociologist Vicky Paraschak utilizes the idea of "racialized spaces" to refer to those sites where the Aboriginal sport system remains distinct from the mainstream system. Contrary to the negative connotations normally associated with race and space (i.e., segregation), the concept of "racialized spaces" refers to the enabling features that segregation can provide (Paraschak, 1996a). Thus, in Canada at least, all-Aboriginal sporting events provide Aboriginal people with opportunities to structure their own possibilities for sport and express their identities in their own preferred manner.

Conclusion

Think about the literature on Aboriginal leisure practices in Canada. How are Aboriginal people and Aboriginal issues positioned within this body of knowledge?

Students should keep in mind that the emphasis on Aboriginal agency; that is, the ability of people to act on the priorities they set for themselves, is qualitatively different than focusing on what non-Aboriginal people have done to help Aboriginal people achieve their goals. Furthermore, students should take into account the gendered lens through which Aboriginal leisure is analyzed (i.e., Paraschak, 1995b). Are the experiences of Aboriginal women distinguished from those of Aboriginal men? What are the ramifications for leisure practice when female experiences are neglected? Taking into account the history of Aboriginal leisure in Canada, as well as contemporary practices, should lead us to ask more pertinent questions about leisure and, as a consequence, help us to make more informed decisions about

Is there evidence of the various ways that Aboriginal people are exerting control over their leisure practices and defining what leisure means to them? Does it provide insight on the various constraints limiting the ability of Aboriginal people to implement their vision for leisure? Are "best practices"—as determined by Aboriginal people—included in the texts?

policy and practice. The information presented in this chapter has shed light on implications for practice including: using historical analysis to gain a better understanding of contemporary issues, working with Aboriginal people to implement their vision for leisure, and creating opportunities to learn about Aboriginal games and events.

Key Terms

Agency
All-Aboriginal
Gender
History
Integration
Self-determination

References

Canada. (1996). *Report of the Royal Commission on Aboriginal Peoples: Looking forward, looking back, Vol. 1.* Ottawa, ON: Minister of Supply and Services Canada.

Cosentino, F. (1975). A history of the concept of professionalism in Canadian sport. *Canadian Journal of History of Sport and Physical Education, 6*(2), 75–81.

Cosentino, F. (1998). *Afros, Aboriginals and amateur sport in Pre-World War One Canada.* Ottawa, ON: Canadian Historical Society.

Dewar, J. (1986). The introduction of western sports to the Indian People of Canada's Prairie West. In J. Mangan & R. Small (Eds.), *Sport, culture, society: International historical and sociological perspectives, proceedings of the VIII Commonwealth and International Conference on Sport, Physical Education, Dance, Recreation and Health* (pp. 27–32). London, UK and New York, NY: E. and F. N. Spon.

Fisher, D. (2002). *Lacrosse: A history of the game.* Baltimore, MD: The Johns Hopkins University Press.

Forsyth, J. (2004). North American indigenous games. In R. King (Ed.), *Native Americans in sports* (pp. 229–231). Armonk, NY: M. E. Sharpe.

Fournier, S. (1997). *Stolen from our embrace: The abduction of First Nations children and the restoration of Aboriginal communities.* Toronto, ON: Douglas & McIntyre.

Giles, A. (2002). Sport Nunavut's gender equity policy: Relevance, rhetoric and reality. *Canadian Woman Studies: Women and Sport, 21*(3), 95–99.

Grant, A. (1996). *No end in grief: Indian residential schools in Canada.* Winnipeg, MB: Pemmican Publications.

Gresko, J. (1986). Creating little dominions within the dominion: Early Catholic Indian schools in Saskatchewan and British Columbia. In J. Barman, Y. Hébert and D. McCaskill (Eds.), *Indian education in Canada, Vol. 1: The legacy* (pp. 93–109). Vancouver, BC: UBC Press.

Heine, M. (1995). Gwich'in tsii'in: A History of gwich'in athapaskan games. Unpublished doctoral dissertation, University of Alberta.

Heine, M. (1998). *Arctic sports: A training and resource manual.* Yellowknife, NWT: Arctic Sports Association & MACA (GNWT).

Heine, M. (1999). *Dene games: A culture and resource manual, traditional Aboriginal sport coaching resources, Vol. 1.* Yellowknife, NWT: The Sport North Federation and MACA (GNWT).

Heine, M., & Young, K. (1997). Colliding Identities in Arctic Canadian Sports and Games. *Sociological Focus, 30*(4), 357–372.

Johnston, B. (1988). *Indian school days.* Toronto, ON: Key Porter Books.

Mitchell, M. (1978). *Tewaarathon (lacrosse): Akwesasne's story of our national game.* Cornwall Island, ON: North American Indian Traveling College.

Miller, J. (1996) *Shingwauk's vision: A history of Aboriginal residential schools.* Toronto, ON: University of Toronto Press.

Milloy, J. (1999). *A national crime: The Canadian government and the residential school system, 1879–1986.* Winnipeg, MB: University of Manitoba Press.

Morrow, D. (1988). The knights of the snowshoe: A study of the evolution of sport in nineteenth-century Montréal. *Journal of Sport History, 15*(1), 5–40.

Paraschak, V. (1995a). The Native sport and recreation program, 1972–1981: Patterns of resistance, patterns of reproduction. *Canadian Journal of History of Sport, 26*(2), 1–18.

Paraschak, V. (1995b). Invisible but not absent: Aboriginal women in sport and recreation. *Canadian Woman Studies: Women and Girls in Sport and Physical Activity, 15*(4), 71–72.

Paraschak, V. (1996a). Racialized spaces: Cultural regulation, Aboriginal agency and powwows. *Avante, 2*(1), 7–18.

Paraschak, V. (1996b). Aboriginal Canadians in sport: A clash of cultural values. In Luke Uka Uche (Ed.),

North-South information culture: Trends in global communications and research paradigms (pp. 99–113). Lagos: Longman Nigeria PLC.

Paraschak, V. (1997). Variations in race relations: Sporting events for Native peoples in Canada. *Sociology of Sport Journal, 14*, 1–21.

Paraschak, V. (1998). 'Reasonable amusements': Connecting the strands of physical culture in Aboriginal lives. *Sport History Review, 28*(1), 121–131.

Paraschak, V. (2001). Native American sports and games. In K. Christensen, A. Guttmann, & G. Pfister (Eds.), *International encyclopedia of women and sports, Vol. 2* (pp. 788–791). New York, NY: Macmillan.

Paraschak, V., & Tirone, S. (2003). Race and Ethnicity in Canadian Sport. In J. Crossman (Ed.), *Canadian Sport Sociology* (pp. 119–138). Toronto, ON: Nelson.

Pettipas, K. (1994). *Severing the ties that bind: Government repression of indigenous religious ceremonies on the prairies.* Winnipeg, MB: University of Manitoba Press.

Chapter 23

Leisure in French Canada

Peter A. Morden, Ph.D.
Concordia University

Robert A. Stebbins, Ph.D.
University of Calgary

Learning Objectives

After reading this chapter, students will be able to

1. Describe the distinct linguistic context of Québec and contrast it with the rest of Canada.
2. Be aware of the dominant policies that have been enacted within Québec to preserve Québécois culture identity and to understand how these have shaped leisure engagement.
3. Understand the distinction between majority, parity, and minority societies.
4. Be aware of the range of linguistically appropriate leisure opportunities within French sub-societies outside of Québec.
5. Be familiar with some of the unique leisure challenges faced by French Canadians outside Québec.

Introduction

French-speaking Canada, with considerably more accuracy than English-speaking Canada, can be separated into regions, each distinguished from the other by a great number and variety of special social, cultural, historical, and geographic qualities. Québec is the most obvious and celebrated example of such distinctiveness yet it is by no means the only one, even though many Anglophone Canadians might be surprised by this assertion. From the typical English-Canadian point of view, Acadia—Francophone New Brunswick, Nova Scotia, and Prince Edward Island—constitutes a much less obvious cultural-linguistic region, while Newfoundland, Ontario, the prairies, and British Columbia, according to that perspective, are merely slightly discernible variations on a theme of Anglo-British culture.

Nevertheless, every Francophone region has evolved far enough to justify calling it a society, or more accurately, a sub-society, where each is an enduring component of the larger Canadian society. Again, Québec is the most evolved, by far the most institutionally complete of the Francophone societies in North America. *Institutional completeness* refers to a level of social and cultural organization of a community or society that, in terms of language use, is sufficiently developed to enable the typical person to sustain a full-scale linguistic lifestyle over the course of a normal year (modified from Breton, 1964). Québec can be described as institutionally complete as a person may meet in French all routine needs, as these arise on a daily, weekly, monthly, or yearly basis. Among those needs are those met through leisure.

By contrast, significant *institutional incompleteness* exists in parts of Ontario and Acadia, and still greater incompleteness marks Francophone life in Newfoundland and the West (Cardinal, Lapointe, & Thériault, 1994; Stebbins, 1994). Thus, in the eyes of Canadians (and Americans too), Québec is the benchmark for comparing all other North American Francophone societies. It will be the reference point for this chapter as well, although only Canada's provincial and regional Francophone societies are examined here. Beginning with an examination of leisure in Québec and subsequently turning to Francophone leisure beyond Québec's borders, the goal of this chapter is to explore and compare how leisure is pursued in Canada's Francophone societies as well as to describe the role of leisure in those societies.

Leisure in Québec

To understand how leisure has evolved within Québec society, it is important to situate the province within the broader Canadian and North American linguistic context. The minority status of French within North America has led to the perception, likely correct, that the French language and the Québécois culture of which it is such a large part, is something that requires support and, at times, protection by way of government policy and practice, often of specific relevance to recreational opportunity and engagement. These governmental efforts have often been contentious but have allowed, in part, the maintenance of a distinct French-speaking society and have also strengthened the unique Québécois identity.

Notwithstanding the specific differences that arise in Québec due to the linguistic context, public leisure provision has been subject to similar strains elsewhere and, as a result, how provincial and municipal governments have supported or assured access to recreational opportunity has followed similar lines. Of particular importance is the increased need to "do more with less" with public funds and the resulting emphasis upon the voluntary sector to assume a large part of the burden for the provision of recreational opportunity.

Focus on Montréal

In Québec, although the majority of the province is predominantly francophone (see *French in Québec and Canada*), the linguistic make-up of Montréal, its largest city with close to two million inhabitants, is far different. Compared to the rest of the province, Montréal has significantly fewer unilingual Francophones (29% in Montréal vs. 62% in the rest of the province), significantly more unilingual Anglophones (12% vs. 2%), and a greater proportion of bilingual individuals (57% vs. 35%) (Statistics Canada, 2001). Montréal is truly institutionally complete for both Francophones and Anglophones; the majority of social services may be accessed in either of Canada's official languages. In fact, of the 27 boroughs that make up the Island of Montréal, 9 have a greater proportion of native Anglophones than Francophones (Service du Dévelopement Économique et Urbain, 2001). In these boroughs, a phone call to the local recreation department is as likely to be greeted with "Hi, may I help you?" as "Bonjour, puis-je vous aider?" The vast majority of commercial recreation providers, as well, offer bilingual services.

In addition, Montréal is expressly committed to the leisure of all its citizens. Montréal's Charter of Rights and Responsibilities (2005) clearly articulates this commitment in the section *Recreation, Physical Activities, and Sport*: "Citizens have rights to recreation, physical activities and sports and participate with the Montréal administration in a joint effort to ensure the continued enjoyment of these rights. They contribute to this effort by performing activities consistent with the commitments stated in this chapter, such as through the appropriate use of community facilities.

To foster the rights of citizens to recreation, physical activities, and sports, Montréal is committed to:

a. Supporting a range of services that meets the public's evolving needs;
b. Developing high-quality parks and facilities for recreational, physical, and sports activities that are fairly apportioned in view of the community's evolving needs;
c. Promoting access to activities and facilities" (Montréal Charter of Rights, p. 8, 2005).

What characteristics of Montréal make leisure engagement potentially different than leisure in the rest of Québec? in the rest of Canada?

Before examining these issues though, let's turn our attention to the linguistic character of Québec and how significantly it differs from the broader society that surrounds it.

French in Québec and Canada

Within Québec, it is a seldom-forgotten fact that the French linguistic majority is surrounded by Anglophone societies—both the Canadian society of which it is a part but also, significantly, the American society to the south. While it is well recognised throughout Canada that Québec represents a "distinct society," exactly how distinct is it? The answer is that when it comes to language, it is very distinct indeed. Of nearly 23 million Canadians that live in provinces other than Québec, somewhat fewer than one million, or less than 5% of the population, report French to be their mother tongue (Statistics Canada, 2006). In contrast, those whose mother tongue is French represent approximately 86% of the population in Québec. Additionally, outside of Québec roughly two-thirds of Canadians are unilingual Anglophones; in Québec, more than five in ten citizens is a unilingual Francophone. Lastly, whereas in the rest of Canada about one in ten people is bilingual about four in ten Québecers have knowledge of both official languages. So, within Québec over 90% of the population is able to function in French.

A last significant detail about the linguistic make-up of Québec is that although English is the second most frequently reported mother tongue of those in Québec, there are more people in Québec whose mother tongue is neither English nor French (Statistics Canada, 2006). Over the years, the provincial government has been preoccupied about whether English or French would be adopted by these allophones, both immigrants as well as Québec-born. The worry has been that should English be adopted, as is almost universally the case elsewhere in Canada, then the status of French within Québec would be diminished in the long run. In response to this and other concerns about the sustainability of Québécois culture, in 1977 the government of Québec enacted Bill 101, the Charter of the French Language (the Charter). While not the first, the Charter is the most significant political attempt to ensure the survival of French society within Québec and one of a number of policies that is of direct relevance to the practice of leisure.

Provincial Policy and Leisure

Béland and Lecours (2004) recommend analyses into how policy is related to, for instance, provincial identity (for instance, I am a Québecer) and the political landscape in Québec provides fruitful terrain for such analyses. Firstly, the Charter is very clearly relevant to the protection of Francophone culture and identity within Québec. The intent behind the Charter was "to make of French the language of Government and the Law, as well as the normal and everyday language of work, instruction, communication, commerce and business" (R.S.Q. c. C-11, Preamble). The Charter established French as the official language of

Québec and among its most significant elements is the requirement that children are educated in French, with some exceptions in the case of children with parents educated in English in Canada. This policy has been to the distinct benefit of the adoption of the French language among allophones (Castonguay, 1999). In the quarter-century following the introduction of the Charter, the proportion of allophone children who have adopted French as the language spoken most often at home (in contrast to their mother tongue) has more than doubled from 21% to 46% (Secrétariat à la politique linguistique, 2006). Such linguistic transfers help maintain the dominant position of the French language within Québec.

Of course, we can't overlook the fact that for young people school is a significant influence upon their leisure lifestyle, and this equally affects all students. Extracurricular activities are provided by the school, free time is allocated within the school day, and the bulk of friendships are formed from within the ranks of one's classmates. Since French is the language of education, this is a very significant influence upon non-Francophones to assimilate into the French mainstream, both in the immediate sense and also in the longer term. The long-term effect is seen in linguistic transfers in the direction of French among allophones as well as the promotion of English/French bilingualism among Anglophones. As such, the education system and by extension the Government of Québec is a significant agent of socialization for both new and historic linguistic minorities in Québécois society.

In addition, there are also important effects seen in the here-and-now. There is some evidence that "allophone children educated in French are speaking French among themselves on Montréal playgrounds" (Lisée, 2001), and it is a certainty the case that French is the dominant language used in linguistically mixed environments such as during extracurricular activities. In short, the Charter shapes the context for leisure engagement, and in doing so, particularly within the school system, it helps assure that maintenance of the French language as a pillar of the Québécois identity. The Charter, however, is by no means the only legislation or policy that has functioned to preserve and protect Québécois culture and identity. The examination of two Acts that have come into force suffice to illustrate this; the provincial Cinema Act and the federal Broadcasting Act.

In 1983, with the enactment of the Cinema Act (Loi sur le Cinéma, L.R.Q., c. C-18.1), the Régie du Cinéma was established and received its mandate (Régie du Cinéma, 2007). The purpose of the Régie is to classify all movies distributed within the province. Although film classification systems exist throughout Canada, the Québec rating system demands that a Régie stamp is affixed to each film print or rental cassette or DVD that is to be distributed. In addition such a stamp (with some exceptions) will not be issued to a film produced in a language other than French unless there are French dubbed or subtitled versions available. As a consequence, although close to three quarters of the films shown in Québec are of American origin (Institute de la statistique du Québec, 2005) attendance at "French" films in Québec far surpasses that of English film. In 2004, a total of 19.6 million tickets were sold for films screened in French, representing close to 70% of all tickets sold in the province (Institute de la statistique du Québec).

Federal legislation, as well, has been enacted that serves the interests of maintaining Québécois culture. Shaped to be in accordance with the federal Official Languages Act, the Broadcasting Act is one such example. Among other stipulations, the Broadcasting Act requires that the Canadian Broadcasting Corporation provide, in both French and English, local and regional "programming that reaches out to and reflects Canadians in all communities and in all their diversity" (Department of Canadian Heritage, 2003, p. 1).

One distinct result of the Broadcasting Act, as it has been applied in combination with other governmental supports to French programming, has been the establishment of a well developed system of French language television production and distribution which has bolstered Québécois consciousness and culture (Fletcher, 1998). Fletcher notes that the impact of the French service upon maintaining a sense of cultural connectedness has been profound given the popularity and market penetration of certain programs. In fact, certain French Canadian dramas attain audience shares (the proportion of people watching television that are tuned to a specific program) of 30% or more, which is far superior to comparable English Canadian programs (Standing Committee on Canadian Heritage, 2003). Such programming provides a sense of common experience and a reflection of, generally speaking, Québec life, and equally as significant is the fact that this provides a countervailing influence to the socializing impact of the English, predominantly American media environment.

While Québecers watch more television than people elsewhere in Canada, and while Francophones in the province watch more TV than Anglophones (Statistics Canada, 2006), television viewing statistics also show distinct differences in the kinds of programming that Canada's Anglophones and Francophones access. According to Statistics Canada, Anglophones watch foreign (essentially, American) programming about 70% of the time—almost the same proportion as Francophones watch Canadian (by and large French) programming. When looking at specific kinds of shows, further differences are evident. Anglophones tend to watch more foreign than Canadian drama and comedy than do Francophones (90% vs. 57%), while Francophones tend to watch considerably more "home-grown" documentaries, news, and public affairs programs than do Anglophones (91% vs. 61%). Given that about two-thirds of all viewing time for both linguistic groups is devoted to these types of programs, it is not an exaggeration to say that Francophones and Anglophones live in vastly different televisual environments, with the former group representing a considerably greater success story as far as Canadian broadcasting policy is concerned.

Given the importance of leisure participation to the development and maintenance of Québécois identity, one may imagine that the Government of Québec would be active with respect to enacting other, leisure-specific policies that support the unique character and identity of Québec; however, such has not been the case. In Québec, as elsewhere, in those rare times when leisure policy has been considered and enacted, it has been shaped with technical and administrative concerns at the forefront. Beginning with the "Green book" (*Prendre notre temps: Livre vert sur le loisir au Québec*, Charron, 1977) and the "White Book" (*On a un monde à récreer: Livre blanc sur le loisir au Québec*, Charron, 1979), the dominant intent and effect of provincial policy has been to accord primary responsibility for leisure to municipalities while the provincial government has maintained the responsibility to play a coordinating and supporting role. With the recognition that local communities are best able to respond to the leisure needs of citizens, the stance taken in the White Book foreshadowed many of the tenets included in the federal National Recreation Statement released in 1987.

The White Book led to the establishment of the Ministère du loisir, de la chasse, et de la pêche (MLCP) in 1979 but, for the next 15 years, scant ministerial attention was paid to the contents of the White Book and "no general outline or delineation of leisure's role and place has been achieved since" (Association Québécois du Loisir Municipal, 2000). In 1994, the MLCP was dismantled and provincial responsibility for leisure became somewhat of a ministerial hot potato; over the past decade, as shown in Table 23.1, responsibility has changed hands, on average, about every two years. This may help explain the level of inattention paid to further developing or implementing provincial leisure policy within Québec.

Table 23.1: Evolution of Provincial Responsibility for Leisure

Year	Responsible Provincial Ministry
1994	Municipal Affairs
1998	Education and Youth
1999	Health and social services
2003	Municipal affairs, sport, and leisure
2005	Education, leisure and sport

Source: Secrétariat au loisir et au sport, 2003

The only significant restatement of the provincial government's position with respect to leisure over the past quarter-century is the document entitled "Towards a renewed partnership: Governmental action framework in the fields of recreation and sport" (Ministère des Affaires Municipales, 1997). This action framework notes "the importance of recreation and sport as a tool for social integration" (p. 14), but remains largely a technical-administrative document that has as its dominant thrust a recommitment to the decentralization of responsibility for leisure services.

Have any leisure policies related to linguistic minorities been enacted in your city or province? Do you think these positively contribute to the leisure lifestyles of members of linguistic minorities? Why or why not?

One important point that must be highlighted with respect to such decentralization is the desire to reduce the costs associated with leisure provision. A first step in this direction is developing a dedicated volunteer workforce, which "makes up the cornerstone of the sports and recreation organizations within Québec" (Ministère des affaires municipales, 1997, p. 22). Public-private co-production, outsourcing, and consolidation of responsibility at the regional and municipal level are also emphasized in the Action Framework to reduce overlap and the duplication of effort and cost. Such efforts appear to have afforded a significant reduction in provincial government expenditures since the era of the White Book. In the past twenty-five years, as a share of Québec's gross domestic product, provincial expenditures in the leisure domain have been more than cut in half (Conseil Québécois du loisir, 2004). While this may be viewed as a budgetary success for the government, the volunteer "cornerstone" of the delivery system is showing signs of strain, expressing worry about the future voluntarism due to the weight of responsibility on their shoulder; the perceived lack of financial, professional, and technical support; and the ever-increasing needs of the population (Laboratoire en loisir et vie communitaire, n.d.).

As will be seen in the following section, an emphasis upon voluntarism is certainly not unique to Québec (see Chapter 39). Indeed, whereas in Québec the emphasis upon the voluntary sector is promoted by provincial leisure policy, elsewhere in Canada civic association is the primary means through which Francophone minorities both forge intra-provincial and inter-provincial ties with other Francophones and also provide significant leisure opportunities to members of linguistic minority communities.

Francophone Leisure Outside Québec

In relation to linguistic structure, societies may be classified according to three different types: (1) majority, (2) parity, and (3) minority societies (Stebbins, 2004). Francophones living in a majority society, seen from their point of view, live in institutional completeness. They carry out their daily, weekly, and yearly rounds in the dominant language of that society, the language of the majority of its people. Although, as we described earlier, Québec is Canada's only majority Francophone society, certain regions and communities within the other Francophone societies in the country can also be described as "majority." These include the city of Caraquet and the Acadian Peninsula in New Brunswick as well as the cities of Hearst and Kapuskasing in Ontario, Saint-Isidore in Alberta, and Notre-Dame de Lourdes in Manitoba. Here, too, Francophones dominate numerically and linguistically.

Outside Québec at the societal level then, Francophones live in either parity or minority circumstances, even if some live in majority regions or communities within those societies. Parity societies are of necessity bilingual, reasonably institutionally complete for both languages, and composed of sufficient numbers of Anglophones and Francophones to force the speakers of the other language to recognize their linguistic counterparts in all public areas of community life. In fact, Canada has no parity societies, though it has many parity communities, and New Brunswick constitutes a parity region. In practice, parity refers to the existence of, at minimum, a substantial minority of Francophones in the region or community. To our knowledge, no one has defined "substantial minority," but it is likely that a three-to-one, English-French ratio in the population is the lower limit of parity (1 to 3 should, then, be its upper limit). Additionally, saying that a parity society is bilingual is not to suggest, however, that everyone in it has "knowledge" of both languages as defined by the Census of Canada (Stebbins, 2004). Rather it suggests only that sufficient numbers of bilinguals fill the main public roles (e.g., shop keepers, politicians, civil servants, leisure service providers) to the point of enabling the individual to operate more or less entirely in French or English. Pointe de l'Église (Church Point), Nova Scotia; Sudbury, Ontario; and Saint-Boniface in Manitoba are three of several parity communities in Canada.

Francophones are numerically inferior in the minority societies. Thus most of them live, linguistically, in institutional incompleteness; in Canada they normally carry out in English a sizeable proportion of their routine daily, weekly, and yearly activities. In general, this occurs in the spheres of commerce, health care, politics, government, and the work place. French in these societies is much more often used, sometimes even exclusively so, in the areas of leisure, education, religion, and the family. The inhabitants of a Francophone majority or parity society are obviously Francophone according to the preceding definition. But, so too are the Francophones who live in minority circumstances, since they also routinely use French, even if they can do so only in certain segments of life. Not surprisingly then, one of the main issues facing the Francophones of Canada who live as a linguistic minority is maintaining one's cultural heritage, including especially the capacity to communicate in the French language. Leisure is a main way of doing this.

Leisure

People living in majority, parity, and minority societies tend to pursue their leisure with linguistically homogeneous partners. Compared with Francophones living in Québec and northern and eastern New Brunswick, however, those living elsewhere have substantially more contact with the English language during leisure. But, in every type of Francophone society in Canada (majority, parity, minority), research (Stebbins, 1994; 1998) suggests that French-speaking Canadians spend significant amounts of leisure time in French, taking part in a variety of activities, such as singing in a chorale or acting in a play (amateurism), skiing with family or hiking with friends (hobbyist activity), or attending a dinner party or meeting for drinks with friends (casual leisure). Some activities are carried out in the world of formal groups and organizations, as theatrical work and choral singing are; some are carried out in the informal world of friendship networks and family relations as exemplified by going on a picnic or watching French television. There is Francophone volunteering as well, exemplified in serving as organizer of the annual provincial Francophone weekend get together (it resembles a community fair) or the annual provincial "sugar shack" (cabane-à-sucre) (both are project-based leisure). Francophone community centres rely heavily on casual volunteers to serve food, take tickets, vend drinks, sell crafts or baked goods, and serve similar functions.

List the Francophone leisure activities of which you are aware in your city or region. Using the telephone book, if need be, identify two Francophone organizations in your community.

These days, because of governmental cutbacks, nearly all Francophone organizational activity in the minority societies is conducted by volunteers, with some of the volunteering being casual leisure and some being serious leisure. Whichever form, these volunteers pursue it primarily in 6 of the 16 types of volunteer organizations: education, religion, recreation, civic affairs, human relationships, and the arts.

Stebbins (1998) found that Franco-Albertans volunteering in the French schools in their communities, most of whom were parents, commonly served as career volunteers on one or two school committees or contributed their time to a parent-teacher organization or, rarely, even did both. Those working in the area of religion were often members of one or more parish committees or helped out in a chapter of the Chevaliers de Colomb (Knights of Columbus).

Turning to recreation, Francophones in nearly every province have formed sporting organizations for their youth, possibly the most developed of which are found in Acadia: Société des jeux de l'Acadie (New Brunswick) and Comité provincial des jeux de l'Acadie (Nova Scotia). One main goal here is to hold annual Francophone games. Annual Canada-wide Francophone games are also held; they, too, offering abundant opportunities for volunteering (Gravelle & Larocque, 2005) and athletic display in a French-language milieu (Dallaire & Denis, 2005). Throughout Canada there are also many local Francophone chapters of the Scouts and Guides. This emphasis on youth is well founded, for they are widely recognized by Francophone adults as the latter's replacements in the local community—la relève—a special resource to be nurtured with great care.

Francophones living in minority circumstances seldom participate in the civic organizations of the larger community in French. Yet in a way, they have their own civic organizations, whose missions, in broadest terms, are to relate local and provincial Francophones to each other, the three levels of government, and the general (mostly Anglophone) public. In every province and territory, an overarching association exists for these purposes, frequently extended through numerous branches (régionales) operating in the larger cities. In Acadia these organizations are the Société des Acadiens et Acadiennes du Nouveau-Brunswick, Fédération Acadienne de la Nouvelle-Écosse, and Société Saint-Thomas d'Aquin (P.E.I.). Elsewhere there is, for example, the Association Canadienne Française de l'Ontario and the Association Canadienne Française de l'Alberta. Managing them and staffing their many projects is a veritable sponge of volunteer time, both casual and career.

Additionally, many Francophone communities in the minority societies also maintain a cultural centre or community centre, sometimes combining the two in the same building and organization. Whereas the director of one of these is likely to be remunerated, his or her staff members are often not (though with federal government support more paid staff are now beginning to appear in large cities). From a classificatory standpoint, these centres are both recreational and civic affairs organizations. Museums and historical sites emphasizing local Francophone history and culture—for example, Musée de la mer (Shippegan, N.B.), Village historique (Caraquet, N.B.), Port-Royal (N.S.), Musée acadien (Miscouche, P.E.I.), Gabriel Roy House (Saint-Boniface, Manitoba)—serve both functions, in addition to being tourist attractions.

A good number of organizations have sprung up in the field of human relationships, most of them being small clubs. Depending on the size of the community, it is common to find Francophone clubs for women (sometimes affiliated with a parish), men (often a chapter of the Chevaliers de Colomb), youth (not infrequently part of a provincial federation of such organizations), senior citizens (usually only a provincial organization), and groups established according to the principles of friendship, good works, and commercial activity, as exemplified in Richelieu International. This organization, at one count, had 246 local clubs in Canada, of which 32 were located in Acadia (Guindon & Poulin, 1996, pp. 44–45). In all these clubs, volunteers are the only source of help, including the executive officers of the group, who are classifiable as career volunteers, and its rank-and-file, who mostly serve as casual volunteers performing a variety of functions (e.g., serving meals, selling tickets, publicizing events).

The arts have given rise to their own set of organizations. Theatre is perhaps the most evolved of them all and therefore plays the most significant role in community structure. Theatre societies are common throughout Francophone Canada, and members are not required to be actors. Furthermore, some communities have musical groups, dance troupes, and writers' organizations, although these tend to restrict membership to the artists themselves. It is likewise with craft groups. These organizations may be linked provincially in an overarching entity that represents them to the Francophone and Anglophone communities and to federal and provincial sources of funding for the arts. In New Brunswick this group is known as the Conseil Provincial des Sociétés Culturelles, in Nova Scotia it is Conseil Culturel Acadien de la Nouvelle-Écosse, and in Ontario it is Alliance Culturelle de l'Ontario. Here, too, there is plenty of scope for volunteer work, both serious and casual.

Should federal or provincial funds be used to support francophone leisure in minority circumstances?

Conclusions

As we have outlined in this chapter, leisure within Francophone communities is a potent contributor to the maintenance of a distinct Francophone culture. Particularly in "institutionally complete" Québec, there is a range of policy aimed at the protection of the French language and these policies have direct implications for context and content of leisure within the province. We have noted, for instance, that both federal and provincial policy come strongly to bear upon the media environment, and insofar as television and movies are dominant leisure pastimes, these policies represent important contributions to the maintenance of a distinct Francophone and Québécois identity. We have also noted the provincial government's policy stance that the bulk of responsibility for leisure provision rests with the municipalities, and that there is a heavy reliance on volunteer workforce. Similarly, there is an emphasis outside of Québec upon civic association among Francophones for a variety of leisure related purposes, and that these too help to develop, strengthen, and maintain a sense of collective identity of Francophones living in environments where governmental supports are less than complete. In short, the realm of leisure is a significant context wherein Francophone identity is bolstered. Through the combined influences and supports of a variety of institutions operating within and beyond the apparatus of government, it is very often at leisure that Francophone culture, and our bilingual Canadian character, is expressed, experienced, and reproduced.

Key Terms

Allophone
Assimilate
Charter of the French Language
Identity
Institutional completeness
Linguistic transfer
Majority society
Minority society
Official Languages Act
Parity society

References

Association Québécoise du Losir Municipal. (2000). *Leisure, local community, & quality of life: Leisure and recreation policy for Québec*. Retrieved from http://www.lin.ca/resource/html/rq12.pdf

Béland, D., & Lecours, A. (2004). Nationalisme et protection sociale: Une approche comparative. *Canadian Public Policy, 30*(3), 319–331.

Breton, R. (1964). Institutional completeness of ethnic communities and the personal relations of immigrants. *American Journal of Sociology, 70*, 193–205.

Cardinal, L., Lapointe, J., & Thériault, J.-Y. (1994). *État de la recherche sur les communautés Francophones hors Québec 1980–1990*. Ottawa, ON: Centre de recherche en civilisation canadienne-française de l'Université d'Ottawa.

Castonguay, C. (1999). French is on the ropes: Why won't Ottawa admit it? *Policy Options, 20*(10), 39–50.

Charron, C. (1977). *Prendre notre temps: Livre vert sur le loisir au Québec*. Québec, QC: Haut-Commissariat à la jeunesse, aux loisirs et aux sports.

Charron, C. (1979). *On a un monde à récreer: Livre blanc sur le loisir au Québec*. Québec, QC: Haut-Commissariat à la jeunesse, aux loisirs et aux sports.

Charter of the French Language (1977). Retrieved from http://www.canlii.org/qc/laws/sta/c-11/ 20041104/whole.html

Conseil Québécois du loisir. (2004). *Le partenariat public-privé en loisir: Témoigner du présent pour réussir l'avenir: Les priorités budgétaires du milieu associatif du loisir*. Avis soumis au Ministère des Finances, monsieur Yves Séguin, lors des consultations prébudgétaires en vue de la préparation du budget du Québec, 2004–2005.

Dallaire, C., & Denis, C. (2005). Asymmetrical hybridities: Youths at Francophone games in Canada. *Canadian Journal of Sociology, 30*, 143–168.

Department of Canadian Heritage (2003). *The government of Canada's response to the report of the standing committee on Canadian heritage, our cultural sovereignty: The second century of Canadian broadcasting*. Gatineau, QC: Department of Canadian Heritage.

Fletcher, F. (1998). Media and Political Identity: Canada and Québec in the Era of Globalization. *Canadian Journal of Communication, 23*(3) [Online]. Retrieved from http://www.cjc-online.ca/viewarticle.php?id=472

Gravelle, F., & Larocque, L. (2005). Volunteerism and serious leisure: The case of the Francophone games. *World Leisure Journal, 47*(1), 45–51.

Guindon, R., & Poulin, P. (1996). *Francophones in Canada: A community of interests*, Cat. No. CH3-2/1-1996. Ottawa, ON: Canadian Heritage, Government of Canada.

Institute de la statistique du Québec. (2005). *Statistiques sur l'industrie du film: Édition 2005*. Sainte-Foy, QC: Les Publications du Québec.

Laboratoire en loisir et vie communautaire. (n.d.). Le bénévolat en loisir, un capital a cultiver! Retrieved from http://www5.mels.gouv.qc.ca/sportloisir/publications/benevolat/LaboLoisirFeuillet2.pdf

Lisée, J.-F. (2001). How to resolve the language dilemma: Invest in Québec's uniqueness. *Inroads, 10*, 168–187.

Ministére des Affaires Municipales (1997). *Towards a renewed partnership: Governmental action framework in the fields of recreation and sport*. Québec, QC: Author.

Montréal Charter of Rights. (2005). Retrieved from http://ville.montreal.qc.ca/pls/portal/docs/page/charte_mtl_en/media/documents/charte_droits_en.pdf

Secrétariat à la Politique Linguistique. (2006). *La dynamique des langues en quelques chiffres*. Retrieved from http://www.spl.gouv.qc.ca/publications/statistiques/tableau.html

Service du Dévelopement Économique et Urbain (2001). *Statistical directory of the boroughs of the new city of Montréat*. Retrieved from http://www2.ville.montreal.qc.ca/urb_demo/chiffres/profils/arrondisanglais2.pdf

Standing Committee on Canadian Heritage. (2003). *Our cultural sovereignty: The second century of Canadian Broadcasting*. Presented to the House of Commons, June 11, 2003.

Statistics Canada. (2006). Television viewing by type of programme, 2003. Retrieved from http://www40.statcan.ca/l01/cst01/arts22a.htm?sdi=television

Stebbins, R. A. (1994). *The Franco-Calgarians: French language, leisure, and linguistic lifestyle in an Anglophone city*. Toronto, ON: University of Toronto Press.

Stebbins, R. A. (1995). Famille, loisir, bilinguisme et style de vie Francophone en milieu minoritaire. *Recherches Sociographiques, 36*, 265–278.

Stebbins, R. A. (1998). Les Francophones de l'Ouest canadien et l'avenir sans travail: l'ère du bénévole." *Cahiers franco-canadiens de l'Ouest, 10*, 257–269.

Stebbins, R. A. (2000). *The French enigma: Survival and development in Canada's Francophone societies*. Calgary, AB: Detselig.

Stebbins, R. A. (2004, December). La connaissance des langues: Une définition du recensement du Canada peu utilisée, mais fort utile. *Etudes canadiennes/Canadian Studies, 57*, 85–94.

Chapter 24
Leisure Across the Life Course

Jerome F. Singleton, Ph.D., CTRS
Dalhousie University

Learning Objectives

After reading this chapter, students will be able to

1. Identify and explain the life course.
2. Identify and explain a leisure repertoire.
3. Identify and explain the interaction between life course and leisure repertoire.
4. Identify and explain how the leisure repertoire changes throughout each stage of the life course.

Introduction

Researchers historically have defined leisure from three theoretical perspectives: (1) a sociological perspective (Dumazedier, 1974; Shaw, 1985a, 1985b); (2) a psychological perspective (Neulinger, 1981; Tinsley and Tinsley, 1986); and (3) a social-psychological perspective (Kaplan, 1975; Mannell & Bradley, 1986). The difficulty in understanding leisure is that no single definition has emerged to understand this phenomenon (see Chapter 1). Although no one definition has emerged for the term "leisure," a variety of scholars, including authors of chapters in this textbook, have identified factors that may comprise the experience called "leisure." Researchers agree that leisure plays a unique role in all our lives, throughout our lives. This chapter focuses on the role played by leisure, and the way in which we might pursue leisure, based on changes over the life course.

Leisure and the Life Course

A variety of terms have been used to understand the process of aging. These terms are life course, life cycle, lifespan development, life stages, and life path. Life course is the term used in this chapter. These terms are used to illustrate the transitions of a person's development related to aging (e.g., from infant to older adult), and possible life stages (e.g., parent, grandparent, spouse, widower; Levinson, Darrow, Klein & McKee, 1978; Zuzanek & Smale, 1999). Of greatest importance to this chapter is how entering and

Think for a moment about how the presence or absence of a partner or child might influence your own leisure patterns.

leaving different stages of the life course may influence leisure opportunities. These opportunities will vary across the life course and activity patterns may change as a result.

This chapter recognizes that different cultures define the terms leisure, aging, and stages of life course, based upon their own particular societal norms (Karlis, 1990; Karlis & Dawson, 1989/1990; Ujomoto, 1991, 1999). For example, culture may influence how leisure is perceived or the extent to which it is valued.

Identify one leisure activity that is sanctioned in the Netherlands but not in Canada?

This chapter further recognizes that individuals may experience aging and leisure in their own ways. For example, the presence or absence of a partner, child, work, or school will influence how one organizes his or her time commitments and leisure activities across the life course (Freysinger, 1999; McGuire, Boyd, & Tederick, 2004). These life conditions will influence what Mobily, Lemke, and Gisin (1991) called our "leisure repertoire." Leisure repertoire refers to opportunities individuals may have acquired across their life course. Gender, culture, the context of family, the cohort in which an individual is born, and the opportunities that are made available to that individual by society all influence this repertoire (Henderson, Bialeschki, Shaw, & Freysinger, 1996; Shaw, 2001; Shaw & Dawson, 2001).

Leisure is often viewed as an "organizing principle," a concept useful in understanding individual and family member development (Orthner & Mancini, 1991). Leisure allows individuals to separate themselves from assigned roles, to experience relationships, to share in experiences which further develop their individual personalities, family interactions, and family role expectations (Orthner, Barnett-Morris, & Mancini, 1993). Kelly suggests,

> Through the life course, the play of leisure is a crucial context in which individuals take action that contributes to their development. Not only the play of children, but also the relatively open action of adults in every life period provides for both the continuity and change of self-definitions and lines of action. Leisure and recreation provide opportunities for self-creation and expression that may be limited in other roles and contexts (Kelly, 1991, p. 420).

While our leisure repertoire undoubtedly changes as we age, leisure researchers rarely discuss age in isolation. As McPherson (1983, p. 417) noted, "In short, the meaning and availability of leisure may change across the life cycle in response to personal needs, interests, and abilities; to institutional (work and family) demands; and to cultural change. For this reason chronological age is a weak predictor of leisure behavior." Scholars have found that the stage of an individual's life course (single, married with no children, married with young children, married with teenagers, empty nest, divorced or widowed) may be more useful in identifying the activity patterns as we age (Horna, 1989, 1993; Zuzanek & Smale, 1999). Zuzanek and Smale (1999, p. 130) recognize the assumption related to categorizing individuals by age:

> It has been suggested, for example, that three 19 to 24 year old women, even though they are the same age, will not necessarily be at the same stage of the life cycle. If the first woman is single, employed, and financially independent, while the second is married with no children, and the third is married with two young children and staying at home, their leisure behaviour can hardly be explained by using the category of "19 to 24 year old." It is much more logical to plan for and to understand people in the context of their life-cycle stages rather than their biological age or marital status alone, since the former approach takes into account the total employment and family situation, including the presence or absence of children and their ages."

Zuzanek (1979) proposed that life cycle (life course) could be operationalized into a combination of four factors: (1) biological age, (2) marital status, (3) presence of children, and (4) employment status. The amount of time devoted to each of these categories will change as individuals enter new stages in their life course (Harvey & Singleton, 1989; Singleton & Harvey, 1995). Much of this "repackaging" of a person's time results from shifting roles and role expectations as the person enters a new life course stage. Individuals often add and drop activities as they assume different roles across their life course (Lounsbury & Hoopes, 1988; Singleton & Harvey, 1995). A person's social role, such as being a parent, requires demands on that person's time. Social roles also affect the hours available for leisure (Patterson & Carpenter, 2003). An individual who has taken on the role of student will likely have more time for leisure during spring break than someone playing the roles of bank manager, parent, homeowner, and commuter. In addition, as Zuzanak and Mannell (1998) noted, the functions inherent or required by the various roles we play can impinge upon one another. A parent may be asked by friends to attend a weekend away at a cottage. The parent's role as caregiver of young children may not permit such a trip due to the children's soccer schedule on that weekend.

Family roles and responsibilities are a major influence on leisure activity participation (Horna, 1989, 1993; Shaw, 1992, 1997; Thiessen & Singleton, 1994). In an attempt to develop an identity, children and adolescents are influenced by their parents and peers, sometimes causing conflict and most times influencing leisure activity participation. Parents' leisure patterns are often altered due to the presence of children. Many activities become home-centred, a characteristic usually maintained throughout the life course. We then leave this environment to go to work, to school, to the dentist, to do shopping, or to engage in leisure activities such as going to the movies or taking children to a sporting activity (Zuzanek & Smale, 1999).

Resources for Leisure

Leisure requires resources yet we may not always have access to those resources. What are the resources needed to experience "leisure"? Kelly (1983, p. 144) indicated that, "The primary resources of leisure are time, space, skill, companions, equipment and money." For example, the decision over whether or not to participate in an activity might be determined by cost and the time that is made available for that activity. If the activity is costly and available only at an inconvenient time, then participation is less likely (see Chapter 9). Furthermore, there are times in our lives when such variables may be more or less constraining.

"Participating in organized sports may require the purchase of equipment, the payment of user fees, contribution to travel costs and so on. Spending can range from tens to thousands of dollars. Although research in the United States has suggested that cost and lack of equipment are not deterrents to child's participation, a recent Canadian survey has strongly suggested that income is a barrier for children from households in lower income groups" (Kremarik, 2000, p. 22).

Have you ever been unable to participate in an activity due to lack of money? If so, what was the activity?

By way of example, consider the game of hockey. It takes a great many resources to take part, yet thousands of hockey players do so each season in Canada. Parents need to find a hockey association in which to register their child, pay the associated fees, and then coordinate schedules of work and hockey times to enable the child to participate in the sport. The ability to juggle all these elements will likely change over the life course as the child or children enter different opportunities. Furthermore, parents may assume different job responsibilities that may affect the flexibility to take children to events as well. Players may be able to travel to a week-long tournament while in high school but likely will not when they become a parent and have a baby at home. They may be able to afford to purchase the gear while working full time, but likely will not while in university and living on student loans.

This suggests to us that the actual decision to participate in an activity is shaped by the person's past experience with the activity, past and present opportunities available to the person, current companions available to participate in an activity with, current role expectations related to family or work requirements, and situational contingencies related to the accessibility of opportunities. Consequently, leisure activity patterns and a person's leisure repertoire may change throughout the life course as individuals assume new roles there within.

Transitions throughout the Life Course

Leisure opportunities change when individuals enter a new life stage. Such changes are particularly dramatic when we add a partner, child, or become a caregiver (Bedini & Phoenix, 2004; Shaw, 1992, 1997; Thiessen & Singleton, 1994). It is important to note too that the relative importance of school, work, and family, will vary at different stages of the life course (Horna, 1989, 1993; McPherson, 2004).

Familial leisure relationships are established over time, allowing for different leisure lifestyles and experiences to emerge. As a result, not every family's leisure is organized in the same way, and the nature and quality of communal leisure experiences may vary dramatically from one family to the next. We know, however, that leisure plays a role in developing and maintaining familial relationships (Orthner et al., 1993). Orthner et al., indicate that "during leisure, individuals are able to step out of their assigned roles, capture the essence of a relationship, and share an experience that can help mold their personalities, personal and family role expectations, and patterns of a relationship interaction" (p. 176).

The nature of the leisure activity may have considerable influence on the way in which family members interact. While certain leisure activities, such as watching television, can stifle communication, family game playing can stimulate interaction. Shared leisure activities offer perhaps the best opportunity to communicate, develop new roles, exchange new ideas, and promote relational cohesion. The benefits enjoyed as a result of such family leisure can be long term. Research suggests to us that both the experiences themselves and the ongoing memories of family-based events can build such cohesion. Consequently, leisure experiences can help families to bond and develop their own personal and relational satisfaction.

As with individuals, families will evolve through a series of stages that comprise a life course of sorts. Over the family life course, activity patterns, settings and constraints will change and family members will seek to respond, as best they can, to continue to enjoy their leisure pursuits. Throughout the process, activity patterns may be influenced by both external and internal factors including gender, race, ethnicity, education, lifelong and present incomes and assets, marital status (past and present), and type and place of residence (McPherson, 2004).

Leisure Development through the Life Course

The inevitability of change for everyone, from individuals to societies, forms the basis of developmental theory. Developmental theory suggests how we all come to be the individuals we are. It tells us that we evolve through learning and taking on new roles throughout our lives. Though such role changing continuously supplements the individual, we all move through the life course with some persistent identity (Carpenter & Murray 2002; McGuire, Boyd, & Tederick, 2004).

Leisure is critical to helping us learn who we are and in helping us become who we want to be. Kelly (1987) suggests that to understand leisure in developmental terms it must be approached from a dual perspective. First, we are socialized through leisure. With such participation, one learns and develops while in the process of identifying the self. We may learn that we are an excellent athlete, a talented musician, or a skilled angler. These are positive developments that help intensify our self-esteem and confidence. Conversely, experience may also suggest that it is not worth trying out for a team or worth pursuing any number of goals that are personally meaningful. In such cases, negative outcomes may hamper our personal growth because they can discourage personal exploration for meaning.

Second, we are socialized into leisure. As Kelly (1987, p. 61) noted, "socialization is the acquisition of knowledge, attitudes, skills, and communication and interpretive competencies to act effectively in social institutions and roles." It is the interaction of these variables in our personal history and experiences, which is predominant in socialization into leisure. We learn and internalize our own leisure style; we develop our respective leisure repertoires.

Much of our leisure socialization occurs through accepting and discarding roles as we progress from one stage of the life course to the next. It is these roles that structure our obligations and responsibilities. For decades, scientists (from Erickson in 1950 to Gordon in 1971) worked to develop models to illustrate how individuals enter and leave different stages of the life course. Many of these models suffer from a striking weakness. They tend to discuss "typical" conditions without really delving into specific conditions faced by any given individual. Bialeschki, Kelly, and Pesavento-Raymore (2004, p. 169) are particularly troubled by the assumptions, implicit in developmental models, that everyone follows a relatively narrow set of options or life choices. They state that:

- Varieties in current family patterns challenge the assumption of nuclear family as normative.
- A majority of women in the work force challenge the assumptions of male dominance in family and leisure as well as the workplace.
- A recognition of sexual diversity challenges the entire "mummy-daddy" assumptions of family structure and household composition.
- The market system challenges concepts of leisure as freely chosen action with fundamentally expressive and developmental meanings.
- These changes challenge the traditional structure of work, family, and leisure with changes that are resistant to formal power relations and question access to resources.

Consequently, the reader may discover that the developmental model in this chapter fails to reflect his or her reality. We introduce it here, not as a guide into what "should be" but rather as way of describing historical trends in the life course.

Gordon (1971) developed a model that suggested that individuals tend to go through eleven stages throughout the life course. Kelly (1987) reduced Gordon's model to four stages: (1) preparation phase, (2) establishment phase, (3) maturity phase, and (4) culmination phase. Passage through each phase influences our leisure repertoire and the satisfaction we gain from our leisure. These four stages are not mutually exclusive. Anyone may exist within two or more stages at any given time given the situations in which one finds oneself. More on this is offered next.

After reviewing the following phases, reflect upon how your leisure changed as you entered a new life course? What opportunities did you participate in as you grew up with your family? What activities do you currently participate in with your partner? How will your leisure participation patterns change if you become a parent?

Stage 1: The Preparation Phase

Children's play can usually be divided into four categories: imitative, exploratory, testing, and model building. The earliest forms of play occur during the three first stages of the preparation phase; infancy (0–12 months), early childhood (1–2 years), and the oedipal period (3–5 years). During the earliest stages play takes a very basic form. For example, a parent may try to duplicate the giggles of the child hoping to encourage further imitation. Through such means, bonds are developed and the child learns to express feelings and emotion. Imitative play in early childhood (1–2 years) and oedipal period (3–5 years) involves more complete roles of imitation.

Later in the childhood phase (6–11 years), children are still influenced by the primary contact of socialization into leisure: the family. However, the influence of other institutions such as school, organized sport and recreational programs, and the arts become more pronounced. A major dilemma in late childhood is participation in expressive versus instrumental activities. The distinction between instrumental and expressive activities is based on the primacy of gratification and/or rewards as a result of the action (activity). Expressive activities are activities offering an end in and of themselves. Through them, goals and desires are fulfilled immediately. Instrumental activities, on the other hand, also consist of goals, desires, and needs, but gratification and/or rewards are to be attained at some future time. For example, swimming or weight training are activities that may be pursued to reach an attainable future goal (e.g., fitness). It is also possible for activities to be both instrumental and expressive. Indeed, it would be almost impossible to describe a certain leisure activity to be purely expressive or purely instrumental. An individual may participate in a certain leisure activity (e.g., read a book or weight train) for immediate gratification (expressivity) or for some future gratification or reward (instrumentality). This individual may decide to read a book for immediate gratification of enjoyment and a quest for knowledge; however, he or she must realize that this book may assist in some future tasks (e.g., giving a presentation or writing a paper).

During the early adolescent period (12–15 years) family and school influences begin to slip. It is in this phase that adolescents may begin experimenting with alcohol and drugs in addition to explorations of sexuality and intimacy in the development of relationships. Gender differences in this

Family Influence on Children's Leisure

According to Kremarik, "Soccer is the king of sports among children ages 5 to 14 with 31% of athletically active kids participating regularly. Swimming and hockey are tied for second and third place at 24% each. At the bottom of the list were figure skating and karate (6% each), volleyball (5%) and cycling (3%). Active kids generally have supportive families: almost two-thirds of them (1.4 million) had at least one parent who was also involved in organized sport. Most often these parents were athletes themselves; they were also volunteer administrators (e.g., coach, manager, fund-raiser); and both athletes and volunteers" (Kremarik, 2000, p. 21).

phase may also influence leisure activity participation, such that opportunities and expectations may have a strong influence on development. Leisure opportunities for girls have often been limited by societal expectations (Deem, 1988; Henderson et al., 1996).

During later adolescence (16–20 years) young people become more involved in life decisions. Concerns over entering post-secondary education or the work force, and patterns of relationships to sustain with family, friends and others following high school, are typical. The question "Who am I?" often arises in this period and the adolescent searches for an answer to this question by experimenting with certain roles, responsibilities, and identities.

Male and female adolescents may use leisure as a way to acquire appropriate male and female adult roles, attitudes, and behaviours. Throughout the adolescent stages of the life course (12–20) the development of a personal identity is a predominant dilemma for individuals, Leisure behaviours are, at least in part, dependent upon the roles that each individual chooses to adopt (see Chapter 20).

How did your peer groups influence your leisure and life decisions through adolescence? What has been the long-term influence of your parents on your leisure choices? List five activities in which your parent or parents enrolled you when you were a child. In how many of these activities do you still participate? Why? Did you discontinue any of these activities? Why?

Stage 2: The Establishment Phase

The establishment phase generally takes place between 21 and 65 years of age. Two themes dominate this central period of the life course; productivity in work and family, and status in the social system. Productivity in the many facets of life such as the family and work is necessary to pave the way for future roles and obligations.

Leisure in the young adult stage (19–29) is influenced by a number of factors. During this stage, the occupational situation, family roles, marriage, parenthood, and health status were crucial variables in shaping leisure choices. Kleiber and Kelly (1980) suggested that social goals continue to direct the leisure involvement of young adults, as is the case in the adolescent stage; however, at the same time, demands of employment schedule and responsibilities associated with new roles require modifications in leisure choices and companions. A partner is typically the main leisure companion during this stage; however, if children are present, they tend to dominate a large majority of available leisure time and become the "new" leisure companions. Work associates may be secondary or tertiary leisure companions for professionals.

The development of careers and families tends to have a constraining effect on leisure opportunities particularly for women (Shaw, 1992, 1997; Thiessen & Singleton, 1994). As children are born, leisure choices and opportunities change to reflect the transition to becoming a family (Thiessen & Singleton, 1994). Kelly (1987) indicated that life and leisure will never be the same when the role of parenthood is taken. Leisure activities, when available, tend to be home-centred, such as, viewing television, visiting friends, or taking children to leisure activities.

Stage 3: The Maturity Phase

A major component of most individuals' lives during the early maturity phase is employment. An individual's occupational status and work environment may influence his or her leisure activities and behaviours (see Chapter 11). Socioeconomic status may also influence the form of leisure activities chosen (see Chapter 26).

The primary value themes in the early maturity phase are stability and accomplishment (Kelly, 1987). Leisure pursuits are directed primarily to family cohesion, child development, and community solidarity. Home and family centred leisure activities dominate this life stage. These activities include television viewing, visiting with family and friends, gardening, home workshop, individual hobbies, reading, and walking or some form of physical activity.

The final phase in is that of full maturity (45–65 years of age). The place of leisure in this stage usually varies from person to person, as in previous stages, but there is typically a pattern change such that there are fewer home-centred activities but more evenings out, more travel, and more personally expressive leisure forms such as music, writing, or painting (Kleiber & Kelly, 1980). Fewer financial responsibilities (e.g., mortgage paid, children left home) and typically higher income levels may provide more economic resources for leisure.

Stage 4: The Culmination Phase

Individuals entering the culmination phase will have to deal with a number of changing roles and identities. Work, family, and leisure roles and identities will change because of retirement and advancing age. Following retirement, roles arising from work responsibilities are diminished drastically. The individual no longer has structured, regimented employment policies to adhere to, and is relatively free to decide how this available time will be spent. Individuals who had earlier devoted so much energy to their occupations, may now have difficulty adapting to this new (non-work) freedom.

There can be considerable continuity in leisure patterns as older adults move into the culmination period (McGuire et al., 2004; Singleton & Harvey, 1995). In general, older individuals are no more interested in special clubs and age-segregated events than they were in earlier adult stages.

Conclusion

Through entering and leaving differing stages in a life course, one's leisure repertoire will be influenced by the social construction of his or her life course. It's advisable to consider the following questions when reflecting upon your leisure repertoire.

Leisure is a dynamic concept that is influenced by the social context of your life course. While it is true that leisure may change over the life course, we know too that leisure activities and preferences can be quite stable over time. For example, we know that leisure preferences can be very stable within the home environment (Crawford, Godbey, & Crouter, 1986; Singleton & Harvey 1995). Someone who enjoys listening to music while reading may be able to engage in these leisure activities from childhood through advanced age. Individuals add and drop opportunities based upon the presence or absence of a partner, child, or occupation characteristics (obligations, commitments, demands). Participation is primarily in experiences related to the home and individuals only leave the home based upon opportunities such as work, church, health care provider visits, or participation (or the enabling of participation) in leisure opportunities.

> ? How have your leisure opportunities been influenced by your parents, your culture, your gender, your partner, or by your children? Will you add new opportunities or delete old ones as you enter a new stage of your life course? Are your leisure opportunities independent or inter-dependent upon those individuals present in your life (parents, grandparents, significant others, children siblings, and relatives)?

Acknowledgements

I would like to thank Dr. Ted Tederick, Temple University, Dr. Gaylene Carpenter University of Oregon, Mr. Doug Cripps, University of Regina, and Dr. Pierre Ouellette, Université de Moncton, for their time and insightful comments when writing this chapter.

Key Terms

Culmination phase
Establishment phase
Family
Leisure repertoire
Life course
Maturity phase
Preparation phase
Roles
Socialization
Transitions

References

Bedini, L. A., & Phoenix, T. L. (2004). Perceptions of leisure by family caregivers: A profile. *Therapeutic Recreation Journal, 38*, 366–381.

Bialeschki, D., Kelly, J. R., & Pesavento, L. C. (2004). Women, leisure and the family in the USA: A critical review. In N. Samuel (Ed.), *Women, leisure and the family in contemporary society: A multinational perspective*. Paris, France: CAB International.

Carpenter, G., & Murray, S. (2002). Leisure behaviours and perceptions when mid-life death is imminent: A case report. *Journal of Park and Recreation Administration, 20*, 12–36.

Crawford, D. W., Godbey, G., & Crouter, A. C. (1986). The stability of leisure preferences. *Journal of Leisure Research, 18*(2), 96–115.

Deem, R. (1988). Feminism and leisure studies: Opening up new directions. In E. Winmbush & M. Talbot (Eds.), *Relative freedoms: Women and leisure* (pp. 5–17). Milton Keynes, UK: Open University Press.

Douglas, J. D. (1970). Understanding everyday life. In J. D. Douglas' (Ed.), *Understanding everyday life: Toward the reconstruction of sociological knowledge* (pp. 3–43). Chicago, IL: Aldine.

Dumazedier, J. (1974). *Sociology of leisure*. New York, NY: Elsevier North Holland.

Erickson, E. (1950). Growth and crises of the healthy personality. In E. Erickson (Ed.), *Identity and the lifecycle*. New York, NY: International Universities Press.

Freysinger, V. (1999). Life span and life course perspectives on leisure. In E. L. Jackson & T. L. Burton (Eds.), *Leisure studies: Prospects for the twenty-first century*. State College, PA: Venture Publishing, Inc.

Friedmann, J. (1992). *Empowerment: The politics of alternative development*. Cambridge, MA: Blackwell.

Gordon, C. (1971). Role and value development across the lifecycle. In J. W. Jackson (Ed.), *Role: Sociological studies IV* (pp. 65–105), London, UK: Cambridge University Press.

Harvey, A. S., & Singleton, J. F. (1989). Activity patterns across the lifespan. *Canadian Journal on Aging, 8*(3), 268–285.

Henderson, K. A., Bialeschki, M. D., Shaw, S., & Freysinger, V. J. (1996). *Both gains and gaps: Feminist perspectives on women's leisure*. State College, PA: Venture Publishing, Inc.

Horna, J. (1989). The leisure component of the parental role. *Journal of Leisure Research, 21*, 228–241.

Horna, J. (1993). Married life and leisure: A multidimensional study of couples. *World Leisure and Recreation, 35*(3), 17–21.

Kaplan, M. (1975). *Leisure: Theory and policy*. New York, NY: John Wiley and Sons.

Karlis, G. (1990). Aged immigrants: Forgotten clients in the provision of recreation services. *Recreation Canada, 48*(4), 36–43.

Karlis, G., & Dawson, D. (1989/1990). Ethic maintenance and recreation: A case study. *Journal of Applied Recreation Research, 15*(92), 85–99.

Kelly, J. R. (1983). *Leisure*. Englewood Cliffs, NJ: Prentice Hall.

Kelly, J. R. (1987). *Freedom to be: A new sociology of leisure*. New York, NY: MacMillan.

Kelly, J. R. (1991). Leisure and quality: Beyond the quantitative barrier in research. In T. L. Goodale & P. A. Witt (Eds.), *Recreation and leisure: Issues in an era of change* (3rd ed., pp. 397–411). State College, PA: Venture Publishing, Inc.

Kleiber, D. A., & Kelly, J. R. (1980). Leisure, socialization and the lifecycle. In S. E. Iso-Ahola (Ed.), *Social psychological perspectives on leisure and recreation* (pp. 91–127). Springfield, IL: Charles C. Thomas.

Kremarik, F. (2000). A family affair: Children's participation in sports. *Canadian Social Trends* (No. 11-008), 20–24. Statistic Canada.

Levinson, D., Darrow, C., Klein, F., Levinson, M., & McKee, B. (1978). *The seasons of a man's life*. New York, NY: Alfred A. Knopf, Inc.

Lounsbury, J. W., & Hoopes, L. L. (1988). Five year stability of leisure activity and motivation factors. *Journal of Leisure Research, 20*(2), 118–134.

Mannell, R. C., & Bradley, W. (1986). Does greater freedom always lead to great leisure? Testing a person x environment model of freedom and leisure. *Journal of Leisure Research, 18*(4), 215–230.

McGuire, F. A., Boyd, R., & Tederick, R. E. (2004). *Leisure and aging: Ulyssean living in later life*. Champaign, IL: Sagamore Publishing.

McPherson, B. D. (1983). *Aging as a social process*. Toronto, ON: Butterworths.

McPherson, B. D. (2004). *Aging as a social process: Canadian perspectives* (4th ed.). Don Mills, ON: Oxford University Press.

Mobily, K. E., Lemke, J. H., & Gisin, G. J. (1991). The idea of leisure repertoire. *Journal of Applied Gerontology, 10*, 208–223.

Neulinger, J. (1981). *The psychology of leisure* (2nd ed.). Springfield, IL: Charles C. Thomas.

Orthner, D. K., Barnett-Morris, L., & Mancini, J. A. (1993). Leisure and family over the life cycle. In L. L'Abate (Ed.), *Handbook of developmental family psychology and psychopathology* (pp. 176–201). Malden, MA: Wiley.

Orthner, D. K., & Mancini, J. A. (1991). Benefits of leisure for family bonding. In B. L. Driver, P. J. Brown, & G. L. Peterson (Eds.), *Benefits of leisure* (pp. 289–301). State College, PA: Venture Publishing, Inc.

Patterson, I., & Carpenter, G. (2003). By the decade: An exploration of the leisure perceptions and preferences for two mid-life adults over time. *Annals of Leisure Research, 6*(2), 153–168.

Shaw, S. M. (1985a). The meaning of leisure in everyday life. *Leisure Science, 7*(1), 1–24.

Shaw, S. M., & Dawson, D. (2001). Purposive leisure: Examining parental discourses on family activities. *Leisure Science, 23*(4), 217–231.

Shaw, S. M. (2001). The family leisure dilemma: Insights from research with Canadian families. *World Leisure Journal, 43*(4), 53–62.

Shaw, S. M. (1985b). Gender and leisure: Inequality in the distribution of leisure time. *Journal of Leisure Research, 17*(4), 266–282.

Shaw, S. M. (1992). Dereifying family leisure: An examination of women's and men's everyday experiences and perceptions of family time. *Leisure Sciences, 14*(4), 271–286.

Shaw, S. M. (1997). Controversies and contractions in family leisure: An analysis of conflicting paradigms. *Journal of Leisure Research, 29*(1), 98–112.

Singleton, J. F., & Harvey, A. (1995). Stage of life cycle and activity patterns across the life span. *Journal of Occupational Science Australia, 2*(1), 3–13.

Thiessen, V., & Singleton, J. (1994). *Becoming a family and losing leisure: Is there subjective equity? Winnipeg area study #53.* Winnipeg, MB: University of Manitoba.

Tinsley, H. E. A., & Tinsley, D. (1986). A theory of the attributes, benefits, and causes of leisure experience. *Leisure Sciences, 8*(1), 1–45.

Ujomoto, V. K. (1991). Ethnic variations in the allocation of time to leisure activities. *Loisir et Société/Society and Leisure, 14*, 557–573.

Ujomoto, V. K. (1999). Time budget methodology in social science research ethnicity and aging. In W. E. Pentland, A. S. Harvey, M. P. Lawton, & M. A. McColl (Eds.), *Time use research in the social sciences* (pp. 231–244). New York, NY: Kluwer Academic.

Zuzanek, J. (1979). Leisure and cultural participation as a function of life cycle. Paper presented to the annual general meeting of the Canadian Sociology and Anthropology Association, Saskatoon, Saskatchewan.

Zuzanek, J., & Mannell, R. (1998). Life-cycle squeeze, time pressure, daily stress and leisure participation: A Canadian perspective. *Loisir et Société/Society and Leisure, 21*(2), 513–544.

Zuzanek, J., & Smale, B. J. A. (1999). Life cycle and across the week: Allocation of time to daily activities. In W. E. Pentland, A. S. Harvey, M. P. Lawton, & M. A. McColl, (Eds.), *Time use research in the social sciences* (pp. 127–154). New York, NY: Kluwer Academic.

DESCENTE
DESCENTE

Chapter 25
Leisure and Disability

Peggy Hutchison, Ed.D.
Brock University

Learning Objectives

After reading this chapter, students will be able to

1. Be aware of the differences among various terms, including impairment, disability, and handicap.
2. Recognize how current perceptions of disability have been influenced by the way disability was historically constructed or interpreted.
3. Understand how construction of disability has impacted leisure and other participation opportunities.
4. Identify current attitudes, trends, and approaches that reflect attempts to reconstruct disability in ways that are more consistent with inclusion and citizenship.

Introduction

People with disabilities make up a significant sector of Canadian society. Canadian statistics indicate that approximately 12% of the population has some sort of disability (Statistics Canada, 2003). As you may be witnessing in your own communities today, many of these individuals are beginning to experience a quality of life in the community not dissimilar to other citizens. People with disabilities, however, have not always been accorded the opportunities we now believe to be the right of every citizen. Although much progress has been achieved in recent years, people with disabilities continue to face many challenges to full participation and citizenship. Understanding more about this situation is very important for the field of recreation and leisure. The vital role recreation and leisure plays in enhancing quality of life for all citizens, including people with disabilities, is now being recognized (Hawkins, 1997).

Social Construction

Today we understand how individuals with disabilities were afforded few rights and opportunities in the past. It goes back to the very way society viewed the idea of "disability." The World Health Organization (WHO) provides a starting point for this thinking.

WHO Definitions

- *Impairments* are described as physiological abnormalities.
- *Disabilities* are limitations in functional performance stemming from impairments.
- *Handicaps* are resulting disadvantages that may take the form of arbitrary barriers constructed, consciously or unconsciously, by society. (McNeil, 1993)

WHO's descriptions of impairment, disability, and handicap as distinct concepts help us understand how social conditions affect people's perceptions and experiences of disability. A process known as social construction can help us further understand the significance of these terms. This concept explains how knowledge is created and assumed to be true. Through our interactions in society, we learn to behave in certain ways based on the meanings we have attached to certain concepts like impairment (Douglas, 1970). This meaning is reflected in our behaviour, language, and attitudes. So when we reflect on the lack of opportunities historically afforded people with disabilities, we now know that this is because of the way "disability" was socially constructed.

Consider the concrete example of a person who has a spinal cord injury and is in a wheelchair, or another person who has a mental health problem such as depression, to see how our understanding of the term "handicap" affects our perception of disability. If having "impairments" such as a spinal cord injury or depression are viewed negatively by society, rather than positively or at least neutrally, then the meaning attached to the impairments that will be created will be negative. This negative interpretation affects attitudes and behaviours accordingly. Any number of things can then occur, from labelling, lowered expectations, segregation, congregation, to isolation. The person with the spinal cord injury or depression may now be seen as helpless, incompetent, and a burden, not capable of learning or contributing to society in any meaningful way. This vicious cycle, which results in a major social handicap, has often been done unconsciously and in the name of rehabilitation. This is the situation in society in which many people with disabilities have found themselves.

On a more optimistic side, social construction theory clearly shows that if the context changes, the meaning can also change, for the better (Berger & Luckmann, 1966). Many people fear becoming disabled, but disability is a part of normal human experience. Every ethnic, cultural, and religious group includes people with disabilities. The longer one lives, the greater the chances are that one will live with some form of disability. So, is it not time to change the meaning associated with having an impairment? Later the mechanisms that have contributed to improving conditions will be explored.

Historical Understandings of Disability

Many historical factors have contributed to a perception of disability as negative or undesirable. These factors are very relevant today because they continue to influence the meanings we attach to the concept of disability. Early work exploring these historical factors focused more on the concept of devaluation, rather than social construction. Devaluation was seen as a process of relegating someone to low social status based on having a significant characteristic that is not valued by society (Wolfensberger & Thomas, 1983). The role of imagery in promoting devaluation of people with disabilities, such as portraying an adult in a child-like way, was exposed. In the cases of people with disabilities, this work showed that these images are often based on unconscious negative historical role perceptions. For example, an adult with Down syndrome might be seen as an eternal child. It can now be seen how this concept of *devaluation* is an integral part of the construction of disability.

In the 19th century, industrialization and urbanization both contributed to the view that some people could not be productive and had limited capacity to participate in community life. For people who were not cared for by their families or were left to wander the streets, poorhouses were operated by churches to take care of the handicapped, the poor, and criminals. These historical role perceptions resulted in the unconscious belief that it was acceptable for these "undesirable" people to be poor, unemployed, segregated from the rest of society, and denied basic human rights.

The most extreme and devastating impact of these historical negative images was the creation of institutions intended to "care" for these individuals. In the later part of the 19th century, people with developmental disabilities were placed in hospitals specifically for them. The images of people with disabilities that originated during this period portrayed these people as incapable, worthless, vegetable-like, sexually deviant, and even dangerous and unable or undeserving of leisure opportunities. People with mental health problems in asylums or psychiatric hospitals were viewed as "sick," thus beginning the deep entrenchment of the medical model during the early 20th century. All needs were addressed within the medical model, with doctors and nurses prescribing treatments such as restraints and even sterilization in the late 19th century and early 20th century (Wolfensberger, 1980). Later in the 20th century, use of shock therapy and medications also became widespread. Institutionalization of people with physical disabilities did not gain widespread acceptance until much later, after World War II, when the government wanted to make a contribution by creating hospitals for war veterans (Simmons, 1982). These rehabilitation hospitals soon became available to other persons with physical disabilities. Leisure counselling was one of several therapies, which were aimed at helping people cope with their disability and gain skills and awareness to return to the community.

Regardless of the type of institution, *institutionalization* reinforced a belief that people with similar labels firstly had the same needs and that those needs were best addressed in large congregated settings like institutions. Several other themes were also dominant: low expectations, limited choice, restricted opportunities to learn, isolation from family and community, stigmatization, and entrenchment in the medical model.

Shortly after the mid-20th century, society was beginning to realize the ills of institutions and that institutionalization as a social policy was socially unjust (Goffman, 1961; Hutchison & Potschaske, 1998). This was in part due to the psychology movement, which reversed earlier misconceptions: that certain people were incapable of learning and simply needed to be warehoused in institutions. If people were not going to be living in institutions, they would need services in the community to keep them occupied and to provide opportunities for growth. A variety of voluntary advocate associations such as the Canadian Association for the Mentally Retarded, the Canadian Association for the Blind, the Canadian Mental Health Association, the March of Dimes, and the Canadian Rehabilitation Council for the Disabled were created during this period.

So what did these community services look like as they developed in the 1950s and 1960s? Because society was still in a very segregated frame of reference due to a century of institutions, many services that were created were special or separate. For example, housing was in the form of large group homes, where residents participated informally with other residents in their home or as a group during community outings. Employment was mostly training in the form of sheltered workshops, where recreation activities were offered at lunchtime or after work. Education typically included special education schools and classes. Special Olympics programs began first in the United States and then in Canada to demonstrate that people with disabilities had the right to recreation opportunities in the community (Storey, 2004). Programs such as field hockey and swimming were available. Many voluntary associations, such as the March of Dimes, also provided residential camping programs in the summer.

While many of these early services that began in the 1950s were seen as an important step away from institutionalization, today we now understand that participation in these formal services led to entrenchment in a new role of "clienthood." Clienthood implies that people with disabilities are dependent on an array of human services, professionals, and volunteers for most of their support. It has come to be understood that many of these traditional services assumed segregation and compliance, focussed on deficits, encouraged professionals as the decision makers, stressed congregation rather than individualization, and led to learned helplessness. Unconsciously, new negative images of people with disabilities as "clients" and "special" were being created by many services and supports that were supposedly designed to make life better for people. In other words, community services began to treat people similarly to the way people living in institutions were being treated. This concept, whereby people's lives in community have many characteristics of life in an institution, became known as *community institutionalization*. Is it any surprise then that the construction of disability is linked with the image of clienthood?

Community Institutionalization and Its Impact on Quality of Life

Institutions are not defined by "brick and mortar" but by people's way of thinking. People living outside institutions generally show better quality of life than those within. Still their quality of life outside is not guaranteed. In Canada, in recent years, most individuals leaving institutions return to communities where they are part of a formal human-service system. Research illustrates that living in a community service system does not necessarily enhance quality of life. Community-based services do not, by definition, mean that people are connected with the community or that people have more control in their lives. We must be careful not to simply replace large institutions with smaller community institutions. In other words, *in* the community did not mean *of* the community. People still find themselves doing segregated recreation activities and being only with other labelled people. The move from institutional to community-based services can best be seen, not as an end point, but rather as part of the evolution toward the creation of supportive communities that will be truly empowering for citizens with disabilities. Such empowerment will enable people to engage in hobbies, attend sports events, join community clubs, visit friends, and so on (Hayden, Soulen, Schleien, & Tabourne, 1996; O'Brien & O'Brien, 1991; Walker, 1999).

Why People with Disabilities Needed Even Better Lives and How This Began to Happen

Social change movements are generally responsible for advocating rights and improving conditions for the citizenry. Social change processes usually involve people gradually becoming aware of their inequality, having glimpses of possibilities for a more socially just society, developing new frameworks through conversation with leaders and participants, and advocating for policy change (Zoerink & Rosegard, 1997). Social justice is a vision of society where distribution of resources is equitable, participation is valued for all, and members are safe and secure.

As the *disability movement* evolved over many years, it was influenced by a wide range of social movements summarized below (adapted from Hutchison & McGill, 1998, p. 20).

Since the 1960s, the civil rights movement in the United States provided the impetus for other marginalized groups to address their inequities. If persons of colour were addressing their inequality, then was it not possible that persons with disabilities themselves could begin to address their inequality and work towards human rights? This was a significant shift, because previous efforts in the disability field were mostly initiated by parents and professionals. This was the origin of the *consumer disability movement*, where people with disabilities began to take control of their own lives.

Normalization and integration also began to influence Canada in the late 1960s. These philosophies, Scandinavian in origin, built on the civil rights movement, but were specifically focused on disability. Normalization is "the use of culturally normative means to offer persons life conditions

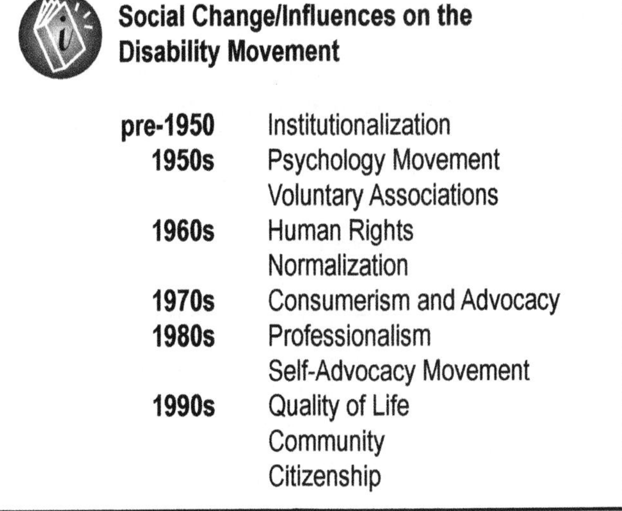

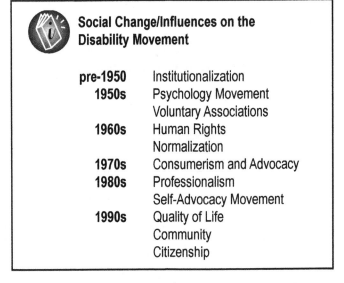

Social Change/Influences on the Disability Movement

pre-1950	Institutionalization
1950s	Psychology Movement
	Voluntary Associations
1960s	Human Rights
	Normalization
1970s	Consumerism and Advocacy
1980s	Professionalism
	Self-Advocacy Movement
1990s	Quality of Life
	Community
	Citizenship

at least as good as that of average citizens, and as much as possible enhance or support their behavior, experiences, status, and reputation" (Flynn & Nitsch, 1980, p. 8). Use of culturally normative implied integration was happening. This was the first time the idea of integration was introduced and promoted. Normalization provided a way of analyzing the myriad of segregated services that had evolved since the 1950s, making them better, and creating more integrated programs in the community. While normalization did not spell the end of segregated services, in most communities there emerged a "continuum of services" from segregated to more integrated options. In recreation, this gave parents and people with disabilities more choice (Dybwad, 1990). In many municipalities, an "integration coordinator" was hired to oversee agency policy development, accommodation, and coordination (Hutchison & Lord, 1979). Leisurability Publications, and its feature publication, the *Journal of Leisurability* were started in Canada in 1974 to promote integration for people with disabilities and others seen as vulnerable in recreation and leisure.

The 1980s and 1990s brought Canada yet another change that impacted the disability movement. Known as the *community movement*, its intent was to balance the earlier focus on services, professionals, and clienthood. The community movement focused on people with disabilities becoming an integral part of community life, not simply integration into recreation programs. This focus on community appeared to be doing a better job of constructing citizenship by focusing on the gifts and capacities of people with disabilities as contributors to community life (Kretzmann & McKnight, 1993).

Collectively, these philosophies and movements have responded to the call for improved quality of life in the community for people with disabilities, essentially lives that are more inclusive and in a new paradigm than in the past (Pedlar & Hutchison, 2000).

Current Trends in Leisure and Disability

This evolution essentially brings us to today, where an inclusion philosophy is being promoted. In other words, the gradual social construction of disability over the past few decades has led us to a paradigm shift that has as a goal the concept of inclusion. A paradigm shift is basically a significant change in the way of viewing the world—social reconstruction. The shift from institution, to community institution, to community is illustrated. The paradigm shift we have been discussing is illustrated in the Social Construction of Disability *i*-box (adapted from Hutchison & McGill, 1998, p. 19; Lord & Hutchison, 1998, p. 409). We can see that institution and community institutionalization are part of the traditional paradigm of devaluation, whereas community is part of the new paradigm of inclusion.

Self-determination is the core of the person-centred approach. The independent living (IL) movement in Canada is a good example of this approach because it emphasizes that people with disabilities can best identify their own needs and can have productive lives in the community via self-help, empowerment, advocacy, and the removal of environmental, social, and economic barriers. (Hutchison, Pedlar, Dunn, Lord, & Arai, 2000)

These new paradigm concepts are fundamental to the social reconstruction of disability. Old paradigm values related to clienthood and services that promoted segregation are being deconstructed and more positive images, values of citizenship, participation, and community are emerging. This new construction of disability in many ways continues to be a "work in progress." The Canadian landscape is dotted with numerous projects and groups that embrace the new paradigm. Several provincial governments across the country are also beginning to transform their service systems to be more in line with new paradigm values.

So what does this new life in community look like? Examples of new paradigm approaches can give us insight into ways that people are reconstructing disability. Disability supports are gradually becoming more person-centred, ensuring that individuals are not dumped in the community without adequate support or clumped together with others with disabilities (Bullock & Mahon, 2000). A person-centred approach sees the person with a disability as a unique individual, someone with unknown and unexplored potential, and a person whose diversity needs to be respected

Recently, the concept of individualized funding for disability supports has been seen as a necessary part of

Social Constructionism of Disability

Paradigm Shift

Traditional Paradigm *(devaluation)*		**New Paradigm** *(inclusion)*
Institution	Community Institutional	Community
• Segregation • Medical • Labelling • Patient role • Limitations	• Integration • Rehabilitation • Clienthood • Services • Learned helplessness • Volunteers/staff	• Citizenship • Empowerment • Full participation • Individual & community capacity-building • Relationships

this approach. In many cases, individualized funding, which goes directly to the individual rather than the service, ensures that persons with disabilities have a textured life—a full, rich, inclusive life in the community (Pedlar, Haworth, Hutchison, Taylor, & Dunn, 1999; Lord & Hutchison, 2003). These mechanisms are essential for grounding today's supports in the new paradigm and building a new construction of "disability."

There has been a growing emphasis on intentionally building support networks with people with disabilities (Heyne, Schleien, & McAvoy, 1993). Real friendships with valued members of society are an important part of the reconstruction of disability (Devine & Lashua, 2002). Most children, living with disability, now live at home, attend neighbourhood schools, and are given supports to make friends with peers (Sciberras & Hutchison, 2003/4). Friendships are important for both adults and children because they make people feel valued, give people the chance to take risks, make it possible to rely less on services, significantly increase the possibility of the person living a normal life, and on the other side, help non-disabled people learn acceptance (Hutchison, 1990). A variety of approaches, such as support circles and community connecting, are now available to guide this process within a new paradigm (Hutchison & McGill, 1998). Recreationists are beginning to see relationship building as an important part of their domain and are determining ways to make changes within programs to be facilitative of friendships (Schleien, Green, & Stone, 1999).

Technological advances are enabling participation in ways never before imagined. The field of assistive devices (AD) is taking on a life of its own as evidenced in journals specifically focusing on technology (Weiss, Bailik, & Kizony, 2003). Ways that people with disabilities can access the Internet, e-mail, and virtual reality through computers is now being explored (Liverton, 2000). New designs in power wheelchairs mean people are on the move, and new approaches such as facilitated communication are making communication possible for individuals with autism and other disabilities. Doing assistive-devices research in ways that support the values of the independent-living movement will ensure that these supports are done within the spirit of the new paradigm (Blanck, Ritchie, Schmeling, & Klein, 2003).

All these trends reflect what has become known as the new paradigm. Accordingly, these values are beginning to inform the way the disability movement and social policy interpret disability within a leisure context. A thorough summary and analysis of this period can be found in the *Journal of Leisurability*'s celebration of 25 years (Hutchison, 2000; McGill, 2000).

Outstanding Issues on Leisure and Disability

> We've arrived! With fanfares of fireworks circling the globe, electronically bringing cultures and humanity together like never before, we've entered a new century and a new millennium. It's our chance to create a universe of communities where people with "differences" can truly belong. (King, 2000, p. 3)

"We've come a long way baby, but we still have a way to go," seems to be the message of Audrey King, Canadian consumer author, advocate, and speaker. Realizing all the components of the new inclusion paradigm is a slow process. Progress has been made, but challenges remain. What are those challenges and what contribution does recreation and leisure need to make in addressing these constraints? This chapter began with a discussion about social construction as a framework for understanding the past and present and will end with a challenging question:

> Should social construction continue to be the framework for future agendas? To begin, you could ask the question "What leisure constraints for people with disabilities do you witness today in your community?"

Donning a lens of inclusion and taking a close look around any given community's citizenry with disabilities reveals the many constraints and struggles that people have to overcome to live fully in the inclusive paradigm. Far too many people are unemployed or underemployed, working in sheltered work or part-time employment. Many people with disabilities still rely primarily on disability pensions. What this means is that they are living at the poverty level, which in turn means that their leisure constraints are intricately linked to economic constraints. They cannot afford a YMCA membership or a week's holiday in Mexico, as many of the general public can, or to have a car which might provide expanded leisure options. Many people still have a large percentage of their lives in a service paradigm, making it impossible to have a voice, or to experience empowerment and full citizenship; and many people still have weak social networks, of which many recreation providers still neglect to see within their mandate. Finally, many people with disabilities are participating in so-called "inclusive recreation pursuits"; however, the degree to which these go beyond integration and contribute to stronger social networks, capacity building, and empowerment are questionable. At the same time, it is also possible to see many examples of people, projects, and programs which are clearly making progress in the new paradigm.

It is no wonder that this quick survey of people's lives has painted a picture of mixed blessing in the lives of people with disabilities. In some ways, the use of social construction in leisure and recreation is just beginning, which might explain why we still have so far to go. For example, leisure studies using the concept of social construction and inclusion only first appeared in the late 1990s (Devine, 1997). This work, carried out by Mary Ann Devine and her colleagues, continues today bringing the inclusion lens to the recreation field through studying social construction of disability, inclusion, social acceptance in leisure environments, and constraints to inclusive leisure (Devine, 2003/2004; Devine, 2004; Devine & Dattilo, 2001; Devine & Lashua, 2002). All of this work reflects an assumption that reconstruction of our concept of disability lies in our ability to create an inclusive society and that many challenges still remain.

The new paradigm talks about empowerment and full participation. Research on empowerment of people with disabilities began to appear in research and dialogue in the 1990s (Friedmann, 1992; Labonte, 1996). To narrow the gap between what we know about the new paradigm and what currently exists, a stronger oppression analysis will be needed to frame disability issues. Empowerment refers to the process that people who have been devalued go through to gain or regain the power and control over their lives, which is necessary for dignity and self-determination. Sometimes oppression has been framed in terms of dominating groups (those with power), subordinated groups (those without power), historical reinforcers (root cause), and change movements as forms of resistance (Carniol, 1995). Oppression theory and empowerment research together contribute to the idea that people with disabilities can resist compliance and segregation and work toward full participation. Empowerment work that best contributes to a new paradigm, however, builds on oppression and empowerment theory but includes the broader concept of participation (Pedlar et al., 1999). Many people with disabilities are participating in our communities; however, they have a long way to go before they can be described as having full participation with a textured life.

A textured life implies that inclusion needs to be understood in its broadest possible sense. Inclusion is about full participation in all aspects of life. Many people in society do not take the recreation and leisure field seriously enough because of our preoccupation with recreation programs rather than a focus on broad inclusion issues such as citizenship. The reality is that citizenship is often based in leisure participation, whether it be neighbourhood association participation, cultural participation, or sports involvement.

The other challenge is that many people in society still do not know the difference between integration and inclusion. The recreation and leisure field needs to do much more about this problem. If we would listen more to the consumer voice in our communities, we would see that people with disabilities know the difference and can best speak to this issue. The recreation field and society in general have not been *really listening* to our many Canadian consumer leaders who are writing, lecturing, and teaching about different aspects of inclusion. There are many such leaders and their message is an important one. Patrick Worth (1999) writes about his own experience with community living, friendships, and leisure. Audrey King (2000) talks about her own and other's experiences with deinstitutionalization. Judith Snow (1994) talks about love, friendship, and inclusion. Catherine Frazee (2003) discusses inclusion, rights, and equality experienced by youth with disabilities. Finally, Kathryn Church (1995) discusses mental health reform, her own personal experience, and the differing voices of consumers and policy-makers. While only the last one, or perhaps two, might be considered as having a social construction theory as the foundation, we can recognize the other authors' voices for what they are—an honest attempt to shift the paradigm.

These contributions of consumer leaders raise the whole question of the role of people with disabilities in providing leadership that might further assist in the shift to the new inclusion paradigm (Powers, Ward, Ferris, Nelis, Ward, Wieck,

Judith Snow: Leader, Mentor, and Conscience

In 1983, the first documented support circle was about the life of Judith Snow and her "Joshua Committee." At the time, Judith, a woman who is a quadriplegic, was living in a chronic-care hospital, ready to die due to loneliness, frustration, and malnutrition. A Toronto professor, Dr. Marsha Forest, visiting with her students, met Judith and immediately developed a bond. It took some time, but a circle of friends was developed around Judith. Soon the group had secured funding from an Order in Council to get her out of the hospital and living in her own place. Judith has fulfilled many of her dreams since that time, including completing a Master's degree in psychology, getting married, working, and teaching people about the importance of friends and circles. Most importantly, Judith has been a leader in the inclusive field, a mentor for others with and without disabilities, and a conscience for our often unwelcoming society. (Forest & Snow, 1983; Lord & Hutchison, 1998)

et al., 2002). Much of the leadership that we see coming from people with disabilities is most noticeable through their contribution in consumer disability organizations such as the Council of Canadians with Disabilities, People First of Canada, and the National Network on Mental Health (Hutchison et al., 2000). However, we have to ask ourselves whether the model of "consumers as leaders" is filtering down to the recreation field. None of the consumer authors noted earlier is in the leisure studies field and there is no leisure literature which is looking at this—which might provide a clear indication as to where the inclusion paradigm work might go next.

In the leisure context, this might mean people with disabilities as leaders in inclusive recreation policy-making, program development, and research. Currently, people with disabilities are providing leadership through consumer disability social movements (Enns & Neufeldt, 2003). It might be useful for the field of recreation and leisure to forge more partnerships with these movements. For example, the Active Living Alliance for Persons with Disabilities has a partnership with the Canadian Association for Independent Living Centres. Both of these organizations focus on participation and inclusion. If recreation and leisure practitioners could see themselves as a movement for change, they might have the vision of working with other broader social movements for change.

Listening to consumers and promoting consumers as leaders might also help us address another issue that has plagued our field for years and limited inclusion. The controversy about what to do about our many *special* programs, like Special Olympics (Storey, 2004) will take on a new light. Some suggest getting rid of them because thousands (millions in the United States) of people attending segregated programs distracts from the momentum that people with disabilities need to move fully to the new paradigm (Giangreco, 1996). There may be some merit to this argument. For example, Claire Tregaskis (2004), a consumer researcher from Britain, has been studying the interface between people with and without disabilities at Greenways Leisure Centre to learn more about construction of disability, inclusion, and leisure and how to move more fully inside the new paradigm. Tregaskis's (2004) insightful work suggests that people in segregated community programs at her centre remain the objects of negative stereotypes and do not benefit from being treated "in an ordinary way" as did people with disabilities who were integrated.

In conclusion, the challenge for the future is to continue to dialogue with people with disabilities, build positive partnerships in all areas of society, create welcoming settings in all parts of society, and work with others to continue to reconstruct our views and concepts of difference.

Key Terms

Devaluation
Disability
Handicap
Impairment
Inclusion
Institutionalization
Integration
Labelling
Medical model
Perceptions
Social construction
Social movements

References

Berger, P. L., & Luckmann, T. (1966). *The social construction of reality: A treatise in the sociology of knowledge.* Garden City, NJ: Doubleday.

Blanck, P., Ritchie, H., Schmeling, J., & Klein, D. (2003). Technology for independence: A community-based resource centre. *Behavioral Sciences & The Law, 21*(1), 51–62.

Bullock, C., & Mahon, C. (2000). *Introduction to recreation services for people with disabilities: A person-centred approach* (2nd ed.). Champaign, IL: Sagamore.

Carniol, B. (1995). *Case critical: Challenging social services in Canada* (3rd ed.) Toronto, ON: Between the Lines.

Church, K. (1995). *Forbidden narratives: Critical autobiography as social science.* Luxembourg, Germany: Gorden and Breach.

Devine, M. A. (1997). Inclusive leisure services and research: A consideration of the use of social construction theory. *Journal of Leisurability, 24*(2), 3–11.

Devine, M. A. (2003/2004). Constraining and freeing: The meaning of inclusive leisure experiences for individuals with disabilities. *Leisure/Loisir, 28*(1–2), 27–48.

Devine, M. A. (2004). "Being a 'doer' instead of a 'viewer'": The role of inclusive leisure contexts in determining social acceptance for people with disabilities. *Journal of Leisure Research, 36*(2), 137–159.

Devine, M. A., & Dattilo, J. (2001). Social acceptance and leisure lifestyles of people with disabilities. *Therapeutic Recreation Journal, 3*(4), 306–322.

Devine, M. A., & Lashua, B. (2002). Constructing social acceptance in inclusive leisure contexts: The role of individuals with disabilities. *Therapeutic Recreation Journal, 36*, 65–83.

Douglas, J. D. (1970). Understanding everyday life. In J. D. Douglas (Ed.), *Understanding everyday life: Toward the reconstruction of sociological knowledge* (pp. 3–43). Chicago, IL: Aldine.

Dybwad, R. (1990). *Perspectives on a parent movement: The revolt of parents of children with intellectual impairments.* Cambridge, MA: Brookline.

Enns, H., & Neufeldt, A. (2003). *In pursuit of equal participation: Canada and disability at home and abroad.* Calgary, AB: Captus.

Flynn, R. & Nitsch, K. (Eds.). (1980). *Normalization, social integration and community services.* Baltimore, MD: University Park Press.

Forest, M., & Snow, J. (1983). "The Joshua Committee": An advocacy model. *Journal of Leisurability, 10*(1), 20–23.

Frazee, C. (2003). *Thumbs up! Inclusion, rights and equality as experienced by youth with disabilities.* Toronto, ON: The Laidlaw Foundation.

Friedmann, J. (1992). *Empowerment: The politics of alternative development.* Cambridge, MA: Blackwell.

Giangreco, M. (1996). "The stairs didn't go anywhere!" A self-advocate's reflections on specialized services and their impact on people with disabilities. *Physical Disabilities: Education and Related Services, 14*(2), 1–12.

Goffman, I. (1961). *Asylums.* Garden City, NJ: Anchor and Doubleday.

Hawkins, B. (1997). Promoting quality of life through recreation and leisure. In R. L. Schalock & G. N. Siperstein (Eds.), *Quality of life, vol. II: Application to persons with disabilities* (pp. 117–129). Washington, DC: AAMR.

Hayden, M. F., Soulen, T., Schleien, S. J., & Tabourne, C. E. (1996). A matched, comparative study of the recreation integration of adults with mental retardation who moved into the community and those who remained at the institution. *Therapeutic Recreation Journal, 30*(1), 41–63.

Heyne, L., Schleien, S., & McAvoy, L. (1993). *Making friends: Using recreation activities to promote friendship between children with and without disabilities.* Minneapolis, MN: Institute on Community Integration, University of Minnesota.

Hutchison, P. (1990). *Making friends: Developing relationships between people with a disability and other members of the community.* Toronto, ON: G. Allan Roeher Institute.

Hutchison, P. (2000). The evolution of integration research: Celebrating 25 years of the *Journal of Leisurability. Journal of Leisurability, 27*(4), 32–43.

Hutchison, P., & Lord, J. (1979). *Recreation integration: Issues and alternatives in leisure services and community involvement.* Toronto, ON: Leisurability.

Hutchison, P., & McGill, J. (1998). *Leisure, integration and community* (2nd ed.). Toronto, ON: Leisurability.

Hutchison, P., Pedlar, A., Dunn, P., Lord, J., & Arai, S. (2000). Canadian Independent Living Centres: Impact on the community. *International Journal of Rehabilitation Research, 23*(2), 61–74.

Hutchison, P., & Potschaske, C. (1998). Social change and institutions: Implications for recreationists. *Therapeutic Recreation Journal, 32*(2), 130–156.

King, A. (2000). From institutionalization to community: How far have we come? *Journal of Leisurability, 27*(1), 3–9.

Kretzmann, J., & McKnight, J. (1993). *Building communities from the inside out: A path towards finding and mobilizing a community's assets.* Chicago, IL: ACTA.

Labonte, R. (1996). Community empowerment and leisure. *Journal of Leisurability, 23*(1), 4–20.

Liverton, J. (2000). Computer game play as a potential catalyst for the social integration of people with high physical support needs. *Journal of Leisurability, 27*(2), 35–44.

Lord, J., & Hutchison, P. (1998). *Living with a disability in Canada: Toward autonomy and integration. Determinants of health: Settings and issues.* Papers commissioned by the National Forum on Health (pp. 375–431). Ottawa, ON: Les Editions MultiMondes.

Lord, J., & Hutchison, P. (2003). Individualised support and funding: Building blocks for capacity building and inclusion. *Disability and Society, 18*(1), 71–86.

McGill, J. (2000). A retrospective: Twenty-five years of practice in the field of leisure and persons with disabilities. *Journal of Leisurability, 27*(4), 9–31.

McNeil, J. M. (1993). *Americans with Disabilities, 1991/92: Data from the survey of income and program participation.* Washington, DC: US Dept. of Commerce, Economics, and Statistics Administration, Bureau of the Census.

O'Brien, J., & O'Brien, C. L. (1991). *More than just a new address: Images of organizations for supported living agencies.* Lithonia, GA: Responsive Systems Associates.

Pedlar, A., Haworth, L., Hutchison, P., Taylor, A., & Dunn, P. (1999). *A textured life: Empowerment and adults with developmental disabilities.* Waterloo, ON: Wilfrid Laurier University Press.

Pedlar, A., & Hutchison, P. (2000). Restructuring human services in Canada: Commodification of disability. *Disability and Society, 15*(4), 637–651.

Powers, L. E., Ward, N., Ferris, L., Nelis, T., Ward, M., Wieck, C., & Heller, T. (2002). Leadership by people with disabilities in self-determination systems change. *Journal of Disability Policy Studies, 13*(2), 125–133.

Schleien, S., Green, F., & Stone, C. (1999). Making friends within inclusive recreation programs. *Journal of Leisurability, 26*(3), 33–43.

Sciberras, J., & Hutchison, P. (2003). Close friendships of integrated youth: Parents as partners, *Leisure/Loisir, 28*(1/2), 87–114, DOI: 10.1080/14927713.2003.9649941

Sciberras, J., & Hutchison, P. (2004). Friendships of youth with disabilities: Parents as partners. *Leisure/Loisir, 28*(1/2), 87–114.

Simmons, H. G. (1982). *Asylums to welfare*. Toronto, ON: National Institute on Mental Retardation.

Snow, J. (1994). *What's really worth doing and how to do it: A book for people who love someone labeled disabled (possibly yourself)*. Toronto, ON: Inclusion Press.

Statistics Canada. (2003). *A profile of disability in Canada*. Ottawa, ON: Human Resources Development Canada.

Storey, K. (2004). The case against the Special Olympics. *Journal of Disability Policy Studies, 15*(1), 35–42(8).

Tregaskis, C. (2004). *Constructions of disability: Researching the interface between disabled and non-disabled people*. London, UK: Routledge.

Walker, P. (1999). From community presence to sense of place: Community experiences of adults with developmental disabilities. *Journal of the Association for Persons with Severe Handicaps, 24*(1), 23–32.

Weiss, P., Bialik, P., & Kizony, R. (2003). Virtual reality provides leisure time opportunities for young adults with physical and intellectual disabilities. *Cyber Psychology & Behavior, 6*(3), 335–342.

Wolfensberger, W. (1980). In R. J. Flynn & K. E. Nitsch (Eds.), *Normalization, social integration, and community services* (pp. 7–30, 71–115, 117–129). Baltimore, MD: University Park Press.

Wolfensberger, W., & Thomas, S. (1983). *PASSING (Program analysis of service systems' implementation of normalization goals: Normalization criteria and ratings manual)* (2nd ed.). Toronto, ON: National Institute on Mental Retardation.

Worth, P. (1999). Friends make a difference. *Journal of Leisurability, 26*(3), 3–9.

Zoerink, D. A., & Rosegard, E. J. (1997). Social justice through inclusive leisure services. In D. M. Compton (Ed.), *Issues in therapeutic recreation: Toward the new millennium* (pp. 17–37, 2nd ed.). Champaign, IL: Sagamore.

Chapter 26
Social Class, Poverty, and Leisure

Heather Mair, Ph.D.
University of Waterloo

Learning objectives

After reading this chapter, students will be able to

1. Understand the concepts of social class and poverty with the Canadian context.
2. Appreciate how issues of social class and poverty are important for understanding all aspects of leisure, from issues of diversity to programming and management.
3. Be able to apply the concepts of social class and poverty to the study of leisure.
4. Understand that much research still needs to be done in the area of leisure and social class and poverty in order to enhance our understanding of the impact of these issues and to improve practice.

Introduction

We tend to use the word "class" as a way of locating people or things within larger groups. For instance, you may think of *class* as the group of students with whom you attend the lectures for this course or as a way of organizing biological classifications. We may even think of those with an elegant sense of style as being "classy" as compared to others in society. This chapter focuses, in particular, on *social class*. Social class represents any important means of expressing distinctions within society. This chapter will help clarify some of the confusion that might exist around discussions of social class and suggest why it is an important notion for our study of leisure.

This chapter also introduces the concept of poverty. Like "class," the term "poverty" is also used in many ways. Typically it generates images of having no income or wealth. When we think of poverty is this way, we may even think about it as being a condition that exists in other parts of the world but not here in Canada or North America. This is certainly a perception that will be addressed in this chapter. We also use the term "poverty" to denote a lack of something besides income, such as resources or opportunity to access power, education, or even leisure services. These issues are all central to any discussion of poverty in Canada. In this chapter, we'll be linking social class, poverty, and the study of leisure. Before getting started, it is important to get a recent picture of social class and poverty here in Canada.

A Picture Of Canadian Poverty

While poverty rates have been declining in this country, there are still significant and persistent problems as millions are poor and hundreds of thousands of Canadians are living on incomes that cannot bring them out of poverty. The National Council of Welfare (2010a) argues the gap in average incomes between the rich and poor is *increasing*, and in 2007, "the average after-tax income was $13,900 for the poorest 20% of families and $126,700 for the richest 20%—a difference of $112,800." Moreover, women continue to have consistently higher poverty rates than men, especially if they are unmarried or are single parents. Women over 65 are also nearly twice as likely as men to live in poverty. Child poverty in Canada is also a serious and growing concern. While the Canadian government passed a resolution to end child poverty by 2000, the rates continue to increase. Access to employment, of course, offers some relief for those living in poverty but low-waged employment, especially where only one person is working in a household, can also mean poverty for some families. Further, as the National Council of Welfare has shown, even families where a member is employed full time can still be living below the poverty line (NCW, 2010b). We'll talk more about poverty and how it is measured in Canada a little later in the chapter.

What Do We Mean By Social Class?

Max Weber, a preeminent sociologist who lived between 1864 and 1920, developed some of the most influential and long-lasting ideas about social class and the components that create it. He suggested that people could be grouped into a specific social class when there were similarities in their ability to access resources such as food, clothing, shelter, education. He wrote about the similar interests and lifestyles that sprung from their class grouping in this way. He described a *hierarchy* (a series of ordered groupings) of class groups in the following way:

- upper or capitalist class
- upper-middle class
- middle class
- working class
- working poor
- underclass

You can see that we still use much of this terminology today. While issues of distinguishing between classes in society are sometimes subtle and even unsettling to some, it is important to consider that there are many ways to think about these social divisions. For instance, some people may think of society as having essentially two classes—the "haves" and the "have-nots"; others may divide society into "lower-," "middle-," and "upper-" class citizens. You may hear people refer to "the professional class" or "the working class," and there is even a book by Richard Florida called *The Rise of the Creative Class* (2003).

For sociologists, social class is a very useful way of thinking about how people live and act in the world because it highlights issues of social status and power. It draws our attention to hierarchy, as some classes have more wealth and power than others and therefore have a different level of social status than others in society, not to mention a different style of living and leisure interests.

One of the ways to measure or define social class is by dividing society into groups based upon *socioeconomic status*. This allows us to see where the majority of people fit into society and to make general assumptions about their leisure practices and needs. While socioeconomic status is generally determined by a person's occupation, level of education and income, there are other components that come into play. For instance, some components that may be considered as important to our definition of social class include:

- what a person does for a living
- his or her level of education
- income level
- reputation or status
- possessions such as property
- family history

It is clear that these components are related. For example, the higher a person's level of education, the more likely she or he is to have a job that pays a high level of income and that holds high standing in society.

Raymond Williams (1983) noted that while there have been a wide variety of meanings of social class over time, the way we think about this idea today (i.e., in the sense of socioeconomic divisions) began with the Industrial Revolution, particularly in Britain (1770 to 1840), when there were great divisions within society in relation to how we produced material goods (that is, divisions between the factory owners and the labourers working in the factories). As the Industrial Revolution continued and greater numbers of workers became labourers in the factories, the relationships between social classes became very clearly demarcated. Moreover, members of this growing industrial society became increasingly conscious of their social position. Instead of land and property, once a primary determinant of class, social power and status were determined by what jobs, income and even how much free or leisure time one possessed. Thus, while social class may often be defined by socioeconomic status, its social meanings and how it influences leisure choice, behaviour, and access are probably the most interesting for those who study leisure.

Is everyone equal? Can you tell the social class of someone just by how they dress or their mode of transportation? What about their choice of leisure activity?

Why Are Issues of Social Class Important To Our Study of Leisure?

In his famous book, *The Theory of the Leisure Class*, Thorstein Veblen (1899) argued that the upper classes were in fact the only classes who could truly have leisure. Even further, Veblen argued that the lower classes sought to emulate or copy the upper classes by pursuing upper-class leisure activities in order to gain status. By introducing the terms *conspicuous consumption* and *conspicuous leisure*, Veblen argued that leisure was a way for members of society to distinguish themselves through their activities. Conspicuous consumption is the deliberate consumption of goods or services as a way to draw others' attention. For example, a person buys an expensive and flashy vehicle in order to suggest wealth and status. Conspicuous leisure, then, is engaging in leisure activities that suggest wealth and status. Examples of high-status leisure activities might include spending a weekend at the spa or taking a long and expensive holiday to a remote and exotic location. Instead of defining leisure as freedom from obligation (as did many of the authors writing during Veblen's time), this economist-turned-social-critic drew attention to the social meanings of leisure and their role in conveying class status. In Veblen's writing, then, we are encouraged to think about leisure as a way of signifying social class in that leisure choices can convey taste, difference and status. Related to these ideas, French sociologist Pierre Bourdieu developed the notion of distinction. In his book, *Distinction: A Social Critique of the Judgement of Taste* (1984), Bourdieu argued that social meanings were attached to the ways that members of society try to distinguish themselves from one another. In short, people sought to enhance their social position by expressing expensive and refined tastes in everything from goods (think of the flashy car example noted above) to food, wine, and cultural activities.

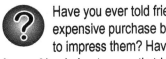

Have you ever told friends about a trip or an expensive purchase because you were hoping to impress them? Have you ever heard a story from a friend about an exotic trip and felt envious or impressed by their tale?

What Is Poverty?

As with concerns about how to define and understand social class, the notion of poverty is also not as straightforward as it might seem. Poverty is generally thought of as the absence of access to something essential—either in material form (such as food or clothing) or in service form (such as health care or education). Economists and sociologists use the terms *relative poverty* and *absolute poverty* in order to distinguish between those who have less or more than those around them and those who have absolutely nothing. Absolute poverty occurs when people are not receiving enough resources to support and maintain their physical health over time. This includes living in a safe place and having access to adequate nutrition. The notion of relative poverty refers more to the social context and can vary over time and in different places.

Measuring Low Income and Poverty in Canada: Two Main Approaches

The National Council of Welfare (2001–2002) and many other groups concerned with issues of poverty and low income in Canada frequently use two measures for determining who is living in poverty in this country. The *low-income cut-off* or *LICO* is the official, Statistics Canada measure of poverty. Generally, LICOs mark income levels where people have to spend disproportionate amounts of their incomes on food, shelter, and clothing. For example, if a family spends more than 20% of its income on these three necessities, then it is considered to be near the low income cut-off point. It should be noted that because it is more expensive to live in some places than others, LICOs are very complicated measures and take into account the geographical location of the families being studied. The *market basket approach* estimates the cost of a specific "basket" of goods and services that are required to reach a minimum standard of living. As with the LICO, the market basket approach tries to take into account the varying cost of goods and services in communities across the country. While many people argue about the utility of these measures, they are often used to get a sense of poverty in Canada.

Understanding the Causes of Poverty

When we talk about poverty, we often discuss its causes. Like definitions of poverty, its causes are also wide-ranging and varied and are not always universally agreed upon by researchers and policymakers. Some of the more frequently cited causes of poverty include the following:

- *individual, or "pathological" causes*: poverty as the result of the behaviour, choices, or abilities;
- *familial causes*: poverty is a result of family history or upbringing;
- *agency causes*: poverty as the result of the actions of others, including war, government, and the economy;
- *structural causes*: poverty is the result of not having access to power and resources in society.

Read through this list of "causes" of poverty. Which make sense to you? Why? Is there a factor that you can think of that is not on this list? As noted above, the National Council of Welfare notes that gender may be an important factor when considering poverty and low-income status. Where do you think gender falls in the list of causes above? For example, is it a structural issue? Why or why not?

Why Are Issues of Poverty Important To Our Study of Leisure?

In 1970, the World Recreation and Leisure Association declared that leisure was a *basic human right*, regardless of one's economic, educational, or employment situation. To this end, leisure researchers and leisure service providers feel a sense of obligation to be aware of and attendant to, issues of equality when considering access to leisure opportunities. This means understanding the impact of both social class and poverty upon leisure choices and opportunities.

As Dawson writes:

> Sometimes we forget that our recreation service delivery system emerged in large measure out of the recognition that leisure is a *right for all citizens*, not just for a privileged few from the wealthy "leisure class." (Dawson, 2000, p. 100; emphasis added)

One important aspect of poverty is its impact upon a person's social life. For the most part, when we consider issues of poverty and social class, we need to be aware of the impact of *social exclusion* and *marginalization*. As leisure has a strong social component, being socially excluded or marginalized means, literally, that one has no or limited opportunities to participate in the leisure activities of mainstream society. In many cases, people are unable to take part in many common leisure activities in society such as sports or cultural activities because they lack the time or the financial resources to participate. Social exclusion and marginalization are notions that describe the impact of being poor or living in poverty and, unfortunately, are part and parcel with concerns about access to leisure activities in Canada. As the National Council of Welfare (2001–2002) notes:

> poverty can also mean loneliness and exclusion from sports, recreation, culture and other activities around which individual confidence, friendships and other positive social relationships are built. For children especially, this can have long-lasting effects. (p. 4)

For children living in poverty, social exclusion is a serious concern. As the Canadian Parks and Recreation Association notes:

> 1.1 million or 1 in 6 children in Canada live in poverty and research shows that children in low-income families are far less involved in sport, cultural and recreational pursuits than in families with average and above average incomes. (2011)

These places are all important areas, especially for children. This is where they can interact, develop skills, and play with other kids while feeling part of the wider community. Related to this is the notion of *social stigma* as people who do not have much money may feel that other members of society are judging them because of their financial situation. This may lead them to feel uncomfortable in social settings

Focus on a leisure researcher: Dr. Don Dawson and the 'democratization' of leisure

Dr. Don Dawson is a Canadian researcher whose provocative work on social class and the challenges it presents to the provision of leisure services, while undertaken a while ago, stands the test of time as it set the stage for research in this area. He described not only the need to be aware of differential access to leisure opportunities that comes from being less wealthy in Canada, he identified some ways that we could meet what he called "the opportunities and obligations of the recreation profession" (Dawson, 2000, p. 106). In short, Professor Dawson identified five major components to be considered to meet this obligation and opportunity:

1. *Undertaking ongoing and routine needs assessment:* finding out what the particular needs are of low income groups and those living in poverty as well as building trust relationships.
2. *Having a commitment to long-term political change:* meeting the needs of the poor is not a one-time exercise but should be part of a long-term commitment to help change their situation.
3. *Providing sufficient resources (people, time, and money)*: providing affordable access to services such as transportation, equipment, and programs.
4. *Increasing knowledge and awareness:* making sure that leisure providers are aware of members of low-income groups in the community and making sure that the members of these groups are aware of leisure services.
5. *Fostering a sense of ownership:* people are more likely to access programs and services that they feel some connection to, or ownership of, so gathering and implementing the ideas of these groups will foster their involvement and will make for more relevant programs.

Some of his most influential works in this area include:

Dawson, D. (1985). On the analysis of class and leisure. *Loisir et Société/Society and Leisure, 8*(2), 563–572.

Dawson, D. (1986). Unemployment, leisure, and liberal-democratic ideology. *Loisir et Société/Society and Leisure, 9*(1), 165–182.

Dawson, D. (2000). Social class and leisure provision. In M. T. Allison & I. E. Schneider (Eds.), *Diversity and the recreation profession: Organizational perspectives* (pp. 99–114). State College, PA: Venture Publishing, Inc.

Dawson, D., Andrew, C., & Harvey, J. (1991). Leisure, the local state and the welfare state: A theoretical overview. *Loisir et Société/Society and Leisure, 14*(1), 191–217.

Dawson, D., & Harrington, M. (1996). "For the most part, it's not fun and games": Homelessness and recreation. *Loisir et Société/Society and Leisure, 19*(2), 415–435.

and they may be unwilling to participate in activities, even if they are free or affordable.

Now that we have presented a discussion about the definition and impact of social class and poverty in Canada, it is important to consider what this means for the past, current and future study of leisure.

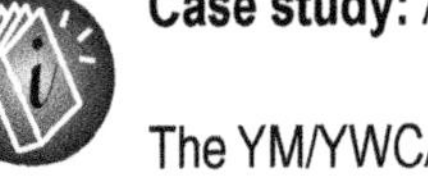

Case study: A question of policy?

The YM/YWCA defines itself as: A charitable association dedicated to the development of people in spirit, mind, and body as well as the improvement of local, national, and international communities. To this end, they have programs available to assist people in lower social classes through a Membership Assistance Program. The program has the following components:

1. [Participants] are unable, not unwilling, to pay the full fee for a general membership.
2. Because memberships are not government funded, the Y needs everyone to pay as much as they can towards the membership fee. No one is denied a Y membership because of an inability to pay, but some decide they are not willing and so do not become Y members.
3. Applicants for Membership Assistance need to make a commitment to use the Y on a regular basis and to pay the agreed portion of the membership fee.
4. All information provided by members is kept confidential. The Y expects the same confidentiality of its assisted members.
5. If a participant is interested in applying for Membership Assistance, a tour of the facility and a confidential interview are held.
6. During the confidential interview, the following is questions are asked: Why you would like to become a member of the YMCA-YWCA? Which programs and services interest you? [What is] the net monthly income for your household from all sources? Applicants are asked to bring monthly income slips, rent/mortgage payment receipts, utility bills and proof of other fixed monthly expenses.

Source: (http://www.ymca.ca)

What do you think about this program? Can you see a reason why a potential participant who cannot afford membership would be uncomfortable with this interview process?

What Do Students of Leisure Know about Social Class and Poverty?

Issues of poverty and social class, while not frequently studied, are important to our understanding of leisure because they speak to concerns about equality, equity, and access. Early research into the relationship between leisure and social class considered differences in leisure and other behaviours. William G. Mather published a study in 1941 that investigated the relationship between income and "social participation" as defined by membership in social groups, church groups, political and other cultural organizations. He found that membership and involvement in these groups was extremely limited for those in the lower classes (defined in his article as those earning under $100 [U.S.] a month). In 1969, Rabel J. Burdge investigated the connection between social-class status and leisure activity and concluded that members of the upper and middle classes were nearly always more likely to participate in leisure activities. Certainly, where income is an important part of leisure pursuits (either through entrance or membership fees or equipment), the ability to participate in leisure activities has generally been thought to be class-dependent.

More recently, researchers investigating the relationship between social class, poverty and leisure have been concerned with whether social class (particularly lower-class status) was a barrier or a limitation to pursuing leisure activities. The Canadian Recreation and Parks Association (2001), for example, looked at the leisure activities of youth in relation to the income of their families. They found that the lower the family income, the less likely a child is to participate in nearly all forms of organized recreation from art, drama, and music, to community groups, organized sports, and youth camp activities (p. 61). Other related research has broadened these questions by considering the relationship between race, gender, and social class within the context of leisure. Kelly (1999) argues that by looking at the relationship between social class and leisure, we can become more aware of the different kinds of leisure expectations and needs of people in different social class groupings. For example, for individuals in lower-class strata, issues of resource availability as well as access to publicly provided environments where leisure activities are taking place may be fundamental concerns. For individuals in other classes, however, more attention might be given to considering the private provision of leisure services. Researchers and leisure service providers, however, must always be aware of the imbalance that exists among classes and what this means for equitable leisure-service provision. Dr. Don Dawson is one of the foremost researchers in this area. Some of his work is described in the *i*-box on p. 246. Trussell and Mair (2010) conducted a project with people living in poverty and experiencing homelessness in the Waterloo Region of Ontario and found that leisure service providers must consider providing "judgment-free spaces" for people who are among the most marginalised and judged in our society. In addition, central to our understanding of leisure, of course, is work. In this way, understanding the leisure opportunities that exist (and those that do not exist) for people who must work long hours, who are unemployed, or who are part of the working poor is essential (See Hilbrecht's chapter on leisure and the changing workplace). Mair, Reid, and Arai's recent book (2010) brings together some of Canada's foremost thinkers on these issues.

For the most part, leisure researchers can do much more to take into account issues of social class and poverty, both in regards to the challenges they present to ideas of constraints to participation, but also to the meanings we attach to leisure activities and what that tells us about ourselves and our changing values.

Chapter Summary

Issues of social class and poverty are important to consider when thinking about leisure as well as Canadian society more generally. This chapter has provided definitions of both social class and poverty while emphasizing that these are complex terms. Further, we suggest the need to continue to work to improve our understanding of these issues. We've discussed how keeping issues of social class and poverty in mind when researching leisure or providing leisure services is essential for meeting the diverse needs of members of different class groups and especially for providing equitable access for those who are marginalized in society. Future research must continue in this area, as the gap between rich and poor in Canada is ever-widening.

Outstanding Issues and Questions

- Do all Canadians, regardless of social class, have a right to leisure? If so, how do we provide for those who cannot access leisure on their own due to financial constraints?
- Despite the declaration by the World Leisure and Recreation Association in 1970 that leisure is a basic human right, notions of poverty do not generally include adequate access to leisure. Why not? Do you think leisure is important enough to be included in definitions of poverty? Why or why not?
- How can we determine whether issues of social stigma are important factors in determining the kinds of leisure that people choose? How might leisure service providers address these issues?

Key Terms

Absolute poverty
Conspicuous consumption
Conspicuous leisure
Relative poverty
Social stigma
Socioeconomic status

References

Burdge, R. J. (1969). Levels of occupational prestige and leisure activity. *Journal of Leisure Research, 1*(3), 262–274.

Bourdieu, P. (1984). *Distinction: A social critique of the judgment of taste.* Cambridge, MA: Harvard University Press.

Canadian Recreation and Parks Association (2011). Everybody gets to play. Retrieved from http://www.everybodygetstoplay.ca

Campaign 2000—End child poverty in Canada. Retrieved from http://www.campaign2000.ca/

Dawson, D. (2000). Social class and leisure provision. In M. T. Allison & I. E. Schneider (Eds.), *Diversity and the recreation profession: Organizational perspectives* (pp. 99–114). State College, PA: Venture Publishing, Inc.

Florida, R. (2003). *The rise of the creative class.* New York, NY: Basic.

Kelly, J. R. (1999). Leisure and society: A dialectical analysis. In E. L. Jackson & T. L. Burton (Eds.). *Leisure studies: Prospects for the twenty-first century* (pp. 53–68). State College, PA: Venture Publishing, Inc.

Mair, H., Arai, S. M., & Reid, D. G. (Eds.). (2010). *Decentring work: Critical perspectives on leisure, social policy, and human development.* Calgary, AB: University of Calgary Press.

Mather, W. G. (1941). Income and social participation. *American Sociological Review, (6)*3, 380–383.

National Council of Welfare (NCW). (2001–2002) The cost of Poverty. Volume 115 [Data retrieved from http://publications.gc.ca/collections/collection_2011/cnbncw/H68-53-2002-eng.pdf

National Council of Welfare (NCW). (2010a). *Poverty Profile 2007: Bulletin No. 10, Income inequality.* Retrieved from http://www.ncw.gc.ca

National Council on Welfare (NCW). (2010b). *Poverty Profile 2007: Bulletin No. 7, Poverty and paid work.* Retrieved from http://www.ncw.gc.ca

Trussell, D. E., & Mair, H. (2010). Seeking judgment-free spaces: Poverty, leisure, and social inclusion. *Journal of Leisure Research, 42*(4), 513–533.

Veblen, T. (1899). *The theory of the leisure class.* Amherst, NY: Prometheus.

Williams, R. (1983). *Keywords.* (revised ed.) New York, NY: Oxford University Press.

PART II: Leisure Delivery in Canada

Section D: Traditional Leisure Delivery

Chapter 27

A History of Leisure Provision in Canada

Susan Markham-Starr, Ph.D.
Acadia University

Elsie McFarland's Statement about Young People

As Canadians move into a leisure-oriented century, young and vigorous leaders will be required in increasing numbers. The young people entering the field of recreation will need considerable faith in themselves and in their profession. Knowledge of earlier development, of the progress that has been made, and of the men and women who made it possible may provide future leaders with roots from which to grow in strength and wisdom to face the challenges that lie ahead (McFarland, 1970, p. 1).

Sanderlin Re: Significant Communications

History is an academic discipline in which people living in a present time seek to understand the significant communications of people in past societies (Sanderlin, 1975, p. 1).

Learning Objectives

After reading this chapter, students will be able to

1. Appreciate the complexity of our field's history.
2. Identify the key advocates for leisure provision in Canada—our heroes.
3. Identify why and how park and recreation services began in their home community.
4. Identify why and how recreation services began in their home province.
5. Identify why and how national parks were established in their home province.

Introduction

The idea of leisure provision is not new to Canadians. After all, the oldest social club in North America, L'Ordre de Bon Temps—The Order of Good Cheer—was founded four centuries ago in 1606 by Samuel de Champlain and his men at Port Royal in what is now Nova Scotia. The purpose of the club was to "improve [the] health and morale" of the men in this French colony (Parks Canada, 2004)—doesn't this sound like leisure? Relatively new to leisure (with barely 120 years of history) is the phenomenon of organized, mandated, legislated leisure provision, often delivered by government agencies. Many students will be either working as leisure service providers in some part of the field or participating in programs offered—this is an opportunity to inquire about an agency with which you have some experience. Why was the agency established? Who were the passionate advocates for it? Who were the heroes in recreation and parks? What arguments convinced the decision makers that this field was worthwhile? Why do certain jobs exist? These are all questions whose answers will help in understanding and appreciating your position and your community.

One of the key figures in the history of leisure provision in Canada is Elsie McFarland. She was not only the first chronicler of Canada's municipal recreation history, she was a passionate advocate for recreation and for recreation education—she was one of the first women to hold a senior government position in recreation (Alberta); she wrote the first comprehensive history of public recreation in Canada; she was one of the first Canadians to achieve a doctoral degree in recreation administration; she was the first woman to be president of the Canadian Parks/Recreation Association; and she was the chair of one of the first university programs in recreation education (University of Alberta). She believed passionately in both the importance of recreation in the community and the need to appreciate the roots of recreation to sustain our beliefs as we work in the field. This chapter is dedicated to her.

The way to find out about and investigate the history of the parks and recreation field is by taking a look at the "significant communications of the time." Through digging for, and inspecting and interpreting memos, letters, reports, legislation, manuscripts, pictures, and maps, attempts are made to understand why our predecessors did what they did as they responded to the social, economic, and political conditions of their day. They were passionate advocates for social reform and for civic enhancement. They saw recreation as a way to improve the conditions for children, youth, and adults. They saw parks as a way to bring breathing spaces into the cities, to make cities more attractive, and to preserve the natural environment. Many of their values were similar to the values in the twenty-first century. Different jargon may be used, and today it may be the benefits of recreation that are discussed (Canadian Parks/Recreation Association, 1997), but the core values are similar.

The field's history is like a huge, multi-dimensional jigsaw puzzle covering the length and breadth of Canada, over several centuries, with many advocates for leisure services. Each piece in the puzzle is unique and represents one part of the field's national history. Each piece can be explained by local and national conditions, and each piece has been affected by the changing social, economic, political, and physical environments (Edginton & Williams, 1978). The next pages will highlight some of the puzzle's pieces and aid in illustrating how they fit into the big picture.

Municipal Parks—Air and Exercise

Today's parks can be traced to the early days of Canada's British colonial past. In St. John's, Newfoundland, the Garden "was used as a public space by 1583. It was full of wild roses, strawberries, and other fruits" (Wright, 1983, p. 55). Later, the Common was established in Halifax in 1763, but not purely for park purposes. While that Common has been called "Canada's First Park" (Markham & Edginton, 1979), it was actually established to be "a perpetual common for pasturage for the sole use and benefit of the... inhabitants" of Halifax (Lawrence, 1760)—it was a pasture, not a park. Many of our parks began for very utilitarian purposes such as military reserves, battle sites, cemeteries, quarries, or landfills.

Parks, as they are thought of today—land set aside primarily for public recreation purposes—began in Canada in the 19th century. Advocates of these parks hoped that they would improve many negative conditions in cities: conditions that were overwhelmingly evident in British cities but not yet in Canada. The statement made in 1859 by the Chairman of Toronto's Committee on Public Walks and Gardens is an eloquent example of just such hopes, declaring that parks were an inestimable blessing of incalculable advantage, an inspiration, and that they would improve the condition of all (cited in McFarland, 1970, p. 14). What were these blessings, these advantages, these improvements? The Eloquent Orations *i*-box shows examples of what they might be—at least in the minds of their staunch advocates.

The eloquent statements that follow were made by people who fervently hoped that parks and playgrounds would improve all conditions in the city—from the physical and mental health of individuals, to the social welfare of groups, to the physical and economic well-being of the city. Most of the examples cited in the text box focus on the "health" benefits of parks; but, what of the supposed "economic" benefits of parks? Civic boosters often promoted establishing and developing parks as a way to increase the wealth of the city. For example, in Halifax in 1864, the Committee of Common recommended that the Common be developed as a park and pleasure ground, not only "as it would add materially to the health and comfort of our residents," but also as it would add to "the prosperity of our city" (Halifax Committee of Common, 1864, p. 38). More of the Committee's ideas about economic prosperity are shown in the *i*-box about civic boosterism in Halifax. Decades later, in 1911, Winnipeg politicians were urged to improve "health conditions by providing boulevards, parks and other breathing spaces. These in turn attract strangers to the city and accordingly the city prospers" ("City planning," June 10, 1911).

Eloquent Orations

- Parks were to be "the lungs of the city" (claimed by many authors).
- Parks and playgrounds would "develop the child physically, intellectually, and morally" (Brown & Hughes, 1910, p. 72).
- Parks would provide examples of "rational enjoyment" while encouraging "vigorous exercise" for "physical development and health" in the interests of national defence (Kelso, 1908, pp. 181–183).
- Playgrounds would provide the opportunity to "grow character" and prevent juvenile delinquency (Riis, 1913, pp. 273–274).
- "Recreation facilities pay ample dividends in humanity by promoting the health and happiness of the people" (Harkin, 1914).

Civic Boosterism in Halifax

In every city where there are parks and pleasure grounds for promenading, it also makes an attraction for strangers and frequently induces gentlemen of skill and capital to come and settle... to establish manufactories and... build handsome residences... give employment... and their capital will circulate through the whole community and be likewise the means of increasing the population (Halifax Committee of Common, 1864, p. 40).

The rhetoric of the civic boosters defies any time period boundaries. For example, on April 14, 1983, the *Edmonton Journal* ran an article referring to downtown beautification entitled, "City Too Ugly to Attract Firms" in which an alderman made the comment, "One of the reasons we are losing [white-collar firms] is that I don't think we have a city of enough attractions with which to compete. What attracts these people is the quality of life in a city."

The attractions to which the alderman referred included the parks. A survey of any contemporary local newspaper will yield more examples, often related to major sport or cultural facilities or downtown redevelopment.

Nineteenth-century "parks and pleasure grounds" were often modelled on formal English gardens. Parks were for promenading, strolling, sitting, looking at horticultural displays, listening to band concerts, and various genteel activities such as tennis that were not vigorous or physically active. While "recreation use" was part of the rationale for most parks, active use was discouraged by park managers. In addition to the formal, manicured parks, several cities conserved part of their natural environment in parks. Examples of this that have withstood most encroachments over the century are Stanley Park in Vancouver, Mt. Royal Park in Montréal and Point Pleasant Park in Halifax.

As Canadian cities progressed through the twentieth century, each was subject to the influences from the social, economic, and political environment. Some influences were countrywide, but some were unique to their particular locales. For example, cities on the Prairies grew dramatically in physical size and in population before World War I. Each of these cities competed intensely to emulate the major metropolises of the east and to attract settlers and institutions. Each city's decision makers permitted their land bases and services to expand substantially. After a pre-war depression, the war, and a slow post-war recovery, each city found itself holding a large supply of land forfeited due to property taxes not being paid—land that was now a valuable resource. When each city became committed to the idea that it needed parks and playgrounds, it designated part of these lands for such purposes. The challenge of the recession became the opportunity of the 1920s (Markham, 1991).

Cities in Eastern Canada and in British Columbia did not experience the dramatic cycles of boom and bust like those in the Prairies during the early part of the century; however, Canadian cities were all subject to the effects of the economic depression of the 1930s. The Depression led to dramatic reductions in revenues for the cities that could have resulted in the elimination of park and recreation services. There were incidents, however, where recreation and park services actually grew because of the recognized need to provide leisure opportunities or work for the unemployed. The BC Pro-Rec Movement (and its spin-offs) is just one example of this, and it will be discussed later in relation to the development of recreation services. Among the programs funded by the Federal Government as part of its "make work" efforts was a relief project program that several cities used to build recreation and park facilities. Most notable among these relief projects was the work done in Montréal,which employed over a thousand men, in the construction of recreation facilities such as a beach and swimming pool on St. Helen's Island, Beaver Lake in Mt. Royal Park, and roads in both parks (McFarland, 1970, p. 48). Thus, while the country was suffering through the Depression, some cities were able to add to their recreation infrastructure at minimal cost to that city.

After the Depression and World War II, post-war population growth—the baby boom—led to considerable pressure for leisure services. These pressures included increased demand for parks and recreation services in the 1960s, increased awareness of matters related to the physical environment in the 1970s and 80s, followed by dramatic fiscal restraints imposed as North America's economic recession forced cutbacks in public sector services in the 1980s and early 1990s. These cutbacks have come in many forms including: reductions in transfer grants from the provincial to the municipal levels of government; reductions in base-level services provided to the public; increased fees to provide revenue to fund recreation services; and the downgrading of recreation and park programs from municipal government to local community volunteer groups without the commensurate financial support to operate these programs. Understanding the history of each of your communities can help you to understand and appreciate the state of the leisure services that exists today.

Discover Your Community's Park and Recreation History I

1. What is the oldest park in your home community?
2. When was it established?
3. Why was it established?
4. Were there civic boosters in your community?
5. What recreation uses have been developed in that park?
6. Who donated land for parks in your community?
7. Who were the advocates for parks in your community?
8. How has your community dealt with fiscal restraint? of restructuring? of downgrading?
9. How has your community dealt with the challenges and opportunities that it has faced?
10. How has it responded to changes in the social, economic, political, and physical environment?

Municipal Recreation—Beginning with Vacation Schools

The National Council of Women of Canada (NCW) is an umbrella organization for a collection of groups advocating social reform. The NCW became involved in leisure provision in 1901 when it became the national advocate promoting supervised playgrounds. The motion that led the NCW into its lengthy commitment to recreation called on them to lead the campaign for playgrounds—in the language of the day the motion was termed, "Vacation School and Playgrounds." The following *i*-box shows the complete 1901 motion.

National Council of Women's 1901 Motion

Whereas the agitation for Vacation Schools and Playgrounds where children may find organized recreation having become so wide-spread that it is now known as the Playground Movement, and whereas the establishment of such Vacation Schools and Playgrounds is acknowledged by educators and philanthropists to be desired in every community, and whereas the necessity for such schools and playgrounds to improve the condition of children in the cities of Canada is obvious, therefore be it resolved that this National Council of Women of Canada declare themselves in favour of the establishment of Vacation Schools and Playgrounds, and pledge themselves to do all in their power to promote their organization. (National Council of Women of Canada, 1901, p. 152)

The underlying motive for the establishment of these playgrounds was social reform. The words of Mabel Peters shown in the *i*-box below sound very much like some of the twenty-first century rationale for proactive programs for youth at risk that will keep them out of trouble—and out of the criminal justice system!

National Council of Women and Youth at Risk

This National Council of Canada cannot bring into the lives of Canadian children a greater boon than by organizing vacation schools and public playgrounds. All methods of reform that do not begin with childhood, strike only at leaves and branches of evil, and fail to touch the root. Train the child correctly and the adult will not need reformation. (National Council of Women of Canada, 1901, p. 152)

Being an advocate for playgrounds did not necessarily mean being the operator of such playgrounds. The NCW preferred to be a catalyst for their establishment and supporter from afar (McFarland, 1970). The actual provision of the playgrounds was handled at the level of the Local Councils of Women. Here they would first create a local council Playgrounds Committee, and then establish a few summer playgrounds with games and arts and crafts programs. The council helped with fund raising, but did not staff the playgrounds; often local school teachers were hired for this—usually women. School boards were very often involved at this stage, as they possessed two essential ingredients for a playground program—land and buildings. Eventually most cities created a local playground association that was more broadly based than the Local Council for Women, in which citizens and representatives of various groups, such as school boards or town and city councils, could assist. The next step in many cities was often the creation of a playground commission as a part of civic government, with the final step being the incorporation of playgrounds into a part of a civic department that might be responsible for both parks and recreation. In many cities, the occurrence of these final two steps happened as the municipal governments became committed to the idea of recreation through playgrounds.

As previously mentioned, staff members hired by a Local Council or its successors were typically local school teachers, and they were often women. There was a recognized need for training in recreation, and it was to this end that, in 1912, the National Council advocated that the provincial Normal Schools (teachers' colleges) develop courses to train playground teachers and supervisors. Unfortunately, the requested training was usually very slow in coming. There were, however, isolated examples, such as the Normal School in Nova Scotia, that provided its trainee teachers with information about recreation and leisure in the late 1920s in hopes that they would, in the words of the time, "help to spread the gospel of 'a wise use of leisure'" (Canadian Council on Child Welfare, March 16, 1929). It took several more decades before the first university recreation programs were established at the University of British Columbia in 1960 and the University of Alberta in 1962 (McFarland. 1970).

Playgrounds moved, from the early years of hiring female teachers to be playground leaders, to more inclusive hiring; however, McFarland concludes that:

> With the advent of male supervisors a much greater emphasis on physical activities and competitions became apparent and the concept of the arts as unmanly grew to plague later attempts to establish broad recreation programs. (1970, p. 9)

Mabel Peters was the driving force pushing the National Council of Women to do something about playgrounds. As a zealous campaigner at the local, national, and international scene for supervised playgrounds for children, she may be called the "Mother of the Canadian Playground Movement." Miss Peters and her colleagues viewed playgrounds as a way to "overcome the evils of enforced idleness," by providing children with opportunities of "rational activity and healthy play" (National Council of Women of Canada, 1901, pp. 152, 154). Such thoughts were classic examples of the social reformers' agenda of uplifting pursuits.

Peters travelled widely throughout Canada and the United States, speaking both to those who were committed to the playground movement and those who were not yet convinced. Her travels in the United States brought her in contact with Jane Addams, a key social activist in Chicago (Clarke, 1979, p. 96), and the members of the Playgrounds Association of America, of which she was an early member. She was also a member of the National Council in 1907 and 1908, and one of the Honorary Vice-Presidents of that association's 1908 congress in New York City ("National council," 1907, p. 11; "Honorary vice-presidents," 1908; "Council and board of directors," 1908, p. 15; and National Council of Women of Canada, 1908, p. 39).

One of her ambitions was to form a Canadian association similar in mandate to the Playgrounds Association of America, but focusing on the Canadian situation (Saint John Playgrounds Association, 1913, p. 2). In 1913 she reported that there was strong support for the proposed National Canadian Playgrounds Association (National Council of Women of Canada, 1913, pp. 44-45); however, that strong support dwindled when she died, and the idea also died. It was not until 1945 when the Ontario Parks Association transformed itself into the Parks and Recreation Association of Canada (PRAC) that such an association came into being (Markham, 1995). PRAC is now CPRA—the Canadian Parks and Recreation Association.

Discover Your Community's Park and Recreation History II

1. When was the first playground established in your home community?
2. Where was that playground? in a park? at a school?
3. What group established that playground?
4. Who did they hire as staff?
5. Did your community establish a playgrounds association? a playgrounds commission? a recreation commission?
6. When was the recreation department established in your community?
7. Who have been the advocates for recreation in your community?
8. How has your community dealt with the challenges and opportunities that it has faced?
9. How has it responded to changes in the social, economic, political, and physical environment?

Provincial and National Recreation Services—BC Pro-Rec and Beyond

One initiative of provincial and federal governments in Canada is promoting well-being, including health, wellness, and active living. But how did the services that contribute to that well-being develop? Throughout the 1930s, surrounded by economic, political, and social turmoil, both nationally and internationally, the federal government was being urged to promote and support activities that are now believed to contribute to the well-being of Canadians. During this decade, the Canadian federal government was preoccupied with economic depression, unemployment, and social and political unrest. Consequently it did not view leisure and recreation as top priorities. There were several groups of social reformers and practitioners, however, who promoted that recreation be given both financial and moral support—groups such as the Canadian Council on Child Welfare, the Young Men's Christian Association, the Cadet Service, the Canadian Physical Education Association, the Canadian National Parks Association, and the National Council of Women (Markham, 1994). Each group focussed on a different aspect of recreation, such as play, sport, fitness, or outdoor recreation. The motives that drove each of these advocates were based on their perceptions of individual, societal and national needs. The British Columbia Provential Recreation Programme (BC Pro-Rec) appears to have been the group that had the most impact.

The work of BC Pro-Rec, with its dynamic proponent, Ian Eisenhardt (see photo, p. 256), began in 1934 (Schrodt, 1984). While Eisenhardt was in charge of the Pro-Rec programme, he also worked on the national front as a consultant to the Youth Employment Committee (YEC) of the National Employment Commission (NEC). He convinced the YEC to recommend physical training schemes for the unemployed, and to promote federal funding for provincial projects such as Pro-Rec. His ideas were subsequently included in the Commission's attempts to provide programs to make the young and unemployed people fit for work. The most well-documented program is the Dominion-Provincial Youth Training Program, which funded the training of physical recreation leaders in British Columbia, Alberta, Saskatchewan, Manitoba, and New Brunswick by 1940.

Eisenhardt's first appearance on the national recreation scene was certainly not his last. The influence of the BC Pro-Rec movement spread eastward. His speeches and articles were cited in numerous publications. Finally, as the 1943 National Physical Fitness Act was proclaimed and the National Council on Physical Fitness was developed, Eisenhardt, now Major Ian Eisenhardt, was hired as National Director of Physical Fitness in 1944. Eisenhardt's contributions were firmly based on the principle of recreation for well-being and

Major Ian Eisenhardt, 1944 National Director of Physical Fitness

recreation making people fit for work, in recreation leadership and other fields (McFarland, 1970).

There were many advocates for national and provincial recreation services. Recreation was intended to improve people's general well-being, make them fit for work, or fit for war. However, by the end of the 1930s, the overriding concern of recreation was to make men fit for war. The war effort superseded all other activities. After the war, faced with the post-war baby boom, the provincial governments finally began to recognize that they needed to provide recreation services. But did they all establish Recreation Departments? No. In most provinces, the first step was to establish some unit related to recreation in the Department of Education; this happened in Ontario, British Columbia, and Alberta in 1945, 1953, and 1955, respectively (McFarland, 1970). It was not until 1972 that Nova Scotia became the first province to create a Department of Recreation—a department whose primary responsibility was to create and facilitate recreation service for its citizens. Across the country, most provinces established similar departments in the 1970s; however, just as a government can establish a recreation department, it can then change it. The following *i*-box relates the saga of this department's name changes in Nova Scotia. Other provinces have gone through similar amalgamations and disintegrations with partners that include community services, tourism, culture, parks, environment, agriculture, and forestry, all in the interests of efficiency, effectiveness, and political expediency.

Provincial Recreation in Nova Scotia

1972	Department of Recreation
1978	Department of Culture, Recreation, and Fitness
Fall 1987	Government reorganization: Recreation disappears from any department's mandate for 3 weeks
Late 1987	Sport and Recreation Commission
Early 1993	Department of Tourism, Culture, and Recreation
Mid 1993	(post election) Sport and Recreation Commission
2003	Sport and Recreation Commission within the Office of Health Promotion
2006	Physical Activity, Sport, and Recreation Program area in the Department of Health Protection and Promotion

Discover Your Community's Park and Recreation History III

1. What is the name of the department responsible for recreation in your province?
2. When was the first department responsible for recreation in your province established?
3. Has that department had other names and mandates since the first one?
4. Who were the advocates for provincial recreation services in your province?
5. Was your province part of the Dominion-Provincial Youth Training Program?
6. What role do programs sponsored by Health Canada have in your province?

National Parks—It All Started at Banff

The area we now call Banff National Park was originally 10 square miles reserved by the federal government in 1885 to protect the land from sale or settlement or squatting (Canada House of Commons, 1885). The motives for this reservation were not entirely altruistic or aiming to conserve or preserve the natural environment; rather they stemmed from the desire to control use of the hot springs, as noted in the first legislation shown in the National Parks in Canada *i*-box.

Over the next two years, the idea of what this parcel of land might become for Canadians expanded, from the 1885 conception of hot springs and their sanitary advantage, to a more broad definition of park use, established through the 1887 Rocky Mountain Park Act, which stated that the land was to be "a public park and pleasure ground for the benefit, advantage, and enjoyment of the people of Canada" (Lothian, 1976, citing Statutes of Canada, 1887, 50–51 Victoria, c32).

National Parks in Canada, 1885

That whereas near the station of Banff on the Canadian Pacific Railway, in the provisional District of Alberta, North West Territories, there have been discovered several hot mineral springs which promise to be of great sanitary advantage to the public, and in order that proper control of the lands surrounding these springs may be vested in the Crown, the said lands in the territory including said springs and in their immediate neighbourhood, be and they are hereby reserved from sale or settlement or squatting (Canada House of Commons, 1885).

The Park's boundaries have changed many times (see Byrne, 1968, p. 143). Through the years of expansion and contraction there were many disputes over the role of the Park: should it conserve the natural environment or should that natural environment be used for the economic benefit of the region and the country? When the Park was established, John A. Macdonald, the Prime Minister of the time, declared that parts of it would be "a perennial source of revenue, and if carefully managed it will more than many times recuperate [visitors] or recoup the Government for any present expenditure" (Canada House of Commons, 1887, p. 233). There were various ways to recoup the Government's treasury: tourism was one such way, as were timber, mineral, and water resources. (See Brown, 1970 regarding the idea of the "Doctrine of Usefulness" of resources in the national parks.) These debates continued throughout the history of Canada's national parks into the present. Are they to be preserved and pristine, or are the resources to be used? Who will benefit from either scenario? Or will we try to create a typically Canadian compromise?

What began as a handful of parks in western Canada, attracting tourists to the spectacular mountain scenery, eventually expanded into a pan-Canadian system of national parks. The expansion, however, was not a smooth, steady process; there were bursts of activity followed by periods of very slow or no growth. Bella's 1979 explanation of the growth pattern draws upon events in the economic and political environment. She shows that by 1929, 11 of the 14 national parks were in the four western provinces: Manitoba, Saskatchewan, Alberta, and British Columbia. The remaining three parks, all in Ontario, were very small and accounted for only 0.04% of the land base of the national park system—99.96% was in the west. There were no national parks east of the St. Lawrence Islands. Bella asserts that when the federal government's control over the land and natural resources in the western provinces was broken, the federal government lost its ability to establish parks in the west unilaterally. That political situation, combined with the stagnation of the economy in the 1930s and the host of other priorities in the war and post-war years, led to the addition of a mere four parks to the system between 1929 and 1957, with no further agreements for parks until *1967*. Then things changed.

Bella attributes the newfound interest in the 1960s of expanding the national parks system to the election of Pierre Trudeau and the Liberal party in 1968. With Trudeau as Prime Minister, and with another avid outdoorsman, Jean Chrétien, as minister responsible for national parks, lobbying for national parks by groups such as the National and Provincial Parks Association of Canada fell on sympathetic ears (Bella, 1979). The number of national parks grew. The notion of a system of national parks with representation from 39 natural regions began with the creation of the first system plan in 1977 (Parks Canada, 2005).

So what is the state of our national parks today? There are 38 national parks and reserves representing 24 of the 39 natural regions (Parks Canada, 2005). Organizationally, the Parks Canada Agency, operating at arms length from government, is responsible for the national parks. The Parks Canada Charter says that they "are guardians… guides… partners… storytellers" committed to protecting and celebrating our natural and cultural heritage (Parks Canada 2006). The system is growing, but it is suffering growing pains as the pressures to add new parks must be balanced with the pressures to maintain the existing parks. Within each park there are tensions about the degree of development (or non-development) that will be permitted. This is all part of the process wherein rational system planning encounters the political process. As Pierre Trudeau might say "the universe is unfolding" (Valpy, 2004).

Discover Your Community's Park and Recreation History IV

1. What national parks have been created in your home province?
2. When were they created?
3. Why were they created?
4. Who were the advocates promoting the creation for the parks?
5. Who were the opponents of the creation of these parks?
6. What natural regions based on the Parks Canada System Plan are represented by these parks?
7. What are the tensions about development or preservation in these national parks?

Concluding Remarks

After reading this historical overview, it is now up to you to add pieces from your home communities or your provinces. Who were the advocates? Who were the heroes? Have fun.

Key Terms

BC Pro-Rec
Civic boosters
Elsie McFarland
Ian Eisenhardt
Mabel Peters
National Council of Women
National parks
National Physical Fitness Act
Natural regions
Park
Social reformers
System plan
Vacation schools

Further Resources

Canadian Parks and Recreation Association website http://www.cpra.ca/
Health Canada website http://www.hc-sc.gc.ca/
Mabel Peters entry on the Dictionary of Canadian Biography website http://www.biographi.ca/EN/ShowBio.asp?BioId=41770
National Council of Women website http://www.ncwc.ca/
Parks Canada website http://www.parkscanada.ca/

References

Bella, L. (1979). Partisan politics and national parks north of 60. *Park News, 15*(3), 6–12.

Brown, C. A. B., & Hughes, J. L. (1910). Municipal playgrounds. In *Addresses delivered before the Canadian Club of Toronto 1909-1910* (pp. 69–74). Toronto, ON: Canadian Club.

Brown, R. C. (1970). The doctrine of usefulness: Natural resources and national park policy in Canada, 1887–1914. In J. G. Nelson (Ed.), *Canadian parks in perspective*. Montréal, QC: Harvest House.

Byrne, A. R. (1968). *Man and landscape change in the Banff National Park area before 1911*. Ottawa, ON: Parks Canada.

Canada House of Commons. (1885). Order in Council No. 2917.

Canada House of Commons. (1887). Debates of the House of Commons.

Canadian Council on Child Welfare. (1929) Records in MG28 I10, National Archives of Canada (NAC). Ottawa, ON.

Canadian Parks/Recreation Association (1997). *Benefits of recreation*. Ottawa, ON: Canadian Parks/Recreation Association.

City planning scheme will transform Winnipeg into beautiful metropolis. (1911, June 10). *Winnipeg Telegram*.

City too ugly to attract firms—Wright. (1983, April 14). *Edmonton Journal*.

Clarke, M. E. (1979). *The Saint John Women's Enfranchisement Association, 1914–1919*. University of New Brunswick, Fredericton.

Council and board of directors of the Playground Association of America. (1908, October). *The Playground*, 13–16.

Edginton, C. R., & Williams, J. C. (1978). *Productive management of leisure service organizations*. New York, NY: John Wiley & Sons.

Halifax Committee of Common. (1864). *Annual report, 1863–64*. Halifax, NS: City of Halifax.

Harkin, J. B. (1914, January 24). Memorandum re: Dominion parks. In University of Alberta Archives, Pearce Papers f429.1.

Honorary vice-presidents. (1908, September). *The Playground*.

Kelso, J. J. (1908). The play spirit and playgrounds in Toronto. In *Empire Club of Canada, Toronto, addresses, 1907–1908* (pp. 178–187). Toronto, ON: Empire Club.

Lawrence, C. (1760, March 28). Letter from the Governor to the Chief Surveyor. In *Public Archives of Nova Scotia, Allotment Book, 1760*, p. 71.

Lothian, W. F. (1976). *A history of Canada's national parks* (Vol. 1). Ottawa, ON: Parks Canada.

Markham, S. E. (1991). The impact of prairie and maritime reformers and boosters on the development of parks and playgrounds, 1880 to 1930. *Loisir et Société/Society and Leisure, 14*(1), 219–233.

Markham, S. E. (1994). Advocates for national recreation services in the 1930s: Well-being? Work? War? In F. I. Bell & G. H. V. Gyn (Eds.), *Access to active living: Proceedings of the 10th Commonwealth and International Scientific Congress* (pp. 87–92). BC: University of Victoria.

Markham, S. E. (1995). The early years. *Recreation Canada, 53*(3), 6–16.

Markham, S. E., & Edginton, C. R. (1979). The Common of Halifax: Canada's first park. *Recreation Canada, 37*(1), 12–17.

McFarland, E. M. (1970). *The development of public recreation in Canada.* Ottawa, ON: Canadian Parks/Recreation Association.

National council of the Playground Association of America. (1907, June). *The Playground*, 11.

National Council of Women of Canada. (1901). *Yearbook.* Ottawa, ON: Taylor and Clark.

National Council of Women of Canada. (1908). *Yearbook.* Toronto, ON: G. Parker and Sons.

National Council of Women of Canada. (1913). *Yearbook.* Toronto, ON: Parker Brothers.

Parks Canada. (2004). Port-Royal national historic site. Retrieved from http://www.pc.gc.ca/lhn-nhs/ns/port royal/index_e.asp

Parks Canada. (2005). *National parks system plan* (3rd ed.). Retrieved from http://www.pc.gc.ca/docs/v-g/nation/index_e.asp

Parks Canada. (2006). *National parks system plan* (3rd ed.). Retrieved from http://www.pc.gc.ca/agen/index_E.asp

Riis, J. A. (1913). The value of playgrounds to the community. In *Canadian Club of Toronto proceedings, 1912–1913* (pp. 271–279). Toronto, ON: Canadian Club.

Saint John Playgrounds Association. (1913). *First annual report.* Saint John, NB: Saint John Playgrounds Association.

Sanderlin, D. (1975). *Writing the history paper.* Woodbury, NY: Barron's Education Series, Inc.

Schrodt, B. (1984). Federal programmes of physical recreation and fitness: The contributions of Ian Eisenhardt and BC's Pro-Rec. *Canadian Journal of the History of Sport and Physical Education, 15*(2), 45–61.

Valpy, M. (2004, June 25). The universe is unfolding as it should. *Globe and Mail*, p. A4.

Wright, J. R. (1983). *Urban parks in Ontario: Part 1: Origins to 1860.* Ottawa, ON: University of Ottawa.

2

Chapter 28
Private Sector Providers

Laurene Rehman, Ph.D. & Nila Ipson, Ph.D.
Dalhousie University

Learning Objectives

After reading this chapter, students will be able to

1. Define private or commercial recreation.
2. Identify some reasons for the increase in commercial ventures in Canada.
3. Define entrepreneurship and factors contributing to the increase of recreation entrepreneurship in Canada.
4. Describe some key trends and research questions facing commercial recreation services.

Introduction

So what have you done for fun lately? Chances are you have been using private or commercial recreation services. For example, have you been to a movie, bought new running shoes, bought an iPod or new CD, been to a fitness club or sport game, whitewater rafted or kayaked, rock-climbed, been snowboarding or skiing, or been out for coffee or a meal? In many cases, these are all examples of private recreation. Often commercial recreation providers are people who have recognized a need that, as Holly Bond (Bulldog Interactive Fitness, Dartmouth, NS) says, is "staring you in the face." So now that you've realized how widespread these services can be, let's review some of the key concepts and issues the industry is facing.

Private vs. Public Recreation: What Are the Similarities and Differences?

Both the public and private sector work together towards improving people's lives through recreation. Indeed, recreation delivery in Canada is based on a continuum of service delivery, with public recreation on one end and private recreation on the other. Major differences exist between these two sectors (e.g., the philosophic approach, service delivery, and financial base). For example, in the public sector, funding usually is obtained from government sources, while the private sector receives little if any revenue from the tax base. Instead, private recreation is largely dependent on membership fees, grants or subsidies, registration, and/or funding from other organizations (e.g., sponsoring businesses). Another example of the differences between the public and private spheres is the philosophic approaches used in each. Public recreation, at least in its roots, has been focused on providing "recreation for all," while private recreation is centered on meeting unique niche markets. Despite the existence of such a continuum, most of what you read and study about recreation tends to be public delivery. In fact, Suzie Woodruff Giddy (previous owner of Northcliffe Tennis Club, Halifax, NS) explained that we tend to prepare students in undergraduate recreation programs to be municipal recreation directors and not to consider going into business or operation for oneself (see case study below on Ms. Woodruff Giddy). Instead, we focus mainly on the public sector.

Deciding to Become a Recreation Entrepreneur!

Suzie Woodruff Giddy had never really considered opening her own recreation business. She earned her recreation undergraduate degree from Dalhousie University and felt most prepared to work in municipal recreation. However, when the opportunity arose to purchase a nearly bankrupt indoor tennis club (Northcliffe Tennis Club, Halifax, NS), she decided to take a chance. She explained that being your own boss is not something for everyone. "You need to be passionate about what you're doing and the money will follow," says Ms. Woodruff Giddy. If you want a regular pay cheque, job stability, regular vacations, and a fixed schedule, then the public sector is probably for you. If, however, you enjoy creativity, you have a tolerance for risk, you care passionately about your customers, and you enjoy being accountable only to yourself, then the private sector is the only place to work. Ms. Woodruff Giddy loves what she does and her enjoyment for being an entrepreneur is evident when you meet her. Most recently, she has sold her business and expanded into a new niche market—supporting at-risk women in developing countries. This is an example of how one opportunity can lead to others. Her previous business continues to thrive as a great example of private recreation, and she has now developed a new avenue for her energy and passion.

Definition of Commercial Recreation

Commercial recreation is offered by the private sector, and although many consider commercial or private recreation to be relatively new, its existence predates that of organized public recreation. Commercial recreation can be defined as the provision of "recreation-related products and services by private enterprise for a fee with the long-term intention of being profitable" (Jamieson, 2006, p. 164). For example, bowling alleys charge for the rental of the lane, shoes, and birthday party room. These fees are used to offset the costs of their facility operation. In order for the owner to maintain the facility, s/he will need to obtain a profit in the long term. This additional revenue could then be used, for example, to replace a leaking roof, purchase new bowling balls, add neon lighting, hire additional staff, and so forth. One of the leaders in the growing economy is private entrepreneurship. When such service delivery is carried out in an entrepreneurial or innovative way, it is also called entrepreneurial recreation (Jamieson, 2006). So, what does "entrepreneurial" really mean? How can someone be entrepreneurial? Think of a time when you or someone you know acted in a really innovative or creative manner. This could have been problem-solving in a way that you would never have thought of but that came up with an amazing solution. Or it could be finding something that no one had thought of before that people would like to do in their leisure time. It could also be identifying or recognizing a trend before it becomes popular.

Perhaps one of the main reasons why private recreation has tended to be neglected in the leisure field is its perceived focus upon making a profit—its being "pay to play." Sometimes we assume that making money means we forget the "common or public good" in favour of the "bottom line" or "almighty dollar" (Bullaro & Edginton, 1986; Crossley, Jamieson, & Brayley, 2001; Karlis, 2004). One of the outcomes of such thinking has been that we know far less about the experiences of commercial recreation providers and the realities of working in this sector. Trying to understand these experiences and realities will form the basis of this chapter. Let's now consider the wide range of types that exist in Canada.

How can you be entrepreneurial?

Think of something that people could do in their leisure time to reduce physical inactivity among youth to tackle the obesity epidemic. Any ideas?

The Private Recreation Industry

For-profit oriented businesses provide the largest variety of leisure opportunities in Canada and the United States. They include a wide range of businesses, including sports organizations, outdoor-recreation providers, social and adult service clubs, wholesale and retail outlets, hospitality and tourism organizations, entertainment facilities, and health and wellness facilities. The commercial recreation industry continues to be an important part of the Canadian leisure services system, and it represents one of the most rapidly expanding market sectors in the Canadian economy (Bullaro & Edginton, 1986). Johnson and Johnson Tew (1999), in a study of commercial recreation providers in Ontario from 1988–1998, found a constant increase in the number of providers. Statistics Canada (2009b) reported that the average Canadian household spent $3,840 of their annual household income on recreation and recreation-related activity (e.g., food, recreation, clothing, tobacco and alcohol, games of chance, and reading materials). Revenues for the amusement and recreation industry in Canada totaled $7.7 billion this same year (Statistics Canada, 2009a).

Types of Commercial Recreation Providers

The specific types of commercial recreation providers can be grouped into three main categories (Crossley et al., 2001). These include **local commercial recreation, hospitality**, and **travel industries** (See Figure 28.1). Each of these categories has "purist" organizations as well as "sub-industries" that overlap with several categories (Crossley et al., 2001, p. 16).

- **The local commercial recreation industry's** primary function is to provide "retail products, entertainment and recreation programs for people in their home communities." Examples of entrepreneurial businesses that could relate to this sector include: sport retail stores, fitness centres, and sport/recreation clubs.
- **The hospitality industry's** primary function is to provide "accommodations, food and beverage, and related amenities." Examples of businesses in these industries include: bed and breakfast facilities, tours, coffee shops and Internet cafes, etc.
- **The travel industry's** primary function is "the movement of people and the provision of travel-related services" (Crossley et al., 2001, p. 16). Some examples of these businesses could include: ski resorts, kayak tours, bus/sport tours, etc.

There are also facilitators for each of the above categories that support the industries. For example, the local commercial recreation industry is supported by equipment wholesalers, and publishers and writers of leisure-related magazines and books. The hospitality industry is supported by convention and visitor information bureaus; while the travel industry is supported by travel trade businesses such as travel agencies, tour operators, schools, and vacation time-share services.

The overlapping circles in Figure 28.1 highlight the diversity, interconnectedness, and complexity of the commercial recreation industry. For example, the travel industry (for more on this topic see Smith's chapter on tourism) is based on the provision of travel-related service (e.g., airlines, bus lines, trains and rental cars). The travel industry, however, can overlap with local commercial recreation and hospitality when retail products, recreation activities, food, lodging and amenities (e.g., souvenir shops, heli-skiing, cruises, meetings, and conventions) are provided for residents and tourists. The hospitality industry involves businesses that "cater to travelers and the special needs of residents" (Jamieson, 2006, p. 165) and is based on the provision of accommodations, food and beverages, and other related

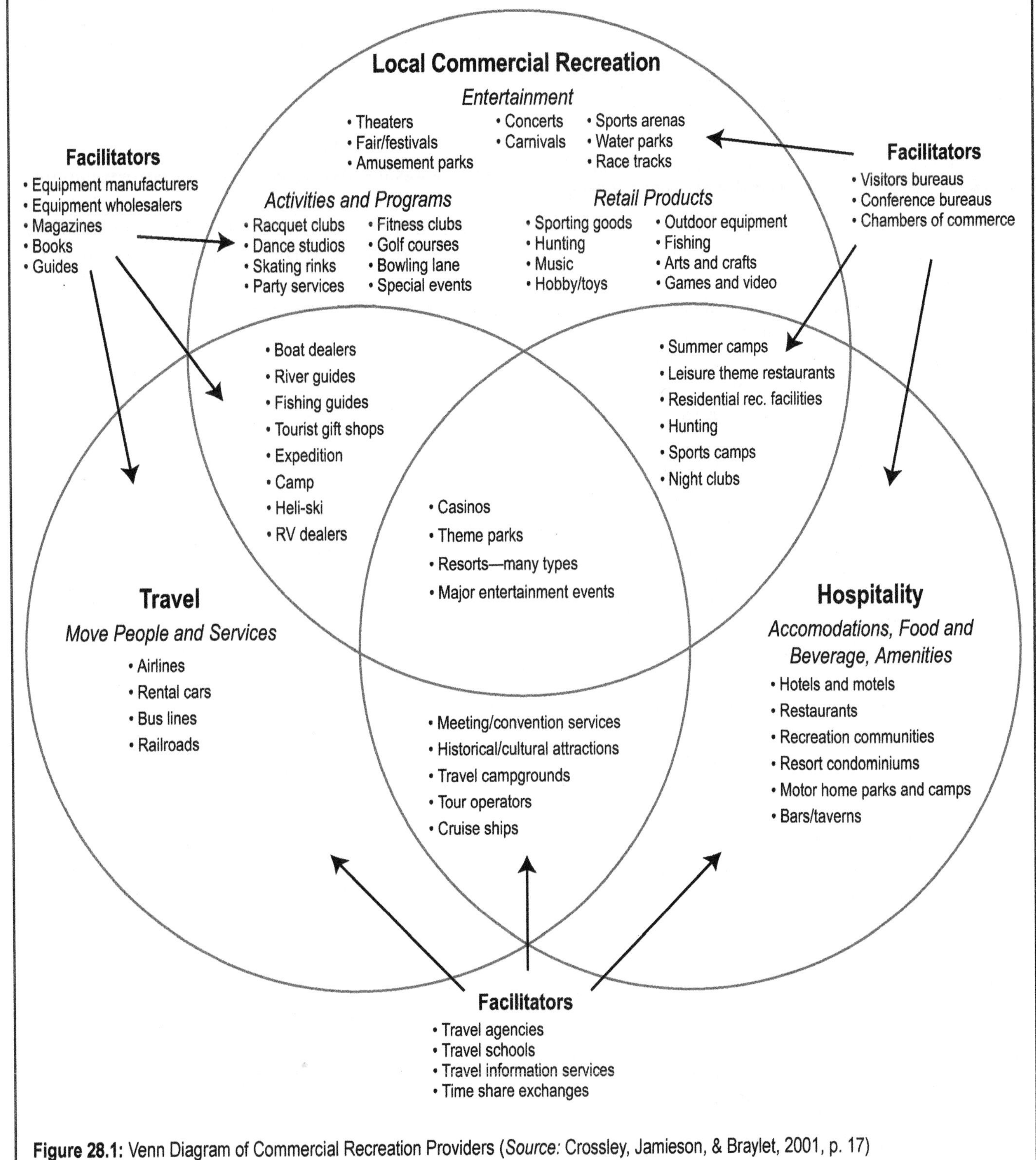

Figure 28.1: Venn Diagram of Commercial Recreation Providers (*Source:* Crossley, Jamieson, & Braylet, 2001, p. 17)

An interesting example of a combination of activities is a bus tour that included a combination trip with three national sport teams competing (i.e., basketball, football, and hockey) in three days. The tour included all travel, accommodation, and event tickets. This was focused on a niche market for men and could be considered a "mancation." The trip was marketed primarily to men through their workplace in a region where national sport teams were not competing.

Small- to medium-sized businesses in Canada are defined as those with fewer than 100 employees and comprise 98% of workplaces. Micro-businesses (fewer than five employees) make up 56.6% of businesses in Canada (Industry Canada, 2005a).

A prominent researcher in the area of recreation-based small businesses, Dr. Trevor Slack (at the University of Alberta), suggests more research on management-related topics (e.g., organizational theory, organizational structure, power and politics) needs to be conducted and applied within leisure studies to examine the implications of traditional management theories to leisure/recreation settings.

amenities (e.g., hotels, campgrounds, resorts, restaurants) but overlaps with travel (as mentioned above) and commercial recreation when recreation activities are provided in such settings as hunting lodges, themed restaurants, and sports day camps. The commercial recreation industry provides retail products, entertainment, and recreation programs (e.g., fitness centres, theatres, dance studios, water parks, music stores) and can overlap with both the hospitality and travel industries. Finally, some business categories (casinos, theme parks, resorts) exist within all three industry categories. As leisure and recreation businesses bridge a variety of industries, the Standard Industrial Codes (SIC) (used in the United States to classify businesses) are difficult to apply, as the businesses may fall within several divisions.

One thing that is important about the types of commercial recreation providers within Canada is the increasing number of small businesses operating in each of these categories and sub-industries. Most of the businesses are small- to medium-sized (operating with a small number of employees and often with a small number of operators or owners).

Recreation-based Small Businesses

Leisure-based small businesses are becoming important at an international level (Berrett, Burton, & Slack, 1993). For example, in 2001, 54 of the world's top 500 companies were categorized as leisure companies (Byers & Slack, 2001). So who are these entrepreneurs and small-business owners who are contributing to employment and economic growth?

A great example is Holly Bond (previous owner of Bulldog Interactive Fitness, see Figure 28.2). She started her own business after having recognized a need for youth fitness. She creatively combined the interests of youth in both video games and "fun." See how she solved her own son's physical inactivity dilemma in the case study. The ability to solve a problem creatively—or "see a need, fill a need" is a key

Thank you for your interest in Bulldog Interactive Fitness Inc®.

I started Bulldog Interactive Fitness® for several reasons. I have a computer-loving teenage son who was overweight and needed help, and I was at wits end trying to find a place where he would feel comfortable, get results, and most importantly, have fun. At the same time, I was working as a pharmaceutical representative and speaking to physicians on a daily basis about cardio vascular health, the shocking increased rates of childhood obesity, diabetes and hypertension in youth. I didn't want my son to be a casualty of our technological age. With the alarming decrease in physical education in the school system, I realized that something had to be done. I tried to figure out how to combine my son's love of computers and interactive games with fitness, and I found a combination that works!

After many, many months of searching and testing, we found a combination that keeps teens coming back for more! Our son has lost 20 pounds and is now a healthy, self-secure individual with more confidence and self-esteem. His grades have shown a marked improvement and he knows that this accomplishment is because he put his mind to it. As he danced and biked through video games, the weight melted off…the whole family is thrilled.

We are dedicated to helping youth lose weight while they gain self-esteem. We are committed to making each workout a fun, positive and safe experience. We are passionate about what we do, and who we do it for each and every day. Bulldog Interactive Fitness® is now a successful company – our membership has exceeded our predictions. We have many members that have experienced positive results; whether the member lost weight, increased self-esteem and independence, or made the "A" team in soccer…we have dozens of testimonials to share with you!

As the health crisis of our youth becomes increasingly apparent throughout North America, Bulldog Interactive Fitness® offers franchisees a revolutionary business opportunity to bring solutions to children and teens as well as their parents. We are actively seeking franchisees and area developers throughout North America, and we look forward to hearing from you.

We hope that you will share in our vision, and join our team…a team that makes a difference in the dreams and futures of young Canadians. We invite you to request additional information, and welcome the opportunity to speak to you one-on-one. You can contact me, Holly Bond, for more information on how to share in our success while transforming the lives of the youth of today.

Holly Bond

Holly Bond
President and Owner
Bulldog Interactive Fitness Inc.®

Figure 28.2 Case Study of an Entrepreneur

skill of recreation entrepreneurship. So what is driving individuals to start their own business in the recreation field?

Why Are People Starting Recreation Businesses?

Why would you start a business in the recreation field? Recreation small-business owners have identified several reasons. Some have started a business because they really enjoy a certain recreational activity and are highly skilled at it. Others want more autonomy and control in their working lives. Yet others are more interested in having greater freedom to balance work, leisure, and family time (Rehman et al., 2005). The need to escape unemployment has driven some owners to look for interesting ways to create new jobs. For example, with increased downsizing of many manufacturing companies and challenges faced by traditional resource sectors (e.g., closing mines, cod moratorium, decreased logging), people are looking for different forms of work. Recreation-based small businesses have provided one viable alternative. There are really three options available to people interested in operating a recreation-based small business.

Tanya Colburne is one such example of a creative entrepreneur who moved back to Nova Scotia after working in the head office for several years with a national sport team. She used her work experience and expertise to develop a consulting business. Not only is she providing the knowledge gained in that sport, but also she has been able to leverage it to other sports in the area of event planning and entertainment.

One option is to purchase an existing business (such as a family business). This option is becoming more enticing as fewer family-based businesses are remaining within the "family." As children and siblings are not as interested in working within the family business, some owners are selling their businesses. Another option is to start a new business. This is increasingly the case in the recreation industry. A person "sees a need or niche" and develops a business around the concept or hobby. The final option is to purchase a franchise. This option brings both opportunities and headaches. Franchises provide preexisting business plans, as well as shared marketing or promotional opportunities; however, the franchise owner has less flexibility in business operation and decision making.

Within each of the above small-business options, there are different types of business structures. These include sole proprietorship, partnership, corporation, and the cooperative.

What is a corporation? It is defined as a "legal entity that is separate from its owners, the shareholders" (Canada Business Service Centre, 2005). The primary benefit of a corporation is that shareholders are not personally liable for the debts, obligations or acts of the corporation. Do you know of any corporations in the recreation field? What are some examples?

The sole proprietorship consists of the owner as primary or "sole" owner and decision maker. This option provides the most flexibility, but also the greatest level of risk as the owner is responsible for all liabilities of the business. The partnership option provides an opportunity to share start-up costs, but also means joint decision making and profit sharing. Setting up a corporation provides legal protection to the owners, but also requires the greatest amount of paper work and the owner is accountable to shareholders. An increasing number of recreation-based businesses are seeking corporation status to protect the owners from legal liability related to clients' recreational participation. A cooperative is the last type of business structure. This type is operated and administered by members. These members share in the decision making and profits of the organization. A recreation-based example is Mountain Equipment Co-op where shoppers are also "members." Another example is a pottery cooperative, where clients are members and share materials and supplies and can choose to sell their products to each other. To obtain a better understanding of the realities of recreation-based business operation, in the next section we will explore some challenges typically faced by operators.

What is a cooperative? According to the Canada Business Service Centre (2005), it is a business organized and controlled by members based on a system of one membership, one vote. The key is a focus upon a democratic approach to business operation with members sharing in the key decision making.

Challenges for Private Recreation Providers

Working for oneself is often seen as a great opportunity to have "the job of one's dreams"! Unfortunately the job of one's dreams may become the job of one's life—entire life, that is, as the business obligations consume your time and energy!

What Happened to My Leisure?

Participating in an activity you love is often one of the things driving an owner to start a business, especially in the recreation field—"I just love sea kayaking, so I should teach others to kayak!" This eco-tourism concept is one example of how a business can develop from a recreation activity or hobby. The challenge, however, is that when you participate in your hobby, 24 hours a day, 7 days a week, 365 days a year, is it still a hobby? Rehman et al. (2005), in a study of recreation-based business owners operating in Nova Scotia, Canada, found one of the biggest concerns identified by owners was diminishing personal leisure. As one participant explained, "my work is my leisure." Another observed, "you don't get a lot of leisure time in this business ... you have to look at your job as something you totally enjoy." Pickard (2004) found similar results through interviews with sole proprietors running small outdoor recreation companies. In her study, owners often sacrificed commitments in other life spheres (e.g., family, leisure, and other employment) to make their businesses successful.

The demands of being self-employed can lead not only to a decrease in time for self or leisure, but also decreased desire to participate in your favourite hobby—or at least what used to be your favourite! As you become so intimately involved in one activity for so much of your life, the need to escape through leisure or to become the patron of another type of recreational business owner may become overwhelming.

Negotiating Work, Leisure, Family

Trying to balance the rest of your life alongside a business operation is also a challenge. Small-business owners note that work–life balance is a huge problem. While there can be a tremendous amount of flexibility in terms of the hours you work and the days of the week, as the business is "your own," trying to take time away can be daunting. Operating a business operation is not a traditional nine-to-five occupation, so building in time for others is challenging. The recreation-based business owner tends to be working when others are participating in leisure. Vacations or breaks away from the business tend to be taken in slow seasons or "down times," which are not usually the traditional holidays. In fact, your recreation will often be providing it for everyone else. Suzie Woodruff Giddy (see previous case study) highlighted that if you are interested in having a regular pay cheque and vacations, then small-business operation is not for you! In spite of these apparent negatives, for Ms. Woodruff Giddy, the opportunity to **be your own boss**, escape "red tape," and be accountable only to yourself, meant there was **no** other option for her.

The challenge of negotiating a work–life balance may reduce slightly over the life cycle of the business. In particular, time away from the business may be more a challenge during the start-up or early phase of the business. During a start-up period, the owner is focused on ensuring the business has a good track record. Later on, it may be possible to take more time away from the business, especially if the owner is confident in his/her staff/employees.

Strategies for Success of Private Recreation Providers

Recreation-based small-business owners have identified a variety of factors which they feel have contributed to their success. Within the following section, we will explore some of these to get a sense of what to consider when operating a financially feasible private recreation business. These factors include developing a business plan; finding "good" people; nurturing the growth of the business; setting an appropriate price; and enjoying what you're doing.

At the heart of a good business is a solid *business plan* (Jamieson, 2006). A business plan serves as a map for a business and considers a number of important elements of business administration (see insert below). It allows the business owner to communicate his/her vision with potential investors, potential partners, and even employees.

> **What is a business plan?**
>
> It is the "heart of a business enterprise because it determines the way in which the business will receive and use fiscal resources to gain a profit over a projected period" (Jamieson, 2006, p. 171). Parts of the plan include: description of the business and owner, marketing plan, financial plan, and operations plan.

A business plan can be used by a recreation-based owner to justify the need or unique "niche" for a commercial venture, and why s/he should be allowed to charge a fee for the new service. In some cases, public recreation may not be able to afford to meet specific leisure needs and a business plan can be used to justify how the business is different from those already in operation. For example, bungee jumping may not be affordably offered in a public recreation environment, especially given the risk management concerns, but a commercial venture could fill this need. Skateboard parks provide another such example of where a public facility may not be able to afford to provide the opportunity for their consumers due not only to the issue of risk, but also the specialized equipment needed (e.g., half pipe, ramps). The business plan can outline how a private owner could afford to offer such recreation but also make it financially lucrative.

Another strategy for achieving business success is ***finding "good" people*** to assist with the business. Within the recreation industry, relationships with people are critical to the participant's leisure experience. The service literature calls such relationships "rapport." One of the main reasons a person will either stay with a program or organization is because they like the people who are working there. Conversely, a key reason to quit is because you had a bad experience with the coach, the program leader, the front office staff, etc. Therefore, a recreation-based business needs to have employees that can establish a positive rapport with fellow workers and with clients. This is one of the characteristics of "good" employees. Another characteristic of a good employee is technical skill. Staff members may be asked to undertake any variety of tasks ranging from programming and training to bookkeeping and promotions. While not every staff member can have all the necessary skills, "good" staff understands their roles and are able to carry them out. Much of the role of the small-business owner is to ensure that all staff members are "good." This will help employees recognize they are working for the good of the business—or one common cause.

Once a recreation-based business is in operation, a critical challenge for success is continuously thinking of ways to ***nurture the business***. This may or may not involve increasing the size of the business; indeed, many owners favour operating and retaining a smaller business presence. Rehman et al. (2005) found that increasing the size of the business often meant that the owner no longer had sole control over the quality of the business service/product. Growth meant the introduction of more partners and greater complexity. Many who took part in the study reported that they wished to avoid such complexity and were happy to simply "pay all the bills." Doing so signaled to them that they were a success.

One way to nurture the business is to emphasize the importance of quality service as critical to business success and growth. Pickard (2004) found that a focus on quality service needed to be considered as separate from financial gain. Other entrepreneurs have highlighted that satisfying customers means the business will prosper. Another way to nurture the business is to develop partnerships or relationships with key players ranging from other businesses to venture capitalists. Such relationships can serve to provide a source of funding, marketing, information sharing, and, potentially, customers. Working in the recreation industry, owners highlight that they are continually relying on the connections they can develop with others.

One way of enhancing relationships in today's technological society is through social networking and usage of this process. For example, Tanya Colburne (see previous case study) has used social networking—such as Facebook and Twitter—extensively to announce new advances in her business, upcoming events and services, and simply to update her ever-expanding network of contacts. She explained, though, that using such networking requires constant nurturing to ensure "friends" are updated regularly, or they will become rapidly disinterested. Social networking allows recreation business owners to share their information at a much more rapidly and can also allow direct users to interact with each other. This creates a platform easily accessible to others and encourages greater awareness of the business product/services.

A challenge for achieving a successful recreation-based business is ***setting appropriate prices***. Before being able to set prices, it is important to determine exactly how much it will cost for each program/service provided. In the commercial sector, knowing this information allows prices to be set that recover the full cost plus a percentage for a profit margin. Other pricing strategies are demand-oriented (based on how much people are willing to pay) or competition-oriented (what others are charging). Any price set by a small business owner will probably reflect all three variables (cost to produce, willingness to pay by the user, and existing prices within the marketplace). This is why pricing experts often suggest that price setting as much an art as it is a science.

In the final analysis, the best strategy for having a successful recreation-based business is to make sure you ***enjoy what you're doing!*** Recreation-based business owners truly live by the philosophy that "in the beginning I lived for recreation, but now recreation is my life"!

Words of Wisdom

Success is... knowing when to stop and play! (Anonymous)

Future Directions of the Commercial Recreation Industry

After reading this chapter you should have an understanding of the scope of the commercial recreation industry, and issues to consider if you are interested in pursuing a career in this field. Lastly, we note key trends that will be driving the field into the future.

Forecasting the future is often a challenge; however, in order to be successful it is necessary to anticipate future trends. One of the leading trends that will continue to drive the commercial recreation industry is the entrance of small businesses. Small businesses are uniquely positioned to respond to customer needs. Byers and Slack (2001) explain that more understanding is needed of small businesses in the leisure industry in order to be able to support them in the industry. In 2001, small businesses accounted for just over 1 million companies, and this number has increased to 2.7

million in 2009 (or 16% of the workforce) (CFIB, 2001, 2011).

One particular aspect of customer needs that recreation businesses need to continue to address in the future is quality service. A focus on quality will allow commercial recreation operators to attain a competitive advantage. As consumers will be increasingly taxed with trying to make decisions over where to spend their leisure dollars, those operators who are seen as providing a "quality service" will be more competitive.

Another trend that will drive the commercial recreation industry is the continuous advancements in technology. "The entrepreneurial spirit, which has been the core of those who excelled at leisure services, will become even more important in the coming era; an era in which things will never be the same" (Godbey, 1997, p. 14). In order to avoid being left behind, businesses need to stay at the cutting edge of technology and communication. Finding unique ways to incorporate new technologies (e.g., advanced product materials, unique and new equipment, advancements in facility design) into the recreation field will allow owners to position themselves against others.

A final trend to consider for the future of commercial recreation is the development of niche markets. Identifying potential customers is critical to the commercial industry. At the centre of private recreation is the ability to identify and respond to niche markets. Niche markets represent not only unique groupings or segments of people, but also unique interests or needs of those groups. This has been a key principle behind the industry and will become even more critical in the future as new businesses enter the industry. Owners will need to identify who their potential customers entail and find unique methods of meeting their needs. Of particular interest at present are the baby boomers, or "zoomers." They represent a large and vast number of future clients with leisure needs, especially as they enter retirement (Foot & Stoffman, 1998). Another issue with respect to niche markets will be considering the replacement of current owners as they themselves face retirement (see *i*-box below).

Dr. Nicole Vaugeois, a researcher on tourism-based small businesses, notes more research is needed to determine useful strategies for replacing entrepreneurs when nearing retirement. She highlights that successful strategies for assisting the transition into business operation are also needed.

In summary, the commercial recreation industry holds many prospects for employment in the leisure field. It is often not the first avenue of employment considered by students, yet should be seriously explored as there is a wealth of opportunities available.

Sources of Additional Information

Canada Business Service Centre (http://www.canadabusiness.ca)

A Guide for a Feasibility Study of recreation enterprises (http://web1.msue.msu.edu/msue/imp/modtd/33119707.html)

Trade Show Week (http://www.tradeshowweek.com/)

Successful Meetings.com (http://www.successmtgs.com)

Social media for marketing resources (http://www.whitepapersource.com/socialmediamarketing/report/)

Key Terms

Private/commercial recreation
"Pay to play"
Entrepreneurship
Strategies
Challenges
Business plan
Social networking

References

Berrett, T., Burton, T. L., & Slack, T. (1993). Quality products, quality service: Factors leading to entrepreneurial success in the sport and leisure industry. *Leisure Studies, 12*, 93–106.

Bullaro, J. J., & Edginton, C. R. (1986). *Commercial leisure services: Managing for profit, service, and personal satisfaction.* New York, NY: Macmillan.

Byers, T., & Slack, T. (2001). Strategic decision-making in small businesses within the leisure industry. *Journal of Leisure Research, 33*(2), 121–136.

Canada Business Service Centre. (2005). *Forms of business organization.* Retrieved from http://www.cbsc.org

Canadian Federation of Independent Business (CFIB). (2001). Small business. Retrieved from http://www.cfib.ca/default_E.asp?1=E

Canadian Federation of Independent Business (CFIB). (2011). Small business facts. Retrieved from http://www.cfib-fcei.ca/english/research/canada/33-small_business_facts/1148-small_business_facts.html

Crossley, J. C., Jamieson, L. M., & Brayley, R. E. (2001). *Introduction to commercial recreation and tourism: An entrepreneurial approach* (4th ed.). Champaign, IL: Sagamore.

Delamere, T., & Wright, A. (n.d.). Chapter nine: Commercial recreation resources. Unpublished manuscript.

Foot, D. K., & Stoffman, D. (1998). *Boom, bust, and echo: Profiting from the demographic shift in the new millennium.* Toronto, ON: Macfarlane, Walter, & Ross.

Godbey, G. (1997). *Leisure and leisure services in the 21st century.* State College, PA: Venture Publishing, Inc.

Industry Canada. (2005a). Survey of regulatory compliance costs. *Small Business Quarterly, 79*(2), 1–8. Retrieved from http://strategis.ic.gc.ca/

Industry Canada. (2005b). Small business research and policy: Key small business statistics–July 2005. Retrieved from http://strategis.ic.gc.ca/epic/internet/insbrp-rppe.nsf/en/rd01229e.html

Jamieson, L. (2006). Commercial recreation and tourism. In G. Kassing (Ed.), *Introduction to recreation and leisure* (pp. 163–176). Champaign, IL: Human Kinetics.

Johnson, R., & Johnson Tew, P. (1999). A longitudinal study of leisure opportunities in three Ontario communities. *Book of Abstracts: 9th Canadian Congress on Leisure Research* (pp. 187–189). Wolfville, NS.

Karlis, G. (2004). *Leisure and recreation in Canadian society: An introduction.* Toronto, ON: Thompson Educational.

O'Sullivan, E. (1991). *Marketing for parks, recreation, and leisure.* State College, PA: Venture Publishing, Inc.

O'Sullivan, E., & Spangler, K. J. (1998). *Experience marketing: Strategies for the new millennium.* State College, PA: Venture Publishing, Inc.

Pickard, T. (2004). *Management strategies used within small outdoor recreation businesses and its effect on the owner's health and leisure participation.* (Unpublished Master's thesis). Dalhousie University.

Rehman, L., Ipson, N., Pickard, T., & Richardson, L. (2005). Exploring experiences of recreation-based small business owners. *Book of abstracts: 11th Canadian Congress on Leisure Research.* Malaspina, BC.

Statistics Canada. (2009a). Service bulletin: Amusement and recreation. Service Industries Division. Retrieved from http://www.statcan.gc.ca/pub/63-248-x/63-248-x2011001-eng.pdf

Statistics Canada. (2009b). Spending patterns in Canada. Retrieved from http://www.statcan.gc.ca/pub/62-202-x/62-202-x2008000-eng.pdf

Section E: Strategies for Leisure Delivery

centre

Chapter 29
Models of Public Leisure Services Delivery

Bryan Smale, Ph.D.
University of Waterloo

Learning Objectives

After reading this chapter, students will be able to

1. Understand the basic principle underlying the provision of leisure services by parks and recreation departments in Canadian communities.
2. Understand the different approaches to equitable provision of leisure services and the rationale underlying each of them.
3. Understand the role and influence that local government has in the provision of leisure services in communities.
4. Recognise the challenges facing parks and recreation departments when trying to implement an approach to providing leisure services equitably.

Introduction

Residents of most communities across Canada enjoy a wide array of publicly provided leisure services, programs, and facilities. Local government agencies responsible for the delivery of these leisure services have long embraced a rather simple principle to ensure that residents can take advantage of these recreational opportunities—*the equitable provision of leisure services to all members of the community*. Essentially, public leisure services agencies want to ensure that everyone in the community has full and equal access to the various services and facilities provided. By doing so, local government can contribute to the quality of individual and community health and well-being.

The principle of equitable provision is almost universally accepted by recreation professionals and expected by community residents, and is regarded as both appropriate and desirable. Such broad acceptance of the principle is the result of leisure services being thought of as a "public good," which means that they are deemed to be of social value, are not subject to market forces, are not exclusionary, and they generate benefits to the community that exceed the costs to provide them. Of course in recent years, leisure services have increasingly been treated as marketable products which may or may not be offered by the local parks and recreation department depending on public demand, ability to pay, and/or political expediency. The exceptions to this trend are recreation opportunities, such as parks and trails, that the commercial sector is unlikely to provide because they provide primarily social and environmental benefits rather than economic ones.

Despite widespread support for the principle, equitable provision is extremely difficult to implement. Consequently, the focus of attention for both practitioners and analysts has not been whether the principle is an appropriate policy for the delivery of leisure services, but rather, how to go about achieving it. This task has become even more challenging. With public resources to support social services continuing to dwindle (Baines, 2006) and greater calls for accountability in the performance of local government, parks and recreation departments across Canada must adopt strategies for the delivery of leisure services to all community residents that are not only equitable, but effective and efficient.

The first task is, of course, to define what we mean by "equitable provision." Even though a number of different approaches have been adopted to deliver leisure services to the community, each of them still attempts to adhere to the principle of equitable provision. Once an understanding of equitable provision is in place, we need to critically examine the advantages and disadvantages of the ways in which each approach has been put into practice to determine if the leisure needs of the residents of a community are indeed being met.

Basic Approaches to Equitable Provision

The idea most often used to address the principle of equitable provision is equity. By definition, equity is "the quality of being equal or fair" and is based on notions of "fairness, impartiality, or justice" (*Oxford English Dictionary*, 1997). From this perspective, some individuals or groups in the community might receive the same, more, or perhaps even less service than others if such a disproportionate provision results in a delivery system that would be judged as being fair in the provision of access to public recreation opportunities. In other words, departures from equal treatment are justifiable if those departures are seen as being more fair or just.

Much of the interest in how public services are provided was guided by the theoretical literature on social justice, which discussed a general moral philosophy that the overall fairness of a society was reflected in the way in which it divided and distributed resources. Most prominent among the early writers on social justice was Rawls (1971). His work was very influential in shaping the perspectives taken in the political science and public administration literature during the 1970s and early 1980s. According to Rawls, justice depends upon two principles: equality for all and recognition of difference. While equality is an essential starting point for justice (and hence, fairness) to prevail, some recognition of differences must also be present to ensure that those disadvantaged groups have access to the same rights and privileges as everyone else in a just society. Consequently, adoption of these principles brought about systems of "distributive justice" where resources might not necessarily be distributed equally to all residents, but rather be redistributed to the least advantaged so they are not denied access to opportunities. Following Rawls, authors such as Lineberry (1974 with Welch; 1977), Mladenka and Hill (1977), Rich (1979, 1982), and Lucy (1981) focused on issues related to the distribution of public services, including recreation, and conducted some of the earliest empirical research examining distributions of public resources in communities. Their work set the stage for leisure researchers, and Wicks and Crompton in particular, who produced a series of papers that described four basic approaches used by local government in the effort to achieve equity in the provision of leisure services: (1) equality, (2) need, (3) demand, and (4) market (Crompton & Wicks, 1988; Wicks & Backman, 1994; Wicks & Crompton, 1986, 1987, 1989). These basic approaches and the ways in which they are implemented are illustrated in Figure 29.1. As originally stated by Laswell (1958) and reiterated by Crompton and Wicks (1988), whichever approach is adopted by a local parks and recreation department, its decision essentially comes down to which approach best answers the question, "who gets what, when, and how?" In fact, the better question is "who gets what, *where,* and why?" [emphasis added] (Harvey, 1973; Smith, 1994) because the allocation of resources in the community is inherently a spatial problem, too.

Provision Based on Equality

The first approach to equity is based on equality of provision. The premise underlying this approach is that each individual within the community will receive the same amounts of services or the same benefits from those services as everyone else. Equality of provision can therefore be thought of in terms of either inputs or outputs. *Equality of inputs* means that the same amount is provided to everyone and no distinctions are made on the basis of social, cultural, or economic differences among residents. Using equality in services provision is the easiest approach to take and has traditionally been used in most communities, especially for neighbourhood parks and recreation facilities. It is worth noting that equality of provision focuses on equal access to and not equal use of the services and facilities provided by the local parks and recreation department. Clearly, not everyone in the community will choose to use the resources with which they have been provided, but they must at least have equal opportunity to make that choice.

The means by which equality is implemented has relied on the "standards approach," which is a set of widely held guidelines that prescribe the minimum amount of service to provide to the community based on population size. Standards are most often used in decision making on the provision of parks and facilities as part of a larger community recreation planning exercise. The Ontario Ministry of Culture and

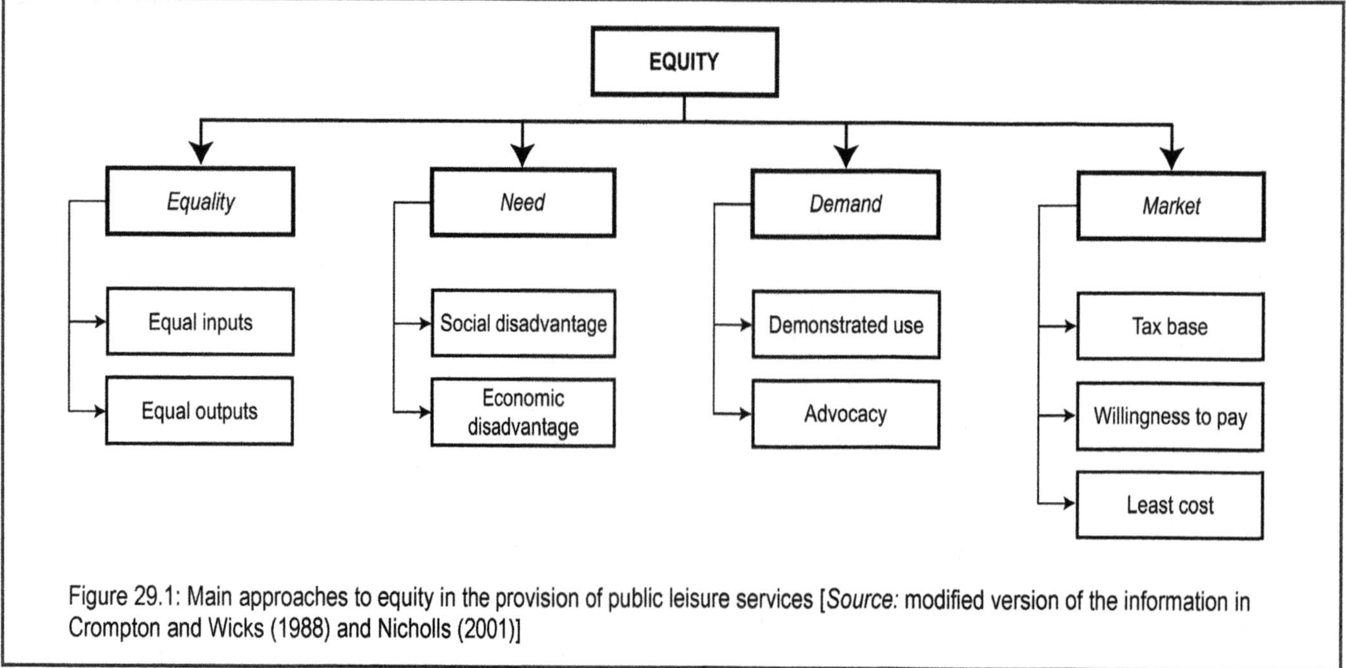

Figure 29.1: Main approaches to equity in the provision of public leisure services [*Source:* modified version of the information in Crompton and Wicks (1988) and Nicholls (2001)]

Recreation produced a manual in 1976 that detailed, for example, the minimum area in hectares of parkland required to service each 1,000 residents in the community, the numbers of facilities needed to support communities of various population sizes, and the distances residents should be expected to travel to take advantage of these facilities. In this latter instance, these distances—called *service radii*—represent that part of the community the park or facility is intended to serve. As the facilities become larger and serve greater numbers of the residents in the community, the distances people would be expected to travel will correspondingly increase. Some examples of these standards, which are still widely relied upon today, are shown in Table 29.1.

The use of standards typifies the equality of inputs approach, especially because using standards makes no distinctions among residents regardless of differences in their age, sex, ethnicity, income, or any other characteristics. Hence, an underlying assumption of this approach is that there is no distinction in the *desire* for access to public recreation opportunities among the diverse populations in our communities. Nevertheless, everyone is treated equally in what they receive.

In contrast, *equality of outputs* means that residents in the community are to receive the same benefits from the provision of leisure services. This perspective on equality means that even though everyone might not be provided with the same amount of service, they are ultimately intended to receive the same level of benefit from whatever services they are provided. For example, two neighbourhoods might be provided with precisely equal levels of service (i.e., inputs), but derive quite different benefits (i.e., outputs).

Table 29.1: Selected examples of standards for provision of public recreation services and facilities

A. Standards for Open Space

Type	*Hectares per 1,000 population*	*Service radii*	*Typical Size*
Tot-lot	0.10 to 0.20 ha	0.20 to 0.40 km	0.25 to 0.80 ha (average 0.20 ha)
Parkette	0.20 ha	0.20 to 0.40 km	0.25 to 0.40 ha (average 0.20 ha)
Neighbourhood park	0.40 to 0.80 ha	0.40 to 0.80 km	0.10 to 8.0 ha (average 2.5 ha)
Local park or playfield	0.40 to 0.80 ha	0.80 to 5.0 km (average 1.5 km)	1.5 to 40 ha (average 3 to 10 ha)
Community-wide park	2.0 ha	0.80 to 5.0 km (average 3.0 km)	10 to 80 ha (average 40 ha)
Regional park	1.5 to 4.0 ha	within 30 km	10 to 400 ha (average 40 to 100 ha)

B. Standards for Facilities

Type	*Description*	*Standard*
Arena	One arena with spectator seating and others for recreational purposes with limited seating	One location per 20,000 residents
Sports field	For soccer, rugby, or football, combined with local park or secondary school	One location per 20,000 residents
Golf course	Regulation length (18 holes) including driving range, on minimum of 50 to 70 hectares	One location per 30,000 residents
Swimming pool	Year-round use, combined with recreation centre or school, minimum capacity of 200 persons	One location per 20,000 residents
Tennis courts	Lighted, combined with schools, with minimum of three courts per location	One location per 5,000 residents

The reasons underlying these differences might be attributable to the different character of the neighbourhoods and the degree to which each one perceives or has a greater or lesser desire for the types of opportunities afforded by the services provided. Conversely, two neighbourhoods might receive different amounts of service if it can be determined that the benefits derived would be the same. This is a first step towards recognising differences among residents in terms of what level of service might be provided by the local parks and recreation department in order for all residents to obtain equal levels of benefits. This represents, of course, an enormous challenge for leisure services agencies because of the difficulty in accurately determining the benefits actually received by residents.

Provision Based on Need

The second approach to equity is based on need. In this approach, sometimes referred to as *compensatory equity*, services are provided to those groups and/or those areas within the community that are deemed to be socially or economically disadvantaged. In essence, the leisure provider offers programs and services based on perceived need in the community. Its role is to redistribute resources in a way that assists or compensates groups that might not otherwise have the capability to access recreation opportunities.

For leisure services agencies, determining "need" represents a particularly difficult challenge. How does the local parks and recreation department decide who is in greater need of leisure services and should therefore be compensated? Providing additional services to groups that are economically disadvantaged might appear to be the easiest strategy to adopt as it is consistent with Rawls's difference principle. The economic circumstances of some groups, such as low income levels or low property values, suggest that they are less able to access recreation services and programmes. Furthermore, people with lower incomes are forced by circumstances to live in areas that are typically much higher in density, less well developed, and hence, less well-provided for. Under such conditions, the need for assistance might seem obvious.

Residents' access to leisure opportunities might also be influenced by a variety of needs that are more subtle than purely economically based ones. Need may be based on population characteristics such as ethnicity, age, or gender, which are characteristics frequently linked to social disadvantage. In a multicultural society like Canada, many groups have cultural ties that might not be consistent with the types of programs and services traditionally provided by the local parks and recreation department. By focussing on sports programs, especially for youth, many local leisure services agencies may not be adequately providing for the interests of people, for example, from different ethnic backgrounds or in the later years of their lives (see Chapters 20, 21, 22, & 24).

Regardless of the difficulty in determining need, provision of leisure services based on need has long-standing support among parks and recreation professionals. As an approach that attempts to identify where need exists and to redistribute resources to compensate, provision based on need has traditionally been embraced by leisure providers and community members alike because of its emphasis on principles of fairness and justice.

Provision Based on Demand

The third approach to equity is based on demand. Provision of service is deemed to be most equitable if it responds according to the demand expressed by residents—those who desire the services most will receive more of them. Demand is expressed by residents in a couple of different ways. Quite simply it can be expressed as levels of participation in the community; with those groups or areas that demonstrate the highest levels of participation receiving greater amounts of services and programs. Demand can also be expressed through advocacy; that is, those groups within the community that lobby most effectively for resources are more likely to receive them.

An approach to provision based on demand provides local agencies with a simple means of determining where provision of leisure services can most effectively respond to the apparent desires of the community's residents. Basically, this approach looks for patterns of consumption expressed by the community's residents. By identifying those groups or areas in the community that are showing higher levels of participation in certain recreational pursuits or making greater use of specific types of recreation facilities, the local parks and recreation department can channel more resources to those groups to ensure they receive adequate support and access.

Arguably, this approach to equity is regarded as fair because those residents have clearly demonstrated their demand for public recreation services and programs through their participation. Why provide resources to residents who are not even using them? One of the problems with this assumption, of course, is that demand is very often created by providing services. For example, the use of a recreation facility is typically highest among those residents who live closest to that facility; in other words, their demand is in part simply reflecting the higher availability and access of existing resources. What remains unclear is whether the residents in other areas would participate more if they too received similar levels of provision. So, the question remains whether or not responding to *demand* has necessarily addressed the leisure service *needs* of the community equitably.

Another way in which the community's residents can express demand for leisure services and programs is through advocacy or appeals. By responding to residents' direct appeals, the local parks and recreation department provides people with an opportunity to indicate what services, and in what amount, they wish to receive. Such an approach releases the parks and recreation department from assuming that levels of participation are indicative of the need for such services, because by advocating, residents are vocalizing their desires directly. Responding to advocacy is also politically attractive, because the department can show quite clearly that it is responding to the expressed demands of the community and is thereby being accountable.

Unfortunately, resident advocacy can blur the distinction between demands by and needs of residents. While it can be argued those residents who successfully lobby for additional resources are effectively demonstrating their "need" for those resources, they are often not members of groups in the community typically defined as being "in need." Highly effective advocacy groups, such as neighbourhood associations, are often the most highly informed, resourced, and privileged segments of a community—"insiders" in the system—as opposed to more disadvantaged groups, which are the intended target groups for provision based on need. Indeed, advocacy efforts by residents are not necessarily judged on the basis of economic or social considerations, so greater provision could be the result of effective lobbying rather than need.

Provision Based on the Market

Finally, the fourth approach to provision is one based on the market. In the commercial sector, resources are distributed in the market place based on people's ability or willingness to pay for the products on offer. By adopting this perspective for public recreation, services and programs can be allocated based on three different strategies: (1) the amount of taxes paid by residents; (2) the willingness of residents to pay for services; (3) and a least cost approach.

Within a market model, the tax base becomes a surrogate indicator of revenue generation. In other words, those residents who pay higher taxes effectively have paid more for public services and should therefore receive proportionately more of them. Using this perspective, the tax base in a community can be used to help in deciding where and what quantity of recreation services and facilities should be allocated. To be seen as an equitable approach to provision, one must accept that allocation is directly tied to the tax base—those who pay more, get more. Indeed, residents may even use this argument in a demand approach to provision by advocating for increased service provision based on the taxes that they pay in their neighbourhood.

A related market strategy to provision is based on residents' willingness to pay for the services they receive. Under this strategy, while the parks and recreation department would continue to provide a basic infrastructure of parks, open space, and facilities, residents who were interested in receiving greater amounts and/or quality of services and programs would pay for them. Supporters of this approach regard it as fair, because those residents not interested in using public leisure services would not be required to pay for them, beyond their contributions through the tax base. In effect, this approach is based on *efficiency* of provision because resources are only allocated to those who will use them to the extent to which they pay, and hence, no resources are wasted by allocating them to those who are not interested in using them.

The third strategy in the market approach is based on a least cost principle. This strategy also focuses on efficiency in the provision of leisure opportunities, because it is driven by a desire to minimise the costs associated with providing services and programs. For example, a parks and recreation department might choose to provide programs at a school or facility that charges the lowest rental rather than at a site closest to the intended users; or a new park might be planned for an area of the community of no interest to developers. This market approach is seen as equitable, because rather than targeting resources to a limited number of groups or areas within the community, they can be distributed more widely to everyone in the community. Similarly, with the potential savings accrued from adopting a least-cost strategy, resources might still be available to allocate where they are thought to be most needed. Unfortunately, the least costly locations are typically the least desirable in terms of attractiveness and, importantly, accessibility. Consequently, even though resources might be distributed more widely, they are distributed without consideration to those who might be willing—or able—to use them.

A market approach to providing recreation resources in the community can be further complicated by how the parks and recreation department regards its relationship to the commercial sector. If the public agency feels it can better serve the community by providing less costly alternatives to those residents who cannot afford similar services in the commercial sector, it has effectively entered a competitive market and is therefore subject to the same market forces that dictate whether services survive or not. Furthermore, the agency opens itself up to the criticism that the public sector should not be directly competing with the commercial sector. Alternatively, the parks and recreation department might simply choose to provide services that the commercial sector does not provide, thereby serving that part of the community that has a need for such services, but that the commercial sector views as unprofitable. The danger here, of course, is that the public sector is simply reacting to the market and is not making targeted resource allocation decisions to serve its residents.

Nevertheless, a market approach to allocating parks and recreation resources is attractive to many agencies because it is seen as fiscally responsible during times when accountability is a priority and financial resources are much harder to come by. Even though there is some debate whether local parks and recreation departments have been as seriously affected by cut-backs as other local services (see for example, Connolly & Smale, 2002), in times of fiscal restraint, the market approach has gained political support. Many parks and recreation departments now struggle to maintain a balance between adopting a market approach along with operational approaches based in the commercial sector and adapting those approaches to fit the public sector's desire for equity in the provision of leisure services. The greatest criticism of the market approach is that those residents who are economically disadvantaged and who live in poorer areas of the community—and are by definition in the greatest need of services—are least likely to be allocated resources based on the market model. The market approach is, in this respect, completely contrary to an approach based on need.

This criticism of the market approach is not applicable for all public recreation resources. The commercial sector typically does not provide parks and other open space opportunities such as soccer fields or baseball fields, nor do they provide, with the very rare exception, major recreation facilities such as swimming pools or skating and hockey arenas. Consequently, the local parks and recreation department relies primarily on the local tax base to develop and operate such resources. Nevertheless, even though there is no need to consider a competitive market in the distribution of open space and facilities, the amount of taxes paid still provides a strong political incentive under this approach to provide more resources to those areas that have contributed the most to the tax base.

Which of the various approaches to the delivery of public leisure services do you think is currently being used in your home community? Do you think it is working well? Why?

Regardless of which approach to the delivery of leisure services is adopted, local parks and recreation departments are faced with allocating resources within an ever changing social and political environment. An approach supported at one time might no longer be supported by a government with a different social and/or political agenda. Consequently, the way in which resources get allocated might be a compromise between a desire to adhere to the principle of equitable provision within one perspective while trying to accommodate alternate perspectives. For example, the parks and recreation department might be more sympathetic to a needs-based approach to the provision of its services and programs, but the local government might be concerned with fiscal responsibility and wish to emphasise a more market-based approach to all of its service delivery decisions, including leisure. The inevitable result then, is a combination of approaches being employed in most communities. Some services and programs impose fees when the groups using them are regarded as willing and able to pay (market approach), other programs are offered for free to groups perceived as having limited access (need-based approach), and neighbourhood parks are planned and distributed based on the standards approach (equality approach). The approach receiving greater emphasis, however, is frequently determined by the political environment in which the local parks and recreation department operates.

Theoretical Models of Leisure Services Delivery

As noted previously, the choice of a particular model for the delivery of leisure services is ultimately linked to the political orientation in place within the community or even the society at large. For example, if the approach taken by the community parks and recreation department is based on equality, this is a natural response to a philosophy of social justice, which is typically associated with a liberal democratic society.

Unlike North America where most of the discussion has focused on specific ways of achieving equitable provision, in Europe, early debates focused on different political orientations and their associated economic perspectives that gave rise to different approaches of allocating leisure resources. In particular, Beckers (1989) put forth a typology of six models for the creation and delivery of public leisure services, which he derived based on the perspectives offered by Bramham, Henry, Mommass, and Van der Poel (1989). In each case, similarities can be drawn between Beckers's models based on political orientation and the previously discussed approaches based on equitable provision.

1. *Minimalist model*: as the name implies, the minimalist model provides the least provision of leisure services possible by the local government. Instead, this approach presumes that recreation is principally the responsibility of either or both the commercial or volunteer sectors.

2. *Welfare model*: the welfare model operates within the local government under a traditional social welfare policy. With this approach, only specialised leisure services are provided in an effort to counteract gaps not served by the commercial sector. Typically, these specialised services are targeted at disadvantaged groups in the community or those least able to pay.
3. *Entrepreneurial model*: an entrepreneurial model positions local government to engage in the provision of leisure activities and programs to generate profits, which in turn, could be used to subsidise services that on their own are not self-supporting, but are socially desirable in the community.
4. *Therapeutic model*: the therapeutic model regards the provision of leisure services primarily as a tool for community development, especially for special populations such as individuals with physical or intellectual disabilities.
5. *Economic model*: under the economic model, recreation provision on the part of local government is essentially a means for attracting outside investors and industries to the community. If successful, the model results in producing economic benefits to the community as a whole.
6. *Cultural model*: the cultural model views leisure as an integral ingredient of local cultural or leisure policy, and as such, leisure services provided by the public sector allow for the expression of the prevailing societal and community culture.

Which of the approaches described earlier share similarities with the models described by Beckers?

Beckers recognised that just one of these models is rarely implemented on its own by the leisure services agency for two principal reasons. First, different models are often employed to deliver different kinds of services, depending in part on the perceived need within the community. For example, a municipal golf course might be seen as fitting within the entrepreneurial model because of its ability to generate revenues in support of other services, whereas local parks might fit more closely with the cultural model because of the overarching belief in the many benefits that parks and public open space offer to the community as a whole.

Second, and perhaps more importantly, the model adopted is subject to the prevailing political orientation within local government and within the broader political environment. Depending on whether the sociopolitical landscape emphasizes a market orientation or a social welfare orientation very much influences, if not dictates, the perspective taken towards the provision of leisure services. For example, a municipal council that embraces the political perspective that it is primarily the responsibility of the market to supply goods and services, including recreation, is likely to see local government's role in the provision of leisure services reflected in the minimalist model (which has similarities to the least cost strategy of the market approach). In contrast, a municipality that embraces a more social democratic perspective is likely to see an active role for local government in the provision of leisure services; in other words, the welfare model (which has similarities to an equity approach based on need). Whether done intentionally or not, local leisure services agencies tend to adopt more than one model of service delivery simply because all of its programs and facilities cannot realistically be provided by a single approach.

Which of the different approaches to the delivery of public leisure services do you think would be the most effective? Which one do you think would be most efficient? Can one approach achieve both effectiveness and efficiency?

In recognition of this influence, Henry (1988) developed a typology that attempted to reflect how the political ideologies of local government become reflected in the way in which leisure services are provided. He first identified five idealized models of local government and then described the economic and political circumstances under which each model emerged. Finally, Henry speculated on the role that a public leisure services agency might take on as a result of these influences arising from the local government (see Table 29.2, p. 280).

In Henry's typology, the role adopted by local government extends from one that is highly removed from the market place unless it is needed to provide essential services (i.e., a contract management role) to one where government takes an active role in local economic development with an eye towards building a healthier community (i.e., a municipal socialist role). More often, local governments fall somewhere in between these two extremes and adopt different roles as the circumstances demand. For example, parks and open space are the sole responsibility of the public sector, so local government feels some obligation to ensure that these resources are provided and maintained at satisfactory

Table 29.2: Henry's (1988) idealized models of local government and public leisure services provision

Idealised Model	Role of Local Government	Role of Public Leisure Services Agency
Contract Management	Local government is the provider of last resort. Only services regarded as essential are delivered to the public. Individuals take responsibility for their own physical and mental well-being and pursue interests through the market place.	Leisure services agency must determine what the leisure needs of the community are and directly provide those services that cannot or will not be provided by the commercial or voluntary sectors (e.g., urban parks).
Financial Stringency	Local government makes practical responses to increasingly strained economic conditions in the community. Local government does not embrace an ideological view of its enabling role.	With no political commitment to leisure as a community need, leisure services agencies have difficulty justifying expenditures on the provision of services under conditions of increasing economic pressures. Similar to Becker's minimalist model where government reduces services provision to the lowest expenditure possible.
Keynesian	Local government serves as a manager of the equilibrium between the supply and demand of services. Increased investment in local goods and services is made to stimulate the demand and the acquired financial resources are redistributed in order that those individuals most in need are provided for.	Leisure services agency identifies the needs of the community and expands resources in those areas to bring about greater community well-being. A community's latent needs for leisure services must be determined by expert assessment—especially in financially constrained times—rather than through community self-determination.
Post Industrial	Local government invests in the local economy and redistributes resources to reduce inequalities, like the Keynesian model, but differs in that its involvement is aimed at facilitating change in an information and service economy.	Leisure services agency moves away from central delivery of services and towards facilitating citizen involvement by creating and implementing recreation services in local areas. This role promotes greater citizen self-determination and emphasis on the needs of disadvantaged groups.
Municipal Socialist	Local government actively intervenes in community economic development to serve the interests of the community as a whole. Typically, the focus is on counteracting social problems produced by the market (e.g., high rates of unemployment, social unrest). Heavy investment in social services such as education, housing, and leisure is seen as essential in maintaining a healthy, educated community and restoring the local economy.	Leisure services agency expands into areas typically held by the commercial sector in order to use the profits to subsidise needed and desirable programs and services that are provided to foster the community good.

levels in the community. While this view appears consistent with a contract management role, the local government might regard its commitment to parks and the benefits they provide as essential parts of its role as custodian of the community's well-being, which is more consistent with a Keynesian role (see Table 29.2 for details). In each instance, the parks and recreation department will use approaches to the provision of leisure resources that reflect these government roles.

Traditionally, local governments have influenced the provision of leisure services in two principal ways, both of which are suggested in Henry's typology. The first way is in its response to what it regards as "market failure." If the commercial sector is unable or unwilling to provide needed services, local government may step in and provide it to its residents. Of course, as we have seen, deciding what services are *needed* in the community is frequently the subject of debate. This debate is in part the centrepiece of the second way in which local government influences leisure services provision—determining what services can be regarded as a "public good" and therefore having inherent *social* value. Local government ensures that services deemed to be a public good are accessible to the residents without any of the restrictions that the market may impose. If the costs to provide a service are greater than the revenues they return, the market will not provide them. However, if the collective, social benefits generated by the services are deemed to be of greater value than the costs to provide them, even if those costs exceed revenues generated from their provision, then they are considered to be a public good (McConnell, Brue, & Pope, 1990). When leisure services are regarded as a public good, they are accepted as being of sufficient interest that they must be provided by local government. In principle, this would ensure that all residents in the community will benefit from the provision of such services. Hence, this view is inextricably linked to the principle of equity.

Ironically, most parks and recreation departments now offer at least some programs and opportunities (e.g., golf courses) that arguably only provide benefits to those individuals who pay the fees to use them. By definition, these types of offerings are private goods, which are typical of the market place and operate under the exclusion principle—those who can or will pay, receive the benefits, and those who cannot or will not pay, do not receive them (McConnell, Brue, & Pope, 1990). For the most part, leisure services agencies offer both public and private goods, even if some residents will not have access to certain opportunities. Rather, they simply see the mix of programs, services, and facilities they provide as contributing collectively to the overall benefits received by the community as a whole. Such is the complexity of attempting to achieve equitable provision.

Challenges in Achieving Equitable Provision

Regardless of the good intentions a parks and recreation department might have in achieving equitable provision, it faces a number of challenges. Not only does the prevailing political environment exert a significant influence on the approach adopted, but one approach is unlikely, on its own, to achieve equity. Consequently, in practice, apparently conflicting approaches might be adopted if they are seen as collectively achieving equitable provision of resources. Indeed, the approaches described here are really reflections of current practice as opposed to consciously selected courses of action by local parks and recreation departments. The local agency rarely if ever has the authority to act on a particular model based on some shared philosophical perspective of the "right way" to provide its leisure services to the community. Rather, as noted earlier, what we tend to see is the application of different models of provision depending on the nature of the services being provided and the needs of that part of the community they are intended to meet.

Furthermore, communities continue to grow and evolve. Neighbourhoods mature and change as people of different ages, different ethnicities, and family structures move in, around, and out of the community. Public facilities such as swimming pools and arenas, however, cannot be moved about the community, and what was once a favoured venue for recreation by a neighbourhood might become a less well used site by that neighbourhood as its residents evolve. This is why a recreation space standards approach based on equality of provision is traditionally implemented, because a standards approach is insensitive to social and economic differences among residents. As the community changes, the even distribution of parks and facilities is arguably equally accessible to everyone, regardless of where they live. Consequently, approaches to leisure services delivery can be more easily changed and effectively implemented for services and programs, which can be moved around the community in response to residents' demands or needs.

Finally, despite the argument that leisure services are a public good, parks and recreation departments are increasingly being pressured by local governments to generate more revenue for their services. This has resulted in the introduction and/or raising of user fees for many programs and services, as well as increased participation in promoting special events, such as sports tournaments and festivals, to attract revenue through tourism. Embracing these strategies has both obvious and more subtle consequences to achieving equitable provision. The greatest impact of introducing or raising fees for programs is the limitations it might place on certain groups in the community, such as the poor. In particular older adults and single parent families may be placed at a disadvantage because they are frequently among the most economically disadvantaged members within our population. When emphasis is placed on the financial viability of the parks and recreation department rather than on the protection of the public good, critical leisure services that might have been operating at a loss are in serious danger of being eliminated irrespective of the social benefits they provide. The challenge then, is to find a balance between responding to the pressures that could change the face of public recreation and reaffirming leisure services as a public good and maintaining a commitment to equal opportunity in their provision.

If you were in charge of the local parks and recreation department, which approach or combination of approaches to providing leisure services to the community would you adopt? Why?

Key Terms

Accessibility
Demand
Equality
Equitable provision
Equity
Market
Need
Public good
Service provision

References

Baines, D. (2006). "Whose needs are being served?" Quantitative metrics and the reshaping of social services. *Studies in Political Economy, 77*, 195–209.

Beckers, T. (1989). Integrating leisure policies in advanced societies: The squaring of the circle. Cities for the future: The role of leisure and tourism in the process of revitalization. *Post-Congressbook, Recreatie Reeks Nr. 7* (pp. 55–61). Den Haag: Stiching Recreate.

Bramham, P., Henry, I., Mommaas, H., & van der Poel, H. (Eds.). (1989). *Leisure and urban processes: Critical studies of leisure policy in Western European cities.* London, UK: Routledge.

Connolly, K., & Smale, B. (2002). Changes in the financing of local recreation and cultural services: An examination of trends in Ontario from 1988 to 1996. *Leisure/Loisir, 26*(3/4), 213–234.

Crompton, J. L., & Wicks, B. E. (1988). Implementing a preferred equity model for the delivery of leisure services in the U.S. context. *Leisure Studies, 7*, 287–304.

Harvey, D. (1973). *Social justice and the city.* London, UK: Edward Arnold.

Henry, I. (1988). Alternative futures for the public leisure service. In J. Bennington & J. White (Eds.), *The future of leisure services* (pp. 207–243). Essex, UK: Longman.

Howell, S., & McNamee, M. (2003). Local justice and public sector leisure policy. *Leisure Studies, 22*, 17–35.

Laswell, H. O. (1958). *Politics: Who gets what, when, how.* New York, NY: Meridian Books.

Lineberry, R. L. (1977). *Equality and urban policy.* Beverly Hills, CA: Sage.

Lineberry, R. L., & Welch, R. E., Jr. (1974). Who gets what: Measuring the distribution of urban public services. *Social Science Quarterly, 54*, 700–712.

Lucy, W. (1981). Equity and planning for local services. *Journal of the American Planning Association, 47*, 447–457.

McConnell, C. R., Brue, S. L., & Pope, W. H. (1990). *Micro economics.* Toronto, ON: McGraw-Hill Ryerson.

Mladenka, K. R., & Hill, K. (1977). The distribution of benefits in an urban environment: Parks and libraries in Houston. *Urban Affairs Quarterly, 13*, 73–94.

Nicholls, S. (2001). Measuring the accessibility and equity of public parks: A case study using GIS. *Managing Leisure, 6*, 201–219.

Ontario Ministry of Culture and Recreation. (1976). *Guidelines for developing public recreation facility standards.* Toronto, ON: Sports and Fitness Division, Ministry of Culture and Recreation.

Oxford English Dictionary. (1997). London, UK: Oxford University Press.

Rawls, J. (1971). *A theory of justice.* Cambridge, MA: Harvard University Press.

Rich, R. C. (1979). Neglected issues in the study of urban service distributions: A research agenda. *Urban Studies, 16*, 143–156.

Rich, R. C. (Ed.). (1982). *Analyzing urban-service distributions.* Toronto, ON: Lexington Books.

Smith, D. M. (1994). *Geography and social justice.* Oxford, UK: Blackwell.

Wicks, B. E., & Backman, K. F. (1994). Measuring equity preferences: A longitudinal analysis. *Journal of Leisure Research, 26*(4), 386–401.

Wicks, B. E., & Crompton, J. L. (1986). Citizen and administrator perspectives of equity in the delivery of park services. *Leisure Sciences, 8*(4), 341–365.

Wicks, B. E., & Crompton, J. L. (1987). An analysis of the relationship between equity choice preferences, service type, and decision making groups in a U.S. city. *Journal of Leisure Research, 19*(3), 189–203.

Wicks, B. E., & Crompton, J. L. (1989). Allocating services for parks and recreation: A model for implementing equity concepts in Austin, Texas. *Journal of Urban Affairs, 11*(2), 169–188.

Chapter 30
Leisure Planning

Donald G. Reid, Ph.D.
University of Guelph

Learning Objectives

After reading this chapter, students will be able to

1. Have a basic understanding of the fundamentals of leisure planning.
2. Gain a greater understanding of the mechanics of leisure planning and the fundamental values that underlie each of the approaches presented.
3. Learn the basic concepts on which planning for leisure is based.

Introduction

Fundamentally, leisure planning is the direct intervention and organization of a recreation system. It is the expression of future aspirations built around a set of values that become expressed through an implementation strategy. Exactly whose values get incorporated into the plan is among the important questions to be addressed in this chapter. Fundamentally, leisure planning is about the creation of a vision for the future and then deciding how that future will be achieved. This chapter contrasts the basic models of planning and discusses their implementation and the consequences of making choices among alternatives.

Planning is defined and viewed in a variety of different ways. Some authors (Chadwick, 1971) see planning as a basic human activity of thought or forethought and as a process leading to satisfying some predetermined goal. The Rational Choice Model (Davidoff & Reiner, 1962) and Linking Knowledge to Action (Freidmann, 1987) are variations on that theme. Each of these models takes a slightly different approach to planning activity. The approaches to planning outlined above depend on different types of data-collection methods, and on giving additional weight to certain kinds of information over others.

The Rational Choice Model for example, depends on quantitative information and is intent on linking expenditure data to use or participation statistics. It tries to maximize participation as efficiently as possible in consideration of the expenditure of funds required to produce that activity. Efficiency is a prime motivator for the selection of this model as the basis of planning. In the Rational Choice Model, behaviour is thought to be the sole indicator of the needs and goals of the participant. The activity is considered to be an end in itself rather than a means to some other, perhaps larger, social goal.

Linking knowledge to action, on the other hand, emphasizes people reflecting on their values and goals, and then determining the appropriate path to achieving those ends. Activity in this model is considered a means to some larger social or psychological goal. This latter approach usually favours qualitative information gathering and reflexive analysis over quantitative and deterministic data. The focus here is on the effectiveness of the program or activity for those who are interested and engaged, and, while cost may be of concern, it is not the determining factor, nor is it weighted as heavily as in the Rational Choice Model. In each case, the model offers the planner an alternative way of thinking about and solving the problem at hand.

The basic models of planning described above are based on the notion that planners and decision makers must intervene in the social environment to achieve goals created by society. Others believe that the market, if left alone, is the best method for allocating resources including recreation and leisure. The ways of viewing planning as described above must be examined in opposition to the more economic deterministic view of the world that leaves decision making (planning) to the market mechanism. In some ways, the Rational Choice Model noted above can be viewed as a bridge between the pure market model and the more value-centered approach of those that link knowledge to action, as seen, for example, in the social learning model discussed later in this chapter. While some might not describe the pure market approach to service development and delivery as planning, it is undoubtedly the making of conscious decisions that propose how the future world should be constructed.

Fundamentally, then, society has at least two choices in how it conducts its affairs, including the provision of leisure and recreation, and those are through human intervention in the social system embracing a planned approach, or through the "invisible hand" of the market. Both of these distribution and choice mechanisms are at play in the leisure and recreation field producing two very different results, as will be discussed later in this chapter.

Needless to say, just about everything humans do is planned in some way or another. It may be through a formal planning process or a less formal decision-making procedure, but it is planned nonetheless.

The Classical Planning Process

Grand and sophisticated theories have been developed over the decades to help guide the planning process, but when one thinks of a classical planning process for recreation purposes it generally looks similar to the one described by Freidmann (1987, p. 78) presented below:

1. *The formulation* of goals and objectives for recreation built on a vision of statement.
2. *The identification and design* of major alternatives for reaching the goals identified.
3. *The prediction* of consequences that would be expected to follow upon adoption of each alternative.
4. *The evaluation* of consequences in relation to desired objectives and other important values.
5. *The decision* based on information provided in the preceding steps.
6. *The implementation* of this decision through appropriate institutions and strategies.
7. *The feedback* of actual program results and their assessment in light of the new decision situation.

The question of what gets planned is a major consideration that needs to be addressed. Traditionally, planning in the leisure and recreation field has concentrated on a couple of well-defined areas. Certainly, areas and facilities, including the built and natural environment, have figured prominently in the planning of leisure and recreation development. Program development is also a major area of focus. Indeed, municipal recreation departments and non-governmental organizations (NGOs) develop a schedule of programs using a planned approach similar to the one described above. Operational reviews that centre on examining administrative practices and decision making have also emerged as a subject for attention in planning activity. Marketing studies and market segmentation are often considered planning activity in the subfield of tourism development. So, planning, in some form or other, plays a large role in the development and presentation of services throughout the entire recreation and leisure delivery system.

Macro Approaches to Planning

In his book, *Planning in the Public Domain: From Knowledge to Action,* Friedmann (1987) describes four macro approaches to planning. They are:

1. *Social Reform*: essentially control from the top. It views those in authority as experts who have special knowledge of the situation or of society generally, which allows them to direct the plan and its outcome. In leisure and recreation this approach to planning generated the traditional master plan concept. It embraced the idea of rational choice, that is, that the plan was comprehensive in scope and based on logic and wisdom.
2. *Policy Analysis*: also a top-down planning model but is seen as being much more scientific in its development than some of the other theories to be discussed here. It depends on the collection and analysis of data, which, it is felt, will lead to rational choices. Data for analysis are typically quantitative. Friedmann (1987, p. 139) suggests that policy analysis embraces three traditions: "systems engineering with its strong bias for quantitative modeling; management science with its leanings toward a general-systems theory…; and political and administrative sciences with their behavioral orientation."
3. *Social Learning*: links action to knowledge and discovery. This approach is viewed as bottom-up and places those who will be the recipients of the plan squarely in a highly participatory role. It is often characterized as learning by doing. The focus of this type of planning may slide its focus from plan as product to plan as process. With such a focus, the emphasis is on learning as much as on what gets produced. In recreation and leisure planning, needs assessments are often undertaken and completed based on this model.
4. *Social Mobilization*: an extension of the social learning model. It embraces the focus on agency (citizen) control and the bottom-up approach but adds a radicalization component to the model. Again, Friedmann (1987, p. 225) suggests that it "encompasses three great oppositional movements of Utopianism, social anarchism, and historical materialism." Unlike social learning, social mobilization may start with a political position or an agenda that some group in the community wishes to be realized through the plan. An example of this in our field could be found in an athletic group (e.g., swimmers) who are pushing the community to develop a facility (e.g., pool).

The discussion above points out the different approaches to planning that require planners, in this case recreation planners, to think about the rationale that is suitable to drive the plan and then to select an appropriate framework on which to conduct that activity. It is a prescription for failure to misdiagnose the circumstances driving the plan and then to adopt an inappropriate approach to the activity. Friedmann (1987, p. 76) sets out the options in Figure 30.1.

Figure 30.1 provides a tentative classification, as Friedman calls it, to indicate the place where each of the approaches to planning is situated on the political spectrum. This gives us additional information that helps us decide which macro approach would be best suited for a task at hand. Framing it in this way also indicates that planning is a part of the body politic and should be viewed in that context.

Knowledge to action	Conservative	Radical
Societal guidance	Policy analysis	Social reform
Social transformation	Social learning	Social mobilization

Figure 30.1 The politics of planning theory

Prevailing Types of Leisure Planning

Community recreation planning has been very successful in guiding leisure development over the years. Historically, it has been driven by the commitment to distribute areas and facilities equitably among the population. Initially, governments provided the recreation field with such planning instruments as "standards for development" based on facility-to-population ratios. As time went on, other devices were added to the repertoire of assessing needs for program and facility development. Themes such as historical demand, latent demand (potential future), social development (recreation's role in building community), and ameliorating the social deficit (e.g., delinquency) became part of the analysis in addition to the standards approach.

An initial focus for community leisure planning is to create a short- and long-term vision that recreation development can work towards. To that end, most community recreation plans begin with research that attempts to uncover individual and community needs that require attention. Community leisure research utilizes such methods as survey research, which seeks to question in detail a random sample of community members about their present and anticipated recreation needs and aspirations. It also tries to determine the constraints and barriers in the system (see Chapters 9, 26, and 34). Additionally, it undertakes interviews with key members of the community for the purpose of obtaining their enlightened perspective, focus-group meetings and workshops with non-governmental organizations (NGOs) that have a recreation interest either as suppliers or consumers, and community service organizations who often contribute their fundraising expertise and effort to community projects.

All public input gained through this research activity is usually fed back to the community by way of public presentations that focus on the outcome and interpretation of the results of the study, by the planner. Most community recreation plans today do not deal solely with the sponsor's interests (usually the municipal recreation department) but, to varying degrees, with the concerns of other actors in the recreation system, including non-governmental (NGO) interests, and, in some cases, private-sector issues as well. In addition to focusing on traditional and mainstream issues, community recreation planning includes a focus on all segments of society, including the socially marginalized and other groups in society who are viewed as being challenged or disadvantaged in some way or other (see Chapter 31).

In addition to concentrating on the need for constructed recreation facilities and programming of activities in them, all levels of government have engaged in park and protected area planning as well. Senior-level governments, such as federal or provincial jurisdictions, often provide a national or regional park system that includes historic sites and unique natural features in the landscape. Local or municipal governments generate and provide a system of recreation facilities and programs for their local constituents including culture and arts, as well as physical activities.

Creation of these systems is often a marriage between environmental and social planning. Perhaps a good example of the union of the environmental with the social is offered by Parks Canada in their Visitor Activity Management Plan (VAMP) (Environment Canada, 1987). Each individual park site undertakes research that examines environmental considerations along with surveys of visitor perceptions about, and satisfaction with, park services. VAMP is dedicated to protecting the environment while providing maximum satisfactions to the users of the park.

Additionally, senior-level governments also plan at the macro level to determine and develop new sites in and for the entire inventory. In Parks Canada's case, there is great interest in providing sites that ecologically represent the major features of the Canadian landscape.

National and local governments, likewise, develop plans for adding new parks to the inventory as well as designing uses for sites once obtained. At all levels of government, site design plays a large role in planning parks and green space (Pigram, 1983) in addition to the planning that goes on to establish the park as part of the overall system. This can be as large in scale as determining what areas inside the park will be used for what activity (e.g., camp sites vs. nature areas) or as micro as determining vegetation planting.

Tourism planning is also a distinct subject area of leisure planning. Mill and Morrison (1985) outline four major parts to the tourism system: (1) the market which is the process by which a traveller makes a buying decision; (2) the process by which travel suppliers present their product to the purchasing public; (3) travel options available to the destination site; and (4) the destination site itself, including the supporting infrastructure. It is this last part of the system on which leisure planners focus most of their attention. Of course there are planning issues with regard to product design and creation of the supporting infrastructure, but, perhaps more importantly, recent attention has broadened the scope of planning to include examining the needs of the wider community and those who, while not directly benefiting from tourism development, are directly affected both positively and negatively by it (Reid, Mair, George, & Taylor, 2001). This community assessment often includes some effort at raising awareness among citizens with regard to the positive and negative aspects of tourism development, examining and discussing community values (outlining those that the community wants to share with the rest of the world and those they wish to protect against outside influence), and the identification of environmental and social impacts of the proposal before development begins.

The process by which these and other issues get explored in planning is through the creation of a vision for development (often accomplished through some form of public forum); goal and objective setting that is designed to accomplish the vision, examination of the strengths and weaknesses of the present tourism attraction; taking inventory of the physical and human assets in the community that could potentially lend themselves to tourism development, product creation and recommendations for action; and some discussion about organizing the system so that the appropriate amount of developmental control remains in the hands of the citizens affected. This latter point is generally accomplished by the creation of an agreed-upon process for continued monitoring and evaluation of the development between community officials and the development proponent.

Planning as Managed or Stimulated Change

The way in which planning for leisure and recreation is approached often dictates the trajectory or outcome of the planning process. In the first instance, planners must decide if their activity ought to focus on managing change or whether it is more appropriately devoted to stimulating change. If it is the former, then plans usually involve more formal documents dedicated to accomplishing some important future goal. That goal may be to design (or redesign) the entire recreation system, including areas and facilities, as well as major program segments that the planning authority intends to develop over some period of time. Usually these types of large-scale plans include proposals for funding the physical and natural infrastructure they intend to develop and the fiscal requirements for all major activities that are contained within the plan. Traditionally, these types of plans and planning activities have been described as "master plans." Often master plans suggest the construction of a large facility or the development of a new program area or endeavour. In such a circumstance, a feasibility study is often required to examine that particular recommendation in greater detail. The feasibility study answers the fundamental question: are the proposed actions practical from a fiscal perspective and, if so, will they accomplish the objective sought in the most efficient and effective manner possible?

Leisure and recreation planning is often as much concerned with stimulating change as it is in developing and managing a complex system. The needs of society are becoming so complex and numerous that individual agencies, whether governmental or not, cannot simply act on their own in providing service as if there were no other players in the system. Indeed, even individual citizens demand input into the planning activities of government agencies, including those devoted to leisure and recreation, and especially in the case of private development that has the potential to alter or affect their environment.

Being involved in the recreation planning process can be as much a recreation activity as participation in any of the products of that plan. In this case, the process of planning is as much focused on the planning activity itself as it is on the substance or eventual outcome of the plan. Planning with the intent of stimulating change rather than managing it is seen more as an instrument of education and coordination than it is in concentrating on developing new physical infrastructure or program, although often that can result from the process as well. The goal is often devoted to constructing a multi-provider system of leisure delivery, where all the parts of that system coordinate their activity jointly yet remain autonomous and independent, to realize goals that would not be able to be accomplished by any single agency acting entirely on its own. That being said, there is a delicate balance between being part of a system through coordination and cooperation, and losing one's independence through abandonment of the agency's original mandate and raison d'être. Working together in planning that focuses on coordinating activity should result in strengthening the individual autonomy of agencies rather than diminishing it.

Stimulating change often requires focus on the system rather than the individual departments and agencies that constitute the system. You might think of the system as a symphony orchestra. The orchestra is made up of several sections like the woodwinds, percussion, brass, etc. The orchestra also has a leader who makes music out of what would otherwise simply be noise. The plan in this case is the orchestra leader that first prescribes and then coordinates the activities of all the players in the system. Planning to stimulate change, either in society generally or in the leisure system specifically, can also be directed at the individual agency as it struggles to become more relevant to its constituency and to society in general. This type of planning activity is often described as the "operational review." The goal of this category of planning is to reallocate resources away from areas that are seen as redundant to new areas of interest that are necessitated by changes in the demographic structure of society, newly discovered needs for services, or a change in mandate. The emphasis in operational review planning is on both effectiveness of the organization and the efficiency of its operations.

Citizen Participation in Leisure Planning

The issue of citizen participation is a wide-reaching concern for many aspects of leisure studies generally and is discussed by many authors contributing to this book. Nevertheless, this issue is of such great importance to leisure planning specifically that a short discussion needs to be presented here on community participation in the planning process. Not only is input into the process and outcome of the leisure plan important to all citizens, but it also represents an opportunity for those involved to reflect on their own leisure lives as it relates to the accomplishment of their personal life goals.

The issue of citizen participation in the planning process must deal with the matter of power. For example, Habermas (Guess, 1987) tells us that society can be dominated by various groups (he called this hegemony). Gramsci (1971) suggested that, in particular, society is often dominated by the state apparatus and this domination is supported by the institutions that the state creates or supports. Perhaps the largest of these institutions is the powerful corporations, including the media that dominate our daily lives.

Others have suggested how we might seek freedom or emancipation from such hegemony (McCarthy, 1978; Warren, 1995). Freire's (1990) concept of conscientization offers one example. Conscientization through planning is the process leading to the reduction of hegemony. An important goal of the planner is to educate the public with regard to their own needs and aspirations in their lives. Conscientization of a public is different than allowing the public into the world of the planner. The goal is to enter the world of the citizen, not to have the citizen enter the world of the planner or those whom the planner represents (the state). The planner does not plan for others but instead helps the members of society plan for their own communities.

Freire's concept of conscientization is built on the principle of citizen involvement. This involvement represents more than simply asking citizens for input on projects being planned. It is intended to provide an important avenue for self-discovery and self-education. As citizens are made more aware of their own needs and interests, hegemony of the state is reduced. This is a very facilitative process which in turn suggests that leisure planners need to have a skill set beyond the technical aspects of planning and be well versed in human and group dynamics and community consultation and animation. Fundamentally, planning leisure is more than simply arranging leisure encounters. Leisure planners must view leisure as more than simply the creation of activities for the sake of individual consumption and economic development. Such planning is an in-depth examination of the needs of individuals in the system, their goals and aspirations, and the development of strategies to achieve that future.

The benefits to social and psychological expansion must also be considered in the goals of planning. Planning is a tool for community capacity building in addition to leisure-goods production. It encourages citizens to learn new skills that can be carried forward to other community or individual projects. Additionally, social networks become more widespread by individual involvement in leisure planning. While these benefits may seem somewhat intangible when compared to the creation of a new facility, for example, they are equally beneficial to advancing the general capabilities of a community over time. They provide the fabric for future community problem solving and often spawn leadership skills that would have otherwise gone undiscovered or untapped. For some in the community, involvement in leisure planning provides another avenue for self-development and for creating feelings of self-empowerment.

What Does the Future Hold?

Planning for leisure involves the ongoing need to determine the philosophy on which community leisure will be based. Is it simply the commodification of activity (creating activities so they can be purchased or consumed) and hence, a commercial venture, or does it have some redeeming social value that is dedicated to the advancement of the human and social condition? At the present time, much of what gets planned and how we plan has been the result of choices that have been dictated by market and political forces outside the leisure domain. The practice of leisure and recreation in association with the academic community needs to implement a discussion about what is of value to the advancement of society and how leisure and recreation will contribute to those goals. The philosophies and techniques for future leisure planning can then be constructed around those decisions.

Key Terms

Citizen participation
Conscientization
Goals, objectives, implementation, evaluation and feedback
Hegemony
Managed and stimulated change
Mobilization
Planning
Rational Choice Model
Social reform
Policy analysis
Social learning
Social mobilization

References

Chadwick, G. (1971). *A systems view of planning*. Oxford, UK: Pergamon.

Davidoff, P., & Reiner, T. (1962). A choice theory of planning. *Journal of the American Institute of Planning, 28*(3), 103–115.

Environment Canada, Parks. (1987). *Getting started: A guide to service planning*. Ottawa, ON: Environment Canada.

Freire, P. (1990). *Pedagogy of the oppressed*. New York, NY: Continuum.

Friedmann, J. (1987). *Planning in the public domain: From knowledge to action*. Princeton, NJ: Princeton University Press.

Guess, R. (1987). *The idea of critical theory: Habermas and the Frankfurt School*. Cambridge, UK: Cambridge University Press.

Gramsci, A. (1971). *Selections from the prison notebooks*. London, UK: Lawrence & Wishart.

McCarthy, T. (1978). *The critical theory of Jurgen Habermas*. Cambridge, UK: Polity.

Mill, R. C., & Morrison, A. (1985). *The tourism system: An introductory text*. Englewood Cliffs, NJ: Prentice Hall.

Pigram, J. (1983). *Outdoor recreation and resource management*. London, UK: St. Martin's.

Reid, D. G., Mair, H., George, W., & Taylor, J. (2001). *Visiting your future: a community guide to planning rural tourism*. Guelph, ON: Ontario Agriculture Training Institute.

Warren, M. (1995). The self in discursive democracy. In S. K. White, (Ed.), *The Cambridge companion to Habermas* (pp. 167–200). Cambridge, UK: Cambridge University Press.

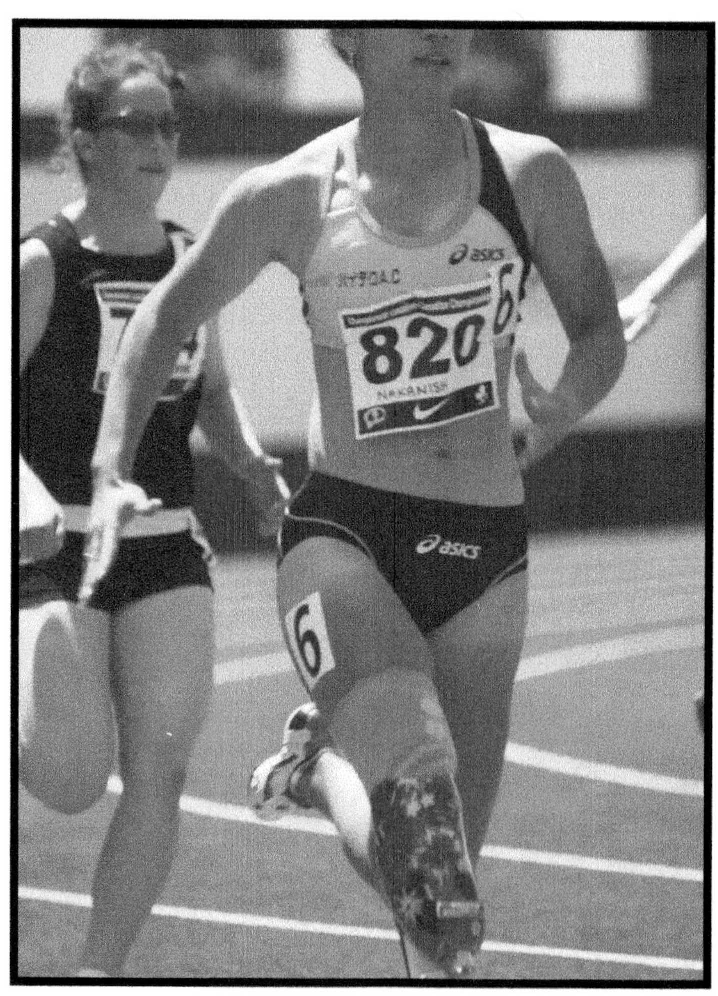
asics
820
asics
6

Chapter 31
Mapping the Recreation and Leisure Landscape for Canadians with a Disability

Jennifer B. Mactavish, Ph.D.
Ryerson University

Michael J. Mahon, Ph.D.
University of Lethbridge

Learning Objectives

After reading this chapter, students will be able to

1. Recognize and use the basic terminology used in recreation and leisure services that include people with a disability.
2. Recognize and use "people first" language.
3. Understand the difference between words such as impairment, activity limitation, and participation restrictions.
4. Understand the significance and meaning of key concepts that are foundational to this area, and how they relate to social justice and human rights.
5. Recognize and be familiar with the major approaches to services based on their main purpose, and their distinguishing features.

Introduction

In today's fast-paced world with its many competing demands for time and attention, people must juggle work, school, family responsibilities, and the like. The commonality of this experience fuels a multi-million dollar industry dedicated to combating the "time famine" and re-claiming life balance by engaging in activities and pastimes that are personally meaningful and enjoyable.

Many Canadians find this balance in informal, self-organized recreation and leisure experiences, and in the vast network of options also available through private (e.g., Shapes), not-for-profit (YM-YWCA), and public (e.g., community recreation departments) service delivery sectors (Statistics Canada, 2003). Among public sector organizations, most are responsible for serving all members of our communities. As Hutchison chronicled in Chapter 6 of this text, significant gains in fulfilling this mandate have been made, however, full and equal access to formally structured public options remains an ongoing challenge for many Canadians.

Disadvantaged segments of our communities continue to be marginalized and underserved as planning and delivery priorities are predominated by demands for public recreation programs and services for the "norm" (Smith, Austin, & Kennedy, 2001). Focusing on individuals at the margins of mainstream interest in this system, our purpose in the present chapter is to provide an overview that maps the contemporary landscape and emerging directions in systems, services, and practices in recreation and leisure in Canada.

Defining Our Focus

As in many professional fields, it is sometimes difficult to navigate all of the "insider" terminology when you are just starting out. To guide your introduction, this section of the chapter covers key terms and ideas that are needed for learning the basics.

Canadians at the "Margins"

Having read about recreation and leisure in other textbooks or other chapters in this book, familiarity with the phrase, "people with special needs" may have been created. This used to be a popular way of describing individuals who fell "outside" mainstream society (Austin & Powell, 1981). Traditionally, special needs was the catch all label used in reference to older adults, people from socially and economically disadvantaged backgrounds, and individuals with disabilities.

In Canada and other Commonwealth countries (e.g., Australia, New Zealand) this term has gradually fallen out of favour, as it has more recently in the United States (Smith, Austin, & Kennedy, 2001). Greater interest and sensitivity by researchers, practitioners and policy makers to the unique needs and interests of the individuals formerly subsumed within this single categorization, and the populace in general have contributed to this shift in perspective.

Have you ever been at a party, surrounded by people laughing and talking with one another, yet no one seems to notice you or make any effort to include you in the fun? There you are, sitting on your own, stuck in time, events unravelling before your eyes—all the while you seem to be invisible. How do you feel? What do you think? What do you do?

Specific to Canadians with disabilities, the Jasper Talks, which took place in Jasper Alberta in 1986, played a key role in this change. The Blueprint for Action, an outline of objectives and initiatives for promoting active living among individuals with disabilities, was a groundbreaking contribution and its effects are still evident in this area today (e.g., the Active Living Alliance). Another outcome with lasting impact was the *Words with Dignity* publication. Created in partnership with people with disabilities, this document outlines a common language in referring to disability that is respectful and rejects terms or labels that perpetuate stereotypes ("the disabled," "the retarded"), lumps people with widely different abilities into convenient boxes, and—most of all—fails to acknowledge the individual first and foremost. These guidelines are the basis for what is called *people first language* (PFT).

More on PFT...

If it is necessary to mention a person's disability, here are some tips:

- Focus on the person first (e.g., Mike has cerebral Palsy, or in general references, use phrases like "individuals or people with a disability");
- Avoid words that evoke pity (e.g., "suffers from," "is afflicted with," "confined to");
- When in doubt, ask the person with a disability for guidance.

The World Health Organization's International Classification of Functioning, Disability, and Health (2001), known as the ICF, also offers a useful framework for promoting common understanding of the various terms used when discussing disability related issues. Simply put, this framework advances the idea that human functioning is defined by how our minds and bodies work—independently and together as an integrated system—to meet requirements of daily living.

Adopting this view on human functioning and knowing some of the key terms in the ICF is important as many students, professionals, and members of the general public do not fully understand what it means to have a disability and, often are unsure of proper terminology, which leads to concerns that they might, in the words of many of our students, "say the wrong thing and offend somebody." Among the important details in the ICF are three key terms: (1) impairment; (2) activity limitations; and (3) participation restrictions. *Impairment* refers to underlying differences in the way a person's body works (i.e., body functions: physiological, psychological, and cognitive) and/or how it looks (i.e., body structures: anatomical parts of the body). When differences in body function and/or structures (i.e., impairment) interfere with activities of daily living, an individual is said to have *activity limitations* or what some continue to refer to as *disability*. *Participation restrictions*, once called *handicaps*, describe the added barriers (e.g., social stigma, lack of accessibility, supports) people might encounter as a result of environmental factors (e.g., with other people, organizations, institutions).

Beyond acting as a guide to thinking about appropriate terminology, the ICF is a reminder that everyone, independent of whether they have a recognizable impairment or not, may encounter activity or participation restrictions at some point in their lives. This "new" way of thinking is critical to creating more inclusive communities and, by extension, inclusive recreation and leisure service systems. In highlighting recreation and leisure services for Canadians at the margins, we concentrate on organized, public and not-for-profit systems and services that include individuals with a disability. With recent population estimates indicating approximately 24% or 6.5 million Canadians over the age of 12 having some form of activity limitation, this is a sizable sub-segment of our population (Statistics Canada, 2003).

ICF: Key Terms and Definitions

Body and Functions ➠ "Impairment" in these areas, person may look or perform "differently"

Activity Limitations ➠ Occur if "impairment" interferes/limits activities of daily living

Participation Restrictions ➠ Barriers that result from external/environmental factors encountered by the individual (e.g., social stigma, exclusion)

Note: Adaptation of the World Health Organization's (2001) International Classification of Functioning, Disability, and Health (ICF) model (p. 18).

In keeping with the principles of people first terminology, we are not using the term "disability" to categorize individuals, but rather to describe current and emerging directions in the delivery of recreation and leisure to this highly diverse segment of our society. Additionally, we use the term *at the margins* to acknowledge that despite tremendous strides in greater inclusion of individuals with disability within these contexts, there remains room for further advances (Pedlar, Hutchison, Arai, & Dunn, 2000; Raphael, 2004). It is important to acknowledge, that while focusing on people with disabilities in this chapter, much of the discussion can be applied to other marginalized groups (e.g., Aboriginal people, ethnic minorities, people living in poverty) that traditionally have not been fully served by community recreation and leisure service systems.

Recreation and Leisure Service System

In Canada, recreation and leisure services that include people with disabilities are offered by a number of different organizations and agencies, most of which are public (e.g., community parks and recreation program) or run by not-for-profit groups (e.g., Society for Manitobans with Disabilities). Loosely categorized according to their main purpose—participation or rehabilitation—Figure 31.1 includes an overview of different modes of service provision we will cover. Sport for development (SFD), which does not fit neatly into this dichotomy, is included based on its status as an emerging tool in international development and conflict resolution and the pivotal role Canadian-based organizations have played in its growth.

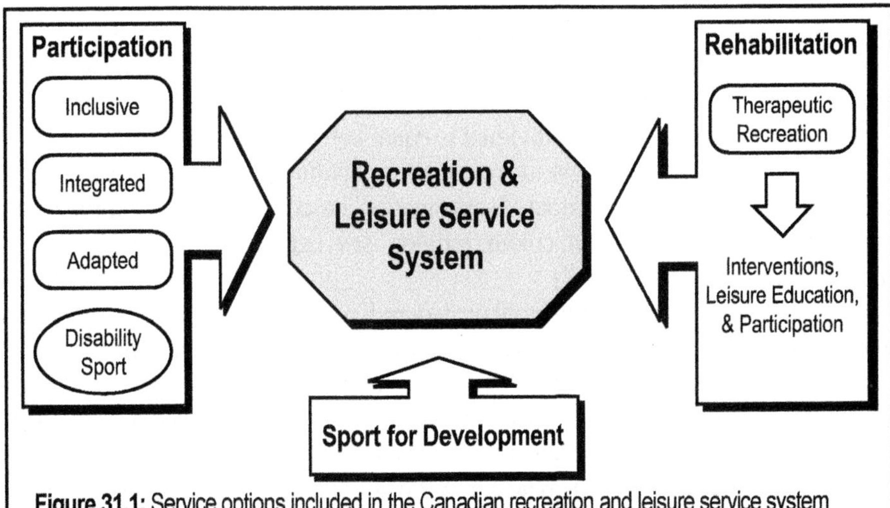

Figure 31.1: Service options included in the Canadian recreation and leisure service system

Conceptual Foundation

One of the distinguishing features of professional practice is the use of theories and concepts to ground what we do in practice and to substantiate the rationale for our actions (Rossman & Schlatter, 2000). In delivering recreation and leisure services that include people with disabilities, there are a number of core concepts that work together in setting this foundation. Examples of these core concepts or values are highlighted in Table 31.1. The principle of normalization, which is largely credited with starting the move towards greater inclusion of people with disabilities in all facets of life has given way, or more precisely, been extended by efforts to elevate life quality (Schalock, 2000). These key ideas and the others listed (e.g., self-determination, integration) readily fit into a social justice framework and are entrenched in the human rights movement. What does this mean and how are these notions brought to life in Canadian society broadly and recreation and leisure services specifically?

Broadly defined, social justice is about ensuring that all members of a society have the same basic rights, security, opportunities, obligations and social benefits (http://www.polity.org.za/html/govdocs/white_papers/social97gloss.html). This notion captures embedded values—human dignity, autonomy, equality, and solidarity—that most human rights legislation and law reflect (Quinn & Degener, 2002). Social justice and its related values are incorporated in the Canadian Charter of Rights and Freedoms, adopted on April

Table 31.1: Examples of core concepts in the provision of recreation and leisure services that include people with a disability

Core Concept	Definition
Humanism	A philosophy or world-view that recognizes and respects the uniqueness of human beings to be self-directed, to make wise choices, and to realize their potentials (Austin & Crawford, 2001).
Normalisation	Ensuring that the life patterns and conditions experienced by people with disabilities are as close as possible to, or indeed the same as, those enjoyed by other citizens (adaptation, Nirje, 1992).
Self-determination	The opportunity and freedom to make decisions (define & set goals) and to take actions based on those decisions (Ward, 1988).
Integration	Includes two elements physical and social integration. That is the sharing of physical space and time and social interactions between people with and without disabilities (Bullock & Mahon, 2000).
Quality of life	A person's desired condition of living related primarily to home and community living, school or work, and health and wellness (Schalock, 1997).

17, 1982, which is a core component of our Constitution and laws of governance. Section 15, subsections 1 and 2, specifically address the rights of individuals with disabilities, noting, in short, that: "Every individual is equal before and under the law and has the right to the equal protection and equal benefit of the law without discrimination based on race, national or ethnic origin, colour, religion, sex, age, or mental or physical disability."

Historically, many not-for-profit providers of recreation and leisure services for people with disabilities filled the gap in accessible public opportunities, and continue to fill this role today; however, the Charter clearly indicates the responsibility of public providers to meet the needs and interests of all Canadians (McPherson, Wheeler, & Foster, 2003).

The Recreation and Leisure Service System: Approaches to Program Delivery

As mentioned above, recreation and leisure services that include individuals with disability are organized and delivered in a number of different ways. To simplify this complex system, we have loosely grouped offerings by their major purpose: (1) participation; (2) rehabilitation; and (3) sport for development. The vast majority of community leisure programs and services focus on participation to promote positive outcomes such as personal enjoyment, skill development, health and fitness, and social relationships. The delivery of these programs and services is largely the responsibility of public and not-for-profit groups at the local, municipal, or provincial level. Within Canada, involvement at the National level typically includes policy development, advocacy, and overall systems coordination.

Participation

In the delivery of programs that emphasize participation, there are three basic approaches:

- Adapted recreation
- Integrated recreation
- Inclusive recreation

Adapted recreation usually takes place in segregated settings (i.e., the program is only open to people with disabilities) and is designed to provide accommodations (e.g., activity modification) and supports (e.g., one-to-one instruction) that facilitate participation. This method of delivery is sometimes referred to as special recreation, not because of the participants involved but the types of services and supports offered (Meyer, 1981).

Adapted programming, while evident in many municipal recreation departments across Canada, has been criticized for separating people from other members of the community because of their disability (e.g., Hutchison & McGill, 1998). Consequently, we are witnessing a gradual shift away from this traditional approach.

Integrated recreation is one response to this criticism. This approach brings people with and without disabilities together in the same program at the same time, with social interaction among participants being an essential feature. Accommodations and supports are provided as necessary to maximize participation of individuals with disabilities. Integrated approaches to service delivery also continue to be used across Canada; however, they too have been less than successful in fostering social interactions among participants with and without disabilities. While a variety of factors (e.g., absence of structured efforts to promote social interaction) contribute to the isolation and social disconnection experienced, negative public attitudes and lack of understanding are the main obstacles (Condeluci, 1995).

Inclusive recreation is advanced as the future direction in dealing with past concerns about the delivery of recreation and leisure services (Lord & Hutchinson, 2003). Inclusive and integrated recreation share social acceptance as a core value, with the former being distinctive in that it:

1. Recognizes the unique needs and interests of all participants, which are not exclusively defined by whether or not a person has a disability;
2. Fosters equal and joint benefits for all participants;
3. Provides accommodations and supports as needed to maximize participation (i.e., not simply based on someone having an identifiable disability).

The subtle but important shift from focusing on a person's disability to concentrating on enhancing meaningful and shared benefits for *all* participants is the hallmark of inclusive recreation. Considering recreation from this perspective adds impetus to viewing people, as people first, and our professional responsibility to serve all members of our communities.

Disability Sport

In describing recreation and leisure services to this point, we have not differentiated any of the many forms of activities and experiences—creative arts, theatre, music, outdoor recreation, physical recreation pursuits, and the like—subsumed within these different approaches. Disability sport, which fits best within the adapted recreation tradition, is one area that warrants closer consideration. There are over a dozen organizations in Canada dedicated to advancing sport opportunities for individuals with disabilities. Most of these groups belong, via affiliations with national sport governing bodies, to one of two international sport movements: the Paralympics or Special Olympics (see Table 31.2 for summary of the differences between these movements).

The Canadian Paralympic Committee (CPC) is the coordinating body that represents and promotes sport for athletes with various forms of disability (e.g., cerebral palsy, visual impairments, spinal cord injury, intellectual disability) nationally. The CPC is a member of the International Paralympic Committee (IPC), which, in turn, is a member of the International Olympic Committee that serves elite athlete and sport development worldwide. The word *Paralympics* denotes that the IPC movement parallels or mirrors the Olympic movement, but their main focus is on athletes with disabilities. International, multi-sport winter and summer games are organized by the IPC and are usually hosted at the site of the Olympic Games at a different time during the same year. For example, the Athens Olympic Games (2004) were followed several weeks later by the Athens Paralympic Games, and the Paralympic Winter Games in Torino (2006) took place two weeks after the Olympic Games hosted at the same location.

Table 31.2: The main differences between the Paralympics and the Special Olympic Movements

Key differences	IPC	SO
Philosophy	Elite competition	Sport for all
Eligibility	Athletes with various forms of disability (e.g., cerebral palsy, spinal cord injury, amputation, visual impairments, intellectual disability)	Exclusively for athletes with intellectual disability
Competition structure	By classification based on function in relation to demands of the sport, or in "open" competition (i.e., one "winner" as per the Olympics)	Divisioning (groupings) based on age, sex, and "ability" (based on performance times, multiple sections of the same event based on differences)
When	Quadrennial cycle as per the Olympic Games (same year, same location, different time)	Quadrennial cycle with World Games falling one year before Olympic and Paralympic Games

Special Olympics (SO) is an international sport body with an exclusive mandate to serve individuals with intellectual disability. This body also organizes multi-sport, international "World Games" every four years in both summer and winter sports. Typically, these games are hosted the year before the Olympic Games and Paralympic Games.

Although not well known, the work of a Canadian researcher—Dr. Frank Hayden—played a pivotal role in establishing this movement with his groundbreaking research in the 1960s that demonstrated the value of participation in physical activity and sport for individuals with intellectual disability (Mactavish & Dowds, 2003). Special Olympics Canada, which was the first accredited SO body outside of the United States, is a not-for-profit group that presently includes chapters in all 10 provinces and 2 territories (Yukon, Northwest Territories). These chapters, via volunteer coaches provide ongoing programming to over 17,000 members, which culminate every four years with National Winter and Summer Games.

Disability sport, especially Special Olympics, is frequently criticized for providing segregated programming in which membership is based on a person's disability. Of the many arguments raised, the contention that SO undermines the emergence of other, non-segregated options in the community is heard most often (Hourcade, 1989; Wehman, & Moon, 1985). Interestingly, these critiques seldom devote equal attention to the providers of recreation and sport services who are mandated to, but do not always, offer viable and attractive alternatives. Additionally, the inherent exclusivity of sport at the elite level does not make its way into this debate.

Have you ever dreamed about being an Olympian and even trained to the best of your ability, only to be faced with the harsh realisation that you simply were not "good enough" to meet the standards demanded at this level? Well, imagine you have a disability and have the skill and talent to be an international calibre athlete. Do you think you should have the chance to showcase your talents or should objections about the segregated nature of Paralympic Sport close this window of opportunity?

Rehabilitation

Recreation with a rehabilitation emphasis also is an important delivery system element, albeit relatively new in Canada. While often associated with institutions (hospitals, senior's care centres), the setting does not define whether recreation is therapeutic or rehabilitative. Programs and services of this nature can take place in acute care and rehabilitation hospitals, as well as community based settings such as independent living programs. The use of recreation for rehabilitation or therapy is most often described as *Therapeutic Recreation* (TR) or *Recreation Therapy*. In Canada, as in other jurisdictions, debates are ongoing over which of the aforementioned titles is most appropriate, but the essence of this service remains consistent—the purposeful use of recreation as a form of treatment or intervention that has a specific goal or set of goals in mind. As such, it is rather different from recreation engaged in for the purpose of participation. The Canadian Therapeutic Recreation Association (CTRA, 2006) describes Therapeutic Recreation as:

> Therapeutic Recreation is a profession that recognizes leisure, recreation and play as integral components of quality of life. Service is provided to individuals who have physical, mental, social or emotional limitations which impact their ability to engage in meaningful leisure experiences.

CTRA identifies functional interventions, leisure education and participation as key elements in therapeutic recreation programming. Table 31.3 includes descriptions of these distinct approaches.

A final element of therapeutic recreation, not included in the CTRA definition is what Bullock and Mahon (2000) call planning for transition. In this step, the individual is guided through a self-assessment of goals and accomplishments achieved, and identifies challenges that may emerge in the future and supports for ensuring desired leisure participation. This personalized plan is crucial in bridging the transition from therapeutic recreation (i.e., recreation as a tool for achieving rehabilitation objectives) to recreation and leisure that serves broader individual interests (e.g., personal satisfaction, fun, recreation for "its own sake").

Table 31.3: Common approaches in therapeutic recreation programming

Approach	Definition
Functional intervention	Address daily living skills important for independent functioning such as money management, transportation skills, or using the telephone. These interventions are done within the context of recreation. For example, a therapeutic recreation specialist might teach an individual with an intellectual disability how to take the bus to a recreation centre. The ultimate goal of this intervention might be to enable this individual to independently travel to participate in a recreation program at the centre.
Leisure education	Is "an individualized and contextualized educational process" (Bullock & Mahon, 2000, p. 332) that usually includes three components: (1) awareness of self in leisure, (2) skill learning and rehearsal, and (3) self-determination. Activities in each component are designed to enhance a person's ability to engage in and benefit from leisure.
Participation	Functional interventions and leisure education are critical in rehabilitation process, with participation in personally meaningful recreation being an ultimate aim. This component provides the link between therapeutic recreation and the participation focused approaches (adapted, integrated, inclusive recreation, disability sport) noted previously.

Sport for Development

The United Nations recently acknowledged sport as a unique tool for building social capital and development—one that inspires people to work individually, collectively, and collaboratively to address social, economic, and political concerns with the ultimate aim of fostering peace (United Nations, 2003). Sport for all is a central idea in this movement, which emphasizes inclusion of all community members regardless of age, sex, ability, or race. Called *sport for development* (SFD), this is an emerging area of interest in recreation and leisure service delivery. As home to three distinct organizations, Canada is a leader in this area.

Right to Play (RTP) is a Canadian based non-governmental organization (NGO) with offices and programs in various regions of the world. Founded by Johann Koss, a four-time Olympic gold medallist from Norway, RTP is an athlete-driven organization that brings sport and play opportunities to children and youth in the most disadvantaged areas of the world. RTP delivers two types of programs. Sportworks focuses on child and community development through sport, whereas Sporthealth programs use the power of sport to provide health education and encourage healthy lifestyle behaviours.

The *Commonwealth Games International Development* (IDS) through Sport Program, based in Canada since 1993, uses physical activity and sport to create positive social change in the Caribbean and Africa. Since its inception IDS has worked with local partners in Barbados, Benin, Botswana, Dominica, Gambia, Grenada, Guyana, Jamaica, Kenya, Lesotho, Malawi, Namibia, St. Kitts and Nevis, St. Lucia, St. Vincent and the Grenadines, Trinidad and Tobago, Turks and Caicos, South Africa, Seychelles, Swaziland, Tanzania, Uganda, Zambia, and Zimbabwe.

Play Around the World (PAW), started by the Faculty of Physical Education and Recreation at the University of Alberta in 2000, is a unique student driven SFD initiative that operates for three months each summer in Thailand. Through this program, PAW students bring sport to diverse settings and groups such as orphanages, schools, and residences that include children with disabilities and run an outreach project for street kids.

What Is Social Capital?

It is an old idea that emphasizes the importance of connections among individuals—social networks—as the glue for translating an "I" mentality into a "we" mentality (Putnam, 1993). Social capital promotes trust, mutual understanding, shared values and behaviours that bond people together and make cooperative action possible (Cohen & Prusak, 2001).

Conclusion

This chapter includes key ideas and concepts that relate to recreation and leisure services that include Canadians with disabilities. A good way to remind yourself of the main points of importance is to go back and think about whether you have achieved the learning objectives. A quick review of the boldfaced items and *i*-boxes will also be helpful in this reflective self-learning assessment.

In mapping the recreation and leisure landscape for Canadians with a disability, we have emphasized the mandate of public systems for serving all members of our community. While equal access to systems and services are critical, so too are the attitudes and acceptance of people. As an active participant or a future professional, we hope you will move forward with heightened awareness and a willingness to do what it takes to ensure that all people benefit from meaningful recreation and leisure.

Key Terms

Adapted recreation
Disability
Inclusive recreation
Integrated recreation
Leisure education
Paralympics
Recreation and leisure
Service delivery system
Special Olympics
Sport for development
Therapeutic recreation

References

Austin, D. R., & Powell, L. G. (1981). What you need to know to serve special populations. *Parks and Recreation, 16*(7), 40–42.

Austin, D., & Crawford, M. (2001). *Therapeutic recreation: An introduction* (3rd ed.). Boston, MA: Allyn & Bacon.

Bullock, C., & Mahon, M. J. (2000). *Introduction to recreation services for people with disabilities: A person-centered approach.* Champaign, IL: Sagamore Publishing.

Canadian Therapeutic Recreation Association Philosophy (n.d.). Retrieved from http://www.canadian-tr.org/

Cohen, D., & Prusak, L. (2001). *In good company. How social capital makes organizations work.* Boston, MA: Harvard Business School Press.

Condeluci, A. (1995). *Interdependence: The route to community.* Winter Park, FL: GR Press.

Hourcade, J. (1989). Special Olympics: A review and critical analysis. *Therapeutic Recreation Journal, 23*, 58–65.

Hutchison, P., & McGill, J. (1998). *Leisure, integration, and community* (2nd ed.). Toronto, ON: Leisurability Publications.

Lord, J., & Hutchison, P. (2003). Individualised support and funding: Building blocks for capacity building and inclusion. *Disability and Society, 18*(1), 71–86.

Mactavish, J., & Dowds, M. (2003). Physical activity and sport for individuals with intellectual disability: Concepts, strategies, opportunities, and issues. In R. Steadward, G. Wheeler, & J. Watkinson (Eds.), *Adapted physical activity* (pp. 559–588). Edmonton, AB: University of Alberta Press.

McPherson, G., Wheeler, G. D., & Foster, S. L. (2003). Sociopolitical influences on adapted physical activity. In R. Steadward, G. Wheeler, & J. Watkinson (Eds.), *Adapted physical activity* (pp. 75–95). Edmonton, AB: University of Alberta Press.

Meyer, L. (1981). Three philosophical positions of therapeutic recreation and their implications for professionalization and NTRS/NRPA. *Therapeutic Recreation Journal, 15*(2), 7–16.

Nirje, B. (1992). *The normalisation papers.* Sweden: Uppsala University Centre for Handicap Research.

Pedlar, A., Hutchison, P., Arai, S., & Dunn, P. (2000). Community services landscape in Canada: Survey of developmental disability agencies. *Mental Retardation, 38*(4), 330–341.

Putnam, R. D. (1993). *Making democracy work.* Princeton, NJ: Princeton University Press.

Quinn, G., & Degener, T. (2002). *Human rights and disability: The current use and future potential of United Nations human rights instruments in the context of disability.* Geneva: Office of the United Nations High Commissioner on Human Rights.

Raphael, D. (2004). *Social determinants of health: Canadian perspectives.* Toronto, ON: Canadian Scholars' Press.

Rossman, J. R., & Schlatter, B. E. (2000). *Recreation programming: Designing leisure experiences* (4th ed.). Champaign, IL: Sagamore.

Schalock, R. L. (1997). The concept of quality of life in 21st century disability programmes. In R. I. Brown (Ed.), *Quality of life for people with disabilities: Models, research and practice* (pp. 327–340). Cheltenham, UK: Stanley Thornes.

Schalock, R. L. (2000). Three decades of quality of life. In M. L. Wehmeyer & J. R. Patton (Eds.), *Mental retardation in the 21st century* (pp. 335–356). Austin, TX: Pro-ed.

Smith, R. W., Austin, D. R., & Kennedy, D. W. (2001). *Inclusive and special recreation* (4th ed.). Boston, MA: McGraw-Hill.

Statistics Canada. (2003). *Canadian community health survey* (Health Indicators Catalogue no. 82-221, Vol. 2004, No. 1). Government of Canada.

Ward, M. J., (1988). The many facets of self-determination. *National Information Center for Children and Youth with Handicaps, 5*, 2–3.

Wehman, P., & Moon, M. S. (1985). Designing and implementing leisure programmes for individuals with severe handicaps. In M. P. Brady & P. L. Gunter (Eds.), *Integrating moderately and severely handicapped learners.* Springfield, IL: Thomas.

World Health Organization (2001). *International classification of functioning, disability and health* (ICF). Geneva: Author.

Chapter 32
Community Development

Alison Pedlar, Ph.D.
University of Waterloo

Learning Objectives

After reading this chapter, students will be able to

1. Have an understanding of the evolution of community development in recreation in Canada.
2. Recognize the major community development approaches used within recreation.
3. Appreciate the relevance of citizen participation and community involvement in community development initiatives.
4. Understand the importance of community development in recreation practice.

Introduction

Community development efforts are characterized by citizen participation, community initiative and social change that benefit the individual and the community as a whole. Recreation provides an excellent opportunity to work within a community development framework, for it is within the spaces where recreation occurs that people come together in ways that are uniquely conducive to building community; and it is within these same spaces that people are able to celebrate one another's ability to work together to enhance both individual and collective quality of life.

The Evolution of Community Development in Canada

In the early part of the 20th century, some communities were extremely impoverished and had no sense of a future. There was little or nothing to engage community members. However, with strong community leadership, some organized and fought to change their dominant identity from depressed or marginal areas to communities that offered people something to feel proud about. Some of the earliest roots of community development in Canada can be found in communities that have gone through this process. Important movements, like the cooperative movement in the Maritimes and elsewhere, have long and proud histories of working to improve situations of entire communities. In many parts of Canada, from the Maritimes to the Prairies, the cooperative movement encouraged community mobilization through adult education. Local democratic control and citizen participation were critical features of cooperatives that developed in the Antigonish tradition (Lotz, 1997), a movement that emerged in eastern Canada in the 1920s and focussed on adult education of disadvantaged groups of people in order to address their social and economic needs in a cooperative and collaborative manner.

Other early efforts to improve people's circumstances included the settlement house and the playground and park movements. The settlement movement emerged from the need to provide shelter and food for people who were coming to Canada, principally from Europe, in search of a new and better life. Established citizens concerned for the welfare of new Canadians began to develop houses where a number of families could live under one roof, share a kitchen and resources, and work cooperatively to provide food and sustenance to their families and others who lived in the house. St. Christopher's House in Toronto is a model of community development that is rooted in settlement houses where people have worked together to improve their life situation since the early 1900s. St. Christopher House is still in operation and their web site indicates:

> From the beginning, participants in St. Christopher's House have been given a "hand up" rather than a "hand out." This effective approach has resulted in the creation of numerous programs including the following:
>
> - the Music School
> - a summer camp
> - childcare and parent support
> - Meals on Wheels
> - employment counselling
> - adult literacy programs
>
> (http://www.stchrishouse.org/st-chris/history/)

Similarly, the playground movement marked a significant contribution to community development from within the recreation field, as efforts were made to provide a place for the children to gather and play in safety in the less affluent urban neighbourhoods. The public playground movement, out of which grew the Boys and Girls Clubs of Canada, was founded in 1900 in St. John, New Brunswick, and marked the beginning of efforts to ensure that children who had very little, would at least have a safe place to play (http://www.bgccan.com/content.asp?L=E&DocID=3). The playground movement and the park movement are evidence of the connection that the recreation and leisure field has to community development and social movements. In each case the goal is to enable citizens to work collectively, to gain a voice and to take actions to enhance their everyday situations.

During the latter half of the 20th century, there were periods when communities were involved in aspects that affected everyday life. Certain periods—the 1950s, for example—saw little attention being paid to citizen participation. The 50s were a time of expansion and rebuilding after the Second World War and people looked to their governments to help that happen. Expressions of citizenship that are manifest in self-determination, choice, and political action by community members were less of an issue during this time of recovery and rapid urban and suburban expansion. In contrast, during the 1960s and again in the 1990s, the idea of citizenship became more prominent in many people's thinking. The movement of people out of central cities to newly built suburbs accelerated the decay of inner cities (Jacobs, 1961). When initiatives were taken by governments to regenerate the inner cities by developing large housing projects and corporate office buildings, these often led to the dislocation of the poor who lived in the houses and apartments that were destroyed to provide room for the new projects (Hodge, 2003; Rubin & Rubin, 1992; Rubin, 2000). By the 90s, communities were facing related issues, often centred on unemployment and poverty (Popham, Hay, & Hughes, 1997).

Can you describe a community that you have known, read or heard about that has worked to overcome a history of marginalization? What do we know about its history and how people came to be ready and willing to change their situation?

Upon entering the 21st century, the relevance of community development again caught the attention of governments and citizens, and there was an increased sensitivity to issues around sustainability of initiatives designed to improve people's quality of life and the health of communities (Arai, 1996). Indeed, the involvement of communities in community development and social learning processes (Friedmann, 1987), which enable citizens and municipalities to work in partnership around important decisions that affect people's everyday lives, is recognized as important to the future of healthy communities (Arai & Pedlar, 1997; Hancock & Minkler, 2005; Rubin & Rubin, 1992).

Leisure Research and Community Development

During the past decade, Canadian leisure studies researchers and practitioners have addressed a number of important considerations in relation to community development practice. In 1996, the *Journal of Applied Research* (JAPR) published a number of articles dealing with community development issues, including the following: what community development means in the context of recreation and leisure practice (Pedlar, 1996); the different ways practitioners, researchers and citizens think about community development (Hutchison & Nogradi, 19996); the variation in community development practice according to size and structure of recreation service delivery organizations (Karlis, Auger, & Gravelle, 1996); the role of recreation and leisure in bringing low-income communities together to make positive change (Reid & van Dreunen, 1996); and citizen action in improving the environment and social health of their community (Arai, 1996). Almost 10 years later, Karlis (2004) published a fairly extensive account of community development and leisure and recreation.

Researchers interested in community and the role of recreation and leisure in community development continue to push us forward into increasingly expansive ways of thinking about community development. Many are focusing on the added value that can accrue from community development efforts. Some examples of this more recent communitarian thought bring attention to individual rights and respect, but equally stress the importance of a strong commitment to the well-being of the community as a whole, which can occur when using community development in recreation and leisure (Arai & Pedlar, 2004).

There is also an interest in social capital which generally refers to the energy and capacity generated through people working together for the individual and collective good. Glover, Shinew, and Parry (2005) looked at this in the context of social capital development through gardening and festivals. Others have examined the role of recreation in community building and social capital development among children (Yuen, Pedlar, & Mannell, 2005). Important work has also been done with community development and inclusion in local sport and recreation of women and children living in poverty (Frisby & Millar, 2002). The use of recreation within a community development framework was also part of collective action and citizen engagement in preserving family life in an inner city neighborhood (Conolly, 2002/2003).

Awareness of this research is important to fully understanding how community development and recreation come together, especially if we aim to apply community development principles as recreationists.

For the purposes of this chapter, the concept of *community* needs to be explored before looking more closely at community development, because without understanding this, foundations of community development within recreation and leisure studies cannot be fully appreciated.

What Is Community?

Many agree that it is not possible to talk in any detail about community development without first clarifying what we mean by *community.* Community can take many different forms, including, for instance, a social grouping (e.g., the philanthropic community), an ethnic grouping (e.g., the Francophone community), people who live in the same physical or geographical location (e.g., the Vancouver community), people who share a special interest (e.g., the horticultural community), people who join together to seek equity with other citizens (e.g., the community of people with a disability), and people who never meet but who come together via the Internet (e.g., a virtual community). These are only a few of the many kinds of groupings that we refer to as communities. None of us would claim to be part of such communities unless we felt like we belonged, that others in the community were accepting and welcoming of us (McKnight, 1986), and that we were interested in the same general goal or purpose for which the community existed. Key aspects of knowing that we belong to a community include a psychological sense of attachment, a spatial or geographical location in which we feel rooted, and association by virtue of a shared or common interest. Hence, community means social networks. As Etzioni wrote, "Communities are webs of social relations that encompass shared meanings and above all shared values" (1998, xiii).

Think about the communities to which you belong and describe how you know it is a community and that you belong?

Community is not automatically inclusive. Moreover, community is not inherently good, since it can have negative outcomes for people and can work in ways that exclude some, especially those who may be viewed as *different* and who are marginalized because of their difference. Communities become *closed* to those who are seen as not conforming to the dominant norms, such as gated neighbourhoods that work to exclude certain people who are not regarded as suitable members (Pedlar & Haworth, 2006). People with disabilities and visible minorities exemplify those who have lots of experience with this sort of exclusion from community (see Chapter 6). Community development can work in ways that help break down the barriers to inclusion and foster community building in positive ways. Recreation can play a powerful role in that process. In the following section community development itself will be looked at more closely.

What Is Community Development?

Community development can refer to both a *process* and an *outcome.* Often (and ideally) a community development initiative can involve both a process and an outcome. Process refers to the actual learning to work together for a common objective. For example, a group of people might be interested in learning ways to improve the sorts of recreation opportunities that are available to them. Their learning to work together, to identify problems and possible solutions, represents a learning process. This is often referred to as development *of* community (Wilkinson, 1989). Recreation offers fertile ground for the development of community and for such learning and skill enhancement processes.

Development as an outcome is more generally associated with development *in* community. An example might be the development of a new hockey arena within a neighbourhood—the community will gain a place to recreate, but the actual development of the arena may happen with little or no input from the citizens. Development *in* community may also mean that jobs are created as a result—as may be the case in building an arena—so a clear economic element would likely exist to development in community as well. Economic development is generally associated with development in the community, and includes strategies aimed at addressing poverty and improving employment opportunities (Lewis, 1997).

Many would argue that development in community without, or in the absence of, development of community is not community development. Similarly, there is a long-standing debate about whether community development ought to refer to purely economic development or whether the focus ought to be primarily aimed at social development initiatives. Some have suggested that real social change and the improvement of people's lives, which is what community development is essentially about, can only happen when both social and economic changes occur within a community. Ethnic festivals offer one example of an initiative that could link both the social and economic goals of community development and result in both development of and development in community. Within these festivals, people might gather to sell artifacts associated with their culture. These artifacts, in turn, bring visitors into the community who leave behind money they brought to purchase such goods. In this way both social and economic goals are met. Visitors are given valuable insight into the marginalized group and they leave behind money the group can use to strengthen its own sense of identity.

An especially important point to reiterate here is that community development ought to offer people the opportunity to grow and to experience a better quality of life than might otherwise be had; this can happen through recreation and leisure activities that bring people together in ways that improve their personal and collective situations. Later in this chapter some examples of recreation and leisure initiatives will be looked at where people have been centrally involved in community development.

Community development, then, may have several slightly different meanings. Nevertheless, there is a core theme that runs through the various meanings of community development: change and improvement in a person's circumstances and in the quality of community life are central to community development. The definitions of community development, contained in the following *i*-box, further reflect this central point. The way we work toward that change and improvement may differ; in other words there are different methods of achieving community development.

Definitions of Community Development

"Community development can be tentatively defined as a process designed to create conditions of economic and social progress for the whole community with its active participation and the fullest reliance upon the community's initiative" (UN, 1955, p. 1).

"Community development is a strategy of change grounded in an ethos of equality and social justice. It is a process anchored in the conviction that all affected by a particular action or decision should have an opportunity to participate" (Wharf & Clague, 1997, p. 307).

"Community development within recreation and leisure services represents a type of service approach that is highly dependent on citizen participation, particularly of citizens who are vulnerable. Overall, community development aims to support and encourage both individuals and local communities through becoming involved, educating themselves, developing skills, and making changes to life conditions they find intolerable" (Hutchison & McGill, 1998, p. 168).

As suggested by these definitions, values that are associated with community development include social justice, social change, self-determination, and sustainability. Citizen participation is another key characteristic of community development. Without community mobilization and citizen participation, it is doubtful that community development will have much of an impact on a community. Sometimes traditional service delivery that is planned and developed in isolation of citizens is represented as community development. However, community development in a pure sense stresses the centrality of community involvement, the participation of citizens working closely perhaps with municipal or other staff, but sometimes working quite independently of staff, using resources and skills indigenous to the community.

In the following section the different approaches to community development will be addressed in order to begin to see more explicitly what it is about recreation that lends itself so well to community development, both in terms of development *of* and development *in* community.

Approaches to Community Development

As suggested previously, without citizen participation there can be no *true* community development; however, participation is not a matter of "either/or" but of "more or less." Arnstein talked about this in her seminal article on citizen participation in the 1960s. She drew the analogy between different levels of participation and a ladder of participation and power, suggesting that different levels of participation resulted in different outcomes for individuals and in turn the collective. It is generally agreed, that if community development is genuinely going to alter people's situations, then citizens have to be part of the process of pursuing change—they have to be on that ladder of participation. There are several ways this can happen, and a number of researchers and practitioners have set out approaches to community development that provide for differing degrees of citizen involvement. One of the most frequently cited approaches comes from the work of Rothman (1995). He sets out what he calls "community intervention approaches" and discusses them in terms of three primary types of intervention. These three—locality development, social planning, and social action—are most often applied in social work community development initiatives. They are summarized as follows:

- *Locality development*, otherwise known as self-help, is generally regarded as first and foremost concerned with process—that is people coming together and learning to work cooperatively to bring about change in their circumstances. An assumption of the self-help approach is that people have the will and can develop the skill to help change their circumstances. Citizens come together around a common purpose or interest, and as Rothman notes, the self-help approach is concerned with "building the capacity of a community to make collaborative and informed decisions" (1995, p. 45).

- *Social planning*, sometimes referred to as technical assistance, is more concerned with the outcome or task at hand than is the self-help approach. As a result of the focus on task, communities that employ social planning are more likely to use the services of an expert or professional to get the results they want, rather than work through a process of learning how to take the matter into their own hands.
- *Social action* is concerned with both process and task, but is more frequently characterized by conflicting interests and a less cohesive community perspective. Due to conflicting interests, which will often involve power differentials, people may employ more radical approaches to getting public attention focused on the problem.

While these three approaches to community intervention are presented as distinct, often the lines that separate them are blurred. As a result we may see an overlapping or intermixing of these strategies, depending on the circumstances and structures that communities are facing at the time. These circumstances are rarely static and consequently communities will (or at least should) adapt and utilize whatever methods or approaches fit the changed circumstances. For a detailed account of the three foundational principles of community development, it is strongly recommended that the reader refer to Rothman's (1995) discussion.

Within recreation and leisure, practitioners may not necessarily use the Rothman terminology or typologies when referring to strategies employed in community development work. Instead, they may refer to the *direct service approach* or the *indirect service approach*. The first of these is similar to the social planning or technical assistance approach, in that a professional, possibly not associated directly with the community, is brought in to assist in the delivery of a program that serves the interests of the community. The indirect service approach became more prominent in recreation and leisure services in the latter part of the 1970s through to the present. It may echo some of the principles of self-help if, for example, the community, while working in partnership with the local municipal recreation department, organizes and runs its own recreation activities or programs, such as using a local community centre for badminton or basketball games. An alternative approach that has been used by communities to create and develop recreation opportunities is referred to as the *self-sufficiency approach* (Karlis, 2004). This is more in line with the principles of community development that suggest stronger communities develop when citizens identify their own issues or problems and devise solutions that are compatible with their values, resources and preferences. A difficulty with this approach can be, of course, that a community needs the support, fiscal or otherwise, of the greater community and the traditional leisure service providers within the municipality, to begin developing their own opportunities.

Community Recreation in Community Development

There is a significant, albeit subtle, difference between services that operate from a *community-based* perspective and those that work from a community *development* perspective. Labonté (1993, 1996, 2005) drew our attention to this in his work on individual health, the health of the community, recreation and community empowerment. He pointed out the importance from a community development perspective of the community itself identifying the problem it faces and of organizing a method of responding to the problem. When this occurs the community has a vested interest and genuine participation in what and how things operate. In contrast, community-based services comprise those that are planned and managed from outside the community, and generally with much less insider knowledge and commitment to working together to find solutions. Community-based services reflect a weaker understanding of the strengths, needs, and preferences of the community members. For instance, community-based recreation would be the result of the decisions that have been made wholly outside the community, in the recreation department at city hall, perhaps. While the end result may be a recreation program located in the community, members of the community will have had little or no input into what that looks like, and the program may not reflect the needs and preferences of those who are to use it.

In contrast, community recreation that employs community development practices is grounded in the values, preferences, choices, and energies of the citizens who reside there. It is important to note that efforts have been made in recent years to replace the more traditional community-based approach to service delivery with approaches that more closely resemble community recreation (Glover, 2004). Assuming the availability of appropriate public resources to foster and sustain community recreation, then community development will be more feasible when citizens drive the development of the activity, potentially producing development of and development in community with the full participation of citizens.

While communities need support in terms of human and economic resources, it has been argued that community development should be carried out by communities themselves, without outside resources. This is not always practical, of course, and often those resources are very important to help kick-start community initiatives. Indeed, community development should not be seen as an excuse or a way for governments to take a totally hands-off approach to community initiatives (Pedlar, 1996; 2006). Community development will be stronger and any change that happens will last and be more sustainable when there is collaboration and partnership with outside groups, including government.

Recognizing Community Capacity and Community Building

Authentic community development recognizes the relevance of all interests in building community capacity to take ownership of its own problems and find its own solutions (McKnight & Kretzmann, 2005). The McKnight and Kretzmann model of community building involves citizens, governments, community organizations, and public and corporate interests joining together to maximize their resources and increase the likelihood that improvements in people's opportunities and participation will happen. It may mean that a strong leader from the community or a forward-thinking practitioner has to step forth to initiate the processes of bringing those various interests together and identifying the resources that can come into play to solve a problem, like a lack of recreation opportunities for children within a low-income neighbourhood.

Case Study: Mapping Community Capacity

A good example of this sort of community building in recreation happened when recreation researcher and mother, Elizabeth van Druenen, living in a low-income neighbourhood, realized that children there did not have access to safe after-school or weekend recreation. She set about mapping the community's capacity to respond to this problem by first contacting as many people as possible in the neighbourhood, working from the grass roots to establish how widespread the issue was and how much interest there was among people in the neighbourhood to address the problem. Ultimately, residents of the area, municipal recreation staff, social welfare workers, the local school, local businesses, and the children whose lives were most affected, worked to organize recreation opportunities for the children within the school (after hours). In the process of discovering the capacities of the community, a neighbourhood association was formed and members set about dealing with a range of issues confronting the area. In this process, people contributed their skills to the overall well-being of the neighbourhood, with neighbours participating in a reciprocal arrangement that enabled the wide range of resources and capacities in the neighbourhood to be applied to solving problems and generally improving the quality of community life. Here the segmentation that sometimes exists within community was overcome and recreation was influential in people paying attention not simply to a recreation program, but to many other aspects of life in the neighbourhood as well. Recreation then became a vehicle for community development and social change (Reid & van Dreunen, 1996).

Case Study: Women Organizing for Women

Another example of the way recreation has been used in conjunction with community development is contained in what was essentially a research project to try to ensure "access to community-based recreation programs for women on low income" (Frisby, Trif, Millar, & Hoeber, 2005, p. 369). This project is called Women Organizing Activities for Women (WOAW). Frisby and her colleagues spent several years working with women in Vancouver, BC, who had experienced a life of social exclusion and marginalization stemming from poverty. The researchers employed many community development strategies in their research project, which was structured around active participation of the women at every stage of the project, partnerships with community agencies, and a research team. The initiative, like many social action endeavours, is ongoing and change happens gradually, but there have been major outcomes along the way, including most especially changes in the ability of the women and their children to access recreation and participate in the community in ways that they once would not have even considered to be a possibility.

Case Study: Community and Recreation Staff Form an Alliance

One final example of a community and municipal recreation staff coming together reinforces the importance of encouraging ownership of the initiative to remain with the community. In the Christie Pits Park neighbourhood of Toronto residents worked very closely with the recreation staff at the community centre, and have successfully reclaimed space for recreational purposes. Through community building activities such as festivals and baseball, the Christie Pits area is now a vibrant, safe, and active community. This case study has been captured on video and is well worth accessing to see that it is indeed possible for practitioners to work with communities in ways that foster self-determination in the community and result in accessible recreation opportunities for members of all ages (Asterisk Productions, 1997). Like the WOAW project, it demonstrates the importance of a participatory process, which means that the practitioner must be prepared to relinquish his or her power position so that the community is able to identify its own wishes and grow its own solutions.

The Future for Community Development in Recreation

An important first step in ensuring that recreation practitioners are prepared for the challenges of community development is to understand fully the issues of power that rest in the hands of the professional. A central tenet of community development is that change can only happen with a redistribution of power, and although power is never totally eliminated, in community development it has to be shared. This sharing and redistribution of power needs to happen in ways that allow the community to be knowledgeable about its situation, to have a voice, and to act on that voice. Indeed, just as knowledge is power, having the ability to exercise that knowledge and power is essential to communities bringing about change. The implications of this for a practitioner include training in democratic and participatory planning practices. The practitioner needs to understand and apply group facilitation techniques, and must be well-informed regarding community resources. Most important is the ability to work with and respect diverse cultural groups and the encouragement of inclusion in those instances where inclusion is actually desired by members of the community. With care and reflective practices, the recreationist who builds trust and confidence among community members will be well situated to facilitate the development of community.

Key Terms

Citizen participation
Community capacity
Community development
Cooperative movement
Community recreation
Locality development
Playground movement
Professional power
Settlement houses
Social planning
Social action

References

Arai, S. (1996). Benefits of citizen participation in a healthy communities initiative: Linking community development and empowerment. *Journal of Applied Recreation Research, 21*, 25–44.

Arai, S., & Pedlar, A. (1997). Building communities through leisure: Citizen participation in a healthy communities initiative. *Journal of Leisure Research, 29*(2), 167–182.

Arnstein, S. R. (1969). Ladder of citizen participation. *American Institute of Planners*, July, 1969, 216–224.

Boys and Girls Clubs of Canada, History. Retrieved from http://www.bgccan.com/content.asp?L=E&DocID=3

Connolly, K. (2002/2003). Do women's leadership approaches support the development of social capital? Relationship building in a voluntary neighbourhood initiative. *Leisure/Loisir, 27*(3/4), 239–264.

Etzioni, A. (1998). *A Responsive Society: Collected essays on guiding deliberate social change.* San Francisco, CA: Jossey-Bass.

Friedmann, J. (1987). *Planning in the public domain: From knowledge to action.* Princeton, NJ: Princeton University Press.

Frisby, W., & Millar, S. (2002). The actualities of doing community development to promote the inclusion of low-income populations in local sport and recreation. *European Sport Management Quarterly,* (3), 209–233.

Frisby, W., Reid, C. J., Millar, S., & Hoeber, L. (2005). Putting "participatory" into participatory forms of action research. *Journal of Sport Management, 19*, 367–386.

Glover, T. D. (2004). The 'community' center and the social construction of citizenship. *Leisure Sciences, 26*(1), 63–83.

Glover, T. D., Shinew, K. J., & Parry, D. C. (2005). Association, sociability, and civic culture: The democratic effect of community gardening. *Leisure Sciences, 27*(1), 75–92.

Hancock, T., & Minkler, M. (2005). Community health assessment or healthy community assessment: Whose community? Whose health? Whose assessment? In M. Minkler (Ed.), *Community organizing and community building for health.* (pp. 138–157). Piscataway, NJ: Rutgers University Press.

Hodge, G. (2003). *Planning Canadian communities: An introduction to the principles, practice, and participants.* Toronto, ON: Nelson Canada.

Hutchison, P., & McGill, J. (1998). *Leisure, integration and community.* Toronto, ON: Leisurability Publications, Inc.

Hutchison, P., & Nogradi, G. (1996). The concept and nature of community development in recreation and leisure services. *Journal of Applied Recreation Research, 21*(2), 93–130.

Jacobs, J. (1961). *The death and life of great American cities*. New York, NY: Random House.

Karlis, G. (2004). *Leisure and recreation in Canadian society: An introduction*. Toronto, ON: Thompson Educational Publishing, Inc.

Karlis, G., Auger, D., & Gravelle, F. (1996). Three approaches to community development in recreation organizations: The development of a theoretical model. *Journal of Applied Recreation Research, 21*(2), 131–141.

Labonté, R. (1993). *Health promotion and empowerment: Practice frameworks*. Toronto, ON: Centre for Health Promotion/Participation.

Labonté, R. (1996). Community empowerment and leisure. *Journal of Leisurability, 23*(1), 4–20.

Labonté, R. (2005). Community, community development, and the forming of authentic partnerships: Some critical reflections. In M. Minkler (Ed.), *Community organizing and community building for health*. (pp. 82–96). Piscataway, NJ: Rutgers University Press.

Lewis, M. (1997). Community economic development: Making the link between economic development and social equity. In B. Wharf & M. Clague (Eds.), *Community organizing: Canadian experiences* (pp. 164–180). Toronto, ON: Oxford University Press.

Lotz. J. (1997). The beginning of community development in English-speaking Canada. In B. Wharf & M. Clague (Eds.), *Community organizing: Canadian experiences*. (pp. 15–28). Toronto, ON: Oxford University Press.

McKnight, J. (1986). Regenerating Community. In K. Church (Ed.), *From consumer to citizen* (pp. 15–22). Toronto, ON: CMHA.

McKnight, J., & Kretzmann, J. P. (2005). Mapping community capacity. In M. Minkler (Ed.), *Community organizing and community building for health* (pp. 158–172). Piscataway, NJ: Rutgers University Press.

Pedlar, A. (1996). Community development: What does it mean for recreation and leisure? *Journal of Applied Recreation Research, 21*(1), 5–23.

Pedlar, A. (2006). Practicing community development and third way politics: Still faking it? Special issue of *Leisure/Loisir, 30*(2).

Pedlar, A., & Haworth, L. (2006). Community. In C. Rojek, S. Shaw, & T. Veal (Eds.), *The handbook of leisure studies*. London, UK: Palgrave and Macmillan.

Popham, R., Hay, D., & Hughes, C. (1997). Campaign 2000 to end child poverty: Building and sustaining a movement. In B. Wharf & M. Clague (Eds.), *Community organizing: Canadian experiences*. (pp. 248–271). Toronto, ON: Oxford University Press.

Reid, D., & van Dreunen, E. (1996). Leisure as a social transformation mechanism in community development practice. *Journal of Applied Recreation Research, 21*(1), 45–65.

Rothman, J. (1995). Approaches to community interventions. In J. Rothman, J. Erlich, & J. Tropman (Eds.), *Strategies of community intervention* (pp. 26–63). Itasca, IL: F. E. Peacock Publishers, Inc.

Rubin, H. J. (2000). Renewing hope within neighbourhoods of despair: The community-based development model. Albany, NY: State University of New York Press.

Rubin, H. J., & Rubin, I. (1992). *Community organizing and development*. Columbus: Northern Illinois University.

St. Christopher House, *Our history of Social Innovation and Community Mobilization*. Retrieved from http://www.stchrishouse.org/st-chris/history/

United Nations. (1955). *Social progress through community development*. New York, NY: Author.

Wharf, B., & Claque, M. (1997). Lessons and Legacies. In B. Wharf & M. Clague (Eds.), *Community organizing: Canadian experiences* (pp. 302–325). Toronto, ON: Oxford University Press.

Wilkinson, K. P. (1989). The future for community development. In J. A. Christenson & J. W. Robinson (Eds.), *Community development in perspective* (pp. 337–354). Ames, IA: Iowa State University Press.

Yuen, F. C., Pedlar, A., & Mannell, R. C. (2005). Building community and social capital through children's leisure in the context of an international camp. *Journal of Leisure Research, 37*(4), 494–518.

Video: *Reclaiming Community* (1997). From Asterisk Productions, Vision TV and British Columbia Film.

Overland & Underfoot
Regards grandioses

Chapter 33
Leisure Education

Brenda J. Robertson, Ph.D.
Acadia University

Learning Objectives

After reading this chapter, students will be able to

1. Gain an appreciation for the concept of leisure education.
2. Understand elements of leisure functioning.
3. Acquire knowledge about approaches to leisure education delivery.

Introduction

Leisure education is the process through which individuals acquire the knowledge, skills, and attitudes that motivate and facilitate their leisure functioning. *Leisure functioning* is the method by which an individual experiences leisure. In 1993, the Charter on Leisure Education was adopted by the World Leisure & Recreation Association. The purpose of the Charter was to provide international acknowledgement not only of the importance of leisure within society, but also the need for governments, educational institutions, and communities to facilitate leisure education opportunities (Ruskin & Siven, 1995). The Charter acknowledges the following: that leisure knowledge and skills must be acquired for individuals to become fully participating members of society and for enhanced quality of life; that leisure education is required to ensure equal access by all to leisure opportunities and resources; that leisure education is a lifelong process; that both formal and informal leisure education opportunities are required within society; and that those involved with the leisure services delivery system must take responsibility for providing innovative leisure education opportunities integrated with other leisure services.

Who Can Benefit from Leisure Education?

Traditionally, leisure education has fallen within the realm of therapeutic recreation, and hence has been viewed as a structured process made necessary through the advent of catastrophic disease or disability. Leisure education however, is a process that begins at the earliest stages of cognitive development and can continue until death. At every stage of the life cycle and through every life event experienced, there are things to learn and understand about leisure.

Through Leisure Education, One Can Learn to:

- Value free time/leisure
- Understand the benefits that accrue from certain leisure activities
- Be able to overcome stereotypes about certain activities
- Assume self-responsibility for leisure
- Acquire specific activity skills
- Know where the opportunities to participate in leisure exist
- Possess certain personal skills required for leisure functioning
- Understand barriers and learn to overcome them
- Be able to identify and access resources to facilitate leisure
- Possess-planning, decision-making, and problem-solving skills
- Value personal/community wellness
- Respect others
- Learn how to live a balanced lifestyle

Life Cycle Transitions

There are standard life transitions that most people experience which impact leisure functioning. At each milestone, environmental factors impact regular leisure lifestyle patterns. These include such events as starting school, transitioning from elementary into high school and then into either the working world or university, ending one type of work and beginning another, and retirement. Times of transition result in changes in leisure functioning and leisure education during those times can facilitate leisure transition.

Adolescence: Adolescents require particular attention with regards to leisure education. Frequently, adolescents are considered too young for certain behaviours, but too old for others. As such, during adolescence when individuals are encouraged to abandon the carefree lifestyle of a child, assistance is often required to transition successfully into adulthood and to appropriate adult-type leisure behaviours (Holmes & Robertson, 2006).

Adulthood: Adults generally are assumed to be able to facilitate their own leisure functioning in addition to shouldering the responsibility to facilitate leisure for others. In spite of this, leisure seems elusive for many adults today.

Many people require assistance to value leisure, to plan for leisure, and to make personal decisions that facilitate personal leisure functioning. Adults need to feel a sense of entitlement to leisure, which will enable them to help others such as children, aging parents, and employers to understand and respect the need that they, as adults, have for leisure (Simmons, 2000).

Older Adults: Older adults possess the greatest amount of life experience but may often find themselves underappreciated and alienated from the world that surrounds them. As a society that tends to value work over leisure, Canadians appear to value those who are working and making contributions to society in that way, over those who are not. This holds true even if an individual has earned retirement through a lifetime of occupational sacrifice and commitment. Creating a satisfying leisure lifestyle upon retirement, in a society that does not value or respect aging, is a challenge for many. Through leisure education, older adults can be assisted to discover and embrace satisfying leisure-based lifestyles (Binkley & Seedsman, 1998).

Family Change: Leisure education can be a useful means of exploring leisure compatibility as a couple prior to marriage; preparing for changes in leisure functioning prior to having children or when facing an empty nest; when changes in work patterns by either partner impacts leisure functioning; or at the time of a catastrophic illness or death of a spouse who was, in many cases, the primary leisure partner. Also, in cases where family structures breakdown resulting in divorce and then reinvent themselves (e.g., step parents and blended families), leisure education processes can assist all individuals involved with the transition and the establishment of new family leisure lifestyles (Shannon & Morrison, 2006).

Gender: Despite many advances for women in terms of aspects such as acceptance in the work force and changing roles within the household, many women still do not enjoy the same access to leisure as do men. Women often put the needs of others before their own and dedicate their lives to the service of others including their spouse, children, and parents (see Chapter 20). Leisure education can assist women to value themselves, recognize their own needs, and seek to satisfy those needs through their personal leisure without guilt.

Life Events: Life events such as contracting a serious illness, loss of a loved one, loss of employment, moving to a new community, experiencing a dramatic change in financial status, or developing an addiction can all impact leisure functioning. Such life events, whether sudden or expected, disrupt leisure patterns such that assistance is often required to make appropriate adjustments (Carpenter, 1993).

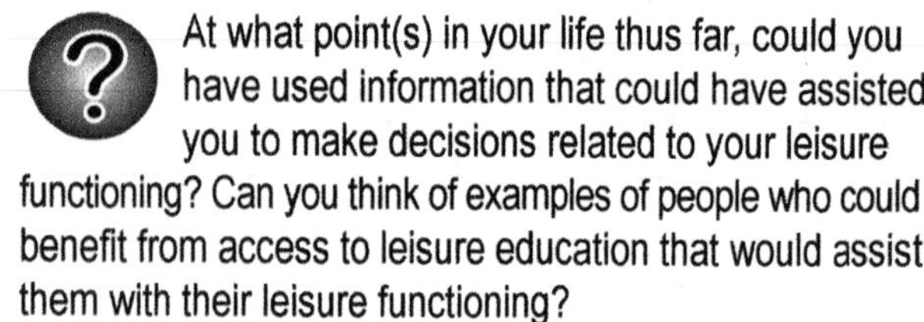

At what point(s) in your life thus far, could you have used information that could have assisted you to make decisions related to your leisure functioning? Can you think of examples of people who could benefit from access to leisure education that would assist them with their leisure functioning?

Sources of Leisure Education

Many sources influence leisure beliefs, knowledge, attitudes, and behaviours. In the past, structured leisure education has existed primarily within therapeutic settings where it was considered a component of the rehabilitation process. Little attention has been given by the profession, or within the literature, to the sources of leisure education for children. Yet, leisure education is an important aspect of the developmental socialization process. Education for leisure seems to be taken for granted, yet there is no one sector of society that acknowledges responsibility for the leisure education of children. Families and schools are most frequently cited as the appropriate sources; however, there is little evidence to suggest that any institution universally accepts this responsibility. Although some parents and teachers are well-equipped to serve as effective leisure educators, others do not possess the necessary knowledge to serve in that role. As such, there is no recognized system that ensures the transference of core leisure knowledge from one generation to the next.

Dr. Jean Mundy, recently retired from Florida State University, is considered by many to be the mother of leisure education. In her book *Leisure Education: Theory & Practice* (1998), she discusses the philosophical underpinnings of leisure education, leisure related challenges facing various segments of the population, leisure education program models, and program planning.

Leisure Education within the Family Unit

Within leisure studies, family is often identified as the first context of leisure learning and tends to provide the primary socialization of leisure values (Barnett & Chick, 1986). As the primary developmental relationship, the interaction between a child and his/her parents is the vehicle for the developmental process. Therefore, most leisure participation during these early years involves and is shaped by family. Changing family structures in recent years have created a myriad of new challenges for families and a shifting of roles and priorities. With the creation of new types of family units such as single parent families, same-sex families, and blended families, many adults are committing time to satisfying their needs through relationship development, which takes time and energy. In these new family units, roles and responsibilities are not always clear and evidence exists that indicates the leisure education of children within the family unit is not always receiving adequate attention.

With more women entering the work force, adult roles and functions within family units are changing. This has influenced the extent to which parents engage in leisure education with their children. In many families, as work and career take on greater priority for adults, the leisure education of children often appears to have become a diminished responsibility. Parents frequently look to organized activities to occupy their children rather than spending the time themselves. Through involvement in such activities, youth may be exposed to leisure values and attitudes that are not in keeping with those of the family. It is through spending time engaged with ones children that parents are able to teach the leisure knowledge, attitudes, and skills that youth require to engage in positive leisure functioning.

In what ways did members of your family provide leisure education for you? Is there one type of family unit that would be best suited to provide leisure education to the children?

Leisure Education within the School Setting

Changes in family structures have also had a major impact upon the school system (Ruskin & Sivan, 2002). Some of these changes have left children experiencing insecurity, low self-esteem, and facing other issues that have negatively impacted their behaviour and school performance. Not only are schools challenged to help youth address such issues, but also technological advances are changing and challenging traditional learning paradigms. Meanwhile, school administrators are being given fewer resources and expected to provide a quality education. This has lead to curricular cuts in areas considered less essential, which often include leisure education based programs such as art, music, drama, and physical education as well as extra curricular offerings in such areas. The result is that schools are not necessarily always a source of positive leisure education.

What did you learn about leisure, either positive or negative, through the schools that you attended? Should families or schools assume primary responsibility for the leisure education of youth in Canada today?

A study by Robertson (2002) sought to understand from the perspective of youth ages 12 to 16, where they learned about leisure. For male youth, the most frequently cited sources of leisure education reported in order of decreasing frequency include: friends, television, mothers, coaches, and fathers. For female youth, the most frequently identified sources included: friends, mothers, school, coaches, and summer camps. In this study, recreation leaders were not frequently reported as being a significant source of leisure education. The role of recreation practitioners, who are guardians of leisure knowledge, in providing education for society must be carefully considered.

Caldwell, Baldwin, Walls and Smith (2004) developed a leisure education program designed to promote healthy use of free time among middle school adolescents. *TimeWise: Learning Lifelong Leisure Skills* curriculum was designed to increase positive free time use to curb substance abuse. Preliminary results indicate that participants are better able to restructure boring situations into something more interesting; have improved decision-making skills, take greater initiative, demonstrate increased community awareness; and have increased participation in new interests, sports, and nature-based activities.

Understanding Leisure Functioning

During the past 30 years, various leisure education models have been developed, each one representing the critical elements of the process as determined by their authors (e.g., Mundy & Odum, 1979; and Peterson & Gunn, 1984). Research conducted to develop most of these models focused on individuals with special needs, in particular those facing mental and physical challenges.

To develop leisure education initiatives that will facilitate positive leisure functioning, one must first understand the decision process relating to the use of free time (see Jackson, 2005, and Mannell & Kleiber, 1997). The following model illustrates the process that determines decision making around leisure engagement. Individuals are not generally aware that such a cognitive process is occurring and guiding leisure decision making. The purpose of leisure education is to create a conscious awareness of this process so that one might intervene in ways that will enhance leisure functioning. The next section describes the components of the model (Figure 33.1, p. 316).

Needs

Engagement in a specific activity is motivated by the intention to satisfy a particular need. In the same way that messages

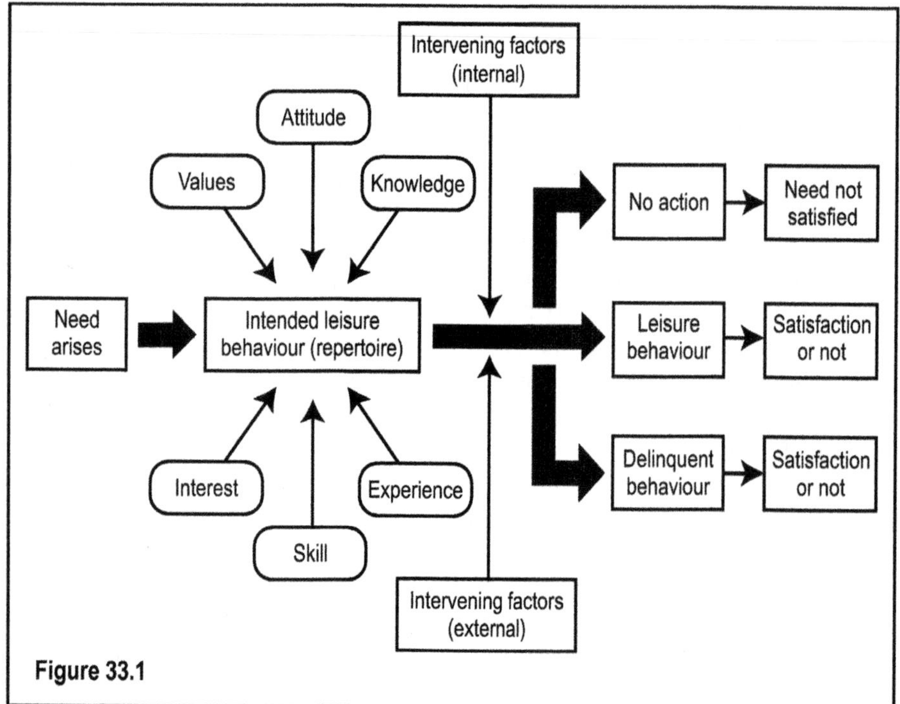

Figure 33.1

going for a run after work, the mother who escapes from the family by locking the bathroom door and soaking in the tub, or the older adults who live alone but meet regularly for a card game with friends are all examples of individuals with certain needs that in turn motivate their free time behaviours. Life is such that for a variety of reasons, all needs do not get acted upon and so are not satisfied. See Common Reasons *i*-box.

Once a need arises, there are usually a number of activities in which the individual could engage to satisfy the need. There are a multitude of activities that could satisfy a specific need but no activity will necessarily satisfy the same need for every individual. For example, the desire to connect with the past could be met through reading historical works, talking to one's grandparents, visiting a museum or historic site, or becoming an historic re-enactor to name but a few. So how does an activity become an intended behaviour or part of an individual's leisure activity repertoire?

The leisure activity repertoire represents all the activities that one may choose to engage in during free time to satisfy a need. In order for an activity to become part of an individual's leisure activity repertoire, the conditions described below must exist.

Values: The activity reflects the individual's personal values. For example, those who value preservation of the natural environment are not likely to ride on motorized vehicles that damage the forest floor. An individual who values physical fitness and time with family may go for a bike ride as a means of spending time with his or her partner and children.

Knowledge: In order for an activity to become part of a leisure repertoire one must not only have awareness of the activity, but also specific knowledge of aspects relating to it. Spelunking, train surfing, or origami will not be in one's repertoire if the individual has no knowledge of what these activities are or that they exist. If one has an awareness of spelunking (caving), but does not know how to become involved in the activity, where to go to engage in spelunking, or what equipment is required then she or he is not likely to have an intention to participate.

Attitudes: Attitudes represent how we think, act and feel toward an issue, a person, or a recreation program. We are not likely to engage in activities that we dislike. It may be, for example, that we tried the activity and did not enjoy it. Such an experience could very well lead to a negative

from our body inform the brain that we need to eat, drink, or sleep so that specific actions follow, our brains are constantly receiving messages about our social psychological needs. These messages motivate all behaviours, not only those associated with leisure. Within the context of work, we are often constrained by our ability to pursue actions to satisfy immediate needs. For example, a clerk at a busy grocery store is not free to act immediately should the need for solitude arise. Certain work provides greater flexibility and the opportunity to satisfy a myriad of needs within the context of the job. It is that factor that draws certain individuals to certain types of occupations. During free time individuals have far greater opportunity to act in a manner that will satisfy their dominant needs at that particular time.

All persons have the capacity to experience similar needs; however, individual life experiences cause certain needs to become more dominant than others in certain individuals at certain times. For example, an individual raised in a competitive home environment may learn to value competition and therefore seek it in their lives. Some individuals crave adventure and challenge, while others are driven by the need for creative expression. There are people who constantly search out opportunities for social interaction, while others prefer their solitude. Most people express these needs through what we call motives. They are motivated to satisfy the more dominant needs as they arise. That is why we sometimes seek out the company of others while at other times we prefer to be alone. Our daily activities, many of which are beyond our control, cause certain needs to arise at certain times that motivate activity choices during free time. The young professional who relieves the job stress by

Common Reasons for Leisure Behaviour

- To acquire knowledge—to increase one's level of knowledge about topics of interest
- To be adventurous—to engage in experiences that are mysterious and exciting
- To be challenged—to test one's mental and or physical skills
- To commune with nature—to experience a sense of connectedness with nature
- To compete—attempt to acquire victory over another
- To connect with the past—to gain an understanding and appreciation of past times
- To be creative—to use personal resources to create something that is unique
- To discover—to make new cognitive connections about aspects of our environment
- To be entertained—to gain stimulation from observing an external stimuli
- To escape—to have mental and or physical separation from undesirable situations
- To achieve fitness—to acquire positive sense of self through physical exertion
- To have fun—to feel elation from living completely in the moment
- To experience mastery of skill—to gain satisfaction through developing a competency
- To be playful—to act out emotions with reduced inhibition
- To gain recognition—to experience acknowledgement for an ability or accomplishment
- To relieve stress—to shift away mentally from thoughts that create feelings of anxiety
- To get a rush—to experience sensory arousal from external stimuli
- To express oneself—to externally project inner feelings
- To have social connection—to experience a sense of comfort connection to a group
- To experience solitude—to access positive feelings associated with being alone
- To have a spiritual connection—to appreciate the existence of a creator guiding one's life.

attitude. Often times, however, negative attitudes are formed against activities based upon assumptions or stereotypes. When asked whether they would like to try sausage making for example, many people react negatively, even though they have never tried the activity. When properly introduced to this culinary pursuit, however, people often develop a different attitude—a more positive and informed one that helps them to be more open to adopting sausage making as part of their leisure repertoire.

Interest: Certain activities capture our interest and others do not. If we are not interested in a specific activity, we wouldn't be likely to pursue it even though it may hold the potential to satisfy a specific need. We may all wish to be fit, but some may reject long distance running to achieve fitness. We may all desire excitement, but not all will seek skydiving as a hobby. Such lack of interest may be caused by a number of factors. For example, certain activities fit better with our self-concept than others. Often stereotypes associated with specific pursuits may foster or prevent interest from developing.

Skills: To engage in any activity, a certain set of skills is required. In all cases there are the technical skills such as being able to shuffle and deal a deck in card games, read a map and use a compass in orienteering, or deliver a rock and sweep in curling. Leisure pursuits may require a wide variety of skills ranging from teamwork and communication to negotiation. Without at least minimal skills, participation in most activities is unlikely to be much fun so skill set often determines which activities will and will not be included in one's leisure activity repertoire.

Experience: Previous experience with activities may determine whether or not we intend to continue to pursue them. Even if our knowledge is somewhat limited, and our skills not particularly well honed, if the experience we have with an activity is positive, chances are we will pursue it again. Negative experiences, particularly of a traumatic nature, may prevent us from engaging in that activity in the future. A hiker who gets pursued by a bear, a boy scout who is taunted by other youth, or a skier who gets trapped in an avalanche may all cease involvement in the activity.

Intervening factors: The greater the number of activities contained in one's repertoire, the better the chances that when a need arises the individual will be able to identify an activity to pursue to satisfy the need. Once an activity that can satisfy the need is identified, certain factors may intervene, which unless negotiated, may prevent participation in the intended behaviour. These are called internal and external intervening factors or constraints (see Chapter 9). An internal intervening factor is psychologically rooted while an external one arises from the environment.

Constraint Negotiation: Constraint negotiation is the process through which ways and means are found to overcome constraints that arise. In most cases, ways can be found to work around a constraint. In cases where this is not possible,

Common Internal Factors that Can Intervene between Intending to Engage in a Certain Activity and Actually Doing So:

- no one with whom to engage in the activity
- low self-esteem
- social role constraint
- low self-efficacy
- sense of entitlement
- inappropriate level of challenge
- ethic of care

Common External Factors that May Be beyond Our Control that Can Prevent Us from Engaging in Certain Activities:

- lack of free time
- lack of partners with whom to engage
- scheduling of activities
- expense involved in participation
- over-regulation that limits enjoyment and access
- access to appropriate transportation

if the leisure activity repertoire is sufficiently large and diverse, another activity may need to be pursued to satisfy a need. The key to negotiating constraints is self-responsibility. Self-responsibility is the process through which individuals acknowledge that they are responsible for identifying and facilitating activities during their free time to satisfy their own needs. Others may assist through the provision of opportunities, but it is the individual who must initiate action to take advantage of the opportunities. Through leisure education, specific strategies can be developed to overcome constraints.

Leisure Participation: Depending upon one's ability to negotiate constraints, there exist three possible outcomes related to leisure participation. The first is that an individual is not able to negotiate the constraints and therefore no action results and so the individual's needs will not be satisfied. For those who are able to negotiate the constraints successfully, engagement in leisure behaviour will result, which will hopefully satisfy the need depending upon the quality of the experience. In certain cases, the individual may not be able to negotiate constraints to socially accepted forms of leisure pursuit; however, they may find delinquent activities accessible, given that such activities typically exist outside of societal control and as such involve fewer social constraints. Involvement in delinquent activities as leisure may or may not satisfy the participant's needs, depending upon the nature of the experience (see Chapter 18).

Leisure Education Delivery Models

There are a variety of options for structured leisure education program delivery. The selection of a delivery model depends upon the nature of the participants as well as availability of resources including facilities, leaders, equipment, transportation, and time. The basic content of any program includes the following: leisure awareness; an understanding of the leisure behaviour model (needs, values, attitudes, knowledge, interests, experience, skills, and constraints/negotiation); and personal planning.

Several models are described here. Each offers its own unique approach to helping individuals build their own leisure repertoire and their capacity to enjoy activities within that repertoire. This discussion is not comprehensive, but rather is intended as an overview of the many means through which leisure educators explore leisure education. Further detail on the models and their effectiveness can be found in a report entitled *The Interface Between Leisure Education and Youth Justice Renewal* (Robertson, 2002).

Activity Sampling: This is an experiential-based approach where participants learn specific lessons about leisure through participation in a variety of activities. Along with exposure and an opportunity to participate, appreciation for the activity is fostered. Individuals learn how to pursue each activity and how it can be incorporated into their personal leisure lifestyle. This is a highly interactive program. Throughout the sessions, various short activities and exercises are carried out to help participants to understand the broader lessons about leisure that are reflected in the specific steps of learning the specific activity. For example, in a cooking lesson, participants learn that they need to plan ahead by ensuring that they have all the required ingredients. In a more general sense, discussion could ensue about making better use of free time on a weekend by planning ahead with discussion of what those considerations might be.

Adventure Based Model: This model strives to take participants outside their personal comfort zones. Such experiences are challenging and facilitate personal assessment and reflection. Participants are guided through a series of progressive activities such that inhibitions are reduced, trust is fostered, and communication is increased. Once appropriate levels of trust and communication are established, the group is presented with a series of challenge initiatives. Each step of the delivery is intended to focus more broadly on aspects of participants' individual leisure functioning. For example, participants may be challenged to work together to complete a task such as crossing a stream or climbing over a wall. The techniques used to work together to complete the task could be debriefed in terms of playing on a sport team and why it is important to have teamwork to be successful in sport.

Entrepreneurship Model: This model recognizes and acknowledges that leisure does not exist in isolation from other components of one's life. It is based upon the Entrepreneurial Cycle, which includes personal visioning, leisure visioning, internal assessment, external assessment, and strategic planning. Using personal values, abilities, and interests, participants are assisted to identify resources they can access to make informed choices about how to spend their free time. For example, an individual lacking confidence in his or her abilities may not be motivated to pursue many forms of leisure pursuit; however, by identifying something that the individual does well, such as math in school, it could be used to foster interest in new leisure pursuits such as being a sport statistician for example.

Marathon Model: In this model, a group of participants meets with a facilitator for an extended period of time. In a leisure education marathon, the facilitator leads the group through the various phases of the prescribed process at a pace acceptable to the group. As such, if the group is discussing a particular topic such as leisure values, they may decide to stay focused on that topic for hours. This type of process is useful if gaining long-term commitment or sustained interest of the individuals over time is difficult. The sense of group involvement and momentum that is built through active discussion is not disrupted by time constraints. For example, it would be challenging to get a group of street youth together every week at the same time for a structured set of leisure education sessions; however, attracting them once and running the session over several hours could be effective as long as they become engaged in the process.

Peer Mentoring Model: In certain cases, individuals learn best from their peers. This model positions individuals who have had basic training in leisure education content and delivery techniques within a group of their peers. Their challenge is to then seek out opportunities to enhance the leisure functioning of others through a variety of means including targeted discussions, activity facilitation, and advocacy. This approach is particularly effective with adolescents. For example, having one or more students in a school in order with their peers as well as with teachers and administrators working to promote and facilitate leisure is a more effective approach then having a recreation professional from outside the school attempt to do so.

Structured Cognitive Model: This model generally employs a classroom-based approach in which individuals participate in series of presentations, activities, exercises, and discussions on components of leisure education. This approach is expert driven, but relies upon active involvement of participants who are challenged to explore aspects of their own leisure functioning through self-assessment and analysis. For example, 4-6 session programs could be offered for a broad range of groups with similar leisure issues and interests ranging from expectant parents to at-risk youth to persons with addictions to those about to retire. The focus of the specific program depends upon the common issues and challenges that each group might be facing with regards to their leisure functioning.

Wellness Model: This model addresses the various components of life that constitute overall wellness, such as nutrition, physical activity, stress management, and addiction. Through a series of activities and exercises, participants gain information that can assist them to make healthier leisure and lifestyle choices. Participants gain an appreciation for the inter-relatedness of the physical, social, intellectual, emotional, and spiritual dimensions of wellness. Individuals examine their leisure lifestyles from a wellness perspective.

A Canadian study *The Interface Between Leisure Education Delivery Models and Youth Justice Renewal* involved delivering leisure education to groups of incarcerated youth and high school students, testing seven different approaches: activity sampling, adventure based, entrepreneurship, marathon, peer mentoring, structured cognitive, and wellness. With data collected prior to the programs, upon completion, and at three and six months post intervention, positive results were reported. The results include increases in the following areas: involvement in pro social recreation, openness to try new activities, desire to develop relationships based upon shared leisure interests, self responsibility for leisure, and leisure planning and decision making (Robertson, 2002).

Conclusions

To live a satisfying and balanced lifestyle, individuals require certain knowledge, attitudes, and skills. These must be acquired, initially through childhood socialization with continual retooling throughout the lifespan. Leisure education is an ongoing process that can take place in myriad of ways. Recent societal changes have resulted in no one institution assuming the primary role for this function. Although not always well positioned to provide direct leisure education, those in the leisure services field are the ones who do possess the knowledge required to help facilitate leisure education within a variety of settings. This can be achieved by working with families and community service providers assisting them to become leisure educators. Leisure providers themselves can also approach the provision of leisure services from more of an educational perspective, than simply service provision. The goal is to foster a greater sense of self responsibility for positive leisure functioning.

Key Terms

Leisure education
Leisure functioning
Life cycle transitions
Program delivery models

References

Barnett, L., & Chick, G. (1986). Chips off the ol' block: Parents' leisure and their children's play. *Journal of Leisure Research, 18*, 266–283.

Bedini, L. A., & Bullock, C. C. (1988). Leisure education in the public schools: A model of cooperation in transition programming for mentally handicapped youth. *Journal of Expanding Horizons in Therapeutic Recreation, 3*, 5–11.

Binkley, A., & Seedsman, T. (1998). Issues in leisure education for older adults. In J. Mundy (Ed.), *Leisure education: Theory and practice* (2nd ed.). Champaign, IL: Sagamore Publishing.

Bullock, C. C., & Howe, C. Z. (1991). A model therapeutic recreation program for the reintegration of persons with disabilities into the community. *Therapeutic Recreation Journal, 25*(1), 7–17.

Caldwell, L. L., Baldwin, C. K., Walls, T., & Smith, E. A. (2004). Preliminary effects of a leisure education program to promote healthy use of free time among middle school adolescents. *Journal of Leisure Research, 36*, 310–335.

Carpenter, G. (1993). Leisure and health during middle adulthood: A case study. In D. M. Compton & S. E. Iso-Ahola (Eds.), *Leisure and mental health*. Park City, UT: Family Development Resources, Inc.

Dattilo, J. (1999). *Leisure education program planning: A systematic approach* (2nd ed.). State College, PA: Venture Publishing, Inc.

Holmes, O., & Robertson, B. J. (2006). *Leisure behaviour transition patterns*. Paper presented at the 88th National Association of Student Personnel Administrators, Washington, DC.

Howe-Murphy, R., & Charnoneau, B. G. (1987). *Therapeutic recreation intervention: An ecological perspective*. Englewood Cliffs. NJ: Prentice Hall.

Jackson, E. L. (Ed.). (2005). *Constraints to leisure*. State College, PA: Venture Publishing, Inc.

Mannell, R. C., & Kleiber, D. A. (1997). *A social psychology of leisure*. State College, PA: Venture Publishing, Inc.

Mundy, J. (1998). *Leisure education: Theory and practice* (2nd ed.). Champaign, IL: Sagamore Publishing.

Mundy, J., & Odum, L. (1979). *Leisure education: Theory and practice*. New York, NY: John Wiley & Sons.

Peterson, C. A., & Gunn, S. L. (1984). *Therapeutic recreation program and design: Principles and procedures*. (2nd ed.). Englewood Cliffs. NJ: Prentice Hall.

Robertson, B. J. (2002). *The interface between leisure education and youth justice renewal*. Wolfville, NS: Acadia University Press.

Ruskin, H., & Sivan, A. (2002). *Leisure education in school systems*. Jerusalem: The Hebrew University of Jerusalem.

Ruskin, H., & Sivan, A. (Eds.). (1995). Leisure education: Towards the 21st century. *Proceedings of the international seminar of the world leisure and recreation commission on education held in Jerusalem*. Provo, UT: Brigham Young University.

Shannon, C., & Morrison, K. (2006, May). *Leisure education: Making it a family matter*. Paper presented at the Canadian Therapeutic Recreation Conference, Halifax, Nova Scotia.

Simmons, F. A. (2000). *Education for leisure: Its practice and purpose in the adult education market*. Unpublished master's thesis, University of New Mexico, Albuquerque.

Section F: Managing Leisure Services

Chapter 34
Program Planning and Program Evaluation: Practice and Principles

Susan M. Arai, Ph.D.
University of Waterloo

Learning Objectives

After reading this chapter, students will be able to

1. Define program planning and program evaluation.
2. Identify five steps in program planning.
3. Understand the differences between summative, formative and process evaluation.
4. Understand the relationship between program evaluation and program planning and implementation.
5. Identify five steps to developing a program evaluation.

Introduction to Program Planning and Evaluation

Why does a recreation centre offer a drop-in centre for youth and a woodworking program for adults? Why does a recreation program focus on the development of self-esteem and body image for young women between ages 13 and 15? These decisions are often the outcome of a process of program planning. With program planning, recreation and leisure professionals make a series of decisions based on a wide range of information that is gathered and analyzed about people and their communities. Leisure programs and services are planned in order to provide positive benefits for individuals and communities, but how do we know if we are achieving our goals? The people we work with change, and the needs and assets of the communities that we work in will change over time. Will a program or service that we plan and implement also be required to change? Answering these questions requires an understanding of three pillars: program planning, program implementation, and program evaluation.

Program planning is a process of gathering information about the situation and environment being planned in and the resources that are available to work with, and making decisions about the goals and objectives for the program, the program content, and the indicators of the program's success. Program implementation is putting the stated program into action. A program evaluation is then used to determine whether a program or service produced the intended result; in other words, it addresses the question, "Did it work?" It is important to create a built in program evaluation from the beginning of program design, rather than as an afterthought. Program evaluation should be considered in relation to program planning and design, and the planning should be for the implementation of the program itself. The relationship between these three aspects of the program is shown in the diagram of the "program logic model" (W. K. Kellogg Foundation, 2003) that appears in Figure 34.1.

Through evaluation it may be determined whether a program or service is meeting the objectives stated in the program plan. In the case of Healthy Leisure Living *i*-box (see p. 322) the answer to this question is essential to the survival of the program in times of budgetary constraints. In some instances, we may also wonder if our program or service is still working, such as the case identified in the Hamptonville Recreation Centre *i*-box (see p. 324).

In the remainder of this chapter we will explore program planning and program evaluation in more detail. As we do so, we will further explore the cases of the Hamptonville Recreation Centre and the Healthy Leisure Living program, and answer some critical questions about the planning and evaluation process.

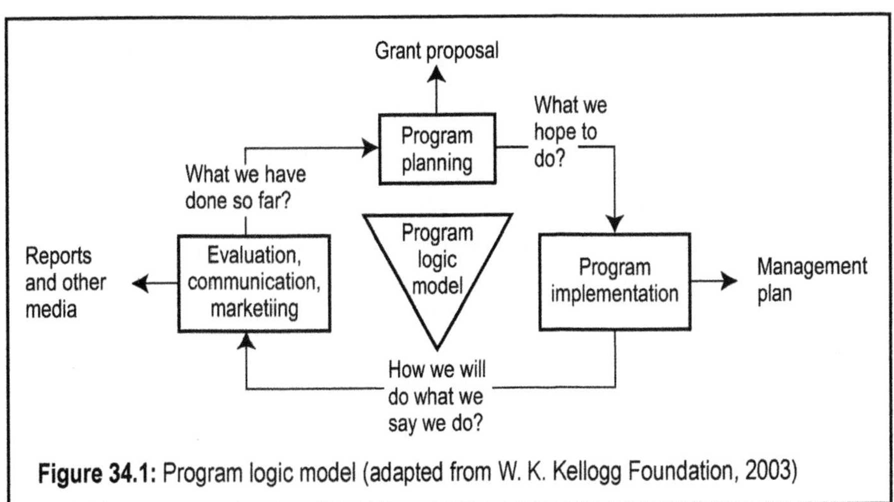

Figure 34.1: Program logic model (adapted from W. K. Kellogg Foundation, 2003)

The Hamptonville Recreation Centre

In the town of Hamptonville, the recreation centre has been in existence since the 1970s. Over the years it has provided programs for children and youth including swimming, leadership, and physical activity programs. It provides adult recreation programs such as a drop in volleyball night, adult swim and aquafit programs. In addition to the pool, there is a small fitness facility, rooms for programming, and a large multi-purpose auditorium and meeting space.

Over the last ten years the community of Hamptonville has been changing. Many of the youth have been leaving the community for College and University and have not been returning. Over time the proportion of the population over the age of 40 has steadily increased, and the population of the children is approximately half of the size that it was in the late 1980s.

The Director of the program has noticed that participation levels in the programs offered have been decreasing. She wonders whether the recreation and leisure needs of the community have changed.

"Healthy Leisure Living"

Healthy Leisure Living is an eight-week leisure education program, designed for adults who experience a chronic illness, to explore leisure opportunities that will enhance their health and well-being.

There are two main objectives of the program: (1) to increase knowledge about the connections between leisure and health among adults who experience a chronic illness, and (2) to increase awareness of leisure opportunities available in the community for adults who experience a chronic illness.

This program is offered through a partnership created by the local hospital and the municipal recreation department. It is delivered by a recreation therapist. Each year the program is offered five times, and the program has been running for about eight years. In the last year the budget for the hospital has been decreased and management is looking for programs that are no longer required. Your manager would like a program evaluation to be conducted to help to show the benefits that Healthy Leisure Living provides for the participants.

Steps to Program Planning

> Good plans shape good decisions. That's why good planning helps to make elusive dreams come true (Bittle, 1972).

Program planning is a way of making a vision, or what was hoped to be achieved in the program, come to life. It is about making decisions and developing a way to put those decisions into operation. Program planning can be approached in a number of different ways; however, common to these processes are five core steps shown in Figure 34.2.

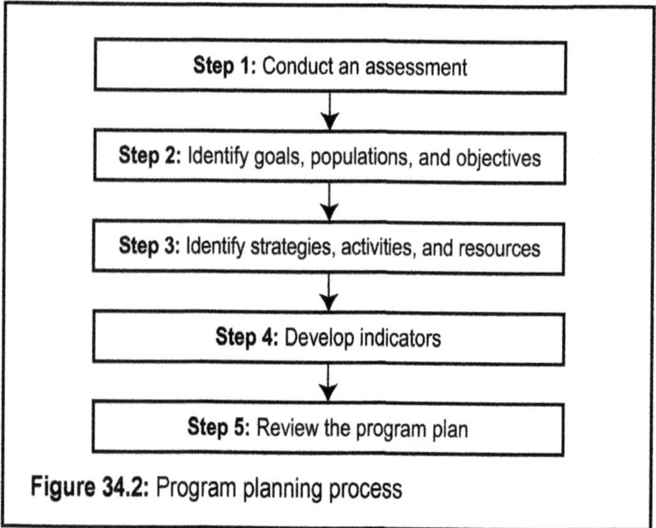

Figure 34.2: Program planning process

Should the program planning be proceeded with? This is the question that is asked in Step 1 of the program planning process. Answering that question involves gathering information about the needs of the populations that the program will serve, identifying the assets of the community, identifying the stakeholders, exploring the literature and knowledge that will help in making program decisions. For the Hamptonville Recreation Centre this may include reading the literature on trends in recreation and leisure services, reading municipal reports about the changing demographics of the community, talking to stakeholders in the community, and conducting an assessment of the strengths and assets of the community. If another organization in the community offers, or is able to offer a program (e.g., aquafit) there may not be a need for the Hamptonville Recreation Centre to offer this service. This step also involves looking at the resources (time, money, facilities) that are available to contribute to the program, and the vision or mandate of the organization to ensure that there is a match.

Step 2 involves answering the question, what will the program hope to achieve? In this step, the goals and objectives of the program are established. A goal is a statement of the purpose or desired accomplishment of the program. Most recreation programs will have a single goal. The objectives then, are brief statements that identify the impact or effect that the program will have. There are five principles to keep in mind when designing objectives. A useful acronym reminds us that objectives should be SMART; that is:

- Specific: clear and precise
- Measurable: able to be evaluated
- Appropriate: to the population and the need
- Reasonable: realistic
- Timed: specific time frame provided for achievement of objective (Health Communication unit, 2001).

In the Healthy Leisure Living program two main objectives of the program were identified: (1) to increase knowledge about the connections between leisure and health, and (2) to increase awareness of leisure opportunities available in the community. To develop program goals, objectives, and indicators, knowledge from courses in the social psychology of leisure, leisure theories, and leisure and community development comes in handy.

Step 2 also involves identifying the key group or segment of the community that requires attention to achieve the goal and objectives; sometimes this group is referred to as the population of interest, or the target group. For the Healthy Leisure Living program the population of interest is adults who experience a chronic illness.

In the case of the Healthy Leisure Living Program, do the objectives stated meet the criteria of SMART objectives?

Step 3 involves identifying and developing the strategies, activities and resources that will be used to achieve the objectives of the program. Choosing the strategy involves deciding how the program will be delivered (e.g., one day workshop or an eight week program meeting one hour a week) and whether the recreation professional will be a leader, broker or facilitator. A leader will deliver the program and help the participants to learn or engage in a series of activities. A broker will organize other people in the community (health promoters, doctors, nurses, fitness instructors) to deliver the program components. A facilitator may train previous program participants to provide peer support to new program participants; or, in the case of a self-help group, he or she may support a group of people to come together to solve their own problems. The program will then involve a series of activities such as introductions and ice-breakers, delivering a lecture, or involving the group in an experiential exercise, a discussion group, or a group task. A review must then be done of the resources available to implement the program (e.g., human resources, financial resources, equipment and facilities). Decision making about the location of the program involves considering issues of accessibility, or perhaps limited resources will require that an organization partner with another organization to provide the required space in order to implement the program.

Step 4 involves the development of indicators, specific measures, for each objective or strategy to identify the point at which goals or objectives have been achieved (Health Communication Unit, 2001). This step addresses the question, "How will you know if your program has achieved its objectives?" For example, if a program objective is that by the end of the program participants will be able to identify how leisure improves their health, the indicator could be the percentage of participants who can identify at least four positive health impacts of a leisure activity.

Step 5, is the review of the program plan; a way to ensure that there is a logical relationship between the goal(s), population of interest, objectives, strategies, and activities, and that the resources are in place to implement the program. This step provides an opportunity to refine steps 1 through 4 as required to ensure that they fit together. For anyone developing the program plan, Step 5 is an opportunity to share the plan with others and to gather feedback that may help to further refine the plan, or to fit the program plan with other initiatives in the organization and community.

What Is a Program Evaluation?

Communities and individuals have a right to relevant and effective programs, services, and activities. A *program evaluation* is the "systematic collection of information about the activities, characteristics, and outcomes of programs to make judgments about the program, improve program effectiveness, and/or inform decisions about future programming" (Patton, 1997, p. 23).

As shown in Figure 34.1, planning for the evaluation is the final phase of the program logic model. The main purpose for doing a program evaluation is to develop information that will help guide program decision making. A program evaluation may be designed to examine specific programs or services. For example, it may be desirable to gather feedback from participants about the benefits of their participation in a leisure education program such as Healthy Leisure Living. The evaluation of whether a program promotes the social inclusion of all participants may also be desired. Program evaluations help to explore the strengths and weaknesses of programs/services, and whether programs achieved the planned goals or outcomes. Results of the evaluation may be used to market programs and the benefits that they provide to individuals and/or the community (see Figure 34.1, p. 323).

Organizations may also be evaluated. For example, at the Hamptonville Recreation Centre the evaluation of client satisfaction with the array of services, or the quality of service may be desired. If the Centre is engaged in community development work, evaluation of how the Centre is helping to build community capacity including local leadership, network development, and shared information may be a good idea. An evaluation of an organization will help to determine the benefits the organization provides to its clients, and the challenges that prevent the organization from meeting its mission and goals. An evaluation may also answer the question: What are the benefits the organization provides to the community?

In answering these questions, decision makers can identify support for decisions to keep, modify or delete a program/service, or to change the way in which programs and services are delivered by the organization. If an evaluation is designed properly, it will be able to narrow the gap between the world of research and the world of management practice.

In the cases of the Healthy Leisure Living program and the Hamptonville Recreation Centre look at Figure 34.1 and discuss how the evaluation will be used.

Why Should We Do Program Evaluations?

Evaluation helps to develop effective programs, services and activities. The outcome of every program evaluation should be useful information that will enable people to modify aspects of the program for improvement, and to make decisions about the program. In the end, the focus should be on "narrowing the gap between generating evaluation findings and actually using those findings for program decision making and improvement" (Patton, 1997, p. 6). The three main types of evaluations are: (1) *summative* (outcome) *evaluations,* (2) *formative evaluations*, and (3) *process evaluations*. Each type of evaluation provides a different answer to the question, "Why should we do program evaluation?" They also differ in when they are used (timing) in relation to the program's history and development.

Summative evaluations are the most commonly understood form of evaluation. This form of evaluation focuses on the outcomes of the program and attempts to answer questions such as: Did the clients get better? Did the program achieve its goals? Did things improve after a new policy was implemented?

Summative evaluations are completed at the end of a program or service and the main intent is to determine program effectiveness (Patton, 1990, 1997). When a new program develops, it is important to run the program a few times to allow the staff to refine and change the program, and to work out issues related to staffing and resources before conducting a summative evaluation. Once the program has been running for a few years and program implementation is happening smoothly, then it is likely time to do a summative evaluation.

Summative evaluations address changes in program participants that happen over a shorter period of time such as changes in their leisure awareness, knowledge or beliefs, or leisure behaviours. Summative evaluation may also measure how participation in a program (service utilization) has increased over a five year period. Looking at changes over a longer time period, a program evaluation may also attempt to measure how the health status of the program participants has changed.

Summative Evaluations

Used when a program has been running for a few years and things are going smoothly.

Summative evaluation—short term

- changes in awareness, knowledge, beliefs
- changes in behaviours
- benefits to participants
- removal of barriers to participants
- increase in number of people reached

Summative evaluation—intermediate

- changes in service utilization
- changes in behaviour

Summative evaluation—long term

- changes in service utilization
- morbidity/mortality
- health status

Formative evaluations provide information to improve the program or service. The evaluation describes, and is an attempt to understand, the dynamic program processes and their holistic effects on participants (Patton, 1990). Formative evaluations are conducted at various points throughout the delivery of the program or service.

Formative evaluations may be used when in the process of developing a program, restarting the program after it has not been offered for a long period of time, or redesigning programs when the needs of the community change. A formative evaluation can include a needs assessment that looks at service utilization, including waiting lists for a program, gaps in service provision, and the stakeholders' perception of their needs. If working from a foundation of community development, a formative evaluation may also be used to conduct a capacity assessment of the community. This may include the available resources (people, buildings, organizations) and other aspects such as local leadership, existing networks of communication and resource distribution, and the amount of community cohesion that exists.

Formative Evaluation

Use when developing or restarting a program

Needs assessment

- use of services, waiting lists
- gaps in services provided
- stakeholder perceptions of needs
- stakeholder perceptions of desired programs

Capacity assessment

- stakeholder identification of assets and capacities of the community

Process evaluations are used when attempting to understand the internal dynamics of how a program, organization, or relationship operates. Some of the program-related questions that a process evaluation will help to address include: What are the things that people experience that make this program what it is? How are clients brought into the program and how do they move through the program once they are participants? What is the nature of staff-client interaction (Patton, 1990)? Process evaluations will often look at how the program or service was implemented, and attempt to identify ways that the delivery of the program or service may be improved.

Process Evaluation

Use during the first few years of implementation

- work performed
- staff time, staff turnover
- expenditures/costs
- promotion/publicity
- participation
- inquiries
- resources distributed
- groups performed/training sessions held
- contacts made
- client satisfaction

What type of evaluation approach do you think is needed in the cases of the Healthy Leisure Living Program and the Hamptonville Recreation Centre?

Who Is the Program Evaluation For?

Knowing the intended audience is essential when designing effective evaluations. Program evaluations may be done to provide information to a number of different stakeholders. A program evaluation may provide information for staff for program development. It may provide evidence of outcomes and information for the people who fund the program or services, for example, government or a community foundation. Program evaluations may also provide information for the clients who use the programs and services, or people who make referrals to the program or service.

Knowing who will be interested in the results of a program evaluation is important. The way in which the evaluation is designed and the way the results are disseminated will depend on the intended audience which may include one or more of the following noted in Table 34.1.

Table 34.1: Evaluation decisions

Audience	Evaluation information will be used to...	Type of evaluation used
Your program participants and you and your team	Make decisions for program planning	• Formative evaluation • Process evaluation
Funders (local, provincial, or federal government; foundations, etc.)	Make decisions to continue to fund your program, or not.	• Summative evaluation • Process evaluation (e.g., participation rates, costs)
Your Board and senior management	Make decisions to continue the operation of the program staffing decisions	• Summative evaluation • Process evaluation (e.g., participation rates, costs) • Process evaluation (e.g., staff time, participation rates, costs)
The community	Provide an accountability mechanism to the community	• Summative evaluation • Process evaluation (e.g., participation rates, costs)
The research community	Contribute to the literature on evaluation and effectiveness	• Summative evaluation

Who is the audience for the results of the evaluation of the Healthy Leisure Living Program and the Hamptonville Recreation Centre?

Conclusions

Program planning, implementation and evaluation are central to the success of recreation and leisure services. Program planning ensures that programming decisions are based in logic using available information. Evaluations provide feedback about whether the delivered programs and services are benefiting the people being served. This information may then be used to revise the program plan (see Figure 34.3) in a feedback loop between program planning and evaluation. Based on the evaluation data, improvements to the program strategies and activities may be mad, and resources may be used more efficiently in the delivery of the program; it may even be possible to modify the objectives of the program.

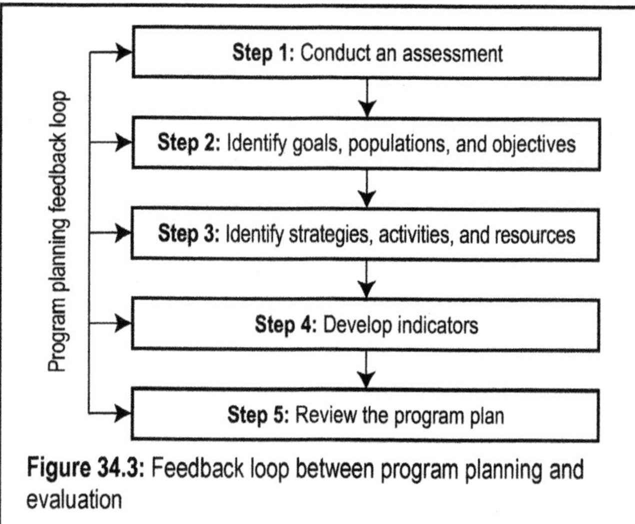

Figure 34.3: Feedback loop between program planning and evaluation

In this chapter different types of evaluations were explored (summative, formative, process) as were the types of questions that can be addressed with evaluation. The demand for information-based decision making in program planning and for outcome (summative) evaluations has been increasing over the last decades as government funding has become scarce. Staff persons are consistently being asked to prove why the program they offer should be continued. Often, program evaluation are not thought of until it is too late. It is important to plan for evaluation as an ongoing aspect of the cycle of program planning and implementation, as explored in Figure 34.1. In addition, it is important that future recreation and leisure professionals develop the broad range of skills required for program planning, implementation and evaluation.

Through such actions, strides can be made toward ensuring that programs address a fundamental principle of the recreation and leisure profession; that communities and individuals have a right to programs, services, and activities which are relevant and effective.

Key Terms

Capacity assessment
Formative evaluation
Needs assessment
Process evaluation
Program planning
Program evaluation
Summative evaluation

References

Bittel, L. R. (1972). *The nine master keys of management.* New York: McGraw-Hill.

Health Communication Unit. (2001). *Introduction to health promotion program planning.* Retrieved from http://www.thcu.ca/infoandresources/publications/planning.wkbk.content.apr01.format.oct06.pdf

Patton, M. Q. (1990). *Qualitative research.* Thousand Oaks, CA: Sage Publications.

Patton, M. Q. (1997). *Utilization-focused evaluation: The new century text* (3rd ed.). Thousand Oaks, CA: Sage Publications.

W. K. Kellogg Foundation. (2003). *Logic model development guide.* Battle Creek, MI: W. K. Kellogg Foundation.

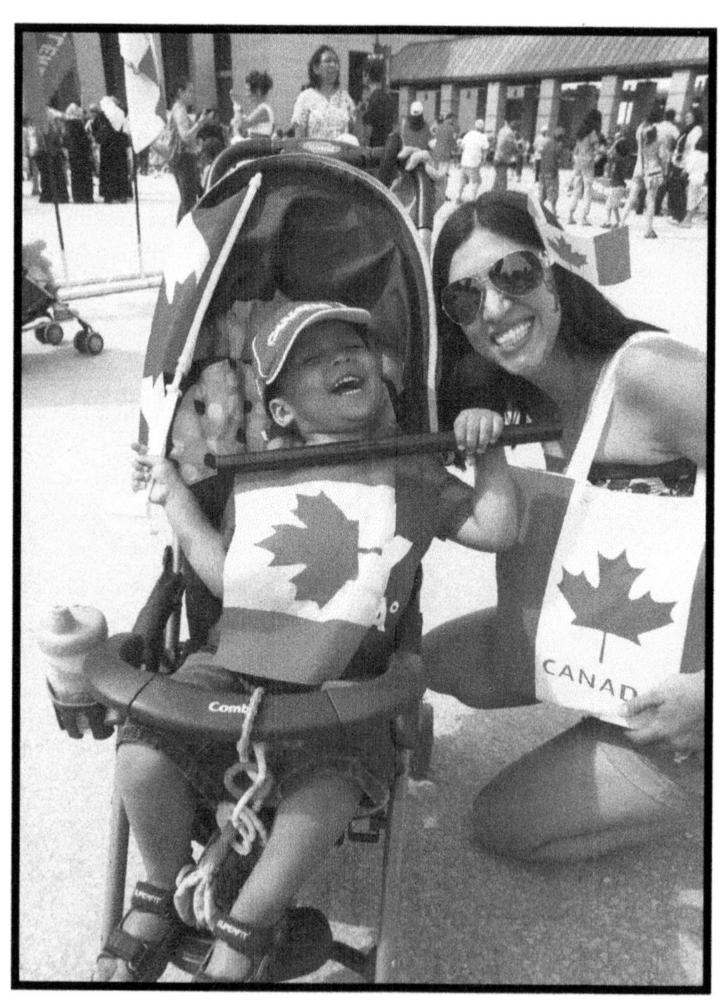
CANAD
Comb

Chapter 35
People-Centred Management

John Meldrum, Ph.D.
University of Victoria

Learning Objectives

After reading this chapter, students will be able to

1. Understand the historical evolution of management theory and practice.
2. Know the difference between managing and leading.
3. Understand the role of organizational culture in the workplace.
4. Know the role of employee reward and recognition programs.

The Most Critical Resource

Leisure service organizations have many resources with which they pursue their respective mandates. These resources can be financial, material, or human. Human resources are the people that make up an organization. They may be managers, employees, partners, or volunteers. It is they who plan strategies, manage and put all the other resources that an organization has at its disposal into action; and it is they who are the vital link between an organization and its clients (McCarville, 2002). Given the importance of people to any organization it seems axiomatic that "if management wants to deliver an outstanding level of service to its customers then it must be prepared to do a great job with its employees" (Reynoso & Moores, 1995, p. 65).

Although people are central to the success of any organization, few organizations are able to capitalize consistently on the strength of their people (Pfeffer & Veiga, 1999). This chapter will help the reader understand the importance of people in any organization and offer some insight on how best to manage human resources. It will focus less on the "mechanics" of human resource management and more on the concept of developing and maintaining a leisure service workplace that is employee and results focused. Let's begin with a short journey through the foundations of management theory.

Thinking about Employees—A Look Back

During the late 18th century, the development of the steam engine started what we now call the Industrial Revolution. Like any revolution it led to significant changes, in particular, in the way goods were produced. Large factories began to emerge for the first time creating numerous challenges that organizations and their managers had not seen before. Early efforts to understand and improve management techniques were directed primarily toward increasing efficiency. Perhaps the most famous of those who sought efficiency in the workplace was Frederick Winslow Taylor. The father of what is now called "scientific management," Taylor was one of the first to attempt to systematically analyze human behaviour at work. His model was the machine, with its cheap, interchangeable parts, each of which performs one specific function. Taylor attempted to do with complex organizations what engineers had done with machines. His goal was to make individuals into the equivalent of machine parts: easily interchangeable, consistent, cheap, and passive.

Taylor's work involved breaking down each task to its smallest unit to discover the one best way to do each job (Taylor, 1947). Taylor's overall goal was to remove human variability and the worker's judgment from the system. Taylorism, as his ideas came to be known, worked; productivity increased dramatically in many factories where his ideas were adopted. Of course, this did not come about without resistance. There was, and continues to be, great human cost when control is taken from the workers.

While scientific management produces impressive results, critics draw attention to the emotional costs of this approach. Labour-management conflict and increasing employee apathy, boredom, and in turn, wasted human resources seemed also to result from scientific management. Concerns over the emotional costs of Taylorism led a number of researchers to examine the discrepancy between how workers were supposed to work and how they actually behaved. The result was the behavioural school of management, or the *human relations movement*. Emerging in the 1920s and 1930s, this movement arose from increasing concern over the dehumanizing and alienating effects of scientific management in the workplace (Mayo, 1946).

A key turning point in the behavioural movement came with a research project conducted at the Hawthorne Plant of the Western Electric Company in Cicero, Illinois. This series of studies, first led by Harvard Business School professor Elton Mayo, began by examining the physical and environmental influences of the workplace (e.g., brightness of lights) and later, moved into the psychological components of the work setting (e.g., number and length of breaks, the role of group pressure). The major finding of the study was that workers were pleased to receive attention from the researchers who expressed an interest in them. A term arising from these studies was the *Hawthorne effect*, a phenomenon where one sees an increase in worker productivity produced by the psychological stimulus of being singled out and made to feel important.

Four General Conclusions Drawn from the Hawthorne Studies:

1. Aptitudes of individuals are imperfect predictors of job performance. Although they give some indication of the physical and mental potential of the individual, the amount produced is strongly influenced by social factors.
2. Informal organization affects productivity. The studies also showed that the relations that supervisors develop with workers tend to influence the manner in which the workers carry out directives.
3. Work-group norms affect productivity. The Hawthorne researchers were not the first to recognize that work groups tend to arrive at norms of what is "a fair day's work," however, they provided the best systematic description and interpretation of this phenomenon.
4. The workplace is a social system. The Hawthorne researchers came to view the workplace as a social system made up of interdependent parts (Franke, R. H. & Kaul, J. D, 1978).

Insights from this and other studies began to push managers away from the notion that workers were working at full capacity when following instructions provided by managers. They began to explore workers' response to various stimuli, and in particular, their willingness to problem solve. The emphasis shifted from a focus on the manager to an exploration of the role of work groups in solving organization problems. Much of the management research over the next few decades focused on the role of more open and trusting work environments with a greater emphasis on group dynamics. This chapter is based largely on insights from this research tradition.

New(er) Ways of Thinking about Workers

Douglas McGregor is often credited with popularizing the Human Relations approach with his Theory X and Theory Y. He discovered that although many managers understood the importance of workers and work groups, their actual behaviours seemed to undermine the efforts of workers and the groups in which they worked. McGregor blamed these behaviours on the assumptions managers were making about their workers. He called these assumptions Theory X (see *i*-box). These assumptions suggested generally that workers were not particularly happy to be working. Consequently, managers believed that their job was composed largely of watching and controlling their workers. This perspective is generally consistent with Taylor's work.

McGregor's review of decades of research suggested to him that these assumptions were simply not valid. Instead he developed a new set of assumptions (Theory Y), which seemed to offer a more accurate and helpful view of the worker within the workplace (Dessler, Starke, & Cyr, 2001).

Theory X Assumptions

- Work is inherently distasteful to most people.
- Most people are not ambitious, have little desire for responsibility, and prefer to be directed.
- Most people have little capacity for creativity in solving organizational problems.
- Motivation occurs only at the physiological and security levels.
- Most people must be closely controlled and often coerced to achieve organizational objectives.

Theory Y Assumptions

- Work is as natural as play if the conditions are favourable.
- Self-control is often indispensable in achieving organizational goals.
- The capacity for creativity is spread throughout organizations.
- Motivation occurs at affiliation, esteem, and self-actualization levels, not just security, physiological levels.
- People can be self-directed and creative at work if properly motivated.

Does classical management theory offer anything of use to future leisure service managers and professionals? Assess your own ideas about workers. Do you agree with Theory X or Theory Y? Why?

The management literature has moved on since these early debates. The classical view of Taylor is still very much in evidence in high volume settings, for example, where workers must create thousands of objects through highly prescribed processes. The assembly line, the fast food outlet, and even many large instructional recreation classes all demand that procedures be carried out in set ways. The lifeguard at a swimming pool cannot decide when and where the job might best be accomplished. The many tasks, such as where to stand or how to carry out a rescue, are prescribed down to the finest detail.

Managers understand too that workers are thinking, feeling individuals who can be very involved in the work place. They can be active problem solvers who search for meaning and satisfaction from their work. They may work alone but are also very much influenced by the social environment in which they find themselves. The manager plays a central role in establishing and maintaining that environment. The literature continues to explore the role of the manager in helping the worker succeed. The rest of this chapter outlines some of the insights they have discovered over the years.

Working with Employees—Managing vs. Leading

The drive for efficiency came to us long before Taylor popularized his scientific management techniques. It has been with us for centuries, and continues to dominate managers' thinking and actions. Peter Drucker (2001), a renowned management professor, noted that efficiency is doing things right while effectiveness is doing the right things. He goes on to say that many of today's work spaces rely on knowledgeable workers. Knowledgeable workers are those who can solve complex problems, deal with changing and dynamic work spaces, and work independently as well as in groups. For them, getting the job done well is as important as getting it done efficiently. As Drucker tells us, for managers of these knowledge based workers the focus must be on effectiveness rather than on simple efficiency.

In what ways are leisure services knowledge based workplaces? When do some leisure organizations focus more on efficiency (doing things right) than on effectiveness (doing the right things)?

Warren Bennis, a leadership theorist, was also concerned with efficiency and effectiveness but discussed them in terms of management roles and responsibilities. He thought of effectiveness (doing the right things) and doing things right (efficiency) as a key distinction between managers and leaders. He believed that managers were most concerned with efficiency, whereas leaders were concerned with effectiveness. He thought of those concerned with effectiveness as being transformational leaders. That is, managers do things right and leaders do the right things. For example a manager usually administers, maintains, focuses on systems and controls, asks how and when, and keeps an eye on the bottom line. Conversely, a leader, innovates, develops and focuses on people, inspires trust, asks what and why, and has a long-term view with an eye on the horizon (Bennis, 1989).

Management is the process of setting and achieving the goals of the organization through the functions of management: planning, organizing, directing (or leading), and controlling. A manager is hired by the organization and is given formal authority to direct the activity of others in fulfilling organization goals. Thus, leading is a major part of a manager's job. Yet, a manager must also plan, organize, and control. Generally speaking, leadership deals with the interpersonal aspects of a manager's job; whereas planning, organizing, and controlling deal with the administrative aspects of that same job. Leadership deals with change, inspiration, motivation, and influence. Management deals more with carrying out the organization's goals and maintaining the status quo (Kotter, 1990).

The key point in differentiating between leadership and management is the idea that employees willingly follow leaders because they want to, not because they have to. Leaders may not possess the formal power to reward or sanction performance; however, employees give the leader power by complying with what he or she requests. In the 1920s and 1930s, leadership research focused on trying to identify the traits that differentiated leaders from non-leaders. These early leadership theories were *content theories*, focusing on what an effective leader is, not on how to lead effectively. The trait approach is one example of a content theory. This approach assumes that leaders share certain physical, social, and personal characteristics. Although this theory continues to receive wide support, years of research have not been able to identify a set of traits that will consistently distinguish leaders from followers. It seems as if no two leaders are alike, nor does any one leader possess all of the traits thought to create a leader. Furthermore, traits leading to leadership roles seem to vary with the situation. In other words, traits that create a leader in one setting may not work in another setting.

Research began to suggest that it was not a given trait that created leaders but rather, the types of techniques used by individuals as they worked with other people. We now realize that different situations may call for different leadership styles. A second set of theories, called *contingency theories* argue that the "right" or effective leadership style varies according to the demands of any particular situation or context. This approach has garnered considerable support over the years and continues to inform and direct management thinking. It suggests that leaders must respond to ever changing work conditions if they plan to be effective. In the fast-paced settings that characterize leisure service delivery, employees must be ready and able to problem solve, sometimes hundreds of times each day. The manager's role is not to think for the employee but instead to work with the employee in achieving mutually desired goal. Managers cannot assume that workers will simply carry out tasks assigned by the manager. They cannot assume that workers need only be told what to do to ensure success. Instead, managers must create conditions that help their own workers succeed. By doing so, they and their organizations will succeed.

There has been some effort here in Canada to establish the skills needed to perform successfully as a manager of park and leisure services. For example, the British Columbia Recreation and Parks Association (BCRPA, 2005) suggested that the skills one requires for the position of parks and recreation director can be placed into several broad categories: for example, administrative, leadership, and communication skills as well as experience and knowledge of organized recreation in a community or public environment. Hurd and McLean (2004) found similar categories of competencies in their examination of the skills needed to be a leader at the senior or CEO level of a parks and recreation department in the United States. They found six competency categories: business acumen, communications and marketing skills, community relations, leadership and management skills, planning skills, evaluation skills and professional experience.

Building on this work McLean, Hurd, and Jensen (2005) grouped senior leadership in leisure service organizations into three broad categories: the Practical CEO, the Structured CEO, and the Traditionalist CEO. The *Practical CEO* is a problem solver who listens to his or her people and involves them in decision making. These individuals take a very humanist approach to management. Their focus is on helping the worker perform well. The *Structured CEO* focuses more on the structure of the organization using a pragmatic approach to management. These individuals focus more directly on specific techniques like program and service evaluation and are likely to lead by example. The *Traditionalist CEO* is clearly more concerned with formal skill sets and is very closely connected to parks and recreation as a profession. She or he values external validation of credentials through education or certification and holds long held views of organizational management such as a respect for authority.

This research group discovered that five factors were shared by two or more of the different types of CEOs: (1) the ability to recruit and train staff; (2) the ability to treat people fairly and with respect; (3) the ability to make decisions; (4) currency with professional trends; and (5) acting in an honest and ethical manner. Note that all these dimensions involve "softer" management skills as opposed to technical knowledge such as planning, budgeting, or marketing. The emphasis, in this study at least, was very much on the manager as leader, not the manager as technician.

Which type of the three CEOs described would you want to work for? Why?

The rest of this chapter is concerned with those techniques managers and leaders have been using to create successful workplaces. Although there are many such techniques, this chapter focuses on the following two: organizational culture and recognition/reward structures.

Creating a Positive Work Environment—Organizational Culture

Organizational culture is perhaps best described as the personality of an organization. It is the shared characteristics, traditions, and values held by members of an organization. As such, it guides the everyday behaviour of all employees. It offers them a way of thinking about and acting toward daily decision making. If the culture is one of teamwork, then workers will automatically think of working with others as they seek solutions to problems. If the emphasis is on revenue, then that is the test they will apply as they make programming decisions. Culture tells workers what is right and wrong, good and bad, desirable and undesirable.

Culture is created and perpetuated by cultural artifacts, patterns of behaviour and values and beliefs. You can learn much of the culture of an organization by looking at the arrangement of furniture, at what staff members wear and how they act. Office spaces adorned with toys or funny slogans and personal pictures tell of a culture that encourages fun, one that understands that work doesn't have to be work like. Spaces in which everyone wears formal office attire send another message. In the latter culture there is less relaxed and more serious in its approach to daily operations. Managers spend a great deal of time helping create and perpetuate corporate culture. This is because they know that they can't (and shouldn't) tell people how to act each moment of the day. Instead they help create a culture in which good things are more likely to happen. They create a culture that helps guide all the workers in ways that move the organization forward.

Managers play a key role in creating and maintaining organizational culture. Their job is to clarify expectations through the use of signs, symbols, stories, rites and ceremonies. For example, a new manager at a swimming pool noticed that all the signs posted around the pool focused on those things the patrons were *not* supposed to do. There was to be NO running, NO splashing, NO shouting, and so on. The culture that had emerged in the pool was very formal and almost adversarial between staff and patrons. These signs were symbolic of this culture. The manager wanted to create a more positive culture in the facility, so signs were changed to reflect that new perspective. The "NO running" sign was changed to "For your safety, please walk on deck."

This pool manager was also aware of the power of symbols. Staff members were encouraged to smile when they met patrons on deck, to kneel down to eye level when chatting with children, to play with children in the water while off duty. These were all symbolic gestures intended to build a positive culture within the workplace of the pool. Stories and rites were also important to rebuilding the culture of this workplace. We tend to tell stories about events that are worth remembering. We tend to repeat actions that prove successful. This manager tried to find stories that helped everyone understand the new culture and ensured that these stories were told and retold. The stories chosen for this purpose dealt with a lifeguard who went out of her way to help a patron who had a flat tire in the parking lot and with an instructor who never failed to surprise and delight his pupils with a bit of imagination and lots of class preparation. Each of these stories not only inspired fellow employees but also helped suggest how they too might act in the same situations. These stories were repeated at all new staff training sessions. It is in such ways that stories build culture. New instructors were also placed in a swim class and asked to do things that were, by nature, very difficult to master. Like any new student they struggled with the challenges of this class, but senior instructors (they called them *mentors*) were on hand to support, teach, and encourage. Through such rites culture is built and maintained from one generation of instructors to the next.

Communicating Organizational Culture

As an example let us look at how culture can be communicated to a new an employee in a municipal leisure service department. Pat has just graduated from the most prestigious recreation and leisure studies program in the country and is about to begin her first day on the job as the new aquatics programmer. Even before she is officially on the payroll she has already been learning about the culture. During her interview she noticed that all senior managers' doors were open, and many of them were engaged with other employees. Chatting before her interview, she took note of how many times her future boss used the word *team* and constantly referred to the important role their agency played in serving the needs of the community. She noticed pictures on the wall recognizing "service super heroes" from the past weeks, dressed in crazy capes and costumes; she briefly wondered what she might be getting herself into! On her way in she was greeted by Director of Leisure Services who introduced herself as "Jane" who then walked Pat around to meet all the other employees. The next part was somewhat unexpected. Pat was told her first day would be spent participating in the programs she would soon be responsible for. Jane said this was something all new employees did because "we can never forget who we are here to serve."

How would describe this organization's culture? How has culture been demonstrated or encouraged in an organization, team or group of which you've been part? How might the organizational cultures differ in organizations led by the three types of CEOs raised by Mclean, Hurd, & Jensen, 2005?

Recognition and Reward

Managers enhance performance by rewarding, often informally as well as formally, the behaviours they wish to see continue in the organization. When one speaks of rewards, it is often things like pay and benefits that come to mind. This is fair because these are indeed important and essential to most employees; however, in many public sector settings, pay and benefits are formally negotiated through unions or other such agreements, and thus fall outside the control of most managers. Consequently, the focus here will be on soft rewards, the often forgotten "pats on the back" that most of us appreciate and need to continue in order to feel appreciated in the workplace.

The key to rewards and other forms of compensation is often not the amount of the reward but rather, how the reward is administered. First, rewards must be allocated in a "fair" or "just" manner (Davenport & Roberts, 2005). Justice is conceptualized as having two primary dimensions, those of distributive justice and procedural justice. Distributive justice is based on equity theory (Adams, 1963), which states that employees compare their effort (job inputs) to the reward they receive in return. Fairness also applies to procedural justice, which as the name implies, focuses on the process used to make reward allocations (Alexander & Ruderman, 1987). Procedural justice is an evaluation of how decisions are made and their perceived fairness. For example, an employee may evaluate how rewards are distributed or, more precisely, perceived to be distributed. Procedural justice seems to be more important than distributive justice over the long run (Folger & Konovsky, 1989).

Second, communication must support any reward initiative. Such communication must be open and two-way in nature (Erikson, 2004). Those being rewarded must be well-informed about the timing of rewards, how the reward is tied to performance, and most of all they must be able to deal with any issues that arise during the administration of rewards. In all these cases, front-line managers and supervisors are keys to successful reward programs. They must work with employees to ensure that rewards are actually operating as intended.

Putting It All Together

As a new manager how does one put it all together? On the surface it seems pretty straightforward. You treat people well and they are more likely to perform well. This chapter has attempted to illustrate that although the goal may be simple, getting there requires constant work and a solid commitment to the philosophy that it's the people that are the key to fulfilling any organization's mission. Pfeffer and Veiga (1999) may have put it best when they said, "In the end, the key to managing people in ways that lead to profits, productivity, innovation, and real organizational learning ultimately lies in the manager's perspective" (p. 47). It all comes down to how an organization and its leadership view the people who make up that organization. Viewing employees as assets is the essential first step. Without this perspective most managerial actions may be taken as gimmickry and with cynicism from employees. Mutual trust between employer and employee must be the foundation of any employee centred enterprise. It helps create an environment where employees have the opportunity to develop and test their skills and knowledge and to be recognized for it. Trust, involvement, opportunity and recognition provide the basis for a strong employee centred work place. By focusing on, and freeing the talents of their employees, leisure service organizations can develop an environment where committed and engaged employees are better able to deliver the quality services and programs to the members of its community.

Key Terms

Human relations movement
Leadership
Organizational culture
Scientific management

References

Adams, J. (1963, November). Toward an understanding of equity. *Journal of Abnormal and Social Psychology*, 422–436.

Alexander, S., & Ruderman, M. (1987). The role of procedural and distributive justice in organizational behavior. *Social Justice Research, 1*(2), 177–198.

Bennis, W. G. (1989). *On becoming a leader*. Reading, MA: Addison-Wesley.

British Columbia Recreation and Parks Association. (2005). *Parks and recreation competencies and standards review project: Summary report*. Retrieved from http://www.bcrpa.bc.ca/about_bcrpa/resources.htm

Davenport, T., & Roberts, D. (2005). Managers—The missing link in the reward change process. *Journal of Organizational Excellence, 24*(2), 3–16.

Dessler, G., Starke, F., & Cyr, D. (2001). *Management: Leading people and organizations in the 21st century*. Toronto, ON: Prentice Hall.

Drucker, P. F. (2001). *The essential Drucker: Selections from the management works of Peter F. Drucker*. New York, NY: Harper Business.

Erickson, B. (2004). Nature times nurture: How organizations can optimize their people's contributions. *Journal of Organizational Excellence, 24*(1), 21–30.

Folger, R., & Konovsky, A. M. (1989). Effects of procedural and distributive justice on reactions. *Academy of Management Journal, 32*(1), 115.

Franke, R. H., & Kaul, J. D. (1978). The Hawthorne experiments: First statistical interpretation. *American Sociological Review, 43*, 623–643.

Hurd, A. R., & McLean, D. D. (2004). An analysis of the perceived competencies of CEOs in public park and recreation agencies. *Managing Leisure, 9*(2), 96–110.

Kotter, J. (1990). *A force for change*. New York, NY: Free Press.

Mayo, E. (1946). *The human problems of an industrial civilization*. Boston: Division of Research, Graduate School of Business Administration, Harvard University.

McCarville, R. E. (2002). *Improving leisure services through marketing action*. Champaign, IL: Sagamore Publishing.

McLean, D. D., Hurd, A. R., & Jensen, R. R. (2005). Using Q-methodology in competency development for CEOs in public parks and recreation. *Managing Leisure, 10*(3), 156–165.

Pfeffer, J., & Veiga, J. F. (1999). Putting people first for organizational success. *The Academy of Management Executive, 13*(2), 37.

Reynoso, J., & Moores, B. (1995). Towards the measurement of internal service quality. *International Journal of Service Industry Management, 6*(3), 64.

Taylor, F. W. (1947). *The principles of scientific management*. New York, NY: Norton.

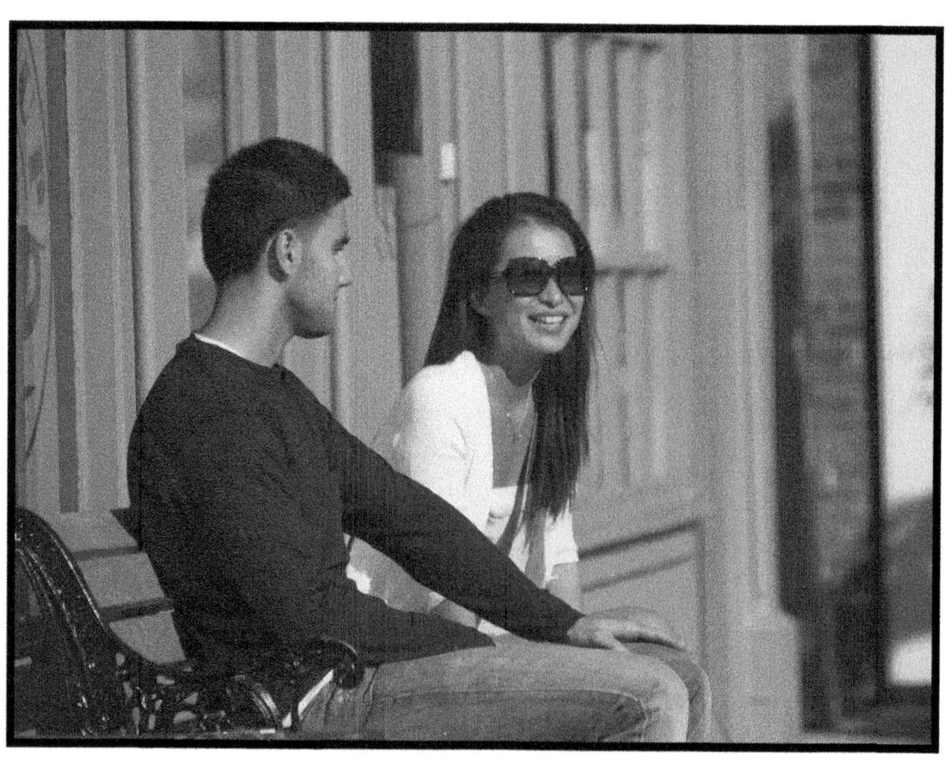

Chapter 36
Marketing Recreation and Leisure Services

Andrew T. Kaczynski, Ph.D.
University of South Carolina

Luke R. Potwarka, Ph.D.
University of Waterloo

Learning Objectives

After reading this chapter, students will be able to

1. Define marketing.
2. Understand sources of confusion surrounding the role of marketing in public, private, and not-for-profit contexts.
3. Describe the six activities involved in the process of marketing.
4. Be aware of alternative marketing philosophies.

Introduction

Marketing is being done all around us. We encounter advertisements for ski vacations in winter, baseball games in summer, and brochures for community recreation programs arrive in our mailboxes periodically throughout the year. Marketing, however, encompasses much more than just advertising. Indeed promotion, the particular element of marketing under which advertising is subsumed, is comprised of several other strategies that can also be used to communicate with potential clients and participants. As Figure 36.1 shows, marketing consists of six main activities, each of which will be described in this chapter. Most marketing effort occurs "below the surface" though, which is why the terms marketing and promotion are often, but incorrectly, used interchangeably. Some elements of marketing (e.g., program development, pricing) have achieved widespread use, though perhaps not to their full potential, in all sectors of leisure service delivery. Other elements (e.g., research, segmentation), however, are ignored far too often, sometimes to the detriment of participants and the community.

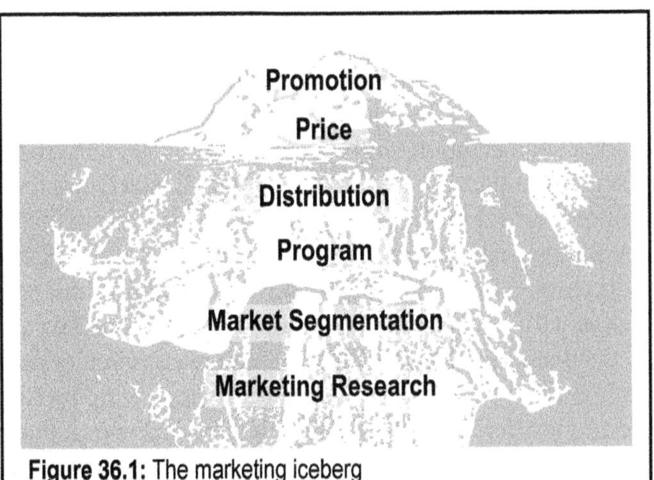

Figure 36.1: The marketing iceberg

Do you buy a product or use a service just because you like the advertisements for it, or do you also take into account how well it meets your needs, how much it costs, and how convenient it is, among other factors?

Another misconception is that marketing is undertaken solely to sell a product or service and its main goal is profit generation. In this chapter we explain how marketing simply provides a set of neutral tools or activities, which can be applied equally and appropriately to achieve a wide range of organizational and participant objectives (McCarville, 1999). The "Is Marketing Synonymous with commercialism?" *i*-box (p. 338) describes an early article by Schultz, McAvoy, and Dustin (1988) that expressed concern about the use of marketing and other business tactics in recreation and leisure services. The rebuttal by Havitz (1988) argued that marketing did not apply solely to commercial objectives and could just as easily be used to promote positive societal outcomes. Unfortunately, confusion about the true nature and purpose of marketing continues to linger, including within the field of park and recreation services.

To help alleviate some of these misunderstandings, we begin this chapter by defining marketing. The middle section of the chapter includes a description of the six activities generally involved in the process of marketing. Finally, alternative marketing philosophies that incorporate emphasis on enhancing beneficial societal outcomes are described.

What Is Marketing?

In their widely adopted social services marketing text, Crompton and Lamb (1986) stated: "Marketing is two things. First, it is a philosophy, an attitude, and a perspective. Second, it is the set of activities used to implement that philosophy. Acceptance of the philosophy is a prerequisite for successful implementation of the activities" (p. 1). As Figure 36.1 shows, these activities include research, segmentation, product or program development, distribution, pricing, and promotion. It is the philosophy behind these actions, however, that separates marketing from other less client-focused methods of providing services. These authors further asserted that "the marketing concept... holds that the social and economic justification for an organization's existence is the satisfaction of customer wants" (Crompton & Lamb, 1986, p. 3). Kotler, one of the pioneers of marketing in the business literature, defines marketing as "a social and managerial process by which individuals and groups obtain what they need and want through creating and exchanging products and value with others" (Kotler, Armstrong, Cunningham, & Warren, 1996, p. 6). These definitions suggest that marketing is an interactive process between a provider and its clients (Figure 36.2). By understanding the wants and needs of participants and providing services that satisfy them, a park and recreation organization in the public, private, or not-for-profit sector can gain their support in the form of user fees, taxes, and related monetary and non-monetary expenditures (Crompton & Lamb, 1986).

Is Marketing Synonymous with Commercialism?

During the 1980s, business principles, including the tools of marketing, gained in popularity among parks and recreation managers as they learned to deal with the new climate of fiscal austerity in government services and elsewhere. The appropriateness of these changes in operating philosophy and methods were debated in Parks and Recreation magazine, a popular publication for professionals in the United States.

In their article entitled, "What are we in business for?" Schultz, McAvoy and Dustin (1988) lamented: "Our professional magazines, journals, and conferences formerly focused on strategies to better serve the leisure needs of people. Those same [sources] now feature marketing and merchandising strategies designed to cater to the recreation wants of customers who choose to pay" (p. 52). They suggested that by integrating such strategies into the delivery of parks and recreation services, the profession might become more focused on the bottom line than on promoting the public good.

In response to some of the perceived misconceptions within that original article, Havitz (1988) argued that, "marketing is not synonymous with commercialism" (p. 34) and that using the two terms interchangeably is inaccurate. He went on to say, "certainly, we do not want to copy the worst characteristics of the commercial sector, but we shouldn't be above borrowing from the commercial sector's strengths" (p. 36). Marketing, he claimed, can actually improve the quality of public services by designing programs (as well as the distribution, pricing, and promotion of those programs) that are more tailored to the needs of participants and the community.

This debate was indicative of the uncertainty at the time about whether new business-related ideas like marketing were appropriate for leisure service delivery, and, if they were, how to effectively implement them. Similar discussions still arise today, but perhaps with less regularity and vigour given that the terminology and tools of marketing have generally been accepted, if not perfectly integrated, into the operations of parks and recreation agencies.

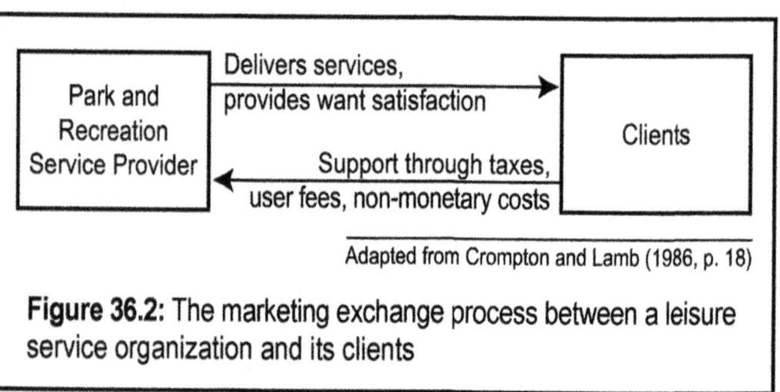

Figure 36.2: The marketing exchange process between a leisure service organization and its clients

In summary, although some professionals and academics still associate it with generating profits for individuals or corporations, the process of marketing is actually centred around identifying the needs and wants of participants and segmenting them into groups so that these desires might be fulfilled efficiently and effectively. Sometimes this will be done with the goal of making money, but in other situations, betterment of the community may be the primary motivation for engaging in marketing efforts.

Marketing Activities

The set of marketing activities will be the focus of discussion in the next several sections of this chapter. More specifically, we will explore the marketing activities of research, market segmentation, and each element of the marketing mix (i.e., product or program development, place/distribution, price, and promotion) in more detail. Indeed, many people associate marketing solely with the activities of the marketing mix. However, effective marketing strategy begins with a solid understanding of the needs and wants of the community, and with dividing the community into groups that share similar characteristics and product or program preferences. Consequently, the initial two sections below describe research and segmentation, the foundations of good marketing practice.

Foundations of Marketing

Research

In order to meet the diverse leisure needs of citizens, providers must first collect and evaluate marketing information from their community. In other words, leisure service marketers must first establish what is known as *marketing intelligence*. Marketing intelligence consists of two principal components: *needs assessments* and *environmental analyses*. The information that is gathered from these research activities can be used to develop marketing strategy more aligned with the needs and wants of potential clients.

Every marketing decision should begin by considering the needs and wants of potential clients. Acquiring information on what services citizens want the organization to deliver is a primary goal of conducting needs assessments. For example, based on needs assessment survey results, a service provider may determine that the leisure needs of young families, older adults, or some other segment in the community are not being met with current program offerings. In addition, conducting a community needs assessment can help leisure service providers determine what types of programs potential client groups seek, their reasons for accepting or rejecting a specific service, and their location preferences for facilities (Crompton & Lamb, 1986).

Knowledge of uncontrollable forces external to the organization is also important to the development of effective marketing strategy. For example, external social factors such as significant demographic changes (e.g., an aging population, declining birth rates) can greatly influence how leisure service providers design and implement programs that meet changing citizen demands. Moreover, leisure service marketers should be attuned to changing economic conditions in their community. Changes in disposable income levels, interest rates, inflation, and unemployment levels can influence demand for certain service offerings and may lead providers to revise their current pricing strategies. The legal-political sector is also an important external force affecting many leisure service agencies. Government can establish laws that enable, limit, or regulate people's leisure behaviour in some way, thereby influencing what services an agency can offer, to whom, and when (Crompton & Lamb, 1986). For example, municipal governments usually require that housing developers set aside parkland or build recreation amenities during the construction of new neighbourhoods.

Market Segmentation

Most leisure service organizations operate within heterogeneous communities comprised of individuals with unique sets of needs and wants. As such, market segmentation strategies attempt to break communities into meaningful client groups to meet the diverse leisure needs of citizens (McCarville, 2002). More specifically, market segmentation can be defined as, "the process of dividing a total clientele into groups consisting of people who have relatively similar service needs, for the purpose of designing a marketing mix (or mixes) that more precisely matches the needs of individuals in a selected segment (or segments)" (Crompton & Lamb, 1986, p. 113). In this way, organizational resources can be directed at developing marketing mix strategies (e.g., creating new programs, setting suitable prices, determining where the service will be offered, establishing communication efforts) that are aligned with the specific target group(s) a provider wishes to serve. It is important to note that not all market segments can be targeted, so leisure service marketers must know how to select appropriate market segments within a community to ensure effective and efficient service delivery.

Leisure service providers should consider three separate criteria when making decisions about whether or not to target specific market segments. First, before committing organizational resources towards the development of programs and services aimed at relatively homogenous client groups, a manager must determine if the market segment is *sufficiently large and/or important* to warrant servicing. In many cases, the size of the potential market (i.e., the estimated number of individuals in a given market segment) may need to be large enough to ensure the economic practicality of the initiative. However, not all decisions about whether or not to target specific client groups have to be made solely on the basis of the economic feasibility of the program. For example, a market segment consisting of just a few individuals may be appropriate in some therapeutic recreation contexts, such as rehabilitation programs for persons recovering from serious injuries.

Second, leisure service marketers need to determine whether or not a market segment is *measurable*. In other words, a service provider should be able to quantify the size of potential client groups they wish to target with service offerings. For example, many communities possess data relating to the sociodemographic characteristics of citizens (e.g., age cohorts, income groups, population by geographic region). This information can be easily obtained and used to estimate the size of potential market segments. Once again, without a fairly accurate estimation of how many individuals make up a potential client group, it may be difficult for a service provider to justify the commitment of marketing resources.

Third, leisure service marketers need to determine whether or not the market segment is accessible. Indeed, it is of utmost importance for a service provider to be able to communicate (via advertising and other promotional efforts) with targeted client groups. For some providers, reaching a specific market segment may pose some challenges. For example, Crompton and Lamb (1986) suggested that older adult groups, especially those with reading and hearing disabilities, and minority groups who do not speak the first language of the community/country in which they reside, require unique, creative, and imaginative efforts to ensure effective communication.

Figure 36.3 outlines three strategies that leisure service marketers can use when selecting market segments using the programs offered at a swimming pool as an example. First, marketers can utilize an *undifferentiated strategy* for selecting target markets. For this approach, one single marketing mix (e.g., program, time and location at which the program will be offered, price, and methods of promotion) is developed for everyone. Typically, this strategy works best when a large portion of the total market has common service needs (Crompton & Lamb, 1986), although this strategy is the least client-oriented of the three options described here. Second, leisure service marketers can employ a *differentiated strategy* for selecting target markets. Essentially, this strategy enables a service provider to adapt its service to the wants of each selected client group by developing different marketing mixes for each segment. However, this strategy may cost providers much time, effort, and monetary resources to implement. Third, leisure service marketers can adopt a *concentrated strategy* when selecting target markets. Under this approach, marketing efforts are focused on one or a small number of client groups which are considered the most important or most responsive.

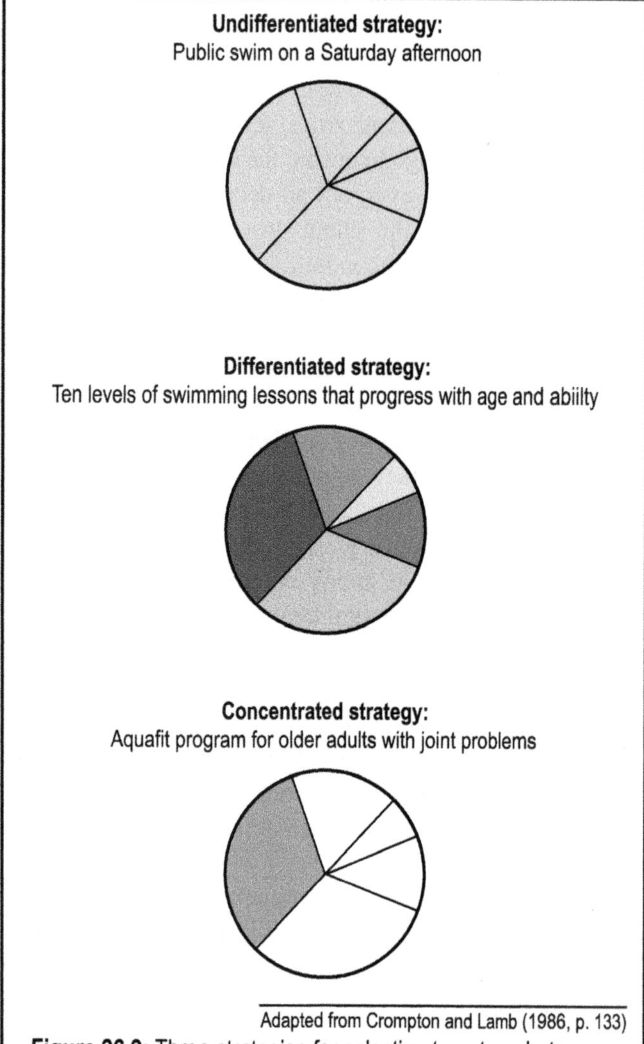

Undifferentiated strategy:
Public swim on a Saturday afternoon
Differentiated strategy:
Ten levels of swimming lessons that progress with age and abiilty
Concentrated strategy:
Aquafit program for older adults with joint problems
Adapted from Crompton and Lamb (1986, p. 133)

Figure 36.3: Three strategies for selecting target markets

Once an appropriate segmentation strategy has been selected, leisure service marketers should then attempt to describe the market segments they wish to serve in detail. Potential market segments are typically described in terms of their underlying sociodemographic, geographic, behavioural, and psychographic characteristics. *Sociodemographic* descriptors include age, stage in life cycle, gender, income, education level, occupation and ethnicity. *Geographic* descriptors focus on location, travel time, and general accessibility. *Behavioural* descriptors relate to the rate of use, level of skill, and stage of readiness in the participation process. *Psychographic* descriptors focus on opinions, attitudes, or benefits sought by participants (McCarville 2002).

The first three categories describe client groups in terms of easily-measurable life conditions. However, psychographic characteristics are more concerned with an individual's lifestyle. Unlike sociodemographic, geographic, and behavioural descriptors, psychographic descriptors attempt to describe who people are in terms of their personality, participation motives, interests, beliefs, and values (Schiffman & Kanuk, 2000). This data can then be used to design programs and services that are more in tune with individuals' lifestyles. Often, more than one descriptor should be used to describe potential client groups. For example, a leisure service provider may wish to focus marketing efforts on developing programs or services for females, ages 15 to 18 (i.e., two sociodemographic descriptors), who live within walking distance of a provider's fitness facility (i.e., a geographic descriptor), who wish to participate in a cardiovascular fitness program (i.e., a behavioural descriptor), and who seek to develop and maintain a healthy lifestyle (i.e., a psychographic descriptor).

Pick a recreation program with which you are familiar and describe the potential market segment(s) it attempts to attract.

The Marketing Mix

Once a leisure service provider selects a target client group, marketers must design and implement programs and services that cater to the unique needs and desires of the group's members. The *marketing mix* is typically used for this purpose. The mix is best described as a set of tactical tools which marketers can manipulate and blend together to influence the demand for a particular product or service (Kotler, Armstrong, & Cunningham, 2005). More specifically, to tailor service offerings that meet the needs of potential client groups, leisure service marketers must make decisions regarding the four elements in the marketing mix: (1) products and services, (2) place/distribution, (3) price, and (4) promotion. When making marketing mix decisions, leisure service marketers should maintain an outward focus by considering the needs and wants of clients, as opposed to an inward focus, which considers the needs of the provider (Johnson Tew, Havitz, & McCarville, 1999). The following discussion examines each element of the marketing mix as it relates to leisure service providers.

Products and Services

Products are typically defined as "anything that can be offered to a market for attention, acquisition, use, or consumption that might satisfy a want or a need" (Kotler, McDougall, & Armstrong, 1988, p. 208). Traditional marketing mix literature (e.g., Kotler et al., 2005; Schiffman & Kanuk, 2000) is primarily concerned with the design and development of consumer products for commercial sector market segments; however, most leisure organizations provide programs and services for client groups as opposed to tangible consumer products. Unlike manufactured goods, leisure services represent experiences, and therefore, are usually not able to be touched, smelled, tasted, or returned.

The *intangible* nature of leisure services can pose some potential challenges for marketers when they attempt to design programs that meet the diverse needs of client groups. For instance, leisure service marketers may find it difficult to convey the unique characteristics of their service offerings. Think of how challenging it may be for a Caribbean tour operator to actually convey information about an evening sunset, the smell of the ocean, or the feeling of refreshment one receives from diving into a pool on a hot afternoon. Indeed, leisure marketers may have trouble attracting potential participants because of the intangible nature of many service offerings (Zeithaml, 1991). Therefore, one of the most difficult tasks facing service providers is to be able to "tangiblize the intangible" (Levitt, 1983).

Unlike products, services are produced and consumed simultaneously. In other words, the production and consumption of services are *inseparable* (Parasuraman, Zeithaml, & Berry, 1985). For example, when we go to a movie theatre, the movie is being produced (i.e., displayed on the screen) and consumed (i.e., watched) at the same time. The notion of inseparability highlights the importance leisure service providers should place on fostering positive staff-client interactions when designing programs and services (McCarville, 2002). Often, these interactions are the only source of information clients use when they evaluate and/or form opinions about a program or service. In addition, leisure service marketers must also acknowledge that services are *heterogeneous* (Parasuraman et al., 1985). Services are often described as being heterogeneous because no two service encounters are ever exactly the same. For instance, a trip down a river during a whitewater rafting adventure will never be the same twice. Each trip will have its own unique properties, such as different weather and river conditions, composition of participants, equipment, and tour guides. Service offerings will differ from one provider to the next, as well as on a daily basis. Therefore, leisure service marketers should aim for consistency in service delivery so that the needs and wants of clients can be met on a continual basis.

What strategies can leisure service marketers use to ensure that programs are developed with the needs and wants of potential clients in mind?

Place/Distribution

Kotler et al. (1988) define *distribution* as the process of presenting products or programs to clients. More specifically, in many leisure contexts, distribution (i.e., place) refers to questions such as when, where, and by whom a program or service will be offered (Johnson Tew et al., 1999). Once again, it is important for leisure service marketers to consider the needs and wants of clients when making scheduling and location decisions. For example, information on where potential clients are travelling from and what times of the day individuals are free from obligations can be used to offer more convenient program or service offerings.

Traditionally, most leisure organizations have adopted the role of a direct provider with respect to service provision as opposed to delivering them in partnerships with others (Crompton, 1999). Such approaches have been on the decline in recent years, perhaps in response to the high costs associated with providing all services "in house." In addition, the direct provider approach to service delivery has been criticized (e.g., Crompton, 1999; Osborne & Gaebler, 1992) for being unable to meet the leisure needs of everyone in a community or market segment. More recently, some providers are adopting the facilitative approach to leisure service delivery (Johnson Tew et al., 1999). The facilitative approach involves forming partnerships with other public or private sector organizations to meet the leisure needs of the community more effectively. For example, leisure service organizations can refer clients to other providers in a community or co-produce a program or service with another organization.

What would be some advantages and disadvantages of forming partnerships with other organizations to deliver programs or services?

Price

According to McClosky (1982), price refers to *any cost an individual must forego to enjoy a product or service.* Clients may face a number of *non-monetary* costs when attempting to participate in leisure programs or services. For example, costs related to the amount of time (e.g., travel time) and effort (e.g., acquiring the necessary resources to participate) that participants must invest may need to be taken into account when setting prices (Walsh, 1986).

Before establishing a price for a particular program or service, leisure service marketers should determine their pricing objectives and strategies. Typically, commercial sector organizations set prices with the goal of turning a profit. Conversely, public and not-for-profit agencies normally set prices to pursue a variety of goals. They may wish to encourage participation levels so they may offer some programs at low cost. In other cases, they may wish to discourage participation (for example, they may wish to limit use of wilderness settings). Consequently, their fees may be set to either break even (i.e., only recover the agency's costs and expenses), to generate revenue needed for operations, or in some cases, to lose money. Public sector agencies may base pricing decisions on equity and fairness as opposed to profit generation and will offer price subsidies (i.e., discounts) to encourage participation from marginalized or disenfranchised groups of citizens (e.g., persons who are unemployed, older adults). Subsidizing individuals' leisure participation may not always be viewed as fair pricing practices. For example, the Should Leisure Service Providers Subsidize Older Adults? *i*-box highlights some arguments in favour of and against providing fee subsidies for older adults in recreation settings. If, however, leisure service providers choose to offer price subsidies for certain client groups, efforts should be made to minimize the amount of embarrassment that individuals may experience from the initiative (Emmett, Havitz, & McCarville, 1996).

In recent years, the notion of charging user fees for public leisure service offerings has become a fairly contentious issue among academics and practitioners alike. Many critics (e.g., Kyle, Absher, & Chancellor, 2005; More, 2002; Shultz et al., 1988) have argued that charging user fees for public leisure services is exclusionary and should not be done for services that are considered a public good (i.e., services that benefit the entire community). Notwithstanding these arguments, it is important for leisure service marketers in all sectors to set prices that are appropriate for the market segment(s). Whenever possible, leisure service marketers should involve clients in pricing decisions.

Should Leisure Service Providers Subsidize Older Adults?

Arguments in Favour:

- Society should show older adults appreciation for a lifetime of work.
- Many older adults have low incomes.
- Older adults may have a lot of free time to engage in leisure activities.
- Increased participation in leisure activities may lead to positive health benefits, and therefore, can help reduce health care costs.

Arguments Against:

- In many cases, older adults have few expenses (e.g., no mortgage).
- Taxpayers may have to "pay the difference" resulting from provision of the subsidy.
- Other segments of the population may need the subsidy more than older adults.
- Public money could be better spent on providing certain segments with subsidies for other social services (e.g., health care).

Can you think of any other arguments in favour of or against subsidizing recreation participation among older adults? What about some arguments for and against subsidizing children's participation?

Promotion

Promotion can be defined as a *set of activities that communicate the merits of a product or service and persuade target clients to use it* (Kotler et al., 2005). The purposes of promotional activities such as advertising, publicity, personal contact, and incentives are to inform, educate, persuade, and remind potential clients about program or service offerings (Crompton & Lamb, 1986). First, promotional activities can *inform* potential participants about the program or service by providing them with basic information regarding the date, location, time, price (if any), and any other pertinent information about the event. Second, promotional activities can *educate* potential participants about the value of programs and services (e.g., improved health benefits, development of new skills). Third, promotional activities can *persuade* potential clients to participate in a program or service. For example, many commercial sector fitness organizations advertise seasonal discounts and other incentives in an effort convince individuals to purchase memberships. In addition, concrete evidence of the benefits that can result from participation in a particular program or service (e.g., improved cardiovascular functioning) can be communicated to potential clients to encourage participation. Finally, promotional activities can *remind* participants about the personal and community benefits that can accrue from their participation. Leisure service providers also need to demonstrate appreciation for participants' support and/or patronage so as to positively influence future participation decisions.

The key challenge facing leisure service marketers is to move potential participants along a continuum from awareness of program or service offering to action (participation) by carefully crafting and applying a unique *promotional mix*. The promotional mix consists of tools such as advertising, publicity, personal contact, and incentives that can be used to communicate with target client groups. For example, advertisements (e.g., seasonal program brochures) and publicity (e.g., newspaper articles) can be used to make participants aware of program or service offerings, incentives can be used to stimulate program trials and encourage participation, and personal contact (e.g., presentations to school classes) can help the provider to begin to develop a relationship with clients.

In summary, the marketing mix consists of a set of neutral tools which leisure service marketers can use to design programs and services that are aligned with the needs and wants of potential client groups. Effective marketing strategy is only possible after a leisure service provider first conducts extensive marketing research (e.g., community needs assessments, environmental analyses), and then attempts to break the community into meaningful, homogenous client groups. Indeed, without a firm understanding of what potential participants desire with respect to service offerings, it may be challenging for a service provider to satisfy their leisure needs effectively.

Alternative Marketing Philosophies

To this point, we have characterized marketing as a process involving the use of a set of neutral tools for the purpose of satisfying clients' and participants' wants and needs. However, taken too far, this "client-first" orientation can provoke some concerns. For example, an outdoor recreation tour company might offer expensive nature-viewing trips into the wilderness areas of northern Canada. If the targeted clientele for such excursions desire gourmet meals and comfortable sleeping accommodations, the company might elect to construct elaborate facilities to fulfill the participants' wishes. Doing so, however, would likely cause environmental and perhaps cultural damage through the building and ongoing operation and maintenance of those facilities. Such an approach is obviously unacceptable in many ways for parks and recreation organizations. Speaking about leisure services, Havitz (2000) argued, "pure marketing—simply giving people exactly what they want—is a hopelessly inadequate model in public sector contexts because it ignores possible negative consequences to both the individual in question and to long-term community and societal interest" (p. 46). Two alternatives to pure marketing include societal and social marketing. Figure 36.4, depicts these three marketing philosophies along a continuum ranging from pure through societal to social, while also adding the selling orientation for the purpose of comparison.

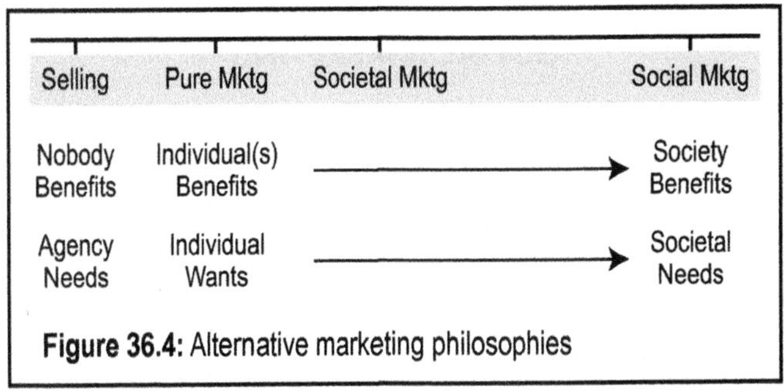

Figure 36.4: Alternative marketing philosophies

The upper row in Figure 36.4 compares a selling orientation and the three marketing philosophies based on who derives benefits from the product or service being marketed. The second row describes whether the marketing actions are focused on meeting wants or needs. A selling orientation is driven by the agency's need to sell the goods or services it has produced. Unfortunately, when this approach is adopted, neither the agency nor its clients benefit because people are unlikely to partake of services that do not fulfill their needs or wants. The nature trip example described above embodied pure marketing characteristics because the company was heavily focused on satisfying the participant's nature-viewing preferences, and the forays into the backcountry would generally benefit only those people who went on the trip. As mentioned above, adopting a pure marketing perspective for parks and recreation services is likely to be inappropriate without some important modifications (Crompton & Lamb, 1986).

Societal Marketing

Societal marketing maintains the pre-eminent focus on satisfying the wants of the participant, but aims to achieve this goal in a way that also maintains or improves the individual's or society's well-being (Kotler, Armstrong, & Cunningham, 2002). For example, mountain bikers in British Columbia may be permitted access to certain wilderness terrain, but may be assessed an additional fee to be used for the conservation of other sensitive areas. In this way, societal marketing compares to pure marketing in its emphasis on meeting clients' needs; but by manipulating one or more marketing mix variables (in this example, price), it mediates this participant-first philosophy with one of protecting the greater good.

How would each of the three philosophies just discussed look in practice in the area of parks and recreation in which you would like to work? (e.g., How would a golf course change its marketing mix variables to adopt a pure, societal, or social marketing philosophy?)

Social Marketing

Social marketing, on the other hand, places the primary emphasis on improving society, with secondary consideration given to what is desired by individuals (Kotler, Roberto, & Lee, 2002). For this reason, the gap between pure and societal marketing in Figure 36.4 is shown as smaller than the gap between social marketing and either of these other marketing philosophies. Social marketing can be defined as:

> the application of commercial marketing technologies to the analysis, planning, execution, and evaluation of programs designed to influence the voluntary behavior of target audiences in order to improve their personal welfare and that of the society of which they are a part (Andreasen, 2003, p. 296).

For instance, programs and accompanying promotions aimed at redressing child obesity through recreation are prime examples of social marketing. Bright (2000) suggested, "social marketing is consistent with the social welfare philosophy that drives the work of public recreation professionals" (p. 16). As Figure 36.4 suggests, social marketing is often about giving an individual or the community something it needs, rather than something it necessarily wants. However, this is always done with as much attention to maintaining a marketing orientation as possible (Andreasen, 1995). For example, to assist people to become more healthy, parks and trails can be created to promote active transportation (a program/service strategy), efforts can be made to offer fitness classes at workplaces rather than at a traditional gym (a distribution strategy), or discounts could be offered to reduce at least one potential cost of participation (a pricing strategy). In conclusion, social marketing aims to improve/change the behaviour of some target population to address the needs of that group or the larger community, *but* it manipulates the various marketing mix variables to make the desired behaviour as convenient as possible.

Summary

This chapter has described the philosophy and activities of marketing. We have also discussed several alternative marketing philosophies that surfaced over the past few decades in response to concerns surrounding the adoption of a pure marketing philosophy to guide the provision of parks and recreation and other services. Marketing continues to evolve and take on different forms. For example, relationship marketing, experience marketing, and internal marketing have all been developed to address the particular challenges of delivering services, rather than products (Lovelock & Wirtz, 2004). As well, public sector leisure services marketing has recently been redefined to emphasize the importance of satisfying the concerns of policymakers and non-users (Novatorov & Crompton, 2001a, 2001b). Unfortunately, despite a general acceptance of marketing among leisure service professionals, lingering confusion about the true nature of marketing and its full array of activities continues to confound its integration into effective practice (Johnson-Tew et al., 1999). With increased exposure and education, however, marketing can assist recreation professionals to understand and deliver leisure services that better satisfy the wants and needs of participants as well as the broader community.

Key Terms

Marketing
Market research
Market segmentation
Marketing mix
Societal marketing
Social marketing

References

Andreasen, A.R. (1995). *Marketing social change.* San Francisco, CA: Jossey-Bass.

Andreasen, A. R. (2003). The life trajectory of social marketing: Some implications. *Marketing Theory, 3*(3), 293–303.

Bright, A. D. (2000). The role of social marketing in leisure and recreation management. *Journal of Leisure Research, 32*(1), 12–17.

Crompton, J. L. (1999). *Financing and acquiring park and recreation resources*. Champaign, IL: Human Kinetics.

Crompton, J. L., & Lamb, C. W. (1986). *Marketing government and social services*. New York, NY: John Wiley & Sons.

Emmett, J. L., Havitz, M. E., & McCarville, R. E. (1996). A price subsidy policy for socio-economically disadvantaged recreation participants. *Journal of Park and Recreation Administration, 14*(1), 63–80.

Havitz, M. E. (1988). Marketing is not synonymous with commercialism. *Parks and Recreation, 23*(5), 34–36.

Havitz, M. E. (2000). Marketing public leisure services: Some (temporarily) pessimistic perspectives from an unrepentant optimist. *Journal of Leisure Research, 32*(1), 42–48.

Johnson Tew, C. P. F., Havitz, M. E., & McCarville, R. E. (1999). The role of marketing in municipal recreation programming decisions: A challenge to conventional wisdom. *Journal of Park and Recreation Administration, 17*(1), 1–20.

Kotler, P., Armstrong, G., & Cunningham, P. H. (2002). *Principles of marketing: Canadian edition* (5th ed.). Scarborough, ON: Prentice Hall.

Kotler, P., Armstrong, G., & Cunningham, P. H. (2005). *Principles of marketing: Canadian edition* (6th ed.). Scarborough, ON: Prentice Hall.

Kotler, P., Armstrong, G., Cunningham, P. H., & Warren, R. (1996). *Principles of marketing: Canadian edition* (3rd ed.). Scarborough, ON: Prentice Hall.

Kotler, P., McDougall, G., & Armstrong, G. (1988). *Marketing: Canadian edition*. Englewood Cliffs, NJ: Prentice Hall.

Kotler, P., Roberto, E., & Lee, N. (2002). *Social marketing: Strategies for changing public behavior*. Thousand Oaks, CA: Sage Publications.

Kyle, G. T., Ashber, J. D., & Chancellor, C. (2005). The experience of psychological reactance in response to encountering fees for public land recreation. *Leisure/Loisir, 29*(2), 355–378.

Levitt, T. (1983). The marketing myopia. *Harvard Business Review, 38*(4), 45–56.

Lovelock, C. H., & Wirtz, J. (2004). *Services marketing: People, technology, strategy*. Upper Saddle River, NJ: Prentice Hall.

McCarville, R. E. (1999). Marketing public leisure services. In E. L. Jackson & T. L. Burton (Eds.), *Leisure studies: Prospects for the twenty-first century* (pp. 415–433). State College, PA: Venture Publishing, Inc.

McCarville, R. E. (2002). *Improving leisure services through marketing action*. Champaign, IL: Sagamore.

McClosky, D. (1982). *The applied theory of price*. New York, NY: MacMillan.

More, T. A. (2002). The marginal user as the justification for public recreation: A rejoinder to Crompton, Driver, and Dustin. *Journal of Leisure Research, 34*(1), 103–118.

Novatorov, E. V., & Crompton, J. L. (2001a). A revised conceptualization of marketing in the context of public leisure services. *Journal of Leisure Research, 33*(2), 160–185.

Novatorov, E. V., & Crompton, J. L. (2001b). Reformulating the conceptualization of marketing in the context of public leisure services. *Leisure Studies, 20*, 61–75.

Osborne, D., & Gaebler, T. (1992). *Reinventing government: How the entrepreneurial spirit is transforming the public sector*. New York, NY: Addison-Wesley.

Parasuraman, A., Zeithaml, V. A., & Berry, L. L. (1985). A conceptual model of service quality and its implications for future research. *Journal of Marketing, 49*(4), 41–50.

Schiffman, L. G., & Kanuk, L. L. (2000). *Consumer behaviour* (7th ed.). Englewood Cliffs, NJ: Prentice Hall.

Schultz, J. H., McAvoy, L. H., & Dustin, D. L. (1988). What are we in business for? *Parks and Recreation, 23*(1), 52–54.

Walsh, R. (1986). *Recreation economic decisions*. State College, PA: Venture Publishing, Inc.

Zeithaml, V. (1991). How consumer evaluation processes differ between goods and services. In C. H. Lovelock (Ed.), *Services marketing* (2nd ed., pp. 39–47). Toronto, ON: Prentice Hall.

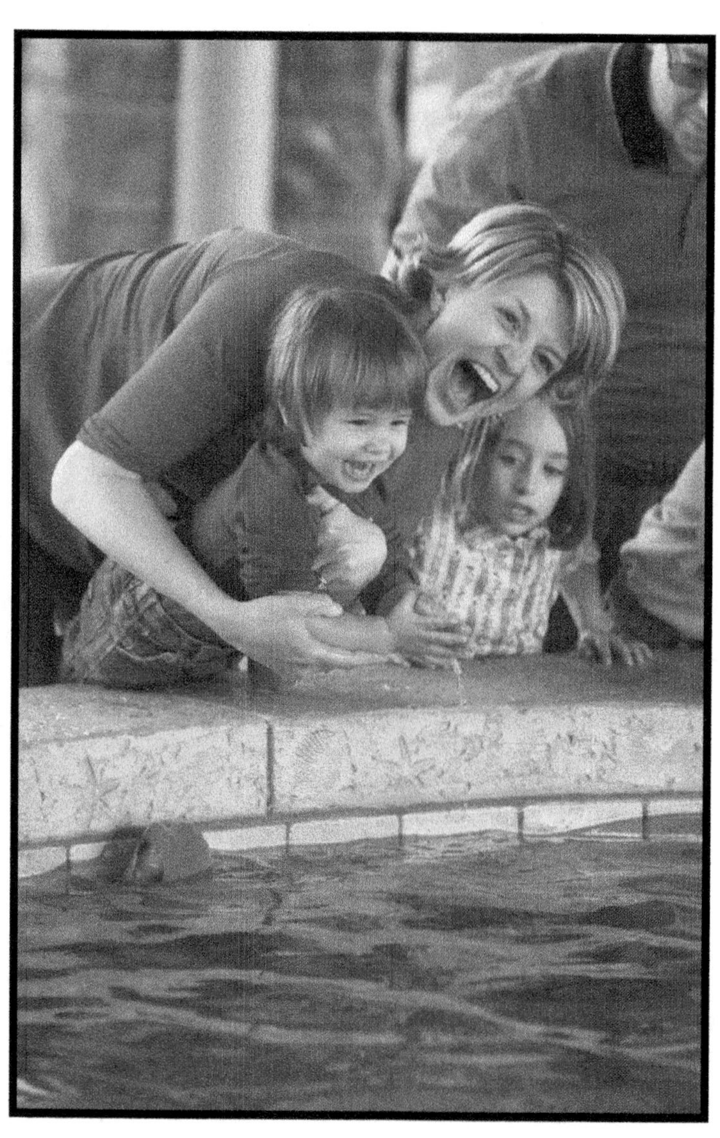

Chapter 37
Offering More Than Programs: Creating Solutions for Your Clients

Ron McCarville, Ph.D.
University of Waterloo

Learning Objectives

After reading this chapter, students will be able to

1. Understand the importance of the value proposition in creating sport and leisure services.
2. Recognize the importance of both benefits and costs to programming success.
3. Understand the process of leveraging and how it might be used to improve program quality.
4. Understand some of the mechanisms through which emotional connections might be nurtured between clients and sport or leisure.

Introduction

Sport providers create and promote products. All sport products exist along a continuum ranging from very tangible goods (like team paraphernalia or sports equipment) to very intangible services (the best example might be the emotional connection with favourite teams or the personal sense of accomplishment enjoyed when that team wins). This chapter focuses on the intangible-service end of the sport product continuum. To begin, *services* are "any activity or benefit that one party can offer to another that is essentially intangible and does not result in the ownership of anything. Its production may or may not be tied to a physical product" (Kotler & Bloom, 1984, p. 147).

The emphasis here is on helping readers create services that improve the lives of target groups. The concept I will use to do this is the *value proposition*. The value proposition represents a way to think about your role as service provider. As the title of this chapter suggests successful programmers must think beyond simply offering programs. The goal is to find more and better ways to serve clients. Thinking in very intentional ways about the value proposition can help make that happen.

A value proposition outlines the desires you hope to fulfill for your clients, as well as how they are to be satisfied. It is a "detailed description of what is to be done for the customer (what needs and wishes are to be satisfied), and how this is to be achieved" (Edvardsson & Olsson, 1996, p. 149). The value proposition needs to be both clear and compelling. Every decision you make, every policy you generate, and every event you promote must be assessed against that proposition.

It may help to think of a value proposition as a *solution*. What solution do you wish to create for your clients? The best solutions offer all that the clients are seeking *and* help them avoid things they dislike. For example, fans attending a soccer match seek excitement but wish to avoid uncomfortable seats; they seek to be entertained but hope to avoid traffic and parking problems. Your job, as a service provider, is to discover what clients seek and help them find it. Just as importantly, though, your job is to discover what they dislike and help them to avoid it. This chapter is devoted to helping you create meaningful value propositions; to offer more of what people want and eliminate those things they dislike. The emphasis will be on building solutions around your clients' emotional commitment to sport.

Organization of the Chapter

The chapter has two primary sections. Consistent with the notion of "solutions," the first section "Building Benefit into the Value Proposition," focuses on providing benefits to sport participants, spectators, and fans alike. This section suggests that all successful programming starts with clients' desires.

There are many things your clients may seek from a sport-related experience. The benefits they seek range from entertainment and diversion to affiliation and identification (Walters & Lancaster, 1999).

The second section, "Reducing Costs," suggests that we must provide more than benefits. The best providers spend a great deal of energy eliminating things their clients don't want. This section deals directly with many of the costs that our clients dislike. The goal is to find ways to help them avoid those costs. These costs can be monetary, physical, or even emotional. In all cases, the chapter offers steps to creating solutions, and then provides leveraging activities for discussion purposes. *Leveraging* is the process of using existing resources to better effect. When providers leverage, they amplify the effects of a given action. Through leveraging, the sport marketer turns a game into an event, a building into a sport shrine, and elevates a simple team logo to the status of an icon. I encourage you to develop your own leveraging ideas as you create your own programming solutions.

Section 1: Building Benefit into the Value Proposition

Much of the benefit gained from sport emerges from emotional connections between the client and the overall sport experience (Funk, Filo, Beaton, & Pritchard, 2009). We know that this emotional connection can be encouraged and nurtured by the actions of the provider (Funk & James, 2001). We do this in three basic ways. First, we create what is called the *servicescape* (sport providers also call this a "sportscape"). Next we *encourage identification* with the activity and its participants. This will also help us to *entertain* those we hope to serve. Let's consider each of these activities in some detail.

Creating a Servicescape

Marketing guru Phillip Kotler once observed that one of the most important features of the total product is the *place* where it is bought and/or consumed (Kotler, 1983). In service delivery this place is called the *servicescape*. The servicescape is the setting in which the activity takes place. This setting is essential to supporting the actions on the field of play. We know, for example, that when providers create successful servicescapes, clients are more likely to report improved service quality and increased perceptions of value (Hightower, Brady, & Baker, 2002).

Your task is to create a space that facilitates delivery of the sport product. For example, it is difficult to build a positive emotional connection if participants can't find parking spots or if seats are uncomfortable. The provider must create a service environment that supports the value proposition. It might help to compare sport settings to a stage play. Those who manage and stage a play go to a great deal of effort to set a mood that supports what happens on the stage. The same is true in sport and leisure. The importance of *tangible cues* is common to all servicescapes (Al-Sabbahy, Ekinci & Riley, 2004). Tangible cues are those things the clients can hear, see, smell, and so on (Zeithaml, Parasuraman, & Berry, 1990). Clients may assess facilities, scenery, and even fellow spectators and competitors as they evaluate their surroundings. In this way, clients act like detectives (Berry, 1995) as they look for clues deciding whether or not the surroundings are appropriate—whether or not the setting makes them feel welcome. The better service providers know this and ensure that all the cues support their value proposition. At one golf course, for example, managers offered to paint all the private homes that could be seen from their fairways and greens. They painted each in a way that added to the idyllic landscape they wished to create. In this way, they were assured of a common look and feel, and one that was consistent with the experience sought by their clients. The managers of this course understood the importance of tangible cues in creating a servicescape.

The servicescape has several dimensions. In terms of spectator sports, the servicescape is comprised of variables like stadium access, aesthetics and cleanliness, layout, crowding, food service, and fan control (Chelladurai & Chang, 2000). Relevant factors may be general (like availability of parking) or specific (like the comfort of seating) in nature (Hall, O'Mahony & Vieceli, 2010). From the participants' perspectives, the emphasis is more on performance variables like field conditions and protection from the elements.

The challenge in creating an appropriate servicescape is in understanding the desires of your clients group(s). In some cases, the situation may demand convenient parking and comfortable seats for thousands of spectators. In other cases, clients may seek muddy trails for running, pristine fairways for golf, or open roads for cycling. The needs of the activity blended with the desires of participants and spectators will determine the appropriate servicescape characteristics.

Leveraging Activities

- Create a servicescape for your favourite sport or leisure activity. Think about the image you wish to project. How will the servicescape be used by your clients?
- Build the look and feel of the servicescape around the experience you wish to create.
- Create a setting that anticipates clients' desires and offers convenient solutions.

We must understand those things our clients seek before we can provide them. Funk, Filo, Beaton, and Pritchard (2009) wrapped up all these insights into a concept they labelled SPEED (Socialization, Performance, Esteem, Excitement, and Diversion). SPEED encompasses many of the dominant benefits sought within the sport experience. While the relative importance of all these variables is still being established, the concept of SPEED does offer a useful way to think about delivery of sport products. It helps us think about the various elements of sport so that we can program accordingly.

Encouraging Identification

In many ways, sport represents a performance (Funk, Filo, Beaton, & Pritchard, 2009). It brings us together in powerful ways. As a result, fans and participants may identify a great deal with a sport and its participants.

We use the term *identification* when describing personal commitment and emotional involvement (Sutton, McDonald, Milne, & Cimperman, 1997) and such identification is critical to building support for your sport product. The influence of this identification can be profound offering a win–win opportunity for fans and providers alike. For the fan, identification has been related to feelings of positive self-esteem and increased social ties (Branscombe & Wann, 1991; Johnson, Groothuis, & Whitehead, 2001). For providers, fan identification has been linked to reduced price sensitivity and a reduced emphasis on performance/outcomes (Sutton et al., 1997).

Identification can be enhanced by creating a connection between the sport and its followers. The challenge is to build an association between brand elements and beliefs and preferences already held by your client groups. In this way, the connection remains intact regardless of performance of individuals or of outcomes on the field of play.

Leveraging Activities

- Focus on cherished values that resonate with your clients. Words like success, pride, desire, or skill all reflect deeply held beliefs about what is desirable in friends, family, community, and self. Suggesting that they also exist in your sport offering creates an immediate connection between the client and the sport.
- This connection can be very emotional. Sport providers often enhance the emotional nature of the connection by building a sense of community around a sport and its various characteristics. They describe the team as "your" or "our" team. It is no coincidence that they use the term "home team" when referring to local participants as they play in host communities.
- Offer/sell clothing and any other objects that help fans advertise their loyalty and help participants declare their commitment. Remember, though, that research suggests these objects must offer good value if they are to be accepted by fans.
- Create online communities that give clients the opportunity to share their ideas and concerns about their sport or team/favourite player.
- Create opportunities where clients can play, watch, talk about, or otherwise enjoy the sport or team they love.

It is the nature of sport and games that outcomes are uncertain. Neither the participant nor the spectators know the outcome in advance. For this reason, the appeal of sport is largely aspirational in nature. Sport is entirely concerned with what clients want to happen. It focuses on the goals that participants and spectators hope will be achieved. They hope to score, want their team to win, hope their favourite player will succeed. The uncertainty that is part of all sport helps build anticipation. This anticipation, in turn, helps build identification.

Leveraging Activities

- It may seem ironic, but you can help build future aspirations by looking backward. Tell the fans of the team or sport's traditions, of noteworthy moments in its history, of past glories. That too will help clients picture the future they hope to enjoy.
- Focus on those qualities and outcomes clients value. Winning is an obvious conclusion that is much valued, but remember that the team won't always win.
- Mastery is one of the great motivators in sport and leisure settings. Find ways to help clients enjoy success in their chosen activities.
- It helps when clients identify with the sport itself and with those who are part of our sport offering (players, coaches, even mascots). If we care about those who perform for us, we are more willing to accept their actions, to believe in what they are trying to do. This insight is critical for the sport provider. Clients must believe that the performance is important, that the athletes' efforts are worthwhile. They must be able to relate to the athlete's performance, to identify with the task. As providers help create this connection, they are creating value.

Leveraging Activities

- Frame the event. Framing refers to offering a context through which to appreciate what you are seeing. This new context builds interest, enthusiasm, and even respect. Tell fans how many hours the players have spent practicing to get to this moment, or the speed of that last fastball. You can even focus on the size of the crowd, the temperature on game day, the youngest participant, or anything that sparks interest among those in attendance.

- People often relate as much to a sport as to the actual game they are witnessing. Discover trivia about the activity or sport itself and tell them about it.

Providing Entertainment

We are best entertained when we open ourselves to an event or activity. In order to be entertained, we must let down our guard, accept that which is placed before us. To enjoy movies, we must accept that superheroes can fly, that genies pop out of bottles, that dogs can play basketball.

In order to entertain, providers create opportunities for people to open themselves to the experience. They must provide reasons for fans to celebrate and embrace the moment. It is easy to see how we might build entertainment value around a home run or a win, but these golden moments are not predictable. As suggested above, one of the great challenges in sport marketing is uncertainty. In sport, we cannot be certain if a team will win on the field. Sport providers support "winning moments" by leveraging entertainment value in everyday activities. They must seek to build entertainment around those things they can control.

Providers often enhance the entertainment potential of an event by encouraging active involvement on the part of the spectator. We know that, while involved in sport, people are often willing to "suspend the everyday." They are willing to revel in the special conditions that surround them at the event. They will participate in a wave, cheer with complete strangers, chant songs and slogans in ways that would never be part of their regular lives. It is these types of special moments upon which entertainment is built.

Leveraging Activities

- Encourage fans to actively support the team. Fans participating in "the wave" at an event, those who wave towels, wear uniforms, or paint themselves or signs with slogans are all opening themselves to the moment. Circulate towels for spectators to wave, encourage them to wear special shirts, and to take part in group displays of support.
- Create rituals—those acts that we repeat over and over. With repetition they develop their own special meaning. Ritual helps deal with the uncertainty inherent in sport. Players might wear lucky clothing or they may act in special ways. Fans also find comfort in ritual. They might touch a particular statue for luck. Have contests to discover favourite rituals and have everyone try to repeat them in order to support the team.
- Use sponsors to contribute to the entertainment value through in-game promotions. Fans expect that the game ball will arrive without fanfare. Why not have a sponsoring courier company "deliver" the game ball to centerfield?

Section 2: Reducing Costs

The value proposition must outline how you plan to minimize cost as well as provide benefits. There are many such costs, but I focus here on three that offer a particular challenge to your clients. They are *monetary price*, *inconvenience*, and *uncertainty*. These are the costs that chip away at the value proposition you hope to offer. Your task is one of minimizing these costs because they irritate and constrain your clients.

Cost 1—Monetary Price

Monetary price is the amount in dollars and cents that clients are asked to pay for your services. A fundamental point you must remember in all your pricing activities is that clients compare the price you charge to a reference price they hold in memory. This price may be the price they last paid or an average of several prices they have paid in the past. It is this comparison that tells them how acceptable or unacceptable your price might be.

Regions of acceptance develop around expected price levels (Rao & Sieben, 1992). In other words, your clients are much more likely to pay the price they expect to pay. As price levels deviate from the expected levels, the individual is less likely to accept your price. We know too that beginners may possess larger regions of acceptability. They simply don't have the experience to establish what is acceptable from what is not. As a result, they may be more accepting of whatever price you charge. On the other hand, experienced users may have more precise expectations regarding desired price levels (McCarville, 1996). Specifically, they often expect to pay the amount they paid last time and resist price increases.

Leveraging Activities

- If prices are rising, your regular clients will notice. Provide information that justifies the increase. It is best to focus on the added benefit they will receive as a result of the increase.

- Coupons can be used to reduce unhappiness over price increases. As a bonus, coupons can also be used to encourage trial of new sport programs and opportunities.

Cost 2—Inconvenience

Inconvenience is one of those constraints or costs that clients hope to avoid. Unfortunately, service delivery always demands something from our clients. Clients must "co-produce" whatever product they hope to enjoy (Prahalad & Ramaswamy, 2004). Participants must have the requisite skills, and fans must be both knowledgeable of and "connected" to the sport (Green & Jones, 2005). If they are unprepared or uncertain, the event can be ruined and its value compromised. They must be ready, willing, and able to carry out whatever task is assigned them. The sport provider's goal, then, is to assist the client in co-producing the service. In this way, value is enhanced.

Leveraging Activities

- Break consumption down into its component parts and consider how each stage challenges the client and how this challenge might be reduced.
- Find ways to simplify each stage of the event. Start with any planning the client might have to do and end with post-event recollections.
- Help clients with problem solving; tell them what to expect, when to arrive to ensure a good seat, where to park, and what to wear to better enjoy the venue. Answer all their questions so their next step is always obvious.

Another inconvenience-related issue is that of the queue or line. People hate to wait in line. When asked to wait in this way, clients are faced with a dilemma. Those who choose to wait are essentially held captive, so waiting in line can be seen as a form of entrapment (Colenutt & McCarville, 2000). Freedom is limited because the individual has no power to reduce the delay. Resulting perceived lack of control may lead to increased levels of stress and dissatisfaction.

Queuing need not always result in dissatisfaction, however. Factors that "shrink" perceptions of time duration are associated with more positive experiences (Csikszentmihalyi, 1975; Flaherty, 1991). The key is to keep clients occupied or distracted while in a queue. Mannell and Bradley (1986) found, for example, that participants believed that delays were of shorter duration when they were offered greater choice and control during the wait.

Leveraging Activities

- Distract (engage, enlighten, and entertain) clients while they are waiting in queue
- Use queues as an opportunity to build sense of belonging and community. Distribute sport/team related paraphernalia, hold contests, encourage interaction.
- Identify locations where queues might occur (street corners leading to a stadium, entrances, ticket booths, etc.) and find ways to engage those in line. Jugglers might toss out sport-specific paraphernalia, or a stilt walker might greet those arriving at the game.

Cost 3—Uncertainty

There are several types of uncertainty that your clients face. You improve the value proposition when you reduce that uncertainty. For example, participants (and especially new participants) might wonder if they can handle the demands of programs that were physical in nature (fitness classes and so on). They might wonder if the program yields the promised benefits. They might worry they won't know the other participants.

Leveraging Activities

- Make the benefits of participation clear
- Make the demands clear so clients will know what is expected
- Make options available (rentals, instruction, reservations, etc.) so clients can pick and choose those offerings they feel they need to make the most of their participation.

Clients are also uncertain of the "deal" they are getting. They must perform often very sophisticated calculations concerning all they must give up in order to take part in the programs you offer (Bowman & Ambrosini, 2000). These calculations can require considerable cognitive energy because there are few clear answers to the questions they are pondering. How much will I enjoy attending a tennis match with an old friend? It has great potential but I dislike stadium seating, the weather is not promising, and the match is scheduled late in the day. Is it worth it? Does it matter who is playing in the match? Does it matter that the next day is a workday? Does it matter that the seats were on sale, that they are well placed, or that I have attended this same match for the past 10 years? There are many variables to ponder, and clients often give up without having taken part. In overcoming these uncertainties, the provider should simplify the process for the decision maker.

Leveraging Activities

- When making decisions, clients often focus first on the costs they believe they must endure so help clients make the cost/benefit comparison. Make the benefits clear before outlining costs (price, location, etc.).
- Provide ways of thinking about the dilemma being faced by the client. Provide your own heuristics. Nike's "Just do it" slogan told clients to overcome the obstacles and get on with it.
- Remind clients of those variables that should most influence their sport-related decisions. Focus on the fun they will have.

Concluding Comments

This chapter offers a customer-service perspective. In it I assumed that the provider's role is largely one of discovering the desires of consumer segments, then mobilizing resources to fulfill those desires. The key is being client-centred. This is all the more important, given that clients help co-produce the service with the provider. Such co-production is common to all service delivery. The client (participants, spectators, and volunteers) and the provider come together during what is often called the "moment of truth" in order to create an event. Players must be willing and able to meet the demands required of the sport. Spectators and volunteers must also do their part in order to enjoy the event. Customer service is about helping all our clients optimize that event.

Remember that the key to all successful programs is the perception of your clients. Clients focus on the benefits they feel they gained and the costs they believe they endured. This is perhaps the greatest insight a provider can have when dealing with sport and leisure services. The provider must be concerned with the clients' feelings and beliefs, concerns and cares, desires and dilemmas. Your job is to understand the client, and then help that client solve all the challenges of participation. We do this by creating a compelling value proposition and then building solutions for our clients.

Remember that much of sport's success relies on its ability to deliver memorable experiences. Such experiences, in turn, create emotional attachment to an intended product. In this chapter, I have focused on building a connection between the client and the sport product. By doing so, the provider gains access to deep-seated values and beliefs. A sport product that connects with these beliefs can offer a profound sense of personal meaning and can influence behaviour over the lifetime of the individual. From connections come satisfaction; from satisfaction comes value. The sport provider must continually seek opportunities to make this connection.

Key Terms

Value propositions
Solutions
Leveraging
Benefits
Servicescape/sportscape
Identification
Entertainment
Tangible cues
Costs
Monetary price
Inconvenience
Uncertainty

References

Al-Sabbahy, H., Ekinci, Y., & Riley, M. (2004). An investigation of perceived value dimensions: Implications for hospitality research. *Journal of Travel Research, 42*, 226–234.

Berry, L. (1995). *On great service*. New York, NY: The Free Press.

Bowman, C., & Ambrosini, V. (2000). Value creation versus value capture: Towards a coherent definition of value in strategy. *British Journal of Management, 11*, 1–15.

Branscombe, N., & Wann, D. (1991). The positive social and self-concept consequences of sports team identification. *Journal of Sport and Social Issues, 15*, 115–127.

Chelladurai, P., & Chang, K. (2000). Targets and standards of quality in sport services. *Sport Management Review, 3*, 1–22.

Colenutt, Christina, E., & McCarville, R. E. (2000). The effect of a queue-type delay on recreationists' mood and satisfaction levels with a leisure provider. *Journal of Park and Recreation Administration, 18*(2),1–20.

Csikszentmihalyi, M. (1975). *Beyond boredom and anxiety*. San Francisco, CA: Jossey-Bass.

Edvardsson, B., & Olsson, J. (1996), Key concepts for new service development. *The Service Industries Journal, 16*, 140–164.

Flaherty, M. G. (1991). The perception of time and situated engrossment. *Social Psychology Quarterly, 54*(1), 76–85.

Funk, D., & James, J. (2001). The Psychological Continuum Model: A conceptual framework for understanding an individual's psychological connection to sport. *Sport Management Review, (4)*2, 119–150.

Funk, D., Filo, K., Beaton, A., & Pritchard, M. (2009). Measuring the motives of sport event attendance: Bridging the academic-practitioner divide to understanding behavior. *Sport Marketing Quarterly, 18*, 126–148.

Green, C., & Jones, I. (2005). Serious leisure, social identity and sport tourism. *Sport in Society, 8*(2), 164–181.

Hall, J., O'Mahony, B., & Vieceli, J. (2010). An empirical model of attendance factors at major sporting events. *International Journal of Hospitality Management, 29*, 328–334.

Hightower, R., Brady, M., & Baker, T. (2002). Investigating the role of the physical environment in hedonic service consumption: An exploratory study of sporting events. *Journal of Business Research, 55*, 697–707.

Johnson, B., Groothuis, P., & Whitehead, J. (2001). The value of public goods generated by a major league sports team: The CVM approach. *Journal of Sports Economics, 2*, 6–21.

Kotler, P. (1983). *Principles of marketing* (2nd ed.). Englewood Cliffs, NJ: Prentice Hall.

Kotler, P., & Bloom, P. (1984). *Marketing professional services*. Englewood Cliffs, NJ: Prentice Hall.

Mannell, R. C., & Bradley, W. (1986). Does greater freedom always lead to greater leisure? Testing a person x environment model of freedom and leisure. *Journal of Leisure Research, 18*, 215–230.

McCarville, R. (1996). The importance of price last paid in developing price expectations for a public leisure service. *Journal of Park and Recreation Administration, 14*(4), 52–64.

Prahalad, C. & Ramaswamy, V. (2004). Co-creating unique value with customers. *Strategy & Leadership, 32*(3), 4–9.

Rao, A., & Sieben, W. (1992). The effect of prior knowledge on price acceptability and the type of information examined. *Journal of Consumer Research, 19*, 256–270.

Sutton, W., McDonald., M., Milne, G., & Cimperman, J. (1997). Creating and fostering fan identification in professional sports. *Sport Marketing Quarterly, 6*(1), 15–22.

Walters, D., & Lancaster, G. (1999). Value and information: Concepts and issues for management. *Management Decision, 37*(8), 643–656.

Zeithaml, V., Parasuraman, A., & Berry, L. (1990). *Delivering quality service: Balancing customer perceptions and expectations*. New York, NY: The Free Press.

Chapter 38
Financing Leisure Services I: Traditional and Emergent Funding Sources

Mark E. Havitz, Ph.D.
University of Waterloo

Learning Objectives

After reading this chapter, students will be able to

1. Understand the role and scope of five types of mandatory funding common to public sector leisure service agencies.
2. Appreciate the potential associated with emergent funding resources which are available to supplement traditional funding sources for public sector leisure service agencies.
3. Critique the efficacy and equity of both traditional and emergent funding sources.

Introduction

Although acquisition of resources is paramount to our ability as professionals to provide benefits to society, finance is both mystifying and intimidating to many people. A fundamental theme of these chapters is that financing is a personal issue as well as a professional issue. Every financial "mechanism" or "tool" has negative baggage as well as positive benefits. Views of a particular financial tool will be shaped not only by one's professional standing, but by personal and political beliefs and position in society, and may evolve over time. For example, tools like property taxes, partnerships, or corporate sponsorships may be viewed differently by various recreation professionals, elected officials, recreation participants, non-participants, and competitors.

As the business of marshalling resources goes on in order to provide recreation and leisure services, the questions must continually be asked: How great is demand for these services? What are the trends in leisure and recreation participation? These seemingly simple questions are often difficult to answer. If demand is rising, then more resources are generally needed to provide adequate services. Indeed, long-term projections made regarding North Americans' recreation participation in the mid-20th century were often exceeded, creating a mindset among contemporary leisure services professionals that growth is almost inevitable (Crompton, 1999). For example, Eagles and Wilkie (1998) documented that combined Canadian national and provincial park visitation skyrocketed nearly 50% during the nine-year period from 1988 to 1996. Research also suggests that demand for leisure services may be uneven—growing in some ways and stabilizing or even declining in others. Barber and Havitz (2001) found that the percentage of Canadian adults participating in seven of ten selected recreation activities (cross-country skiing, hockey, ice skating, jogging/running, squash, swimming, and tennis) declined by 5% or more in the 10-year period examined. Participation in two activities, bicycling and downhill skiing, was basically stable and for only one activity, golf, did participation rates rise by more than 5%. Numerous factors influence such trends, including an aging population, sedentary lifestyles among many people, and increasing multiculturalism, which encourages participation in a broader variety of activities. Future studies of this type will likely show disparate growth and decline patterns for those and other activities.

What are your positions on the various financial tools? Can you defend them? Continually ask yourself these questions as you read these financing chapters.

The bottom line is that financial planning is complicated by the complex forces influencing leisure participation patterns as well as by shifting political preferences regarding how leisure services should be funded. How much money is really needed? How many facilities are appropriate? Is more land needed, or are existing reserves adequate to serve current and future demand? How many professional staff are necessary to meet the needs of constituents?

If demand for a particular recreation activity is dropping in our community or at our facility, what should be our professional response? Should we provide more resources (e.g., money, staff, facility upgrades, marketing) to reverse the trend? Or should we decrease the resources allocated to that activity and, in extreme circumstances, abandon it? What is the basis for your position?

Our Financial Cornerstone: Understanding Taxes and Taxation

Property Tax

Property taxes are the major tax source for local governments including towns, cities, regions, counties, and schools. They account for about 80% of local government revenue in North America (Crompton, 1999). Taking a longitudinal approach, Connolly and Smale (2002) reported that, contrary to popular perceptions that property tax revenues were declining, they actually rose steadily over their nine-year study period. They added that about 10% of municipal spending was attributable to recreation and culture in the Ontario communities they studied. Taken together, these studies confirm that property taxes are an important revenue source for leisure service agencies. Crompton argued that "Theoretically, the property tax is consistent with both the ability-to-pay principle and the benefit principle of taxation. To the extent that the value of property owned increases with income, those with greater ability to pay will pay higher taxes. Property tax serves as a benefit to those who pay it because its revenues are used to finance local government expenditures on services that benefit property owners and increase the value of their properties" (p. 18).

Property taxes are a function of two numbers: the assessed value of a property X the local tax rate. Canadian municipalities generally use a form of "market value" assessment, which, in simple terms, refers to the approximate value for which the property would sell on the open market. If a property is worth $250,000 it should be assessed at approximately that value, though actual assessments tend to be on the low side to minimize landowner initiated complaints and formal appeals. Residential property tax rates usually range from just under 1% to as high as 3%. For example, 2005 rates in Waterloo, Ontario, were about 1.33%. By contrast, they were just 0.89% 100 kilometres away in Toronto.

One possible reason for this discrepancy is that there are three levels of government in Waterloo (Region, City, and Schools), whereas there are only two levels (City and Schools) in Toronto. Despite these differences in levels of government and tax rates, it is entirely possible that a Toronto homeowner may pay a similar (or even higher) property tax bill as her Waterloo counterpart. How can this be? The likely reason this case would be that property values tend to be higher in larger cities than they are in smaller cities, and lower still in most small towns and rural areas.

As a general rule, business property tax rates tend to be higher than are those for residential properties. For example, in 2003 average municipal residential property tax rates were 0.57% in British Columbia, 1.18% in Alberta, and 1.48% in Nova Scotia. By contrast, average municipal business property tax rates in those provinces were 1.39%, 1.42% and 2.93% respectively (Bish, 2004). Why are business taxes higher than residential taxes? The short answer is that businesses, by definition, operate to generate revenue whereas residences, unless they are sold, do not.

Leisure services agencies (broadly defined to include agencies dealing with recreation, parks, fine and performing arts, libraries, tourism, and sports) account for a fairly modest percentage, usually less than 20%, of total property taxes received in Canada. That said, property taxes account for a large percentage of many leisure services

---

Assume you own a residential property valued at $200,000 and your property tax rate is 1.5%. That means that your annual property taxes are $200,000 x 0.015 or $3,000. Also assume that 15% of your property taxes ($450) are designated for leisure facilities and services.

What are you likely getting for your $450? Brainstorm for a few minutes and compile a list then compare it to Table 38.1.

Table 38.1: Sample park and recreation amenities funded primarily with property tax revenues

Neighbourhood parks	Arenas
Regional parks	Soccer/football fields
Paved trails	Ball diamonds
Natural trails	Municipal golf courses
Canoe/boat liveries	Driving ranges
Wetlands/wildlife habitat	Skate parks
Historic markers/sites	Hockey rinks
Picnic shelters	Cricket pitches
Play areas/structures	Basketball courts
Community centres	Ropes courses
Older adult centres	Lawn bowling pitches
Band shells/stages	Curling rinks
Community gardens	Tennis courts
Flower gardens/arboretums	Swimming pools
Waterfronts/beaches	Wading pools
Shuffleboard courts	Volleyball/badminton court

Do the facilities and services on your list represent a fair value for your dollar? When formulating your response, consider the following questions: Do these amenities affect your (and your family's) quality of life and health? Do these amenities affect quality of life and health of others in the community? Does the existence of these amenities affect (for better or for worse) your property value? Would these amenities exist without the property tax? If so, how would they be financed?

agencies' operating budgets, normally in the range of 35% to 50%. Property taxes normally account for over 90% of school district revenues. Why does this discrepancy occur? It exists largely because, in comparison to other municipal services such as schools, police and fire departments, leisure services agencies have a broader range of financial support from which to draw. User fees, which will be discussed later in this chapter, represent the funding mechanism that has grown the most over the past several decades.

Municipalities often fund capital projects, such as arenas and community centres, using debentures. Municipal debentures are sold on the market and represent the Canadian equivalent of American municipal general obligation bonds. Debentures are a safe and secure form of investment. The security is provided by the government's unconditional pledge of full tax support. At the municipal level, this security is provided by the property tax. Capital projects are often paid off over an extended period of years, generally 10 to 25, to spread the burden on municipal taxpayers. Canadian federal and provincial governments sell bonds rather than debentures, using the same underlying principle.

One fundamental way in which Canadian property tax laws differ from those in other countries is with respect to the prohibition of tax abatements or bonuses. A bonus occurs when an individual property owner is given a property tax break, not available to others, as an incentive to move to a particular community or to remain in a community. It is common practice for American cities to compete in this manner to lure or retain industry and high profile businesses such as professional sport franchises. Pressure to consider bonuses in Canada reached a climax in the late 1990s as NHL franchises such as the Québec Nordique and Winnipeg Jets relocated south of the border. Amid fears that others might follow, especially small market teams like the Edmonton Oilers and Ottawa Senators, a measure to consider bonuses was tabled in Parliament. Public outrage quickly quelled the debate, however, and bonusing remains illegal in Canada (Havitz & Glover, 2001).

Assuming that bonusing might mean that property tax revenues would be reduced in the community offering a tax break to a professional sport franchise, what is your opinion on this issue? Argue both pro and con.

Sales Tax

We pay sales tax on almost everything we buy. Exceptions to this rule include purchases of unprepared food (e.g., from a grocery store) and medicine. Such exceptions represent attempts to reduce the regressive nature of sales taxes. A regressive tax is one that bears most heavily on people with low incomes. In Canada the majority of sales taxes are collected by the federal and provincial governments. If you shop at the local mall and purchase $100 of goods, your total bill would likely be in the neighbourhood of $114, with the $14 representing the impact of various sales taxes. This amount will vary from province to province.

The federal Goods and Services Tax (GST) was first levied in 1991 and set at 7%. It was reduced to 6% in the summer of 2006. The 7% GST generated approximately $30 billion in revenues per year; roughly $1,000 per person (Policy Channel, 2006) so the 6% GST might be expected to generate just over $25 billion per year. Ironically, the first provincial sales tax (PST) was first in 1936 by Alberta, presently the only province that does not charge a PST. Current PST rates range from 7% in British Columbia and Manitoba to 9% in Québec and Saskatchewan, and 10% in Prince Edward Island. PST rates are effectively 8% in the remaining provinces. Given that the PST rates have been historically similar to GST rates, it is plausible to hypothesize that province by province PST revenue totals also approximate $1,000 per person. Similar to the exclusion for food and medicine, many recreation services and rentals are exempt from PST; for example, rental of ice time at arenas and of picnic shelters and campsites at parks in Ontario. Rules often seem random and contradictory however. Rentals of skiing, hockey, canoeing, tennis and golf equipment are charged PST in Ontario, whereas rentals of bowling shoes, ice skates, and boot-type roller skates are exempt.

Local governments normally do not collect sales taxes in Canada. As such, municipal governments do not generally rely on sales tax as a source of direct revenue; however, they often benefit indirectly in the form of transfer payments from the federal and provincial governments. For example, to encourage fitness participation or environmental awareness, a provincial government may provide money to municipalities as a means of supporting local initiatives to those ends. One aspect of recreation/tourism taxed above and beyond PST rates in most provinces is the rental of hotel and motel accommodations. These taxes vary greatly from location to location. For example, Alberta enforces a province-wide 4% hotel tax (Alberta Government, 2006), while British Columbia mandates 8% but operations with fewer than four rental units, such as bed and breakfast inns and campgrounds of any size are exempt (Accommodations BC, 2006). Other provinces such as Ontario and Nova Scotia allow individual municipalities to set their own rates. The rate in Niagara Falls, a prime tourism destination, is 12% while many other Ontario municipalities collect no hotel tax. It is easy to see why hotel taxes may be relatively popular among local residents, because the fees, which go to support local infrastructure and programs, are paid primarily by visitors. They can also be controversial, however, as some business owners view hotel taxes as potentially destructive to the local tourism industry. For example, as this chapter was going to press, many Cape Breton hotel and motel operators were actively opposing a legislature approved, but not yet implemented, 2% room tax on those very grounds (CBC News, 2006).

Income Tax

The largest revenue source for Canadian federal and provincial governments is the income tax. The average Canadian family pays just under $9,000 in income taxes each year. Individual amounts vary, of course, depending on a variety of factors including a person's gross (before tax) income, the province in which he or she lives, the method of filing (single or joint), and which of numerous possible legal deductions and credits are figured into the mix.

To make them less regressive, federal tax rates and those of most provinces are "graduated" (Table 38.2). That is, people pay an increasing amount, and percentage of income, as gross income rises. Because the first $8,000 of annual income is tax exempt and because the average Canadian adult makes about $30,000 per year (average household income was about $66,000 in 2005), it is not surprising that the majority of people are taxed only at the 16% and 22% rates and at the comparably appropriate provincial rates (Canada Revenue Agency, 2006). As already stated, provincial income tax rates vary from province to province (Table 38.3). Although the financial impact of income taxes is profound, their impact on leisure services programming is not very visible. Most income tax funds applied to leisure services come in the form of provincial and federal transfer payments to local government infrastructure.

High profile exceptions to this statement include Parks Canada and the various provincial park agencies that receive substantial income tax support in their base operating budgets.

Table 38.2: Canadian federal tax rates (2005)

Basic Personal Amount (non-taxable income):
$8,012

Federal tax rates:
16% on the first $35,595 of taxable income;
22% on the next $35,595 of taxable income;
26% on the next $44,549 of taxable income; and
29% of taxable income over $115,739

Retrieved 8 November 2005 from www.cra-arc.gc.ca/tax/ individuals/faq/taxrates-e.html#provincial

Table 38.3: Provincial income tax rates (2005)

Alberta: 10% of taxable income

British Columbia: 6.05% on the first $33,061 of taxable income, + 9.15% on the next $33,062, + 11.7% on the next $9,794, + 13.7% on the next $16,268, + 14.7% on the amount over $92,185

Manitoba: 10.9% on the first $30,544 of taxable income, + 14% on the next $34,456, + 17.4% on the amount over $65,000

New Brunswick: 9.68% on the first $32,730 of taxable income, + 14.82% on the next $32,732, + 16.52% on the next $40,965, + 17.84% on the amount over $106,427

Newfoundland and Labrador: 10.57% on the first $29,590 of taxable income, + 16.16% on the next $29,590, + 18.02% on the amount over $59,180

Nova Scotia: 8.79% on the first $29,590 of taxable income, + 14.95% on the next $29,590, + 16.67% on the next $33,820, + 17.5% on the amount over $93,000

Ontario: 6.05% on the first $34,010 of taxable income, + 9.15% on the next $34,010, + 11.16% on the amount over $68,020

Prince Edward Island: 9.8% on the first $30,754 of taxable income, + 13.8% on the next $30,755, + 16.7% on the amount over $61,509

Québec: 16% on the first $28,030 of taxable income, + 20% on the next $28,040, + 24% on the amount over $56,070

Saskatchewan: 11% on the first $36,770 of taxable income, + 13% on the next $68,286, + 15% on the amount over $105,056

Québec information retrieved 26 June 2006 from: http://www.revenu.gouv.qc.ca/documents/eng/formulaires/tp/tp-1.d.gr-v(2005-12).pdf. Other information retrieved 8 November 2005 from: www.cra-arc.gc.ca/tax/individuals/faq/taxrates-e.html#provincial

Other Taxes

Revenue Canada, the provinces, and municipal governments collect a variety of other taxes including those on capital gains, land transfers, and so forth. These taxes are relatively specific to individual circumstance and are, for many people and businesses, sporadically if ever applied. As such, they are not discussed in this chapter. Others, such as the manufacturers excise tax, are not used in Canada but provide interesting possibilities for funding leisure service facilities and programs.

Exactions

An *exaction* or *development charge* is a local government requirement imposed on developers or builders, mandating

Though not common to Canada, manufacturers' excise taxes are used to fund some outdoor recreation activities, for example fishing and hunting in the United States. Manufacturers' excise taxes are levied when equipment is purchased and they represent an attempt to allocate the costs of providing recreation amenities to the participants in those activities (Crompton, 1999). Proponents essentially say, "Let's charge an extra tax on products used for a specific activity and use the money to develop and improve facilities and programs directly related to those activities." Like hotel taxes, this tax would be levied in addition to the applicable PST and GST. If such a tax were implemented for hockey equipment, it would be enforced when skates, pads, sticks, tape and the like were sold, and funds raised would go specifically to the construction and renovation of hockey facilities and to support hockey programming. In comparison to traditional funding mechanisms currently used to fund hockey in Canada, do you think this would be an equitable and effective tax? Explain your position.

that they dedicate park land or pay a fee to be used by the government entity to acquire and develop infrastructure including park and recreation facilities. Exactions represent the most important land acquisition vehicle for municipal governments. Conceptually, it makes sense that new residents in a community pay the majority share of new facilities, such as neighbourhood parks, facilities and services for which they will be the primary beneficiaries. Indeed, the costs associated with exactions are normally passed on to homebuyers by developers.

Although there are several types of exactions used in Canada, the two most common are *land dedication* and *fees-in-lieu*. Developers most often choose one or the other or a combination of the two. Land dedication means that a certain percentage, normally a fixed percentage such as 5%, of the property to be developed is set aside as parkland. Some jurisdictions also allow the use of population density formulas, for example requiring that one hectare of parkland be set aside per 300 housing units created (Kaczynski, Charette, John, & Yuja, 2001). Exacted land must be used as parkland in Canada, not for other purposes such as water treatment facilities, fire stations, or city maintenance garages. That said, exacted parkland can be, though this is rarely the case, sold at the discretion of the government. Floodplain land is considered acceptable for exactions. Indeed floodplains often make excellent parkland for recreation activity; however, ravines and steep sloped land can only be included in the exaction if it is above and beyond the normal fixed percentage. If a fee-in-lieu option is chosen the developer provides the municipality with cash instead of land, usually equal to fair market value of land as just described with respect to the population density approach, or a percent of the fair market value of the land being developed. One advantage of the fee-in-lieu option is that, if desired, exacted resources can be pooled to create a smaller number of larger parks instead of a large number of small parks. Fee-in-lieu options are available in most provinces, except British Columbia and Newfoundland (Havitz & Glover, 2001).

Taxation Summary

The objectives of the first section of this chapter have been twofold: (1) to introduce the importance of taxes and exactions as means of financing government supported leisure services programming and infrastructure and (2) to generate awareness regarding why many citizens feel overburdened with regard to taxation. Tax limitation movements have become common in the past 25 years and resistance to this traditional funding mechanism is especially prevalent among citizens, for non-participants, for example, who perceive little benefit from the taxes they pay. In that sense, the "benefits of recreation movement" started in the 1990s becomes particularly salient as professionals strive to better connect value for the dollar in the minds of the citizenry. At the same time, leisure service professionals have become more entrepreneurial in seeking alternative fund-raising sources and delivery strategies, while trying to maintain equitable and effective facility and program options for their communities. The remainder of this chapter speaks to those issues.

Emergent Funding Sources

User Fees

The existence of user fees can be traced back to some of the earliest recreation programs; however, there is no doubt that user fees are higher and more widely applied at present than they were prior to 1980. Marketing texts generally suggest that public sector leisure service agencies generate between 20 and 40% of their revenue from user fees. They are not universally applied however. For example, municipal agencies rarely charge fees of any kind for general park, playground, or trail use. When fees are in effect, certain user groups, most often children and older adults, are usually subsidized. Likewise certain program offerings, especially those with a substantial education component, are often subsidized. Other offerings such as municipal golf courses, community festivals, and sport leagues often charge break-even or revenue generating prices, especially to adult participants. Equity issues related to the pricing of leisure services are discussed in greater depth by Kaczynski and Potwarka in Chapter 36.

Do you believe that municipal recreation programs should be supported solely with tax revenue, solely with user fees, or some combination of taxes, fees, and other revenue sources? Justify your response and include some discussion of which people are being served by the program and what participation benefits might accrue to them and to society.

Support from Sponsorships

The International Event Group defines sponsorships as "a cash and/or in-kind fee paid to a property in return for some access to the exploitable commercial potential associated with that property" (IEG, 2003, p. 1). Acknowledged as the fastest growing form of marketing communication, companies spend over $10.5 billion annually on sponsorships in North America (IEG, 2003). Based on the relative population size of the U.S. vis-à-vis Canada, a realistic estimate is that between $1 and $2 billion is spent in Canada. A majority of the $10.5 billion accrues to leisure agencies and contexts: 70% to sports, 9% to charitable causes, 8% to attractions and entertainment tours, 8% to festivals fairs and events, and 5% to the arts (IEG, 2003).

The obvious benefits for the receiving agency are the financial or in-kind resources brought by the sponsor; however, in the sense that sponsors generally expect a return on their investment. Reciprocity is important in sponsorship contexts. Some commonly touted benefits accruing to sponsors include increased awareness of programs and products, image enhancement, product or program trial, hospitality opportunities, team building, and creation of social capital (Crompton, 1999). An important challenge for leisure services agencies in the future will be measuring sponsorship effectiveness from the perspective of those putting forward the financial and in-kind resources. Many variables could be explored including: message exposure (how many people hear about a sponsorship), impact on awareness of the company and its products, impact on the company's image, impact on potential customer's intent to purchase the company's products or services, and the actual influence on sales. These all seem relatively straightforward, but are difficult to quantify in practice.

Leisure services professionals must also be mindful of how sponsorships affect agency image and effectiveness, and how citizens feel about them (Mowen & Havitz, 2002). Tobacco and alcohol company sponsorships serve to illustrate this issue. Sponsorship of recreation events in Canada by tobacco companies has been banned since the Tobacco Act took effect in 1998; although the Act is, as of this writing, under review by the Supreme Court of Canada (CTV, 2006). Sponsorship by alcohol companies continues to thrive. While it is true that long-term responsible alcohol consumption is not likely as lethal as long-term tobacco use, critics point to the often tragic consequences of drunk driving and alcoholism as reasons why alcohol sponsorships should also be banned.

Compile a list of reasons in support of alcohol company sponsorships of leisure services programming and weigh it against a similarly constructed list of downsides. What is your professional position on this issue?

Support from Donations

Canadians collectively donate between $3 and $4 billion to charitable organizations each year. Over 90% of Canadians made financial or in-kind donations to charitable and not-for-profit organizations in 2000 (see Chapter 40). Donations differ fundamentally from sponsorships in that they are generally made on altruistic grounds. Revenue Canada specifies donors cannot reap tangible rewards, financial or otherwise, as a result of their donation. The exception to this rule is that donors can claim income tax deductions for their donations. Indeed, Revenue Canada charitable giving guidelines have been adjusted in recent years to make charitable giving more attractive.

Prior to 1996, tax deductions on charitable giving were limited to 20% of net income. That limit has since risen to 75% of net income, and as further incentive, donations in excess of that amount can be carried forward for up to five years. Of course, the reality is that few Canadians make donations anywhere near this magnitude. The average annual charitable donation claim was just over $250 in 2000 (Imagine Canada, 2005). Nevertheless, even people of modest means occasionally make large donations. For example, a recently retired person making $50,000 per year but living comfortably in good health and mortgage free may decide to donate proceeds from the sale of his mother's $150,000 house received via her will rather than pocket or invest the money. In this case the donation would have to be claimed over a period of years subject to the Revenue Canada guidelines summarized above. Though the amounts vary slightly from province to province, over time the donor would receive federal and provincial income tax deductions worth approximately half of the charitable donation, or nearly $75,000.

Attempts to calculate the impact of donations on leisure services agencies are complex. Only 3% of charitable donation dollars are given directly to support arts, culture and recreation. The plurality of donations goes to religious organizations, which account for 49% of dollars donated (Imagine Canada, 2005). Other popular giving categories include health (20%), social services (10%), philanthropy and volunteerism (7%), and the environment (2%). The reality is that a portion of the activities carried out by each of the latter five types of agencies are likely related to recreation, parks, sport, and tourism.

Public and not-for-profit sector leisure services agencies increasingly look to charitable donations to supplement traditional revenue sources. The cultivation of donors is a long-term process, but one which can pay large, if sporadic dividends. Potential donors are relatively easy to identify as over 80% of donation dollars come from just 25% of charitable givers, and nearly 50% come from the most generous 5%. Two common methods of cultivating donors include planned donation workshops and gift catalogues. The former method involves identifying the aforementioned potential large donors, developing personal relationships between them and your staff, and engaging them with professional presentations designed to highlight effective ways in which their donations could be used by your agency. By contrast, gift catalogues are often distributed broadly throughout a community in hope of reaching a broad cross section of potential donors. Gift catalogues are especially effective in "making tangible" the effect of each donation. Figure 38.1 depicts some content of a gift catalogue recently used in Cambridge, Ontario.

Support from Foundations

Foundations, not-for-profit corporations that are organized and operated for the benefit of the general public, are increasingly used as sources of funding for park and recreation services and facilities. In Canada, foundations fall under the broader heading of registered charities. There are over 78,000 registered charities in Canada (Charity.com, 2006). Recreation directly accounts for just 4.5% of all charities and 0.7% of all charitable revenue (Havitz & Glover, 2001); however, these figures are deceptively low because foundations classified as supporting arts and culture, education, health and well-being initiatives, the environment, religion, and various social services often include leisure services programming within their respective mandates.

Foundations are attractive resource acquisition mechanisms for several reasons. For example, land donors often prefer to donate land to municipalities via foundations rather than directly to

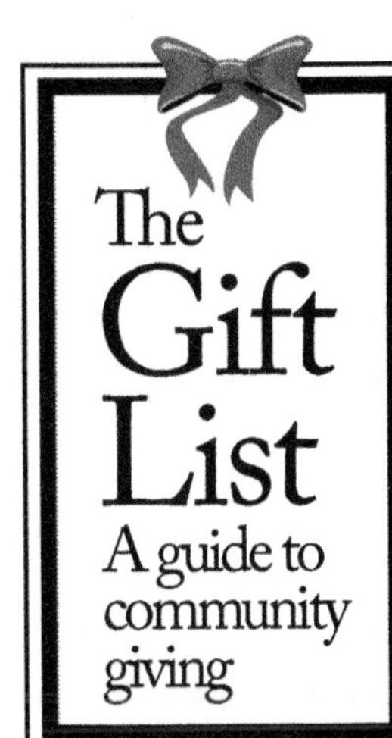

The Corporation
of the City
of Cambridge

Community
Services Department
73 Water Street North
PO Box 669
Cambridge, Ontario
N1R 5W8

No act of kindness, no matter how small, is ever wasted.
Aesop

"Quality of Life" is a term often used to describe the collective well-being of a community. We all do our share through the payment of taxes and support of local charitable organizations to maintain the "quality of life" to which we have become accustomed.

There are times, however, when one is presented with the opportunity to enhance the "quality of life" in a community by making a specific contribution. This guide presents such an opportunity.

NICETIES vs NECESSITIES

In times of restraint, budgeted funds often provide only for essential services in the City and the collective quality of life tends to diminish. Your generosity in a contribution will provide a great deal of satisfaction to you, the giver, and to the community.

LET YOUR HEART DO THE WALKING

The items listed are suggestions for your consideration. You may want to contribute a specific item or contribute with others towards a larger item. Let your heart do the walking through this guide. If you do not find a gift this is of interest to you, department staff will be pleased to discuss other items with you.

DONATIONS IN KIND

Financial donation may be beyond the realm of many individuals or groups who wish to assist the community. Another valuable commodity is you. We can use your time and talents in constructive ways. Maybe you'd like to assist with a special event, help maintain a neighbourhood park, or donate your time in graphic art. The possibilities are boundless. But first we must know about you, your interests and skills, to put them to work effectively.

He doubles his gift who gives in time.

YOUR GIFT RETURNS THE FAVOUR

For every gift to the City, you may receive a gift in return - appropriate recognition and assured satisfaction. Recognition is available and may include an engraved donor plaque, an officially signed and recorded certificate or a public news media announcement. Confidentiality will also be respected should that be the wish of the donor.

REMEMBER THIS: Give the gift that returns the favour, the gift that satisfies. May we hear from you?

PARKS & CEMETERIES

Trees	$ 200	Plus
Park Benches	$ 130	
Playground Equipment	$ 500	Plus
Picnic Tables	$ 150	Plus
Drinking Fountains	$ 2,500	Plus
Outdoor Bleachers	$ 2,000	
Ball Diamond Backstops	$ 4,000	Each
Spray Pad	$ 20,000	Plus
Tennis Courts	$ 15,000	Each
Creative Play Structures	$ 6,000	Plus
Washroom Building	$ 30,000	
BBQ Grills	$ 300	Each
Trucks	$ 15,000	Plus
Picnic Shelters	$ 4,000	Plus
Tractors (Farm Type)	$ 20,000	
Ground Compactor	$ 5,000	
All Purpose Asphalt/Concrete Pads	$ 1,000	Plus
Softball Diamond	$ 30,000	Plus
Information Kiosks	$ 7,000	
Foul Weather Tarp for Playing Fields	$ 2,000	
Playing Field Lighting	$ 25,000	
Grounds Maintenance Equipment	$ 300	Plus
Lighting (Roads, Walkway, Security)	$ 2,000	Plus
Portable Canteens	$ 20,000	Plus
Sculptures	$ 2,000	Plus

ARENAS & POOLS

Ice Resurfacing Machine	$ 25,000	
Swimming Pool Equipment (deck furniture, lane markers)	$ 500	Plus
Audio-Visual Equipment (projectors, record players, tape recorders	$ 250	Plus
Ice Hockey Goal Nets	$ 2,500	/Set
Floor Scrubber	$ 3,000	
Arena Sound System	$ 6,000	
Indoor Pool Sound System	$ 2,000	
Compressor (Arena)	$ 13,000	
Banquet Tables	$ 150	Each
Banquet Chairs	$ 25	Each
Security Lockers (change rooms) (set of three)	$ 1,000	/Set
Canoes	$ 600	Each
Pool Heat Blanket	$ 1,000	
Tot Docks (Pools)	$ 1,600	Each
Inflatable Water Structures	$ 700	Each
Water Polo Nets	$ 400	/Set
Water Basketball Nets	$ 1,300	/Set
Diving Boards	$ 2,000	Each
Life Jackets	$ 50	Plus
Concession Equipment	$ 500	Plus
Indoor Alarm Systems	$ 3,000	Plus
Programme Schedule Boards	$ 3,000	Each
Facility Lighting	$ 20,000	Plus

TRANSIT

Bus Shelters	$ 15,000	Each
Bus Route Maps	$ 10,000	
Buses	$ 210,000	
Van for Disabled	$ 35,000	
Transit Garage Equipment	$ 500	& up

Provincial Ministry of Transportation and Communication provides a subsidy on all transit items

Figure 38.1: Sample pages from the Cambridge, ON gift catalogue public sector agencies because of the mechanics related to reversionary clauses. That is, foundations are more likely, over the long term, to ensure that donated property is used for the purpose intended, such as parkland or open-space, than it might be if decisions are left up to heirs or public bureaucrats. They can also be flexible when circumstances call for that. Foundations often provide pre-acquisition or bridge-financing to preserve facilities or open space until park and recreation agencies are ready to receive them.

Foundations take many forms (Crompton, 1999). Umbrella foundations are formed when coalitions of not-for-profit and public organizations pool resources to develop facilities or services. Facility-specific foundations are just that; they allow people to make donations to support a specific park or recreation facility. Local agency-specific foundations are similar to facility-specific foundations except they can accept a broader range of donations in support of the affiliated leisure service agency's operations. Corporate foundations often target their efforts toward a specific cause. For example, TD, Canada Trust's "Friends of the Environment" foundation supports a range of local and larger scale environmental projects. Community foundations operate in a geographically specific area but support a broad range of initiatives including, but not limited to, leisure services. There are over 140 active community foundations in Canada (Community Foundations of Canada, 2006). Now over 50 years old, the Vancouver Foundation is the largest community foundation in Canada. It supported $30 million of projects in 2005 using income generated from assets, which are currently worth over $600 million.

> ? Using your community as an example, what recreation facilities and programs are supported, at least in part, by private donations or foundations? Would these facilities and programs exist without this type of support? If so, how would they likely be funded? Would they be of comparable quality (better, worse, or about the same)?

This chapter focused on acquiring financial resources. The next finance chapter will focus on minimizing costs, foraging effective partnerships, and managing financial assets in the form of budgetary decisions.

Key Terms

Donations
Exactions
Foundations
Sponsorship
Taxes

References

Accommodations BC. (2006). *Online accommodations.* Retrieved from http://www.accommodationsbc.com/visitor.html

Alberta Government. (2006). *Tourism Levy Act.* Retrieved from http://www.qp.gov.ab.ca/documents/Acts/T05P5.cfm?frm_isbn=0779735757&type=htm

Barber, N., & Havitz, M. E. (2001). Canadian participation rates in ten sport and fitness activities. *Journal of Sport Management, 15*, 51–76.

Bish, R. L. (2004). *Property taxes on business and industrial property in British Columbia.* Vancouver, BC: Fraser Institute. Retrieved from http://www.fraserinstitute.ca/admin/books/files/Property-Taxes.pdf

Canada Revenue Agency. (2006). *What are the income tax rates in Canada for 2006?* Retrieved from http://www.cra-arc.gc.ca/tax/individuals/faq/taxrates-e.html#provincial

CBC News. (2006). *Province shelves Cape Breton hotel tax.* Retrieved from http://www.cbc.ca/ns/story/ns-hotel-levy20060331.html

Charity.com. (2006). *Canadian registered charities.* Retrieved from http://www.charity.com/canadiancharities.shtml

Connolly, K., & Smale, B. J. A. (2002). Changes in the financing of local recreation and cultural services: An examination of trends in Ontario from 1988 to 1996. *Leisure/Loisir, 26*, 213–234.

Crompton, J. L. (1999). *Financing and acquiring park and recreation resources.* Champaign, IL: Human Kinetics.

Community Foundations of Canada. (2006). *Welcome to Community Foundations of Canada.* Retrieved from http://www.cfc-fcc.ca/faqs.cfm

CTV. (2006). *Supreme Court to rule on tobacco sponsorship ban.* Retrieved from http://www.ctv.ca/servlet/ArticleNews/story/CTVNews/20060323/Tobbacco_ban060323/20060323?hub=Health

Eagles, P. F. J., & Wilkie, K. (1998). Canadian provincial and national park use. In M. E. Havitz & T. D. Glover, *Financing and acquiring public park, recreation and open space resources in Canada* [Online, Chapter 1]. Champaign, IL: Human Kinetics.

Havitz, M. E., & Glover, T. D. (2001). *Financing and acquiring public park, recreation and open space resources in Canada* [On-line]. Champaign, IL: Human Kinetics.

Imagine Canada. (2005). *Managing an organization.* Retrieved from http://sectorsource.ca/managing-organization

International Event Group (2003). *IEG's guide to sponsorship.* Chicago, IL: IEG, Inc.

Kaczynski, A. Charette, J., John, A., & Yuja, E. (2001). Acquiring resources through exactions. In M. E. Havitz & T. D. Glover, *Financing and acquiring public park, recreation and open space resources in Canada* [Online, Chapter 1]. Champaign, IL: Human Kinetics.

Mowen, A., & Havitz, M. E. (2002). Signs of trouble: Citizen-driven guidelines for sponsor and donor recognition in park and recreation settings. *Parks and Recreation, 37*(9), 82–90.

Policy Channel. (2006). GST. Retrieved from http://goo.gl/iCSgA5

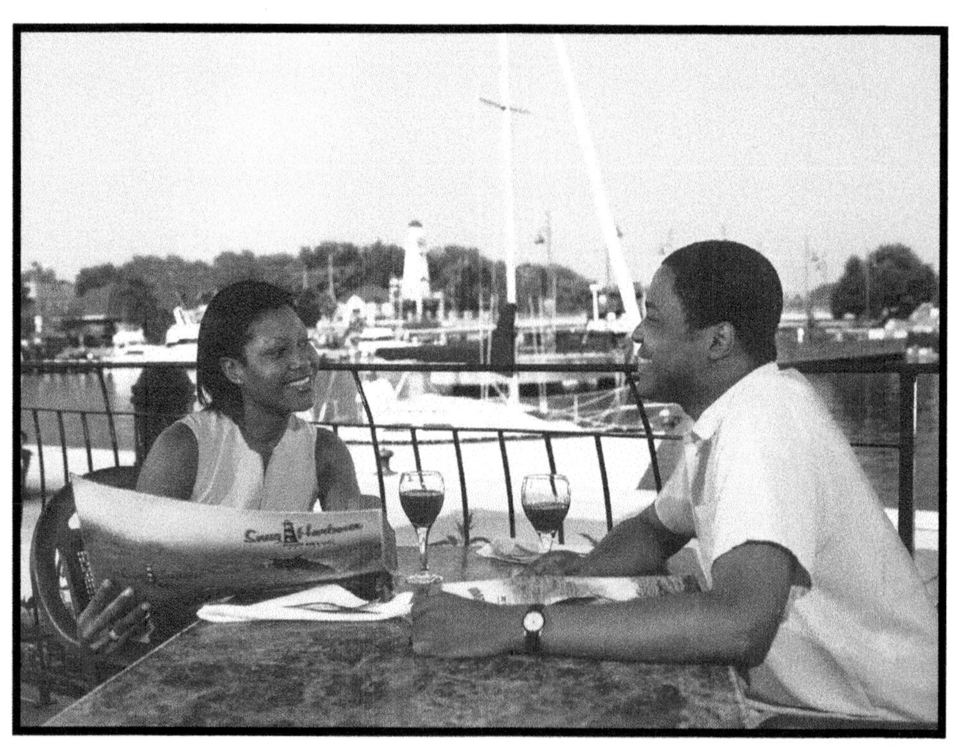

Chapter 39
Financing Leisure Services II: Cost Control and Budgeting

Mark E. Havitz, Ph.D.
University of Waterloo

Learning Objectives

After reading this chapter, students will be able to

1. Understand the strengths and weaknesses of various partnership arrangements.
2. Be aware of arrangements for acquiring land resources without outright purchase of property.
3. Be able to differentiate between basic budgetary options and know some strengths and weaknesses of various approaches.

Introduction

The financial discussion in the previous chapter focussed on raising revenue. Another important consideration faced by leisure service providers involves controlling costs while striving to ensure that high quality and effective leisure options are available to citizens. Because issues related to health and well-being, physical activity, culture and the environment are often complex and interrelated; and because recreation and leisure services are offered by the full range of not-for-profit agencies, public agencies and commercial businesses, it often makes sense for stakeholders, including participants and the general citizenry, to pool resources to solve problems and serve society. Four alternative service delivery strategies are introduced in this chapter: (1) co-production through facilitation, (2) co-production through community development, (3) partnerships of various types, and (4) less-than-fee simple arrangements.

Facilitation and Co-production

Traditionally, leisure services agencies gather financial (e.g., taxes, user fees, sponsorships) and human resources (e.g., paid staff, volunteers) and build and maintain facilities (e.g., parks, arenas, community centres) to provide services to their constituents. This form of operation is called *direct provision.* Three alternative models to direct provision are described in this section. Facilitation is the least radical of these alternative leisure services delivery strategies. Different types of facilitation, wherein one agency helps another agency or business provide services, are available. Referrals represent a fairly simple form of facilitation. For example, the city of Kitchener, Ontario, encourages other organizations and businesses to advertise in its seasonal recreation brochures (Figure 39.1, p. 368). This type of arrangement is possible if agencies and businesses view each other less in competitive terms and concentrate instead on making as many services as possible available to citizens. Some people have argued that leisure services agencies should go even farther, and systematically explore, categorize, and promote options within their communities (Figure 39.2, p. 369). This type of exercise could be done with various constituent groups in mind, including, but not limited to tourists, children, adolescents, and older adults.

After reviewing Figures 39.1 and 39.2, consider the following: What barriers exist that might inhibit or prevent public sector leisure service agencies from working with not-for-profit or commercial sector "competitors"? How might these barriers be minimized or eliminated?

A second type of facilitation occurs when a leisure services agency offers technical assistance to other organizations. Perhaps the most common form of this type is when municipal agencies assist minor sport organizations with scheduling, training officials and coaches, running safety clinics, and so forth. In addition, agencies that operate new state-of-the-art facilities often grant requests from other agencies to explain programming advantages, energy efficiency, and other benefits accruing as a result of the new physical plant. Finally, a leisure services agency may adopt a brokering posture. Rather than directly provide services, an agency operating under this philosophy will serve as the go-between between agencies and businesses that provide leisure services (e.g., bowling alleys, fitness clubs, golf courses, theatre troops, and music and art schools) and the potential clients looking for those services.

Co-production of Leisure Services and Community Development Approaches

The hallmark of these types of service delivery approaches is that citizens, volunteers, and paid professionals work together to provide services and/or experiences. Six advantages of co-production over traditional direct provision have been cited in the literature (Crompton, 1999). Co-production: fosters a "do-it-yourself" ethos among participants; encourages citizen empathy for government; may reduce the cost of providing services; makes agencies more responsive to the needs of citizens because citizens are actually involved in the process; allows citizens to be creative and develop talents; and provides additional socialization opportunities as citizens are not simply passive receptors of services.

The most radical form of co-production is community development. Community development, in contrast to traditional leisure services programming, focuses on a process of involving citizens in decision making and results in changes in individual lives and in the community itself (Hutchison & Nogradi, 1996). Pedlar (1996) added that under a community development model, reflective practitioners find larger purpose in identifying with the communities they support, and recreation is seen more clearly as praxis than product. In other words, the process of engaging and empowering citizens is viewed as being equally or more important than the actual program development and participation outcomes. Many authors have argued that community development models are most appropriate in contexts characterised by social and economic distress (Arai, 1996; Reid & van Dreunnen, 1996; see Chapter 32.)

Leisure and recreation services are normally subsidized at the supply-side in Canada. That is, taxes are collected and used as the primary basis to develop facilities and programming for the community. Vouchers represent another radical departure from this mode. Voucher systems take the opposite tact by putting money directly into the hands of citizens and letting them spend as they wish. In other words, a voucher system places emphasis on individual citizens' judgment rather than on the expertise and good intentions of agency personnel. That is, they would subsidize the demand side. Although voucher systems are not currently used in public sector Canadian recreation contexts, this concept has been proposed in other contexts. For example, a "plank" in the Conservative Party's successful 2006 federal election campaign platform was that child care should be subsidized by giving individual families a choice of whether to spend money on those services rather than by using tax dollars to create and sustain a government-run child care system. Voucher systems tend to be controversial. The question box on page 370 provides an example of the potential such systems have as well as the challenges that might face a leisure services agency considering a voucher approach.

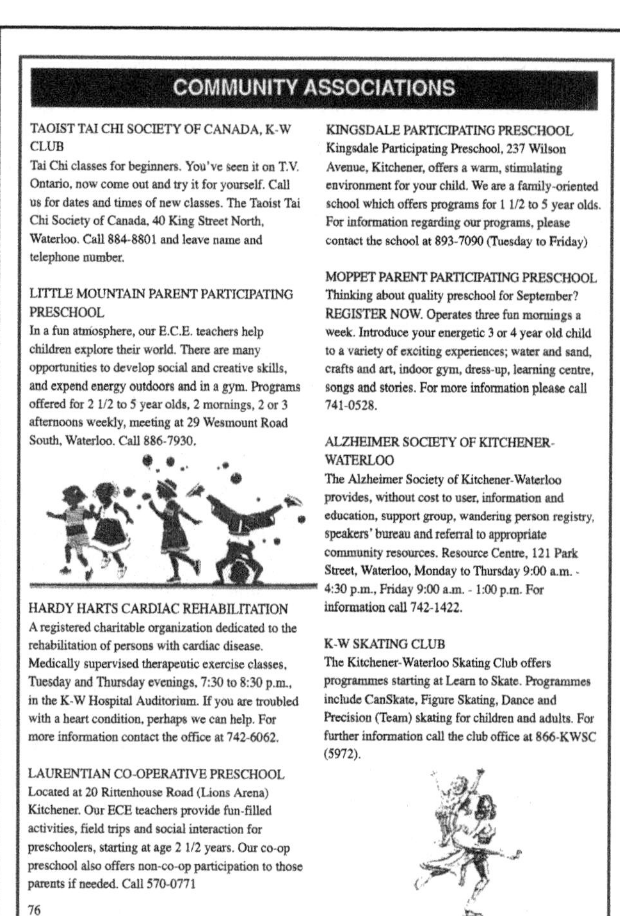

COMMUNITY ASSOCIATIONS

TAOIST TAI CHI SOCIETY OF CANADA, K-W CLUB
Tai Chi classes for beginners. You've seen it on T.V. Ontario, now come out and try it for yourself. Call us for dates and times of new classes. The Taoist Tai Chi Society of Canada, 40 King Street North, Waterloo. Call 884-8801 and leave name and telephone number.

LITTLE MOUNTAIN PARENT PARTICIPATING PRESCHOOL
In a fun atmosphere, our E.C.E. teachers help children explore their world. There are many opportunities to develop social and creative skills, and expend energy outdoors and in a gym. Programs offered for 2 1/2 to 5 year olds, 2 mornings, 2 or 3 afternoons weekly, meeting at 29 Wesmount Road South, Waterloo. Call 886-7930.

HARDY HARTS CARDIAC REHABILITATION
A registered charitable organization dedicated to the rehabilitation of persons with cardiac disease. Medically supervised therapeutic exercise classes, Tuesday and Thursday evenings, 7:30 to 8:30 p.m., in the K-W Hospital Auditorium. If you are troubled with a heart condition, perhaps we can help. For more information contact the office at 742-6062.

LAURENTIAN CO-OPERATIVE PRESCHOOL
Located at 20 Rittenhouse Road (Lions Arena) Kitchener. Our ECE teachers provide fun-filled activities, field trips and social interaction for preschoolers, starting at age 2 1/2 years. Our co-op preschool also offers non-co-op participation to those parents if needed. Call 570-0771

KINGSDALE PARTICIPATING PRESCHOOL
Kingsdale Participating Preschool, 237 Wilson Avenue, Kitchener, offers a warm, stimulating environment for your child. We are a family-oriented school which offers programs for 1 1/2 to 5 year olds. For information regarding our programs, please contact the school at 893-7090 (Tuesday to Friday)

MOPPET PARENT PARTICIPATING PRESCHOOL
Thinking about quality preschool for September? REGISTER NOW. Operates three fun mornings a week. Introduce your energetic 3 or 4 year old child to a variety of exciting experiences; water and sand, crafts and art, indoor gym, dress-up, learning centre, songs and stories. For more information please call 741-0528.

ALZHEIMER SOCIETY OF KITCHENER-WATERLOO
The Alzheimer Society of Kitchener-Waterloo provides, without cost to user, information and education, support group, wandering person registry, speakers' bureau and referral to appropriate community resources. Resource Centre, 121 Park Street, Waterloo, Monday to Thursday 9:00 a.m. - 4:30 p.m., Friday 9:00 a.m. - 1:00 p.m. For information call 742-1422.

K-W SKATING CLUB
The Kitchener-Waterloo Skating Club offers programmes starting at Learn to Skate. Programmes include CanSkate, Figure Skating, Dance and Precision (Team) skating for children and adults. For further information call the club office at 866-KWSC (5972).

76

Figure 39.1: Sample pages from the Kitchener, Ontario leisure guide

WATERLOO REGION

We're not promoting our attractions

Let people know about good hiking trails, and our museums

BY HOWARD BURTON
FOR THE RECORD

Each week, staff at Perimeter Institute for Theoretical Physics in Waterloo spend a considerable amount of time putting together a list of interesting events in Waterloo Region and beyond for our team of visiting and permanent scientists.

The staff members add updates to our standard visitor packages that include features on regional hiking, camping, sports, music, dance, transportation links to Toronto and other information of interest to our well-traveled, international clientele who may be in Waterloo, if not Canada, for the first time.

You might wonder why a theoretical physics institute should have to do this. So do we.

Waterloo Region does not do the best job promoting itself. That's rather curious for an environment so dependent on attracting and retaining young, sophisticated professionals. Competing for top talent is a difficult business in all sectors, and particularly so in the internationally competitive fields of high-tech, insurance and academe that clearly drive essential aspects of the local economy.

If it is hard enough to recruit dynamic, cosmopolitan people to a small community in southwestern Ontario; it is considerably harder without established community support to highlight all the attractive features that can be enjoyed.

Now that municipal and regional elections are behind us, it is time to make a concerted promotional effort, with all three cities and the region addressing the issue. There is an overwhelming need for slick, coherent regional information packages geared to young professionals, dynamic, informative websites of upcoming events and activities, and coordinated activities to better recruit doctors and other essential workers to the area.

Such people are generally not interested in quilt festivals or bake sales. But they are invariably impressed by the remarkable quality of the local classical music scene, the developing theatre scene, attractive surrounding countryside with cycling and hiking trails, unique regional attractions, such as the Waterloo Regional Children's Museum and Langdon Hall, and stimulating aspects of the greater area, ranging from Toronto to Stanford, Niagara and north to Bruce Peninsula.

Many people do recognize that much more could be done to promote the region coherently.

In Waterloo, for example, there is a group of people who support the creation of a local tourist office. This is a very positive idea and efforts on this front should be co-ordinated with similar initiatives from Kitchener, Cambridge and the region to eliminate redundancy and strengthen the case for the entire area.

Unfortunately, however, there is a notion to locate this tourist office in the old Waterloo train station near Waterloo Park. This would be a large mistake.

One benefit of being involved in regional promotion is the need to look afresh at one's home town from an outside perspective, thereby exposing not only its strengths and possibilities, but also its weaknesses.

Let us look at Waterloo, the city I call home personally and professionally. What impression does a visiting scientist typically have when she arrives in uptown Waterloo for a stay at the Perimeter Institute?

Here is a small university town with one main street somewhat removed from both campuses, a few isolated coffee shops (virtually none with an outdoor patio in the summer), a rather surprising number of enjoyable restaurants in fairly close proximity, an old, uninspiring '50s-style shopping centre significantly breaking up the flow of the core, a plethora of parking lots, some interesting shops on Regina Street and a good repertory cinema. That's about it.

This is Waterloo's reality. People don't come here and gasp at the beauty of the environs, even by regional standards. It is not as attractive as Galt and doesn't have nearly the appeal of Stratford.

But Waterloo has two very important aspects: the dynamism of the nearby universities and the sense of overarching potential for an exciting and vibrant future.

Back now to the Waterloo train station. Examine the surroundings: a location directly between two new, well-funded, international institutes (Centre for International Governance Innovation and Perimeter Institute) and a national gallery (The Canadian Clay and Glass gallery), with an enormous tract of land for development to the west, a parking lot to the immediate south and a beautiful park a short walk away which naturally links the uptown core to both the University of Waterloo and Wilfrid Laurier University.

What an opportunity. It's not too hard to imagine this entire area as a spectacular destination spot, complete with several cafés and public spaces. Not to take advantage of this once-in-a-lifetime opportunity would be absurd—most cities would be green with envy.

Yet this is precisely where some believe we should simply put down a tourist kiosk—at the expense of potential cafés, shops and the possibility of creating a delightful magnet for both residents and visitors.

The irony is devastating. By slapping a tourist booth in the most promising area of the city, we are actually denying that area a chance to achieve its promise. The phrase "build it and they will come" only works if the "it" is something people will want to come to.

The notion that hordes of tourists will flock to a tourist information booth just because it is there is almost Kafkaesque. Let us instead give people a reason to come to the locale and then capitalize on their presence with a tourist office.

So build the tourist office—but move it there after the area has developed appropriately. Build it adjacent to the public spaces, the cafés, the new galleries and boutiques.

This is not a pipe dream. The Waterloo train station and its immediate environs have been eyed by several private-sector interests for quite some time. They are not looking for handouts or subsidies, merely a chance to capitalize on a well-recognized opportunity. And they are not getting a chance to contribute to something that would benefit all of us.

This is a big opportunity, but it is hardly a mega-project. No large expenditures of public monies are involved. Quite the contrary. The City of Waterloo stands to gain considerably from the added tax revenue and economic growth.

What is needed now is strong vision and guidance from city officials to ensure the locale can fulfill its potential.

Let's promote our region as coherently and as intelligently as we can, putting our best foot forward to attract top talent in diverse fields from around the world. But let's also not forget to move forward aggressively to seize the opportunities to ensure that we always have something special to promote.

Figure 39.2: Plea from a citizen regarding more systematic promotion of leisure attractions

In a bold move, the leisure services board of the fictional community of Singleton, NS has decided to implement a recreation voucher scheme. The City Council has decided that instead of directly providing $100 of tax-supported recreation services for each city resident, that it will provide $75 in recreation services per resident and rebate the remaining $25 to each resident in the form of a recreational voucher. Residents can apply their $25 to defray the cost of participation at any eligible outlet (public or private). Eligible outlets were chosen from the range, broadly defined, of recreation agencies and businesses operating in the municipality.

Critique the list of redeemable options. Who else should be eligible? Why? Who should not be eligible? Why? What other positive and negative aspects of this system are apparent? Can you come to a reasonable resolution that would allow you to support this system and make it viable over the long term?

Healthylife Fitness Centre	Jerry's Winning Bingo Parlour
Susan T's School of Music and Art	Women's Fitness Club
Evangeline Golf and Country Club	Celtic Music House
The YMCA of Singleton	Acadian Heritage Dance Studios
Yellow Rose Garden Supplies	Backman Racquet Club
Burger Queen Restaurant	Singleton Syncro Swim Centre
Jerome's Studio of Jazz	Tap Dawg's Dance Studio
Singleton Recreation Complex	Ballet World Dance Studios
Campus Billiards	Grinder's Hockey Skating School
Amy's Escort Service	Lighthouse Fish and Chips
Yuen Wa Chinese Restaurant	Alberta Steak House
Woodley's Alternative Cinema	Rita's Highlands Pub
Rollerama Rollerskating	Nila's Sporting Goods Emporium
Singleton Pool and Fitness Centre	Singleton Figure Skating Club
Paul's Outdoor Recreation Gear	Singleton Symphony Orchestra
Maritime Ski Club	Hockman's Seaside Resort
Singleton Arena	Revolutionary Night Club
Ronnie Mac's Waterpark	Magic Sun Tanning Spa
Sky Taxi Balloon Rides	Moose and Elk Pub
Galactica Movie Plex	Laurene's Art and Craft Supply
MacKay's House of Scallops	Smith's Paintball Palace
Sandstone Curling Club	Seaside Campground
Marcia's Mini-Putt Golf	C. DeMar Track and Field Club
Ron's Bicycle Shop	Singleton Community Theatre

The Complementary Assets of Public Agencies and Business Enterprises

Partnerships and collaborative efforts often make sense because different partners possess different strengths. Crompton (1999) argued that the primary assets of public sector agencies include their extensive land holdings, their ability to raise capital at low costs, and their control over zoning and permit processes. By contrast, commercial sector strengths include their ability to raise money (capital), specialized management expertise, reduced labour costs, and their ability to adapt to change.

Partnerships between Public Agencies and Business Enterprises

The Canadian Municipal Public-private Partnerships (1996) inventory identified 163 projects with collective capital budgets of $3.16 billion and operating budgets of $232 million. Recreation was the largest category, accounting for 30% of these projects, though they tended to be much smaller in financial scope than were projects in categories related to water, transportation, and solid waste. Public-private partnerships were disproportionately concentrated in Ontario, British Columbia, and Nova Scotia. Common venues for partnerships of this type include arenas, sport and entertainment complexes, golf courses, indoor athletic fields (e.g., soccer), marinas, aquatics centres, and ski areas. Davies (2001) documented an exemplary case of an innovative London, Ontario skate park in which citizen groups, unions, businesses, and public sector leisure service agencies worked together for the common good.

As you might expect, venues such as arenas, sports complexes, and concession services that lend themselves to revenue generation are the most likely candidates for public-private partnership consideration. More radical ideas have been explored, however. In the 1990s, one Canadian community, Ingersol, Ontario, developed an arrangement whereby its entire recreation program was contracted to a private sector company. The private operator believed that profit could be made by operating these programs and the city believed it could save money by operating through that company. This arrangement is no longer in effect, however (Havitz & Glover, 2001).

The most common criticism of public-private partnerships generally relates to issues of equity and access. Private sector companies are typically less concerned than the public sector in ensuring access to programs for citizens. While revenue generation and cost savings are often paramount concerns for the private sector, they may be secondary for public sector providers. For example, the public sector may knowingly lose money on a facility or program to ensure that it is available at fee levels that most citizens can pay. While this is a legitimate measure for the public sector, it would be frowned upon by most private sector operators because their livelihood is not subsidized by tax revenue.

Intergovernmental Partnerships

It is sometimes advantageous for multiple government agencies to work together to provide services. These arrangements can take many forms. For example, a leisure services agency might partner with a police agency to deal with youth crime, partner with a long-term care facility to provide services for older adults, and partner with a school district to encourage community access to school facilities. Leisure service agencies sometimes partner with other leisure service agencies. Based on his work with a number of rural and small-town agencies in Alberta, Glover (1999) developed four guidelines for success in such arrangements. First, a municipality should enter an inter-municipal partnership only when it requires the assistance of another municipality to achieve its aims. Partnerships may be time-consuming and difficult to implement so agencies should be selective in this regard. Second, municipalities should only consider forming inter-municipal partnerships with municipalities that are located within close proximity. In urban contexts, recreation participation that requires daily travel of more than 15–20 minutes each way is difficult to maintain over the long term. Although these time frames may be stretched a bit in rural contexts, time and travel costs are consistently among the most frequently cited constraints to recreation participation especially when factored in with the broader array of time constraints stemming from perceptions of the pace of life (Scott, 2005; also see Chapter 9). Third, a municipality should form an inter-municipal partnership only if it has something that its partner(s) value(s) and which it can afford to share. This could take the form of a recreation facility, staff resources, or any number of things. Finally, a municipality should have the approval of its municipal council and broad support from its citizens/residents before entering an inter-municipal partnership. It is much better to build these relationships from the bottom-up than to impose them from the top-down.

Less-Than-Fee Simple Arrangements

Ownership of a parcel of land can be thought of as a "bundle of rights." Owners may sell or bequeath land, restrict access, erect buildings and structures on it, and use it for recreation, crop production, mineral extraction and so forth. Taken as a group, these rights constitute ownership in fee simple. Most private property in Canada is owned in fee simple. For example, a fee simple home owner who wishes to paint her house, cut down a tree, set up an outdoor clothesline, build a deck, prohibit people from snowmobiling across her back lawn, or sever a lot off of her side lawn to sell to another individual can normally do so unless there are specific by-laws in her community prohibiting those things. A less-than-fee interest consists of one or more rights or specifically defined parts of rights (Crompton, 1999). As such, less-than-fee simple arrangements in the context of leisure service delivery refer to rights given up by a private landowner for the benefit of society or (special) rights given to the general citizenry to which they would not normally be entitled with respect to private property. For example, the woman may sign a 100-year agreement with the municipality which allows members of the general citizenry to cross her property on snowmobiles. She no longer owns the property in fee simple, because she has given up the right to prohibit people from crossing certain parts of her property. Likewise, the next owner of the property will also own it in less-than-fee simple, because the 100-year agreement is likely to span most or all of his or her lifetime as well. The municipality does not own the property in fee simple either. All they own is the right to allow members of the general citizenry to cross what would normally be private property.

Sometimes leisure services agencies cannot afford to acquire desired parkland in fee simple (by purchasing the property or through exactions or so forth). In these cases, less-than-fee simple arrangements may be the only feasible way to achieve desired goals. Less-than-fee-simple ownership of public open space is often desirable because: the cost of fee-simple acquisition may be prohibitive, maintenance of fee-simple property is at taxpayer expense whereas land remains on tax roles if less-than-fee-simple methods are used, and less-than-fee-simple is less disruptive to existing uses. From among the many options available, three will be introduced here: zoning, easements, and differential taxation.

Zoning is perhaps the most visible form of less-than-fee simple control of land for leisure purposes, among other things. Zoning is a type of by-law passed for land use control in Canadian municipalities. Canadian zoning by-laws have three general functions (Town of East Gwillimbury, 1997): (1) they implement the objectives and policies of a municipality's official plan; (2) they provide a legal way of managing land use and future development (e.g., environmental restrictions on residential property adjacent to creeks and rivers for the health of those watercourses); and (3) they protect citizens from conflicting and possibly dangerous land uses in the community (e.g., placement of truck terminals adjacent to schools or parks).

Zoning by-laws are not necessarily permanent. Indeed, all Canadian municipalities have the right to amend their zoning by-laws unless doing so interferes with vested rights inherent in land ownership or if statutory restrictions prohibit such changes. The power to rezone, for example, cannot be used to enable councils to acquire property for a park or other public purposes at advantageous prices (Rogers, 1996). Citizens are also afforded the right to appeal zoning laws. In fact, some zoning by-laws have been challenged in the courts. For example, by-laws that controlled the establishment of group homes by allowing their conditional use in certain areas have been determined unconstitutional according to the Canadian Charter of Rights and Freedoms because they discriminated against disadvantaged people (Rogers, 1996).

Another less-than-fee simple approach is the purchase easement. Easements can be perpetual (indefinite in length) or set for a fixed term (normally a period of 5–15 years in Canada). They can also be "affirmative" or "negative." An affirmative easement allows people to do something they might not normally be able to do. For example, a park agency could purchase an affirmative easement from a private landowner allowing the general public to cross the property to access a boat launch site on a lake or river. By contrast, the agency may purchase a negative easement from some land owners to prevent them from doing something that would normally be within their power such as removing a stand of mature trees, thus preserving the character of the privately owned open space adjacent to a park. Although not always the case, easements tend to reduce the value of private property because they restrict the rights of current property owners and potential purchasers with respect to what they can do with the land.

Differential tax assessment involves situations when the government chooses to tax private property at a level less than what might be expected to preserve open space. This is usually done to prevent landowners, for example farmers, from converting land at the edge of a growing city into forms, such as housing developments, that would make more money but could potentially mean that valuable open space might be lost. There are three types of differential tax assessment. Under pure preferential taxation, property is assessed on current use, not market value. This is extremely popular among landowners because there is no penalty for conversion to development. The second option, differential taxation, is similar to pure preferential taxation in that the private property is assessed on current use, but taxes are deferred. The penalty for early withdrawal normally requires a landowner to pay full taxes for the past for two to five years, plus interest. Finally, under restrictive agreements, land is assessed on the basis of current use. Land must remain in the program for the term of the contract, usually 10 years. Differential taxation, whatever the form employed, is often criticized because it encourages speculation, given that developers usually purchase years in advance anyway. Critics argue that differential taxation just gives land owners an unwarranted tax break in the meantime.

The creation of greenways represents one of the current trends in park planning at both the national and local levels. "One of the most fundamental principles of conservation is that there should be a system of natural corridors across the landscape, interspersed with large core natural areas. These core and corridor areas provide an inter-connected web of natural habitats" (Ontario Nature, 2006). Greenways would be prohibitively expensive for a city or province to develop exclusively using public funds for at least two reasons: the money involved in acquiring and maintaining the land, and the loss of tax revenue if huge tracts of urban land are preserved as public property. Therefore, greenways are often constructed by cobbling together public lands and private lands using easements, differential taxation and the like, to create contiguous recreation space. The most common application of greenway principles in Canada has been with respect to the development of urban trails linking parks, subdivisions, and transportation corridors. The now under-construction Trans Canada Trail, which will be the longest trail in the world, is a spectacular example of a greenway on a large scale. Greenways are not without controversy, however. The Ontario Greenbelt, intended to guide development in the area surrounding metro Toronto, has been simultaneously praised and criticized by various communities, business interests, and citizens (Toronto Star, 2004a, 2004b).

Think of your own community. Identify a piece of "undeveloped" property that might be useful for some type of recreation facility or service, potential parkland, playing fields, community centre, etc. Assume that the municipality does not have the means to purchase the property in fee simple. Which of the less-than-fee simple options outlined above would be the best "acquisition tool" in this case? Why?

Putting It All Together: Budgeting

Budgeting is perceived as very important by recreation professionals (Crompton, 1999), but professionals have traditionally felt that their competency in this area is low (Smale & Frisby, 1992). In simple terms, budgets are projections of how and where resources will be allocated, most often expressed in terms of how much money will be spent, over a given time period. Most agencies and businesses have at least three types of budgets with which they are simultaneously concerned: (1) *cash budgets,* which depict inflows and outflows of cash, and for which issues like seasonality are especially critical for many recreation agencies and businesses; (2) *capital budgets,* which are developed for major equipment purchases, facility construction and renovation and normally spread over a number of years; and (3) *operating budgets,* which guide the affairs of an agency or business (program development and implementation, salaries and wages, taxes, hydro, etc.) and are usually developed on an annual basis. The major focus of this section will be on operating budgets.

Budgetary monitoring and control is important. Most agencies and businesses review operating budgets on a monthly or quarterly basis. Because each type of budget has its own time-schedule, cash, capital and operating budgetary outcomes may not always be in sync. For example, sometimes it happens that major facilities (say an arena or community centre) near completion in a year when the agency's operating budget is being scaled back and personnel are being cut. This may occur because the capital budget for the project was developed some five to ten years prior, when the economy was strong and demand projections high.

The remainder of discussion in this chapter will focus on operating budgets. Personnel generally represent the largest line item (or set of line items) in service industry and agency contexts. Personnel issues such as wages, salaries and benefits may account for between 50 to 90% of the expenses for many agencies. It is important to note that this would be for the agency as a whole unit, however. Individual facilities, such as arenas, would likely have a much lower ratio if staffing requirements are minimal and operating expenses such as hydro and gas costs are high. Most agencies' operating budgets will include both a listing of expected expenses and a listing of expected revenues. In the interest of conserving space, however, the sample budgets presented here will include only the expenses side of the ledger.

Line-item budgets include a detailed listing of each expense or revenue source anticipated by an agency or facility. Figure 39.3 depicts a line-item budget for the arena in the fictional town of Howeville, SK. An actual line-item budget for a facility of this type would likely be longer and more detailed than depicted here. For example, the "Facility external (landscaping)" line could be broken down to include separate lines for trees, flowerbeds, lawns and so forth. Each of those could be broken down further by specifying costs for planting, watering, trimming, and so forth.

Line-item is the simplest form of budgeting. Like most forms of budgeting, line-item budgets are generally "incremental" because they use the previous budget as a point of departure. For example, Figure 39.3 allows comparisons of the previous year's budget with the future budget. Assuming objectives are static, it is easy to add or cut budgets using a line-item format (–2 or +3% "across the board" and so forth). The "line-item veto" may make budget cutting more "efficient" and are often preferred by executives because it allows them to delete budget items literally line-by-line. The line-item veto tends not to be as popular among lower level managers and staff. Line-item budgets are poor at revealing the "big picture," that is, how budget cuts or additions might affect the agency's programs and services. For better or worse, because they are incremental they also tend to perpetuate the status quo. In this case, no across the board additions were made. Rather, some items were adjusted upward or downward to reflect changing budget priorities or inflationary pressures. Likewise, there is no evidence of a line-item veto in Figure 39.3.

Program budgets go by several names (e.g., program-based, program planning based). Program-based budgets are similar to line-item budgets in form, with the exception that the resultant line-items are subdivided by program (Figure 39.4, p. 374). Program budgets can provide performance measures related to employee workload, efficiency, and effectiveness. Program budgets are superior to line-item budgets in that they focus better on the "big picture" and/or outputs. As such, they are a more effective management tool because they more clearly show the effect of additions and cuts than do line-item budgets. Like line-item budgets, program budgets are incremental in nature and, because they take more time and effort to develop, are more costly to produce than are line-item budgets.

Rather than relying on staff to submit a wish list of program needs every year and building the budget to an unknown level, many agencies now use target-base budgeting (TBB), also called envelope or entrepreneurial budgeting.

Line Item	Year A Actual	Year B Estimate
Manager salary (1 full-time)	$ 60,000	$ 62,000
Salary (custodian)	$ 40,000	$ 41,000
Salary (programmer)	$ 42,000	$ 43,000
Salary (full-time equipment operator)	$ 38,000	$ 38,500
Wages (2 part-time equipment operators)	$ 18,000	$ 19,000
Wages (6 part-time rink guards)	$ 30,000	$ 31,000
Benefits (OMERS)	$ 5,800	$ 6,000
Benefits (CPP—Canada Pension Plan)	$ 4,500	$ 4,800
Benefits (UI—Unemployment Insurance)	$ 4,900	$ 5,300
Benefits (EHT—Employer Health Tax)	$ 2,900	$ 3,000
Benefits (Extended Health)	$ 2,400	$ 2,500
Benefits (Long Term Disability)	$ 900	$ 1,000
Benefits (Dental)	$ 2,400	$ 2,600
Benefits (Group Life)	$ 400	$ 400
Utilities (electricity and water)	$195,000	$210,000
Utilities (natural gas)	$ 50,000	$ 58,000
Facility internal (insurance)	$ 13,700	$ 14,500
Facility internal (market research)	$ 4,000	$ 3,500
Facility internal (promotion)	$ 12,500	$ 13,000
Facility internal (uniforms)	$ 1,000	$ 1,000
Facility internal (programming supplies)	$ 2,000	$ 2,500
Facility internal (maintenance supplies)	$ 15,000	$ 16,000
Facility internal (equipment/materials)	$ 27,700	$ 27,000
Facility external (parking/signage/snow removal)	$ 15,500	$ 15,000
Facility external (landscaping)	$ 8,200	$ 2,000
Totals	**$596,800**	**$622,600**

Figure 39.3. Line-item budget for Howeville, SK's "Mr. Hockey Arena"

Under a TBB system, the executive director sets a budget ceiling for the agency then turns authority for developing and implementing programs and services to agency staff members, who operate within the established budget limits.

Most operating budget cycles are annual in nature although they don't necessarily follow the calendar year (Figure 39.5). For example, a leisure services agency or business may choose to start the budget year just prior to the busiest season similar to the way that school systems often start the budget year with the onset of fall term. The budget process should include both visioning components and practical components. There is a tendency to allow the latter to take precedence as details are worked out with an eye on the all-important bottom line, though in reality the former is critical to maintaining the integrity and relevance of an agency because a budget represents not only financial policy but also a political plan.

After reviewing the information provided in Figures 39.3 and 39.4, which budget format, Line Item or Program-Based, would you prefer if you were manager of the Howeville Arena? Support your answer in as much detail as possible.

Summary

The past two chapters have outlined how agencies traditionally receive or collect financial resources (taxes, exactions, user fees), supplement them with non-traditional sources (sponsorships, foundation grants), minimizing expenditures while maximizing effectiveness (partnerships and facilitative approaches with a variety of private and public agencies). Achieving the optimal balance is difficult because political, economic, and social forces are constantly in a state of flux. Nevertheless, it is important that potential leisure services professionals have a solid understanding of the aforementioned variables, tools, and mechanisms and that this knowledge is integrated with the personal and professional values that guide decisions.

Line Item	Public Skate ***	Minor Hockey***	Men's Hockey	Women's Hockey***	Figure Skating
Manager salary (1 full-time)**	6,200	31,000	16,500	3,100	6,200
Salary (custodian)	4,100	20,500	10,250	2,050	4,100
Salary (programmer)	4,300	21,500	10,750	2,150	4,300
Salary (full-time equipment operator)	3,850	19,250	9,625	1,925	3,850
Wages (2 part-time equipment operators)	1,900	9,500	4,750	950	1,900
Wages (8 part-time rink guards)	31,000	—	—	—	—
Benefits (Provincial retirement plan)	600	3,000	1,500	300	600
Benefits (CPP—Canada Pension Plan)	480	2,400	1,200	240	480
Benefits (UI—Unemployment Insurance)	530	2,650	1,325	265	530
Benefits (EHT—Employer Health Tax)	300	1,500	750	150	300
Benefits (Extended Health)	250	1,250	313	125	250
Benefits (Long Term Disability)	100	500	250	50	100
Benefits (Dental)	260	1,300	650	130	260
Benefits (Group Life)	40	200	100	20	40
Utilities (electricity and water)	21,000	105,000	52,500	10,500	21,000
Utilities (natural gas)	5,800	29,000	14,500	2,900	5,800
Facility internal (insurance)	1,450	7,250	3,625	725	1,450
Facility internal (market research)	350	1,750	875	175	350
Facility internal (promotion)	1,300	6,500	3,250	650	1,300
Facility internal (uniforms)	100	500	250	50	100
Facility internal (programming supplies)	250	1,250	625	125	250
Facility internal (maintenance supplies)	1,600	8,000	4,000	800	1,600
Facility internal (equipment/materials)	2,700	13,500	6,750	1,350	2,700
Facility external (parking/signage/snow removal)	1,500	7,500	3,750	750	1,500
Facility external (landscaping)	200	1,000	500	100	200
Totals	**90,160**	**295,800**	**147,900**	**29,080**	**59,160**

* In-house expenses only. Does not include budgets for voluntary organizations (e.g., Howeville Minor Hockey, Skate Howeville, Howeville Adult Hockey Association).

** Pro-rated, where appropriate, on the basis of ice-time used by each program.

*** These three programs are partially subsidized by tax dollars. Men's Hockey and Figure Skating are not directly subsidized, so user fees must cover all costs as noted.

Figure 39.4: Program-based budget for the Howeville Arena, year B*

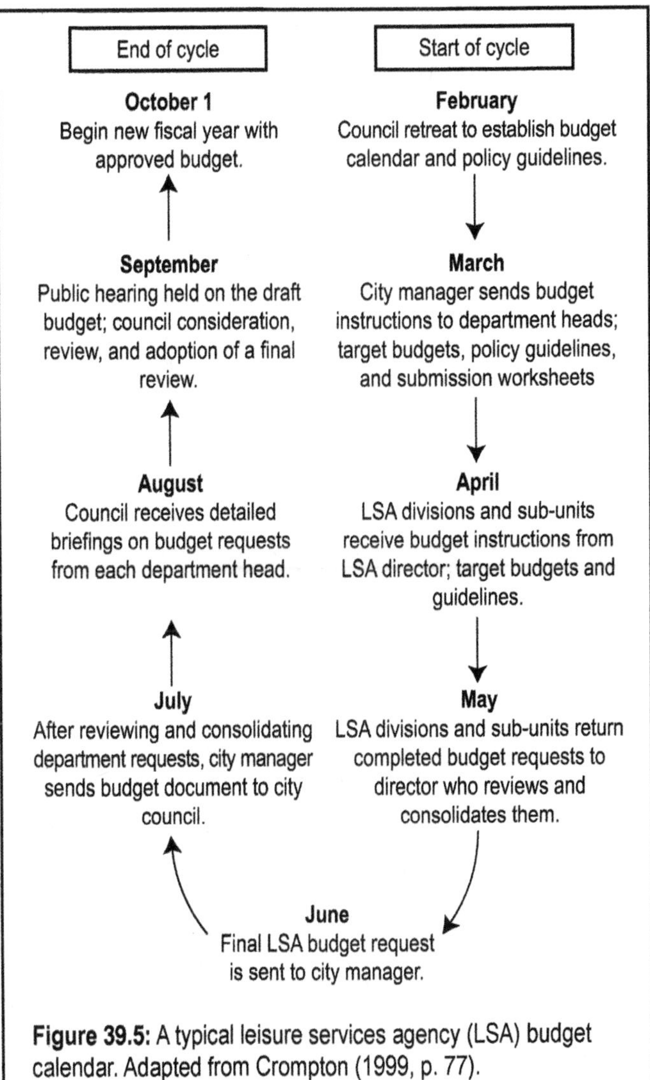

Figure 39.5: A typical leisure services agency (LSA) budget calendar. Adapted from Crompton (1999, p. 77).

Key Terms

Co-production
Facilitation
Less-than-fee simple
Line item, program-base
Partnerships
Target-base budgeting

References

Arai, S. (1996). Benefits of citizen participation in a healthy communities initiative: Linking community development and empowerment. *Journal of Applied Recreation Research, 21*, 25–44.

Canadian Municipal Public-Private Partnerships. (1996). *An inventory* (97 pp.). Halifax, NS: Government of Nova Scotia Press.

Crompton, J. L. (1999). *Financing and acquiring park and recreation resources*. Champaign, IL: Human Kinetics.

Davies, C. (2001). Community, union, and city government: Partners in skatepark building—London, Ontario [Online, Chapter 8]. In M. E. Havitz & T. D. Glover, *Financing and acquiring public park, recreation and open space resources in Canada* [On-line]. Champaign, IL: Human Kinetics.

Glover, T. D. (1999). Municipal park and recreation agencies unite! A single case analysis of an inter-municipal partnership. *Journal of Park and Recreation Administration, 17*(1), 73–90.

Havitz, M. E., & Glover, T. D. (2001). *Financing and acquiring public park, recreation and open space resources in Canada* [On-line]. Champaign, IL: Human Kinetics.

Hutchison, P., & Nogradi, G. (1996). The concept and nature of community development in recreation and leisure services. *Journal of Applied Recreation Research, 21*, 93–130.

Ontario Nature. (2006). Greenway: Breath easy, greenway ahead! Retrieved from http://www.ontarionature.org/enviroandcons/greenway/index.html

Pedlar, A. (1996). Community development: What does it mean for recreation and leisure. *Journal of Applied Recreation Research, 21*, 5–23.

Reid, D., & van Dreunnen, E. (1996). Leisure as a social transformation mechanism in community development practice. *Journal of Applied Recreation Research, 21*, 45–65.

Rogers, I. M. (1996). *The law of Canadian municipal corporations* (2nd ed.). Toronto, ON: Carswell.

Scott, D. (2005). The relevance of constraints research to leisure service delivery. In E. L. Jackson (Ed.), *Constraints to leisure* (pp. 279–293). State College, PA: Venture Publishing, Inc.

Smale, B. J. A., & Frisby, W. (1992). Managerial work activities and perceived competencies of municipal recreation managers. *Journal of Park and Recreation Administration, 19*(4), 81–108.

Town of East Gwillimbury. 1997. Citizen's Guides: Zoning by-laws. Retrieved from http://www.town.eastgwillimbury.on.ca/municipl

Toronto Star. (2004a, November 7). Greenbelt project good for Ontario. Editorial, p. A12.

Toronto Star. (2004b, November 8). Opposition to Greenbelt plan grows. Opinion, p. A17.

Chapter 40
Volunteering in Canada

Sandra J. Corbin, B.E.S., M.A.
University of Waterloo

How Important Are Volunteers?

Volunteers contribute their time to perform a wide variety of tasks including food bank packers, sports coaches, special event workers, hospital visitors, board members and fund-raisers. What volunteers do you know and what impact have they had on your life?

Learning Objectives

After reading this chapter, students will be able to

1. Appreciate the scope of volunteering in Canada.
2. Understand the influence of demographic characteristics on rates of volunteering.
3. Identify the kinds of organizations and activities in which Canadians volunteer.
4. Be aware of the motives and benefits reported by Canadian volunteers.
5. Appreciate the role of volunteers in the provision of leisure services.
6. Have knowledge of some current trends in volunteering.

Introduction

Volunteering is an important topic for leisure students and future practitioners because of its dual function as a leisure activity and a method of recreation and leisure service delivery. Whether they are operating sports clubs, delivering art programs, providing hands-on care or advocating for social change, volunteers touch virtually all aspects of community life in Canada. According to the 2000 National Survey on Giving, Volunteering and Participating (NSGVP), 6.5 million Canadians or 27% of the population ages 15 and older volunteered through an organization in the year preceding the survey (Hall, McKeown & Roberts, 2001). Canadians reported volunteering more than 2 billion hours to non-profit and voluntary organizations in 2003, an equivalent to more than 1 million full-time jobs (Statistics Canada, 2005). This makes Canada's voluntary sector the second largest in the world (Hall, Barr, Easwaramoorthy, Wojciech-Sokolowski, & Salamon, 2005). More than half of the approximately 161,000 Canadian non-profit and voluntary organizations are run entirely by volunteers. The value of volunteer work amounted to 1.4% of Canada's gross domestic product in 2000 (Statistics Canada, 2004).

What Is Volunteering?

Just as researchers have struggled with defining the concept of leisure, there are differences in attitudes and beliefs about volunteering. Traditionally, volunteering refers to any activity that is freely undertaken to benefit another person, group or cause (Johnstone, 2004; Van Til, 1988; Wilson, 2000). This view of volunteering emphasizes that it is an act of free will. Individuals volunteer because they choose to do so, and, for many, there is no expectation of remuneration or financial gain.

Recent changes in provincial legislation across Canada, and in other countries, however, have begun to challenge the traditional definition of volunteering. In Ontario, for example, provincial legislation requires students to complete 40 hours of community service as a condition of their graduation. Other legislation has created work for welfare schemes wherein recipients must undertake some form of work to collect their welfare benefits. For both students and welfare recipients, service in voluntary organizations has become a practical way of fulfilling their commitments. In addition, many jurisdictions offer people found guilty of minor criminal offences the choice of undertaking unpaid "community service" in lieu of serving time in an institution. Individuals who are mandated to volunteer for reasons such as these represent 8% of all Canadian volunteers (Lasby & McIver, 2004). While purists may challenge the notion that these individuals are in fact volunteering in the traditional sense, the contribution they make to the voluntary sector cannot be ignored.

Volunteering as Leisure

Volunteering and leisure share a number of common characteristics. Both are based on activities that are freely chosen, primarily intrinsically motivated and that can provide individual benefits such as self-actualization (Henderson & Presley, 2003) and increased self-esteem (Clary et al., 1998). However, the identification of an activity as leisure is subjective, so not everyone thinks of their volunteering as leisure. This perspective may stem, in part, from the view that leisure is simply for fun (Stebbins, 2001) or is linked to idleness or selfish behaviours (Bedini & Phoenix, 1999; Juniu, 2002). Those who hold these views may feel their volunteering would be trivialized if they called it leisure (Stebbins, 1998a). In spite of these perceptions, many people do experience their volunteering as leisure activity, and as such, it is important for us to understand who volunteers are, what they do, and why they do it (see Chapter 8).

Is Volunteering Leisure?

According to a study of volunteer community activists (Mair, 2002) the answer to this question is yes, no, and maybe. Most participants reported that their "real" leisure involved relaxing activities that refueled them for their volunteer activist work. Others suggested that their activist volunteering could sometimes be leisure because some events were enjoyable. As with many kinds of activities, volunteering may or may not be viewed as leisure depending on who is being asked and how they experience the activity.

Types of Volunteering

In *After Work: The Search for an Optimal Leisure Lifestyle*, Stebbins (1998b) identified 16 types of organizational volunteers, including those he called career volunteers, who engaged in the activity as serious leisure (see Chapter 9). More recently, Arai (2000) suggested a typology of volunteers based on factors such as the individuals' understanding of their volunteer organization and their involvement in decision-making processes. Formal or organizational volunteering is activity undertaken through a voluntary group or through a public or private institution. Coaching a minor league baseball team or being a volunteer member of a local Parks Board are two examples of this type of volunteering. Volunteering may also be informal and refers to any unpaid work a person undertakes on his or her own to support another. Almost 77% of Canadians contributed their time informally to assist others. The most commonly reported activities of this type were shopping and driving others to appointments, performing housework, baby-sitting, and doing home maintenance or yard work for others (Hall et al., 2001).

A Profile of Canada's Volunteers

In 2000, Statistics Canada's National Survey on Giving, Volunteering and Participating (NSGVP) provided us with a profile of the contributions Canadians made to one another and to their communities. The results of this survey reflect how the extent of involvement in volunteering by individuals is influenced by a variety of factors including gender, age, marital status, household status, education, employment status, and income. The following section will explore some of the differences between Canadian volunteers based on these factors (Hall et al., 2001).

According to the 2000 NSGVP survey, Canadian women volunteered at a slightly higher rate than men (28% versus 25%) but contributed fewer hours on average (155 versus 170 hours). Comparing these findings to those in the previous NSGVP survey, both men and women were volunteering in smaller numbers than in 1997. However, those who were choosing to volunteer were contributing more hours than before.

In 2000, the rate of volunteering was higher for youth (29% for those aged 15-24) and those in mid-adult years (30% for those aged 35-54) than for other age groups. Canadians aged 64 years and over volunteered at the lowest rate (18%), but contributed the highest number of hours, on average, over the year. Generally, the average time spent volunteering increased with age from a low of 130 hours for those ages 15 to 24 to a high of 269 hours for those 65 and over. Compared to the 1997 NSGVP, the volunteer rate has declined for all age groups. These trends indicate that while some people were spending more hours on their volunteering, not as many people were choosing to volunteer. In 2000, married people reported the highest rate of volunteering (28%) and widowed Canadians the lowest (17%). Volunteers who were widowed, or who were separated or divorced gave more hours (253 and 181 hours respectively) than those who were married (175) or single (126).

Since 1997, fewer people have been choosing to volunteer; however, those people who do are volunteering more hours. What factors might be influencing this trend?

Households with children tend to have higher rates of volunteering. Almost one of every three Canadians (32%) in a household with children under the age of 18 years volunteered. Canadians without children in the household volunteered at a lower rate (24%). Volunteers with children in the household, however, contributed fewer hours on average (150) compared to those without children (168).

The 2000 NSGVP survey also suggested that volunteering participation tends to increase with years of formal education. Canadians with at least some post-secondary education volunteered at a higher rate than those with less education. Individuals with a university degree reported the highest rate of volunteer participation, at 39%. One-third of Canadian volunteers who reported having at least some post-secondary education contributed the most hours on average (173 hours). In the years between 1997 and 2000, all but one education group reported an increase in the average number of hours volunteered. The exception was individuals who reported having a high school diploma; they decreased their volunteering time by an average of nine hours between 1997 and 2000.

The majority of volunteers in Canada are employed; however, according to the NSGVP 2000, part time workers reported volunteering at a higher rate than those who worked full time. While those volunteers not in the labour force, such as students and retirees, had lower rates of participation, they contributed, on average, the most number of hours (193). Between 1997 and 2000, the employment group with the largest change in volunteer hours was the unemployed, who reported an average increase of 54 hours.

Higher levels of household income increase the likelihood of volunteering. Only 17% of people with household incomes under $20,000 volunteered compared to 39% of those with incomes of $100,000 or more. Conversely, the average number of hours volunteered tended to decline with income. With an average of 207 hours, individuals with the lowest level of income volunteered the greatest amount of time. This group also reported the greatest change between 1997 and 2000, showing an average increase in volunteering time of 59 hours. Individuals with a household income of between $80,000 and $99,999 reported an average decrease in volunteering time of 1 hour during the same three-year period.

Volunteering in Rural Ontario

Where one lives can also have an impact on rates of volunteering. A recent report on volunteering in rural Ontario revealed that people who lived in small towns and rural areas had higher rates of volunteering than people who lived in urban areas. For example, 35% of rural volunteers contributed to culture, arts and recreation organizations compared to 24% in urban areas. (Barr, McKeown, Davidman, McIver, & Lasby, 2004)

Why might rural individuals volunteer more than people who live in larger communities?

How Do Volunteers Contribute?

Most of Canada's volunteers contribute their time to five major types of organizations: arts, recreation, and culture; social services; religious; education and research; and health. As shown in Table 40.1, arts, recreation, and culture organizations rank at the top of the list with the highest percentage of both volunteers and hours contributed. The 2000 NSGVP survey found that women are more likely to volunteer for health-related organizations (25%) while men are more attracted to arts, recreation, and culture organizations (39%).

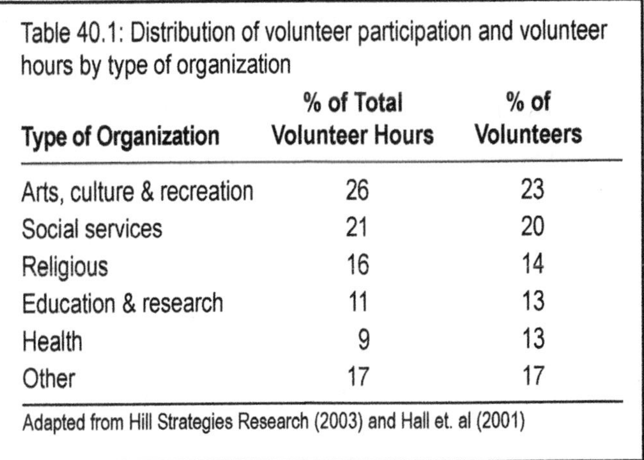

Table 40.1: Distribution of volunteer participation and volunteer hours by type of organization

Type of Organization	% of Total Volunteer Hours	% of Volunteers
Arts, culture & recreation	26	23
Social services	21	20
Religious	16	14
Education & research	11	13
Health	9	13
Other	17	17

Adapted from Hill Strategies Research (2003) and Hall et. al (2001)

In the 2000 NSGVP, volunteers were asked about their contribution to a number of general types of activities. More than half of all volunteers (57%) reported that they helped organize or supervise events or activities for an organization. Other activities that reported high participation included sitting as a board member (41%), canvassing, campaigning, and/or fund-raising (40%) and providing office assistance in an organization (30%). As shown on Figure 40.1, other categories (e.g., teaching, coaching, support, and information

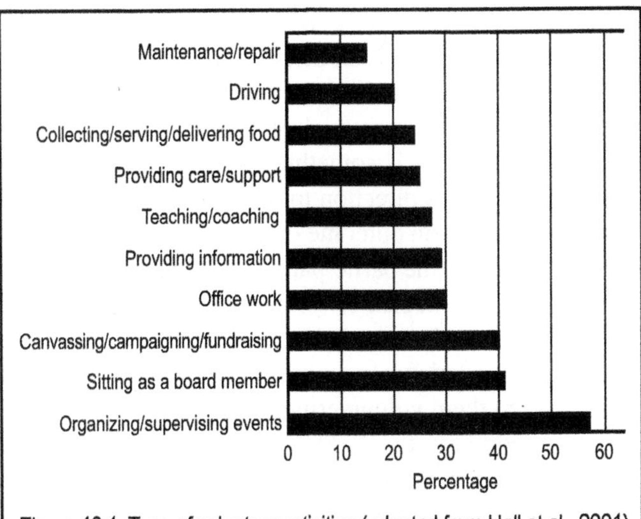

Figure 40.1. Type of volunteer activities (adapted from Hall et al., 2001)

services), reported less than 30% participation by volunteers (Hall et al., 2001).

While men and women tend to participate in the same kinds of volunteer activities there are some differences worth noting (Canadian Centre for Philanthropy, 1998).

Women, for example, are more likely than men to:

- Canvass, campaign or fund-raise (47% versus 39%)
- Provide care or support (25% versus 21%)
- Collect service or deliver food (25% versus 21%)

Men on the other hand are more likely to:

- Teach or coach for an organization (30% versus 22%)
- Maintain, repair or build facilities (23% versus 9%)
- Drive for an organization (21% versus 17%)

How might gender expectations impact the activities men and women choose for their volunteering?

Why Do People Volunteer and How Might They Benefit from the Experience?

Individuals benefit from volunteering because it enhances their feelings of self-efficacy, self-worth and self-esteem (Omoto & Snyder, 2002), provides a sense of fulfillment (Tang & Weatherford, 1998), and helps to buffer depression and increase personal life satisfaction (Wilson, 2000). Volunteering also provides opportunities for self-determination, recreation, personal growth, and service to others (Twynam, Farrell, & Johnston, 2003). When exploring the specific benefits that individuals can derive from volunteering, it is important to examine their motives for volunteering as well. As Stebbins (2001) suggests, they are different sides of the same coin. A motive is something that drives a person to action and provides direction to that action once it is activated. A benefit is an outcome of that action that is identified as positive by the participating individual (Mannell & Kleiber, 1997). In the case of volunteering, motives are what drive people to volunteer and benefits are those outcomes that make the experience meaningful and satisfying for them and that keep them volunteering.

As reported in the 2000 NSGVP survey (Hall et al., 2001), the most common motivation for Canadian volunteers (95%) was that they valued the work being done by a particular organization and decided to help in that work. Other motives reported by volunteers included the desire to use their skills and experience (81%), being personally affected by the cause of the organization they support (69%), and the promise of acquiring job-related skills and improving job opportunities (23%). As noted previously, some (8%) individuals are motivated by extrinsic factors such as providing community service in exchange for a reward or to avoid punishment.

Benefits reported by volunteers in the 2000 NSGVP survey (Canadian Centre for Philanthropy, 2004a) included improved interpersonal skills (79%), improved communication skills (68%), and increased knowledge about issues related to their volunteering (63%). Also reported were increases in managerial, fund-raising, and technical or office skills.

Age Differences Related to Volunteer Motives and Benefits

Improving job opportunities through volunteering is a motive that decreases with age. In the 2000 NSGVP, 55 percent of volunteers 15–24 years of age reported it as a motive for their volunteering while only 6% of those over 65 did. Half of the volunteers over 65 years of age reported that their religious beliefs were an important motive (Canadian Centre for Philanthropy, 2004b). The 15 to 24 year age group was also more likely than older volunteers were to report improving their interpersonal (82%) and communication skills (77%) through their volunteering (Canadian Centre for Philanthropy, 2004a).

Why Do Some People Get Involved While Others Don't?

Lack of time is a major limiting factor to participation in many leisure activities and volunteering is no exception. In the 2000 NSGVP, 76% of volunteers reported lack of time as the primary reason they did not volunteer more. When non-volunteers were asked why they did not volunteer, 69% responded similarly, noting they did not have the time to volunteer. Many volunteers (34%) and non-volunteers (46%) are not willing to make a year round commitment to a voluntary organization (Hall et al., 2001). Non-volunteers also reported that they did not volunteer because they had not been personally asked (37%), or because they did not know how to get involved (20%). These two constraints are particularly strong for new Canadians (Canadian Centre for Philanthropy, 2004c) and those volunteers between the ages of 15 and 24 (Canadian Centre for Philanthropy, 2004d).

Volunteering as a Method of Leisure Service Delivery

For those practitioners and managers working in the arts, recreation, and culture sector, volunteers are an important part of the service delivery system. Whether it is setting up for a community festival or helping with neighbourhood leisure programming, many public sector agencies rely heavily on volunteer workers (Silverberg, Marshall, & Ellis, 2001). The public sector, however, is not the only provider of recreation and leisure services that depends on volunteers. Not-for-profit and voluntary organizations such as service clubs, minor sports groups, and recreation organizations also provide a wide variety of recreation and leisure services, especially in rural areas. In the not-for-profit and voluntary sector, reliance on volunteers is substantial with 63.1% of arts and culture organizations and 73.5% of sports and recreation groups having no paid staff (Hall et al., 2004). From the perspective of recruiting and managing these arts, recreation, and culture volunteers, it is essential that practitioners know who these volunteers are and in what ways, if any, they differ from volunteers in general.

Thinking back to your home community, what kind of organizations utilized volunteers to achieve their goals? How significant a part did those volunteers play in the organizations?

Who Are Canada's Arts, Recreation, and Culture Volunteers?

In 2003, arts, recreation, and culture organizations made up 39.4% of all non-profit and voluntary organizations (Statistics Canada, 2004). Volunteers in arts, recreation and culture organizations account for 32.5% of all Canadian volunteers and contribute 31.3% of all volunteer hours (Hall et al., 2004). In Where Canadians Volunteer, Lasby and McIver (2004) provide a profile of arts, recreation, and culture volunteers. They found that men make up 58% of the volunteers in arts, recreation, and culture organizations and individuals between the ages of 35 and 54 accounted for almost half of the volunteers in this sector. The impact of marital status and household income on volunteering in the arts, recreation, and culture sector mirrors the pattern these factors have on volunteering in general. That is, volunteers in arts, recreation, and culture were more likely to be married than not, and their rate of volunteering increases with income. Arts, recreation, and culture volunteers were slightly more likely than the general population of volunteers to volunteer because their friends did. Volunteers in this sector, especially those involved in sports organizations were also much more likely to say they became involved because of the involvement of their own children (Parks and Recreation Ontario, 2005). Rather than suggesting they have no time to volunteer, arts, culture, and recreation volunteers were more likely to say they did not want a year-round commitment to an organization.

Even within the arts, culture, and recreation volunteer sector, there are differences in volunteers based on the kinds of organizations for which they volunteer. Women make up a greater percentage of arts and culture volunteers than they do in the general volunteer population and they outnumber male volunteers in this sector by 16%. Arts and culture volunteers, on average, tend to be older (54% are 45+) and better educated than the general volunteer population (Hill Strategies Research Inc., 2003). The typical community sport volunteer has been described as male, aged 35-44, college or university educated, married with dependents, employed full time with a household income of $60–90,000 (Parks and Recreation Ontario, 2005).

Sport Volunteers in Saskatchewan

A 2002 survey of sports volunteers in Saskatchewan reported eight primary motives for volunteering. In order of importance the motives were: helping the community, helping others, social interaction, recognition and/or status, a belief that it was "the right thing to do," diversion from everyday activity, career advancement, and obligation. Motives of social interaction, diversion, recognition, and career advancement were stronger among younger volunteers (ages 15–24) than in older volunteers. Social interaction and helping others were stronger motives for women sport volunteers than for men. Men were slightly more likely than women to volunteer in sports organizations because they felt pressured by others (Canadian Centre for Philanthropy, 2002a).

Trends in Volunteering

As society changes so to do the values, interests, motives, and constraints experienced by volunteers. According to Linda Graff (2005), organizations that do not track changes in volunteering and adjust their volunteer management practices accordingly are doomed to suffer from myriad problems related to recruitment and retention of volunteers. The next section will examine a number of current trends that will impact volunteers and volunteer management in the near future.

Volunteering in Decline

From 1997 to 2000, the rate of volunteering in Canada decreased from 31% to 27% and the total number of hours volunteered declined by 5% (Hall et al., 2001). Volunteer organizations have reported that over the last 5 to 10 years, they have seen a considerable shrinking within the volunteer pool (Hall et al., 2003). Driven by the desire to achieve a balance between the numerous demands on their lives, many individuals are becoming increasingly thoughtful about why and with whom they volunteer (Graff, 2005).

Virtual Volunteering

Technological changes continue to have a significant impact on our lives and volunteering has not been immune to this trend. Volunteer based organizations are just beginning to examine how they can utilize information and communication technology to offer opportunities for virtual volunteering. Virtual volunteers are those who contribute their time and effort with an organization through an online connection rather than, or in addition to, onsite activities (Canadian Centre for Philanthropy, 2002b; Murray & Harrison, 2005). Virtual volunteers may undertake activities such as designing logos or posters, creating web pages or databases, research and fund-raising. While not yet widely used in Canada, virtual volunteering offers participation potential for individuals who might not be able to volunteer because of time constraints, the inability to travel, or a disability that excludes traditional volunteer opportunities.

Family Volunteering

Family volunteering describes volunteer activities that are carried out by members of a family as a joint activity. While family volunteering has been practiced for many years, it has only recently been acknowledged as a specific type of volunteering. Family volunteering is an attractive option for many time-crunched individuals because it allows them to contribute to the community while still spending time with their families (Reilly & Vesic, 2003). The distinction between family volunteering and "regular" volunteering is that family volunteering relates to volunteer work that is explicitly designed to accommodate either a group of people or adults and children together (Bowen & McKechnie, 2003). Family leisure activities, such as family volunteering, are said to be an important aspect of the overall quality of life for families and many parents believe that they play an important role in the socialization and development of their children (Shaw, 2001).

Research has shown that individuals who see their parents volunteer or who volunteer as children are more likely to care about others and to volunteer as adults (Flanagan, Bowles, Jonsson, Csapo, & Sheblanova, 1998; Hall et al., 2001; Wilson, 2000). As a result, for many organizations, accommodating family volunteering may be seen as an investment in a future pool of volunteers. Family volunteering can also be used as a mechanism to increase the diversity of an existing volunteer pool, especially in terms of broadening the age of its volunteer base (Bowen & McKechnie, 2003). Many organizations have realized, however, that implementing family volunteering programs may be costly to undertake because of the need to revisit and revamp existing volunteer management processes and structures that are based on the needs and interests of more conventional volunteers (Hegel & McKechnie, 2002).

Episodic Volunteering

Individuals are increasingly choosing not to tie themselves down to a long-term commitment through their volunteering. This has resulted in an increase in episodic volunteering. MacDuff (2005) identifies three main types of episodic volunteering: temporary, interim and occasional. Temporary volunteers are those who serve for only a short time, often a few days or hours. Interim volunteers work for the organization regularly but for a term of less than six months. Finally, the occasional volunteer works regularly but for short periods of time. All three types of episodic volunteering reflect a desire for more flexibility on the part of the volunteer to control their time commitment to the organization. Many organizations can and do accommodate many different levels of participation by volunteers. For organizations whose volunteers require extensive training or an extended commitment, this increase in episodic volunteering may be a challenge to ongoing recruitment efforts.

Conclusions

While the profiles of volunteers provided in this chapter reflect only a small portion of the information available from the NSGVP survey, they do underscore the necessity of viewing volunteers as individuals with specific needs and interests. As this chapter has shown, volunteers encompass a broad spectrum of backgrounds, contribute their time for a wide variety of reasons, and seek many different experiences and benefits. Whether encountered as leisure participants or leisure service providers, volunteers are most often seeking experiences that are both meaningful and satisfying. It is the role of a leisure practitioner to provide the opportunities and environment for volunteers to achieve an optimal leisure experience.

Key Terms

Episodic volunteering
Family volunteering
Virtual volunteering
Volunteering

References

Arai, S. M. (2000). Typology of volunteers for a changing sociopolitical context: The impact on social capital, citizenship and civil society. *Loisir et Société/Society and Leisure, 23*(2), 327–352.

Barr, C., McKeown, L., Davidman, K., McIver, D., & Lasby, D. (2004). *The rural charitable sector research initiative: A portrait of the non-profit and voluntary sector in rural Ontario*. Toronto, ON: Canadian Centre for Philanthropy.

Bedini, L. A., & Phoenix, T. L. (1999). Addressing leisure barriers for caregivers of older adults: A model leisure wellness program. *Therapeutic Recreation Journal, Third quarter,* 222–240.

Bowen, P., & McKechnie, A. (2003). *Family volunteering: A discussion paper*. Ottawa, ON: Volunteer Canada.

Canadian Centre for Philanthropy. (1998). *Gender differences in giving and volunteering*. Toronto, ON: Canadian Centre for Philanthropy.

Canadian Centre for Philanthropy. (2002a). *Volunteer motivation: What drives sports volunteers?* Toronto, ON: Canadian Centre for Philanthropy.

Canadian Centre for Philanthropy. (2002b). *Virtual volunteering in Canada*. Toronto, ON: Canadian Centre for Philanthropy.

Canadian Centre for Philanthropy. (2004a). *The benefits of volunteering*. Toronto, ON: Canadian Centre for Philanthropy

Canadian Centre for Philanthropy. (2004b). *Motivations and barriers to volunteering*. Toronto, ON: Canadian Centre for Philanthropy.

Canadian Centre for Philanthropy. (2004c). *The giving and volunteering of new Canadians*. Toronto, ON: Canadian Centre for Philanthropy.

Canadian Centre for Philanthropy. (2004d). *The giving and volunteering of youth*. Toronto, ON: Canadian Centre for Philanthropy.

Clary, E. G., Snyder, M., Ridge, D., Copeland, J., Stukas, A. A., Haugen, J., et al. (1998). Understanding and assessing the motivations of volunteers: A functional approach. *Journal of Personality and Social Psychology, 74*(6), 1516–1530.

Flanagan, C. A., Bowles, J. M., Jonsson, B., Csapo, B., & Sheblanova, E, (1998) Ties that bind: Correlates of adolescents' civic commitments in seven countries. *Journal of Social Issues, 54*(3), 457–477.

Graff, L. (2005). *Best of all: The quick reference guide to effective volunteer involvement*. Kemptville, ON: JTC, Inc.

Hall, M. H., Andrukow, A., Barr, C., Brock, K., de Wit, M., Embuldeniya, D., et al. (2003). *The capacity to serve. A qualitative study of the challenges facing Canada's non-profit and voluntary organizations*. Toronto, ON: Canadian Centre for Philanthropy.

Hall, M. H., Barr, C. W., Easwaramoorthy, M., Wojciech Sokolowski, S., & Salamon, L.M. (2005). *The Canadian non-profit and voluntary sector in comparative perspective*. Toronto, ON: Canadian Centre for Philanthropy.

Hall, M. H., de Wit, M. L., Lasby, D., McIver, D., Evers, T., Johnston, C., et al. (2004). *Cornerstones of community: Highlights of the national survey of non-profit and voluntary organizations*. Catalogue no. 61-533-XIE, Ottawa, ON: Statistics Canada.

Hall, M. H., McKeown, L., & Roberts, K. (2001). *Caring Canadians, involved Canadians: Highlights from the 2000 national survey of giving, volunteering and participating*. Catalogue no. 71-542-XIE, Ottawa, ON: Statistics Canada.

Hegel, A., & McKechnie, A. J. (2002). *Family volunteering: The final report*. Ottawa, ON: Volunteer Canada.

Henderson, K., & Presley, J. (2003). Globalization and the valuing of volunteering as leisure. *World Leisure, 45*(2), 33–37.

Hill Strategies Research, Inc. (2003). *Volunteers in arts and culture organizations in Canada*. Hamilton, ON: Hill Strategies Research Inc.

Johnstone, G. (2004). Volunteerism in Canada. In L. Kelly (Ed), *Management of volunteer services in Canada* (pp. 1–16). Kemptville, ON: JTC Inc.

Juniu, S. (2002). Perception of leisure in Latino women immigrants: Global consideration. *World Leisure, 44*(1), 48–55.

Lasby, D., & McIver, D. (2004). *Where Canadians volunteer: Volunteering by type of organization*. Toronto, ON: Canadian Centre for Philanthropy.

MacDuff, M. (2005). Societal changes and the rise of the episodic volunteer. In J. L. Brudney (Ed.), Emerging areas of volunteering. *ARNOVA Occasional Paper Series, 1*(2), 49–61.

Mair, H. (2003). Civil leisure? Exploring the relationship between leisure, activism and social change. *Leisure/Loisir, 27*(3/4), 213–237.

Mannell, R. C., & Kleiber, D.A. (1997). *A social psychology of leisure*. State College, PA: Venture Publishing Inc.

Murray, V., & Harrison, Y. (2005). Virtual volunteering. In J. L. Brudney (Ed.), Emerging areas of volunteering. *ARNOVA Occasional Paper Series, 1*(2), 31–48.

Omoto, A.M., & Snyder, M. (2002). Consideration of community: The context and process of volunteerism. *The American Behavioural Scientist, 45*(5), 848–867.

Parks and Recreation Ontario. (2005). Community sport volunteer profile: Fact sheet. Retrieved from http://216./13.76.142/PROntario/PDF/SPORTVOLUNTEER-factSheet/pdf

Reilly, R. C., & Vesic, V. (2003). Family volunteering: Making a difference together. *Leisure/Loisir, 27*(3/4), 305–332.

Shaw, S. M. (2001). The family leisure dilemma: Insights from research with Canadian families. *World Leisure Journal, 43*(4), 53–62.

Silverberg, K. E., Marshall, E. K., & Ellis, G. D. (2001). Measuring job satisfaction of volunteers in parks and recreation. *Journal of Park and Recreation Administration, 19*(1), 79–92.

Statistics Canada. (2005). *Non-profit institutions and volunteering: Economic contribution*. Retrieved from http://www.statcan.ca/Daily/English/051212/d051212b.htm

Statistics Canada. (2004). *National survey of non-profit and voluntary organizations*. Retrieved from http://www.statcan.ca/Daily/English/049020/d040920b.htm

Stebbins, R. A. (1998a). Volunteering: A serious leisure perspective. *Non-profit and Voluntary Sector Quarterly. 25*(2), 211–224.

Stebbins, R. A. (1998b). *After work: The search for an optimal leisure lifestyle*. Calgary, AB: Detselig Enterprises.

Stebbins, R. A. (2001). *New directions in the theory and research of serious leisure*. Mellen Studies in Sociology, 28. Lewiston, NY: Edwin Mellen Press.

Tang, T. L., & Weatherford, E. J. (1998). Perception of changing self-worth through service, The development of a service ethic scale. *The Journal of Social Psychology, 138*(6), 734–743.

Twynam, G. D., Farrell, J. M., & Johnston, M. E. (2003). Leisure and volunteer motivation at a special sporting event. *Leisure/Loisir, 27*(3/4), 363–377.

Van Til, J. (1988). *Mapping the third sector. Voluntarism in a changing political economy*. New York, NY: Foundation Center.

Wilson, J. (2000). Volunteering. *Annual Review of Sociology, 26*, 215–240.

LIFE

Chapter 41
Event Management

Christine Van Winkle, Ph.D.
University of Manitoba

Learning Objectives

After reading this chapter, students will be able to

1. Distinguish between various types of events.
2. Recognize the unique qualities of the event experience.
3. Understand the special issues to consider when planning and managing events.
4. Consider the impacts and outcomes of events.

Introduction

People have been planning and managing parties, meetings, and large celebrations throughout history, and many of us have some experience managing events. While event management is not new, the increasing professionalization within this field and the academic study of events are more recent phenomena. You might be wondering what is unique about managing events compared with other forms of recreation. This chapter will delve into the unique aspects of managing events but will begin by reviewing what qualifies as a special event.

Defining Events and Event Typologies

"Event" and "special event" are often used interchangeably within the field of event management. According to the Oxford English Dictionary (Stevenson, Elliott, & Jones, 2001), "special" is defined as "better or different from what is usual" (p. 675), whereas "event" is defined as "a public or social occasion" (p. 240). Using these definitions, a "special event" can be described as a public or social occasion that is different from what is usual. While this dictionary definition is accurate, it does not describe events from the event provider, attendee, or host community's perspective.

From an organization's perspective, an event is considered an activity or program that takes place outside of the normal range of services (Getz, 1991). For example, a community centre might offer a recreational badminton league as part of their usual activities; therefore this would not be considered a special event. However, if they were to host an annual weeklong badminton competition, this would be considered a special event. For the event attendee, a special event provides time and space for a leisure, cultural, or social experience that is not usually available (Getz, 1991). For example, many rural communities host harvest-related events where residents get together once a year at a community venue to celebrate their rural culture and local food production. From the host community's point of view, the event might be considered both a unique leisure opportunity for residents and a tourist attraction. Events are often used to attract visitors to a community. While the majority of attendees are typically local residents, the ability for events to draw outsiders to the community is often a reason used in support of hosting the event. Throughout this chapter, "event" and "special event" will be used to refer exclusively to events within the broad field of leisure.

Table 41.1: Event Classification

Size/scale	• Number of Attendees • Local, national, international
Form	• Multi-venue, single venue • Multi-purpose, single purpose • Multi-genre, single genre
Area/topic/genre	• Sport, art, culture, recreation, business, lifestyle
Function	• Fundraising, promotion, participation, presentation, celebration, competition, recreation
Audience	• Public, private • Participatory, spectator • Residents, tourists
Presenter	• Public, private, not-for-profit • Event as primary function, event as secondary function
Regularity	• Regular, periodic • One-time, biannual, annual, biennial, decennial, bicentennial, centennial
Accessibility	• Free, paid admission • Remote, accessible location
Venue	• Indoor, outdoor • Urban, rural • Natural, built environment

? Think about an event you've attended recently. Using Table 41.1 as a guide, identify the size, form, area, function, audience, presenter, regularity, accessibility, and venue to classify the event.

A number of different classification systems have been used to categorize events. Common ways of categorizing events are presented in Table 41.1, p. 387.

No single classification of events exists, because categorization depends on the reason events are placed into groups. For example, government agencies might classify events into public or private to determine which events should receive money from a funding program. A destination-marketing professional might group events into their topic area (sport, art, etc.) and develop specific promotional materials for each type. Alternatively, a researcher interested in understanding the environmental impacts of events might place events into categories based on the size (number of attendees) or location (natural or built environment).

Hallmark: internationally significant and inseparable from the host community (e.g., The Running of the Bulls in Pamplona, Spain, which marks the beginning of the Pamplona Festival).

Mega-event: internationally significant event that typically acts as a tourist attraction (e.g., The Winter Olympics are held in different locations every 4 years and attract a large number of visitors to the host city).

Festival: themed cultural celebration (e.g., Winnipeg International Fringe Festival celebrates theatre in its various forms and offers over 1,300 free and paid performances at over 20 venues in Winnipeg, Manitoba, for two weeks each summer).

Fair: multi-purpose (exhibition, trade, recreation, education, competition) community gathering where local goods are available for sale (e.g., At the Norfolk County Fair and Horse Show in Simcoe, Ontario, attendees can purchase goods, participate, watch various competitions, and can go on amusement rides).

Tradeshow: members of a specific industry gather to exhibit, sell, or buy goods (e.g., The Halifax RV show exhibits the newest models of recreational vehicles to consumers).

Conference: a meeting where people discuss and exchange ideas (often through presentations) on a particular topic (e.g., The Travel and Tourism Research Association hosts an annual conference where researchers can share their ideas related to travel and tourism).

Convention: formal gathering of people who share a common interest and meet for a common purpose (e.g., G.I. Joe fans and collectors can attend the G.I. Joe Canadian Convention to hear speakers, get autographs, and trade collectors' items).

Many specific types of special events have been identified and differ based on the characteristics described in Table 41.1. While no single classification system for events exists, there are some types of events that have been given their own names because of their unique characteristics.

The Special Event Experience

As noted above, special events provide people with the opportunity to experience leisure. Understanding why people attend events is useful to event managers who want to attract attendees. Motivation for attending events has frequently been studied and has been informed heavily by leisure and tourism motivation research. Research examining festival motivation reveals that escape, excitement/thrills, novelty, entertainment, socialization, group togetherness, and family togetherness are often needs that people feel will be met by attending special events (Uysal, Gahan, & Martin, 1993). Tourism research exploring push-and-pull motives (Dann, 1977), has helped event scholars and professionals to understand motives for attending international events (Wamwara-Mbugua & Cornwell, 2010). Pull factors are external forces that draw a person to an event, while push factors are internal forces that motivate the person to attend the event. Novelty-seeking and hedonism (pleasure-seeking) are examples of push factors for festival attendance, while culture, shopping, and meeting unique people are examples of pull factors (Wamwara-Mbugua & Cornwell, 2010).

Satisfaction is a commonly studied outcome of event attendance. Unsatisfied event attendees may not return to an event in the future, which can affect the long-term viability of an event (Getz, 2007). Satisfaction research can typically be classified as either "appraisal satisfaction" or "need satisfaction" (Mannell, 1999). Need satisfaction is based on the event meeting the needs or motives that led a person to attend the event. Alternatively, appraisal satisfaction is an evaluation of the quality of an experience and requires people to reflect on their perception of the quality of the overall event or specific components of the event (such as facilities, food, and entertainment). Whether or not people are satisfied depends partly on their expectations for the event experience.

The experience economy, first described by Pine and Gilmore (1999), refers to how experiences have become valued economic offerings. Today, products and services are being repackaged as experiences to enhance their economic worth. The experience economy is a useful perspective to help understand the various factors affecting personal and memorable experiences. Pine and Gilmore have identified a number of principles that can be used to design memorable experiences, and event managers should consider how these can be integrated into the event experience (Hayes & McLeod, 2006). The principles are 1) create a compelling theme, 2) provide positive cues to reinforce the theme, 3) offer tangible memorabilia to remind people of the experience, and 4) engage all senses (touch, taste, smell, and sight). Furthermore, experience-economy literature suggests that experiences can be enhanced by engaging attendees as co-producers of their own experiences (Mossberg, 2007).

How can an event manager engage attendees as co-producers of their own experiences?

Leisure-constraints research is key to understanding why people don't engage in recreational activities. Chapter 9 provides an overview of the constraints research, theories, and models and reviews three types of constraints (intrapersonal, interpersonal, and structural) that people must negotiate to participate in an activity. A study by Milner, Jago, and Deery (2003) revealed that event non-attendees were likely to be older, retired, and widowed, and the reasons for not attending events included lack of interest, lack of time, hassle, age, and cost. By understanding the reasons some individuals do not attend events, event managers can find ways to help non-attendees negotiate these constraints.

How can event producers help event non-attendees to overcome constraints to participation? Can event producers do anything about lack of interest in an event? If so, what can they do?

Planning and Managing Events

Planning and managing events is not entirely different from recreation, tourism, or sport management, but events do possess some unique qualities that require additional consideration when planning and executing the event. Unlike typical recreation programs, events often involve managing large crowds, ticketing, queue management, safety and security, animation, working with dignitaries and celebrities, developing and implementing ticketing systems, booking and managing numerous venues, and working with vendors.

Crowd Management

The public nature of many events often results in large crowds. While some events, such as meetings and private social events like anniversary parties, involve a limited number of invited guests, other events are open to the public and can attract hundreds of thousands of people. This presents a range of challenges for the event coordinator, including ticketing, site access, and restrictions, queue management, safety, security, animation, and managing crowd behaviour.

Ticketing

Requiring tickets to an event is a form of crowd management. By issuing a limited number of tickets, the event coordinator can know in advance how many people to expect at the event. Tickets can be sold or given away for free, and they can also be available in advance or at the door. When tickets are reserved in advance but are picked up at the door on the day of the event, they are often at a "will call" box office. "Will call" is a term that originated in theatre to refer to pre-purchased tickets on hold at the box office, but it is a term now used by many events.

Queue Management

Event attendees often wait in many line-ups. Sometimes managing these line-ups is quite simple, but when you have large crowds gathered it could become complicated. Line-ups are also known as queues, and queuing theory applies mathematical algorithms to understand line-ups and waiting times (Gross & Harris, 1998). There are many queuing theories that suggest how people behave in queues, and these can be useful to event managers. Tum, Norton, and Wright (2006) offer a formula that can be used by event managers to understand time to access a site.

Safety and Security

Events take place in complex social and physical environments and should be made as safe and secure as reasonably possible to ensure attendees are able to enjoy the event. A safe environment is one that does not present hazards. Event managers take many precautions to reduce and eliminate possible hazards. Examples include ensuring proper food preparation to reduce incidences of food-born illness, proper sanitation by providing waste bins, reducing site hazards by clearly marking uneven ground, and proper site drainage.

Event security is multifaceted and aims to protect both people and property from harm. Event organizers will often involve private security firms, on- and off-duty police officers, and volunteers in security efforts. All event areas are typically included in the security plan. Security screening at the gates to some events is used to ensure unsafe objects (weapons, glass) are not allowed on site. Reducing unsafe behaviour is another aspect of security, and eliminating or reducing access to alcohol is an option considered by many event managers to minimize unsafe behaviour.

On rare occasions, a crowd can become a mob or turn into a riot. Mobs are crowds with heightened, shared emotion. Riots, which often evolve out of mobs, are characterized by violent acts towards people or property (O'Connell & Cuthbertson, 2008). A number of theories have been used to understand how people behave in crowd settings (O'Connell & Cuthbertson, 2009). For example, deindividuation theory predicts that people join crowds because they can escape socially accepted behaviours and norms (O'Connell & Cuthbertson, 2009). Understanding how crowds behave is important for event security efforts.

Animation

Program animation is a key concept in recreation program planning and refers to how program participants are moved through a program (Rossman & Schlatter, 2008). Various techniques are used to animate a program including a leader or emcee, signage, and the program itself. When planning events, considering how attendees will move through the event space and time is key to help to manage crowds. Through careful program animation, you can cause crowds to disperse or come together; also, you can allow guests to experience event elements at the same time or at different times. It is important to consider how program animation impacts the event attendee's experience. If too much direction is given, this could negatively affect people's perception of freedom, which is important when trying to facilitate a leisure experience. Alternatively, too little direction might be frustrating to participants and result in dissatisfaction with the event experience (Rossman & Schlatter, 2008)

Special Guests

Special events often include dignitaries, performers, celebrities, or athletes as attendees, presenters, or performers. Some events exist solely because of the high-profile people in attendance, such as a royal wedding. Working with important people requires additional planning and management.

Hiring performers or celebrities typically involves contacting their representatives, clearly identifying expectations, negotiating, discussing and reviewing a contract with lawyers, and following through on the details contained in the contract. To contact a performer or celebrity, you can use professional associations, agencies, or contact them directly. When stating your expectations, you must articulate whether you expect an appearance (signing autographs, meeting the press), or a performance (specifying the date, time, length, and content), or both. Negotiations will involve discussing the performance, appearances, promotion, travel accommodations, food, payment, and other details of the visit. The contract should be detailed, specific, and accurate. Often, a rider is attached to the main agreement that outlines important elements that support the main contract. Information about performer requirements regarding rehearsals, food, accommodations, and equipment will typically be included in the rider. It is important to know the details of the contract and to follow through on all listed requirements. Finally, there will be additional administrative work when bringing performers from foreign countries, including obtaining work permits and completing tax forms.

If heads of state, political figures, and royalty are part of an event, then it is important to become familiar with the protocol required for hosting the dignitaries you have invited. The provincial government and federal government have protocol offices, which will be able to help you with hosting a dignitary. You will also need to be aware of the styles of address used to speak with these special guests. For example, if Her Majesty Queen Elizabeth II were to attend your event and engage you in conversation, the first time you spoke to her, you would call her Your Majesty, and then Ma'am from that moment on.

Venue

Venues are the spaces used to host the event. Because events occur infrequently, few organizations maintain a permanent venue for their event and must reserve and rent spaces. Site selection is typically based on the type of event, image, the number of people attending, and the facilities needed. Events that take place outdoors in public spaces must have permits from the local government to set up tents, sell food and goods, and to make noise at certain times of day. Indoor venue rentals typically involve signing contracts with the owner of the space, and you must be sure to review what space and equipment is included in the rental. When considering a space to host an event, the event coordinator must complete a site-needs assessment, determine where different event elements will take place, identify any alterations that need to be made to the site, and consider how to create the appropriate ambiance in the site selected.

Vendors

Vendors include those people and businesses that sell food, beverages, crafts, and other goods and services at the event. When including vendors at an event, the event coordinator will need to consider how many and what type of vendors should be part of the event. These decisions will be based on the needs of the event attendees, as well as the following venue and event specifications: space, site access, power distribution, water, cleaning stations, inspections and permits, and security. When working with vendors, a vendor contract that outlines the commitment, rules/regulations and expectations of the vendor and event staff and should be signed by both the vendor and an event representative. Special permits are needed for different types of vendors, including permits to sell and serve food and alcohol, and to sell merchandise.

Event Outcomes

There are many outcomes that result from events. Earlier, we discussed motivations for event attendance and discovered that events provide individuals with opportunities to experience leisure, socialize and meet new people, spend time with friends and family, and experience excitement.

When examining the outcomes of events, research has revealed that a range of economic, sociocultural, and environmental impacts result. The term "impacts" refers to both positive and negative changes in the economy, community, or environment (Pearce, 1989). The economic impact of events result from the new money generated or brought into a community because of the event (Getz, 2007) and can be either positive or negative. Economic impacts are the most well-studied impacts, likely because positive economic outcomes are often used as a rationale for hosting an event (Dwyer, Mellor, Mistilis, & Mules, 2000). An example of positive economic impact is the increased employment opportunities generated by the event. A negative economic impact is the expense of developing and maintaining event facilities. The sociocultural impacts of events are often studied by asking residents about their perceptions. A positive social impact is the opportunity to share the local cultural traditions with visitors, while a negative social impact would be the perception of increased crowding in the neighborhood where the event takes place. The environmental impacts of special events are the least studied outcome of events. Like economic and sociocultural impacts, environmental impacts can be either positive or negative. A positive environmental impact of hosting an event might be increased awareness of a unique environment, whereas a negative impact might be increased litter and waste in the event environment.

The amount and type of impacts that occur depend on a number of factors, including characteristics of the event, the environment, the host community, and visitors. The goal of sustainable event management is to maximize the benefits and minimize the negative outcomes of hosting an event. Tools exist to assist event managers in minimizing their negative impacts.

Can you think of any more examples of positive and negative economic, sociocultural, or environmental impacts of events? List as many examples as possible and discuss how to minimize the negative impacts and to maximize the positive outcomes.

Event professionals and researchers recognize the need to better understand all of the impacts of events. The triple bottom line (TBL) refers to the combination of the social, environment, and economic impacts into one framework.

The David Suzuki Foundation website has information informing event managers about how to host a carbon-neutral event. Visit www.davidsuzuki.org for more information.

The TBL was developed in accounting (Hede, 2008) and is now being applied to event management. The TBL is already often done when evaluating events, but researchers are urging event managers to consider the TBL in the planning stage of event management (Hede, 2008).

Conclusion

Event management is complex and requires an extensive body of knowledge known as the Event Management Body of Knowledge (EMBOK). This includes administration, design, marketing, operations, and risk management know-how (Silvers, Bowdin, O'Toole, & Nelson, 2006). Many event professionals seek higher education to ensure they have the preparation necessary for this demanding field. Studying recreation management can provide a strong foundation for a career in event management. By studying leisure and recreation, students gain an understanding of the experiences people seek, factors affecting experiences, and how to manage leisure experiences.

Key Terms

Special event
Experience economy
Triple bottom line (TBL)
Hallmark event
Mega-event
Festival

References

Dann, G. (1977). Anomie, ego-enhancement and tourism. *Annals of Tourism Research, 6*(4),184–94.

Dwyer, L., Mellor, R., Mistilis, N., & Mules, T. (2000). A framework for assessing tangible and intangible impacts of events and conventions. *Event Management, 6*(3), 175–189.

Getz, D. (1991). *Festivals, special events, and tourism.* New York, NY: Van Nostrand Reinhold.

Getz, D. (2007). *Events studies: Theory, research and policy for planned events.* Oxford, UK: Butterworth-Heinemann.

Gross, D., & Harris, C. M. (1998). *Fundamentals of queuing theory*. Mississauga, ON: John Wiley & Sons.

Hayes, D., & MacLeod, N. (2007). Packaging places: Designing heritage trails using an experience economy perspective to maximize visitor engagement. *Journal of Vacation Marketing, 13*(1), 45–58. DOI: 10.1177/1356766706071205

Hede, A. (2008). Managing special events in the new era of the triple bottom line. *Event Management, 11*(1/2), 13–22.

Mannell, R. C. (1999). Leisure experience and satisfaction. In E. L. Jackson & T. L. Burton (Eds.), *Leisure studies: Prospects for the twenty-first century* (pp. 235–248). State College, PA: Venture Publishing, Inc.

Milner, L. M., Jago, L. K., & Deery, M. (2003). Profiling the special event nonattendee: An initial investigation. *Event Management, 8*(3), 141–150.

Mossberg, L. (2007). A marketing approach to the tourist experience. *Scandinavian Journal of Hospitality & Tourism, 7*(1), 59–74.

O'Connell, T., & Cuthbertson, B. (2008). *Group dynamics in recreation and leisure*. Champaign, IL: Human Kinetics.

Pine, B. J., & Gilmore, J. H. (1999). *The experience economy: Work is theatre and every business a stage*. Boston, MA: Harvard Business School Press.

Pearce, D. (1989). *Tourist development*. New York, NY: Wiley.

Rossman, J. R., & Schlatter, B. E. (2008). *Recreation programming: Designing leisure experiences*. Champaign, IL: Sagamore.

Silvers, J. R., Bowdin, G. A. J., O'Toole, W. J., & Nelson, K. B. (2006). Towards an international event management body of knowledge (EMBOK). *Event Management, 9*(4), 185–198.

Stevenson, A., Elliott, J., & Jones, R. (2001). *Colour Oxford English dictionary*. New York: Oxford University Press.

Tum, J., Norton, P., & Wright, N. (2006). Management of event operations. Oxford, UK: Butterworth-Heinemann.

Uysal, M., Gahan, L., & Martin, B. (1993). An examination of event motivations: A case study. *Festival Management and Event Tourism, 1*(1), 5–10.

Wamwara-Mbugua, L. W., & Cornwell, T. B. (2010). A dialogical examination of Kenyan immigrants' acculturation in the United States. *Journal of Immigrant & Refugee Studies, 8*(1), 32–49. DOI:10.1080/15562940903379118

Index

A

B

C

D

E

F

G

H

N

O

P

Q

R

S

T

U

V

W

Y

Z

Other Books by Venture Publishing, Inc.

21st Century Leisure: Current Issues, Second Edition
by Valeria J. Freysinger and John R. Kelly
Active Living in Older Adulthood: Principles and Practices of Activity Programs
by Barbara A. Hawkins
Adventure Programming
edited by John C. Miles and Simon Priest
Boredom Busters: Themed Special Events to Dazzle and Delight Your Group
by Annette C. Moore
Brain Fitness
by Suzanne Fitzsimmons
Client Assessment in Therapeutic Recreation Services
by Norma J. Stumbo
Client Outcomes in Therapeutic Recreation Services
by Norma J. Stumbo
Conceptual Foundations for Therapeutic Recreation
edited by David R. Austin, John Dattilo, and Bryan P. McCormick
Dementia Care Programming: An Identity-Focused Approach
by Rosemary Dunne
Dimensions of Choice: Qualitative Approaches to Parks, Recreation, Tourism, Sport, and Leisure Research, Second Edition
by Karla A. Henderson
Diversity and the Recreation Profession: Organizational Perspectives (Revised Edition)
edited by Maria T. Allison and Ingrid E. Schneider
Effective Management in Therapeutic Recreation Service, Second Edition
by Marcia Jean Carter and Gerald S. O'Morrow
Evaluating Leisure Services: Making Enlightened Decisions, Third Edition
by Karla A. Henderson and M. Deborah Bialeschki
Facilitation of Therapeutic Recreation Services: An Evidence-Based and Best Practice Approach to Techniques and Processes
edited by Norma J. Stumbo and Brad Wardlaw
Facilitation Techniques in Therapeutic Recreation, Second Edition
by John Dattilo and Alexis McKenney
File o' Fun: A Recreation Planner for Games & Activities, Third Edition
by Jane Harris Ericson and Diane Ruth Albright
The Game Finder: A Leader's Guide to Great Activities
by Annette C. Moore
Health Promotion for Mind, Body, and Spirit
by Suzanne Fitzsimmons and Linda L. Buettner
Human Resource Management in Recreation, Sport, and Leisure Services
by Margaret Arnold, Regina Glover, and Cheryl Beeler
Inclusion: Including People With Disabilities in Parks and Recreation Opportunities
by Lynn Anderson and Carla Brown Kress
Inclusive Leisure Services, Third Edition
by John Dattilo
Internships in Recreation and Leisure Services: A Practical Guide for Students, Fifth Edition
by Edward E. Seagle, Jr., Tammy B. Smith, and Ralph W. Smith
Internships in Sport Management
by Robin Ammon, Jr., Matthew Walker, Edward E. Seagle, and Ralph W. Smith
Interpretation of Cultural and Natural Resources, Second Edition
by Douglas M. Knudson, Ted T. Cable, and Larry Beck

Intervention Activities for At-Risk Youth
by Norma J. Stumbo
Introduction to Outdoor Recreation: Providing and Managing Resource Based Opportunities
by Roger L. Moore and B. L. Driver
Introduction to Recreation and Leisure Services, Eighth Edition
by Karla A. Henderson, M. Deborah Bialeschki, John L. Hemingway, Jan S. Hodges, Beth D. Kivel, and H. Douglas Sessoms
Introduction to Recreation Services: Sustainability for a Changing World
by Karla A. Henderson
Introduction to Therapeutic Recreation: U.S. and Canadian Perspectives
by Kenneth Mobily and Lisa Ostiguy
An Introduction to Tourism
by Robert W. Wyllie
Introduction to Writing Goals and Objectives: A Manual for Recreation Therapy Students and Entry-Level Professionals
by Suzanne Melcher
The Leader's Handbook: Learning Leadership Skills by Facilitating Fun, Games, Play, and Positive Interaction
by Bill Michaelis and John M. O'Connell
Leadership and Administration of Outdoor Pursuits, Third Edition
by James Blanchard, Michael Strong, and Phyllis Ford
Leadership in Leisure Services: Making a Difference, Third Edition
by Debra J. Jordan
Leisure and Leisure Services in the 21st Century: Toward Mid Century
by Geoffrey Godbey
Leisure Education I: A Manual of Activities and Resources, Second Edition
by Norma J. Stumbo
Leisure Education II: More Activities and Resources, Second Edition
by Norma J. Stumbo
Leisure Education III: More Goal-Oriented Activities
by Norma J. Stumbo
Leisure Education IV: Activities for Individuals with Substance Addictions
by Norma J. Stumbo
Leisure Education Program Planning: A Systematic Approach, Third Edition
by John Dattilo
Leisure, Health, and Wellness: Making the Connections
by Laura Payne, Barbara Ainsworth, and Geoffrey Godbey
Leisure in Your Life: New Perspectives
by Geoffrey Godbey
Leisure Studies: Prospects for the Twenty-First Century
edited by Edgar L. Jackson and Thomas L. Burton
Leisure, Women, and Gender
edited by Valeria J. Freysinger, Susan M. Shaw, Karla A. Henderson, and M. Deborah Bialeschki
Making a Difference in Academic Life: A Handbook for Park, Recreation, and Tourism Educators and Graduate Students
edited by Dan Dustin and Tom Goodale
Managing to Optimize the Beneficial Outcomes of Leisure
edited by B. L. Driver
Marketing in Leisure and Tourism: Reaching New Heights
by Patricia Click Janes
More Than a Game: A New Focus on Senior Activity Services
by Brenda Corbett
N.E.S.T. Approach: Dementia Practice Guidelines for Disturbing Behaviors
by Linda L. Buettner and Suzanne Fitzsimmons

Parks for Life: Moving the Goal Posts, Changing the Rules, and Expanding the Field
by Will LaPage
Planning and Organizing Group Activities in Social Recreation
by John V. Valentine
Planning for Recreation and Parks Facilities: Predesign Process, Principles, and Strategies
by Jack Harper
Programming for Parks, Recreation, and Leisure Services: A Servant Leadership Approach, Third Edition
by Donald G. DeGraaf, Debra J. Jordan, and Kathy H. DeGraaf
Recreation and Youth Development
by Peter A. Witt and Linda L. Caldwell
Recreation for Older Adults: Individual and Group Activities
by Judith A. Elliott and Jerold E. Elliott
Recreation Program Planning Manual for Older Adults
by Karen Kindrachuk
Reference Manual for Writing Rehabilitation Therapy Treatment Plans
by Penny Hogberg and Mary Johnson
Service Living: Building Community through Public Parks and Recreation
by Doug Wellman, Dan Dustin, Karla Henderson, and Roger Moore
A Social Psychology of Leisure, Second Edition
by Douglas A. Kleiber, Gordon J. Walker, and Roger C. Mannell
Special Events and Festivals: How to Organize, Plan, and Implement
by Angie Prosser and Ashli Rutledge
The Sportsman's Voice: Hunting and Fishing in America
by Mark Damian Duda, Martin F. Jones, and Andrea Criscione
Survey Research and Analysis: Applications in Parks, Recreation, and Human Dimensions
by Jerry Vaske
Taking the Initiative: Activities to Enhance Effectiveness and Promote Fun
by J. P. Witman
Therapeutic Recreation and the Nature of Disabilities
by Kenneth E. Mobily and Richard D. MacNeil
Therapeutic Recreation: Cases and Exercises, Second Edition
by Barbara C. Wilhite and M. Jean Keller
Therapeutic Recreation in Health Promotion and Rehabilitation
by John Shank and Catherine Coyle
Therapeutic Recreation Practice: A Strengths Approach
by Lynn Anderson and Linda Heyne